ENCYCLOPEDIA OF COLLECTIBLE
Children's Books

IDENTIFICATION AND VALUES

COLLECTOR BOOKS
A Division of Schroeder Publishing Co., Inc.

Diane McClure Jones & Rosemary Jones

ON THE FRONT COVER:

Peter and Gretchen of Old Nuremberg, Viola Jones, Albert Whitman, 1935, oversize, color and b/w illustrations by Helen Sewell, first edition with dust jacket: $40.00

Story-Telling Ballads, Frances Jenkins Olcott, 1920, Houghton collection, green cloth-over-board cover with paste-on-illustration, four color plates by Milo Winter: $40.00

Candy Kane, Candy Kane Series, Janet Lambert, 1943, Grosset & Dunlap reprint with dust jacket: $35.00

Stand by for Mars, Tom Corbett Space Cadet Series, Carey Rockwell, 1952, Grosset & Dunlap, first edition with dust jacket: $50.00

Magic by the Lake, Half Magic Series, Edgar Eager, 1957, Harcourt Brace, illustrated by N. M. Bodecker, first edition with dust jacket: $60.00

Sign of the Twisted Candles, Nancy Drew Series, Carolyn Keene (1933), 1950s, Grosset & Dunlap edition with Bill Gillies dust jacket: $40.00

Pollyanna's Jewels, Glad Books Series, Harriet Lummis Smith, 1925, Page Publications, paste-on-pictorial, six b/w plates, first edition: $50.00

Lost Princess of Oz, Oz Books, Junior Editions, 1939, Rand McNally, 62 pages, shortened adaptations of L. Frank Baum book: $40.00

ON THE BACK COVER:

Tim to the Rescue, Tim and Lucy Series, Edward Ardizzone, 1949, Oxford University Press, first edition with dust jacket: $500.00

Seven Little Sisters Who Live on the Round Ball That Floats in the Air, Jane Andrews, Ginn and Company, 1916 edition: $30.00

Mr. Blue Peacock, Edna Groff Deihl, Just Right Book, Whitman, 1926, 63 pages, color illustrations by C. X. Shinn: $50.00

Motor Boys Bound for Home, Motor Boys Series, Clarence Young, ca. 1920s, Cupples & Leon, hardcover: $30.00

Cover design by Beth Summers
Book design by Ryan Byrd
Cover photography by Charles R. Lynch

COLLECTOR BOOKS
P.O. Box 3009
Paducah, Kentucky 42002-3009

www.collectorbooks.com

The current values in this book should be used only as a guide. They are not intended to set prices, which vary from one section of the country to another. Auction prices as well as dealer prices vary greatly and are affected by condition as well as demand. Neither the authors nor the publisher assumes responsibility for any losses that might be incurred as a result of consulting this guide.

Searching for a Publisher?

We are always looking for people knowledgeable within their fields. If you feel that there is a real need for a book on your collectible subject and have a large comprehensive collection, contact Collector Books.

Proudly printed and bound in the
United States of America

Contents

Introduction

As we finished this book, two very collectible children's books came to market via auction.

The first was a *Harry Potter and the Philosopher's Stone* published by Bloomsbury in 1997, a true first British edition of J.K. Rowling's very first book about the boy wizard. Collectors believe that only 500 to 1,000 copies of this edition exist. The auction house estimated that the book would sell between $10,000 and $20,000. A month later, this particular Harry Potter sold for $18,000.

The second title was the first edition of *Curious George*, a book published almost 50 years before *Harry Potter*. Again the estimated print run for the first edition of this book was small and the demand was known to be high. The auction house determined that this title could go as high as $10,000, although we had seen similar copies of *Curious George* offered for sale less than a year before for $2,000.

So what makes these books so valuable and other children's books, arguably of equal literary merit and artistic beauty, worth $10 on today's market? In the case of both Harry and George, one could argue that heavy merchandising have made both books extremely famous and created literally thousands of collectors eager to own a first edition. And, at the time of the auctions, the auctioneers believed enough of those collectors had thousands of dollars to spend on a single title.

The first and probably most important factor in driving up the price of any collectible book is **desire**. As with all types of collecting, desire can be a very fickle thing. What collectors want today may not be what collectors of the next generation want. Children's books, like children's toys, go through fads. Although it's hard to imagine a time when *Harry Potter* will not rule the bookshelves, J.K. Rowling has brought her successful series to a close. It may be that another book series will rise to equal or greater prominence in the next decade.

In the used book trade, books like *Harry Potter and the Philosopher's Stone* are sometimes called hypermoderns. Collectors and dealers buy them sometimes as a speculative investment, assuming that the desire for these books will continue into the future. It's a gamble. Twenty years into the future, the same book that sold for $18,000 may sell for $1,800 or it may sell for $180,000. It's hard to predict.

To avoid making predictions, we've stayed away from hypermoderns in this encyclopedia and concentrated on children's books published earlier. You'll find a listing for *Harry Potter* in the Series section, but it is the only series from the 1990s listed there. We love reading authors like Garth Nix or series like the *Traveling Pants*, but we find such first editions from the 1990s popping up for a dollar at library sales almost as often as they sell for a higher amount.

At the same time, certain items such as early editions of *Curious George* or *Wizard of Oz*, have become scarce enough and famous enough that even the sorters at library sales know to separate these books out and price them at market values.

The desirability of certain titles have made prices so volatile right now that it was impossible to determine an average price for today's market. Again, that auction estimate of $10,000 for *Curious George* seems to suggest that somebody believes the average price for that first edition should be well above $2,000. When we mention such books, we qualify our listings by saying "one dealer offered it for" or "an auction estimate might be." We tried to stay away from such vague listings but felt certain titles were so famous that we had to address this.

Scarcity is probably the second biggest factor in determining the price of a collectible book. If there are more buyers than items, the price shoots up. Age helps determine scarcity. Books are fragile things and those belonging to children may not survive being hauled to school, left in the sandbox, or dumped under the bed for the puppy to chew. It's one of the reasons why children's books are often deemed collectible even when the condition is less than fine. Unlike adult books, a certain amount of wear is expected and accepted by collectors. Still, a remarkable number of sturdy, well-printed books even from the Victorian age have survived, in part, because many of these books had large print runs to begin with.

Age is not the only factor in scarcity. First editions of books, like the *Harry Potter* mentioned above, can have small print runs as publishers test the market. Of course, if a title proves successful or an author proves popular, later print runs can be quite large. Later editions of the Potter series had print runs into the record-breaking millions for the first editions, which is why the price of a first edition of the fifth or sixth book in the series may be only half the cover price at your average used bookstore. The book will sell for that price, but not for more, given the current supply and demand of the market.

Later books by Kate Greenway, printed more than a hundred years ago, had print runs into the hundreds of thousands, and a remarkable number of these fragile volumes still exist. Still, more buyers than sellers are out there for Greenaway and prices run into the hundreds of dollars for her first editions. Age and a growing number of collectors have broadened the demand for her work, making first editions rise in price.

The same thing may happen to *Harry Potter* or it may not — and the *Encyclopedia of Collectible Children's Books* written 50 or 100 years from now will be a very different book from this volume. This encyclopedia certainly reflects a number of changes, both up and down, in prices since we wrote our first book about collecting children's books in 1997.

Since we began writing about collectible children's books, the internet has become an enormous factor showing the **scarcity** or lack of scarcity for certain titles. You may find a children's book from 100 years ago, and it may be the only copy in your town, but a quick check of internet sales sites may show that literally hundreds of copies are available for sale around the world.

At the same time, a survey just of internet sites does not show the **desirability** of a title. You may not be able to find a match for your book, but at the same time, you may not find a buyer either, even at the lowest price possible. Look at the staggering number of used books being offered for a $1 or less on some sites.

So, in determining prices for this book, we looked at both the scarcity of a title and the desirability of that title. When the book's average price fell below $30 because literally hundreds of copies were available, we dropped it out of the listings for this encyclopedia, although we may have included that title in our earlier books.

We also trimmed a number of early children's books and series whose prices had dropped below $30 per volume, even though only a handful of the books might exist. In the latter case, the low price seems to be determined by the desirability of the title to collectors these days, even though individual titles might well sell to a particular collector.

Sometimes, and this was always the hardest call, we have dropped out series or individual titles because we felt the books were published for and desired more by the "adult" market rather than the collectors of children's books. At the same time, we felt that certain series originally pub-

lished for adults did fall into the children's section of the used bookstore by tradition, and we have listed those.

As always, our listings reflect American market prices, although we have listed a number of British titles, authors, illustrators, and series. Certain books are far more desirable for American collectors than British, and vice versa is true. When dealing with such titles, we tended towards the average American price for the volume.

We expect that almost any book listed in this encyclopedia may come to the market at any time for either less than what we have listed it for or more than the price given. That is the nature of averages. Also, a movie adaptation, a new book referencing an old one, or simply a magazine article can shoot up awareness of a title or author and impact the price dramatically and rapidly. If you are selling a collection, do as much research as possible prior to taking it to a dealer or offering it at auction. When buying, listen to the seller about his or her reasons for prices if the books seem out of the average range to you. Sometimes a book is out of the average in quality and that may well warrant a higher price.

For certain authors and series that have inspired specialized bibliographies, we have listed those reference works under the author's name or series listing. For a more general bibliography of the books used to research this volume, please see the back of this encyclopedia. We always recommend that collectors continue their research into their favorite books and authors, and applaud the many book-collecting magazines, societies, and newsletters that give far more detailed information than can be fitted into this encyclopedia.

As always, our own collection grew as we researched this volume. We buy children's books because we find them beautiful to look at or fun to read. We hope that you also will fill your shelves with the books that you love and, in this encyclopedia, discover even more new and delightful titles for your collection.

Diane McClure Jones
Rosemary Jones

Explanation of Pricing

Prices of collectible books vary dramatically, due to changes in popularity of items. The revival of interest in an old novel for any reason, such as the production of a film based on the story, can create or increase demand.

We have based our prices on suggested prices received from a number of antiquarian book dealers.

All quoted prices are for individual hardcover books in good condition but without dust jackets. When dust jacket pricing information is available, it is included and identified.

Book club editions are usually printed in large quantities and therefore have much lower values. For a few titles, book club editions may be the only hardcover editions available, and in those instances have higher values.

Ex-library editions are not considered desirable by most collectors and book dealers, and therefore are generally sold as reading copies and priced in the $5 to $20 range with a good dust jacket. Exceptions to this rule are books that cannot be found in any other condition.

Good condition means clean, sound cover and spine without breaks or furred edges, clean undamaged pages, all pages and illustrations tightly attached. Price adjustments should be made for fingerprints, small tears, or loose pages. Large reductions are made for broken and seriously damaged covers, loose and missing pages, torn pages, water stains, and mold. In the case of children's books, pencil and crayon marks are other common damages.

Series books often do not identify editions on the copyright page, and so collectors then have to depend on the **list-to-self** method. On the dust jacket flap, or on an interior advertising page in the book, titles of books in the series may be listed. If the book's title is the last title on the list, this is called a "list-to-self" book. (Obviously, if the title is the last book in the series, this method is not helpful.) Because this information is not 100% reliable, collectors and dealers refer to such a book as a "probable first."

A **rare book** is one that is extremely difficult to find, and the price is usually determined at the time of the sale. It will often depend solely on how much an individual collector wants the book. Auction prices can go into the thousands of dollars for a particular sale to a particular customer, but that price may never be paid again for an identical volume and is therefore not a reliable guide to future pricing.

Investments: Because of the fragile nature of paper and the "well-handled" condition of most children's books, most collectors acquire children's books for the joy of finding and owning them. Some of them may be excellent investments. Some may lose value. As we cannot guess which books will increase in value and which will decrease, we have in our own collections books that we acquired and love for their content rather than their potential monetary value.

Defining the Term, Finding the Clues

Because many popular children's books remain in print for decades, identifying first editions can be the trickiest part of collecting. Unlike collectors of modern firsts, the children's book collector cannot rely solely on the information found on the copyright page to identify a first edition. Many new collectors and even some experienced ones also are confused by the different uses of the term "first edition" by publishers and booksellers.

For collectors seeking only first editions of a work, the designation of "first edition" has come to mean a book that was printed during the first run of the press or the "first printing" in the country of original origin. So only a copy of *The Hobbit* printed in the United Kingdom in 1938 would be seen as a "true" first edition and later printings would be later "editions" from the collector's point of view. This same point of view was applied to the *Harry Potter* series, where first edition collectors paid higher prices for the first printing of *Harry Potter and the Philosopher's Stone* from the UK because this was perceived to be more valuable than the later Scholastic first edition of *Harry Potter and the Sorceror's Stone* published in the United States.

Unfortunately, for collectors who only want first printings, this information was not uniformly indicated by most publishers in their books until the 1950s. Even later in the twentieth century, specific printings of children's books were often unmarked or poorly marked, even by publishers who were very careful in marking their adult novels.

For publishers, the term "first edition" often means the first time that their company published an original work. The "edition" would not change until such time as the work was substantially changed, either in a change of text or a change of illustrations. So when J. R. R. Tolkien rewrote *The Hobbit* in the mid-1960s to better fit into the larger *Lord of the Rings* sequence, this 1960s revision was the "second edition" for his publisher. And, from the publisher's point of view, all copies of *The Hobbit* printed from 1938 until those 1960s text changes could be classified as part of the first edition, even though a collector would only consider the 1938 edition as the only "true first." Keeping track of printings or reprintings of a book was largely a matter of internal bookkeeping for publishers and many publishers just didn't bother to mark such information on the copyright page in a standard manner until well into the 1970s.

Booksellers often fall somewhere between collectors and publishers in their definition of first editions. Today, most sellers catalog books as "first editions" if that information is clearly stated on the copyright page. They may also add such information as "first edition, first printing" if that information is available on the copyright page. For books with no clearly stated information on the copyright page, the booksellers will generally look to other factors to identify first editions, but may or may not be able to identify the first printing. In this case, they may still label the book a "first edition" following the publisher's definition of that term (this is the text as it was first published with no substantial changes) but give no indication of printing, or use phrases such as "first edition, early printing." And booksellers may also use the term "first edition thus" to indicate a substantial change in a work such as the addition of new illustrations, change in printing format, new publisher, and so on. A few booksellers even stretch the term "first edition thus" to include reprints by another publisher (i.e., a Grosset & Dunlap reprint of *White Fang* becomes a "first edition thus"). "First American edition" or "First British edition" are also popular terms but may indicate that the book originally was published elsewhere first.

So when exactly is a first edition a first edition and how can you tell if your book is a first? Or how about determining whether a book was printed in the 1890s or the 1910s or even later?

In nineteenth century and early twentieth century books, the best ways to identify a first printing are by errors, incorrect text placement, changes in the binding colors, or other "points" of identification. Fan club publications such as *Oziana Bibliographia*, auction catalogs of well-documented collections, or other specialized reference material list these points for specific titles. Today, even a quick search through websites can turn up a number of collectors who have put up pages documenting the first editions in their collections.

Another useful clue to a book's age can be found in the publishers' advertisements in the back of a book or on the dust jacket. Early editions of a series book generally include advertisements that "list-to-self" (i.e., not going past the title on the cover) or list to the titles published in the same year as the first edition. Collectors should remember that many planned series, such as *Nancy Drew* or *Hardy Boys*, were often started with two or three books. Thus the first book in the series will show an advertisement for all the books that were planned for the first year of publication. Horatio Alger series, such as *Ragged Dick*, often carried information on future titles.

For some books, another good clue to age is the publisher's name. Although many publishers kept the same name for a century or more, some companies, like Scribner's, changed names or shuffled names as business partners quit or died. An *Oz* book with the publisher's name Reilly & Lee cannot have been printed before 1919, no matter what the copyright page says. Some basic information on name changes of major publishers can be found in our Publishers' Histories section.

Cover art can also help date books, especially those of the reprint houses like A.L. Burt, Grosset, Donahue, and Garden City. All of these publishers were very active in reprinting classic works of children's fiction. Many books from these companies (sometimes even using the original publisher's printing plates) show only the original copyright of a work, a date that may be decades different from the year when the book was printed by Burt, Grosset, Donahue, and so on. However, these reprint publishers would change the cover to appeal to the current generation of buyers as well as update ads and other material in the back of the book. If the girl on the cover is wearing a 1920s flapper dress and hairdo, the book wasn't published in 1905, even if the copyright says 1905. A note about a war bond drive in the back of the book may indicate a World War II printing, and so on.

British publishers began consistently distinguishing first editions from later editions with the adoption of the International Copyright Convention of 1957. Like all "rules" of publishing, there are exceptions. The *Amazons and Swallows* series seems to have been clearly labeled by its publisher, Jonathan Cape, from inception, although collectors do look at dust jackets and other information for verification of early editions.

Even after 1957, both American and British publishers were far more casual about identifying editions of children's books than works published for the adult market. So generic guides to identifying first editions may not apply to children's books brought out by a particular publisher.

Starting in the 1970s, American publishers adopted a numeric or alphabetic system such as 1 2 3 4 5 6 7 8 9 or A B C D E to identify printings. This information usually appears on the copyright page. In most cases, the "1" or the "A" indicates a first printing. The "1" was removed, as in 2 3 4 5 6 7 8 9, to indicate a second printing and so on. Sometimes publishers used numbers in a reverse pattern such as 10 9 8 7 6 5 4 3 2 1 or in an alternating pattern of odds and evens. In most cases, the appearance of the "1" or "A" still indicated a first printing, and a line starting or ending with the "2" or "B" a second printing, and so on.

Collectors can also date books through the appearance of publishing codes such as Library of Congress markings (see glossary for dates), ISBN, and bar codes. For example, ISBN numbers started appearing on book jackets or copyright pages in the late 1960s (see glossary for further explanation) and bar codes appeared even later.

Another obvious clue that something is not a first printing is the appearance of the Caldecott or Newbery medal on the dust jacket. These awards are always given after the book has been published and the stickers do not appear on the dust jackets until several months to a year after the first printing.

There are always exceptions to any rule and not all publishers adhered to the same system for all books. If the date of printing makes a significant difference in price, a careful collector should ask for an explanation of dating from the bookseller.

Regular browsing through bookstores and other people's collections can help a collector to get the different "feel" of the books published in the nineteenth century as opposed to those published in the twentieth century. The more examples that you see from a particular era, the easier it becomes to date books at a glance.

Following is an alphabetical listing of many publishers of children's books with general information on the company's history, name changes, and methods of identifying first editions.

Aladdin Books, Aladdin Paperbacks

A popular name for children's books, there is currently a British Aladdin Books (established in 1979) which publishes highly-illustrated nonfiction books for children and an unrelated Simon & Schuster division, Aladdin Paperbacks, which reprints hardcover originals as well as a limited number of original series and single titles. In the 1950s, Aladdin Books reprinted such Bobbs-Merrill nonfiction series as *Childhood of Famous Americans*.

Altemus & Company, Henry Altemus, Henry Altemus Company

The company began as Altemus & Company in 1842 under the ownership of Joseph Altemus. In 1853, Joseph's son Henry inherited the business and the publisher's imprint eventually changed to Henry Altemus (pre-1900) and Henry Altemus Company (post-1900). Under the latter name, the company continued into the 1930s, printing numerous children's series, fairytale collections, and some of the earliest American editions of *Peter Rabbit* in the *Wee Folks* series (ca. 1904). Author Cary Sternick has extensively documented the history of the company and how to identify first editions in *The Henry Altemus Company: A History and Pictorial Bibliography*. Like many Victorian publishers, Altemus did not define editions clearly and books are most easily dated by looking at such information as the company name and advertisements.

D. Appleton & Company, D. Appleton-Century Co., Appleton-Century-Crofts, Inc.

D. Appleton & Company was established in the early nineteenth century and had published their first juvenile title by 1841. In 1933, Appleton merged with the Century Co. (founded in 1881) to form the D. Appleton-Century Co. In 1948, Appleton-Century merged with the F.S. Crofts Co. (founded in 1924) to create Appleton-Century-Crofts, Inc.

Applewood Books

This American publisher reprints rare children's books such as early titles in the *Nancy Drew, Hardy Boys*, and *Tom Swift* series. These reissues are clearly identified as Applewood Books on the title page.

Atheneum

Atheneum Books for Young Readers began in 1961 under the leadership of editor Jean Karl. This New York publisher published a broad range of juvenile fiction by such award-winning authors as E.L. Konisburg, Ursula K. Le Guin, and Judith Viorst. Atheneum identified first editions on the copyright page "First Edition" or "First American Edition." They did not adopt a numeric system for printings until the mid-1980s. Atheneum continues today as an imprint of Simon & Schuster.

Atlantic Monthly Press, Atlantic/Grove

Atlantic Monthly Press was founded in 1917 as a book publisher for the authors and articles found in the *Atlantic Monthly* magazine. This publisher was bought by Little Brown in 1925, although it continued to operate under the title Atlantic Monthly Press. The company later merged with Grove Press (established 1951) in 1993. First editions were usually identified on the copyright page.

Beadle and Company, Beadle & Adams

This early American publisher of dime novels sold more than four million copies of its books during the Civil War. The company's style had a strong influence on such series writers as Gil Patten (pseudonym Burt Standish). By the late nineteenth century, the company operated under the name Beadle & Adams.

Blackie & Son, Blackie & Sons Ltd

Scottish printer John Blackie established his company in 1809, printing books for other publishers, and then began publishing his own titles by 1811. Various business partners and children came into the business, causing name changes from Blackie, Fullerton & Co (ca 1820s) to Blackie & Son (ca 1830s) to Blackie & Sons Ltd (ca 1890s and on). A related company, W G Blackie & Co, was operated by Walter Graham Blackie until it was eventually merged into Blackie & Son. Eventually, the company established the overseas subsidiaries Blackie & Son (India) Ltd, in 1927, and Blackie & Son (Canada) Ltd; and Blackie & Son (Australia) Ltd, in 1926. Many early Blackie books do not have a printing date indicated or may only show the date of the original copyright. Collectors generally rely on publishers' advertisements, inscriptions, or other factors to date books. The words "First published" followed by the year and no other information may indicate a first edition.

Blue Ribbon Books

American publisher Blue Ribbon Books created a number of novelty books during the 1930s and 1940s. According to some researchers, the company coined the term "pop-up" to describe the books of Harold Lenz.

Doubleday purchased Blue Ribbon and Triangle Books (which produced cheap editions of popular books) in 1939 from Reynal and Hitchcock.

Bobbs-Merrill Company

This Indianapolis publisher was founded in 1885 by two booksellers, Silas Bowen and Samual Merrill, and used the imprint, Bowen-Merrill Company. In 1903, the name was changed to Bobbs-Merrill. Early first editions may only show the month of publication on the copyright page. Starting in the 1920s, some books carried the words "first edition," and, in the 1930s, some first editions were identified with a bow-and-arrow symbol on the copyright page. However, for reprints, the copyright dates often refer to the original copyright rather than the year printed by Bobbs-Merrill. In general, this publisher was a reprint publisher, but they did issue first American editions of a few British series.

Bodley Head

This British publisher was first established as an antiquarian bookseller in 1887 and became best known in its early years for publishing The Yellow Book with illustrations by Aubrey Beardsley and James Joyce's *Ulysses*. In the 1960s, Bodley Head editor Judy Taylor created the company's juvenile line and championed such illustrators as Edward Ardizzone. The name was acquired by Random House in 1987 and is currently used as a children's book imprint. First editions of books are usually indicated by "First published" or "First edition published" followed by the date and no further information on the copyright page.

Bowen-Merrill Company

See Bobbs-Merrill Company.

Buccaneer

A reprint house, Buccaneer started reissuing a number of hard-to-find children's books in the 1990s. Their books are clearly marked, lack dust jackets, and generally are priced as modern reprints in the secondary market.

A. L. Burt

Founded by Albert Burt, this house issued many series, was considered a major rival of Grosset & Dunlap, and reprinted numerous "classics" of children's and adult fiction. Their best-selling children's books included the works of Horatio Alger, G. A. Henty, Edward S. Ellis, and James Otis. In 1925, Burt began reprinting the Elsie Dinsmore series in a new fifty-cents format and sold literally thousands of copies. Harry P. Burt sold the company in 1937 to Blue Ribbon Books. In 1939, Doubleday bought Blue Ribbon and the extensive backlist of Burt titles. Like Grosset, Burt books rarely indicated the year of printing (copyright usually refers to the original date that the work was copyrighted, not the date published).

Jonathan Cape

This British publisher began in 1919 as Jonathan Page and Company but changed its name to Jonathan Cape in 1921 after acquiring the backlist of the A.C. Fifield company. Best known to collectors for publishing such series as Swallows and Amazons for children and James Bond for an older audience, the company merged with Chatto and Windus in 1969 and later became part of a conglomerate that included Virago Press and Bodley Head. The entire group became imprints of Random House in 1987. Cape first editions are usually indicated by "first published" followed by the year and on other information on the copyright page.

The Century Co.

Founded in 1880s, this company merged with Appleton in the 1933. The copyright page usually shows the date of first printing as well as any successive printings. First printings should show one date only.

Chatterton & Peck

An early publisher of Stratemeyer's series, Chatterton & Peck's backlist of children series was acquired by Grosset & Dunlap in 1908.

Henry T. Coates

See Porter & Coates.

William Collins & Sons

Founded in 1819, William Collins & Sons published books by J. R. R. Tolkien and C. S. Lewis. The company was acquired by Harper & Row in 1990 and became part of the HarperCollins conglomerate.

Copp, Clark Company, Ltd.

This Toronto publisher issued the Canadian editions of several children's books and series. They often bought printing plates from American publishers, such as Reilly & Lee, and would make only minor changes to cover art and title page (usually substituting their name for the American publisher). Because Copp often had smaller print runs than the American editions, certain collectible titles like the early Oz books may be priced the same or higher than similar American editions.

Coward-McCann

Editor Ernistine Evans helped established Coward-McCann's award-winning juvenile line by publishing such author/illustrators as Wanda Gag (*Millions of Cats*, 1928) and Kurt Wiese. "First edition" or "first edition" followed by the year may indicate Coward-McCann first printings, but other documented first printings from this publisher simply show no additional printings on the copyright page.

Crowell, Thomas Y. Crowell

This New York publisher started in the 1870s with a series of reprints of poetry given the title Crowell's Red Line Poets. In the 1880s, the firm entered the Sunday School market by acquiring the backlist of the bankrupt Warren and Wyman. Early first editions varied, with the publisher using the words "first edition" or no additional printing dates on the copyright page. Starting in the 1940s, first editions were identified with a numerical code.

Cupples & Leon Company

A New York publishing house, Cupples & Leon specialized in series books and reprints of newspaper cartoons such as Buster Brown. The company was started in 1902 by Victor Cupples and Arthur Leon. By the late 1920s, company catalogs listed more than 240 books in 28 series including such titles as *Motor Boys* and *Ruth Fielding*. First editions were not designated from other printings. Periodically the publisher would update artwork on the covers to appeal to the current generation of buyers — it may be easier to identify a book's era from Ruth Fielding's hemline than the copyright page! Advertisements in the back of books or on the dust jackets can also help identify the date of publication.

Dean & Son, Dean & Son, Ltd.

This London firm adopted the name Dean & Son in 1846. The company was one of the first English publishers to make extensive use of lithography and chromolithography for printing illustrations. Starting in the 1840s, it began making movable and flap books for children. The movable books were often published under their own names such as *Dean's New Book of Dissolving Pictures*. According to an article on Robert Sabuda's website, the first "pop-up" ever published may be Dean & Son's *Aladdin & His Wonderful Lamp*, circa 1860, where the paper pictures were made to lift off the page by pulling a hand-knotted string (the company did at least four movable books in this format). Victorian books from Dean & Son are generally dated from inscriptions, company addresses, and other information.

J. M. Dent

This English publisher began printing children's books in the nineteenth century. Prior to the 1930s, Dent did not identify the date of printing. After 1929, books began appearing with the words "first published" followed by the year of publication — although like many British and American publishers, the company's dating of its children's books seems to have been much laxer than other lines.

Dial Press

The Dial Press was an offshoot of the *Dial Magazine* and began publishing books in 1924. In the 1960s, the children's book line was established and Dial went on to publish such leading authors as Judy Blume and to develop such innovations as board books for toddlers illustrated by Rosemary Wells. Eventually the juvenile lines were sold to E. P. Dutton and Dial Press became an imprint of the Penguin USA. First editions are usually clearly identified on the copyright page.

Dodd, Mead & Company (Dodd)

This publisher began as Taylor and Dodd in 1839 and, with the exit of John Taylor, became M. W. Dodd (for Moses Woodruff Dodd). Dodd's nephew Edward Mead joined the firm in 1870, which led to the name Dodd and Mead and later Dodd, Mead & Company. Mead wrote books for children and adults under the pseudonym Richard Markham and the company also published such series as the *Elsie Dinsmore* books. The first Dinsmore title was published 1867. The series lasted for 26 volumes, taking Elsie from childhood to old age, and sold over 5 million copies in a period of 70 years. The Dinsmore titles were reprinted by A. L. Burt in the 1920s. By the twentieth century, Dodd began noting second and later printings on the copyright page. If no such information appears, the book may be a first edition (like most publishers, Dodd seems to be more consistent in how it treated adult fiction than children's novels). The numeric system of identifying printings was adopted in 1976.

M. A. Donohue & Co.

This Chicago publisher generally did not identify the dates of its publications. They bought or leased printing plates of books first published by other publishers. Donohue also issued a number of reprints of Victorian children's series (see Goldsmith and Porter & Coates).

George H. Doran Company

George Doran, a salesman for Fleming Revell, decided to start his own company in the 1890s. Based in New York, he made an arrangement with the British company Hodder & Stoughton in 1908 to reprint its most popular titles for the American market. The company merged with Doubleday in 1927. Early first editions show a "GHD" symbol on the title page or copyright page. After 1921, the GHD symbol appears on the copyright page under the copyright notice.

Dorling Kindersley

Although established in 1974, this British publisher did not start distributing its distinctive white hardbacks in the United States until the 1990s. The DK illustrated books for children have huge print runs, making them easy to find in the secondary market for less than retail price. In 1999, DK wildly overestimated the demand for its *Star Wars* books, printing 13 million copies but only selling 3 million. The company was acquired by Pearson PLC and continues to publish such titles as *How the Universe Works*.

Doubleday

The company started as Doubleday, McClure & Co. in 1897 and later became Doubleday, Page & Co. (ca. 1900). In 1927, Doubleday merged with George H. Doran Company and became Doubleday, Doran. This New York publisher finally consolidated its various holdings as Doubleday & Company in 1945. Prior to the 1920s, a Doubleday first edition might have the same copyright date on title page and copyright page or a single date on the copyright page. After the 1920s, the company usually identified first editions on the copyright page. In the middle of the twentieth century, Doubleday reprinted its titles in cheaper editions through such houses as Garden City Publishing, Blue Ribbon Books, and Triangle Books.

E. P. Dutton & Company

Edward Payson Dutton opened his first bookstore in Boston under the name E. P. Dutton. The company opened a New York branch in the 1860s and eventually began publishing its own titles (an early success was *Life of Christ* in 1874). Publisher E. P. Dutton worked in the firm until 1923 (he died at the age of 92). In 1928, the publishing business was separated from the bookstores and became an independent company under the name E. P. Dutton and Company, Inc. Today, Dutton's Children's Books calls itself "one of the oldest continually operating children's book publishers in the United States." One of the division's biggest hits and continuing bestsellers is the *Winnie-the-Pooh* series by A. A. Milne. In the 1960s, the firm acquired the juvenile line of Dial Books. Dutton was eventually bought by New American Library and then became part of Penguin USA. Until 1928, Dutton first editions generally had a single date on the copyright page. After 1928, the words "first edition" or "first published" may appear on the copyright page.

Faber and Faber

This British publisher was founded in 1929 by Geoffrey Faber, who doubled his name because it sounded more established (but Geoffrey remained the only Faber in the company). This publisher soon became an essential part of the Bloomsbury literary scene with such notable writers as T. S. Eliot serving on the editorial board. The U.S. division of Faber and Faber was sold to Farrar, Strauss and Giroux. The British Faber and Faber continues to publish a wide variety of fiction and nonfiction books, including a complete line of children's books. Like many British publishers, Faber and Faber often used "first published in" followed by the year and no other information to distinguish first editions.

Funk & Wagnalls

This New York publisher began as I.K. Funk & Company in 1876 and became Funk & Wagnalls in 1890. The company became known for its encyclopedia (started in 1912) and dictionaries although it did publish children's books at various times. A Roman numeral I on the copyright page may indicate a first edition or the words "first published" followed by a date and no further information. In the 1970s, the company adopted a numeric system of identifying a book's printings.

Garden City Publishing Co.

This New Jersey publisher reprinted Doubleday's and other publishers' titles on cheaper paper for sale to those seeking a lower-priced book — similar to the type of printing done by book clubs today. Many of the Garden City reprints appear to have been made from the original publisher's printing plates and may not show the actual date of printing. Other Garden City editions may carry the date of publication in the artwork, on the frontispiece, or on the back of the title page.

Golden Press

In the 1940s, Western Publishing's Artist and Writer's Guild created the Little Golden Books line for New York publisher Simon & Schuster. A phenomenal success from the beginning, Western quickly decided that they could make more money if they controlled the books. So, in 1958, Western and paperback publisher Pocket Books established a partnership to buy back Little Golden Books. Golden Press was formed and placed under the control of former Simon & Schuster president A. R. Leventhal. By the early 1960s, Golden Press was selling more than five million books a year. Western bought out Pocket Books' interest and Golden Press became a wholly owned subsidiary in 1964. Golden Press generally uses an alphabetic printing code with an "A" indicating a first printing. See also Little Golden Books and Western Printing & Lithographing Company.

Goldsmith

In the 1930s, this imprint of the M.A. Donahue company produced cheap children's books for the five-and-dime stores. *Five Little Peppers* and *Heidi* were two of their top-selling titles. Goldsmith often tried out new series for their market, designing a colorful dust jacket and putting a series name on the spine. Some were successful, others include the first book only, and several, like the *Herb Kent* series, died after the second title.

Greenwillow Books

This publisher of young adult fantasy began in 1974 and did both original works and many reprints. Their reverse numeric system indicates printing with the "1" indicating a first printing for both originals and reprints. Read the copyright page carefully, as it often starts with the original copyright date, then the date when published by the original publisher, and then lists in small print below that the date of the Greenwillow copyright for reprints. This line is currently an imprint of HarperCollins.

Grosset & Dunlap

Alexander Grosset and George Dunlap launched their company in 1898 by buying the leftover stock of the bankrupt American Publishers Corporation. For the next several decades, cheap editions of popular works remained the mainstay of the company, whether through rebinding other publishers' sheets (pages of a book) in cheaper materials; buying up printers' plates to produce their own editions; or pirating the works of British authors such as Rudyard Kipling. The company's original name was Dunlap & Grosset, but Dunlap left for a brief spell. The company continued as Alexander Grosset & Co. until Dunlap's return in 1900 when the new name of Grosset & Dunlap was adopted. In 1908, salesman John May persuaded the partners to take over the children's line previously published by Chatterton & Peck. Along with C&P's many boys' books came several series by Edward Stratemeyer. From then until the 1970s, Grosset & Dunlap would enjoy enormous success with Stratemeyer's many series including *Tom Swift*, *Hardy Boys*, and *Nancy Drew*. Although called a reprinter of children's books in many histories of American publishing, Grosset & Dunlap actually printed the first editions of the majority of the Stratemeyer titles. The publisher kept the most popular series in print for decades, reprinting titles as quickly as they could sell them (and they sold millions). Following the death of the original partners and eventual decline of the Stratemeyer Syndicate, G&D sold the rights for the *Hardy Boys* and *Nancy Drew* series to Simon & Schuster in the late 1970s. Collectors of G&D books rely on advertisements, changes in binding, and dust jacket art to date their books. The copyright date only refers to the date of original publication and cannot be used to reliably date the work.

Hamish Hamilton Ltd.

James Hamilton served his apprenticeship in publishing at Jonathan Cape and at Harper & Brothers. The half-Scottish, half-American Hamilton established his own London publishing firm in the 1930s, converting his first name James into the Celtic Hamish for the company name. During WWII, Hamilton worked for the American Department of the Ministry of Information, employment that helped him keep the company solvent and obtain the paper (a scarce resource at the time) needed for printing books. Close friendships with many American authors prompted Hamilton to publish the first British editions of numerous American novels as well as expand to a wide variety of literary publishing. In 1965, Hamilton sold the firm to Thomson Organization (a Canadian media firm) but remained the managing director until the 1970s. The firm continues today as a division of Penguin. Like other British publishers, Hamish Hamilton often used "first published in" followed by the year and no other information to distinguish first editions.

Harcourt Brace & Company

Alfred Harcourt and David Brace founded Harcourt Brace & Company in 1919. In 1954, the company merged with World Book Company to create Harcourt Brace & World, Inc. In 1970, company chairman William Jovanovich renamed the company Harcourt Brace Jovanovich (HBJ). In 1993, the publishing division of the corporation went back to using the name Harcourt Brace and, in 1999, further shortened the name to Harcourt Inc.

Harper & Brothers, Harper & Row, HarperCollins

The two eldest Harper brothers published their first book in 1819. Although they'd started out as printers, they quickly realized the potential profit in publishing popular English authors for the growing American market. By 1833, all four brothers were involved in the business, leading to the name Harper & Brothers (who was Harper and who were the Brothers became a standard family joke). In 1962, Harper merged with the textbook publisher, Row, Peterson & Company and began using the imprint Harper & Row. From the late 1800s through 1911, this publisher generally used a single date on the back of the title page to indicate a first edition. From 1912 to 1922, the company used an alphabetic code to identify the first editions. After 1922, the words "first edition" appeared on the copyright page. For the Harper & Row imprint, "first edition" was printed on the back of the title page for firsts published in the early 1960s. Starting in the late 1960s, the company used a numeric code for printings which would appear on the last page of the text. In 1990, Harper & Row purchased the British publisher William Collins and became HarperCollins.

Harper & Row, Peterson.

See Harper & Brothers.

Heineman

British publisher William Heineman started his company in 1890 and published lavish gift books illustrated by Arthur Rackham. Upon Heneman's death in 1920, Doubleday bought a majority interest in the firm. Today, Heineman continues as a subsidiary of Harcourt Education, primarily publishing textbooks for the primary and secondary school trade.

Hodder & Stoughton

In 1868, Matthew Hodder and Thomas Wilberforce Stoughton formed Hodder & Stoughton. Hodder had previously been a partner in Jackson, Hodder & Walford (ca. 1861 – 1868). Although the company began by publishing religious tracts, Hodder & Stoughton expanded its catalog to include all types of adult and juvenile literature. During the Edwardian period, Hodder & Stoughton published many of the most lavishly illustrated gift books including *East of the Sun, West of the Moon* with Kay Nielsen's illustrations, as well as the first editions of J.M. Barrie's *Peter Pan* books. In the 1980s, Hodder bought the English rights to the *Asterix* comics from Brockhampton and continued to publish that series. Since 1993, Hodder & Stoughton has been an imprint of the Hodder Headline group. Like many British publishers, Hodder & Stoughton was fairly inconsistent in how it labeled first editons until the 1970s, when the practice of noting subsequent printings on the copyright page was adopted. The words "first published in" or "first printed in" with a date and no subsequent reprint dates may indicate a first edition in earlier books.

Holiday House

Holiday House has been printing children's books since 1935. This New York publisher commissioned new illustrations for numerous classic works ("first edition thus") as well as publishing original works. Many of the publisher's books have stayed in print for decades and the information on the copyright page often refers to the original copyright by Holiday House rather than the date of printing.

Henry Holt & Company

In 1873, Holt & Leypoldt became Henry Holt & Company. By the 1890s, the company had a strong textbook division as well as published a wide variety of other books. First editions should have no additional printing date on the copyright page or the back of the title page.

After 1944, the words "first edition" or "first printing" may appear on the copyright page.

Houghton Mifflin

Originally called Hurd & Houghton, Hurd retired in 1878 and Houghton went through a number of name changes as he changed business partners, finally settling on Houghton Mifflin in 1880. First editions may have a single date on the title page.

John Martin's Book

This publishing company was founded in 1912 by Morgan Shepard, who had previously written a newsletter for children and signed himself "John Martin." The hardcover publication was sold by subscription as a monthly publication for children and contained stories, puzzles, games, and various illustrations. Shepard hired a variety of freelance artists and writers for his books, and many later achieved fame in their own right. The values of the John Martin books vary according to the talent or later fame of the contributors.

Alfred A. Knopf, Inc.

Starting out as a clerk for Doubleday, young Alfred Knopf quickly decided that he could run his own business. In 1915, he persuaded future wife Blanche Wolf to help him start a publishing company. Until 1933, the first edition's copyright page or the back of the title page would have only a single date or no additional printing dates. After 1934, the words "first edition" may appear on the copyright page with no additional printing dates.

Lee & Shepard Company, Inc.

The company was founded in 1861. See also D. Lothrop & Co.

Frank Leslie

In the 1870s, Frank Leslie's *Boys Library Series* was a popular softcover series for boys, sold through newsstands. Following Leslie's near bankruptcy and death in 1880, his wife took over the business and legally changed her name to Frank Leslie (she also called herself the Baroness de Bazus in later years). Mrs. Leslie launched a number of new books under the Frank Leslie title. She scandalized New York society with her frequent marriages and divorces, and left an estate of $2 million in 1914 to Carrie Chapman Catt to promote the cause of women's suffrage.

J. B. Lippincott and Company, J. B. Lippincott Company

In 1827, thirteen-year-old Joshua B. Lippincott began working in a bookstore. By the 1850s, he owned one of the largest bookselling emporiums in Philadelphia and established his own publishing company under the name Lippincott, Grambo and Company. Grambo retired in 1855 and the name of the firm changed to J.B. Lippincott and Company. The publisher dropped the "and" in the name in 1885, becoming J.B. Lippincott Company. Until 1924,

Lippincott used a single date on the copyright page or copyright date one year later than the title page date to designate a first editions. After 1925, the words "first edition" may appear, or a numerical code, or the words "published" followed by the month and year.

Little, Brown and Company

Established by a pair of Boston booksellers as Charles Little and Company, this publisher then changed the name to Little, Brown and Company in 1847. Through 1929, first editions had only a single date on the back of the title page. Later first editions may be designated by the words "first edition" or "first printing."

Little Golden Books

Originally created for Simon & Schuster's juvenile division in the 1940s, this popular line of early books sold millions of copies of its titles from its earliest years. In 1958, Western purchased the Little Golden line and formed Golden Press. First editions of these books generally had an "A" printed on the first, second or last page. Sometimes the "A" is hidden by the binding. The authors of this book highly recommend Steve Santi's bibliography of Little Golden Books for any serious collector. See also Western Printing & Lithographing Company.

Longmans Green Co.

Established in 1724 in London, Longmans formed a New York branch in 1887. Until the 1920s, first editions generally had the same date on the back of the title page as the front. In the 1920s, the company switched to using the words "first edition" or "first published" to designate first editions.

A. K. Loring

See Porter & Coates.

D. Lothrop & Co., Lothrop Publishing Company, Lothrop, Lee & Shepard Company, Inc.

Founded in Boston in 1850, the company incorporated in 1887 as D. Lothrop & Co. In 1880, Lothrop bought *Five Little Peppers and How They Grew*, a children's book that went on to sell millions of copies. By 1894, the publisher used the name Lothrop Publishing Company. In 1904, Lothrop consolidated with Lee & Shepard. In 1947, the company was purchased by Crown. First editions may be designated in a variety of ways including no additional publishing dates on the copyright page.

Macmillan Company

In 1859, the British publisher Macmillan began distributing popular titles in the United States through arrangements with Scribner & Welford. In 1869, British bookseller George Edward Brett established a Macmillan office in New York. Following his death in 1890, his son George Platt Brett agreed to continue the office if the Macmillans made him a partner. In 1896, the younger Brett reorganized the American branch as a separate company under his control. Through the 1930s, first editions of the American Macmillan generally stated the month and year of publication with a single date on the copyright page. After 1936, the words "first published" may appear on the copyright page.

McGraw-Hill Book Company

James H. McGraw began working in publishing in 1884 and purchased the *American Journal of Railway Appliances* in 1888. At the same time, John A. Hill worked as the editor at *Locomotive Engineer*. McGraw incorporated his publications under the heading of The McGraw Publishing Company in 1899 and Hill followed with The Hill Publishing Company in 1902. Eventually, the two men, who shared a mutual interest in science and technology, joined their book departments to form the McGraw-Hill Book Company while continuing to publish magazines under their separate names. After the death of Hill in 1916, the remaining parts of the companies merged to form the McGraw-Hill Publishing Company and, in 1917, moved into the Hill Building on Tenth Avenue in New York City. Following World War II, the company expanded its college textbook department to offer textbooks for the grade school and high school markets. In the 1960s, the name was changed to McGraw-Hill, Inc. "First Edition" may be indicated on the title page for books printed after 1956 or 1957. Otherwise a single date of printing on the copyright page probably indicated a first. The company started using a numeric system to identify first editions and later printings in the 1970s.

David McKay Company

Like a young Horatio Alger hero, David McKay began working in publishing at the age of 13. Eventually, he founded his own company in 1882. The Philadelphia publisher issued a wide variety of books including both reprints and original children's books. McKay's son Alexander expanded the company's business into comic books, publishing both Walt Disney titles and books based on popular comic strip characters like Little Lulu. In the 1950s, the publisher would usually indicate subsequent printings on the copyright page. A numbering system was adopted in the 1970s.

McLoughlin Bros.

Scottish immigrant John McLoughlin established his New York printing company in 1828. He also wrote and printed sermons for children, which were eventually issued as the series *McLoughlin's Books for Children*. In the 1840s, the firm was known as John Elton and Co. for a time. In 1848, McLoughlin's sons took over the business and renamed it McLoughlin Bros. The company specialized in books for children, first issuing hand-colored picture books and later investing in new methods of printing. In 1869, the company established a major printing plant in Brooklyn and eventually employed a staff of 75 artists to create books and games for children. The company was sold to Milton Bradley in 1920 but continued to publish under the McLoughlin name. In the 1950s, revenues began to dwindle and company was sold again to Kushner & Jacobs. The firm eventually ceased publishing by 1970.

William Morrow and Company

Established in 1926, this New York publisher's books generally have no additional printing dates indicated on the back of the title page of first editions. Occasionally, the words "first printing" may also appear, followed by the year, and with no additional dates indicated. Starting in the 1950s and 1960s, subsequent printings or editions were clearly marked "Second Printing" or "Second Edition" and so on. First printings usually had no additional information on the copyright page. In 1973, the publisher started using a numeric sequence where the "1" indicated a first edition. The company was bought by the Hearst Corporation in 1981 and became an imprint of HarperCollins by 1999.

W. W. Norton & Company

The company's website proudly proclaims that Norton is the "the oldest and largest publishing house owned wholly by its employees." Founded in the 1920s by William Warder Norton and his wife Mary D. Herter Norton, the company strove to "publish books not for a single season, but for the years." The company eventually created a series of *Norton Anthologies* for teaching literature including the *Norton Anthology of Children's Literature* (see http://www2.wwnorton.com/college/english/nacl//index.html). The company publishes a line of annotated classics such as *The Wonderful Wizard of Oz* and *Alice in Wonderland*. W.W. Norton usually indicated first editions on the copyright page or with a numeric code.

Oxford University Press

This British publisher has had an American branch since 1896. In 1958, publisher Henry Z. Walck bought the American OUP's list of juvenile titles. First editions may have the words "first edition" on the back of the title page or may be designated by a single date on the copyright page with no additional dates. Collectors of the British *Biggles* series have reported a number of discrepancies in the labeling of first editions, indicating that OUP may have been more casual about its juveniles.

L. C. Page & Company Publishers, Page Company

This Boston company began in 1892. In 1913, it bought *Pollyanna*, a book that had begun as a serial in the *Christian Herald*. *Pollyanna* and her many sequels, published as the Glad books, cemented the company's financial success. Some estimates put the sale of the first book at more than one million copies. In 1914, the name changed to Page Company, but by 1923, the firm had resumed the L. C. Page name. Page also published other children's series including *Anne of Green Gables* and *Little Colonel*. Company founder L. C. Page often stated that the House of Page owed its long history to the success of *Pollyanna* and *Anne*. He died at the age of 86 at Page

Court in 1956 and the company was eventually sold to Farrar, Straus & Giroux.

Pantheon Books

Acquired by Random House in the 1960s, Pantheon Books continues as an independent imprint of the larger publishing conglomerate. First editions should be clearly marked for any books published after 1965.

Parents' Magazine Press

Many Parents' books were reprints (see also Weekly Reader's Children's Book Club) although the company did some originals as well as the first hardcover editions of works originally published in softcover. Later printings should be indicated on copyright page. A numeric system was not adopted until after 1975.

Platt & Munk

Founded in 1920 by a pair of former Saalfield salesmen, the Munk brothers, and investor George E. Platt, this company focused on colorful books for younger readers. House pseudonym Watty Piper accounted for a number of bestselling titles including the *Brimful Book* and the Piper edition of *The Little Engine That Could*. Although the firm's greatest successes came in the 1920s and 1930s, it continued to publish into the 1970s and eventually became part of the conglomerate that owned Grosset & Dunlap.

Porter & Coates, Henry T. Coates

This Philadelphia publisher issued first editions of several Alger titles as well as acquiring other titles from A.K. Loring. The firm also published other juvenile series. Formed in 1848 as Davis & Porter, Coates became a junior partner in 1866 and eventually the sole owner in 1895. In 1899, Coates began to let Hurst and Donahue reissue the popular but aging Alger titles in cheap 25-cent editions. In 1904, Coates sold the company to John C. Winston and that company took over the publication of Coates' extensive backlist of juvenile titles. Coates' first editions may say "published" followed by the month and year or have only a single date on the copyright page (however, collectors have noted a number of discrepancies over the years).

Prentice-Hall

Founded in 1913 by Professor Charles W. Gerstenberg and his student Richard P. Ettinger (they each used their mothers' maiden names for the company name), the company specialized in textbooks. Prentice-Hall eventually became part of the larger Pearson conglomerate.

G. P. Putnam, G. P. Putnam's Sons

George Palmer Putnam established his New York firm in 1848, publishing both books and magazines like many early American publishers. Financial difficulties forced Putnam to take a job as a collector of internal revenue in the 1860s, but his sons joined the business and the company continued. In the 1890s, Putnam's son, George Haven, was a major sup-

porter of international copyright laws to protect the rights of publishers and authors. France even awarded him a Cross of the Legion of Honor for his work. An American and a British Putnam's were established. The American company designated first editions by the words "first American edition" followed by the year or by showing no additional printing dates on the copyright page. In the 1920s and 1930s, some American books might also state "first edition" on the copyright page. By the 1950s, Putnam also used other systems. If the date on the title page and the date on the copyright page match, it is probably a first edition. Later printings may be indicated by such terms as "second impression" and so on appearing on the copyright page.

Rand McNally

This Chicago firm started in the 1870s as a publisher of business directories and maps. The book division was formed in the 1880s but didn't really start publishing juveniles until later. The *Elf* books and *Elf Junior* books were small books aimed at the same market as the Little Golden Books. Early first editions of Rand McNally chapter books might have the letters "MA" on the copyright page or would show no additional printing dates. After 1937, the words "first published" followed by the year or an alphabetical code might indicate a first edition.

Random House

In the 1950s, New York publisher Random House considerably expanded its juvenile list. The popular *Landmark* series sold more than six million copies in its first five years. Random House editor Bennett Cerf was a major influence on children's publishing in the mid-twentieth century, especially for his promotion of the works of Dr. Seuss and the creation of *I-Can-Read* books. This publisher used a variety of systems for identifying first editions of its children's books. *The Black Stallion* series clearly state "first printing" or subsequent printings on the copyright page. After 1968, the words "First Printed" or "First Edition" appear on the copyright page of many Random House books (and disappear from subsequent printings). The number sequence adopted in the 1970s, unlike that of most publishers, uses the words "First Edition" and a "2" in the number line to indicate first editions (the "1" never appears). Picture books published for the youngest readers may not have editions clearly marked, and collectors rely on advertisements or title lists to date these books.

Reilly & Britton, Reilly & Lee

The Chicago company Reilly & Britton published a variety of children's books and series, including the *Oz* series. In 1919, the company's name was changed to Reilly & Lee. Under the Reilly & Lee name, it continued to publish children's books into the 1960s. For any series book, the publisher's advertisements generally end with or before that edition's title. As both Reilly & Britton and Reilly & Lee, they rarely updated copyright information and most dealers disregard the information on the copyright pages when dating their books.

Roberts Brothers

In 1864, the brothers started publishing children's books as well as their popular photograph albums. In 1868, editor Thomas Niles bought *Little Women* by Louisa May Alcott, which inspired a number of sequels. Niles and Alcott had a long and satisfactory business relationship, partially inspired by Niles' early advice to Alcott to hang onto her copyrights and his highly ethical accounting of her royalties. Little, Brown bought the company and its titles in 1898.

George Routledge & Sons

This British publisher began printing children's books in the 1800s. They are rarely dated.

Saalfield Publishing Co.

Started in 1899 by Arthur J. Saalfield, this firm's early publishing success came from the *White House Cookbook* and other reprint titles. In 1919, Saalfield's son Albert started a children's book division and concentrated on issuing beautiful books to compete with the European imports. However, in the 1930s, the company entered into the "ten cent" trade along with Goldsmith, McLoughlin, and Whitman. The most successful of the Saalfield titles during the Depression featured Shirley Temple. The company also created a line of boxed books and picture puzzles for sale to the toy stores and variety chains. In the 1960s, Saalfield did very well with a Peanuts coloring book, but the company eventually went out of business in the 1970s.

Scholastic

Founded in 1920 by M.R. "Robbie" Robinson, the father of the current Scholastic chairman and CEO Richard Robinson, this publishing firm bills itself as "the world's largest publisher and distributor of children's books." It started out as a much smaller concern — the first Scholastic magazine was only four pages (although Robbie Robinson promised his readers that the next issue would be eight pages). Scholastic did not begin publishing books until 1926 when its first title was *Saplings*, which collected student writings from the Scholastic Writing Awards winners. The Awards program eventually expanded into the Scholastic Arts and Writing Awards, which has distributed more than $25 million in prizes and scholarships and has such distinguished past recipients as Richard Avedon, Robert Redford, Truman Capote, Andy Warhol, and Sylvia Plath, to name just a few. The first Scholastic book club was launched in 1948 and the company has since expanded its clubs and book fairs into an international enterprise that allows students to order inexpensive books and have them delivered directly to their classrooms. In the 1960s, Scholastic scored a big hit with *Clifford the Big Red Dog* books. In 1978, the company started the popular *Goosebumps* series and a number of other paperback series aimed at the middle school market. In 1998, Scholastic published the first U.S. edition of *Harry Potter and the Sorcerer's Stone*. J. K. Rowling's series became a publishing phenomenon with Scholastic selling more than

116 million copies of the first six titles by 2005. The same year, Scholastic also bought The Chicken House, a British publisher of such European fantasy writers as Cornelia Funke. First printings of the *Harry Potter* series and other recent Scholastic books are marked on the copyright page using a numeric system.

Scotts Foresman

This publishing company began in 1889. By 1911, it became the first textbook company for young readers to use four-color printing. In 1930, it began publishing the *Dick and Jane* series. Today the company is part of the Pearson conglomerate.

Scribner & Company, Scribner and Welford, Charles Scribner's Sons

This leading New York publisher had multiple name changes through the nineteenth century. In 1846, Charles Scribner and Isaak D. Baker formed a partnership and bought the publishing business of John Taylor. In 1850, Baker's death and the acquisition of new junior business partners caused the firm's name to change to Scribner, Armstrong and Company. Scribner and Englishman Charles Welford created a second company to import English books under the name Scribner and Welford or Scribner, Welford and Company. The Welford company operated during the same time as the other Scribner company continued to publish original works, primarily by American authors. In 1879, the Armstrong name was dropped in favor of Charles Scribner's Sons. In 1891, Charles Scribner's Sons absorbed the separate company of Scribner and Welford. Mergers and changes continued in the twentieth century, when Scribner mergered with Atheneum in 1978 and became The Scribner's Book Companies. In 1984, the firm became part of the Macmillan Company, which was later bought by Simon & Schuster in 1994. Currently the imprint survives as Scribner. Early first editions of Scribner's own books have a single date on the title page or no additional printings indicated on the back of the title page or copyright page. Starting in 1930, an "A" may be printed on the copyright page to designate the first edition. The company went to a numeric system in the mid-1970s.

Simon & Schuster

This New York publisher started in 1925 and derived its early success from a series of popular crossword books. In 1942, Albert Leventhal launched Little Golden Books, a wise decision that eventually led to him leaving Simon & Schuster to head up Golden Press. See also Western Printing & Lithographing Company.

St. Martin's Press

This publisher began as an imprint of Macmillan in the 1950s. First editions should have no other indication of an additional printing on the copyright page. Like many publishers, St. Martin's adopted a numeric system in the late 1970s.

Stratemeyer Syndicate

Not a publisher, but an important force in children's series books, the Stratemeyer Syndicate was started by Edward Stratemeyer. An early example of a book packager, Stratemeyer would design a series, coming up with titles, plot outlines, and pseudonyms, and then parcel out the work to a large stable of ghost writers. Following Stratemeyer's death in 1930, his daughters continued the company. The majority of Stratemeyer's lines were published by Grosset & Dunlap.

Street & Smith

In 1889, Ormond Smith entered the dime novel trade. This publisher issued a number of magazines and weekly titles. The books had soft cardboard covers, were about 4¼" x 6¼", about 250 pages, and printed on cheap paper. Popular series included the *Frank and Dick Merriwell* series, *Nick Carter* series, *Jack Lightfoot* series, *Young Railroader* series, and novels written by Horatio Alger and Oliver Optic. Popular stories were frequently repackaged into sturdier book formats. Street & Smith went on to become one of the largest publishing firms in the United States, launching a number of famous pulp magazines in the 1930s, such as the *Shadow* and *Doc Savage*, and later creating fashion magazines such as *Mademoiselle*.

Viking Press

In 1925, Harold K. Guizburg and George S. Oppenheimer established Viking Press. In 1933, editor May Massee started Viking's children's book division. First editions published prior to 1937 usually had no additional printing dates on the back of the title page. Later, the words "first published" or "first edition" with no additional printing dates might be used. Viking was an early supporter of the book club idea. Book club editions may have "first edition" printed on the copyright page and may only be identified as book club editions on the dust jacket (front flap).

Henry Z. Walck

Henry Z. Walck was the president of Oxford University Press in New York from 1948 to 1957. In 1958, he purchased Oxford's children's book division and began publishing under his own name. The company was sold to David McKay Company in 1973. Walck's first editions often show the original date on the title page and a matching original copyright date on the back of the title page. Reprints or later printings were noted on the copyright page. Books such as the *Moomin* series list the original date of the Finnish copyright, the date of original English publication, and reprint information on the copyright page.

Frederick Warne & Co. Ltd (Warne)

Frederick Warne began as a bookstore and then started publishing children's books in 1865. During its early years, the company worked with such notable Victorian illustrators as Kate Greenaway and Walter Crane. Frederick Warne's sons Harold, Fruing, and Norman took over the firm and were approached by a young woman named Beatrix Potter to publish her small book about a rabbit. The brothers agreed to publish *Peter Rabbit* (if Potter would provide color illustrations) and the book immediately became a bestseller with 20,000 copies sold in the first year. The youngest brother Norman became engaged to Potter but died in 1905, only a few weeks after their engagement was announced. Norman's brother Harold then became Potter's editor. Potter remained with Frederick Warne for more than 40 years — even helping the "old firm" when Harold was arrested on an embezzlement charge — and eventually willed all her rights to her titles to the publisher. Warne continues to publish all the books in the *Peter Rabbit* series as well as licensing merchandise based on Potter's artwork. Later reprints of its classic titles, such as the Beatrix Potter books, usually stated the date of printing on the copyright page. This publisher has been very inconsistent in marking first editions. Unless the printing is clearly stated on the copyright page, it is extremely difficult to distinguish first printings from later printings. In 1983, Frederick Warne was bought by Penguin and continues today as an imprint of that publishing conglomerate.

Weekly Reader's Children's Book Club

These book club editions show the original publisher on the spine, such as Doubleday or Scribner's, but are clearly marked in several places: back cover, title page, and copyright page. They are considered book club editions (reprints) by collectors and not true first editions, even when this is the first time that the book appeared in hardcover.

Western Printing & Lithographing Company, Western Publishing

As its early name indicates, this publisher started out as a printing plant. In 1916, the partners entered the publishing business when the Hemming-Whitman Publishing Company defaulted on its bills. As the bankrupt company's chief creditor, Western took the Hemming-Whitman's stock and started Whitman Publishing Company to liquidate the assets. As that venture proved profitable, Western continued to expand into the juvenile market. The company formed an agreement in 1933 with Walt Disney Productions for the exclusive right to create books based on the Disney cartoon characters. By 1935, the company opened a second printing plant in New York. In the early 1940s, the Artists and Writers Guild was started to serve as an early book packager. The editors would generate the idea for a book and then hire writers and artists to create it. An early and highly successful venture was the creation of Little Golden Books for Simon & Schuster. Western bought the Golden Books line back in 1958. Western also launched the Golden Key Comics. In 1960, the company went public and changed its name to Western Publishing. See also Golden Press and Whitman Publishing Co.

Whitman Publishing Co.

This Racine, Wisconsin, publisher was formed by Western Printing (see earlier listing). They issued the Big Little Books and the Better Little Books as well as a variety of series books based on comic strip characters or popular movie stars. The early Big Little Books had print runs of 250,000 and 350,000 with no reprints. By the 1960s, changes in endpapers indicate that Whitman would do more than one printing of popular titles. They also reprinted various children's classics. Like Grosset & Dunlap, the copyright date only refers to the original copyright of the material. Collectors rely on other information, such as advertisements and price, to date their books.

John C. Winston Company

Harvard graduate Winston launched his Philadelphia publishing company by creating a subscription book called *The Crown Book of the Beautiful, the Wonderful, and Wise.* Another successful subscription venture was a memorial edition of *Uncle Tom's Cabin* but the company depended on printing nearly 500 varieties of Bibles for financial success. In 1904, Winston bought Henry Coates' backlist of Alger and other juvenile titles and began bringing out its own cheap reprints. In 1940, Winston hit it big again with Eric Knight's *Lassie Come Home*, which sold more than one million copies in various editions.

Throughout the following listings, some book covers and illustrations are shown. To denote which images are featured, the corresponding listings are highlighted in light brown text. The following is an example of said highlighted listings:

Aesop's Fables and Picture Fables, George Routledge, undated nineteenth century, cloth with printed pattern and gilt lettering, about 350 pages, 10 color plates plus numerous b/w drawings, all uncredited: $40.00

──────────── **A** ────────────

AANRUD, Hans

AANRUD, Hans, *Sidsel Longskirt and Solve Suntrap, Two Children of Norway*

Sidsel Longskirt and Solve Suntrap, Two Children of Norway, John C. Winston, 1935, 257 pages, illustrations by Ingri and Edgar D'aulaire, first edition with dust jacket: $450.00

AARDEMA, Verna

Why Mosquitoes Buzz in People's Ears, Dial, 1975 (1976 Caldecott Award), over-size square hardcover, color illustrations by Leo and Diane Dillon, first edition with dust jacket: $50.00. First printing with 1976 Caldecott gold award sticker on dust jacket: $40.00

ABBOTT, Jacob (1803 – 1879), see Series section, ROLLO

ABRASHKI, Raymond, see Series section, DANNY DUNN

ADAMS, Andy, see Series section, BIFF BREWSTER

ADAMS, Eustace, see Series section, ANDY LANE FLIGHT

ADAMS, Frank, illustrator, see Series section, FRIENDS

Babes in the Woods, Blackie & Son, UK, ca. 1915, paste-on pictorial cover, 12 color plates by author: $125.00

Favorite Nursery Rhymes, Blackie, UK, ca. 1910, paste-on pictorial cover, six color

ADAMS, Frank, *Frog Who Would A-Wooing Go*

plates plus numerous full and partial page line drawings by author: $125.00

Frog Who Would A-Wooing Go (first published in 1904 by Blackie, Scotland) Dodge, New York, ca. 1912 edition, oversize, color paste-on-pictorial cover, color endpapers and illustrations by author: $45.00

ADAMS, Richard (1912 – 1988)

Tyger Voyage, Knopf, 1976, oversize hardcover, color illustrations by Nicola Bayley, 30 pages, US first edition with dust jacket: $60.00

Watership Down, Rex Collings, 1972, brown hardcover with gilt rabbit vignette, UK first edition with dust jacket: $1,000.00 and up

Watership Down, Macmillan, 1974, first American edition with dust jacket: $300.00

ADAMS, William T., see Series section, OLIVER OPTIC

ADDAMS, Charles (1912 – 1988)

Charles Addams' Mother Goose, Windmill Books, 1967, illustrations by Addams, first edition with dust jacket: $50.00

Nightcrawlers, Simon & Schuster, 1957, illustrations by author, first edition with dust jacket: $60.00

ADDINGTON, Sarah (1891 – 1940)

Great Adventure of Mrs. Santa Claus, Little, Brown, 1923, color illustrations by Gertrude Kay, hardcover: $50.00

Round the Year in Pudding Lane, Little, Brown, 1924, illustrations by Gertrude Kay, hardcover with dust jacket: $80.00

AESOP (ca. 620 – 560 BC)

Aesop, a Greek, collected fables which were later rewritten and translated into Latin, then modern languages. The stories have been printed as collections in single volumes and as picture books of a single story. Hundreds of variations available. A few examples include:

Aesop, one-volume collections:

Aesop: Fables of Aesop with the Life of the Author, Hurd and Houghton, 1865, small, leather spine and marbelized boards, 311 pages, illustrated with engravings by Herrick, first edition thus: $200.00

Aesop's Fables, undated ca. 1900 – 1915 Raphael Tuck, UK, oversize, dark cover with gilt lettering, color plates plus b/w illustrations by Edwin Noble: $65.00

Aesop's Fables, William Heinemann, 1912, limited edition of 1,450 copies, translation by V. S. Vernon Jones, introduction by G. K. Chesterton, oversize white hardcover with gilt, mounted color plates plus text drawings by Arthur Rackham, first edition: $2,000.00. Later printings ca. 1912 – 1916: $200.00

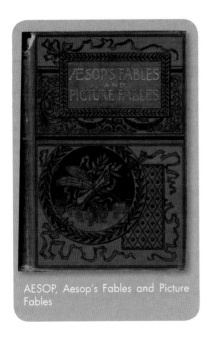

AESOP, Aesop's Fables and Picture Fables

Aesop's Fables and Picture Fables, George Routledge, undated nineteenth century, cloth with printed pattern and gilt lettering, about 350 pages, 10 color plates plus numerous b/w drawings, all uncredited: $40.00

Aesop's Fables: A New Version, Chiefly from Original Sources, Rev. Thomas James, M.A., John Murray, London, 1848, deco-

rated cloth hardcover with gilt, designed and illustrated by John Tenniel. First edition: $800.00. 1848 Collins reprint edition: $175.00

Animals of Aesop, retold by Joseph J. Mora, Dana Estes, ca. 1900, color illustration stamped on hardcover, b/w and color illustrations by Mora, first edition: $250.00

AESOP, Animals of Aesop

Big Book of Fables, Blackie, London, 1912, oversize white hardcover with gilt, top edge gilt, 28 color plates plus b/w illustrations by Charles Robinson, first edition: $1,000.00

Fables of Aesop, Hodder & Stoughton, London, 1909, oversize, cloth-over-board with gilt, oversize, pictorial endpapers, 23 tipped in color plates by Edward J. Detmold, first trade edition: $600.00

Fables of Aesop and Others, E. Walker, 1818, Newcastle, leather with gilt, top edge gilt, 376 pages, marbled endpapers, woodcut illustrations by Thomas Bewick and Robert Elliot Bewick: $1,000.00

Fables of Aesop and Others, W. Kent, London, 1857, oversize, pictorial hardcover, frontispiece and 22 engraved hand-colored full-page illustrations: $600.00

Hundred Fables of Aesop, Bodley Head, London, 1899, decorated hardcover, Sir Roger L. Estrange translation, b/w illus-

trations by Percy J. Billinghurst, first thus: $150.00

Some of Aesop's Fables, Macmillan, London, 1883, brown illustrated hardcover, 79 pages, illustrations throughout by Randolph Caldecott, first thus: $300.00

AIKEN, Joan (1924 – 2004), see also Series section, ARABEL AND WOLVES CHRONICLES. Aiken wrote more than 35 books for children and young adults and more than 100 books for all markets. Below is a sampling of some of the more sought-after, stand-alone titles and anthologies.

All You've Ever Wanted, Jonathan Cape, 1953, illustrations by Pat Marriot, first edition with dust jacket: $200.00

Bundle of Nerves, Victor Gollancz, 1982, first edition with dust jacket: $65.00

Kingdom under the Sea and Other Stories, Jonathan Cape, 1971, illustrations by Jan Pienkowski, first edition with dust jacket: $50.00

Last Slice of Rainbow and Other Stories, Jonathan Cape, 1985, illustrations by Margaret Walty, first edition with dust jacket: $50.00

Necklace of Raindrops, Jonathan Cape (UK) or Doubleday (US), 1968, illustrations by Jan Pienkowski, first edition with dust jacket: $45.00

Not What You Expected, Doubleday, 1974, first edition with dust jacket: $45.00

Smoke from Cromwell's Time, Doubleday, 1970, first edition with dust jacket: $35.00

Tale of a One-Way Street, Jonathan Cape, 1978, illustrations by Jan Pienkowski, first edition with dust jacket: $50.00

Touch of Chill, Victor Gollancz, 1979, first edition with dust jacket: $35.00

Whispering Mountain, Jonathan Cape, 1968, small hardcover, 237 pages, another "Hanoverian novel" loosely tied to the *Wolves* series, first edition with dust jacket: $50.00

ALCOTT, Louisa May (1832 – 1888), see also Series section, LITTLE WOMEN

Alcott's novels were written as individual novels, but gained such wide popularity that they are often added as individual titles to series or bundled into a series of their own, especially the books that contain the same characters.

Old Fashioned Girl, Little, Brown, 1915 edition, color plate illustrations by Jessie Willcox Smith: $75.00

Old Fashioned Girl, Roberts, 1870, Boston, hardcover with gilt: $150.00

ALDERSON, Brian
Cakes and Custard, Heinemann, 1974, oversize, color illustrations by Helen Oxenbury, first edition with dust jacket: $75.00

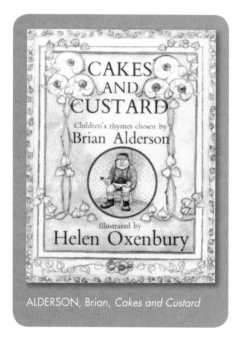

ALDERSON, Brian, *Cakes and Custard*

ALDIN, Cecil (1870 – 1935), see also Series section, FRIENDS

An English illustrator especially beloved for his animal pictures, Aldin is most collectible in the UK where many of his books and pictures remained in print for years or appeared in other mediums such as Royal Doulton's china. Pricing varies on rarity and condition of book, but a good rule of thumb is approximately $10 per color plate for any book illustrated by Aldin. A sampling of early Aldin titles includes:

Dog Day or the Angel in the House, Russell, 1902, first American edition, small, illustrations by Aldin: $125.00

Dozen Dogs or So, Scribner's, 1928 edition, first American edition, oversize, tan cloth-over-board hardcover, 12 color plates plus b/w illustrations by author: $110.00

Gay Dog, the Story of a Foolish Year, Willliam Heinnemann, 1905, oversize, 24 color plates by author: $250.00

Mongrel Puppy Book, Humphrey Milford, London, undated ca. 1900, oversize, illustrated paper-over-board cover, 12 color plates by Aldin: $250.00

Rough & Tumble, Hodder & Stoughton, 1909, paste-on pictorial cover, 24 color plates by author: $250.00

Spot, an Autobiography, Houlston, 1894, Aldin's first published book, 14 monochromatic illustrations: $200.00

Twins, Hodder & Stoughton, 1908, paste-on pictorial cover with gilt title, 24 color plates by author: $250.00

ALDIS, Dorothy (1896 – 1966)
Before Things Happen, G. P. Putnam, 1939, illustrated by Margaret Freeman, first edition with dust jacket: $90.00

Cindy, Putnam, 1942, illustrated by Peggy Bacon, first edition with dust jacket: $50.00

Here, There and Everywhere, Balch, 1928, illustrated by Marjorie Flack, first edition with dust jacket: $70.00

Magic City — John and Jane at the World's Fair, Balch, 1933, illustrations by Margaret Freeman, first edition: $50.00

ALDRICH, Thomas Bailey (1836 – 1907), editor of *Atlantic Monthly*

Story of a Bad Boy, Fields, Osgood, Boston, 1870, bound episodes of serialized story, hardcover with gilt, first edition: $350.00

ALDRIDGE, Alan, and William Plomer
Butterfly Ball and Grasshopper Feast,

Grossman/Viking, 1975, first American edition, pictorial hardcover, color illustrations by Aldridge: $30.00

ALEXANDER, Elsie M., see Series section, SUNNYBROOK MEADOW

ALEXANDER, Lloyd (1924 – 2007), see also Series section, PRYDAIN CHRONICLES, VESPER HOLLY, WESTMARK TRILOGY.

King's Fountain, Penguin Putnam, 1989, color illustrations by Ezra Jack Keats, oversize, first edition with dust jacket: $75.00

ALEXANDER, Martha, author/illustrator
Alexander studied at the Cincinnati Academy of Fine Arts, began her career as an art teacher, and for many years pursued a career in fine arts, crafts, and design. In 1968 she showed some of her light-hearted sketches, which she did for her own enjoyment, to an editor, and was asked to illustrate a children's book. At this point, Alexander has stated, she felt she had found her true calling. She illustrated a few books for others, then wrote many of her own, including the *Blackboard Bear* stories.

ALEXANDER, Martha, *Four Bears in a Box*

Four Bears in a Box, ca. 1980, Dial, 4x5 inch, four miniature hardcover books, each with dust jacket, in a box, color illustrations throughout. These are based on Alexander's picture books. Titles include *Blackboard Bear, We're in Big Trouble, I Sure Am Glad to See You,* and *And My Mean Old Mother Will Be Sorry.* Box with four books in dust jackets: $60.00

ALEXANDER, Theroux
Great Wheadle Tragedy, David Godine, 1975, first edition, purple hardcover

with pictorial paste-on, illustrated by Stan Washburn: $65.00

ALGER, Horatio Jr., see Series section, ALGER BOOKS

ALLEN, Betsy, see Series section, CONNIE BLAIR MYSTERY

ALLEN, Sybil & Roma Tomelty
Guardian Sword, Abelard Schuman, 1970, first edition with dust jacket: $70.00

Lissamor's Child, Abelard Schuman, 1973, first edition with dust jacket: $70.00

ALLINGHAM, William
In Fairy Land, Longmans, 1870, 16 color plate illustrations by Richard Doyle: $600.00

Fairy Shoemaker and Other Poems, Macmillan, 1928, illustrations by Boris Artzybasheff, first edition: $50.00

Rhymes for the Young Folk, Cassell, 1887, illustrations by Helen Allingham, Kate Greenaway, Caroline Paterson, Harry Furniss: $65.00

Robin Redbreast and Other Verses, Macmillan, 1930 edition, illustrations by Greenaway, Helen Allingham, Paterson, Furniss: $45.00

ALMOND, Linda, see Series section, PETER RABBIT

ALTSHELER, Joseph, see Series section, FRENCH AND INDIAN WAR, TEXAN, WORLD WAR

AMBRUS, Victor
Mishka, Oxford, 1975, oversize picture book, color illustrations by author, first edition with same-as-cover dust jacket: $85.00

AMES, Esther Merriam
Circus Put Together Book, undated ca. 1930s Sam Gabriel Publishers, oversize, red cloth spine, six double-page, full-color circus scenes, stickers to add to scenes. Uncut with stickers unused, price is $100.00

Patsy for Keeps, Samuel Gabriel, 1932, oversize, 95 pages, cardboard cover with color illustration, illustrated throughout by Arnold Lorne Hicks, oversize: $100.00

Tinker Town Tom, Rand McNally, 1925, illustrations by Arnold Lorne Hicks, color plate on hardcover, first edition: $150.00

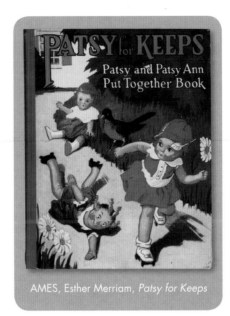

AMES, Esther Merriam, *Patsy for Keeps*

Twistum Tales, Rand McNally, 1929 color paste-on-illustration on cloth-over-board cover, b/w and full-page color illustrations by Arnold Lorne Hicks, first edition: $130.00

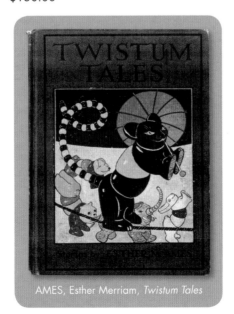

AMES, Esther Merriam, *Twistum Tales*

AMSDEN, Dora
Macaroni Tree, Hebberd, 1927, maroon decorated cover, oversize, blue tinted

plates by Joseph Paget-Fredericks, first edition with dust jacket: $50.00

ANDERSEN, Hans Christian (b. Denmark, 1805 – 1875)
The Hans Christian Andersen Museum in Odense, Denmark, houses many original manuscripts and artworks by Andersen (he was an accomplished papercut artist). This Danish writer's life story and much of the collection can be viewed over the internet. The statue of Andersen's *Little Mermaid* greets all visitors to Copenhagen's main harbor. Literally thousands of English editions of Andersen's stories have been published, with the most collectible being either the earliest known English translations or those with exceptional illustrations or decoration. Pre-1850 copies of Andersen's work in English are difficult to find, rarely in good condition, and prices can vary wildly. Pricing for pre-1850 editions is mostly dependent on the dealer's estimation of value and the condition of the book.

A sampling of Andersen's fairy tales, in order by publication date:

Wonderful Stories, Chapman and Hall, UK, February 1846, translated by Mary Howitt. This book is generally seen as the first major English publication of Andersen's fairy tales (Andersen liked Howitt's translations but had disputes with her over payment for her work), with four hand-colored illustrations, original cloth binding, listed in 2007 by one U.K. dealer for: $15,000.00

Danish Storybook, Joseph Cundalls of London, February 1846, translation by Charles Boner and illustrations by Count Pocci: $300.00

Danish Fairy Tales and Legends, William Pickering, UK, ca. 1846, translated by Caroline Peachey, rebound in contemporary leather: $1,500.00

Dream of Little Tuk, & Other Tales, James Moore and Company, New York, ca. 1848, or Grant & Griffith, London, ca. 1847, translated by Charles Boner (this translator released a number of "pirated" editions of Andersen's work), James Moore edition in publisher's original cloth binding: $1,250.00

Tales and Fairy Stories, George Routledge, London, 1852, translated by Madame de Chatelain and illustrated by Henry Warren: $250.00

Danish Fairy Tales and Legends, Addy & Co, UK, ca. 1853, translated by Caroline Peachey, "Enlarged Edition" with more stories than the 1846 Pickering edition, in original binding: $800.00

Hans Christian Andersen's Story Book, C.S. Francis, New York, ca. 1860, translations by Mary Howitt, in original cloth binding: $250.00

Ice Maiden, Richard Bentley, London, 1863, translated by Mrs. Bushby, illustrations by Zwerker, wood-engraved by Pearson, blue cloth binding with gilt decoration, first edition thus in original binding: $500.00

What the Moon Saw and Other Tales, Routledge, London, 1866, red gilt embossed hardcover, 372 pages, 80 wood engravings by A. W. Bayes, engraved by the Brothers Dalziel: $100.00

Collected Works of Hans Christian Andersen, Author's Uniform Edition, Hurd, Houghton, 1872 – 1878, green cloth-over-board with gilt, illustrations by Stone and Pedersen, 10 volumes. Complete set: $200.00

ANDERSEN, Hans Christian, *Hans Andersen's Fairy Tales*

Stories from Andersen, Hodder & Stoughton, 1911, oversize hardcover with gilt, 28 mounted color plates from drawings by Edmund Dulac, first edition: $650.00

Fairy Tales from Hans Andersen, Frederick A. Stokes, New York, ca. 1905, tan pictorial hardcover, 420 pages, b/w illustrations by Gordon Browne, first edition: $100.00

Hans Andersen's Fairy Tales, undated ca. 1900 – 1915, Raphael Tuck, UK, and David McKay, US, oversize, dark cover with gilt lettering, color plates plus b/w illustrations by Mabel Lucie Attwell: $150.00

Hans Andersen's Fairy Tales, Constable & Co, London, 1913, oversize, red cloth hardcover with gilt and paste-on-pictorial, 288 pages, 16 color plates plus b/w drawings by W. Heath Robinson, first edition: $250.00

Hans Andersen's Fairy Tales, undated, Doran, New York, orange cloth cover, 319 pages, 14 color plates plus b/w drawings by W. Heath Robinson, first Doran edition thus: $50.00

Fairy Tales, Hodder and Stoughton, UK, 1924, oversize, 197 pages, 12 mounted color plates with tissue guards, illustrated by Kay Nielsen, first UK edition: $600.00. 1924 Doran first US edition: $500.00

Fairy Tales by Hans Andersen, George G. Harrap, 1932, rose hardcover with gilt, pink and white endpapers, 287 pages, 12 color plates and numerous b/w drawings by Arthur Rackham, first trade edition: $1,000.00

Complete Andersen, Limited Edition Club, 1949, oversize decorated hardcover, translated by Jean Hersholt, hand-colored Illustrations by Fritz Kredel, six volumes in slipcase, 1,500 limited edition signed by the illustrator and the translator. Complete signed set of six with slipcase: $500.00

Andersen's Fairy Tales, Grosset, 1945, hardcover, color illustrations by Arthur Szyk, with matching slipcase: $70.00

Thumbeline, Simon & Schuster, 1985, ink and watercolor illustrations by Lisbeth

Zwerger, first edition with dust jacket: $80.00

Wild Swans, Horizon, 1988, illustrations by Naomi Lewis, first edition with dust jacket: $80.00

ANDERSON, Anne, illustrator

Fairy Tales of Grimm & Andersen, Collins, 1920, folio with 17 Anderson color plates, b/w line drawings: $900.00

Fairy Tale Book, Nelson, 1930 edition, oversize, blue with gilt lettering, 16 color plates by Anne Anderson, plus many art nouveau style line drawings: $350.00

Funny Bunny ABC, Anne Anderson, undated, ca. 1920, Nelson, oversize coloring book, color illustrated paper-over-board cover, 12 glossy color plates by Anderson of pictures, words and letters, with facing plain paper pages with b/w outlines of color plate illustrations, to paint or color, unmarked: $150.00

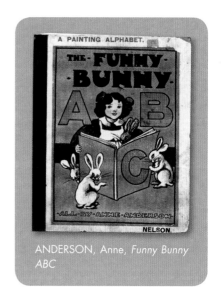

ANDERSON, Anne, *Funny Bunny ABC*

Rosie-Posie Book, Nelson UK, 1911, 12 color plates facing 12 poems plus b/w illustrations by author: $150.00

ANDERSON, Clarence W. (b. Nebraska, 1891 – 1971), author/illustrator, see also Series section, BLAZE

Horses were Anderson's major love, probably due to his Nebraska childhood, and most of this author/illustrator's work revolves around the beauty of having an equine pal. Anderson attended the Chicago Institute of Art, later working in New York and then Boston as a freelance artist. His series, *Billy and Blaze*, concentrates on a boy and his pony, but he also wrote novels for older readers such as *Afraid to Ride* (1957). He was a stickler for accuracy in his drawings and wanted his readers to understand proper horsemanship as well as horses from his illustrations.

Bobcat, Macmillan, 1949, illustrated by Anderson, oversize, first edition with dust jacket: $80.00

ANDERSON, Clarence W., *Heads Up – Heels Down*

Heads Up – Heels Down, Macmillan, 1964, hardcover, illustrated by Anderson, first edition with dust jacket: $30.00

Phantom: Son of the Gray Ghost, Macmillan, 1969, color illustrated cover, illustrated by the author, 86 pages, first edition with dust jacket: $125.00

Thoroughbreds, Macmillan, 1942, lithograph illustrations by author, first edition with dust jacket: $50.00

Tomorrow's Champion, Macmillan, 1946, oversize oblong, 74 pages, lithograph illustrations by author, first edition with dust jacket: $50.00

ANDERSON, Robert Gordon
Eight O'Clock Stories, Putnam, 1923, oversize, 269 pages, illustrated blue cloth-over-board cover with gilt lettering, full-page color illustrations by Dorothy Hope: $50.00

Half Past Seven Stories, Putman, ca. 1922, cloth-over-board cover, 251 pages, color frontispiece, two-tone plates: $35.00

Over the Hill Stories, Putnam, 1925, blue cloth-over-board cover, oversize, illustrations by Nina Ralston Jordon: $30.00

ANDREWS, Jane (1833 – 1887)
Seven Little Sisters Who Live on the Round Ball That Floats in the Air (1861, first published with author listed as "anonymous"), Ginn and Company, 1916 edition, cloth hardcover with gilt, b/w plate illustrations: $30.00

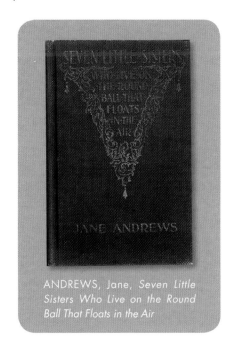
ANDREWS, Jane, *Seven Little Sisters Who Live on the Round Ball That Floats in the Air*

Ten Boys Who Lived on the Road from Long Ago to Now, Lee & Shepard, 1886, small, illustrated by Charles Copeland: $200.00

APPLETON, Victor, see Series section, MOVING PICTURE BOYS, TOM SWIFT

ARDIZZONE, Aingelda
Night Ride, Longmans Young Books, 1973, first edition, oversize oblong yellow pictorial hardcover, color illustrations throughout by Edward Ardizzone: $65.00

ARDIZZONE, Edward (1900 – 1979), see also Series section, TIM AND LUCY

Hunting with Mr. Jorrocks, Oxford, 1956, first edition with dust jacket: $100.00

Paul, the Hero of the Fire, Walck, 1963, b/w and color illustrations by author, US first edition: $50.00

Sarah and Simon and No Red Paint, Delacorte, 1966, oversize, color illustrations throughout by author, US first edition with dust jacket: $170.00

Stories from the Bible, retold by Walter de la Mare, 1961 edition, Faber, London, oversize hardcover, 420 pages, illustrations by Ardizzone, first edition: $100.00

Young Ardizzone, autobiographical, Macmillan, 1971, oversize hardcover, color illustrations by author, US first edition: $60.00

ARMER, Laura Adams
Dark Circle of Branches, Longmans, 1933, illustrations by Sidney Armer, first edition with dust jacket: $40.00

Waterless Mountain, Longmans, 1931 (1932 Newbery Medal), illustrated by author and Sidney Armer, first edition with dust jacket: $100.00

ARMOUR, Richard
Adventures of Egbert Easter Egg, McGraw-Hill, 1965, illustrated by Paul Galdone, first edition with dust jacket: $50.00

Animals on the Ceiling, McGraw-Hill, 1964, illustrated by Paul Galdone, first edition with dust jacket: $65.00

Strange Dreams of Rover Jones, McGraw-Hill, 1973, illustrations by Eric Gurney, first edition with dust jacket: $35.00

Year Santa Went Modern, McGraw-Hill, 1964, illustrated by Paul Galdone, first edition with dust jacket: $65.00

ARNOLD, Henry H., see Series section, BILL BRUCE AVIATOR

ARTZYBASHEFF, Boris (1899 – 1965)
Russian-born illustrator Artzybasheff began illustrating books in the 1920s. He illustrated more than 50 books before 1940.

In his later years, he worked primarily in advertising and magazine covers.

Fairy Shoe-Maker and Other Fairy Tales, Macmillan, 1928, b/w illustrations, first edition: $60.00

Poor Shaydullah, Viking Press, 1931, illustrations by author, first edition with dust jacket: $150.00

Seven Simeons, Viking Press, 1937, 31 pages, b/w illustrations, wood engravings by author, first edition with dust jacket: $150.00

ARUNDEL, Louis, see Series section, MOTOR BOAT BOYS

ASBJORNSEN, Peter and Jorgen Moe
East O' the Sun and West O' the Moon, Hodder & Stoughton, UK, 1914, color plates by Kay Nielsen, first edition: $2,500.00. Limited edition (500 copies printed, signed by Nielsen), auction estimates start at: $20,000.00

East O' the Sun and West O' the Moon, Viking, 1938, illustrations by Ingri & Edgar Parin D'Aulaire, oversize, with dust jacket: $300.00

ASHMUN, Margaret, see Series section, ISABEL CARLETON

ASIMOV, Isaac (1920 – 1992), see Series section, LUCKY STARR

Animals of the Bible, Doubleday, 1978, illustrations by Howard Berelson, first edition with dust jacket: $75.00

Isaac Asimov's Limericks for Children, Caedmon, 1984, first edition with dust jacket: $75.00

ASQUITH, Lady Cynthia
Treasure Ship, Scribner, 1926, oversize, color plates and b/w illustrations by several artists, an anthology of stories for children, first edition: $100.00

ASTURIAS, Miguel Angel (author is a Nobel Prize winner)

Talking Machine, Doubleday, 1971, oblong hardcover, color illustrations by

Jacqueline Duheme, first edition with dust jacket: $60.00

ATWATER, Richard (Richard Tupper, b. Chicago, 1892 – 1948)
Doris and the Trolls, Rand, 1931, illustrations by John McGee, first edition with dust jacket: $200.00

Mr. Popper's Penguins, Little, Brown, 1938, written with Florence Atwater, illustrations by Robert Lawson, first edition with dust jacket: $200.00

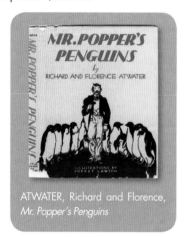

ATWATER, Richard and Florence, *Mr. Popper's Penguins*

ATTWELL, Mabel Lucie (1879 – 1964)
In 1905 Attwell began illustrating books and by 1911 she was illustrating cards and other ephemera for Valentine & Sons of Dundee. Her chubby children, like the Campbell kids in the US, appeared everywhere in Great Britain including more than 1,000 postcards as well as numerous plaques, posters, and other decorative items. In 1943 she began a comic strip titled *Wot a Life* for the *London Opinion.* Her publishers continued to use her artwork for birthday books, illustrated diaries, and annuals for many years. Collectors pay more for the earliest editions of her books and for work with numerous color illustrations. Like other British illustrators, her books command much higher prices in the UK than in the US market. A sampling of titles includes:

Boo-Boos and Santa Claus, undated Valentine, Dundee, hardboard cover, 16 pages with color illustrations and drawings by Attwell, Christmas story, first edition: $300.00

Fairy Tales (the "Attwell Kiddies" Story Book), Valentine, Dundee, undated, ca.

1922, hardboard cover, 16 pages with color illustrations and drawings by Attwell, a collection of classic fairy tales: $500.00

Lucie Attwell's Children's Book, Partridge, London, ca. 1930s, eight color plates, b/w drawings throughout by Attwell, collection of stories, individual volumes priced at: $250.00

ATTWELL, Mabel Lucie, *Lucie Attwell's Children's Book*

Lucie Attwell's Fairy Book, Partridge, London, 1932, 12 color plates and b/w drawings by Attwell: $120.00

Lucie Attwell's Tales for All Times, Partridge, London, 1922, color plates and b/w drawings by Attwell: $500.00

Mother Goose, Raphael Tuck, UK, and David McKay, US, undated, ca. 1900 – 1915, oversize, dark cover with gilt lettering, color plates and b/w illustrations by Attwell: $150.00

For more information on collecting Attwell:

The Collectible World of Mabel Lucie Attwell, John Henty, Richard Dennis Publications, 2001.

AUGUSTA, Josef
Book of Mammoths, Hamlyn, London, 1963, oversize tan hardcover, 92 pages, 20 color plates by Zdenek Burian: $110.00

Prehistoric Animals, Hamlyn, London, undated, ca. 1950s, oversize tan hardcover, 92 pages, 60 color plates by Zdenek Burian: $110.00

AULT, Norman
Dreamland Shores, poems, Milford, London, 1920, oversize, 83 pages, printed illustration on cover, map endpapers, eight color plates plus b/w illustrations by author: $250.00

AUNT ELLA
Wonderful Fan, Dutton, 1882, color illustrated paper-over-board cover, oversize, 96 pages, b/w illustrations: $35.00

AUSTIN, Margot (d. 1990), see also Series section, CHURCHMOUSE

Barney's Adventure, Dutton, 1941, oversize picture book, illustrations by author, first edition with dust jacket: $50.00

Manuel's Kite String, Scribner's, 1943, small, 112 pages, b/w illustrations by author, first edition with dust jacket: $30.00

Willamette Way, Scribner's, 1941, illustrated tan cloth-over-board cover, oversize, 42 pages, color illustrations by author, first edition with dust jacket: $35.00

AVERILL, Esther, see also Series section, CAT CLUB

Hotel Cat, Harper & Row, 1969, illustrations by author, first edition with dust jacket: $80.00

AWDRY, Rev. Wilbert, see Series section, THOMAS THE TANK ENGINE

■ ⋯⋯⋯⋯⋯ **B** ⋯⋯⋯⋯⋯ ■

BABCOCK, Havilah
Education of Pretty Boy, Holt, 1960, illustrations by Arthur D. Fuller, story of a dog and his orphan boy, first edition with dust jacket: $100.00

BACH, Richard
Stranger to the Ground, Harper, 1963, illustrated, first edition with dust jacket: $100.00

BACON, Peggy (1895–1987)
Ballad of Tangle Street, Macmillan, 1929, first US edition with dust jacket: $300.00

Ghost of Opalina, or *Nine Lives*, Little, Brown, 1967, 243 pages, illustrated by author, first edition with dust jacket: $400.00

Good Witch, Franklyn Watts, 1957, illustrations by author, first edition with dust jacket: $75.00

Magic Touch, Little, Brown, 1968, first edition with dust jacket: $60.00

BAGNOLD, Enid, *Alice and Thomas and Jane*

BAGNOLD, Enid (1889–1981)
Alice and Thomas and Jane, Knopf, 1931, illustrations by author and Laurian Jones, first US edition with dust jacket: $200.00

National Velvet, Morrow, 1935, film adaptation starred Elizabeth Taylor, first US edition with dust jacket: $500.00

BAILEY, Alice Cooper
Katrina and Jan, Volland, 1923, color illustrations by Herman Rosse, first edition: $70.00

Skating Gander, Volland, 1927, color illustrated cardboard cover, 93 pages, color illustrations throughout by Marie Honre Myers: $80.00

BAILEY, Carolyn Sherwin (b. NY, 1875–1961)
Finnegan II: His Nine Lives, Viking, 1953, tall hardcover, illustrations by Kate Seredy, first edition with dust jacket: $70.00

BAILEY, Carolyn Sherwin, *Li'l' Hannibal*

Flickertail, Walck, 1962, illustrated by Garry Mackenzie, first edition with dust jacket: $60.00

Li'l' Hannibal, Platt & Munk, 1938, hardcover with pictorial plate, b/w illustrations by George Carlson, first edition: $80.00

Little Rabbit Who Wanted Red Wings, Platt & Munk, 1945, color illustrations by Dorothy Grider, first edition with dust jacket: $50.00

Little Folks' Merry Christmas Book, Whitman, 1948, color and b/w illustrations by Eunice Young Smith, first edition with dust jacket: $30.00

BAILEY, Margery, *Seven Peas in the Pod*

Miss Hickory, Viking Press, 1946 (1947 Newbery Medal), b/w illustrations, lithographs by Ruth Gannett, first edition with dust jacket: $100.00

BAILEY, Margery

Little Man With One Shoe, Little, Brown, 1921, impressed cover, b/w illustrations by Alice Preston: $40.00

Seven Peas in the Pod, Little, Brown, 1919, illustrated cloth-over-board cover with gilt, eight b/w/green plates and numerous b/w line drawings by Alice Bolan Preston: $40.00

BAKER, Cornelia

Magic Image from India, Stern, Philadelphia, 1909, pictorial cloth hardcover, illustrations by Harry Lachman, first edition: $90.00

Queen's Page, Bobbs Merrill, 1905, hardcover, first edition: $50.00

BAKER, Margaret

Ilustrator Mary Baker received her childhood education at home in Runcorn, attended the Chester Art School, and took a correspondence course in commercial illustration. She is best known for silhouettes, drawn to illustrate her sister Margaret Baker's books. Her work also included magazine illustrations and watercolor landscapes.

Dog, the Brownie and the Bramble Patch, Duffield, 1924, silhouette illustrations by Mary Baker, first edition: $90.00

Dunderpate, Dodd, Mead, 1938, cloth-over-board cover, silhouette illustrations by Mary Baker, first edition with dust jacket: $60.00

Four Times Once Upon a Time, Duffield, 1926, silhouette illustrations on colored paper by Mary Baker: $60.00

Little Girl Who Curtsied, Duffield, 1926, cloth-over-board cover, silhouette illustrations by Mary Baker, first edition: $60.00

Lost Merbaby, Duffield, 1927, illustrations by Mary Baker, first edition: $100.00

Mrs. Bobbity's Crust, Dodd, Mead, 1937, illustrations by Mary Baker, first edition with dust jacket: $60.00

Patsy and the Leprechauns, Dodd, Mead, 1933, illustrations by Mary Baker, first edition with dust jacket: $60.00

Three for an Acorn, Dodd, Mead, 1935, cloth-over-board cover, silhouette illustrations by Mary Baker: $60.00

Water Elf and the Miller's Child, Duffield, 1928, oblong picture book, cloth-over-board cover, silhouette illustrations by Mary Baker: $85.00

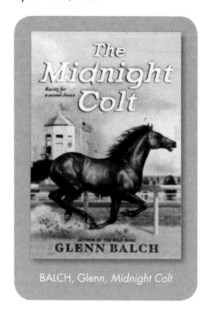

BALCH, Glenn, *Midnight Colt*

BAKER, Margaret J., see Series section, BEARS BOOKS

BAKER, Willard F., see Series section, BOB DEXTER

BALCH, Glenn

Christmas Horse, Crowell, 1949, illustrated by Pers Crowell, first edition with dust jacket: $70.00

Midnight Colt, Thomas Crowell, 1952, hardcover, illustrated by Pers Crowell, first edition with dust jacket: $40.00

Stallion King, Crowell, 1960, illustrations by Grace Paull, first edition with dust jacket: $80.00

Wild Horse, Crowell, 1947, illustrated by Pers Crowell, first edition with dust jacket: $70.00

BALDWIN, Arthur, see Series section, SOU'WESTER

BALDWIN, James (1841 – 1925), see also Series section, SCRIBNER CLASSICS

Titles include:

Sampo, James Baldwin, Scribner, 1912 illustrations by N. C. Wyeth, with dust jacket: $150.00. Without dust jacket: $75.00

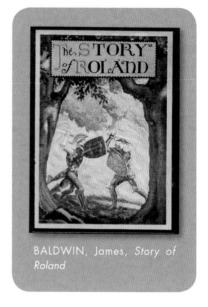

BALDWIN, James, *Story of Roland*

Story of Roland, Scribner Classics, 1930s, paste-on-pictorial, color illustrations by Peter Hurd: $70.00

Story of Siegfried, Scribner, 1882, illustrated by Howard Pyle, first edition: $150.00

Story of the Golden Age, Scribner, 1887, b/w plates by Howard Pyle, first edition: $200.00

BANCROFT, Laura (L. Frank Baum), see Series section, TWINKLE TALES

BANKS, Lynne Reid, see Series section, INDIAN IN THE CUPBOARD

BANNER, Angela, see Series section, ANT AND BEE

BANNERMAN, Helen (1863 – 1946), see Series section, LITTLE BLACK CHILDREN BOOKS

BANNON, Laura

Chicago artist Bannon exhibited at the Art Institute and ran the junior department of the school in the 1930s.

Famous Baby-Sitter, Albert Whitman, 1960, hardcover with paste-on pictorial, color illustrations by author, first edition with dust jacket: $40.00

Gregorio and the White Llama, Albert Whitman, 1944, color, b/w illustrations by Bannon, first edition with dust jacket: $50.00

Katy Comes Next, Albert Whitman, 1959, oversize hardcover, color and b/w illustrations by author, first edition with dust jacket: $50.00

Nemo Meets the Emperor, Albert Whitman, 1957, 48 pages, African boy meets the Emperor of Ethiopia, illustrated by Katharine Evans, first edition with dust jacket: $40.00

Patty Paints a Picture, Albert Whitman, 1946, color illustrations by author, 48 pages, first edition with dust jacket: $35.00

Watchdog, Albert Whitman, 1948, first edition with dust jacket: $60.00

BARKER, Cicely Mary, see Series section, FLOWER FAIRIES

BARKSDALE, Lena, *Milly and Her Dogs*

BARKSDALE, Lena

First Thanksgiving, Frederick Muller Ltd, UK, 1948, illustrated by Lois Lenski, first edition with dust jacket: $30.00

Milly and Her Dogs, Doubleday, Doran, 1942, paper-over-board cover, cloth spine, illustrations by Charlotte Steiner, first edition: $90.00

Treasure Bag Stories and Poems, Knopf, 1947, oversize, 159 pages, color illustrated paper-over-board cover, illustrated endpapers, color illustrations throughout by Maurice Brevannes, first edition: $35.00

BARNABY, Horace

Long Eared Bat, 1929 edition, Saalfield, 60 pages, color plates by Fern Bisel Peat: $65.00

BARNE, Kitty

Secret of the Sandhills, Nelson, ca. 1940, first edition with dust jacket: $50.00

We'll Meet in England, Dodd, Mead, 1944, illustrated by Steven Spurrier, first edition with dust jacket: $60.00

Windmill Mystery, Dodd, Mead, 1950, illustrated by Marcia Lane Foster, first edition with dust jacket: $70.00

BARNES, Elmer, see Series section, MOTION PICTURE COMRADES

BARRIE, James Matthew (b. Scotland, 1860 – 1937)

Alice-sit-by-fire (first published in 1919, London), a play, 1922, Scribner American edition: $35.00

Barrie, Peter Pan: The short work titled *White Bird* introduced Peter Pan, then the play appeared, then the play was rewritten as a novel. The titles are:

Little White Bird, 1902

Peter Pan, the play, 1904

Peter and Wendy, 1911

Peter Pan in Kensington Gardens, 1912

Barrie, Peter Pan, a few of the hundreds of editions, listed alphabetically:

J. M. Barrie's Peter Pan in Kensington Gardens, Scribner, 1932 edition, retold by May Byron, six color plates plus b/w illustrations by Rackham, 123 pages, first edition thus with dust jacket: $100.00

Little White Bird, Hodder & Stoughton, 1902, black and white frontispiece, "Child's Map of Kensington Gardens," Peter Pan character is introduced in this story, first edition: $300.00

Peter and Wendy, Charles Scribner's, 1911, green cloth, gilt decor and lettering, 13 glossy illustrations by F. D. Bedford, first thus: $60.00

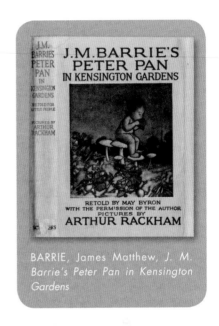

BARRIE, James Matthew, *J. M. Barrie's Peter Pan in Kensington Gardens*

BARRIE, James Matthew, *Peter Pan and Wendy*

Peter Pan, Scribner, 1962 edition, green hardcover, story of the play retold by Eleanor Graham, six color plates by Edward Ardizzone, first thus: $65.00

Peter Pan and Wendy, undated Hodder & Stoughton, "Published by Hodder and Stoughton for Boots Pure Drug Co Ltd." blue hardcover with gilt lettering, 272 pages, illustrated by Gwynedd M Hudson: $75.00

Peter Pan and Wendy, Scribner, 1921, green boards with design in black and gilt showing Peter and Wendy, a treehouse, fairies, 12 color plates plus b/w illustrations by Mabel Lucie Attwell, first edition thus: $400.00

Peter Pan in Kensington Gardens, Hodder & Stoughton, London, 1912, oversize green hardcover with gilt, 50 mounted color plates with captioned tissues plus b/w illustrations by Arthur Rackham, with dust jacket: $3,500.00. Without dust jacket: $600.00

Peter Pan's ABC, Hodder & Stoughton, undated, ca. 1915, oversize hardcover, gold lettering, oval pictorial paste-on, cloth spine, 24 full color plates by Flora White, about 55 pages: $125.00

BARRINGER, Marie

Martin the Goose Boy, Doran, 1932, color and b/w illustrations by Maude and Miska Petersham, first edition with dust jacket: $40.00

Four and Lena, Doubleday, 1938, color and b/w illustrations by Maude and Miska Petersham, first edition with dust jacket: $40.00

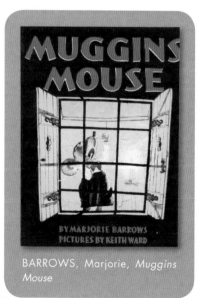

BARROWS, Marjorie, *Muggins Mouse*

BARROWS, Marjorie, see also Series section, GLOWING EYE BOOKS

Chip's Chums, Whitman, 1929, folio, 30 pages, color comic book style illustrations by L. K. Deal, first edition: $50.00

Ezra the Elephant, Grosset, 1936, illustrated endpapers, color and b/w illustrations by Nell Smock: $45.00

Favorite Muggins Mouse Stories: Muggins Mouse, Muggins Takes Off, Muggins' Big Balloon, Rand McNally, 1965, pictorial hardcover, illustrated by Anne Sellers Leaf, first edition: $30.00

Muggins Mouse, Reilly & Lee, 1932, 60 pages, oversize, color illustrations by Keith Ward, first edition: $200.00

One Hundred Best Poems for Boys and Girls, collected by author, Whitman, 1930, illustrations by Paula Rees, first edition: $200.00

Snuggles, Rand McNally, 1935, pictoral hardcover, photo illustrations by Harry Whittier Frees, first edition with dust jacket: $70.00

Who's Who in the Zoo, Reilly & Lee, Chicago, 1932, folio size, color and b/w illustrations by Milo Winter, first edition: $70.00

BARRY, Robert E.
Faint George, Houghton, 1957, oblong oversize picture book, red/b/w illustrations by author: $85.00

BARTHELME, Donald
Slightly Irregular Fire Engine — or the Hithering Thithering Djinn, Farrar, 1971, first edition, green hardcover, illustrated by nineteenth century engravings: $100.00

BARTRUG, C. M.
Blacky, McLoughlin, 1939, small, illustrated paper-over-board cover, illustrated by Charles Bracker: $35.00

Mother Goose Health Rhymes, Whitman, 1942, small oblong, 32 pages, illustrated endpapers, b/w illustrations by Marjorie Peters: $35.00

BARUCH, Dorothy
Day with Betsy Ann, Harper, 1927, b/w illustrations by Winifred Bromhall: $30.00

BARZINI, Luigi
Little Match Man, Penn, 1917, cloth-over-board cover with paste-on-pictorial, 164 pages, color plates by Hattie Longstreet: $50.00

BATES, Katherine Lee, *Once Upon a Time, A Book of Old-Time Fairy Tales*

BASKIN, Esther
Creatures of Darkness, Little, Brown, 1962, oversize hardcover, illustrations by Leonard Baskin. First edition with dust jacket: $65.00

BATES, Katherine Lee, editor
Once Upon a Time, a Book of Old-Time Fairy Tales, Rand McNally, 1921, oversize, cover with color paste-on-pictorial, color illustrations by Margaret Evans Price: $65.00

BAUM, L. Frank (b. Chittenango, NY, 1856 – 1919), see also Series section, OZ BOOKS

Baum wrote under several pseudonyms: Floyd Akers, Laura Bancroft, John Estes Cook, Capt. Hugh Fitzgerald, Suzanne Metcalf, Schuyler Staunton, and Edith Van Dyne. Series that Baum wrote under pseudonyms can be found in the Series section, see: AUNT JANE'S NIECES, BOY FORTUNE HUNTERS, MARY LOUISE, OZ BOOKS

American Fairy Tales, Hill, 1901, b/w illustrations, standard size, b/w illustrations by Ike Morgan, Harry Kennedy, N. P. Hall, with border designs by Ralph Fletcher Seymour, first edition: $500.00

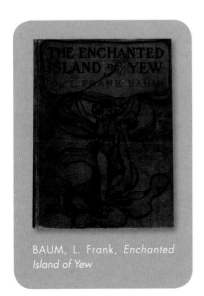

BAUM, L. Frank, *Dot and Tot of Merryland*

American Fairy Tales, Bobbs Merrill, 1908, revised edition, 16 color plate illustrations by George Kerr, first edition thus: $300.00

Army Alphabet, Hill, 1900, oversize, color pictorial boards, color illustrations Harry Kennedy, first edition: $2,000.00

Daring Twins, Reilly & Britton, 1911, first edition: $200.00

Dot and Tot of Merryland, Donohue, 1901, impressed illustration on cover, color illus-

trated endpapers and color illustrations throughout by W. W. Denslow, first edition: $400.00

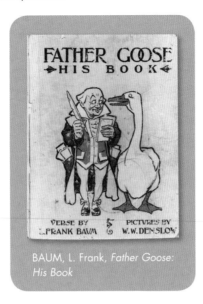

BAUM, L. Frank, *Father Goose: His Book*

Enchanted Island of Yew, Donohue, 1903, impressed illustration on cover, eight color plate illustrations by Fanny Cory, first edition: $500.00

Father Goose: His Book, Bobbs Merrill edition, 1903, hardcover, Denslow illustrations: $200.00

Father Goose: His Book, Donohue edition, 1913, Denslow illustrations: $150.00

Father Goose: His Book, George Hill, 1899, oversize, color illustrations by Denslow: $600.00

John Dough and the Cherub, Reilly Britton, 1906, color plate illustrations by John Neill, first edition: $400.00

Flying Girl (by Edith Van Dyne, a Baum pseudonym), Reilly & Britton, 1911, pictorial cover, 232 pages, four b/w plates by Joseph Pierre Nuyttens, first edition: $250.00

Flying Girl and Her Chum (by Van Dyne, a Baum pseudonym), Reilly & Britton, 1912, pictorial cover, 232 pages, four b/w plates by Joseph Pierre Nuyttens, first edition: $350.00

Last Egyptian, Edward Stern, 1908 (published anonymously), first edition: $200.00

Life & Adventures of Santa Claus, 1902 Bowen-Merrill, color plate and b/w illustrations by Mary Cowles Clark, first edition: $500.00

BAUM, L. Frank, *Magical Monarch of Mo*

Life & Adventures of Santa Claus, later editions with Clark illustrations: $85.00

Magical Monarch of Mo, Bobbs Merrill, 1903, illustrations by Frank Verbeck, first edition: $300.00

Magic Cloak and Other Stories: The Snuggle Tales, 1916 Reilly & Britton, first edition with dust jacket: $600.00

Master Key, Bowen-Merrill, 1901, standard size, paste-on-pictorial on hardcover, color plate illustrations by Fanny Cory: $200.00

Mother Goose in Prose, Way & Williams, 1897, oversize, b/w illustrations by Maxfield Parrish (first children's book for both author and illustrator), first edition: $4,000.00

Mother Goose in Prose, 1901 edition Geo. Hill: $300.00

Mother Goose in Prose, 1905 edition Bobbs Merrill: $200.00

Phoebe Daring: A Story for Young Folk, Reilly & Britton, 1912, 298 pages plus ads, illustrated by Joseph Pierre Nuyttens, pictorial cloth cover, first edition: $240.00

Queen Zixi of Ix, 1905 Century, 16 color plate illustrations by Frederick Richardson: $300.00

Bayley, Nicola, and William Mayne, *Patchwork Cat*

Queen Zixi of Ix, 1919 edition, Century: $90.00

Sea Fairies, 1911, see Series section, OZ BOOKS

Sky Island, 1912, see Series section, OZ BOOKS

BAYLEY, Nicola
Tyger Voyage, Knopf, 1976, glazed pictorial paper covered boards, illustrations by Richard Adams, first edition with dust jacket: $75.00

Patchwork Cat, Jonathan Cape, UK, 1981, Kate Greenaway Award Winner, glossy illustrated boards, illustrations by Nicola Bayley, written with William Mayne, first edition: $100.00

BAYNES, Pauline (England) illustrator
Baynes' illustrations of the *Narnia* series remain her best recognized work, but her career spans five decades now. Trained at the Farnham School of Art, she preferred classes on design to life drawing, and her work often has a very stylized look. Her first illustration job, J.R.R. Tolkien's *Farmer Giles of Ham,* 1949, brought her to the attention of C.S. Lewis (he liked the way that she drew the dragon). She received the Kate Greenaway Medal, the English

equivalent of the Caldecott, in 1968 for *A Dictionary of Chivalry* by Grant Uden.

BEAMAN, S. G. Hulme, see also Series section, TOYTOWN

Seven Voyages of Sinbad the Sailor, retold by Beaman, McBride, 1926, oversize, 70 pages, eight color plates: $45.00

BEATTY, Jerome Jr., see Series section, MATTHEW LOONEY

BEAUMONT, Cyril W.
Strange Adventures of a Toy Soldier, C. W. Beaumont, London, 1926, illustrated hardcover, color illustrations by Wyndham Payne, first edition with dust jacket: $100.00

BEE, Clair, see Series section CHIP HILTON SPORTS

BELASCO, David, and Chas Byrne
Fairy Tales Told by Seven Travelers at the Red Lion Inn, Benesch, 1907, b/w illustrations by George Bleekman: $100.00

BELL, Clare
Tomorrow's Sphinx, Atheneum, 1986, first edition with dust jacket: $50.00

BELL, Lilian
Land of Don't-Want-To, Rand McNally, 1916, cloth with a paste-on-pictorial, illustrations by Milo Winter, first edition: $50.00

Runaway Equator, Stokes, 1910, 118 pages, color paste-on illustration on cloth cover, b/w illustrations by Peter Newell: $50.00

BELLAIRS, John (1938 – 1991), see also Series section, ANTHONY MONDAY, JOHNNY DIXON, LEWIS BARNAVELT

Face In the Frost, Macmillan, 1969, hardcover, illustrations by Marilyn Fitschen, first edition with dust jacket: $45.00

Pedant and the Shuffly, Macmillan, 1966, 79 pages, illustrations by Marilyn Fitschen, first edition with dust jacket: $65.00

Revenge of the Wizard's Ghost, E. P. Dutton, 1985, dust jacket by Edward Gorey, first edition with dust jacket: $50.00

BELLOC, Hillaire (b. France, 1870 – 1953)
Belloc was educated at Oxford and a member of the British Parliament.

Bad Child's Book of Beasts, Duckworth, 1897, pictorial cover, illustration by Basil T. Blackwood, first edition: $200.00

Cautionary Tales for Children, Edward Arnold, 1908, illustrations by Blackwood: $75.00

Moral Alphabet, Edward Arnold, 1899, first edition: $100.00

More Beasts for Worse Children, Edward Arnold, 1897, first edition: $75.00

BEMELMANS, Ludwig (1898 – 1962), see also Series section, MADELINE

Austrian artist Bemelmans emigrated to the US to escape pre-WW2 Europe. His most famous work is his *Madeline* series.

Castle No. 9, Viking Press, 1937, oversize, color illustrations on every page, first edition with dust jacket: $500.00

Golden Basket, Viking Press, 1936, red cloth-over-board cover, illustrated endpapers, 96 pages, color and b/w illustrations by author. Newbery Award book, first edition with dust jacket: $200.00

Italian Holiday, Houghton Mifflin, 1961, oversize hardcover, illustrations by author, first edition with dust jacket: $60.00

Sunshine: A Story about the City of New York, Simon & Schuster, 1950, oversize, pictorial boards, illustrated endpapers, color and b/w illustrations throughout by author, first edition with dust jacket: $200.00

Welcome Home!, Harper & Bros., 1960, oblong oversize, color plates, based on a poem by Beverley Bogert, first edition with dust jacket: $100.00

BENARY-ISBERT, Margot (1889 – 1979)
Wicked Enchantment, MacMillan, UK, or Harcourt Brace, US, 1956, translated from German, hardcover with dust jacket: $45.00

BENCHLEY, Nathaniel, *Feldman Fieldmouse, a Fable*

BENCHLEY, Nathaniel (1915 – 1981)

Feldman Fieldmouse, a Fable, Harper & Row, 1971, 96 pages, b/w illustrations by Hilary Knight, first edition with dust jacket: $100.00

George the Drummer Boy, Harper & Row, 1977, first edition with dust jacket: $50.00

Small Wolf, Harper & Row, 1972, illustrated by Joan Sandin, first edition with dust jacket: $60.00

Walter the Homing Pigeon, Harper & Row, 1981, first edition with dust jacket: $50.00

BENNETT, Anna Elizabeth

Little Witch, Lippincott, 1953, hardcover, illustrations by Helen Stone, first edition with dust jacket: $50.00

BENNETT, Charles H.

Surprising, Unheard of and Never-to-Be Surpassed Adventures of Young Munchausen, Routledge, Warne, 1865, 12 stories, 107 pages, decorative hardcover with gilt lettering, illustrated by author, first edition: $50.00

BENNETT, Dorothy

Golden Almanac, Simon & Schuster, 1944, oversize, 96 pages, color and b/w illustrations by Masha, first edition with dust jacket: $50.00

BENNETT, John

Master Skylark, a Story of Shakespeare's Time, Century, 1897, first edition: $100.00

BENNETT, Rowena

Around Toadstool Table, Rockwell, 1930, small, 109 pages, cloth-over-board cover with color paste-on-pictorial, b/w illustrations by Lucille Holling, first edition: $50.00

Happy Hour Stories, Whitman, 1946, tall, pictorial cover, 382 pages, illustrations by Sally De Frehn, first edition: $80.00

Runner for the King, Follett, 1944, oversize, cloth-over-board cover, 48 pages, color plates by Fiore Mastri, first edition with dust jacket: $50.00

BENSON, E. F., see Series section, DAVID BLAIZE

BERGER, Barbara Helen, author/illustrator
Grandfather Twilight, Penguin Putnam Books, 1984, illustrated by author, first edition with dust jacket: $40.00

BERNARD, Florence Scott

Through the Cloud Mountain, ca. 1922, Lippincott, large, cloth-over-board cover with paste-on-pictorial, gilt lettering, eight color plates by Gertrude Kay, first edition with dust jacket: $300.00

BERRY, Erick (Evangel Allena)

Berry began her career with the Volland company, then illustrated children's books for Harper and Doubleday. In 1928 she and her husband, diplomat Herman Best, began collaborating on children's books based on their experiences in Africa.

Girls in Africa, Macmillan, 1928, first edition, 128 pages, color frontispiece and b/w illustrations by author: $50.00

Humbo the Hippo, Grosset & Dunlap, 1938, color illustrations on every page by author, first edition: $50.00

Mom Du Jos, The Story of a Little Black Doll, Doubleday, Doran, 1931, 116 pages, color and b/w illustrations by author, first edition with dust jacket: $250.00

Penny-whistle, Macmillan, 1930, decorated endpapers, illustrations by author, first edition with dust jacket: $100.00

Seven Bear Skins, Winston, 1948, 275 pages, b/w illustrations by author, first edition with dust jacket: $50.00

Winged Girl of Knossos, Appleton, 1933, illustrations by author, first edition with dust jacket: $50.00

BESKOW, Elsa, author/illustrator

Aunt Brown's Birthday, Harper, 1930, oversize oblong, color illustration on paper-covered boards, color illustrations by author, first US edition: $200.00

Aunt Green, Aunt Brown and Aunt Lavender, Harper & Brothers, 1929, oversize, color illustrations throughout by author, first US edition: $200.00

Buddy's Adventure in the Blueberry Patch, Harper, 1931, oversize oblong, color illustration on paper-covered boards, color illustrations by author: $65.00

Elf Children of the Woods, Harper, 1932, oblong, illustrated boards, color illustrations, 1932 printing with dust jacket: $500.00

Olle's Ski Trip, Harper, 1928, oversize, illustrated paper-covered boards, color illustrations by author, first US edition: $70.00

Pelle's New Suit, Harper, 1929, oversize oblong, illustrated paper-covered boards, color illustrations by author: $45.00

Peter's Voyage, Knopf, 1931, oversize, pictorial boards, printed in Sweden, illustrated in color by Beskow, first edition thus with dust jacket: $250.00. Without dust jacket: $100.00

Tale of the Wee Little Old Woman, Harper, 1930, oversize square, illustrated paper-covered boards, color illustratons by author, US first edition: $200.00

BEST, Herbert

Flag of the Desert, Viking, 1936, western Africa story, illustrated by Erick Berry, first edition with dust jacket: $40.00

Gunsmith's Boy, John C. Winston, 1942, War of 1812, illustrated by Erick Berry, first edition with dust jacket: $35.00

BESTALL, A.E., illustrator, see Series section, RUPERT LITTLE BEAR

In 1936, English illustrator A.E. Bestall took over the *Rupert the Bear* comic strip from orginator Mary Tourtel. He retired from drawing the strip in 1965, but continued doing annuals for the series until 1973. Bestall also illustrated a number of children's books from the late 1920s through 1950.

BETTS, Ethel Franklin, illustrator

Betts studied with Howard Pyle and illustrated stories for *St. Nicholas, McClures,* and *Collier's* magazines.

Complete Mother Goose, Frederick A. Stokes, 1909, color illustrations by Betts: $125.00

BETTS, Ethel Franklin, *One Thousand Poems for Children*

Familiar Nursery Jingles with Illustrations in Colors and in Black and White, Frederick A. Stokes, 1908, illustrated by author, first edition: $80.00

One Thousand Poems for Children: A Choice of the Best Verse Old and New, edited by Roger Ingpen, MacRae Smith, 1923, paste-on-pictorial cover, eight full-page color illustrations by Betts: $100.00

BIANCO, Margery Williams (1881 – 1944)

Hurdy-Gurdy Man, Oxford University Press, ca. 1933, small hardcover, 57 pages, illustrations by Robert Lawson, with dust jacket: $100.00

Poor Cecco, George H. Doran, 1925, pictorial endpapers, gilt lettering, illustrated with full-page color plates by Arthur Rackham, first edition: $150.00

Skin Horse, George H. Doran, 1927, 42 pages, b/w and color illustrations by Pamela Bianco, first edition with dust jacket: $150.00

Street of Little Shops, Doubleday, 1932, b/w illustrations by Grace Paull, first edition with dust jacket: $75.00

Velveteen Rabbit, Heinemann, 1922 (published under "Williams") oversize, pictorial paper boards, illustrations by William Nicholson, first edition with dust jacket: $20,000.00

Velveteen Rabbit, 1926 Doubleday edition, illustrated by William Nicholson: $200.00

BIANCO, Pamela, author/illustrator (daughter of Margery Williams Bianco)

Doll in the Window, Oxford University Press, 1953, square, color illustrations by the author, first edition with dust jacket: $90.00

Little Houses Far Away, Oxford University Press, 1951, 87 pages, b/w illustrations by author, first edition with dust jacket: $60.00

Starlit Journey, Macmillan, 1933, color illustrations by author, first edition with dust jacket: $60.00

Valentine Party, J. B. Lippincott, 1954, color illustrations by the author, first edition with dust jacket: $65.00

BIGHAM, Madge A.

Merry Animal Tales, Little, Brown, 1906, illustrated yellow boards, 200+ pages,

illustrations by Clara Atwood, first edition: $80.00

Overheard in Fairyland, Little, Brown, 1909, green cloth-over-board cover with illustration, gilt lettering on spine, 238 pages, frontispiece, color illustrations throughout by Ruth S. Clements: $60.00

Sonny Elephant, Little, Brown, 1930, cloth-over-board cover, color illustrations by Berta and Elmer Hader, first edition with dust jacket: $150.00

BINGHAM, Clifton, *Let's Pretend*

BINGHAM, Clifton

All Sorts of Comical Cats, Lister, 1902, oversize, cloth spine, pictorial paper-over-board cover, chromolith frontispiece and two-color illustrations throughout by Louis Wain: $450.00

Let's Pretend, Nister, 1859, oversize illustrated boards with cloth spine, b/w and color illustrations by Edith Cubitt, first edition: $400.00

Whirligig Pictures (undated nineteenth century), Nister, London, oversize, pictorial boards, illustrations with Hilda Robinson, 16 pages, six full-page rotating moveable plates with alternating images, first edition and still has dust jacket: $1,000.00

BIRCH, Reginald Bathurst (1856 – 1943)

A prolific illustrator for *St. Nicholas* magazine, Reginald Birch earned the nickname "the children's Gibson" for his detailed pen-and-ink drawings. Like his contemporary Charles Dana Gibson, Birch illustrated a number of novels, including the first edition of *Little Lord Fauntleroy*. His pictures of Fauntleroy were so popular with the

BISHOP, Claire Huchet, *Five Chinese Brothers*

Victorian audience that Scribner later commissioned additional drawings in color for later editions.

BISHOP, Claire Huchet (1899 – 1993)

All Alone, Viking Press, 1953, illustrated endpapers, b/w illustrations by Feodor Rojankovsky, first edition with dust jacket: $50.00

Blue Spring Farm, Viking Press, 1948, jacket and endpapers by Eileen Evans, 183 pages, illustrated boards, music camp in the summer, first edition with dust jacket: $30.00

Five Chinese Brothers, Coward-McCann, 1938, standard size oblong, b/w/yellow illustrations by Kurt Wiese: $50.00

Man Who Lost His Head, Viking Press, 1942, oblong, b/w illustrations by Robert McCloskey, first edition with dust jacket: $120.00

Pancakes-Paris, Viking Press, 1947 (Newbery Honor book, first printing has no award medal on dust jacket), illustrated by Georges Schreiber, first edition with dust jacket: $100.00

BISHOP, Elizabeth

Ballad of the Burglar of Babylon, Farrar, 1968, first edition, hardcover, woodcut color illustrations by Ann Grifalconi: $100.00

BISHOP, Giles, see Series section, UNITED STATES MARINE

BLAINE, John L., see Series section, RICK BRANT

BLAIR, Walter

Tall Tale America, 1944, Coward, illustrated by Glen Rounds: $40.00

BLAKE, Quentin

In 1999, British illustrator Quentin Blake became the first Children's Laureate of Great Britain. Blake lists his major influences as the French illustrator and cartoonist, Honore Daumier, and the English humor magazine, *Punch.* He received his training at the Chelsea School of Art and later became an instructor at the Royal College of Art in London. In collaboration with Russell Hoban, Blake received the Whitbread Literary Award for the picture book, *How Tom Beat Captain Najork and His Hired Sportsmen* (1974). In the late 1970s, he started illustrating the works of Roald Dahl.

Angelo, Jonathan Cape, 1970, oversize pictorial cover, illustrations by Blake, first edition with dust jacket: $200.00

Quentin Blake's ABC, Jonathan Cape, 1988, pictorial boards, first edition: $40.00

BLAKE, Quentin, *Angelo*

BLAND, R. Nesbit

Bunny Tales, ca. 1905, Nister, cloth cover, small, 64 pages, color and b/w illustrations by Edith Cubitt, first edition: $100.00

BLISH, James, see Series section, CITIES IN FLIGHT

BLODGETT, Mabel F.

Magic Slippers, Little, Brown, 1917, small, illustrated cloth-over-board cover, color and b/w illustrations by author, first edition: $40.00

BLUMBERG, Fannie Burgheim

Rowena Teena Tot, Albert Whitman, Chicago, 1934, illustrated in color by Mary Grosjean, Thanksgiving tale, pasted-on pictorial front panel, 32 pages, first edition: $100.00

BLUMBERG, Fannie Burgheim, *Rowena Teena Tot and the Blackberries*

Rowena Teena Tot and the Blackberries, Whitman, 1934, 32 pages, paste-on-pictorial cover, color endpapers, color illustrations by Mary Grosjean, first edition: $100.00

Rowena Teena Tot and the Runaway Turkey, Whitman, 1936, 32 pages, paste-on-pictorial cover, color endpapers, color illustrations by Mary Grosjean, first edition: $100.00

BLUME, Judy

Blubber, Bradbury Press, 1974, first edition with dust jacket: $150.00

Otherwise Known as Sheila the Great, E. P. Dutton, 1972 hardcover, 118 pages, first edition illustration by Roy Doty: $75.00

Pain and the Great One, Bradbury Press, 1984, oversize, first edition with dust jacket: $100.00

BLYTON, Enid (1897 – 1968), see Series section, ADVENTURE, FAMOUS FIVE, FIVE FIND-OUTERS, MALORY TOWERS, MR. TWIDDLE, ST. CLARE

Enid Blyton's Treasury, Evans Brothers, 1947, published for Boot's Pure Drug Co., cloth-over-board cover, oversize, color and b/w illustrations: $35.00

Little Girl at Capernaum, Lutterworth, 1948, color and b/w illustrations by Elsie Walker, first edition with dust jacket: $30.00

Silver and Gold, undated, Nelson, ca. 1927, hardcover with paste-on-pictorial, eight color plates by Ethel Everett: $35.00

BODECKER, N. M., Denmark, author/illustrator

Bodecker studied architecture and economics in Copenhagen, and art at the School of Applied Arts, Copenhagen. He began his career as a writer, on staff at a magazine and freelancing to newspapers, which led to cartooning and then to illustrating. His illustrations appear in children's books and in magazines. In 1972 he was named as one of the ten best illustrators by the *New York Times* for his own book, *Miss Jaster's Garden.*

BODECKER, N. M., *Miss Jaster's Garden*

Hurry, Hurry Mary Dear and Other Nonsense Poems, J. M. Dent & Sons,

London, 1979, 118 pages, b/w illustrations, UK edition with dust jacket: $60.00

It's Raining Said John Twaining — Danish Nursery Rhymes, Atheneum, 1973, first edition with dust jacket: $50.00

Let's Marry Said the Cherry and Other Nonsense Poems, Atheneum, 1974, US first edition with dust jacket: $70.00

Miss Jaster's Garden, Western Publishing, oversize Golden Book, 1972, color illustrated paper-over-board cover, map endpapers, 29 pages, color illustrations throughout by author, first US edition: $65.00

BOND, Michael, see Series section, OLGA DA POLGA, PADDINGTON BEAR, THURSDAY

BOND, Susan McDonald
Tale of a Red Tempered Viking, Grove Press, 1968, first edition, hardcover, illustrated endpapers, illustrations by Sally Trinkle: $50.00

BONHAM, Frank, see Series section, DOGTOWN

BONNER, Mary Graham
Daddy's Bedtime Fairy Stories, Frederick A. Stokes, 1916, illustrated by Florence Choate and Elizabeth Curtis, oval color paste-on-illustration on both cover and dust jacket, first edition with dust jacket: $100.00

BONNER, Mary Graham, *Rainbow at Night*

Madam Red Apple, Milton Bradley, 1929, color plates by Janet Laura Scott, first edition with dust jacket: $70.00

Magic Map, Macaulay, 1927, 238 pages, color frontispiece and 16 blue/b/w illustrations, first edition with dust jacket: $100.00

Miss Angelina Adorable, Milton Bradley, 1928, illustrations by Janet Laura Scott, first edition with dust jacket: $150.00

Mrs. Cucumber Green, Milton Bradley, 1927, color plates by Janet Laura Scott, first edition: $100.00

Rainbow at Night, Lee Furman, 1936, first edition with dust jacket: $50.00

BONTEMPS, Arna Wendell (1902 – 1973)
Golden Slippers: An Anthology of Negro Poetry for Young Readers, Harper & Row, 1941, drawings by Henrietta Bruce Sharon, first edition with dust jacket: $50.00

Lonesome Boy, Houghton Mifflin, 1955, b/w illustrations by Feliks Topolski, first edition with dust jacket: $80.00

BOOTH, Maud Ballington
Sleepy-Time Stories (1899), 1905 edition, Putnam, cloth-over-board cover with impressed gilt design, 17 b/w plates by Maud Humphrey: $100.00

Twilight Fairy Tales, Putnam, 1906, gilt page edge, 16 color plates by Amy Carol Rand: $40.00

BOSSCHERE, Jean de
Christmas Tales of Flanders, Dodd, Mead, 1917, 12 full-page color plates, pictorial endpapers by author, US first edition: $70.00

Folk Tales of Flanders, Dodd, Mead, 1918, gilt lettering on cover, illustrations by author, US first edition: $70.00

Weird Islands, McBride, 1922, 210 pages, illustrated cover, color frontispiece, b/w illustrations by author: $30.00

BOSTON, L. M. (1892 – 1990), see also Series section, GREEN KNOWE

Memory in a House, Macmillan, 1973, first American edition, hardcover with gilt, 142 pages, illustrated from drawn plans and photographs: $50.00

BOVA, Ben, see Series section, EXILES TRILOGY

BOWEN, Sidney, see Series section, RED RANDALL

BOYD, James
Drums, Scribner, 1928, 14 color plates by N.C. Wyeth, first edition: $150.00

BOYLAN, Grace Duffie (1862 – 1935)
Kids of Many Colors, Hurst, 1901, 157 pages, color illustrations by Ike Morgan: $100.00

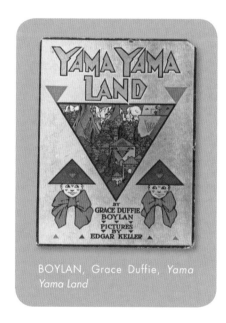

BOYLAN, Grace Duffie, *Yama Yama Land*

Pipes of Clovis: A Fairy Romance of the Twelfth Century, Little, Brown, 1913, pictorial cover, four color plates by Emily Hall Chamberlin, first edition: $40.00

Steps to Nowhere, 1910, color paste-on-pictorial cover, illustrations by Ike Morgan: $50.00

Yama Yama Land, Reilly & Britton, 1909, b/w and two-color and full color, including two double-page color plate illustrations by Edgar Keller: $150.00

Young Folk's Uncle Tom's Cabin, Jamieson-Higgins, 1901, cloth-over-board cover, illustrations by Ike Morgan: $100.00

BOYLAN, Grace Duffie, *Illustration from Yama Yama Land*

BOYLE, Eleanor Vere, illustrator
Beauty and the Beast, Sampson Low edition, 1875, oversize, 57 pages, 10 chromolithographs designed by Boyle: $300.00

BOYLE, Kay
Pinky in Persia, Crowell-Collier, 1968, illustrated by Lilian Obligado, first edition with dust jacket: $75.00

Youngest Camel, Little, Brown, 1939, cloth-over-board cover, illustrations by Fritz Kredel, first edition with dust jacket: $100.00

BOYLSTON, Helen (1895 – 1984), see Series section, SUE BARTON

BOYNTON, Sandra
If at First..., Little, Brown, 1980, illustrations by author, first edition with dust jacket: $70.00

BRADBURY, Ray
Halloween Tree, Knopf, 1972, hardcover, b/w illustrations by Joseph Mugnaini, first edition with dust jacket: $200.00

Something Wicked This Way Comes, Simon & Schuster, 1962, scary young adult book, first edition with dust jacket: $600.00

Switch on the Night, Pantheon, 1955, square hardcover, science fiction author's first children's book, inspired by his infant daughter Susan, color illustrations by Madeleine Gekiere, first edition with dust jacket: $800.00. Hart Davis, first British edition, with dust jacket: $350.00

BRAGG, Mabel C.
Little Engine That Could, ca. 1930, Platt & Munk, *Never Grow Old Stories* series, (from the original title: *Pony Engine*), small, color illustrated paper-over-board cover with cloth spine, illustrated endpapers, color and b/w illustrations throughout by Lois Lenski: $60.00

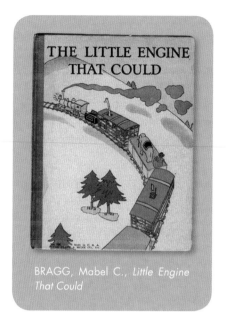

BRAGG, Mabel C., *Little Engine That Could*

BRAND, Christianna
Naughty Children, Gollanz, UK, 1962, illustrations by Edward Ardizzone, first edition with dust jacket: $100.00

Nurse Matilda, Dutton, 1964, illustrations by Edward Ardizzone, US first edition with dust jacket: $60.00

Nurse Matilda Goes to Hospital, Brockhampton Press, UK, 1974, green boards with gilt titles and decoration, color illustrations by Edward Ardizzone, first edition with dust jacket: $150.00

Nurse Matilda Goes to Town, Brockhampton Press, UK, 1967, illustrated by Edward Ardizzone, first edition with dust jacket: $150.00

Welcome to Danger, Foley House Press, UK, 1949, illustrated by William Stobbs, children's illustrated mystery adventure, first edition: $45.00

BRANDEIS, Madeline, film producer

Brandeis wrote and illustrated a series of books with printed illustration on cover, b/w documentary-type photo illustrations from Pathe films, ca. 1930s, Grosset & Dunlap, values range downward from: $100.00

BRELIS, Nancy
Mummy Market, Harper, 1966, illustrated by Ben Schecter, first edition with dust jacket: $60.00

BRENTANO, Clemens
Tale of Gockel, Hinkel & Gackeliah, Random House, 1961, first edition, hardcover, illustrated endpapers, b/w illustrations by Maurice Sendak: $150.00

BRENT-DYER, Elinor, see Series section, CHALET SCHOOL, CHUDLEIGH HOLD, LA ROCHELLE

BRICE, Tony, illustrator

Little Hippo and His Red Bicycle, Rand McNally, 1943, color illustrations by Brice, first edition with dust jacket: $60.00

BRIGHT, Robert, see Series section, GEORGIE THE GHOST

BRIGGS, Raymond (b. 1934 London)
Briggs often combines pictures and text in a comic book format to tell his stories. He earned his first Kate Greenaway Medal for the *Mother Goose Treasury* (1966), which featured a typical Briggs working class look imposed on the classical figures of nursery rhymes. The next Greenaway

BRIGGS, Raymond, *Father Christmas*

was for *Father Christmas* (1973), which tells its story through panels and word balloons as Father Christmas grumps his way through his job of delivering packages. Briggs studied at Wimbledon School of Fine Art, the Slade School of Fine Art, and the University of London.

Father Christmas, Hamish Hamilton, London, 1973, pictorial glazed boards, color illustrations by author, first edition: $45.00

Father Christmas Goes on Holiday, Coward-McCann, 1975, oversize hardcover picture book, cartoon color illustrations by author, US first edition with dust jacket: $50.00

Fee-Fi-Fo-Fum, Coward-McCann, 1964, 40 pages, illustrations by author, US first edition: $45.00

Midnight Adventure, Hamish Hamilton, 1961, illustrated by the author, first edition with dust jacket: $150.00

Ring-a-Ring o' Roses, Coward-McCann, 1962, oversize picture book, 48 pages, color illustrations by Briggs, US first edition: $80.00

Sledges to the Rescue, Hamish Hamilton, 1960, color illustrated dustwrapper and b/w illustrations by author, first edition with dust jacket: $300.00

BRINK, Carol Ryrie (1895 – 1981)
Baby Island, Macmillan, 1937, 172 pages, illustrations by Helen Sewell, first edition with dust jacket: $50.00

Caddie Woodlawn, Macmillan, 1935 (1936 Newbery Medal), illustrations by Kate Seredy, first edition with dust jacket: $100.00

Family Sabbatical, Viking Press, 1956, illustrations by Susan Foster, first edition with dust jacket: $90.00

Mademoiselle Misfortune, Macmillan, 1936, illustrated by Kate Seredy, first edition with dust jacket: $100.00

Magical Melons, Macmillan, 1944, first edition with dust jacket: $70.00

Pink Motel, Macmillan, 1959, illustrations by Sheila Greenwald, first edition with dust jacket: $50.00

Two Are Better Than One, Macmillan, 1968, 181 pages, first edition with dust jacket: $50.00

Winter Cottage, Macmillan, 1939, first edition with dust jacket: $50.00

BRISLEY, Joyce Lankester, see Series section, MILLY-MOLLY-MANDY

BROADHURST, Jean
All through the Day the Looking Glass Way, J. B. Lippincott Company, 1926, silhouette illustrations, words printed backwards and must be read with a mirror, metal reflecting mirror attached by cord, hardcover with original mirror and cord: $60.00

BROADHURST, Jean, *All Through the Day the Looking Glass Way*

BROCK, Betty
No Flying in the House, Harper, 1970, small pictorial hardcover, 139 pages, illustrated by Wallace Tripp, first edition with dust jacket: $60.00

Shades, Victor Gollancz, UK, 1973, illustrations by Victoria De Larrea, first edition with dust jacket: $40.00

BROCK, Charles Edmund (1870 – 1938), BROCK, Henry Matthew (1875 – 1960)
The Brock brothers worked in England

illustrating both periodicals and books from the late Victorian era through the height of the lavish gift books of the Edwardian period. Charles Edmund, who signed his work C.E. Brock, is considered the most collectible; Henry Matthew was the most prolific. A third brother, Richard, was also an illustrator.

Book of Fairy Tales, Henry Matthew Brock, ca. 1900, Warne, gilt decoration on cover, illustrated by Brock: $100.00

BROCK, Emma Lillian, author/illustrator
Beppo, Whitman, 1936, oversize, color illustrations by author: $40.00

Birds' Christmas Tree, Knopf, 1946, hardback, color illustrations by author: $40.00

Hen That Kept House, Knopf, 1933, red decoration on yellow cover, 40 pages, illustrations by author: $40.00

Kristie and the Colt and the Others, Knopf, 1949, color illustrations and b/w illustrations by author, first edition with dust jacket: $60.00

Runaway Sardine, Knopf, 1929, color illustrations by author: $40.00

Then Came Adventure, Knopf, 1941, green cloth-over-board cover, 184 pages, Lake Superior/Gooseberry Bay map endpapers, b/w illustrations throughout: $40.00

BROMHALL, Winifred, illustrator (b. England)

Bromhall studied art in England at Walsall Art School. After her move to New York in the 1920s, she worked in a bookstore, at the New York City library, and the Art Department of a New York Settlement, while building her career as an author/illustrator.

Bridget's Growing Day, Knopf, 1957, first edition with dust jacket: $100.00

Mary Ann's First Picture, Alfred A. Knopf, 1948, oversize, first edition with dust jacket: $100.00

BRONSON, Wilfrid Swancourt
Cats, Harcourt, 1950, first edition, oversize hardcover, illustrations by author: $70.00

Children of the Sea, Museum Press, 1943, London, 248 pages, illustrations by author, first edition with dust jacket: $50.00

BRONSON, Wilfrid Swancourt, *Water People*

Water People, 1935, Wise Parlowe, oversize nature picture book with color illustrations by the author, Rainbow edition: $50.00

BROOKE, L. Leslie (1862 – 1940), illustrator, see also Series section, JOHNNY CROW

BROOKE, L. Leslie, *Illustration from Ring 'o Roses*

Golden Goose Book, Warne, ca. 1920s, oversize, color illustrations by Brooke: $200.00

Nursery Rhyme, undated, Warne, oversize, paste-on color cover illustration of Bo Peep, 16 color plates and b/w illustrations by author: $65.00

Ring 'o Roses, a Nursery Rhyme Picture Book, undated Warne, oversize hardcover, illustrated by Brooke: $70.00

Tailor and the Crow, an Old Rhyme with New Drawings, Warne, 1911, small size, about 50 pages, color paste-on-pictorial, color plates and b/w illustrations by Brooke: $100.00

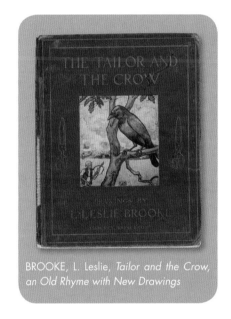

BROOKE, L. Leslie, *Tailor and the Crow, an Old Rhyme with New Drawings*

BROOKS, Walter R. (1886 – 1958), see Series section, FREDDY THE PIG

BROWN, Marcia
During her long career, Brown won three Caldecott Medals and six Caldecott Honors. After graduating from the New York College for Teachers in 1940, she taught English and later worked as an assistant librarian for the New York Public Library. Brown studied art at the Woodstock School of Painting and at the Art Students League in New York, working with such artists as Stuart Davis and Yasuo Kuniyoshi. Her first Caldecott Medal book, *Stone Soup* (1948), was one of Brown's many popular recreations of a classic fairy tale. Brown worked in a

BROWN, Marcia, *Once a Mouse*

variety of mediums ranging from pen-and-ink to woodcuts for *Once a Mouse* (1962 Caldecott) to match the art to the mood. In 1992, she received the Laura Ingalls Wilder Award for her contributions to children's literature.

Backbone of the King, Scribner, 1966, color illustrations, first edition with dust jacket: $70.00

Once a Mouse..., Scribner, 1962, Caldecott Award, hardcover, color illustrations by author, first edition with dust jacket: $125.00

Peter Piper's Alphabet, Scribner, 1959, color illustrations, first edition with dust jacket: $90.00

Skipper John's Cook, Charles Scribner's Sons, 1951, color illustrations, first edition with dust jacket: $90.00

Three Billy Goats Gruff, Harcourt Brace & World, Inc.,1957, pen and ink and watercolor illustrations, first edition with dust jacket: $50.00

BROWN, Margaret Wise (1910 – 1952)

Brown also used the pseudonyms Golden MacDonald, Timothy Hay, and Juniper Sage for children's books.

Big Red Barn, Young Scott Books, 1956, illustrated by Rosella Hartman, first edition: $70.00

Color Kittens, Simon & Schuster, 1949, color illustrations by Alice and Martin Provensen, first edition: $40.00

Goodnight, Moon, Harper, 1947, pictorial hardcover, color illustrations by Clement Hurd, first edition: $150.00

Little Fur Family, Harper & Brothers, 1946, illustrated by Garth Williams, first edition bound in real rabbit fur (later editions used imitation fur) in original cardboard box. With box: $750.00 to $1,000.00. Without box: $500.00

Little Island, Doubleday, 1946, illustrations by Leonard Weisgard (1947 Caldecott), first edition with dust jacket: $60.00

Little Pig's Picnic and Other Stories, D. C. Heath, 1939, illustrations by the Walt Disney Studio, pictorial cover, first edition: $70.00

Noon Balloon, Harper, 1952, illustrations by Leonard Weisgard, first edition with dust jacket: $200.00

Quiet Noisy Book, Harper, 1950, oversize hardcover, 34 pages, color illustrations by Leonard Weisgard, first edition: $50.00

Runaway Bunny, 1942, Harper, illustrations by Clement Hurd: $45.00

Sleepy Little Lion, Harper & Row, 1947, oversize, glossy pictorial hardcover, illustrated by Ylla, first edition: $50.00

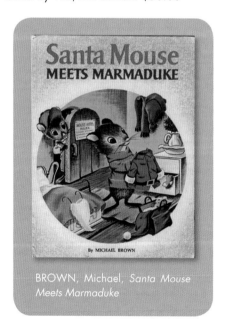

BROWN, Michael, *Santa Mouse Meets Marmaduke*

BROWN, Michael

Santa Mouse, Grosset, 1966, oversize

pictorial hardcover, color illustrations by Elfrieda De Witt, first edition: $50.00

Santa Mouse Meets Marmaduke, ca. 1969, Grosset, oversize pictorial hardcover, color illustrations by George De Santis, with dust jacket: $40.00

Santa Mouse, Where Are You?, Grosset, 1968, pictorial hardcover, color illustrations by Elfrieda De Witt. First edition with dust jacket: $50.00

Treasury of Santa Mouse, Grosset & Dunlap, 1970, Elfrieda DeWitt and George DeSantis, first edition with dust jacket: $40.00

BROWN, Paul, author/illustrator

Crazy Quilt, Scribner, 1934, illustrations by author, first edition: $70.00

No Trouble at All, Scribner, 1940, illustrations by author, first edition with dust jacket: $60.00

Piper's Pony, Scribner, 1935, illustrations by author, first edition with dust jacket: $70.00

Silver Heels, Scribner, 1951, tall, 125 pages, first edition: $100.00

Sparkie and Puff Ball, Scribner, 1954, illustrated by author, first edition with dust jacket: $60.00

BROWNE, Frances

Granny's Wonderful Chair, E. P. Dutton, 1916, illustrations by Katherine Pyle: $80.00

Wonderful Chair and the Tales It Told, 1900 edition, Heath, school edition with instructions for teachers, small, cloth-overboard cover, 192 pages, pen illustrations by Clara Atwood: $30.00

BROWNE, Gordon (1858 – 1922)

A meticulous illustrator, English artist Gordon Browne provided the drawings for a number of Victorian juvenile novels including the works of G.A. Henty and E. Nesbit. He wrote and illustrated his own nonsense tales under the name "A. Nobody."

BROWNING, Robert (1812 – 1889)

Pied Piper of Hamelin, Routledge, 1888,

35 color illustrations by Kate Greenaway: $300.00

Pied Piper of Hamelin, Frederick Warne, 1910, oversize, 48 pages, color illustrations by Kate Greenaway, this edition: $100.00

Pied Piper of Hamelin, London, 1934, limited edition, signed by Rackham, illustrations by Arthur Rackham, slipcase: $1,000.00

BRUCE, Dana, editor

My Brimful Book, Platt & Munk, 1960, oversize illustrated hardcover, illustrations by Tasha Tudor, Margot Austin, and Wesley Dennis: $60.00

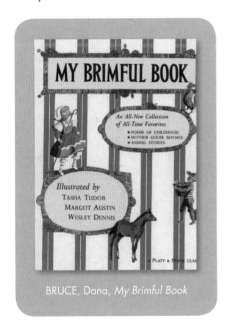

BRUCE, Dana, *My Brimful Book*

BRUCE, Dorita Fairlie, see Series section, DIMSIE

BRYANT, Sara Cone

Best Stories to Tell to Children (first published 1905), 1912 edition, Houghton, Mifflin, 16 color plate illustrations by Patten Wilson: $50.00

Epaminondas and His Auntie, 1938 edition, Houghton Mifflin, silhouette illustrations by Inez Hogan, first edition with dust jacket: $200.00. Without dust jacket: $90.00

Stories to Tell the Littlest Ones, Houghton Mifflin, 1916, first edition: $50.00

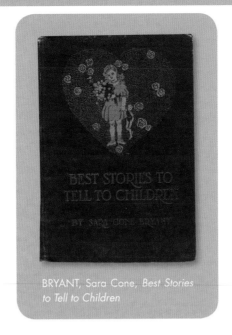

BRYANT, Sara Cone, *Best Stories to Tell to Children*

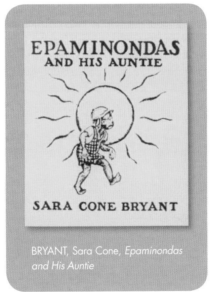

BRYANT, Sara Cone, *Epaminondas and His Auntie*

BUCK, Pearl (1892 – 1973)

Fairy Tales of the Orient, Simon & Schuster, 1965, first edition, hardcover: $50.00

Yu Lan: Flying Boy of China, John Day, 1945, first edition with dust jacket: $50.00

BUCKERIDGE, Anthony Malcom, see Series section, JENNINGS

BUFF, Conrad and Mary

Forest Folk, Viking Press, 1962, illustrations by Conrad Buff, first edition with dust jacket: $30.00

Kemi, an Indian Boy Before the White Man Came, Ward Ritchie Press, 1966,

illustrations by authors, first edition with dust jacket: $60.00

BULFINCH, Thomas (1796 – 1867)

Thomas Bulfinch edited classic mythology and tales of chivalry to make them suitable for children. His books were reprinted many times and illustrated by many artists. A sampling of collectible titles include:

Age of Chivalry, Crosby Nichols, 1859, first edition: $200.00

Age of Fable, Sanborn, 1855, first edition: $200.00

Legends of Charlemagne, Cosmopolitan, 1924, illustrated by N. C. Wyeth, first edition: $175.00

BULL, Peter

Teddy Bear Book, Random House, 1970, oversize hardcover, illustrated, US first edition with dust jacket: $50.00

BULLA, Clyde Robert

Beast of Lor, Crowell, 1977, 55 pages, first edition with dust jacket: $30.00

Down the Mississippi, Crowell, 1954, illustrated by Peter Burchard, first edition with dust jacket: $40.00

Song of Saint Francis, Crowell, 1952, first edition, hardcover, illustrations by Valenti Angelo: $50.00

BUNNY (Carl Schultze, 1866 – 1939), cartoonist

Latest Larks of Foxy Grandpa, Donohue, 1902, oversize oblong, cartoon series in color: $85.00

BUNYAN, John (1628 – 1688), minister

Pilgrim's Progress, Stokes, 1939, retold by Mary Godolphin, illustrated by Robert Lawson, first edition: $50.00

BURCHARD, Peter (b. Washington, D.C.)

Burchard began his art career illustrating army manuals during World War II. After leaving the army, he studied at the Philadelphia Museum of Art's School of Industrial Art. During his career as an artist in New York, he designed book jackets and illustrated more than 100 books. His love of sports, including sailing, can be seen in his brightly colored illustrations of action scenes painted for dust jackets of young adult novels. In the 1970s, he turned to writing historical novels and non-fiction works such as *One Gallant Rush: Robert Gould Shaw and His Brave Black Regiment*, which served as the basis for the 1989 movie, *Glory*.

River Queen, Macmillan, 1957, oversize hardcover, 40 pages, color illustrations by author, first edition with dust jacket: $50.00

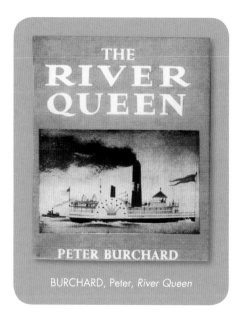

BURCHARD, Peter, *River Queen*

BURGESS, Gelett (1866 – 1951), author/illustrator, see Series section, GOOP

BURGESS, Thornton W. (1874 – 1965), see also Series section, GREEN FOREST, GREEN MEADOW, MOTHER WEST WIND, SMILING POOL, WISHING STONE

Aunt Sally's Friends in Fur, or, *the Woodhouse Night Club*, Little, Brown, 1955, first edition, hardcover, photos by the author: $40.00

Burgess Animal Book for Children, ca. 1920, Little, Brown, full-page color and b/w illustrations by Louis Fuertes: $50.00

Burgess Bird Book for Children, 1919, Little, Brown first edition, color plate illustrations by Fuertes: $100.00

Burgess Flower Book for Children, Little, Brown, color and b/w illustrations: $50.00

Burgess Seashore Book for Children, Little, Brown, color and b/w illustrations: $45.00

Tales from the Storyteller's House, Little, Brown, 1937, color illustrations by Lemuel Palmer: $55.00

While the Story Log Burns, Little, Brown, 1938, first edition: $45.00

Woe Begone Little Bear, Little, Brown, 1929, first edition: $45.00

BURKERT, Nancy (b. Colorado)

Burkert earned her MA degree at the University of Wisconsin. Her delicate use of color and fine ink linework distinguish her illustrations for Roald Dahl's *James and the Giant Peach* (1961), her first book assignment, as well as Randall Jarrell's *Snow White and the Seven Dwarfs* (1972), a Caldecott Honor book. Among other recognitions of her work, she received the 1966 Gold Medal of the Society of Illustrators.

Fir Tree, Harper, 1970, H. C. Andersen story illustrated by Burkert, first edition with dust jacket: $50.00

Scroobious Pip, 1968, Harper, oversize, illustrated by Burkert, first edition with dust jacket: $50.00

BURKERT, Nancy, *Fir Tree*

BURLINGAME, Eugene Watson

Grateful Elephant, Yale Press, 1923, illustrations by Dorothy Lathrop, first edition: $70.00

BURN, Doris

Andrew Henry's Meadow, Coward McCann, 1965, oversize hardcover picture book, b/w illustrations by author, first edition with dust jacket: $80.00

BURNETT, Frances Hodgson (b. England, 1849 – 1924, moved to America in the 1860s), see also Series section, RACKETTY-PACKETTY HOUSE

Editha's Burglar: A Story for Children, Jordan, Marsh, 1888, 64 pages, illustrated by Henry Sandham, decorated brown cloth, first edition thus with dust jacket: $250.00

Giovanni and the Other, Charles Scribner's Sons, 1892, illustrations by Reginald Birch, first edition: $150.00

Little Lord Fauntleroy, Scribner, 1886, gilt-decorated cloth, original illustrations by Reginald Birch, made famous the lace collar for little boys, story first serialized in *St. Nicholas* magazine, first edition: $1,000.00

Little Princess, Warne, 1905, first edition in rewritten book form (originally serialized in *St. Nicholas* magazine), gilt decorations on cover, eight color plate illustrations by Harold Piffard: $300.00

Piccino and Other Child Stories, Scribner, 1894, illustrated cloth-over-board cover, b/w illustrations by Reginald Birch: $70.00

Queen Silver-Bell, Century, 1906, paste-on pictorial, color illustrations: $150.00

Secret Garden, Frederick A. Stokes, New York, 1911, blue cloth, first edition without illustrations: $750.00. Green cloth, first edition thus with frontis and three plates by Maria Kirk: $300.00

Secret Garden, William Heineman, 1911, eight full-page color plates and pictorial endpapers by Charles Robinson, green cloth with gilt decorations, first edition:

$1,500.00. Later editions with eight color plates: $200.00

BURNFORD, Sheila

Incredible Journey, Little, Brown, 1961, Carl Burger illustrations, basis for Disney film, first edition with dust jacket: $80.00

Mr. Noah and the Second Flood, Gollancz, 1963, illustrated by Michael Foreman, first edition with dust jacket: $50.00

BURNHAM, Margaret, see Series section, GIRL AVIATOR

BURNINGHAM, John, author/artist (b. Surrey, England)

Burningham attended the Central School of Art and Craft in London, where he met his wife, illustrator Helen Oxenbury. Following stints as a poster designer for London Transport and an art school instructor, Burningham moved into a regular career as an author/illustrator, winning England's Kate Greenaway Medal for *Borka* (1963) and *Mr. Gumpy's Outing* (1973). He also won a number of international awards including the *New York Times* Best Illustrated Children's Books of the Year Award and the Boston Globe-Horn Book Award for Illustration.

Around the World in Eighty Days (retelling of Jules Verne story), Jonathan Cape, 1972, first edition, oversize hardcover, 95 pages, color illustrations by author: $50.00

BURNINGHAM, John, *Shopping Basket*

Fox Who Went down to the Valley, Bobbs Merrill, 1968, oversize, illustrations by author, US first edition with dust jacket: $80.00

Mr. Firkin and the Lord Mayor of London, Bobbs Merrill, 1967, illustrations by author, first edition with dust jacket: $45.00

Mr. Gumpy's Motor Car, Crowell, 1976, color illustrations by author, US first edition with dust jacket: $40.00

Mr. Gumpy's Outing, Holt, 1970, paper-covered boards, oversize, color illustrations by the author, US first edition with dust jacket: $40.00

Shopping Basket, Jonathan Cape, 1980, large, pictorial boards, picture book, first edition: $40.00

Time to Get out of the Bath, Shirley, Crowell 1978, oblong, oversize, color illustrations throughout, US first edition: $40.00

BURNINGHAM, John, *Time to Get Out of the Bath, Shirley*

BURROUGHS, Edgar Rice, see also Series section, MARS, TARZAN

I Am a Barbarian, Edgar Rice Burroughs, Inc., 1967, first edition, hardcover, gilt-lettered maroon cloth, illustrated by John Coleman Burroughs: $200.00

BURTON, Virginia Lee (1909 – 1968), author/illustrator

Burton intended to be a dancer, but she studied drawing with George Demetrios in Boston and ended up marrying him

and pursuing a career in art. She often looked to her own sons for subjects that they would enjoy when creating picture books. The author/illustrator of *Choo Choo* (1937) and *Mike Mulligan and His Steam Shovel* (1939) became a well-established figure in American picture books in the 1940s. A true perfectionist, she often reworked drawings or stories leading to a revised edition of *Calico the Wonder Horse* or the *Saga of Stewy Stinker* (1950 edition – the 1941 edition calls him Stewy Slinker, not Burton's first choice). Towards the end of her career, she abandoned book illustration in favor of textile design.

Calico, the Wonder Horse or *The Saga of Stewy Stinker,* Houghton Mifflin, 1941, small oblong, printed illustrated cover, black drawings by author printed on series of different colors of pages, first edition: $100.00

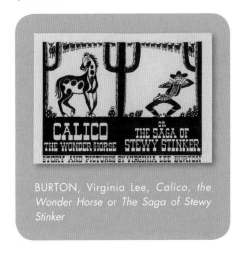

BURTON, Virginia Lee, *Calico, the Wonder Horse* or *The Saga of Stewy Stinker*

Katy and the Big Snow, Houghton Mifflin, 1943, oversize oblong, color illustrations by author, first edition with dust jacket: $200.00

Little House, Houghton Mifflin, 1942 (1943 Caldecott), oversize, color illustrations by author, first edition: $100.00

Maybelle the Cable Car, Houghton Mifflin, 1952, oversize square, color illustrations on every page (Burton studied art in San Francisco) by author, first edition with dust jacket: $300.00

Mike Mulligan and His Steam Shovel, Houghton Mifflin, 1939, oversize, color illustrations by author, first edition: $100.00

BURTON, Virginia Lee, *Little House*

BUSCH, Wilhelm

Max and Moritz, originally written in German, ca. 1865, following are English translations:

Max and Maurice (author's name listed as William Busch on this translated edition), 1898 edition, Little, Brown, small, cloth-over-board cover with impressed illustration, 56 pages, verse, b/w illustrations: $60.00

Max and Moritz: A Story of Seven Tricks, 1925 edition, Braun & Schneider, cloth spine, illustrated paper-over-board cover, 56 pages, illustrations by author: $40.00

BUTTERWORTH, Hezekiah, see Series section, ZIGZAG JOURNEYS

BUTTERWORTH, Oliver

Enormous Egg, Boston, Little, Brown, 1956, illustrated by Louis Darling (numerous reprints of this favorite), first edition with dust jacket: $400.00

Trouble with Jenny's Ear, Little, Brown, 1960, illustrated by Julian de Miskey, first edition: $40.00

BYFIELD, Barbara Ninde, see also Series section, HAUNTED

Glass Harmonica, Macmillan, 1967, over-size hardcover, 160 pages, illustrations by author: $40.00

BYINGTON, Eloise

Wishbone Children, Whitman, 1934, blue cloth-over-board cover with paste-on-pictorial, illustrated endpapers, color illustra-

tions by Kathleen Frantz, first edition with dust jacket: $50.00

BYFIELD, Barbara Ninde, *Glass Harmonica*

·····•·················· **C** ···················•·····

CADY, Walter Harrison (1877 – 1970)

Walter Harrison Cady studied with artist Parker Perkins in his hometown of Gardner, Massachusetts, but his cartoon style seems to be mostly self-taught. In 1913, Cady replaced George Kerr as Thornton Burgess's principal illustrator, a collaboration that lasted for more than 50 years. Because of the popularity of Cady's illustrations, many early Burgess works were reissued with new Cady illustrations.

CAFFREY, Nancy

Hanover's Wishing Star, E. P. Dutton, 1956, b/w photographs, first edition with dust jacket: $40.00

Horse Haven, E. P. Dutton, 1955, b/w illustrations by Paul Brown, first edition with dust jacket: $400.00

Show Pony, E. P. Dutton, 1954, b/w illustrations by Paul Brown, first edition with dust jacket: $200.00

Somebody's Pony, E. P. Dutton, 1951, b/w illustrations by Jeanne Mellin, first edition with dust jacket: $200.00

Scene from the Saddle, E. P. Dutton, 1958, first edition, oblong hardcover, 88 pages,

full-page b/w photos by A. L. Waintrob: $40.00

CALDECOTT, Randolph (1846 – 1886), illustrator

Randolph Caldecott studied at the Manchester School of Art while working at a bank. His earliest sales were to the illustrated newspapers of his day. He moved to London in 1872 to begin a career as an illustrator. A successor to Walter Crane, Caldecott's work was enormously popular during his lifetime and many of his titles received initial print runs of 100,000 books or more. Like Crane and Kate Greenaway, many of Caldecott's early children's books were engraved by Edmund Evans.

CALDECOTT, Randolph, illustration from *Queen of Hearts*

Hey Diddle Diddle Picture Book, Routledge, London, 1882, illustrated paper-over-board cover: $100.00

Queen of Hearts, George Routledge & Sons, London, 1881, pictorial soft cover: $100.00

R. Caldecott's Picture Book No. 1 (1879), 1900 edition, Warne: $100.00

R. Caldecott's Picture Book No. 1, undated edition, ca. 1920s, Warne, 9" x 8", impressed illustration on cloth-covered boards, color illustrations throughout: $55.00

CALHOUN, Mary

Big Sixteen, William Morrow, 1983, oversize, b/w double-page illustrations by Trina Schart Hyman, first edition with dust jacket: $70.00

Daisy, Tell Me!, William Morrow, 1971, illustrations by Janet McCaffery, first edition with dust jacket: $80.00

House of Thirty Cats, Harper, 1965, b/w illustrations by Mary Chalmers, first edition with dust jacket: $80.00

Sweet Patootie Doll, Morrow, 1957, color and b/w illustrations by Roger Duvoisin, first edition with dust jacket: $80.00

Witch of Hissing Hill, William Morrow, 1964, illustrations by Janet McCaffery, first edition with dust jacket: $80.00

Witch's Pig, a Cornish Folktale, Morrow, 1977, color and b/w illustrations by Lady McCrady, first edition with dust jacket: $100.00

CAMERON, Eleanor (1912 – 1996),

see also Series section, JULIA REDFERN, MUSHROOM PLANET

Beast with the Magical Horn, Little, Brown, 1963, illustrations by Joe and Beth Krush, first edition with dust jacket: $200.00

Court of Stone Children, E. P. Dutton, 1973, illustrated by Trina Schart Hyman, first edition with dust jacket: $80.00

Room Made of Windows, E. P. Dutton, 1971, first edition with dust jacket: $100.00

Spell Is Cast, Little, Brown, 1964, illustrations by Joe and Beth Krush, first edition with dust jacket: $40.00

Terrible Churnadyne, Little, Brown, 1959, illustrations by Joe and Beth Krush, first edition with dust jacket: $200.00

CAMERON, Polly

Cat Who Thought He Was a Tiger, Coward-McCann, 1956, illustrated by author, first edition with dust jacket: $50.00

I Can't Said the Ant, McCann, 1961, yellow boards/red lettering, red/white illustrations by author, first edition with dust jacket: $70.00

CAMPBELL, Bruce, see Series section, KEN HOLT MYSTERY

CAMPBELL, Ruth

Cat Whose Whiskers Slipped, Volland, 1925, color illustrations throughout by Ve Elizabeth Cadie: $55.00

Cat Whose Whiskers Slipped, edition Wise-Parslow, 1938, Ve Elizabeth Cadie, color illustrations: $30.00

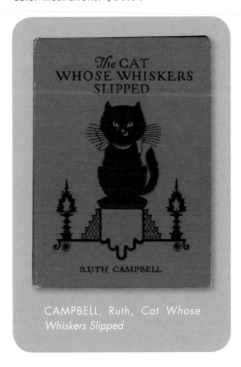

CAMPBELL, Ruth, *Cat Whose Whiskers Slipped*

CANFIELD, Dorothy (1879 – 1958)

Understood Betsy, Henry Holt, 1913, illustrations by Ada Williamson, first edition: $30.00

CARIGIET, Alois, author/artist

Anton and Anne, Walck, 1969, oblong oversize picture book, color illustrations by author, first edition with dust jacket: $100.00

Anton the Goatherd, Walck, 1966, oblong oversize picture book, color illustrations by author: $50.00

Pear Tree the Birch Tree and the Barberry Bush, Henry C. Walck, 1967, illustrated by author, US first edition with dust jacket: $40.00

CARLETON, Barbee Oliver

Benny and the Bear, Follett, 1960, illustrations by Dagmar Wilson, first edition with dust jacket: $40.00

Chester Jones, Holt Rinehart Winston, 1963, illustrated by Gioia Fiammenghi, first edition with dust jacket: $70.00

Secret of Saturday Cove, Holt Rinehart Winston, 1961, illustrations by Geer, first edition with dust jacket: $40.00

Witches' Bridge, Holt Rinehart Winston, 1967, first edition with dust jacket: $40.00

Wonderful Cat of Cobbie Bean, John C. Winston, 1957, color illustrations, first edition with dust jacket: $100.00

CARLSON, Natalie Savage, see also Series section, ORPHELINES

Empty Schoolhouse, Harper, 1965, oversize, b/w illustrations by John Kaufmann, first edition with dust jacket: $80.00

Family Under the Bridge, Harper, 1958, b/w illustrations by Garth Williams, first edition with dust jacket: $60.00

Talking Cat and Other Stories of French Canada, Harper, 1952, red hardcover, frontispiece and b/w illustrations by Roger Duvoisin, first edition with dust jacket: $50.00

CARPENTER, Frank O.

Around the World with Children, American Book, 1917, photo illustrations: $30.00

CARR, Annie Rowe, see Series section, NAN SHERWOOD

CARR, Mary Jane

Peggy and Paul and Laddy, Crowell, 1936, color endpapers, b/w illustrations by Kathleen Voute, first edition with dust jacket: $40.00

CARR, Sarah Pratt, see Series section, BILLY TO-MORROW

CARROLL, Lewis (Revd. C. L. Dodgson 1832 – 1898), see also Series section, ALICE IN WONDERLAND.

With two rather short novels often combined into one, Carroll launched a century of Alice tributes, imitations, and sequels. Hundreds of versions of the original have been published. There are also numerous reference books about the Alice books, available through libraries. This classic has been a favorite of illustrators, including the author, Sir John Tenniel, Peter Newell, Bessie Pease Gutmann, Frank Adams, Maria Kirk, Gertrude Kay, Mabel Lucie Atwell, Margaret Tarrant, Milo Winter, and Gwynned Hudson.

Alice titles:

Alice's Adventures in Wonderland, 1865 (original title: *Alice's Adventures Underground*)

Through the Looking Glass and What Alice Found There, 1899

Alice, a few of the many editions, listed by date of publication:

Alice's Adventures in Wonderland, Appleton, 1866, first American edition. Upon Tenniel's request, Carroll asked his publisher to destroy the first 2,000 copies of *Alice* published in Great Britain in 1865. With the author's approval, the publisher sold the unbound pages to Appleton, a New York publisher, who removed the London title page and substituted its own. Rebound in leather (twentieth century): $7,500.00 to $9,000.00. In original 1860s cloth hardcover: $20,000.00 to $40,000.00

Alice's Adventures in Wonderland, 1870 edition, Lee & Shepard, Boston, small size, red cloth cover, gilt edged pages, Tenniel illustrations: $85.00

Alice's Adventures under Ground, Macmillan, 1886, red cloth cover with gilt lettering and decoration, 37 illustrations by the author: $700.00

Nursery Alice, London, Macmillan and Co., 1890, pictorial boards by E. G. Thomson, Tenniel illustrations in color: $500.00

Alice's Adventures in Wonderland, Altemus, 1897, paste-on cover illustration, four color and over 40 b/w illustrations: $85.00

Alice's Adventures in Wonderland, Harper, 1901, full-page illustrations by Peter Newell: $85.00

Through the Looking Glass and What Alice Found There, Harper, 1902, first edition thus, red hardcover with gilt trim, top edge gilt, frontispiece photograph of illustrator Peter Newell, monochrome plate illustrations by Newell throughout: $300.00

CARROLL, Lewis, *Alice in Wonderland through the Looking Glass*

Alice's Adventures in Wonderland, Heinemann, London, 1907, illustrations by Arthur Rackham: $250.00

Alice's Adventures in Wonderland, Dodge, 1907, illustrations by Bessie Pease Gutmann: $200.00

Alice in Wonderland, Raphael Tuck, 1910, illustrations byl Mabel Lucie Attwell: $100.00

Alice in Wonderland through the Looking Glass, Rand McNally, 1916, tweed cover with paste-on-pictorial, gilt lettering, illustrated endpapers, 14 color plates by Milo Winter: $90.00

Alice in Wonderland, Ward Lock, UK, or Platt & Peck, US, 1916, 48 color illustrations by Margaret Tarrant, first edition thus: $250.00

Alice's Adventures in Wonderland, 1919, New York, illustrations by Maria Kirk: $60.00

Alice's Adventures in Wonderland, 1923 Philadelphia, illustrations by Gertrude Kay: $60.00

Alice's Adventures in Wonderland and through the Looking Glass, ca. 1917, Grosset & Dunlap, illustrations are full-page photos from "moving picture" by Nonpareil Feature Film Co., starring Viola Savoy: $60.00

Alice in Wonderland and through the Looking Glass, Grosset & Dunlap, book undated but is Photoplay edition to promote 1933 Paramount film, 297 pages, 16 photo illustrations, photo montage endpapers, photo dustjacket, photos feature Charlotte Henry as Alice, cast also included Cary Grant, Gary Cooper, W.C. Fields, Edward Everett Horton, Jack Oakie, with dust jacket: $250.00. Without dust jacket: $50.00

Alice's Adventures in Wonderland, Dial Press, 1935, hardcover with gilt lettering and paste-on illustration, b/w illustrations plus 12 color plates by Gwynedd Hudson: $150.00

Alice in Wonderland, Rand McNally, 1938 edition of the 1916 book, black cover with paste-on-pictorial and silver trim, using five of the color plates plus additional b/w in-text drawings by Milo Winter: $30.00

Alice's Adventures in Wonderland, Maecenas Press/Random House, 1969, issued unbound and encased in a linen clamshell box, quarter bound with leather spine and leather clasps with bone closures, three-color etching frontispiece and 12 full-page color lithographs by Salvador Dali. Limited run of 2,500 copies (each copy numbered), signed by Dali on title page at time of publication: $7,500.00. Special edition of same work (200 copies issued) with 13 additional plates on vellum, signed by Dali: $12,500.00

Carroll, Lewis, other:

Hunting of the Snark, Macmillan, 1876, illustrated boards, 83 pages, gilt edged, illustrations by Henry Holiday: $285.00

Hunting of the Snark, Harper, 1903, paper-over-board cover with gilt, 248 pages, 24 b/w plates by Peter Newell, text page decorations by Robert Murray: $225.00

Alice, illustrator reference:

Alice's Adventures in Wonderland: The Ultimate Illustrated Edition, 1989, Bantam, hardcover, color plates, 25 illustrators represented in this beautiful reprinting of classic *Alice* pictures, an interesting reference for *Alice* collectors, with dust jacket: $40.00

CARRYL, Charles E.

Admiral's Caravan, Houghton, 1920 edition, cloth-over-board cover, illustrations by Reginald Birch, first edition with dust jacket: $30.00

Davy and the Goblin (1884), Houghton Mifflin, 1928 edition, Riverside Bookshelf, cloth-over-board cover with paste-on pictorial, illustrated endpapers, color frontispiece, six color plates and b/w illustrations by Bensell and Bacharach: $50.00

Davy and the Goblin or *What Followed Reading "Alice's Adventures in Wonderland,"* Ticknor & Fields, 1885, tan cloth with gilt lettering, picture of goblin on front, illustrations by E. B. Bensell, first edition: $180.00

CARTER, Russell Gordon, *White Plume of Navarre*

CARTER, Russell Gordon (1892 – 1957)

Crimson Cutlass, Penn Publishing, 1933, color frontispiece and four full-page b/w illustrations by Frank Schoonover, with dust jacket: $150.00

White Plume of Navarre, Volland, 1928, paste-on pictorial, color illustrations by Beatrice Stevens: $50.00

CARY, Alice and Phoebe

Clovernook Children, Ticknor, 1885, first edition, small, blue cloth-over-board cover with gilt: $40.00

CAUDILL, Rebecca, (1899 – 1985), see Series section, BONNIE AND DEBBIE

CAVANAH, Frances

Marta Finds the Golden Door, Grosset & Dunlap, 1941, b/w illustrations by Harve Stein, color cover paste-on art by Janice Holland, first edition: $100.00

Secret of Madame Doll, a Story of the American Revolution, Vanguard Press, 1965, hardcover with gilt embossed illustration, b/w illustrations, illustrated by Dorothy Bayley Morse, first edition with dust jacket: $70.00

CAVANNA, Betty (1909 – 2001)

Cavanna wrote the Connie Blair mysteries under the pseudonym Betsy Allen.

Fancy Free, William Morrow, 1961, first edition with dust jacket: $30.00

Ghost of Ballyhooly, William Morrow, 1971, first edition with dust jacket: $50.00

Girl Can Dream, Westminster, 1953, illustration by Harold Minton, first edition with dust jacket: $50.00

Joyride, William Morrow, 1974, first edition with dust jacket: $70.00

Mystery of the Emerald Buddha, William Morrow, 1976, first edition with dust jacket: $30.00

Paintbox Summer, Westminster, 1959, illustrated by Peter Hunt, first edition with dust jacket: $40.00

Runaway Voyage, Morrow, 1978, first edition with dust jacket: $30.00

CAVANNA, Betty, *Stars in Her Eyes*

Stars in Her Eyes, 1958, William Morrow, illustrated by Isabel Dawson, first edition with dust jacket: $40.00

CHADWICK, Lester, see Series section, BASEBALL JOE, COLLEGE SPORTS

CHAFFEE, Allen

Adventures of Twinkly Eyes the Little Black Bear, Milton Bradley, 1919, illustrated by Peter Da Ru, 10 monotone plates, first edition: $50.00

Brownie: The Engineer of Beaver Brook, Milton Bradley, 1925, color plate illustrations by Paul Bransom and color borders by W. Prentice Phillips, first edition: $50.00

CHAFFEE, Allen, *Fuzzy Wuzz Meets the Ranger*

Fuzzy Wuzz, Milton Bradley, 1922, decorated cloth-over-board cover, four b/w illustrations by Peter Da Ru, first edition: $40.00

Fuzzy Wuzz Meets the Ranger, McLoughlin, 1937, hardback, 256 pages, b/w frontispiece illustration, first edition: $40.00

Heroes of the Shoals, Henry Holt, 1935, tales of the U.S. Coast Guard, 20 b/w photo plates, first edition: $50.00

Honk-A-Tonk Takes a Trip, McLoughlin Brothers, 1937, first edition with dust jacket: $40.00

Tawny Goes Hunting, Random House, 1937, cloth-over-board cover, b/w illustrations by Paul Bransom, first edition with dust jacket: $50.00

CHAFFEY, M. Ella
Adventures of Prince Melonseed, Briggs, 1916, first edition, blue cloth-over-board cover, illustrations by Margaret Chaffey: $90.00

CHAMBERLIN, Ethel C.
Minnie the Little Fish Who Lived in a Shoe, Charles E. Graham, 1928, illustrated by Nell Witters, first edition: $30.00

Shoes and Ships and Sealing Wax, Volland, 1928, color illustrated paper-over-board cover, illustrated endpapers, color and b/w illustrations by Janet Lee Scott, first edition: $50.00

CHAMBERS, Robert W.
Cardigan, Harper, 1930, novel set in Colonial period, illustrations by Henry C. Pitz, first edition with dust jacket: $50.00

River-Land, a Story for Children, Harper, 1904, oversize, color and b/w illustrations by Elizabeth Shippen Green: $100.00

CHAPIN, Anna Alice
Babes in Toyland, Dodd, 1924, color illustrations by Ethel Betts: $200.00

Everyday Fairy Book, undated, ca. 1935, Coker, UK, 16 stories, color plates by Jessie Willcox Smith, first edition: $100.00

Janet: Her Winter in Quebec, Little, Brown, 1906, first edition, illustration by Alice Barber Stephens, first edition: $50.00

Now-A-Days Fairy Book, Dodd, 1911, oversize, color plates by Jessie Willcox Smith: $200.00

Toodles of Treasure Town and Her Snow Man, Saalfield, 1908, illustrations by Merle Johnson, first edition: $200.00

True Story of Humpty Dumpty, Dodd, 1905, illustrations by Ethel Betts, first edition: $75.00

CHAPMAN, Allen, see Series section, FRED FENTON, RADIO BOYS, RAILROAD

CHARNAS, Suzy McKee, see Series section, SORCERY HALL TRILOGY

CHASE, Mary (1907–1981)
Chase is the author of the stage play *Harvey.*

Book of Ruth, 1946 edition by Limited Edition Club, oversize hardback with vellum spine, gilt, illustrated boards, illustrated frontispiece, eight mounted color plates by Arthur Szyk, 1,950 copies signed by Szyk, with slipcase: $300.00. Without slip-case: $150.00

Loretta Mason Potts, J. B. Lippincott, 1958, illustrations by Harold Berson, first edition with dust jacket: $100.00

CHASE, Mary, *Loretta Mason Potts*

Mrs. McThing, Oxford University Press,

1952, Helen Sewell illustrations, first edition with dust jacket: $50.00

Wicked Pigeon Ladies, Knopf, 1968, black cloth boards, blue endpapers, b/w illustrations by Don Bolognese, first edition with dust jacket: $150.00

CHASE, Mary Ellen (1887–1973)
Sailing the Seven Seas, Houghton Mifflin Company, 1958, illustrations by John O'Hara Cosgrave, first edition with dust jacket: $50.00

Silver Shell, Henry, 1931, blue moire cover with silver decoration, illustrated by Helen Baker Evers, first edition with dust jacket: $40.00

White Gate, Norton, 1954, 185 pages, imaginary adventure, first edition with dust jacket: $40.00

CHAUCER, Geoffrey
Canterbury Tales, modern verse translation by Frank Ernest Hill, 1946 Limited Edition Club, oversize hardback with vellum spine, illustrated frontispiece, full-page color plates by Arthur Szyk, 1,500 copies signed by Szyk, with slipcase: $300.00. Without slipcase: $150.00.

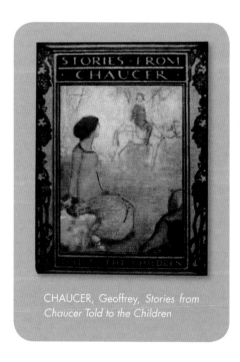

CHAUCER, Geoffrey, *Stories from Chaucer Told to the Children*

Chanticleer and the Fox, 1958 edition, Crowell, illustrated by Barbara Cooney, first edition thus: $50.00

Stories from Chaucer Told to the Children, T. C. & E. C. Jack, UK, 1914, paper boards with paste-on-pictorial, illustrated by W. Heath Robinson: $150.00

CHAUNDLER, Christine

Arthur and His Knights, Frederick A. Stokes, New York, undated, illustrated cloth cover, 312 pages, illustrated endpapers, eight color plate illustrations by MacKenzie mounted on dark gray heavy paper: $90.00

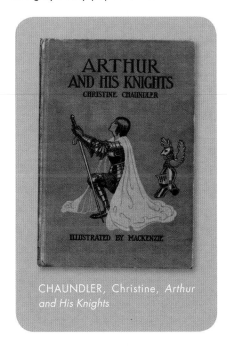

CHAUNDLER, Christine, *Arthur and His Knights*

CHAUNDLER, Christine, illustration from *Arthur and His Knights*

CHISHOLM, Louey, edited stories for *Young Folks* periodical.

CHISHOLM, Louey, *Enchanted Land, Tales Told Again*

Enchanted Land, Tales Told Again, undated, Nelson, cloth-over-boards, 30 color plate illustrations by Katharine Cameron: $200.00

Golden Staircase: Poems and Verses for Children, 1906, T. C. & E. C. Jack, gilt decorative boards, color plates, first edition: $100.00

Hop O' My Thumb, the Wolf and the Seven Kids, 1911, Dodge, 77 pages, color illustrations, first edition: $80.00

CHONZ, Selina

Bell for Ursli, Oxford University Press, 1950, illustrations by Alois Carigiet, first edition with dust jacket: $100.00

Florina and the Wild Bird, Walck, 1953, oversize hardcover, color illustrations by Alois Carigiet, US first edition with dust jacket: $75.00

CHRISMAN, Arthur (b. Virginia, 1889 – 1953)

Shen of the Sea, E. P. Dutton, 1925 (1926 Newbery Medal), first edition with dust jacket: $40.00

CHRISTESON, H. M and F. M.

Tony and His Pals, Whitman, 1934, cloth-over-board cover with photo paste-on-pictorial, b/w photograph, illustrations of Tom Mix and his horse, Tony: $50.00

CHRISTOPHER, John, see also Series section, FIREBALL, SWORD OF SPIRITS TRILOGY, TRIPODS

Guardians, Macmillan, 1970, first edition with dust jacket: $100.00

CHURCH, Peggy Pond

Burro of Angelitos, Suttonhouse, 1931, oversize, cloth spine and illustrated boards, 42 pages, double-page color illustrations and line drawings by Gigi Johnson, first edition with dust jacket: $100.00

CHWAST, Seymour and Martin Stephen Moskof

Still Another Children's Book, McGraw-Hill, 1972, hardcover, illustrated by authors, first edition with dust jacket: $65.00

CIARDI, John (1916 – 1986)

I Met a Man, Houghton Mifflin, 1961, illustrated by Robert Osborn, first edition with dust jacket: $40.00

John J. Plenty and Fiddler Dan, J. B. Lippincott, 1963, illustrated by Madeleine Gekiere, first edition with dust jacket: $40.00

Man Who Sang the Sillies, J. B. Lippincott, 1961, illustrations by Edward Gorey, first edition with dust jacket: $75.00

Monster Den, J. B. Lippincott, 1966, drawings by Edward Gorey, first edition with dust jacket: $90.00

Wish-Tree, Crowell-Collier, 1962, b/w illustrations by Louis S. Glanzman, first edition: $50.00

You Know Who, J. B. Lippincott, 1964, illustrations by Edward Gorey, first edition with dust jacket: $70.00

You Read to Me, I'll Read to You, J. B. Lippincott, 1962, collection of poems illustrated by Edward Gorey, first edition with dust jacket: $100.00

CLARK, Ann Nolan

Looking for Something, Viking Press, 1952, illustrated by Leo Politi, first edition with dust jacket: $50.00

Medicine Man's Daughter, Bell Books, 1963, illustrations by Donald Bolognese, first edition with dust jacket: $40.00

Secret of the Andes, Viking Press, 1965, illustrations by Jean Charlot, first edition with dust jacket: $50.00

CLARK, Joan, see WIRT, Mildred

CLARK, Margery (Mary Clark and Margery Quigley)

Poppy Seed Cakes, Doubleday, 1929, illustrated by Maud and Miska Petersham, first edition with dust jacket: $60.00

CLARKE, Covington
Mystery Flight of the Q2, Reilly & Lee, 1932, first edition: $40.00

Desert Wings, Reilly & Lee, 1930, first edition: $40.00

CLARKE, Pauline, see Series section, FIVE DOLLS

CLAUDY, Carl H., see also Series section, ADVENTURES IN THE UNKNOWN

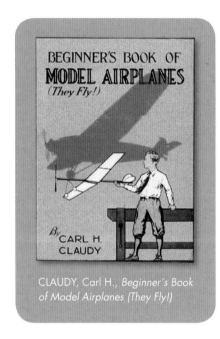
CLAUDY, Carl H., *Beginner's Book of Model Airplanes (They Fly!)*

Beginner's Book of Model Airplanes (They Fly!), Bobbs Merrill, 1930, cloth-over-board cover, 184 pages, explanation and construction directions, first edition: $40.00

Dangerous Waters, Bobbs-Merrill, 1929, first edition: $50.00

Prize Winners' Book of Model Airplanes, Bobbs-Merrill, 1931, cloth-over-board cover, 242 pages, includes folded plans in pockets, first edition: $65.00

Tell Me Why Stories, ca. 1914, McBride, cloth-over-board cover with print illustration, eight color plates by Norman Rockwell: $50.00

Treasures of the Darkness, Doubleday, 1933, Jr. Mystery Club book, cloth-over-board cover, 288 pages, color frontispiece: $30.00

CLEARY, Beverly, *Luckiest Girl*

CLEARY, Beverly, see also Series section, HENRY HUGGINS, RALPH THE MOUSE, RAMONA QUIMBY

Luckiest Girl, Morrow, 1958, first edition, hardcover: $50.00

CLIFTON, Lucille
Don't You Remember?, E. P. Dutton, 1973, square hardcover, color illustrations by Evaline Ness, first edition with dust jacket: $40.00

Everett Anderson's Christmas Coming, Holt, Rinehart and Winston, 1971, oblong hardcover, illustrations by Evaline Ness, first edition with dust jacket: $40.00

My Brother Fine with Me, Holt, Rinehart and Winston, 1975, oversize hardcover, illustrated endpapers, b/w illustrations by Moneta Barnett, first edition with dust jacket: $40.00

Some of the Days of Everett Anderson, Holt, Rinehart and Winston, 1970, hardcover, illustrations by Evaline Ness, first edition with dust jacket: $40.00

Times They Used to Be, Holt, 1974, small hardcover, b/w illustrations by Susan Jeschke, first edition with dust jacket: $60.00

CLINTON, Althea
Treasure Book of Best Stories, Saalfield, 1933, oversize picture book, pictorial cover, b/w illustrations by Fern Bisel Peat, color plates by Eleanora Madsen, first edition: $50.00

CLYMER, Eleanor
Belinda's New Spring Hat, Franklin Watts, 1969, first edition with dust jacket: $50.00

Leave Horatio Alone, Atheneum, 1974, illustrations by Robert Quackenbush, first edition with dust jacket: $70.00

Sociable Toby, Franklin Watts, 1956, illustrated by Ingrid Fetz, first edition with dust jacket: $70.00

Thirty-Three Bunn Street, Dodd, Mead, 1952, illustrations by Jane Miller, first edition with dust jacket: $100.00

Trolley Car Family, McKay, 1947, blue hardcover, first edition with dust jacket: $40.00

CLYNE, Geraldine, see Series section, JOLLY JUMP-UPS POP-UPS

COATSWORTH, Elizabeth (1893 – 1986), see also Series section, SALLY SMITH

COATSWORTH, Elizabeth, *Big Green Umbrella*

Big Green Umbrella, Grosset & Dunlap, A Story Parade Picture Book, 1944, pictorial endpapers, color illustrations by Helen Sewell, first edition with dust jacket: $40.00

Cat Who Went to Heaven, Macmillan, 1930, illustrations by Lynd Ward, first edition with dust jacket: $100.00

Desert Dan, Viking Press, 1960, first edition, orange hardcover, illustrations by Harper Johnson: $40.00

Dollar For Luck, Macmillan, 1951, illustrated by George and Doris Hauman, 154 pages, first edition with dust jacket: $50.00

Mouse Chorus, Pantheon, 1955, illustrated by Genevieve Vaughan-Jackson, first edition with dust jacket: $50.00

Noble Doll, Viking Press, 1961, four color spreads, first edition with dust jacket: $80.00

Wanderers, 1972, Four Winds Press, illustrated by Trina Schart Hyman, first edition with dust jacket: $80.00

COLE, William

Beastly Boys and Ghastly Girls, World, 1964, illustrations by Tomi Ungerer, first edition with dust jacket: $150.00

Folk Songs of England, Ireland, Scotland and Wales, Doubleday, 1961, two-color illustrations by Edward Ardizzone, US first edition with dust jacket: $95.00

COLETTE, *Cat*

That Pest Jonathan, Harper, 1970, pictorial boards, illustrations by Tomi Ungerer, first edition with dust jacket: $70.00

COLETTE

Boy and the Magic, Putnam, 1964, first edition, oblong hardcover, color illustrations by Gerard Hoffnung: $40.00

Cat, Farrar & Rinehart, 1936, 164 pages, translated by Morris Bentinck, illustrations by Susanne Suba, US first edition with dust jacket: $100.00

COLLIER, Virginia

Roland the Warrior, Harcourt Brace, 1934, 237 pages, two-color illustrations by Frank Schoonover, first edition with dust jacket: $80.00

COLLINGWOOD, Harry, see Series section, FLYING FISH

COLLODI, Carlo (Carlo Lorenzini, 1826 – 1890)

Italian author Collodi's story of a wooden puppet who wants to become a real boy, *Le avventure di Pinocchio,* was published as a newspaper serial story from 1881 – 1883. Since then, his work has spawned numerous adaptations and, like most famous children's books, the highest prices are paid for the oldest editions, the most attractively illustrated, or those with famous connections such as the Walt Disney version. See LENTZ, Harold, for pop-up version.

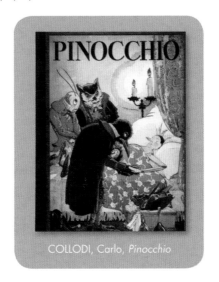

COLLODI, Carlo, *Pinocchio*

Collodi, *Pinocchio,* a sampling of editions in order by date:

Story of a Puppet or the Adventures of Pinocchio..., T. Fisher Unwin, 1892, first English language edition, illustrated by C. Mazzanti, blue cloth, tinted endpapers and edges, first UK edition: $2,000.00

Adventures of Pinocchio, Macmillan, 1927, 12 color plates and b/w illustrations by Attilio Mussino: $55.00

Pinocchio, Doubleday, 1932, illustrations by Maud and Miska Petersham: $35.00

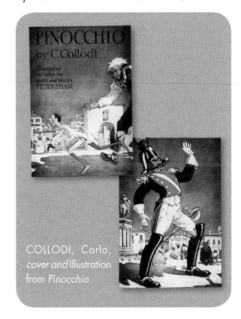

COLLODI, Carlo, *cover and* Illustration *from Pinocchio*

Pinocchio, Limited Edition Club, 1937, illustrated and signed by Richard Floethe, in original slipcase: $55.00

Walt Disney's Version of Pinocchio..., Random House, 1939, color illustrations based on the Disney movie, limited edition (100 copies issued): $2,500.00. First trade edition with dust jacket: $150.00

Collodi, Pinocchio, books by other authors:

Pinocchio's Adventures in Wonderland, with introduction by Hezekiah Butterworth, Jordan, Marsh, 1898, b/w text illustrations, cloth-over-board with gilt: $200.00

Pinocchio under the Sea, Macmillan, 1913, further adventures edited by John Davis, illustrations by Florence Wilde, first edition: $45.00

See also Series section, PINOCCHIO ONCE-UPON-A-TIME

COLUM, Padraic (1881 – 1972)

Adventures of Odysseus and the Tale of Troy, Macmillan, 1918, color and b/w illustrations by Willy Pogany: $100.00

Big Tree of Bunlahy, Macmillan, 1933, 166 pages, color frontispiece, b/w illustrations by Jack Yeats, first US edition with dust jacket: $250.00

Boy Who Knew What the Birds Said, Macmillan, 1918, small, illustrated by Dugald Stewart Walker, first edition: $70.00

Children of Odin, Macmillan, 1920, illustrated endpapers, color and b/w by Willy Pogany, first edition: $80.00

Creatures, Macmillan, 1927, black spine with gilt lettering, silver paper-covered boards, 58 pages, poetry collection, 300 numbered copies signed by Padraic Colum and Boris Artzybasheff: $200.00

Forge in the Forest, Macmillan, 1925, illustrations by Boris Artzybasheff, first edition: $50.00

Frenzied Prince, McKay, 1943, oversize, green hardcover, 196 pages, full-page color plus b/w illustrations by Willy Pogany, first edition with dust jacket: $100.00

COLUM, Padraic, *illustration from Girl Who Sat by the Ashes*

Girl Who Sat by the Ashes, Macmillan, 1919, illustrations by Dugald Stewart Walker, first edition: $50.00

Golden Fleece and the Heroes Who Lived before Achilles, Macmillan, 1921, illustrations by Willy Pogany, US first edition: $50.00

King of Ireland's Son, Henry Holt, 1916, illustrations by Willy Pogany, first edition: $90.00

Peep-Show Man, Macmillan, 1924, illustrated by Lois Lenski, first edition: $50.00

Six Who Were Left in a Shoe, McGraw Hill, 1968, illustrated by Joseph Schindelman, story of the animals left in the old woman's shoe, US first edition with dust jacket: $40.00

COLVER, Alice Mary, see Series section, JOAN FOSTER

COLVER, Anne

Bread-and-Butter Indian, Holt, Rinehart and Winston, 1964, 96 pages, story set in 1770s Pennsylvania, first edition with dust jacket: $70.00

Bread-and-Butter Journey, Holt, Rinehart, and Winston, 1970, illustrations by Garth Williams, first edition with dust jacket: $100.00

Lucky Four, Duell, Sloan & Pearce, 1960, illustrations by Albert Orbaan, first edition with dust jacket: $50.00

COMSTOCK, Harriet

Princess Rags and Tatters, Doubleday, 1912, gray cloth-over-board cover with illustration, small, 112 pages, color illustrations by E. R. Lee Thayer, first edition: $60.00

COOLIDGE, Florence Claudine

Little Ugly Face and Other Indian Tales, Macmillan, 1925, cloth-over-board cover with illustration, small, color illustrations by Maud and Miska Petersham, first edition: $70.00

COOLIDGE, Susan

Little Knight of Labor, 1899, Little, Brown, cloth-over-board cover, illustrated, first edition with dust jacket: $200.00

COOMBS, Patricia, see Series section, DORRIE THE LITTLE WITCH

Lisa and the Grompet, Lothrop, Lee & Shepard, 1970, illustrations by author, first edition with dust jacket: $60.00

Lost Playground, Lothrop, Lee & Shepard, 1963, illustrations by author, first edition with dust jacket: $60.00

Waddy and His Brother, Lothrop, Lee & Shepard, 1963, hardcover, color illustrations by author: $45.00

COONEY, Barbara, illustrator

Cooney attended Briarcliff and Smith College, then studied lithography and etching at the New York Art Students League. Much of her life was spent in New England, and that influence is apparent in many of her drawings. In 1959, her illustrations for *Chanticleer and the Fox* won the Caldecott Award. Early works used scratchboard, but after *Chanticleer*, she experimented with collage, watercolor, acrylics, and other techniques.

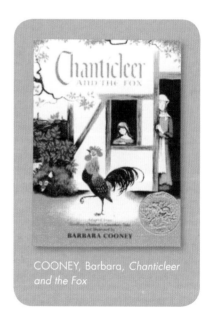

COONEY, Barbara, *Chanticleer and the Fox*

Chanticleer and the Fox, Chaucer story, Crowell, 1958, first edition with dust jacket: $300.00

Chanticleer and the Fox, Crowell, 1959 Caldecott edition with dust jacket: $30.00

King of Wreck Island, Farrar Rinehart, 1941, hardcover, Cooney's first book as both illustrator and author, first edition with dust jacket: $150.00

COOPER, James Fenimore (1789 – 1851)
Although most of Cooper's fiction was meant for adults, titles like *Last of the Mohicans* became known as classic adventure novels for boys.

Deerslayer, Scribner, 1925, illustrated by N. C. Wyeth, paste-on pictorial cover: $75.00

Last of the Mohicans, Macmillan, 1902, illustrated by H. M. Brock, first edition thus: $40.00

Last of the Mohicans, Scribner, 1919, illustrated by N. C. Wyeth, first edition thus: $200.00

COOPER, Susan, see Series section, DARK IS RISING

COPP, Ted, see Series section, STEVE KNIGHT FLYING

CORBETT, Scott, see Series section, DR. MERLIN, ROGER TEARLE

CORY, David, see Series section, BILLY BUNNY, LITTLE JOURNEYS TO HAPPYLAND

CORY, Fanny, illustrator

Mother Goose, Bobbs-Merrill, 1913, oversize picture book, illustrated hardcover with gilt, 73 pages, color plates by Cory: $175.00

COX, Palmer, author/illustrator (b. Canada, 1840 – 1924), see Series section, BROWNIES

COX-McCORMACK, Nancy
Peeps, The Really Truly Sunshine Fairy, Volland, 1918, a Sunny Book, small, color cover illustration, color endpapers, color illustrations throughout by Katherine Sturges Dodge: $70.00

CRAINE, Edith Janice, see Series section, AIRPLANE BOYS, AIRPLANE GIRL

CRANCH, Christopher
Kobboltozo, sequel to *Last of the Huggermuggers*, Phillips Sampson, 1857, orange cloth-over-board cover, 75 pages, b/w illustrations, first edition: $60.00

Last of the Huggermuggers, Phillips, Boston, 1856, cloth-over-board cover, b/w illustrations by author, first edition: $300.00

CRANE, Edith, and Albert Burton
Happy Days Out West, McNally, 1927, blue hardcover with paste-on-pictorial and gilt, small, 129 pages, four color plates by Dorothy Lake Gregory: $30.00

CRANE, Walter (1845 – 1916)
English illustrator Walter Crane was the second son of English portrait painter Thomas Crane, and his early training included an apprenticeship under engraver William James Linton. Crane became one of the first Victorian artists who could sell children's books on the strength of his name alone. Between 1865 and 1876, he produced more than 40 "toy books" (small books approximately 9 inches by 8 inches). In the 1880s, he began to illustrate larger books, including lavish collections of fairy tales. He is considered a major artist of the English Arts and Crafts movement.

Absurd ABC (1874), 1897 "Large Series" edition, John Lane, blue printed wrappers, eight full-page color illustrations by Crane: $600.00

Fable Nook and Story Book, a Collection of Catchy Rhymes and Amusing Stories for Our Little Ones, W. E. Scull, 1901, color pictorial boards, illustrated in b/w and color: $400.00

Red Riding Hood's Picture Book, John Lane, 1898, red cloth cover with black lettering, color illustrations: $400.00

Sirens Three, Macmillan, 1886, oversize, 68 pages, decorated endpapers, illustrated by author, first edition: $400.00

Walter Crane's Painting Book, George Routledge & Sons, 1891, oblong, color pictorial card covers, 12 pairs of pictures, one in color, 11 for child to paint, first edition: $500.00

CRESSWELL, Helen, see Series section, BAGTHORPES

CRESWICK, Paul
Robin Hood, David McKay, 1917, illustrated by N. C. Wyeth, hardcover: $125.00

CROCKETT, S. R.
Red Cap Tales: Stolen from the Treasure Chest of the Wizard of the North, Adam & Charles Black, UK, 1904, pictorial cloth with gilt, 16 color plates by Simon Harmon Vedder, first edition: $90.00

Sir Toady Crusoe, Wells Gardner, 1905, illustrations by Gordon Browne, first edition with dust jacket: $200.00

Surprising Adventures of Sir Toady Lion, Stokes, ca. 1897, gray cloth-over-board cover with color illustration, 314 pages, 69 b/w illustrations by Gordon Browne: $85.00

CROCKFORD, Doris
Flying Scotsman, Oxford University Press, undated, ca. 1937, oblong picture book, color illustrated paper-over-board with cloth spine, full-page color illustrations by Rachel Boger and Henry Cartwright: $35.00

CROCKFORD, Doris, *Flying Scotsman*

CROMPTON, Richmal, see also Series section, WILLIAM BROWN

Jimmy Again, George Newnes, UK, 1951, first edition with dust jacket: $100.00

CROSBY, Ernest
Captain Jinks, Hero, Funk & Wagnalls, 1902, tan cloth-over-board cover with color decorations and gilt on spine, small, 393 pages, b/w illustrations by Dan Beard, first edition: $50.00

CROTHERS, Samuel McChord

Children of Dickens, Scribner, 1925 edition, oversize, 259 pages, black cloth-over-board cover with paste-on-pictorial, illustrated endpapers, 10 color plates by Jessie Willcox Smith, with dust jacket: $200.00

CROWLEY, Maude, see Series section, AZOR BOOKS

CROWNFIELD, Gertrude

Catching up with the Circus, Bouillon-Sanders, 1926, oversize oblong, color illustrated paper-over-board cover, illustrated endpapers, full-page, two-color illustrations by Ethel Pennewill Brown: $50.00

Diantha's Signet Ring, Crowell, 1939, decorative cloth, illustrations by Ervine Metzl, first edition with dust jacket: $40.00

Feast of Noel, E. P. Dutton, 1928, tall, gilt-stamped title, 116 pages, wood-block illustrations by Mary Lott Seaman, first edition with dust jacket: $60.00

CROWNINSHIELD, Mrs. Schuyler

Light-House Children Abroad, Lothrop, 1889, cloth-over-board cover, 446 pages, illustrated with a frontispiece and 27 drawings: $60.00

CRUIKSHANK, George (1792 – 1878), illustrator

The son of painter Isaac Cruikshank, political cartoonist George Cruikshank was an early illustrator of Charles Dickens, including the first edition of *Oliver Twist* in 1838.

Fairy Library, four volumes: *Cinderella and the Glass Slipper, History of Jack and the Beanstalk, Hop-o-My-Thumb and the Seven League Boots, Puss in Boots,* and *Routledge,* 1853, full set with slipcase: $3,000.00

CUFFARI, Richard (1925 – 1978, b. Brooklyn), illustrator

Cuffari studied at the Pratt Institute following service in World War II. For years a freelance commerical artist, he turned to illustrating children's books in the 1960s and later became an instructor of book illustration for the Parsons School of Design. Much of his work centers on historical recreations, such as *Perilous Gard* (1974, Pope), or natural history. With more than 200 books to his credit, Cuffari received a number of design awards including two Citations of Merit from the Society of Illustrators.

CURRY, Jane Louise

Beneath the Hill, Harcourt Brace & World, 1967, illustrated by Imero Gobbato, first edition with dust jacket: $70.00

CURTIS, Alice, see Series section, FRONTIER GIRL

■ · · · · · · · · · · · · · · · · D · · · · · · · · · · · · · · · · ■

DAHL, Roald (1916 – 1990)

Charlie and the Chocolate Factory, Knopf, 1964, b/w illustrations by Joseph Schindelman, US first edition with dust jacket: $2,500.00

DAHL, Roald, *Charlie and the Chocolate Factory*

Charlie and the Great Glass Elevator, Knopf, 1972, hardcover, b/w illustrations by Joseph Schindelman, first edition with dust jacket: $300.00

Gremlins, Random House, 1943, pictorial boards, interior illustrations by Disney Studios, first edition with dust jacket: $4,200.00

James and the Giant Peach, Knopf, 1961, red cloth, four full-page color plates plus other illustrations by Nancy Ekholm Burket, US first edition with dust jacket: $6,000.00

DALGLIESH, Alice (1893 – 1979), see Series section, SANDY COVE

Bears on Hemlock Mountain, Scribner, 1952, small hardcover, b/w/blue illustrations by Helen Sewell: $50.00

Columbus Story, Scribner, 1955, first edition, hardcover, 28 pages, color plates by Leo Politi: $100.00

Thanksgiving Story, Scribner, 1954, first edition, oversize hardcover, illustrations by Helen Sewell: $50.00

DALZIEL BROTHERS

George, Edward, and John were known as the best wood engravers in Victorian England, translating popular paintings by such artists as W.H. Hunt and Dante Rossetti into illustrations for books. The Dalziels were usually credited on the title page as "Engraved by the Brothers Dalziel" or their family name would appear above the title of a work.

DANIEL, Elizabeth

Happy Hours, Rand McNally, 1934, paper-over-board, small, b/w photos with matching verses: $40.00

DANIEL, Elizabeth, *Happy Hours*

DANK, Milton and Gloria, see Series section, GALAXY GANG

DARWIN, Bernard and Elinor, see Series section, MR. TOOTLEOO

D'AULAIRE, Ingri (1904 – 1980) and Edgar Parin (1898 – 1986), authors/illustrators, their books feature colorful, full-page illustrations.

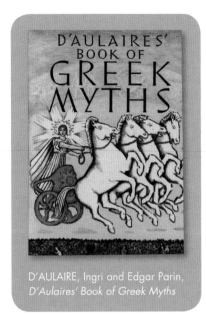

D'AULAIRE, Ingri and Edgar Parin, *D'Aulaires' Book of Greek Myths*

Abraham Lincoln, Doubleday, Doran, 1939, pictorial cover, color illustrations, first edition: $200.00

Buffalo Bill, Doubleday, 1952, illustrated boards, color illustrations by authors, first edition with dust jacket: $200.00

D'Aulaires' Book of Greek Myths, Doubleday, 1962, oversize, first edition with dust jacket: $60.00

D'Aulaires' Trolls, Garden City, 1972, oversize hardcover, color illustrations by authors, first edition with dust jacket: $150.00

Foxie, Doubleday, 1949, lost dog joins rooster and cat as musicians, first edition with dust jacket: $200.00

Leif the Lucky, Doubleday, Doran, 1941, oversize, first edition with dust jacket: $200.00

Magic Meadow, Garden City, 1958, first edition, hardcover, illustrations by authors: $150.00

D'AULAIRE, Ingri and Edgar Parin, *Leif the Lucky*

Nils, Doubleday, 1948, first edition, oversize picture book, color illustrated paper-over-board cover, color and b/w illustrations throughout by authors: $150.00

Norse Gods and Giants, Doubleday, 1967, oversize, first edition with dust jacket: $200.00

DAUZET, Marceline
Forest Friends, Saalfield, 1940, 16 pages, color and b/w illustrations by Fern Bisel Peat: $40.00

DAVIES, Mary Carolyn, poet

Little Freckled Person, Houghton Mifflin, 1919, verse, cloth-over-board cover with printed illustration, 104 pages, color frontispiece, b/w plates by Harold Cue: $35.00

Peter's Trip to Story-Land, Funk & Wagnalls, 1923, story in verse, 10 full-page color illustrations by B. Gray, first edition: $50.00

DAVIS, Lavinia R.
Danny's Luck, Doubleday, 1953, first edition, oblong hardcover, illustrated endpapers, color illustrations by Hildegard Woodward: $60.00

Hobby Horse Hill, E. M. Hale, 1939, first edition: $100.00

Melody, Mutton Bone and Sam, Doubleday, 1947, b/w illustrations by Paul Brown, first edition with dust jacket: $100.00

Plow Penny Mystery, Doubleday, Doran, 1942, illustrations by Paul Brown, first edition with dust jacket: $80.00

Wild Birthday Cake, Doubleday, 1949, oversize, color illustrations by Hildegarde Woodward, first edition with dust jacket: $80.00

DAVIS, Norman
Picken's Great Adventure, Oxford, 1948, first edition, hardcover, illustrations by Winslade: $50.00

Picken's Treasure Hunt, Oxford, 1955, first edition, hardcover, illustrations by Winslade: $50.00

DeANGELI, Marguerite, see also Series section, TED AND NINA

Book of Nursery and Mother Goose Rhymes, Doubleday, 1954, illustrations by author, first edition: $50.00

Elin's Amerika, Doran, 1941, oversize, decorated cloth-over-board cover, 94 pages, litho illustrations by author, first edition: $85.00

Henner's Lydia, Doran, 1936, oversize, 70 pages, litho illustrations by author, first edition: $85.00

Just Like David, Garden City, 1951, pictorial green boards, b/w and two-color illustrations by author, first edition: $40.00

Old Testament, 1960 edition, Doubleday, oversize hardcover, illustrations by DeAngeli, first edition with dust jacket: $65.00

Turkey for Christmas, Westminster Press, 1944, illustrations by author, first edition with dust jacket: $60.00

Yonie Wondernose, Doubleday, Doran, 1944, oversize, illustrated by author, first edition with dust jacket: $40.00

deBOSSCHERE, Jean
Beasts and Men, Folk Tales Collected in Flanders, Heinemann, 1918, oversize, cloth-over-board cover, illustrated endpapers, 12 color plates plus b/w illustrations by author: $120.00

Christmas Tales of Flanders, Dodd, 1917, leather and cloth-over-board cover with gilt, 12 color plates plus two-color and b/w illustrations by author: $200.00

Folk Tales of Flanders, Dodd, 1918, oversize, cloth-over-board cover with gilt, illustrated endpapers, 12 color plates plus b/w illustrations: $110.00

DeBRUNHOFF, Laurent, see Series section, BABAR, SERAFINA THE GIRAFFE

DECKER, Duane

Catcher from Double-A, Morrow, 1950, pictorial hardcover, 188 pages, first edition with dust jacket: $80.00

Fast Man on a Pivot, Morrow, 1951, first edition with dust jacket: $75.00

Hit and Run, Morrow, 1950, first edition with dust jacket: $75.00

Mister Shortstop, Morrow, 1954, first edition with dust jacket: $75.00

Rebel in Right Field, Morrow, 1972, first edition with dust jacket: $80.00

DEFOE, Daniel

Like so many other classics, the 1719 novel *Robinson Crusoe* eventually made its way into the nursery through lavishly illustrated editions.

Life and Strange Adventures of Robinson Crusoe, Ernest Nister, circa 1890, six color plates and multiple black-and-white drawings by assorted artists, picture of Robinson rowing away from wreck printed on cloth cover: $75.00

Robinson Crusoe, Cosmopolitan Books, 1920, illustrated by N. C. Wyeth, 12 color plates and frontispiece, paste-on-pictorial cover: $150.00

DEHN, Paul

Cat's Whiskers, Longmans, Green, 1963, b/w photos by Ronald Spillman, first edition with dust jacket: $40.00

Quake, Quake, Quake: A Leaden Treasury of English Verse, Simon & Schuster, 1961, 109 pages, illustrations by Edward Gorey, first edition with dust jacket: $55.00

DEIHL, Edna Groff, *Mr. Blue Peacock*

DEIHL, Edna Groff

Aunt Este's Stories of Flower and Berry Babies, Whitman, 1924, tan cloth-over-board cover with color paste-on-pictorial, illustrated endpapers, illustrated, first edition: $80.00

Huffy Wants to Be a Pet, Gabriel, 1929, hardback, illustrations by A. E. Kennedy: $40.00

Little Kitten That Would Not Wash Its Face, Gabriel, 1922, oversize, paper boards, color illustrations, in matched box: $60.00

Little Rabbit That Would Not Eat, Gabriel, 1942, hardcover, color and b/w illustrations: $40.00

Mr. Blue Peacock, Just Right Book, Whitman, 1926, cloth-over-board cover with color paste-on-pictorial, oversize, 63 pages, color illustrations by C. X. Shinn: $50.00

Teddy Bear That Prowled at Night, Sam'l Gabriel Sons, 1924, oversize, tall, color picture boards by Mary LaFetra Russell, first edition: $150.00

DeJONG, Meindert (1906 – 1991)

Along Came a Dog, Harper, 1953, pictorial boards, illustrations by Maurice Sendak: $50.00

Good Luck, Duck, Harper, 1950, first edition, oversize, 57 pages, color illustrations by Marc Simont: $65.00

House of Sixty Fathers, Harper & Brothers, 1956, illustrated by Maurice Sendak, first edition with dust jacket: $100.00

Hurry Home, Candy, Harper, 1953, illustrations by Maurice Sendak, first edition with dust jacket: $100.00

Journey from Peppermint Street, Harper, 1968, National Book Award Winner, first edition, illustrations by Emily McCully: $40.00

Little Cow and the Turtle, Harper, 1955, illustrated hardcover, 173 pages, b/w illustrations by Maurice Sendak: $40.00

Singing Hill, Harper & Row, 1962, illustrated by Maurice Sendak, first edition with dust jacket: $100.00

Wheel on the School, Harper, 1954, illustrations by Maurice Sendak, first edition with dust jacket: $100.00

DeLaMARE, Walter (1873 – 1956)

Dutch Cheese, Knopf, 1931, cloth-over-board cover, oversize, four color plates and b/w illustrations by Dorothy Lathrop, first edition: $60.00

Stuff and Nonsense, Constable, 1927, cloth-over-board cover, 110 pages, woodcut b/w illustrations by Bold: $45.00

DENISON, Muriel, see Series section, SUSANNAH

DENNIS, Wesley (1903 – 1966), see Series section, FLIP

Dennis illustrated more than 80 books, primarily horse or animal stories, and is best-known for his illustrations for the books of Marguerite Henry. Dennis attended the New School of Art in Boston. For a short time, he traveled around race tracks, supporting himself by selling portraits of horses to their owners.

DENSLOW, W. W. (1856 – 1915)

The first illustrator of the *Oz* books, artist Denslow held a joint copyright on the

Scarecrow, Tin Man, and other characters of the first *Oz* book. Denslow began his career as a newspaper illustrator and did some cartoon strips that included *Oz* characters. He also did the artwork for postcards, theater posters, and other advertising pieces. He taught art at Elbert Hubbard's Roycroft studios and illustrated several books printed by the Roycroft Press.

DENSLOW, W. W., illustration

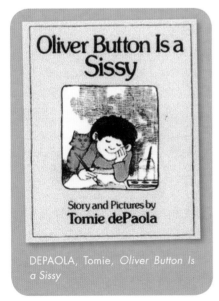

DEPAOLA, Tomie, *Oliver Button Is a Sissy*

DEPAOLA, Tomie (b. Connecticut)

Like many American illustrators of the 1970s, DePaola received his early education at the Pratt Institute in Brooklyn, New York, and also at the Skowhagen School of Painting. During his graduate years at the California College of Arts and Crafts,

he worked as a stage set designer and a muralist. His work often draws upon his own Irish-Italian heritage, including his most famous picture book, *Strega Nona* (Caldecott Honor Award, 1976). His highly recognizable style relies on a strong brown line with color supplied by acrylic, although he occasionally uses colored pencils. The strong use of shapes, rather than photographic renderings, grew out of DePaola's interest in folk art.

Oliver Button Is a Sissy, Harcourt Brace, 1978, illustrations by author, first edition with dust jacket: $40.00

Prince of the Dolomites, Harcourt Brace, 1980, illustrations by author, first edition with dust jacket: $70.00

DeREGNIERS, Beatrice Schenk

Cats Cats Cats Cats Cats, Pantheon, 1958, illustrations by Bill Sokol: $50.00

Giant Story, Harper, 1953, oversize, blue/b/w illustrations by Maurice Sendak, probable first: $65.00

How Joe the Bear and Sam the Mouse Got Together, Parents' Magazine Press, 1965, oversize, pictorial cover, illustrated by Brinton Turkle: $100.00

Red Riding Hood, Atheneum, 1972, 42 pages, two-color illustrations by Edward Gorey, first edition: $75.00

DETMOLD, C. M. (1883–1908)

DETMOLD, E. J. (1883–1957)

The twin brothers Charles Maurice and Edward Julius collaborated on their earliest works and became famous for their careful and realistic animal portraits, done by studying the creatures at the London Zoo. After his brother's suicide in 1908, E. J. Detmold continued to illustrate books through the 1920s.

DICK, Trella, see Series section, TORNADO JONES MYSTERY

DICKENS, Charles

Dickens' classic tales were usually written for a general audience, rather than for children, and usually first appeared in

installments sold at bookshops or newsstands. These were later bound together into books, often with a paper cover, and the buyer could then order an expensive cover, such as leather with gilt trim. All have been reissued constantly, with hundreds of editions featuring a wide range of famous illustrators. A few samples of editions of children's favorites include:

Adventures of Oliver Twist, 1846 Bradbury and Evans, morocco and gilt cover, 24 etched copper plates by George Cruikshank, probably the first edition of this title to be bound in one volume: $500.00

Captain Boldheart/Magic Fishbone, 1964 edition, Macmillan, oversize hardcover, color illustrations by Hilary Knight, first edition thus, with dust jacket: $50.00

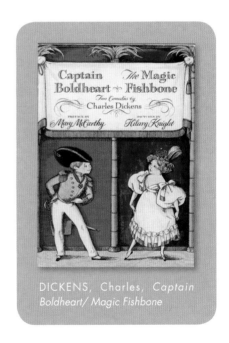

DICKENS, Charles, *Captain Boldheart/Magic Fishbone*

Child's History of England, three volumes, Bradbury and Evans, London, 1852, small, leather covers of polished tan calf with gilt, marbled edges, bound by Riviere: $1,000.00

Christmas Carol, William Heinemann or J. B. Lippincott, 1915, oversize, original full vellum gilt with silk ties, 12 color plates mounted on heavy brown paper. Signed limited edition (525 issued), signed by illustrator Arthur Rackham at time of publication: $4,200.00

Christmas Carol, William Heinemann or J. B. Lippincott, 1915, illustrations by Arthur Rackham, 12 color plates with tissue guards, first edition with original cloth binding: $500.00. With original dust jacket: $2,000.00

Christmas Carol, 1961 edition, World, hardcover, 110 pages, color and b/w illustrations by Ronald Searle, first edition thus: $40.00

Cricket on the Hearth, a Fairy Tale of Home, 1905, J. M. Dent, London, bound by MacDonald in dark green morocco with gilt, holly motif with red onlay of berries on front cover: $800.00

Magic Fishbone, 1953 edition, Vanguard, first edition, oversize pictorial boards with cloth spine, first thus, 36 pages, color and b/w illustrations by Louis Slobodkin: $50.00

Poor Traveller: Boots at the Holly-Tree Inn and Mrs. Gamp, Bradbury & Evans, 1858, small, original green wrappers: $250.00

DICKSON, Gordon R.
Secret under the Sea, Holt, Rinehart and Winston, 1960, illustrated by Jo Ann Stover, first edition with dust jacket: $60.00

Dillon, Leo (b. 1933 Brooklyn), Dillon, Diane (b. 1933 California)
New Yorker Leo and Californian Diane grew up on opposite coasts, then met when they both attended Parsons School of Design. Although they pursued separate freelance careers after marriage, they eventually pooled their talents to create a "third style." From science fiction paperbacks to picture books, the prolific Dillons turned out hundreds of distinct, colorful illustrations often incorporating American-Indian or African motifs. In the 1990s, their son, Lee, joined the family collaboration by creating the borders for the picture book, *Aida.* Due to the beauty of their work as well as its themes, the Dillons' picture books, especially out-of-print works, draw serious interest from collectors.

DINES, Glen, author/illustrator

Tiger in the Cherry Tree, Macmillan, 1958, illustrations by author, first edition with dust jacket: $50.00

Useful Dragon of Sam Ling Toy, Macmillan, 1958, oversize hardcover, color illustrations by author, first edition with dust jacket: $100.00

DISNEY, Walt, Studios
The Walt Disney Studios have issued thousands of publications valued from almost nothing to thousands of dollars. This is such a specialized area, with so much available for the collector, we recommend guide books dealing exclusively with Disney publications. A few examples:

Donald Duck and His Friends, Story Book, Whitman, 1937, 12+ inches tall, stories feature Minnie and Mickey as well as Goofy and Clarabelle: $800.00

Donald Duck Story, Whitman, 1935, the first Donald Duck book, written and illustrated by the Disney staff, folio size, 16 pages, color illustrations throughout, color pictorial wrappers, first edition: $1,200.00

Little Red Riding Hood and the Big Bad Wolf, McKay, 1934, first edition, pictorial boards, full color illustrations from Disney Studios: $250.00

Mickey Mouse in King Arthur's Court, Pop-Up, Dean, 1934, UK edition, oversize, paper covered boards, with brightly colored illustrations of Mickey and Minnie

DISNEY, Walt, Studios, *Three Little Pigs*

Mouse, pictorial endpapers, four full color double-page pop-ups plus b/w drawings, UK first edition: $1,000.00

Mickey Mouse Waddle Book, Disney, 1934, w/cardboard punch-out figures, without waddles: $200.00. With waddles begins at: $5,000.00

Mountaineering Mickey, Collins, UK, 1937, oversize, illustrated boards feature Mickey and Donald Duck, pictorial endpapers, 76 pages, b/w and two-color illustrations, with dust jacket: $1,500.00. Without dust jacket: $300.00

Pop-up Mickey Mouse, Blue Ribbon Books, 1933, pictorial boards, three pop-ups in color plus b/w illustrations: $700.00

Silly Symphony Stories, Whitman, 1936, small, illustrated boards: $250.00

Three Little Pigs (from the Walt Disney Silly Symphony), Blue Ribbon, 1933, oversize, illustrations in color, first edition with dust jacket: $700.00

Thumper, Grosset & Dunlap, 1942, Disney color illustrations with dust jacket: $125.00

Walt Disney's Mickey Mouse Cookbook, Golden Press, 1975 edition, oversize hardcover, color endpapers, color illustrations throughout: $40.00

Walt Disney Thumper Annual, edited by R. H. Taylor, Odhams Press, 1952 oversize hardcover with gilt lettering, 93 pages, illustrated endpapers, color illustrations by studio throughout: $75.00

DIXON, Franklin W., see Series section, HARDY BOYS

DOANE, Pelagie (b. New Jersey, 1906-1996), illustrator
Doane studied at the School of Design, Philadelphia. She began her career in a greeting card company art department, but her stylistic versatility qualified her for a long career in book illustration. She painted sweet illustrations for children's picture books as well as stylish, mysterious dust jackets for the teen *Judy Bolton* mystery series.

Boy Jesus, Oxford University Press, 1953, 56 pages, full-page color illustrations by author, first edition with dust jacket: $45.00

Small Child's Book of Verse, Oxford, 1948, cloth-over-board cover with gilt lettering, oversize, 135 pages, illustrated endpapers, color and b/w illustrations by Doane, first edition with dust jacket: $70.00

DODGE, Louis
Bonnie May, Scribner's, 1916, b/w illustrations by Reginald Birch, first edition with dust jacket: $40.00

Children of the Desert, Scribner, 1917, gray cloth-over-board cover: $30.00

Sandman's Forest, Scribner, 1918, cloth-over-board cover with illustration, 293 pages, six color illustrations by Paul Branson: $50.00

DODGE, Mary Mapes (1831–1905)
Hans Brinker, Winston, 1925 edition, cloth-over-board cover with paste-on-pictorial, 325 pages, illustrated endpapers, four color plates by Clara M. Burd, first thus: $40.00

Hans Brinker, Scribner, 1936, illustrated by Geroge Wharton Edwards, with dust jacket: $40.00

Hans Brinker or The Silver Skates, James O'Kane, NY, 1866, 347 pages plus ads, original cloth cover with gilt lettering: $1,000.00

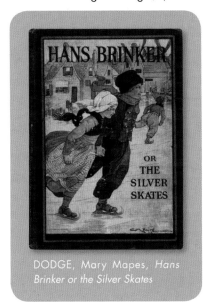

DODGE, Mary Mapes, *Hans Brinker or the Silver Skates*

Land of Pluck, Century, 1894, first edition, cloth-over-board cover, gilt, b/w engraving illustrations: $45.00

Silver Skates, David McKay, 1918, decorated cloth cover with color paste-on illustration, top edge gilt, pictorial dust jacket, color plates and title-page artwork by Maginel Wright Enright, first edition thus, with dust jacket: $150.00

When Life Is Young, Century, 1894, cloth hardcover with gilt, illustrations, first edition of this collection of verses: $100.00

DOLBIER, Maurice
Half-Pint Jinni and Other Stories, Random House, 1948, first edition with dust jacket: $50.00

Lion in the Woods, Little, Brown, 1955, illustrations by Robert Henneberger, first edition with dust jacket: $40.00

Torten's Christmas Secret, Little, Brown, 1951, color illustrations by Robert Henneberger, first edition with dust jacket: $60.00

DONAHEY, William, author/illustrator, see also Series section, TEENIE WEENIES

Children's Mother Goose, Reilly & Lee, 1921, oversize, illustrated hardcover, 12 color plate illustrations by Donahey: $200.00

DOUGLAS, Gilbert
Bulldog Attitude, Crowell, 1957, basketball story, first edition with dust jacket: $100.00

DOW, Ethel C.
Diary of a Birthday Doll, Barse & Hopkins, 1908, cloth-over-board cover with paste-on-pictorial, color plates and b/w illustrations by Florence England Nosworthy and Louise Clark Smith, first edition: $90.00

Mother's Hero, Stern, 1910, 122 pages, color paste-on-illustration on cloth-over-board cover, b/w illustrations by Isabel Lyndall, four color plates by S. Weber: $60.00

Proud Roxanna, Stern, 1909, green cloth-over-board cover with paste-on-pictorial,

color plates and b/w illustrations by Eugenie Wireman: $50.00

DOWNER, Marion
David and the Seagulls, Lothrop, Lee, 1956, illustrations by photos, first edition with dust jacket: $45.00

DOYLE, Arthur Conan
White Company, Cosmopolitan, 1922, illustrated by N. C. Wyeth, pictorial paste-on cover, first edition: $75.00

DOYLE, Richard (1824 – 1957)
The uncle of Arthur Conan Doyle, English artist Richard Doyle was an early Punch illustrator. He is best known today for his fairies, delicate little creatures depicted as being smaller than a leaf or a nut. His magazine work is often signed with the nickname "Dick Kitkat."

DRAYTON, Grace Gibbie Wiederseim (b. Philadelphia), artist/author
Drayton created the round-eyed, chubby cheeked Campbell's Soup kids (ca. 1900), and the Dolly Dingle character in 1913. Dolly Dingle and her friends were featured in full-page color paper doll spreads in *Pictorial Review* magazine for many years. Drayton also wrote and illustrated the *Bobby and Dolly Series,* bestsellers with over a quarter million volumes sold. Her career included book and magazine illustration, advertising illustration, paper doll illustrations, and doll and toy designs for several manufacturers.

DRAYTON, Grace Gibbie Wiederseim, *Tiny Tots: Their Adventures*

Dolly Dimples and Billy Bounce, Cupples & Leon, 1931, 86 pages, illustrated by author. $200.00

Kiddie Rhymes (author name: Wiederseim, Grace G.), George W. Jacobs, 1911, oversize, color illustrated boards, six color illustrations by author: $70.00

Tiny Tots: Their Adventures (author name: Wiederseim, Grace G.), Frederick A. Stokes, 1909, illustrated paper-over-board cover, oversize, b/w illustrations and 12 full-page color illustrations by author: $125.00

DROWNE, Tatiana Balkoff
But Charlie Wasn't Listening, Heinemann, 1961, first edition, oblong pictorial hardcover, 30 pages, two-color illustrations by Helen Meredith: $60.00

DRUMMOND, V. H., see Series section, MRS. EASTER

Du BOIS, William Pène (1916 – 1993),
see also Series section, OTTO THE GIANT DOG

Artist du Bois received the 1948 Newbery Medal for his book *The Twenty-One One Balloons.* His earliest picture books appeared in 1936 when he was only 20. The son of French painter Guy Pène du Bois, he grew up in New York and France, and later worked as the art director for the *Paris Review.* His illustrations often featured animals in human clothing and circus scenes.

Bear Party, Viking Press, 1951, Caldecott Honor Award winner for best illustrated American children's book, illustrated by author, first edition with dust jacket: $100.00

Call Me Bandicoot, Harper, 1970, 64 pages, color illustrations by author, first edition with dust jacket: $50.00

Giant, Viking Press, 1954, 124 pages, b/w illustrations by author, first edition with dust jacket: $125.00

Horse in the Camel Suit, Harper, 1967, square hardcover, 80 pages, color illustrations by author, first edition with dust jacket: $50.00

Lion, Viking Press, 1956, oversize, illustrated endpapers, color illustrations by author, first edition with dust jacket: $50.00

Mother Goose for Christmas, Viking Press, 1973, 40 pages, illustrated endpapers, color illustrations by author, first edition with dust jacket: $50.00

Peter Graves, Viking Press, 1950, oversize, illustrated endpapers, b/w illustrations by author, first edition with dust jacket: $50.00

Du BOIS, William Pène, *Bear Party*

Porko von Popbutton, Harper, 1969, 80 pages, illustrations by author, first edition with dust jacket: $100.00

Squirrel Hotel, Viking Press, 1952, illustrations by author, first edition with dust jacket: $50.00

Twenty-One Balloons, Viking Press, 1947, illustrations by author, first edition with dust jacket: $50.00

DUFFIELD, J. W., see Series section, BERT WILSON

DuJARDIN, Rosamund, see Series section, MARCY RHODES, PAM AND PENNY, TOBY HEYDON

DULAC, Edmund (1882 – 1957)
French artist Edmund Dulac studied at the University of Toulouse and the Ecole

des Beaux Arts. In 1904 Dulac moved to London where he began illustrating books for publisher J. M. Dent and others. Like his contemporaries Kay Nielsen and Arthur Rackham, his works were often issued in various editions, including limited editions with fancier binding and a higher number of color plates.

Edmund Dulac's Fairy Book: Fairy Tales of the Allied Nations, Hodder & Stoughton, 15 color plates tipped in, early edition: $250.00. Easton Press 1996 reprint: $100.00. Other reprints: $35.00

Emund Dulac's Picture-Book for the French Red Cross, Hodder & Stoughton, circa 1915, first trade edition: $175.00

DUNHAM, Curtis
Golden Goblin, or *The Flying Dutchman, Junior,* Bobbs-Merrill, 1906, stamped in green, red, and gilt, duotone textual art and eight full color plates by George F. Kerr: $100.00

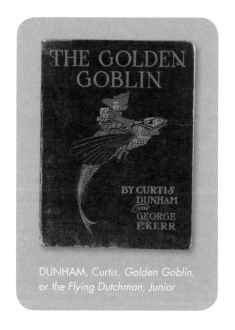

DUNHAM, Curtis, *Golden Goblin, or the Flying Dutchman, Junior*

DUPLAIX, Georges
Animal Stories, 1944 edition, Simon & Schuster, hardcover with illustrated boards, oversize, 92 pages, color illustrations by Feodor Rojankovsky, first edition: $60.00

Gaston and Josephine in America, Oxford, 1934, color illustrated paper-over-board cover, oversize, color illustrations throughout by author, first edition: $95.00

Merry Shipwreck, Harper, 1942, oversize, paper-over-board cover, color illustrations by Tibor Gergely, first edition with dust jacket: $70.00

Pee-Gloo: A Little Penguin from the South Pole, Harper, 1935, hardcover, oversize, 40 pages, illustrated endpapers, illustrated by author, first edition: $75.00

Popo the Hippopotamus, Whitman, 1935, illustrated hardcover, 26 pages, illustrated endpapers, color illustrations by author, first edition: $50.00

Topsy-Turvy Circus, Harper, 1940, oversize, illustrated paper-over-board cover with cloth spine, color illustrations throughout by Tibor Gergely, first edition: $100.00

DUPLAIX, Lily

White Bunny and His Magic Nose, Simon & Schuster, 1945, oversize, paper-over-board cover with color illustration and flocked bunny, interior illustratons full-page color, with flocked characters, illustrations by Masha, first edition: $40.00

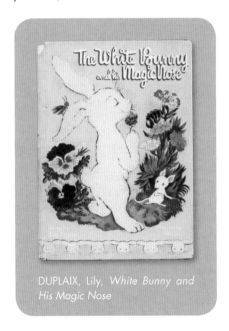

DUPLAIX, Lily, *White Bunny and His Magic Nose*

DUVOISIN, Roger (b. Switzerland, 1904 – 1980), see also Series section, PETUNIA, VERONICA

The son of an architect, Duvoisin studied mural painting and set design at Ecole des Arts, Geneva. His career includes ceramic works, textile design, and in 1932 he wrote and illustrated his first children's book, *Little Boy Was Drawing*. He illustrated his own books, including the popular Petunia stories, and the books of others, winning a Caldecott Medal in 1948.

Christmas Whale, Alfred A. Knopf, 1945, full color illustrations by author, first edition with dust jacket: $50.00

Crocus, Alfred A. Knopf, 1977, oversize, illustrations by author, first edition with dust jacket: $75.00

Day and Night, Alfred A. Knopf, 1960, illustrations by author, first edition with dust jacket: $75.00

Little Boy Was Drawing, Scribner's, 1932, child's drawing comes to life, color illustrations by author, this is Duvoisin's first picture book, hardcover: $200.00

One Thousand Christmas Beards, Alfred A. Knopf, 1955, hardcover, illustrated endpapers, color illustrations by author: $60.00

Three Sneezes, Alfred A. Knopf, 1941, color illustrations by author, first edition with dust jacket: $75.00

■ ·················· **E** ·················· ■

EAGER, Edward (1911 – 1964), see also Series, section HALF MAGIC

Magic or Not, Harcourt Brace, 1959, b/w illustrations by N. M. Bodecker, first edition with dust jacket: $65.00

Mouse Manor, Ariel, 1952, illustrated endpapers, b/w illustrations by Beryl Bailey-Jones, first edition with dust jacket: $65.00

Playing Possum, Putnam, 1955, illustrations by Paul Galdone, first edition hardcover: $70.00

Red Head, Houghton Mifflin, 1951, tall, illustrations by Louis Slobodkin, hardcover: $50.00

EARNSHAW, Brian, see Series section, DRAGONFALL 5 SPACE

EASTMAN, P. D. (Philip Day), illustrator

Massachusetts-born Eastman (1909 – 1986) attended Amherst College and the Art School of National Academy, NY. His career flourished in Hollywood where he worked as animator and producer of animated films for the United Productions of America, after working for Disney Studios and Warner Brothers. He was one of the creators of the Academy Award winning film *Gerald McBoing Boing*. His zany drawings were a good match for Theodore Geisel's stories, and he illustrated learning-to-read books for Random House.

EATON, Anne Thaxter

Animals' Christmas, Viking Press, 1944, color illustrations by Valenti Angelo, first edition with dust jacket: $40.00

Welcome Christmas!, Viking Press, 1955, illustrations by Valenti Angelo, first edition with dust jacket: $35.00

EATON, Seymour, see Series section, ROOSEVELT BEARS

EBERLE, Irmengarde

Apple Orchard, Henry Z. Walck, 1962, illustrated by Ezra Jack Keats, first edition with dust jacket: $50.00

Chipmunk Lives Here, Doubleday, 1966, illustrations by Matthew Kalmenoff, first edition with dust jacket: $90.00

Evie and the Wonderful Kangaroo, Alfred A. Knopf, 1955, hardcover, illustrations by Louis Slobodkin, first edition with dust jacket: $35.00

Good House for a Mouse, Julian Messner, 1940, illustrated by Eloise Wilkin, first edition with dust jacket: $100.00

Robins on the Window Sill, Crowell, 1958, first edition with dust jacket: $50.00

ECKERT, Allan W.

Crossbreed, Little, Brown, 1968, illustrations by Karl E. Karalus, first edition with dust jacket: $40.00

Incident at Hawk's Hill, Little, Brown, 1971, 173 pages, illustrations by John Schoenherr, first edition with dust jacket: $60.00

EDGEWORTH, Maria (1767 – 1849)

Edgeworth wrote educational fiction as well as nonfiction works on education and her "improving stories" for children remained a staple and oft reprinted part of the Victorian library. The value of early UK printings fluctuates with condition and quality of binding. The value of later editions often depends more on the illustrator. A sampling of her titles by date includes:

Parent's Assistant, Joseph Johnson, 1796, Edgeworth's first collection of stories for children. Later editions were expanded into multiple volumes. Early editions (pre-1830), individual volumes in contemporary binding: $125.00

Moral Tales for Young People, Joseph Johnson, 1805, six volumes in set, individual volumes in contemporary binding: $100.00

Parent's Assistant, G. Routledge & Co, 1857, eight illustrations by Phiz, in contemporary binding: $50.00

Simple Susan and Other Tales, 1929 edition, Macmillan, red cloth-over-board cover, 216 pages, four-color plates and 10 b/w illustrations by Clara Burd: $75.00

EDMONDS, Walter D.

Matchlock Gun, Dodd, Mead, 1941, color and b/w illustrations, Newbery Medal winner, first edition with dust jacket: $50.00

Tom Whipple, Dodd, Mead, 1942, illustrations by Paul Lantz, first edition with dust jacket: $100.00

EDWARDS, Leo, see Series section, ANDY BLAKE, JERRY TODD, POPPY OTT, TRIGGER BERG MYSTERY, TUFFY BEAN THE DOG

EHRLICH, Bettina, author/illustrator

Cocolo's Home, Harper, 1950, oversize picture book hardcover, color and b/w illustrations by author, first edition with dust jacket: $70.00

Dolls, Ariel Books, 1963, small, pictorial hardcover, illustrations by author, first edition with dust jacket: $50.00

Goat Boy, Oxford, UK, 1965, oversize, illustrations by author, first edition with dust jacket: $100.00

Pantaloni, Harper, 1957, oversize picture book, color and b/w illustrations by author, US first edition with dust jacket: $40.00

Paolo and Panetto, Watts, 1960, oversize, 32 pages, illustrations by author, US first edition with dust jacket: $75.00

Piccolo, Harper, 1954, miniature size book, color and b/w illustrations by author, US first edition with dust jacket: $40.00

Trovato, Ariel, 1959, oversize picture book, hardcover, color and b/w illustrations by author, US first edition with dust jacket: $60.00

EICHENBERG, Fritz, (1901 – 1990, b. Germany), author/illustrator

As a successful German political cartoonist in the 1930s, Eichenberg annoyed a rising politician named Adolf Hitler. Leaving Germany, where he had studied at the Academy of Graphic Arts in Leipzig, Eichenberg worked in Central America before emigrating to the United States. Much of his work concentrated on illustrating new editions of classics, such as Bronte's *Wuthering Heights,* but the birth of a son inspired a couple of picture books: *Ape in a Cape* and *Dancing in the Moon.*

Ape in a Cape, Harcourt Brace, 1952, oversize alphabet hardcover, illustrated endpapers, color illustrations by author, first edition with dust jacket: $30.00

Endangered Species and Other Fables with a Twist, Stemmer House, 1979, oversize, 128 pages, eight full-color drawings plus b/w illustrations by the author, first edition with dust jacket: $35.00

ELDON, Magdalen

Bumble, Collins, 1950, oversize, 46 pages, illustrations by author, first edition with dust jacket: $50.00

Highland Bumble, Collins, 1952, oversize, color illustrations by author, first edition with dust jacket: $45.00

Snow Bumble, Scribner, 1952, illustrations by author, US first edition with dust jacket: $65.00

ELDRED, Warren, see Series section, ST. DUNSTAN

ELKIN, Benjamin

Gillespie and the Guards, Viking Press, 1956, two-color illustrations by James Daugherty, first edition with dust jacket: $50.00

Loudest Noise in the World, Viking Press, 1954, two-color illustrations by James Daugherty, first edition with dust jacket: $70.00

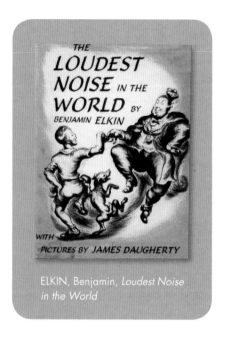

ELKIN, Benjamin, *Loudest Noise in the World*

Six Foolish Fishermen, Watertower, 1957, laminated boards, oversize, illustrated by Katherine Evans, first edition with dust jacket: $35.00

ELLISON, Virginia H.

Pooh Cook Book, E. P. Dutton, 1969, yellow decorated hardcover, Shepard illustrations, first edition with dust jacket: $35.00

Pooh Get-Well Book — Recipes and Activities to Help You Recover from Wheezles and Sneezles, E. P. Dutton, 1973, 82 pages, b/w illustrations, first edition with dust jacket: $50.00

Pooh Party Book, E. P. Dutton, 1971, illustrated by Ernest H. Shepard, first edition with dust jacket: $30.00

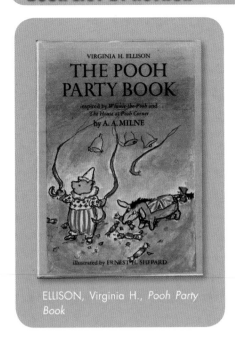

ELLISON, Virginia H., *Pooh Party Book*

Pooh's Birthday Book, 1963, E. P. Dutton, small, color illustrated hardcover, illustrated endpapers, Shepard illustrations, first edition: $40.00

ELMORE, Patricia, see Series section, SUSANNAH AND LUCY MYSTERIES

ELTON, Emily D.

Mince Pie Dream and Other Verses, E. R. Herrick, New York, 1897, printed illustration on cloth-over-board cover, b/w/orange/green color plate illustrations by Blanche McManus: $70.00

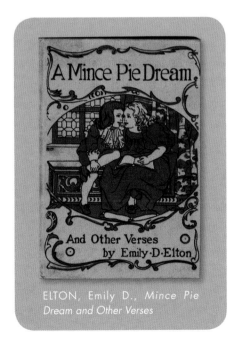

ELTON, Emily D., *Mince Pie Dream and Other Verses*

EMBERLEY, Barbara

Drummer Hoff, 1968, Prentice-Hall, Caldecott Award, color illustrations by Ed Emberley, first edition with dust jacket: $50.00

EMBERLEY, Barbara, *Drummer Hoff*

EMBERLEY, Edward

Emberley studied art at the Rhode Island School of Design and the Massachusetts College of Art. His first art assignment was to paint signs for the army. Following his military service, he worked as commerical artist and cartoonist before becoming interested in children's books. Starting in the 1950s, he produced a number of picture books, often collaborating with his wife Barbara. *Drummer Hoff* received the 1968 Caldecott Award while *One Wide River to Cross* was a Caldecott Honor Book for 1967. In the 1970s, Emberley produced a series of books on drawing, including *Ed Emberley's Drawing Book of Animals* (1970) through *Ed Emberley's Great Thumbprint Drawing Book* (1977).

EMERSON, Alice B., see Series section, RUTH FIELDING

EMERSON, Caroline

Hat-Tub Tale, E. P. Dutton, 1928, first edition, cloth-over-board cover, 185 pages, illustrated endpapers, b/w illustrations by Lois Lenski: $85.00

Little Green Car, Grosset & Dunlap/Artists & Writers Guild First Edition, 1946, pictorial boards, b/w illustrations by Paul Galdone, first edition with dust jacket: $70.00

Merry-Go-Round of Modern Tales, E. P. Dutton, 1927, blue cloth-over-board cover,

oversize, illustrated endpapers, b/w illustrations by Lois Lenski, first edition with dust jacket: $80.00

Mr. Nip and Mr. Tuck in the Air, Dutton, 1946, third book featuring two make-believe animals, illustrations by W. C. Nims (based on the first illustrations by Lois Lenski), 160 pages, first edition with dust jacket: $100.00

School Days in Disneyville, Heath, 1939, illustrations by Disney Studios, first edition: $40.00

EMERY, Anne, see Series section, DINNY GORDON

EMETT, Rowland, author/illustrator
New World for Nellie, Harcourt Brace, 1953, oversize, illustrated by author, first edition with dust jacket: $50.00

ENGDAHL, Sylvia, see also Series section, TOMORROW MOUNTAINS TRILOGY

Journey Between Worlds, Atheneum, 1970, illustrations by James and Ruth McCrea, first edition with dust jacket: $40.00

ENGLE, William, see Series section, G-MEN

ENGVICK, Ed
Lullabies & Night Songs, Harper & Row, 1965, songs set to music by Alec Wilder and illustrated by Maurice Sendak, first edition with dust jacket: $60.00

ENRIGHT, Elizabeth (1909 – 1968), (Daughter of artist Maginel Wright and W. J. Enright), see also Series section, MELENDY FAMILY

Christmas Tree for Lydia, Rinehart, 1951, (story first published in *Woman's Home Companion* in 1947), b/w/red illustrations by author, first edition with dust jacket: $40.00

Gone-Away Lake, Harcourt Brace, 1957, illustrations by Beth and Joe Krush, first edition with dust jacket: $40.00

Kintu, a Congo Adventure, Farrar, 1935, Art Deco color illustrations by author, first edition with dust jacket: $100.00

Return to Gone-Away, Harcourt Brace, 1961, first edition with dust jacket: $30.00

Tatsinda, Harcourt Brace, 1963, illustrations by Irene Haas, first edition with dust jacket: $40.00

Thimble Summer, Farrar & Rinehart, 1938, b/w illustrations by author, first edition with dust jacket: $80.00

ERICKSON, Russell E., see Series section, WARTON THE TOAD

ERNEST, Edward

Animated Circus Book, Grosset & Dunlap, 1943, oversize cardboard illustrated cover, spiral bound, color illustrations and animations by Julian Wehr: $100.00

ERNEST, Edward, *Animated Circus Book*

ERSKINE, Laurie, see Series section, RENFREW

ERWIN, Betty

Aggie, Maggie, and Tish, Little, Brown, 1965, first edition with dust jacket: $40.00

Behind the Magic Line, Little, Brown, 1969, b/w illustrations, first edition with dust jacket: $30.00

Go to the Room of the Eyes, Little, Brown, 1969, b/w illustrations by Irene Burns, first edition with dust jacket: $40.00

Summer Sleigh Ride, Little, Brown, 1966, first edition with dust jacket: $40.00

Where's Aggie?, Little, Brown, 1967, b/w illustrations by Paul Kennedy, first edition with dust jacket: $50.00

Who is Victoria?, Little, Brown, 1973, hardcover, b/w illustrations by Kathleen Anderson, first edition with dust jacket: $30.00

ESTES, Eleanor (1906 – 1988)

Ginger Pye, Harcourt Brace, 1951, 250 pages, b/w illustrations by author, first edition with dust jacket: $70.00

Little Oven, Harcourt Brace, 1955, first edition with dust jacket: $50.00

Lollipop Princess, a Play for Paper Dolls in One Act, Harcourt Brace & World, 1967, oblong pink hardcover, illustrations by author, first edition with dust jacket: $100.00

Miranda the Great, Harcourt Brace, 1967, b/w illustrations by Edward Ardizzone, first edition with dust jacket: $50.00

Pinky Pye, Harcourt Brace, 1958, b/w illustrations by Edward Ardizzone, first edition with dust jacket: $50.00

Tunnel of Hugsy Goode, Harcourt Brace, 1972, drawings by Edward Ardizzone, first edition with dust jacket: $30.00

Witch Family, Harcourt Brace, 1960, b/w illustrations by Edward Ardizzone, first edition with dust jacket: $40.00

ETHERIDGE, Mary Lee, *Mrs. Muff and Her Friends*

ETHERIDGE, Mary Lee

Mrs. Muff and Her Friends, De Wolfe, Fiske, Boston, 1890, blue cloth with red/black/gilt, b/w plates: $40.00

ETS, Marie Hall (1893 – 1984), author/illustrator, see also Series section, MISTER PENNY

Ets began her art career as an interior decorator, then worked as a social worker in Chicago. She studied art at the New York School of Fine and Applied Art and at the Chicago Art Institute, and after a series of personal challenges, began her career as an illustrator of children's books in the 1930s. Much of her work was b/w illustration, but her 1960 Caldecott Medal was awarded for the full color illustrated *Nine Days to Christmas.*

Another Day, Viking Press, 1953, oblong hardcover, b/w illustrations by author, first edition with dust jacket: $40.00

Automobiles for Mice, Viking Press, 1964, picture book, first edition with dust jacket: $60.00

Beasts and Nonsense, Viking Press, 1952, illustrations by author, first edition with dust jacket: $50.00

Cow's Party, Viking Press, 1958, oversize hardcover, 32 pages, illustrations by author, first edition with dust jacket: $50.00

Gilberto and the Wind, Viking Press, 1963, oversize hardcover, color illustrations by author, first edition with dust jacket: $30.00

Just Me, Viking Press, 1965, oblong hardcover, b/w illustrations by author, first edition with dust jacket: $40.00

Nine Days to Christmas, Viking Press, 1959, oversize hardcover, 1960 Caldecott Award book, color illustrations by Ets, first edition with dust jacket: $100.00

Oley the Sea Monster, Viking Press, 1947, picture book, first edition: $60.00

Talking Without Words: I Can. Can You?, Viking Press, 1968, oblong hardcover, b/w illustrations by author, first edition with dust jacket: $45.00

EULALIE (b. London ca. 1895, d. California 1999), illustrator

Eulalie M. Banks began her commercial art career at age 12, selling handmade Christmas cards to family friends. In her early teens she sold card designs and magazine story illustrations, and her first book, *Bobby in Bubbleland*, was published in London in 1913. In 1918 she married Arthur Wilson, moved to Pittsburgh, and began her American art career with illustrations for an edition of *Mother Goose Rhymes*. After divorcing Wilson, Eulalie moved to California with her daughter, Athalie, and became a favorite artist of Hollywood stars. Her work included murals for nurseries in the homes of Harold Lloyd and Charlie Chaplin. She returned to England in the 1940s for a few years, expanding her fame as a book and magazine illustrator, then made California her permanent home. Her illustrated versions for *Child's Garden of Verses* and *Mother Goose* are continually reprinted. Her favorite signature included a sketch of a tiny mouse in blue velvet pants and artist's smock, and Eulalie was fond of telling friends, "I was doing my mouse when Walt Disney was still in diapers." She lived to age 104.

EULALIE illustration

Little Black Sambo, by Helen Bannerman, Platt & Munk, 1928, oversize, red boards, decorated endpapers, color illustrations throughout by Eulalie, one of the best-known illustrations of this story, probable first edition: $500.00

Mother Goose Rhymes, Platt & Munk, 1953, oversize, full-page color illustrations throughout plus b/w drawings, probable first edition with hardcover and paste-on illustrated front: $80.00

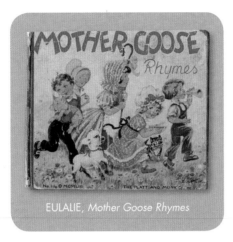
EULALIE, *Mother Goose Rhymes*

Famous Fairy Tales, Platt & Munk, 1923, oversize, brown cloth-over-board cover with gilt lettering and paste-on-illustration, color illustrations throughout, signed Eulalie: $70.00

My First Library: 8 Linenlike Books in a Box, Platt & Munk, Series, 1931, these are the linen-like small books in the 3100 series, titles include *Chicken Little, Little Black Sambo, First Circus, Gingerbread Boy, Little Red Hen, Tale of Peter Rabbit,* and *Three Little Pigs.* Complete set in original illustrated box: $150.00

EVANS, Edmund (1826 – 1905)

Edmund Evans was a Victorian engraver who produced some of the first works in color for children. He began experimenting with color printing as early as 1852 and eventually commissioned such artists as Walter Crane and Kate Greenaway to produce "toy books." These small books aimed at young children contained six pages of text and six pages of colored illustrations and were priced at an affordable sixpence (later the price rose to a shilling). Evans is often credited on the title page of the books that he produced.

EVANS, Katherine, author/illustrator

Flowers for Mother, David McKay, 1948, red/b/w illustrations by author, first edition with dust jacket: $50.00

Ladybug Who Couldn't Fly Home, Wilcox & Follett, 1945, pictorial cover, four-color illustrations, first edition with dust jacket: $40.00

Little Tree, Bruce Publishing, Milwaukee, 1956, first edition: $40.00

Michael Angelo Mouse, Wilcox & Follett, 1945, pictorial cover, first edition with dust jacket: $40.00

EVATT, Harriet, author/illustrator

Davy Crockett, Big Indian and Little Bear, Bobbs-Merrill, 1955, illustrations by author, first edition with dust jacket: $40.00

Mystery of the Alpine Castle, Bobbs-Merrill, 1962, illustrations by author, first edition with dust jacket: $30.00

Papoose Who Wouldn't Keep Her Stockings On, Bobbs-Merrill, 1954, color and b/w illustrations by author, first edition with dust jacket: $40.00

Secret of the Ruby Locket, Bobbs-Merrill, 1943, with gilt lettering, 245 pages, first edition with dust jacket: $60.00

EVERNDEN, Margery

Simon's Way, Henry Z. Walck, 1948, illustrations by Frank Newfeld, first edition with dust jacket: $30.00

Sword with the Golden Hilt, Caxton, 1950, illustrated by William Soles, first edition with dust jacket: $40.00

EVERS, Helen and Alf, authors/illustrators

Benny and His Birds, Rand McNally, 1941, two-color illustrations: $40.00

Fussbunny, Rand McNally, 1944, pictorial boards, first edition: $40.00

House the Pecks Built, Rand McNally, 1940, first edition with dust jacket: $50.00

Merry Mouse, Farrar & Rinehart, 1936, paper-covered illustrated boards, first edition: $60.00

Moonymouse, Rand McNally, 1948, first edition with dust jacket: $70.00

Mr. Scrunch, Rand McNally, 1939, first edition with dust jacket: $200.00

Plump Pig, Rand McNally, 1938, first edition with dust jacket: $50.00

Pokey Bear, Rand McNally, 1942, pink with white polka-dot cover with illustration, first edition: $40.00

Sloppy Joe, Rand McNally, 1947, blue boards, first edition with dust jacket: $70.00

This Little Pig, F. J. Ward, UK, 1935, illustrated paper covered boards, pink and black drawings, first edition with dust jacket: $80.00

EVERS, Helen and Alf, *Pokey Bear*

EWING, Juliana Horatia

Daddy Darwin's Dovecote, Society for Promotion of Christian Knowledge, UK, 1884, pictorial boards, frontispiece in color, illustrations by Randolph Caldecott, engraved and printed by Edmund Evans: $100.00

Dandelion Clocks, Society for Promotion of Christian Knowledge, UK, 1887, yellow ornamental paper boards, frontispiece and illustrations by Gordon Browne and others: $60.00

Grandmother's Spring, Society for Promotion of Christian Knowledge, UK, 1886, chromolithograph illustrations by Richard Andre (16 full-color, 16 two-color), part of series of six books, originally published in *Aunt Judy's Magazine,* 1880, cloth spine and paper backed binding: $200.00

EWING, Juliana Horatia, *Jackanapes*

Jackanapes, Society for Promotion of Christian Knowledge, UK, 1884, first edition in book form, pictorial boards printed in color, frontispiece and text illustrations by Randolph Caldecott: $400.00

Jackanapes, McLoughlin Brothers, 1906, oversize, chromolithograph frontispiece, illustrations by Noble-Ives: $70.00

Jackanapes, Oxford University Press, 1948, color and b/w illustrations by Tasha Tudor, first edition thus, with dust jacket: $250.00

Lob Lie-By-the-Fire or, *The Luck of Linborough,* Society for Promotion of Christian Knowledge, UK, 1885, pictorial boards, first edition with the Randolph Caldecott illustrations: $80.00

Mother's Birthday Review, Society for Promotion of Christian Knowledge, UK, 1885, pictorial cover, small, 82 full-page chromolithographs by Richard Andre, 172 pages, collection of poems, most of them originally published in *Aunt Judy's Magazine* from 1874 to 1883, first edition thus: $100.00

Stories by Juliana Horatio Ewing, Duffield, New York, 1920, 426 pages, color plates by Edna Cooke, hardcover with pictorial paste-on and gilt lettering: $50.00

EYRE, Katherine Wigmore

Song of a Thrush, Oxford University

Press, 1952, illustrations by Stephani and Edward Godwin, US first edition with dust jacket: $50.00

Susan's Safe Harbor, Oxford University Press, 1942, illustrations by Deci Merwin, first edition with dust jacket: $100.00

■ ⋯⋯⋯⋯⋯⋯ **F** ⋯⋯⋯⋯⋯⋯ ■

FABRES, Alice

Anne and Maryke, Holidays in Holland, John C. Winston, 1947, illustrated by Oscar Fabres, 94 pages, first edition with dust jacket: $100.00

FABRES, Oscar, author/illustrator

Fabres grew up in South America, then studied art at the Academie Julian in Paris. His fine art paintings have been exhibited worldwide. His work in commercial art includes magazine and book illustration.

FABRES, Oscar, *Choo-Choo Train*

Choo-Choo Train, John Martin, 1946, paper-over-board cover with spiral binding, color illustrations by author: $40.00

Kwik and Kwak, Methuen, 1945, pictorial coverboard with cloth spine, color illustrations, first edition: $70.00

FALK, Lee, see Series section, PHANTOM

FALKNER, Frederick

Aqualung Twins and the "Iron Crab," Dent & Sons Ltd., 1959, illustrated by Frank Grey, first edition with dust jacket: $30.00

Aqualung Twins and the Vanishing People, J. M. Dent & Co., London, 1957, first edition with dust jacket: $30.00

FALL, Thomas

Eddie No-Name, Pantheon Books, 1963, illustrated by Ray Prohaska, first edition with dust jacket: $50.00

Goat Boy of Brooklyn, Dial Press, 1968, 192 pages, b/w illustrations by Fermin Rocker, first edition with dust jacket: $30.00

FALLS, C.B. (1874 – 1960)

ABC Book, Doubleday, 1923, oversize picture, three-color woodcut illustrations by author, 30 pages: $150.00

Mother Goose, Doubleday, 1924, 96 pages: $350.00

FARALLA, Dana

Singing Cupboard, Blackie and Son Ltd., London, 1963, illustrations by Edward Ardizzone, first edition with dust jacket: $40.00

Swanhilda-of-the-Swans, Blackie, London, 1964, hardcover, illustrated by Edward Ardizzone, first edition with dust jacket: $90.00

Swanhilda-of-the-Swans, J. B. Lippincott, 1964, hardcover, illustrated by Harold Berson, first edition with dust jacket: $50.00

Wonderful Flying-Go-Round, World, 1965, illustrated by Harold Berson, first edition with dust jacket: $40.00

FARJEON, Eleanor (1881 – 1965)

Country Child's Alphabet, Poetry Bookshop, London, 1924, alphabet drawings by William Michael Rothenstein, each accompanied by Farjeon rhymes, first edition with dust jacket: $200.00

Glass Slipper, Allan Wingate, 1946, a play written by Farjeon and her husband Herbert, eight color plates by Hugh Stevenson, first edition with dust jacket: $45.00

Glass Slipper, Oxford, UK, 1955, or Viking Press, US, 1956, novelization of Farjeon's play of the same title, illustrations by Ernest Shepherd, first edition with dust jacket: $75.00

Italian Peepshow and Other Tales, Frederick A. Stokes, New York, 1926, cloth cover with a paste-on pictorial label and gilt lettering, illustrations by Rosalind Thornycroft, first edition with dust jacket: $150.00

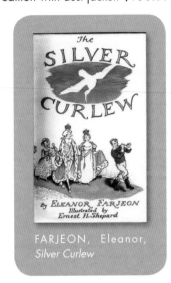

FARJEON, Eleanor, *Silver Curlew*

Little Bookroom: Eleanor Farjeon's Short Stories for Children Chosen by Herself, Oxford, 1956, illustrated by Edward Ardizzone, first edition with dust jacket: $60.00

Martin Pippin in the Apple Orchard, Collins, 1921, illustrated by C. E. Brock, first edition: $150.00. Later Collins printings: $75.00

Martin Pippin in the Apple Orchard, Oxford, 1952, illustrated by Richard Kennedy, with dust jacket: $30.00

Martin Pippin in the Daisy-Field, Michael Joseph Ltd., 1937, illustrated by Isobel and John Morton-Sale, first edition with dust jacket: $150.00

Mrs. Malone, Walck, 1962, illustrated by Edward Ardizzone, first edition with dust jacket: $50.00

Old Nurse's Stocking Basket, Frederick A. Stokes, 1931, pictorial cover, illustrations by Herbert Whydale, first edition: $60.00

Old Nurse's Stocking Basket, Henry Walck, 1965, illustrations by Edward Ardizzone, first edition with dust jacket: $40.00

One Foot in Fairyland, Frederick A. Stokes, 1938, illustrated by Robert Lawson, with dust jacket: $100.00

Perfect Zoo, David McKay, 1929, oblong, color illustrations by Kathy Kruse, first edition: $200.00

Silver Curlew, Oxford University Press, 1953, illustrations by Ernest H. Shepherd, first edition with dust jacket: $200.00

Tale of Tom Tiddler, Frederick A. Stokes, 1930, light cloth-over-board cover with illustration, b/w illustrations by Tealby Norman, US first edition: $100.00

Ten Saints, Oxford, 1936, cloth-over-board cover, illustrations by Helen Sewell, first edition with dust jacket: $60.00

FARLEY, Walter, see Series section, BLACK STALLION

FARMER, Penelope

Castle of Bone, Atheneum, 1972, 152 pages, first edition with dust jacket: $50.00

FARRAR, John

Songs for Johnny-Jump-Up, R. Smith, 1930, verse, small, cloth-over-board cover, 55 pages, line drawings by Rita Leach, printed in brown ink, first edition with dust jacket: $70.00

FARROW, G. E., see Series section, WALLYPUG

FATIO, Louise, see also Series section, HAPPY LION

Christmas Forest, Aladdin Books, 1950, 24 pages, illustrations by Roger Duvoisin, first edition with dust jacket: $40.00

FAULKNER, Georgene

Little Peachling, Volland, 1928, illustrated endpapers, color prints by Frederick Richardson: $75.00

Road to Enchantment, J. H. Sears, 1929, color illustrations by Frederick Richardson: $125.00

White Elephant and Other Tales from India, Volland, 1929, color illustrations by Frederick Richardson: $70.00

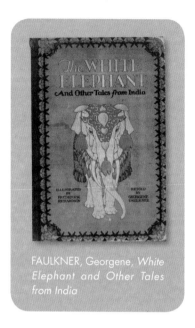

FAULKNER, Georgene, *White Elephant and Other Tales from India*

FAULKNER, Nancy
Journey into Danger, Doubleday, 1966, illustrated by Jon Nielsen, first edition with dust jacket: $40.00

Sword of the Winds, Doubleday, 1957, Arthurian fantasy, illustrated by C. Walter Hodges, first edition with dust jacket: $50.00

FAULKNER, William
Wishing Tree, Random House, 1964, hardcover, illustrated by Don Bolognese, first edition: $70.00

Wishing Tree, Random House, first edition, hardcover, limited edition of 500, in slipcase: $200.00

FEELINGS, Muriel and Tom
Jambo Means Hello, Dial Press, 1974, color illustrations by Tom Feelings, first edition with dust jacket: $30.00

FELTON, Harold
Fire-Fightin' Mose, Being an Account of the Life and Times of the World's Greatest Fire Fighter, Alfred A. Knopf, 1955, illustrated by Aldren A. Watson, first edition with dust jacket: $30.00

FENNER, Phyllis R.
Demons and Dervishes, Alfred A. Knopf, 1946, b/w drawings, first edition with dust jacket: $40.00

Giants and Witches and a Dragon or Two, Alfred A. Knopf, 1943, b/w illustrations by Henry C. Pitz, first edition with dust jacket: $100.00

Giggle Box Funny Stories for Boys and Girls, edited by Fenner, Alfred A. Knopf, 1950, illustrated by William Steig, first edition with dust jacket: $100.00

FENTON, Edward
Fierce John, Doubleday, 1959, illustrations by William Pène Du Bois, first edition with dust jacket: $60.00

Nine Lives or, The Celebrated Cat of Beacon Hill, Pantheon Books, 1951, color illustrated paper over boards, oversize, illustrated by Paul Galdone, first edition with dust jacket: $50.00

Nine Questions, Doubleday, 1959, b/w illustrations by C. Walter Hodges, first edition with dust jacket: $50.00

Penny Candy, Holt, 1970, oblong hardcover, illustrated by Edward Gorey, first edition with dust jacket: $100.00

FERGUSON, Charles W.
Abecedarian Book, Little, Brown, 1964, illustrated by John Alcorn, first edition with dust jacket: $30.00

FIELD, Eugene (1850 – 1895)
Poems of Childhood, Charles Scribner's Sons (1896), 1904 edition, black cover with color pictorial paper label, eight color plates by Maxfield Parrish, first edition with dust jacket: $300.00

Sugar Plum Tree, Eugene Field poem, 1930 edition, Saalfield, oversize picture book, color illustrated paper-over-board cover, b/w illustrations and full-page color illustrations by Fern Bisel Peat: $75.00

Wynken, Blynken and Nod, and Other Child Verses, Charles E. Graham, 1925 edition, illustrated boards, color illustrations, first thus: $100.00

FIELD, Eugene, *Wynken, Blynken and Nod, and Other Child Verses*

Wynken, Blynken and Nod, 1930 edition, Saalfield, oversize, color plates by Fern Bisel Peat: $65.00

Wynken, Blynken and Nod, 1941 edition, Whitman, oversize softcover, color illustrations by Margot Voigt: $50.00

FIELD, Eugene, Margot Voigt illustration

FIELD, Rachel (1894 – 1942)
An Alphabet for Boys and Girls, Doubleday, Page, 1926, small, verse for each letter, watercolor illustrations, first edition: $100.00

Hepatica Hawkes, Macmillan, New York, 1932, woodcuts by Allen Lewis, first edition with dust jacket: $70.00

Hitty, Her First Hundred Years, Macmillan, New York, 1929, illustrated by Dorothy Lathrop, first edition: $100.00

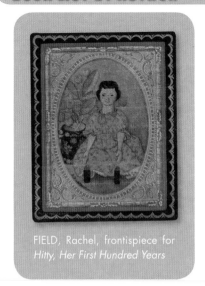

FIELD, Rachel, frontispiece for *Hitty, Her First Hundred Years*

Little Dog Toby, Macmillan, 1928, small, color illustrations, first edition: $90.00

Pocket-Handkerchief Park, Doubleday Doran, 1929, small, color illustrations, first edition: $90.00

Prayer for a Child, Macmillan, New York, 1944, color decorated boards, illustrations by Elizabeth Orton Jones, first edition with dust jacket: $125.00

FINLEY, Jean, see Series section, BLUE DOMERS

FINLEY, Martha, see Series section, ELSIE DINSMORE

FIRMIN, Peter, see Series section, IVOR THE ENGINE, NOGGIN

FISCHER, Hans (1909 – 1958)
Pitschi, Harcourt Brace, 1953, illustrated oblong hardcover, illustrated by author, first edition with dust jacket: $150.00

FISCHER, Hans , *Pitschi*

Rum-Pum-Pum, 1951, Artemis Verlag, Zurich, oversize pictorial boards, 14 pages, illustrated by author: $85.00

FISH, Helen Dean
Four and Twenty Blackbirds, Frederick A. Stokes, 1937, oversize, hardcover, illustrated endpapers, green/b/w illustrations throughout by Robert Lawson: $65.00

FISH, Helen Dean, *Four and Twenty Blackbirds*

When the Root Children Wake Up: A Picture Book, Frederick A. Stokes, 1930, oversize, color illustrations by Sibylle von Olfers, b/w pictorial endpapers, US first edition: $100.00

FISHER, Aileen
Cricket in a Thicket, Scribner, 1963, illustrations by Feodor Rojankovsky, first edition with dust jacket: $50.00

Do Bears Have Mothers, Too?, Crowell, 1973, oversize, illustrated by Eric Carle, first edition: $40.00

Up, Up the Mountain, Crowell, 1968, illustrated by Gilbert Riswold, first edition with dust jacket: $40.00

We Went Looking, 1968 Crowell, illustrated by Marie Angel, first edition with dust jacket: $35.00

FISHER, Paul R., see Series section, ASH STAFF TRILOGY

FITZGERALD, John D. (1907 – 1988), see Series section, GREAT BRAIN

FITZHUGH, Louise (1928 – 1974) see also Series section, HARRIET THE SPY

Bang Bang You're Dead, with Sandra Scoppettone, Harper, 1969, oversize oblong, b/w illustrations by Fitzhugh, first edition: $100.00

Nobody's Family Is Going to Change, Farrar, Straus and Giroux, 1974, first edition with dust jacket: $50.00

FITZHUGH, Percy, see Series section, PEE-WEE HARRIS, TOM SLADE, WESTY MARTIN

FLACK, Marjorie (b. Long Island, 1897 – 1958), see also Series section, ANGUS THE DOG

Flack attended the Art Students League in New York. Although she trained as an artist, her career began with writing a children's book about Eskimos, then expanded as she pursued both writing and illustration.

FLACK, Marjorie, *Story About Ping*

Restless Robin, Houghton Mifflin, 1937, oblong, color illustrations by Flack and Karl Larsson, first edition: $200.00

Story about Ping, Viking Press, 1933, picture book, illustrated by Kurt Wiese, first edition with dust jacket: $300.00

Walter the Lazy Mouse, Doubleday Doran, 1937, oversize, first edition with dust jacket: $200.00

What to Do About Molly, John Lane, London, 1938, oblong, yellow cloth cover, blue pictorial endpapers, illustrated by Karl Larsson, UK first edition with dust jacket: $350.00

FLAHERTY, Frances
Sabu, the Elephant Boy, 1937, Oxford, wraparound photo illustration on paper-over-board cover, full-page photo illustrations facing page of text on each page, first edition with dust jacket: $40.00

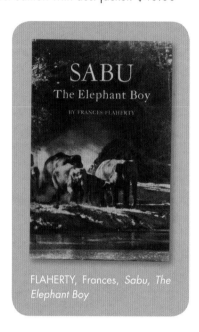

FLAHERTY, Frances, *Sabu, The Elephant Boy*

FLEMING, Ian
Chitty Chitty Bang Bang, the Magical Car, 1964, Random House, illustrated by John Burningham, US first edition with dust jacket: $90.00

FLEMING, Ian, *Chitty Chitty Bang Bang, the Magical Car*

FLETCHER, Robert
Marjorie and Her Papa, Century, 1891, oversize, cloth-over-board cover, b/w plates by Reginald Birch, first edition: $80.00

FLOWER, Jessie Graham, see Series section, GRACE HARLOWE

FOA, Eugenie
Little Robinson Crusoe of Paris, translated by Julia Olcott, Lippincott, 1925, cloth-over-board cover, 160 pages, illustrated endpapers, eight color plates by Marion Mildred Oldham: $30.00

Strange Search, translated by Amena Pendleton, Lippincott, 1929, red cloth-over-board cover with gilt, illustrated endpapers, eight color plate illustrations by Sherman Cooke: $40.00

FORBES, Esther
Johnny Tremain, 1943 Houghton Mifflin (1944 Newbery winner), illustrated by Lynd Ward, first edition with dust jacket: $200.00

FOREST, Antonia, see Series section, MARLOWS

FORSTER, Frederick J.
On the Road to Make-Believe, Rand McNally, Chicago, 1924, oversize blue cloth boards with paste-on pictorial, gilt lettering, pictorial endpages, 128 pages, color illustrations by Uldene Trippe and Milo Winter, first edition: $50.00

FORSTER, Frederick J., *On the Road to Make-Believe*

Tippytoes Comes to Town, Rand McNally, 1926, oversize, 94 pages, cloth-over-board cover with paste-on-pictorial, color and b/w illustrations by Uldenne Trippe: $50.00

FOSTER, Elizabeth
Gigi, Houghton Mifflin, 1943, oversize picture book, 118 pages, illustrated endpapers, color frontispiece, b/w illustrations by Ilse Bischoff, first edition with dust jacket: $45.00

FOSTER, Hal, see Series section, PRINCE VALIANT

FOX, Charles Donald
Little Robinson Crusoe, Charles Renard, 1925, cloth-over-board cover with paste-on-pictorial, illustrated endpapers, illustrated with b/w photo plates from the Jackie Coogan movie, plus seven photo pages of Jackie doing his daily exercises: $65.00

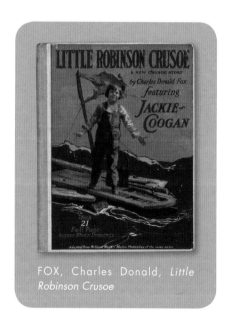

FOX, Charles Donald, *Little Robinson Crusoe*

FOX, Frances Margaret
Angeline Goes Traveling, Rand McNally, 1927, green cloth-over-board cover with paste-on-pictorial, illustrated by Dorothy Lake Gregory, first edition: $30.00

Farmer Brown and the Birds, L. C. Page, Cosy Corner Series, 1900, illustrated by E. B. Barry: $80.00

How Christmas Came to the Mulvaneys, L. C. Page, Boston 1905, cover stamped with decoration of a Christmas tree, b/w drawings by J. H. Appleton, first edition: $40.00

Janey, Rand McNally, 1923, pictorial paste-on cover, illustrated by Dorothy Lake Gregory: $40.00

Little Mossback Amelia, E. P. Dutton, 1939, illustrated by Marion Downer: $40.00

Nannette, P. F. Volland, 1929, red cloth gilt lettering and design, 80 pages, color illustrations by Justin C. Gruelle, first edition: $100.00

Nan's Christmas Boarder, L. C. Page, 1924, 99 pages plus ads, illustrations by Elizabeth Withington and Gertrude E. Martin, US first edition: $50.00

Seven Christmas Candles, L. C. Page, 1909, decorated endpapers, full-page color illustrations by Etheldred B. Barry, first edition: $50.00

Sister Sally, McNally, 1925, cloth-over-board cover with paste-on-pictorial, 105 pages, color and b/w illustrations by Dorothy Gregory: $40.00

Wilding Princess, Volland, 1929, cloth-over-board cover with gilt lettering, color plate illustrations by John Perkins: $100.00

FOX, John Jr.
Little Shepherd of Kingdom Come, Scribner, 1903, oversize, impressed cover illustration, 14 color plate illustrations by N. C. Wyeth, first edition: $50.00

FOX, Paula
Good Ethan, Bradbury Press, 1973, illustrated by Arnold Lobel, first edition with dust jacket: $50.00

Likely Place, Macmillan, 1967, small, illustrated by Edward Ardizzone, first edition with dust jacket: $40.00

Slave Dancer, Bradbury Press, 1973, Newbery Medal for 1974, first printing without medal and with dust jacket: $60.00

Stone-Faced Boy, Bradbury Press, 1968, illustrated by Donald Mackay, first edition with dust jacket: $45.00

FRANCIS, J. G.
Book of Cheerful Cats and Other Animated Animals, Century, 1903 edition, verse, small oblong, illustrated paper-over-board cover, 45 pages, b/w illustrations by author: $40.00

FRANZEN, Nils-Olof, see Series section, AGATON SAX

FRASER, Beatrice and Ferrin
Arturo and Mr. Bang, Bobbs-Merrill, 1963, illustrated, first edition with dust jacket: $45.00

Bennie the Bear Who Grew Too Fast, Lothrup, Lee & Shepard, 1956, illustrated by Roger Duvoisin, first edition with dust jacket: $50.00

FREDERICKS, J. Paget
Miss Pert's Christmas Tree, Macmillan, 1929, oversize, cloth-over-board cover with gilt, color and b/w illustrations by author: $35.00

FREEDLEY, George
More Mr. Cat and a Bit of Amber Too, Howard Frisch, 1962, illustrated by Victor J. Dowling, first edition with dust jacket: $35.00

FREEMAN, Barbara, author/illustrator

Name on the Glass, Faber and Faber, 1964, illustrated by Barbara Freeman, first edition with dust jacket: $45.00

FREEMAN, Don (b. San Diego, 1908 – 1978), author/illustrator

Freeman moved to New York to become a professional musician but he also studied at the Art Students League during the 1920s and 1930s. The loss of his trumpet on the subway led to a career as a freelance artist, covering the New York shows for the newspapers. Freeman illustrated his own picture books as well as many books by other authors.

Come Again, Pelican, Viking Press, 1961, illustrations by author, first edition: $80.00

Corduroy, Viking Press, 1968, hardcover, color illustrations by author, first edition: $30.00

Corduroy's Board Book Collection, Viking Press, 1986, four books in small illustrated lunch box shaped case, with small red catch lock and red handle, first edition: $60.00

Cyrano the Crow, Viking Press, 1960, oversize, color illustrations by author, first edition with dust jacket: $70.00

FREEMAN, Don, *Dandelion*

Dandelion, Viking Press, 1964, two-color illustrations by author, first edition with dust jacket: $30.00

Don Freeman's Newsstand: A Journal of One Man's Manhattan, Associated American Artists, 1941, spiralbound, printed on one side only of heavy stock, drawings of New York people and scenes, three fold-out scenes (includes poem by e.e. cummings), first edition: $120.00

Guard Mouse, Viking Press, 1967, oversize hardcover, pictorial paper covered boards, illustrated by author, first edition with dust jacket: $50.00

Hattie the Backstage Bat, Viking Press, 1970, first edition with dust jacket: $50.00

Mop Top, Viking Press, 1955, first edition with dust jacket: $100.00

Night the Lights Went Out, Viking Press, 1958, 48 pages, color illustrations in yellow and black, first edition with dust jacket: $70.00

Norman the Doorman, Viking Press, 1959, oversize hardcover, 64 pages, color endpapers, full-page or double-page color illustrations on every page, first edition with dust jacket: $50.00

Penguins, of All People, Viking Press, 1971, oblong, first edition with dust jacket: $40.00

Seal and the Slick, Viking Press, 1974, first edition: $40.00

Ski Pup, Viking Press, 1963, cover illustration of St. Bernard pup on ski jump, 56 pages, first edition with dust jacket: $60.00

Turtle and the Dove, Viking Press, 1964, 44 pages, first edition with dust jacket: $50.00

Will's Quill, Viking Press, 1975, oversize hardcover, illustrated by author, first edition with dust jacket: $30.00

FRENCH, Fiona

Jack of Hearts, Harcourt Brace, 1970, oversize, full-color illustrations by author, playing cards represent medieval characters, US first edition with dust jacket: $50.00

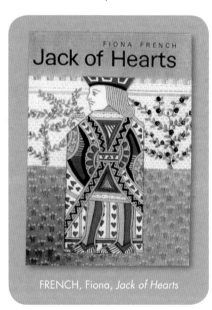

FRENCH, Fiona, *Jack of Hearts*

King Tree, Oxford University Press, 1973, pictorial oversize hardcover, illustrated by author, first edition with dust jacket: $40.00

FRENCH, Paul, see Series section, LUCKY STARR

FRESCHET, Berniece

Bernard Sees the World, Charles Scribner's Sons, 1976, illustrations by Gina Freschet, first edition with dust jacket: $70.00

Owl and the Prairie Dog, Scribner's, 1969, illustrated by Gilbert Riswold, first edition with dust jacket: $35.00

Possum Baby, a See and Read Nature Story, G. P. Putnam's Sons, 1978, line illustrations by Jim Arnosky, first edition: $30.00

FRIEDMAN, Frieda

Bobbie Had a Nickel, John Martin's House, 1946, spiralbound pictorial boards, first edition: $130.00

Janitor's Girl, William Morrow, 1966, illustrations by Mary Stevens, first edition with dust jacket: $40.00

Sundae with Judy, William Morrow, 1949, illustrated by Carolyn Haywood, first edition: $50.00

FRIEDRICH, Otto and Priscilla

Easter Bunny That Overslept, Lothrop, Lee, 1957, illustrated by Adrienne Adams, first edition with dust jacket: $50.00

FRISKEY, Margaret

Mystery of the Gate Sign, Children's Press, ca. 1950, hardcover, illustrated by Katherine Evans: $30.00

Seven Diving Ducks, David McKay, 1940, oversize, illustrated by Lucia Patton, first edition with dust jacket: $35.00

Wings Over the Woodshed, Albert Whitman, 1941, decorated hardcover, illustrations in color and b/w by Lucia Patton, first edition: $35.00

FROEBEL, Friedrich

Mother-Play and Nursery Songs, Lee & Shepard, 1893, edited by Peabody, 192 pages, red cloth-over-board cover, engraving illustrations: $50.00

FROST, Arthur B. (1851 – 1928), author/illustrator

American illustrator Arthur Frost began his career illustrating books for Harper & Brothers and became famous for his work on Joel Chandler Harris's *Uncle Remus* stories. Being red-green colorblind, Frost memorized the position of the paints on his palette to circumvent this handicap.

FROST, Frances (1905 – 1959), see also Series section, WINDY FOOT

Little Whistler, Whittlesey House, 1949, illustrations by Roger Duvoisin, first edition with dust jacket: $40.00

Rocket Away, McGraw-Hill, 1953, illustrated by Paul Galdone, first edition with dust jacket: $70.00

Yoke of Stars, Farrar & Rinehart, 1939, first edition with dust jacket: $150.00

FROST, Lesley

Not Really! Eleven Jolly Stories, Coward-McCann, 1939, illustrations by James Reid, first edition with dust jacket: $35.00

FRY, Rosalie, author/illustrator

Deep in the Forest, Dodd, Mead, 1956, small, 95 pages, b/w illustrations, first edition with dust jacket: $100.00

Fly Home, Colombina, E. P. Dutton, 1960, first edition with dust jacket: $40.00

Mountain Door, J. M. Dent, London, 1960, fairy story, first edition with dust jacket: $40.00

Princess in the Forest, Hutchinson, London, 1961, UK first edition with dust jacket: $150.00

FRYER, Jane Eayer, see Series section, MARY FRANCES

FUJIKAWA, Gyo, illustrator

1 2 3, a Counting Book, Price Stern Sloan, 1981, b/w and color illustrations, hardcover: $50.00

Betty Bear's Birthday, Price Stern Sloan, 1977, illustrated hardcover, watercolor illustrations by author, first edition: $100.00

Sam's All Wrong Day, Price Stern Sloan, 1982, watercolor illustrations, first edition: $60.00

FYLEMAN, Rose (1877 – 1957)

Dolls' House, Doubleday, Doran, 1931, illustrated by Erick Berry, first edition with dust jacket: $50.00

G

GAG, Flavia, author/illustrator

Chubby's First Year, Henry Holt, 1960, picture book, first edition with dust jacket: $40.00

Tweeter of Prairie Dog Town, Henry Holt, 1957, first edition with dust jacket: $50.00

GAG, Wanda (1893 – 1946), author/illustrator

ABC Bunny, Coward-McCann, 1933, oversize picture book, color illustration on paper-over-board cover, red lettering, b/w illustrations by author, first edition with dust jacket: $500.00

Funny Thing, Coward-McCann, 1929, oblong, yellow pictorial cover, Gag's second children's book, illustrated throughout, first edition with dust jacket: $500.00

Gone is Gone, Coward-McCann, 1935, color frontispiece, in-text illustrations, classic folktale retold, first edition with dust jacket: $200.00

Millions of Cats, Coward-McCann, 1928, oblong, 32 pages, yellow and red illustrated endpapers, first edition with dust jacket: $600.00

Nothing at All, Coward-McCann, 1941, oblong, pictorial boards, first edition with dust jacket: $450.00

Snippy and Snappy, Coward-McCann, 1931, oblong hardback, first edition with dust jacket: $200.00

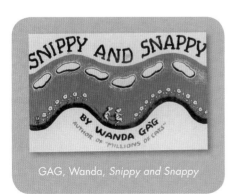

GAG, Wanda, *Snippy and Snappy*

Snow White and the Seven Dwarfs, Coward-McCann, 1938, illustrated paper-over-board cover, small, 43 pages, b/w illustrations by author, first edition with dust jacket: $400.00

Three Gay Tales from Grimm, Coward-McCann, 1943, 63 pages, orange paper-covered boards, first edition with dust jacket: $300.00

GAGE, Wilson
Ghost of Five Owl Farm, World Publishing, 1966, illustrations by Paul Galdone, first edition: $60.00

Miss Osborne-the-Mop, World Publishing, 1963, first edition with dust jacket: $65.00

GALDONE, Paul (1914 – 1986), author/illustrator

Born in Budapest, Galdone came to the U. S. as a teenager with his parents. He learned English in high school, and began sketching as a way of communicating with the other students. His biology class drawings of grasshoppers developed his interest in art. After high school he worked day jobs to help his family and studied art at night school at the Art Students League and the New York School of Industrial Design. His art career began at Doubleday, then expanded to freelance work. Galdone illustrated hundreds of children's books. See also Series section, ANATOLE THE MOUSE, BASIL OF BAKER STREET, MISS PICKERELL, SPACE CAT.

Androcles and the Lion, McGraw-Hill, 1975, oversize picture book, pictorial hardcover, re-telling of classic story, color illustrations: $80.00

Greedy Old Fat Man: An American Folk Tale, Houghton Mifflin, 1983, square, first edition with dust jacket: $100.00

House That Jack Built, McGraw-Hill, 1961, oversize, pictorial hardcover, first Galdone book in which he wrote the text: $40.00

GALE, Leah
Alphabet from A to Z, Simon & Schuster, 1942, square, pictorial boards, 42 pages,

illustrations by Vivienne Blake, first edition with dust jacket: $50.00

Captain Big Bill the Pelican, Samuel Lowe, 1956, a Bonnie "Jack-in-the-Box" book with pop-out features, red/b/w illustrations, illustrated boards: $40.00

GALE, Leah, *Captain Big Bill the Pelican*

Favorite Bedtime Stories, Random House, 1943, oversize, illustrations by Miss Elliot, first edition with dust jacket: $30.00

Favorite Tales of Long Ago, Random House, 1943, oversize, illustrations by Miss Elliot, first edition with dust jacket: $30.00

Hurdy-Gurdy Holiday, Harper & Brothers, 1942, oversize, illustrations by Barbara Latham, first edition with dust jacket: $100.00

Timmy Tiger: The Tale of a Timid Tiger, Samuel Lowe, 1956, a Bonnie "Jack-in-the Box" book, swivel-out head and paws of tiger on cover, pictorial boards, one color plus b/w illustrations: $40.00

GALLICO, Paul
Day Jean-Pierre Was Pignapped, Heinemann, 1964, illustrated by Edmund Dulac, first edition with dust jacket: $50.00

Ludmila, a Story of Liechtenstein, Michael Joseph, 1956, green hardcover with gilt, first edition with dust jacket: $40.00

GALLICO, Paul, *Ludmila, a Story of Liechtenstein*

Man Who Was Magic, Doubleday, 1966, first edition with dust jacket: $50.00

Manxmouse, Coward-McCann, 1968, illustrated by Janet and Anne Grahame-Johnstone, US first edition with dust jacket: $100.00

Snowflake, Michael Joseph, 1952, illustrated paper-on-board covers, 64 pages, decorations by David Knight, US first edition with dust jacket: $90.00

GALLICO, Paul, *Man Who Was Magic*

GALLIENNE, Eva
Flossie and Bossie, Faber, London, 1950, b/w illustrations by Garth Williams, first edition with dust jacket: $80.00

Seven Tales by H. C. Andersen, Harper & Row, 1959, blue boards, gold edge design and title letters, illustrations by Maurice Sendak, US first edition with dust jacket: $100.00

GALT, Katherine, see Series section, GIRL SCOUTS

GANNETT, Ruth Chrisman (1896 – 1979), see also Series section, DRAGON

Katie and the Sad Noise, Random House, 1961, illustrated by Ellie Simmons, first edition with dust jacket: $65.00

Wonderful House-Boat-Train, Random House, 1949, illustrated by Fritz Eichenberg, first edition with dust jacket: $150.00

GARD, Joyce
Mermaid's Daughter, Holt, Rinehart & Winston, 1969, first edition with Vera Bock dust jacket: $60.00

GARDEN, Nancy see Series section, FOURS CROSSING TRILOGY

GARDNER, John
Child's Bestiary, Alfred A. Knopf, 1977, oversize, 70 pages, poems, illustrated by the Gardner family, first edition with dust jacket: $100.00

Dragon, Dragon, and Other Tales, Alfred A. Knopf, 1975, illustrated by Charles Shields, first edition with dust jacket: $100.00

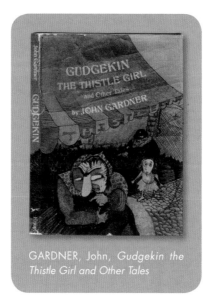

GARDNER, John, *Gudgekin the Thistle Girl and Other Tales*

Gudgekin the Thistle Girl and Other Tales, Alfred A. Knopf, 1976, b/w illustrations by Michael Sporn, first edition with dust jacket: $80.00

In the Suicide Mountains, Alfred A. Knopf, 1977, first edition with dust jacket: $100.00

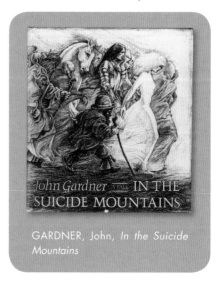

GARDNER, John, *In the Suicide Mountains*

GARIS, Howard R., see Series section, CURLYTOPS, HAPPY HOME, LARRY DEXTER, RICK AND RUDDY, ROCKET RIDERS, UNCLE WIGGILY

GARIS, Lilian, see Series section, MELODY LANE MYSTERY

GARIS, Roger, see also Series section, OUTBOARD BOYS

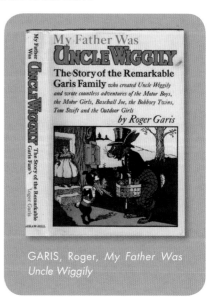

GARIS, Roger, *My Father Was Uncle Wiggily*

My Father Was Uncle Wiggily, 1966, McGraw-Hill, 217 pages, biography of the four writing Garis family members, with dust jacket: $40.00

GARNER, Elvira
Ezekiel, Holt, 1937, half-cloth cover with pictorial boards, 42 pages, color line drawings by author, first edition with dust jacket: $150.00

Little Cat Lost, Julian Messner, 1943, illustrated by Diana Thorne, first edition with dust jacket: $80.00

Sarah Faith Anderson: Her Book, Messner, 1941, color illustrations throughout by author, first edition with dust jacket: $125.00

Way Down in Tennessee, Messner, 1941, color illustrations by Sara Faith Anderson, first edition with dust jacket: $100.00

GARNETT, Eve, see also Series section, ONE END STREET
Book of the Seasons, Oxford, 1952, oversize hardcover, 80 pages, color and b/w illustrations by Garnett, first edition: $35.00

GARRARD, Phillis
Banana Tree House, Coward-McCann, 1938, illustrated endpapers, color and b/w illustrations by Berta and Elmer Hader, first edition with dust jacket: $100.00

Plum Duff and Prunella, Country Life, London, 1938, illustrations by M. E. Rivers-Moore, first edition hardcover: $40.00

Running Away with Nebby, McKay, 1944, oversize, illustrated endpapers, color frontispiece, b/w illustrations by Willy Pogany, first edition with dust jacket: $80.00

GARRETT, Helen
Angelo the Naughty One, Viking Press, 1944, oversize picture book, color illustrations by Leo Politi, first edition with dust jacket: $80.00

Mr. Flip Flop, Viking Press, 1948, color and line illustrations by Garry MacKenzie, first edition with dust jacket: $40.00

Tophill Road, Viking Press, 1950, illustrations by Corydon Bell, first edition with dust jacket: $40.00

GARST, Shannon
Cowboy Boots, Abingdon-Cokesbury Press, 1946, illustrated by Charles Hargens, first edition with dust jacket: $40.00

Rusty at Ram's Horn Ranch, Abingdon-Cokesbury Press, 1951, illustrations by Raymond Creekmore, first edition with dust jacket: $40.00

Wish on an Apple, Abingdon-Cokesbury Press, 1948, illustrated by Jon Nielsen, first edition with dust jacket: $40.00

GARTHWAITE, Marion
Coarse Gold Gulch, Doubleday, 1956, illustrations by Beth and Joe Krush, first edition with dust jacket: $100.00

Shaken Days, Julian Messner, 1954, illustrated by Ursula Koering, first edition with dust jacket: $40.00

GARTNER, John
Sons of Mercury: A Rock Taylor Sports Story, Dodd, Mead, 1956, track and field story, first edition with dust jacket: $200.00

GASKIN, Arthur (1863 – 1926), illustrator

After studying at the Birmingham School of Art, Gaskin followed the arts-and-crafts approach of William Morris to design jewelry and other items as well as illustrate various works. He collaborated with Morris on *The Shepherdess Calendar.*

Good King Wenceslas, with introduction by William Morris, Cornis Brothers, 1895, six illustrations by Gaskin, hardcover: $350.00

GATES, Doris (1901 – 1987)
Becky and the Bandit, Ginn, 1955, school reader, gold cloth hardcover, illustrations by Paul Lantz: $80.00

Blue Willow, Viking Press, 1940, illustrated by Paul Lantz, first edition with dust jacket: $120.00

Cat and Mrs. Cary, Viking Press, 1965, b/w illustrations by Peggy Bacon, first edition with dust jacket: $40.00

Little Vic, Viking Press, 1951, illustrated by Kate Seredy, first edition with dust jacket: $70.00

My Brother Mike, Viking Press, 1948, illustrated by Wesley Dennis, first edition with dust jacket: $70.00

Sensible Kate, Viking Press, 1943, illustrated by Marjorie Torrey, first edition with dust jacket: $40.00

Two Queens of Heaven, Viking Press, 1974, oversize, 94 pages, b/w illustrations by Trina Schart Hyman, first edition with dust jacket: $35.00

GATES, Josephine Scribner, see also Series section, LIVE DOLLS

April Fool Doll, Bobbs-Merrill, 1909, b/w text illustrations and plates by Virginia Keep: $100.00

Land of Delight: Child Life on a Pony Farm, Houghton Mifflin, 1915, b/w plates, first edition: $50.00

Little Girl Blue, Houghton Mifflin, 1910, small, pictorial boards, illustrations by Virginia Keep Clark: $50.00

Little Girl Blue Plays "I Spy!," Houghton Mifflin, 1913, small, color pictorial illustration in oval on front cover and four full-page color illustrations: $50.00

GATES, Josephine Scribner, *Little Girl Blue Plays "I Spy!"*

One Day in Betty's Life, Bobbs-Merrill, 1913, oblong, sketches and margin decorations, plus piano pieces: $80.00

Sunshine Annie, Bobbs-Merrill, 1910, cloth-over-board cover with color paste-on-pictorial, illustrations by Fanny Cory: $40.00

Tommy Sweet-Tooth and Little Girl Blue, Houghton Mifflin, 1911, tall, pictorial cover, illustrations by Esther V. Churbuck: $60.00

Turkey Doll, Houghton Mifflin, 1912, color and b/w illustrations throughout, early Christmas story, first edition: $60.00

GAULT, William Campbell
Gasoline Cowboy, E. P. Dutton, 1974, first edition with dust jacket: $100.00

Speedway Challenge, E. P. Dutton, 1956, first edition with dust jacket: $100.00

Stubborn Sam, E. P. Dutton, 1969, first edition with dust jacket: $100.00

GAY, Romney, author/illustrator

Five Little Playmates, a Book of Fingerplays, Grosset & Dunlap, 1941, small, with paper finger puppets all uncut, first edition with dust jacket: $65.00

Romney Gay Mother Goose, Grosset & Dunlap, 1936, oversize with gilt design of angels on cover, pictorial endpapers, color illustrations by author, first edition with dust jacket: $40.00

Toby and Sue, Grosset & Dunlap, 1937, first edition with dust jacket: $50.00

GAY, Zhenya
170 Cats, Random House, 1939, pictorial cloth cover, first edition: $40.00

Bits and Pieces, Viking Press, 1958, first edition with dust jacket: $35.00

I'm Tired of Lions, Viking Press, 1961, first edition with dust jacket: $35.00

Jingle Jangle, Viking Press, 1953, pictures by the author, first edition with dust jacket: $40.00

Sakimura, Viking Press, 1937, illustrated paper boards, story of a Siamese cat, lithographs by Zhenya Gay, first edition with dust jacket: $70.00

GAY, Zhenya, *Sakimura*

Shire Colt, Doubleday, Doran, 1931, lithographs by Zhenya Gay, first edition with dust jacket: $70.00

Small One, Viking Press, 1958, oversize, illustrated by author, first edition with dust jacket: $50.00

GENDEL, Evelyn
Tortoise and Turtle, Simon & Schuster, 1960, yellow boards with lime green cloth spine, illustrated endpapers, illustrations by Hilary Knight, first edition with dust jacket: $50.00

Tortoise and Turtle Abroad, Simon & Schuster, 1963, illustrated by Hilary Knight, first edition with dust jacket: $50.00

GEORGE, Jean Craighead
American author Jean Craighead George's many novels often feature children pitted against the wilderness. She wrote two sequels to *My Side of the Mountain* almost 30 years after the original was published and several of her books have been repackaged as series.

Julie of the Wolves, Harper, 1972, (Newbery Medal), illustrated by John Schoenherr, first edition with dust jacket (without Newbery sticker): $50.00

Moon of the Owls, Crowell, 1967, illustrated by Jean Zallinger, first edition with dust jacket: $40.00

My Side of the Mountain, Bodley Head, 1962, first British edition with dust jacket: $200.00

My Side of the Mountain, E. P. Dutton, 1959, (Newbery Honor Book 1960), first edition with dust jacket: $500.00

Wounded Wolf, Harper & Row, 1978, oversize, illustrations by John Schoenherr, first edition with dust jacket: $100.00

GEORGIADY, Nicholas P. and Louis G. Romano
Gertie the Duck, Follett, 1959, first grade reader, illustrated by Dagmar Wilson, first edition with dust jacket: $50.00

GERBER, Will
Gooseberry Jones, Putnam, 1947, cloth-over-board cover, 96 pages, b/w illustrations by Dudley Morris, first edition: $50.00

Judishus, Wallace Hebberd, 1945, illustrated by Gwynne Dresser Mack, first edition with dust jacket: $120.00

GERSON, Virginia
Happy Heart Family, Duffield, undated, ca. 1900, oversize oblong picture book, paper-on-board illustrated cover, color plates and line drawings throughout by author: $90.00

GERSON, Virginia, *Little Dignity*

Little Dignity, George Routledge, ca. 1881, oversize with color plates, illustrations by author: $100.00

Rose-Buds, White, Stokes and Allen, 1885, illustrated boards, 64 pages, illustrated, first edition: $100.00

GETCHELL, Margaret C.
Cloud Bird, Davis Press, 1916, hardcover, illustrated by Edith Ballinger Price: $40.00

GETCHELL, Margaret C., *Cloud Bird*

GIBBS, Alonzo
Fields Breathe Sweet, Lothrop, Lee & Shepard, 1963, author's first book, first edition with dust jacket: $80.00

GIBSON, Eva Katharine

GIBSON, Eva Katharine, *Zauberlinda, the Wise Witch*

Zauberlinda, the Wise Witch, Smith, Chicago, 1901, decorated blue cloth-over-board cover, two-tone illustrations throughout, first edition: $80.00

GIDAL, Sonia
Children's Village in Israel, Meier Shfeya Behrman House, 1950, hardcover, 48 pages, photo illustrations by Tim Gidal: $35.00

GILBERT, Paul, see also Series section, BERTRAM

Egbert and His Marvelous Adventures, Harper, 1944, b/w illustrations by H. A. Rey, first edition with dust jacket: $80.00

Elmer Buys a Circus, Grosset & Dunlap, 1941, pictorial cover and illustrated endpapers, illustrations by Anne Stossel, first edition with dust jacket: $50.00

GILBERT, W. S., and Arthur Sullivan
H.M.S. Pinafore, Opal Wheeler adaptation, E. P. Dutton, 1946, illustrated by Fritz Kredel, first edition with dust jacket: $40.00

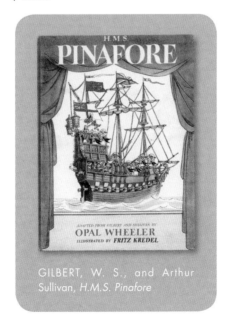

GILBERT, W. S., and Arthur Sullivan, *H.M.S. Pinafore*

Pinafore Picture Book, Macmillan, 1908, first American edition, narrative retelling for children of the operetta, written by Sir W. S. Gilbert, oversize, cloth-over-board cover with impressed illustration, 130 pages, illustrated endpapers, 16 color plates plus b/w in-text illustrations by Alice B. Woodward: $135.00

GILBERT, Sir W. S., *Pinafore Picture Book*

GIOVANNETTI, Pericle
Max, Macmillan, 1954, oversize, illustrated boards with cloth spine, b/w illustrations by author, first edition with dust jacket: $150.00

Nothing But Max, Macmillan, 1959, oversize hardcover, 85 pages, b/w illustrations by author, first edition with dust jacket: $30.00

GIOVANNI, Nikki
Spin a Soft Black Song, Hill & Wang, 1971, oversize square hardcover, illustrated by Charles Bible, first edition with dust jacket: $80.00

Vacation Time, William Morrow, 1980, poems illustrated by Marisabina Russo, first edition with dust jacket: $60.00

GIPSON, Fred (1908 – 1973)
Cowhand, Harper, 1953, first edition with dust jacket: $50.00

Little Arliss, Harper & Row, 1978, sequel to *Old Yeller* and *Savage Sam,* first edition with dust jacket: $75.00

Old Yeller, Harper, 1956, illustrated by Carl Burger, first edition with dust jacket: $200.00

Savage Sam, Harper, 1962, hardcover, 214 pages, b/w illustrations by Carl Burger, first edition with dust jacket: $80.00

Trail-Driving Rooster, Harper, 1955, hardcover, illustrated by Marc Simont, first edition with dust jacket: $150.00

GIPSON, Morrell

Mr. Bear Squash-You-All-Flat, Wonder Book, 1950, small hardcover, color illustrations, mentioned in a Stephen King novel, first edition: $250.00

GIRVAN, Helen

Disappearance at Lake House, Westminster Press, 1959, first edition with dust jacket: $30.00

Down Bayberry Lane, Westminster, 1955, first edition with dust jacket: $50.00

Frightened Whisper, Westminster Press, 1963, first edition with dust jacket: $30.00

Hidden Pond, E. P. Dutton, 1951, illustrated by Albert Orbaan, first edition with dust jacket: $30.00

Mystery of the Unwelcome Visitor, Westminster, Philadelphia, 1961, first edition with dust jacket: $30.00

GLENDINNING, Margarite

Gertie the Horse Who Thought and Thought, Whittlesey House, 1951, oversize, 88 pages, b/w illustrations by Louis Slobodkin, first edition with dust jacket: $80.00

GOBLE, Paul

Girl Who Loved Wild Horses, Bradbury Press, 1978 (Caldecott Medal for 1979), first printing without medal and with dust jacket: $150.00

GOBLE, Warwick (1862 – 1943)

Although not quite commanding the interest of his contemporaries Arthur Rackham or Edmund Dulac, Warwick Goble was a well-known illustrator whose work ranged from the serialized version of H.G. Wells' *War of the Worlds* to numerous elaborate fairytale books.

GODDEN, Rumer

Candy Floss, 1960 edition, Viking Press, hardcover, 65 pages, color and b/w illustrations by Adrienne Adams: $30.00

Dolls' House, 1962 edition, Viking Press, first thus, grey hardcover, 136 pages, color and b/w illustrations by Tasha Tudor, first edition with dust jacket: $200.00

Home Is the Sailor, Macmillan, 1964, color and b/w illustrations by Jean Primrose, first edition with dust jacket: $40.00

Impunity Jane, Viking Press, 1954, illustrated by Adrienne Adams, first edition with dust jacket: $50.00

Kitchen Madonna, Viking Press, 1967, illustrations by Carol Barker, first edition with dust jacket: $50.00

Little Plum, Viking Press, 1963, illustrated by Jean Primrose, first edition with dust jacket: $60.00

Miss Happiness and Miss Flower, Viking Press, 1961, 82 pages, illustrated endpapers, drawings by Jean Primrose, first edition with dust jacket: $90.00

Mouse House, Viking Press, 1957, illustrated by Adrienne Adams, first edition with dust jacket: $50.00

GODDEN, Rumer, *Miss Happiness and Miss Flower*

Mousewife, Viking Press, 1951, b/w illustrations by William Pene du Bois, first edition with dust jacket: $125.00

Mr. McFadden's Hallowe'en, Viking Press, 1975, 127 pages, first edition with dust jacket: $35.00

Old Woman Who Lived in a Vinegar Bottle, Viking Press, 1970, illustrated by Mairi Hedderwick, first edition with dust jacket: $50.00

Operation Sippacik, Viking Press, 1969, illustrated by Capt. James Bryan, first edition with dust jacket: $35.00

Tale of the Tales, the Beatrix Potter Ballet, Warne, 1971, oversize hardcover, illustrated, first edition with dust jacket: $40.00

GODOLPHIN, Mary, see Series section, IN WORDS OF ONE SYLLABLE

GOFFSTEIN, M. B. (Marilyn Brooke)

After graduation from Bennington College in Vermont, Minnesotan Goffstein moved to New York to find work as a children's book illustrator. In the 1960s, she began writing her own books, illustrated with her humorous drawings, such as in *Two Piano Tuners.* She taught book illustration at the Parsons School of Design.

Brookie and Her Lamb, Farrar, 1967, b/w illustrations by author, first edition with dust jacket: $45.00

Goldie and the Dollmaker, Farrar, 1969, illustrated by author, first edition with dust jacket: $45.00

Little Schubert, Harper, 1972, illustrations by author, includes record by Peter Schaaf, first edition and record: $45.00

Me and My Captain, Farrar, 1974, first edition with dust jacket: $60.00

Two Piano Tuners, Farrar, 1970, hardcover, 65 pages, b/w illustrations by author, first edition with dust jacket: $30.00

GOODALL, John S., artist/writer

Adventures of Paddy Pork, Macmillan, London, 1968, small oblong, pictorial boards, b/w illustrations, first edition: $60.00

Jacko, Macmillan, London, 1971, small oblong, pictorial glossy boards, color illustrations by Goodall, first edition: $50.00

GOODALL, John S., *Paddy Goes Travelling*

Naughty Nancy, Atheneum, 1975, mouse wedding, US first edition with dust jacket: $100.00

Paddy Goes Travelling, Macmillan, 1982, illustrated boards, first edition: $70.00

Paddy's Evening Out, Atheneum, 1973, color illustrations by author, US first edition with dust jacket: $70.00

Story of a Castle, Margaret K. McElderry Books, 1986, watercolor illustrations by John S. Goodall, first edition with dust jacket: $100.00

GORDON, Elizabeth, see also Series section, DOLLY AND MOLLY, LORAINE

Billy Bunny's Fortune, Volland, 1919, paper-over-board cover, color illustrations throughout by Maginal Wright Enright: $150.00

Bird Children: The Little Playmates of the Flower Children, P. F. Volland, 1912, color illustrations by M. T. Ross, first edition in its original box: $300.00. First edition without box: $200.00

Butterfly Babies' Book, Rand McNally, 1914, 80 pages, color illustrations by M. T. Ross: $150.00

Flower Children, P. F. Volland, 1910, color illustrations, first edition: $200.00

Four Footed Folk or *the Children of the Farm and Forest,* Whitman, 1914, 45 pages: $100.00

Happy Home Children, Volland, 1924, paper-over-board cover, color illustrations throughout by Marion Foster: $80.00

King Gum Drop or Neddie's Visit to Candyland, Whitman, 1916, illustrated by Hazel Frazee, full-page color plates plus 28 b/w plates and vignettes: $150.00

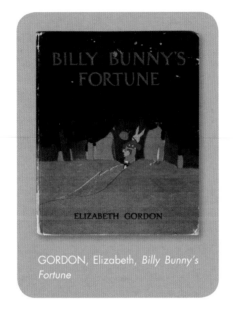

GORDON, Elizabeth, *Billy Bunny's Fortune*

Mother Earth's Children: The Frolics of the Fruits and Vegetables, P. F. Volland, 1914, color illustrated by M. T. Ross, first edition: $300.00

Really So Stories, P. F. Volland, 1924, illustrated in color throughout by John Rae, with original box: $150.00

Some Smiles – A Little Book of Limericks, W. A. Wilde Co., 1911, small, illustrated boards, drawings by M.T. Ross: $150.00

Watermelon Pete and Others, Rand McNally, ca. 1914, small, 70 pages, illustrations by Clara Powers Wilson: $100.00

Wild Flower Children, the Little Playmates of the Fairies, Volland, Chicago, 1918, pictorial hardcover, color illustrations by Janet Laura Scott, first edition: $200.00

GORDON, Harry, see Series section, RIVER MOTOR-BOAT

GOREY, Edward, artist/author

The Gothic tone of Gorey's pen-and-ink drawings is instantly recognizable from his now famous opening credits for the *Mystery* series on PBS. After attending Harvard, Gorey studied at the Art Institute of Chicago. He worked as a freelance artist and later as a staff artist for Doubleday starting in 1953. Besides his own picture books, Gorey provided dust jackets and illustrations for dozens of children's books during the 1960s and 1970s.

Amphigorey, Putnam, 1972, illustrated by author, first edition with dust jacket: $85.00

Amphigorey Too, Putnam, 1975, illustrated by author. first edition with dust jacket: $60.00

Blue Aspic, Meredith Press, 1968, illustrated by author, first edition with dust jacket: $60.00

Doubtful Guest, Doubleday, 1957, illustrated by author, first edition with dust jacket: $200.00

Dwindling Party, a pop-up book, Random House, 1982, glossy pictorial cover, full-color pop-up illustrations by Gorey, first edition: $100.00

Fletcher and Zenobia, with Victoria Chess, Meredith Press, 1967, small square hardcover, first edition with dust jacket: $35.00

GOREY, Edward, *Dwindling Party*

79

Gilded Bat, Simon & Schuster,1966, pictorial hardcover, illustrated by author, first edition with dust jacket: $200.00

Hapless Child, Dodd, Mead,1961, illustrated by Edward Gorey, first edition with dust jacket: $200.00

Haunted Looking Glass, Random House, 1959, 311 pages, stories chosen and illustrated by Gorey, first edition with dust jacket: $50.00

Listing Attic, Duell, Sloan and Pearce, 1954, small hardcover, illustrated by author, first edition with dust jacket: $100.00

Remembered Visit, a Story Taken From Life, Simon & Schuster, 1965, illustrated by Gorey, first edition with dust jacket: $100.00

Unstrung Harp, Duell, Sloan and Pearce, 1953, illustrated by author, Gorey's first book, first edition with dust jacket: $300.00

Utter Zoo, Meredith Press, 1967, 56 pages, illustrations by Gorey, first edition with dust jacket: $150.00

GOREY, Edward, *Willowdale Handcar, or, Return of the Black Doll*

Willowdale Handcar, or, *Return of the Black Doll,* Dodd, Mead, 1979 reissue, small, b/w illustrations on every page, with dust jacket: $40.00

GORHAM, Maurice
Showmen and Suckers, an Excursion on the Crazy Fringe of the Entertainment World,

Marshall, London, 1951, green boards, b/w illustrations by Edward Ardizzone, first edition with dust jacket: $45.00

GORSE, Golden
Mary in the Country, Country Life, London, 1955, 162 pages, illustrated by E. H. Shepard, first edition with dust jacket: $30.00

Moorland Mousie, Country Life, London, 1929, b/w illustrations by Lionel Edwards, first edition with dust jacket: $100.00

Older Mousie, the Life Story of a Child's Pony, Further Adventures, Country Life, London, 1932, illustrated by Lionel Edwards, first edition with dust jacket: $60.00

GOUDGE, Elizabeth
Linnets and Valerians, Brockhampton Press, 1964, first edition with dust jacket: $70.00

Smoky House, Coward-McCann, 1940, illustrated by Richard Floethe, UK first edition with dust jacket: $80.00

GRAHAM, Lorenz (1902 – 1989), see also
Series section, SOUTH TOWN

David He No Fear, Crowell, 1971, illustrated by Ann Grifalconi woodcuts, first edition with dust jacket: $60.00

God Wash the World and Start Again, Crowell, 1971, story of Noah's Ark based on a Liberian story, illustrated by Clare Romano Ross, first edition with dust jacket: $70.00

GRAHAM, Margaret Bloy, illustrator, see
Series section, BENJY THE DOG

GRAHAME, Kenneth (1859 – 1932)
Grahame's most famous children's book, *Wind in the Willows,* first published in 1907, features Toad, Mole, and their woodland and river friends. Over the years, several publishers have turned this single novel into several works by printing individual chapters as picture books.

Dream Days, Dodd, Mead, 1898, b/w illustrations by Maxfield Parrish, first edition: $150.00

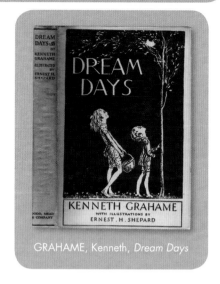

GRAHAME, Kenneth, *Dream Days*

Dream Days, Dodd, Mead, 1931 edition, illustrations by Ernest H. Shepard, first US edition with dust jacket: $50.00

Dream Days, Dodd, Mead, 1953 edition, illustrations by Ernest H. Shepard, with new illustrations, with dust jacket: $30.00

Golden Age, John Lane, 1899, b/w illustrations by Maxfield Parrish, first edition thus: $75.00

Golden Age, John Lane (UK) or Stone Kimball (US), 1895, no illustrations, first edition: $40.00

Walt Disney's Story of the Reluctant Dragon, Garden City, 1941, introduction by Robert Benchley, illustrated, first edition with dust jacket: $150.00

Grahame, *Wind in the Willows,* a sampling of editions by date:

Wind in the Willows, Methuen, 1908, blue cloth, front board decorated gilt design of the "Piper at the Gates" above the gilt title, gilt decorated spine with title and Toad in motoring outfit, frontispiece illustration by Graham Robertson, with tissue guard, first edition: $7,500.00. With original dust jacket: $11,000.00

Wind in the Willows, Scribner's, 1908, illustrations by Ernest Shepard, first American edition: $300.00

Wind in the Willows, Methuen, UK, 1913, color plates by Paul Bransom, first edition thus: $300.00

Wind in the Willows, 1928, 12 color plate illustrations by Nancy Barnhart, with dust jacket: $65.00

Wind in the Willows, Heritage Press, ca. 1940, blue hardcover with gilt, 190 pages, introduction by A. A. Milne, 12 color plates plus b/w illustrations by Arthur Rackham: $50.00

Wind in the Willows, World, 1966, green hardcover with gilt decorations, 16 color plates plus b/w illustrations by Tasha Tudor, first edition thus with dust jacket: $80.00

Grahame, *Wind in the Willows*, related titles:

Toad of Toad Hall, A. A. Milne, Methuen, 1929, the author of Winnie-the-Pooh turned the story into a popular Christmas pantomine play, blue hardcover, 168 pages, top edges gilt, first trade edition with dust jacket: $300.00. Without dust jacket: $150.00

Toad of Toad Hall, A. A. Milne, Scribner, 1929, US first edition with dust jacket: $100.00

GRAMATKY, Hardie (1907 – 1979), see also Series section, LITTLE TOOT

Hardie Gramatky ghosted the comic strip *Ella Cinders* as a young man and also worked for the Walt Disney Studios.

Creeper's Jeep, Putnam, 1948, first edition with dust jacket: $50.00

Happy's Christmas, Putnam, 1970, illustrated by author, first edition with dust jacket: $40.00

Hercules, Putnam, 1940, pictorial endpapers, first edition with dust jacket: $80.00

Nikos and the Sea God, Putnam,1963, illustrated by author, first edition with dust jacket: $40.00

GRANNAN, Mary
Just Mary's Brown Book, Thomas Allan Ltd., Toronto, 1957, hardcover, 150 pages, based on CBC radio program, illustrated by Pat Patience, first edition with dust jacket: $30.00

Just Mary Stories: Just Mary's Green Book, Thomas Allan Ltd., Toronto, 1951, based on CBC radio program, illustrated by Pat Patience, first edition with dust jacket: $40.00

Kim and Katy Circus Day, Thomas Allan Ltd., Toronto, 1956, illustrated by Pat Patience, first edition with dust jacket: $40.00

GRANT, Bruce
Boy Scout Encyclopedia, Rand McNally, 1952, oversize hardcover, illustrated by Fiore and Jackie Mastri, first edition: $60.00

My Cowboy Book (A Start Right Elf Book, Big Edition), Rand McNally, 1967, oversize hardcover, color illustrations by Jack Merryweather (79¢ original cover price): $90.00

GRATTAN, Madeleine
Jexium Island, Viking Press, 1957, 184 pages, illustrated by William Pene du Bois, first edition with dust jacket: $60.00

GRAVES, Robert (1895 – 1985)
Ann at Highwood Hall, Poems for Children, Cassell, London, 1964, illustrated by Edward Ardizzone, first edition with dust jacket: $100.00

Big Green Book, Crowell-Collier, 1962, oversize, illustrations by Maurice Sendak, first edition with dust jacket: $80.00

Penny Fiddle: Poems for Children, Doubleday, 1960, collection of Graves' poems, hardcover, illustrated by Edward Ardizzone, US first edition with dust jacket: $100.00

Poor Boy Who Followed His Star, Garden City, 1968, illustrated by Alice Meyer-Wallace, first edition with dust jacket: $40.00

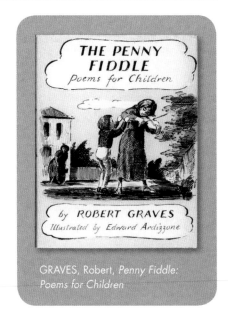

GRAVES, Robert, *Penny Fiddle: Poems for Children*

GRAY, Elizabeth Janet
Adam of the Road, Viking Press, 1942 (winner of 1943 Newbery Medal), illustrations by Robert Lawson, first edition without medal and with dust jacket: $100.00

GRAY, Nicholas Stuart
Apple-Stone, Dennis Dobson, 1965, b/w illustrations by Charles Keeping, first edition with dust jacket: $80.00

Grimbold's Other World, Meredith, 1963, b/w illustrations by Charles Keeping, US first edition with dust jacket: $50.00

Mainly in Moonlight, Meredith, 1967, b/w illustrations by Charles Keeping, US first edition with dust jacket: $50.00

GRAY, Nicholas Stuart, *Over the Hills to Fabylon*

Over the Hills to Fabylon (1954), 1970 edition, Hawthorn, b/w illustrations by Charles Keeping, US first edition with dust jacket: $150.00

Stone Cage, Dobson, 1963, first edition with dust jacket: $65.00

GREENAWAY, Kate (1846–1901)

Kate Greenaway began illustrating books in the 1870s for Edmund Evans, who used a wood block printing process with four colors for her books. She soon became one of England's most popular illustrators with her pictures of children dressed in the earlier Regency style of fashion. By 1883, her first *Almanack* sold more than 90,000 copies. Greenaway's works have been reprinted many times, including many editions by Frederick Warne, who bought the rights for her books from Evans in 1900 and began reissuing her work immediately. Highest prices are paid for her earliest works with the least amount of nursery damage. It is not unusual for corners to be chewed or pages torn in her books. For some extremely rare works, such as an 1885 album engraved by Evans (supposedly only eight copies were printed), prices would be set at auction at the time that the work became available and be equivalent to original artwork. The following is a sampling of early Greenaway titles regularly found in good condition:

A, Apple Pie: An Old-Fashioned Alphabet Book, Routledge, 1886, engraved and color printed by Edmund Evans, pictorial paper-covered boards: $450.00

Almanack, Routledge, issued annually between 1883 and 1895, engraved and color printed by Edmund Evans. A complete set in original bindings was offered by one dealer in 2007 for $6,500.00. Individual volumes with pictorial cover: $100.00

Baby's Birthday Book, Marcus Ward, 1886: $250.00

Children's Songs, Marcus Ward, circa 1875, pictorial boards: $500.00

Kate Greenaway's Alphabet, Routledge, 1885, engraved and color printed by

Edmund Evans, 26 color illustrations: $250.00

Kate Greenaway's Book of Games, Routledge, 1889, engraved and color printed by Edmund Evans. 24 color plates and pictorial cover: $300.00

Language of Flowers, Routledge, 1884, pictorial paper-covered boards, engraved and color printed by Edmund Evans: $150.00

Marigold Garden: Pictures and Rhymes, Routledge, 1885, engraved and color printed by Edmund Evans: $200.00

Mother Goose, or, *The Old Nursery Rhymes*, Routledge, 1881, engraved and color printed by Edmund Evans: $180.00

Painting Book by Kate Greenaway, George Routledge, 1884, engraved and color printed by Edmund Evans: $250.00

Queen Victoria's Jubilee Garland, George Routledge, 1887, engraved and color printed by Edmund Evans. With original ribbon tie: $350.00. Without ribbon: $250.00

Quiver of Love, A Collection of Valentines, Ancient and Modern, Marcus Ward, 1876, four-color plates by Greenaway and four-color plates by Walter Crane: $750.00

Quiver of Love, A Collection of Valentines, Ancient and Modern, Marcus Ward, variant or later edition with plates only by Greenaway or less than four plates by Crane: $350.00

Under the Window, George Routledge, 1879, engraved and color printed by Edmund Evans. More than 100,000 copies of this popular first book by Greenaway were eventually printed by Routledge. First edition: $400.00. Later Routledge printings: $200.00

For more information on identifying Greenaway first editions and rare works:

Schuster, Thomas, and Rodney Engen. *Printed Kate Greenaway: A catalogue raisonné*. T. E. Schuster, 1986.

GREENE, Bette

Summer of My German Soldier, Dial Press, 1973, first edition with dust jacket: $30.00

GREENE, Graham

Little Fire Engine, Max Parrish, London, undated, ca. 1950, oblong oversize, cover cream cloth with red illustrations, pictorial endpapers, blue text, color illustrations by Dorothy Craigie, first edition with dust jacket: $300.00

Little Fire Engine, Bodley Head, 1973, oblong hardcover, 48 pages, illustrated by Edward Ardizzone, first edition thus, with dust jacket: $200.00

Little Horse Bus, Max Parrish, London, 1952, illustrated in color by Dorothy Craigie, first edition with dust jacket: $500.00

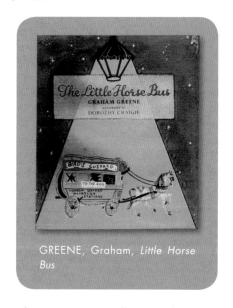

GREENE, Graham, *Little Horse Bus*

Little Horse Bus, Bodley Head, London, 1974, oblong oversize pictorial hardcover, color illustrations by Edward Ardizzone, first edition: $150.00

Little Horse Bus, Doubleday, 1974, color illustrations by Edward Ardizzone, US first edition with dust jacket: $50.00

Little Steamroller, Lothrop, Lee, 1955, square hardcover, 36 pages, color illustrations by Dorothy Craigie, US first edition with dust jacket: $300.00

Little Steamroller, 1974, Doubleday, oversize hardcover, 46 pages, illustrated by

Edward Ardizzone, first American edition thus, with dust jacket: $100.00

Little Train, Eyre & Spottiswoode, undated, ca. 1952, oblong oversize, illustrated by Dorothy Craigie, first edition with dust jacket: $300.00

Little Train, Bodley Head, 1973, pictorial laminated cover, illustrated by Edward Ardizzone, first edition thus: $150.00

GREGG, Alan, see Series section, REED CONROY

GREGORIAN, Joyce Ballou, see Series section, BROKEN CITADAL TRILOGY

GRIMM, Jacob (1785 – 1863) and Wilheim (1786 –1859)

The Grimm brothers collected German fairy tales. Some crossovers occur with other collections. An example is *Red Riding Hood*, recorded from folk tales with a "saved by the huntsman" ending by Grimm, but given a harsh "wolf ate her" ending in an earlier collection by Charles Perrault (1628 – 1703, France). Stories written down by the Grimm brothers have been primarily printed in volumes of collected stories or in picture books of a single story. There are so many versions and editions of these stories, a complete list would require a book limited to the works of the brothers Grimm. A few examples include:

Sets, listed by date of issue:

German Popular Stories Translated from the Kinder und Haus Marchen, collected by M.M. Grimm, from Oral Tradition, C. Baldwin, and James Robins, London, 1823 Vol. 1, and 1826 Vol. 2, first edition in English, brown paper cover with illustration, etched plates by George Cruikshank, two volume set in original paper covers: $60,000.00. Re-bound in leather: $4,000.00

Complete Household Tales, edited by Louis and Bryna Untermeyer, Limited Editions Club, 1962, four volumes include: *Enchanted Beginnings; Hidden Heros* and *Heroines; Magic and Spells;* and *Death and the Devil.* Illustrations by Lucille Cross, four-volume set in slipcase: $150.00

Juniper Tree and Other Tales from Grimm, Farrar, Straus and Giroux, 1973, tan cloth gilt, illustrated throughout with sketches by Maurice Sendak, two volumes. First edition, two-volume set with dust jackets and slipcases: $200.00

Single volume collections:

Grimm Fairy Tales, McLoughlin Brothers, ca. 1897, hardcover, illustrated endpapers, color frontispiece, b/w illlustrations by Johann and Andre: $150.00

Grimm's Fairy Tales, edited by Eric Vredenburg, undated, ca. 1900 – 1915 Raphael Tuck, UK, and David McKay, US, oversize, dark cover with gilt lettering, color plates plus b/w illustrations by Mabel Lucie Attwell: $150.00

Tales from Grimm, Coward-McCann, 1936, oversize square hardcover, color frontispiece plus full-page and in-text illustrations by Wanda Gag, first edition with dust jacket: $250.00

Single titles, listed by date of issue:

King Grisly-Beard, Grimm fairy tale, 1973, Farrar, hardcover, illustrated by Sendak, first edition with dust jacket: $80.00

Little Brother and Little Sister, Constable, 1917, pictorial hardcover with gilt, oversize, illustrated endpapers, 12 tipped-in color plates with tissue guards plus illustrations by Arthur Rackham: $500.00

Sleeping Beauty, Heinemann, 1920, oversize pictorial hardcover, pictorial endpapers, color frontispiece, silhouette illustrations throughout by Arthur Rackham: $700.00

Hansel and Gretel, and Other Tales, E. P. Dutton, 1920, oversize, blue hardcover with gilt, 20 color plates plus b/w illustrations by Arthur Rackham: $400.00

Snowdrop, and Other Tales, 1920, Constable, UK, and E. P. Dutton, US, hardcover with gilt, 20 color plates plus b/w illustrations by Arthur Rackham, first edition: $400.00

Robber Bridegroom, Black Ltd., 1922, oversize blue hardcover, yellow titles,

illllustrated endpapers, 37 pages, eight mounted color plates plus b/w illustrations by H. J. Owen: $200.00

Snow-White and Rose-Red, Rand McNally, 1938, pictorial hardcover, small, illustrations by Clarence Biers, first edition: $300.00

Sleeping Beauty, pop-up, Bancroft, UK, 1961, pictorial covers, blue cloth spine, seven elaborate pop-ups in full color, illustrations by V. Kubasta, first edition: $125.00

Snow White, Little, Brown, 1974, Paul Heins translation, color illustrations by Trina Schart Hyman, first edition with dust jacket: $100.00

GRIPE, Maria (her books are translated from Swedish)

Elvis and His Friends, Delacorte Press, 1973, illustrated by Harald Gripe, US first edition with dust jacket: $50.00

Elvis and His Secret, Delacorte Press, 1976, US first edition with dust jacket: $40.00

Glassblower's Children, Delacorte Press, 1964, first edition with dust jacket: $50.00

Hugo, Delacorte Press, 1970, first edition with dust jacket: $40.00

Hugo and Josephine, Delacorte Press, 1969, illustrated by Harald Gripe, first edition with dust jacket: $40.00

Josephine, Delacorte Press,1970, illustrated by Harold Gripe, US first edition: $40.00

GROVER, Eulalie Osgood, see also Series section, SUNBONNET BABIES BOOKS

Magnolia Primer, Silver, Burdett, 1913, small book with photos and stories based in the South, probable first edition: $100.00

Mother Goose (Volland Popular Edition), M. A. Donohue reprint, Chicago, 1915, color illustrations by Frederick Richardson, green cloth, lettered in silver and with paste-on color illustration, decorated endpapers, first Donohue edition: $250.00

GROVER, Eulalie Osgood, *Overall Boys*

Overall Boys, Rand McNally, 1905, paste-on-pictorial on board covers, illustrated in b/w and color plates by Bertha Corbett: $100.00

Overall Boys — A First Reader, Rand McNally, 1915, illustrations by Bertha L. Corbett, first edition: $100.00

Overall Boys in Switzerland, Rand McNally, 1916, gray cover, illustrated by Bertha Corbett, first edition: $150.00

GROVES-RAINES, Antony
Tidy Hen, Harcourt Brace, 1961, small blue hardcover, full-page color illustrations by author, first edition with dust jacket: $35.00

GRUBB, Mary B.
Our Alphabet of Toys, Harper, 1932, oversize, 28 pages, paper covers, b/w/color illustrations by Carolyn Ashbrook: $35.00

GRUELLE, Johnny (1880 – 1938), see Series section, ALL ABOUT, RAGGEDY ANN

Artist Johnny Gruelle was the son of a professional artist and began his career illustrating comic strips, then Volland picture books. He also designed toys to match his many stories, and created the first Raggedy Ann and Andy dolls. The close-knit Gruelle family included artist son Worth and artist brother Justin, as well as other family members who worked together on projects, then

formed the Johnny Gruelle Publishing Company.

Cheery Scarecrow, Donohue, 1929, small, plain cover, color illustrations throughout: $60.00

GRUELLE, Johnny, illustration from *Cheery Scarecrow*

Friendly Fairies, Volland, 1919, oversize, color illustrations, first edition in original box: $300.00

Funny Little Book, Volland, 1918, small, full color illustrations, characters are wooden toys, early edition: $100.00

Johnny Gruelle's Golden Book, Donohue, 1929, colored boards, color illustrations throughout, first edition with dust jacket: $250.00

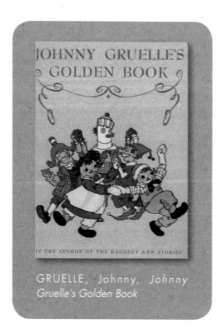

GRUELLE, Johnny, *Johnny Gruelle's Golden Book*

Little Brown Bear, M. A. Donohue & Company, 1920, color and b/w illustrations by Johnny Gruelle, with dust jacket: $200.00

Little Sunny Stories: The Singing Thread; The Way to Fairyland; Mrs. Goodluck Cricket, Volland, 1919, small, about 35 pages, pictorial boards and end papers, collection of stories: $100.00

GRUELLE, Johnny, *Magical Land of Noom*

Magical Land of Noom, Volland, Chicago, 1922, illustrated boards, 12 full-page color plates by Gruelle, with dust jacket: $250.00

My Very Own Fairy Stories, Volland, 1928, pictorial boards, b/w endpapers, color plates by author, first edition: $200.00

Orphan Annie Story Book, Bobbs-Merrill, 1921, illustrated boards, illustrations by author: $200.00

Paper Dragon, Volland, 1926, color pictorial boards, color illustrations, with original box: $250.00

GRUELLE, Justin C., illustrator

Justin was Johnny Gruelle's brother and he illustrated some of the *Raggedy Ann* books.

Mother Goose Parade, Volland, 1929, oversize, rewritten Mother Goose poems by Justin Gruelle, color illustrated paper-over-board cover, color illustrations throughout by author: $100.00

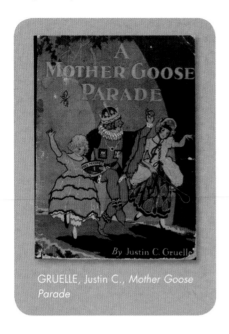

GRUELLE, Justin C., *Mother Goose Parade*

GUILLOT, Rene

Blue Day, Abelard Schuman, 1959, blue/b/w illustrations by Margery Gill, first edition with dust jacket: $70.00

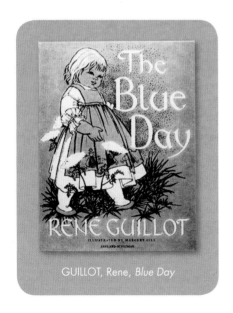

GUILLOT, Rene, *Blue Day*

Kpo the Leopard, Oxford University Press, 1955, illustrated by Joan Kiddell-Monroe, first edition with dust jacket: $200.00

King of the Reindeer, and Other Animal Stories, Odhams Press, London, 1967,

color illustrations by Paul Durand, first edition with dust jacket: $90.00

Pascal and the Lioness, McGraw Hill, 1965, illustrated by Barry Wilkinson, with dust jacket: $60.00

GUIRMA, Frederic

Princess of the Full Moon, 1970, Macmillan, first edition, hardcover, illustrated by Frederic Guirma, first edition with dust jacket: $40.00

GURNEY, Eric

Eric Gurney's Pop-Up Book of Dogs, Random House, easy reader, hardcover, illustrations by author, with pop-up in good condition: $50.00

King, the Mice and the Cheese, with Nancy Gurney, Random House, 1965, illustrated by authors, first edition with dust jacket: $30.00

GURY, Jeremy

Wonderful World of Aunt Tuddy, Random House, 1958, oversize hardcover, color illustrations by Hilary Knight, first edition with dust jacket: $100.00

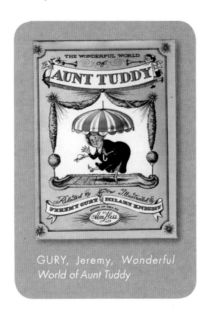

GURY, Jeremy, *Wonderful World of Aunt Tuddy*

GUTMANN, Bessie Pease (b. Philadelphia, 1876 – 1960)

Bessie Pease Gutmann grew up in Philadelphia and attended the Philadelphia School of Design for Women, then continued her art education at the New York School of Art, then the Art Students League of New York. She had already begun her

career when she married Gutmann, a printer. Combining her portraits of their three babies with his printing skills, the Gutmanns built an extremely successful business. Her own book, *Our Baby's Early Days, 1908 Best,* is a collector's item, along with early Gutmann prints. Other children's books illustrated by Gutmann include *Child's Garden of Verses* by Stevenson and *Alice in Wonderland* by Carroll.

GWYNNE, Fred, author/illustrator

Chocolate Moose for Dinner, Prentice-Hall, 1987, illustrations by author, first edition with dust jacket: $60.00

Sixteen Hand Horse, Prentice-Hall, 1980, glazed pictorial boards, first edition with dust jacket: $40.00

Story of Ick, Windmill Books, 1971, first edition with dust jacket: $40.00

◆ ⋯⋯⋯⋯⋯⋯ **H** ⋯⋯⋯⋯⋯⋯ ◆

HAAS, Irene

Little Moon Theater, Atheneum, Margaret McElderry, 1981, oblong, color illustrations by author: $50.00

HADER, Berta and Elmer, authors/illustrators

Berta Hoerner (1891 – 1976) was born in Mexico, educated in Mexico, Texas, and New York, studied art at the University of Washington, Seattle, and at the California School of Design. She began her career in magazine art. Elmer Hader (1889 – 1973) was born in California and also studied art at the California School of Design. After their marriage, they began a lifelong career collaboration on children's books, both writing and illustrating their own stories, as well as illustrating the works of other writers. Their stylistic illustrations show the influences of their California training, often featuring sunshine bright colors and clear, simple forms.

Ding Dong Bell: Pussy's in the Well, Macmillan, 1957, oversize hardcover, illustrated by authors, first edition with dust jacket: $45.00

HADER, Berta and Elmer, *Little Red Hen*

Friendly Phoebe, Macmillan, 1953, hardcover, illustrated by authors, first edition with dust jacket: $45.00

Little Chip of Willow Hill, Macmillan, 1958, oversize hardcover, illustrated by authors, first edition with dust jacket: $50.00

Little Red Hen, Macmillan, 1928, Happy Hour series, illustrated boards, color throughout by authors, first edition with dust jacket: $150.00

Mister Billy's Gun, Macmillan, oversize hardcover, illustrated by authors, first edition with dust jacket: $40.00

Runaways, Macmillan, 1956, oversize hardcover, pictorial paper-covered hardcover, 38 pages, illustrated by authors, first edition with dust jacket: $50.00

Spunky, the Story of a Shetland Pony, Macmillan, 1951, square, 90 pages, color illustrations by authors, first edition with dust jacket: $60.00

Squirrely of Willow Hill, Macmillan, 1950, hardcover, illustrated by authors, first edition with dust jacket: $65.00

Wish on the Moon, Macmillian, 1950, oversize hardcover, color illustrations by authors, first edition with dust jacket: $50.00

HAHN, Lena
Adventures of Baldwin the Penguin, Putnam, 1963, oblong hardcover, color

HAHN, Lena, *Adventures of Baldwin the Penguin*

illustrations throughout by Hans Deininger, US first edition with dust jacket: $50.00

HAILE, Ellen
Three Brown Boys and Other Happy Children, Cassell, 1879, impressed cover illustration with silver and gold gilt, b/w illustrations throughout, some by Kate Greenaway: $45.00

Two Gray Girls, Cassell, 1880, color paste-on-pictorial cover, 258 pages, b/w illustrations listed "by Kate Greenaway, M. E. Edwards and Others": $45.00

HALE, Kathleen, (1898 – 2000, b. Scotland), see also Series section, ORLANDO THE CAT

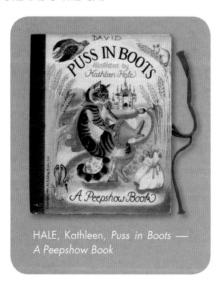

HALE, Kathleen, *Puss in Boots — A Peepshow Book*

Hale began her career doing dust jacket designs for a book publisher and illustrations for *Child Education* publication. As her work gained recognition, she built her reputation as an author/illustrator of children's picture books. Hale is best

remembered for the colorful illustrations in her *Orlando* series, featuring a marmalade cat. Her autobiography is titled *Slender Reputation.*

Manda, John Murray, 1952, color illustrations by author, first edition: $200.00

Henrietta's Magic Egg, George Allen & Unwin Ltd., 1973, paper covered boards with pictorial illustration: $150.00

Puss in Boots — A Peepshow Book, Folding Books Ltd., 1951, pop-up version of the classic children's story in six sections, color illustrations by Hale: $150.00

HALEY, Gail E., author/illustrator

Haley grew up in North Carolina and attended the University of Virginia. Her retelling of the Ananse legends grew out of a year spent living in the Carribbean islands. *A Story, A Story* (1970) won the Caldecott. Haley has used a variety of techniques to illustrate her tales including woodcuts, block prints, and paintings. In the 1980s, she established the Gail Haley Collection of the Culture of Childhood at the Appalachian State University in North Carolina.

HALEY, Gail E., *Post Office Cat*

Green Man, Charles Scribner's Sons, 1980, oblong oversize, folk hero legend, US first edition with dust jacket: $150.00

Post Office Cat, Scribner's, 1976, illustrations by author, first edition with dust jacket: $40.00

Story, a Story, an African Tale Retold, Atheneum, 1970, oblong oversize hardcover, color illustrations by author, 1971 Caldecott Award edition with dust jacket: $40.00

HALLIBURTON, Richard

Adventurer Halliburton was the bestselling author of *Seven League Boots* and *Royal Road to Romance*.

Book of Marvels, the Occident, Bobbs-Merrill, Indianapolis, 1937, pictorial cover, oversize, b/w photo illustrations, with dust jacket: $50.00

Book of Marvels, the Orient, Bobbs-Merrill, 1938, pictorial cover, oversize, b/w photo illustrations, with dust jacket: $50.00

HAMILTON, Virginia

House of Dies Drear, Macmillan, 1968, illustrated by Eros Keith, first edition with dust jacket: $90.00

M. C. Higgins, the Great, Macmillan, 1974 (Newbery Medal winner 1975), no medal sticker to jacket, first edition with dust jacket: $100.00

Time-Ago Tales of Jahdu, Macmillan, 1969, b/w illustrations by Nonny Hogrogian, trickster tales featuring the shape-shifting Jahdu, first edition with dust jacket: $40.00

Time-Ago Lost: More Tales of Jahdu, Macmillan, 1973, illustrations by Ray Prather, first edition with dust jacket: $40.00

Zeely, Macmillan, 1967, illustrations by Shimin Symeon, author's first book, first edition with dust jacket: $100.00

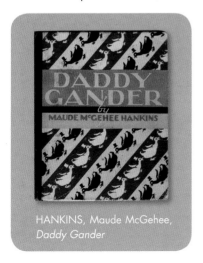

HANKINS, Maude McGehee, *Daddy Gander*

HANCOCK, H. Irving, see Series section, CONQUEST OF THE UNITED STATES, DICK PRESCOTT, MOTOR BOAT CLUB

HANKINS, Maude McGehee

Daddy Gander, Volland, 1928, small paper-over-board cover with cloth spine, color illustrations throughout by Ve Elizabeth Cadie: $80.00

HAROLD, Childe

Child's Book of Abridged Wisdom, Elder, 1905, rope-hinged cover, small, double-pages with color illustrations and decorations: $70.00

HARRADEN, Beatrice

Master Roley, Warner, undated, ca. 1890, cloth with gilt cover: $100.00

New Book of the Fairies, Griffith Farran Browne & Co. Ltd, London, 1897, small, navy boards with gilt illustration, illustrated by Edith Lupton, probable first edition: $50.00

HARRIS, Geraldine, see Series section, SEVEN CITADELS

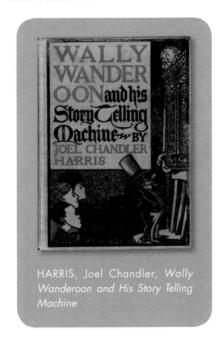

HARRIS, Joel Chandler, *Wally Wanderoon and His Story Telling Machine*

HARRIS, Joel Chandler, see also Series section, UNCLE REMUS

Wally Wanderoon and His Story Telling Machine, McClure Phillips, 1908, cloth hardcover with printed illustration, b/w illustrations by Karl Moseley: $90.00

HARRIS, Rosemary

Child in the Bamboo Grove, Faber, 1971, illustrated by Errol LeCain, first edition with dust jacket: $80.00

Enchanted Horse, UK Kestrel Books, 1981, illustrated by Pauline Baynes, first edition with dust jacket: $40.00

King's White Elephant, Faber, 1973, pictorial boards, color illustrations by Errol LeCain, first edition with dust jacket: $50.00

Lotus and the Grail: Legends from East to West, Faber & Faber, London, 1974, color plates by Errol LeCain, first edition with dust jacket: $80.00

HART, William S., see Series section, GOLDEN WEST BOYS

HARTWELL, James

Enchanted Castle, a Book of Fairy Tales from Flowerland, Altemus, 1906, illustrated endpapers, color illustrations by John Neill, first edition with dust jacket: $200.00

Man Elephant, a Book of African Fairy Tales, Altemus, 1906, pictorial cloth-over-board cover: $35.00

HAVILAND, Virginia

Fairy Tale Treasury, Coward, McCann & Geoghegan, 1972, hardcover, illustrated by Raymond Briggs, first edition with dust jacket: $50.00

Favorite Fairy Tales Told in Greece, Little, Brown, 1970, 90 pages, color and b/w illustrations by Nonny Hogrogian, first edition with dust jacket: $50.00

HAWEIS, Mrs. H. R.

Chaucer for Children, 1882, Chatto, oversize, cloth-over-board cover with decorations, 112 pages, eight color plates by author: $90.00

HAWTHORNE, Nathaniel (1804–1864)

Hawthorne's classics have been reprinted in many editions with many illustrators. Following is a small sample:

Famous Old People: Being the Second Epoch of Grandfather's Chair, E.P.

Peabody, 1841, small, 158 pages, cloth with paper label and gilt, first edition: $600.00

Grandfather's Chair, Wiley & Putnam, Boston and E. P. Peabody, New York, 1841, cloth with paper label and gilt, 140 pages, first book in Hawthorne's trilogy of juveniles, first edition: $800.00

Tanglewood Tales, for Girls and Boys; Being a Second Wonder-Book, Ticknor, Reed and Fields, 1853, ribbed cloth with gilt, full-page engravings throughout, ads are dated one month prior to the date of publication, probable first edition: $4,000.00

Three Golden Apples, 1912 edition, Constable, square pictorial boards, four-color plates by Patten Wilson: $20.00

HAWTHORNE, Nathaniel, *Wonder Book and Tanglewood Tales*

Twice-Told Tales, John B. Russell, 1837, original cloth, Hawthorne's second book and the first to show his name on the title page, limited printing of 1,000 copies: $4,000.00

Wonder Book and Tanglewood Tales, 1928 edition, Duffield, blue cloth-over-board cover with paste-on-pictorial, 399 pages, 10 color plates by Maxfield Parrish: $100.00

Wonder Book and Tanglewood Tales, 1930 edition, Winston, red cloth-over-

board cover with paste-on-pictorial, 358 pages, illustrated endpapers, four-color plates and b/w illustrations by Frederick Richardson: $30.00

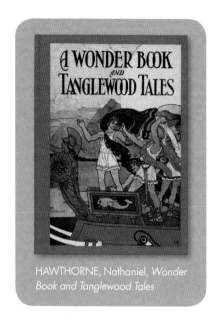

HAWTHORNE, Nathaniel, *Wonder Book and Tanglewood Tales*

Wonder Book for Girls and Boys, Ticknor, Reed and Fields, 1852, cloth with gilt, frontispiece and six engraved plates by Baker from designs by Billings: $4,000.00

HAY, Timothy (pseudonym for Margaret Wise Brown)

Horses, Harper & Brothers, 1944, illustrations by Wag, pictorial boards, 30 pages, first edition with dust jacket: $250.00

HAYES, Clair W., see Series section, BOY ALLIES WITH THE ARMY

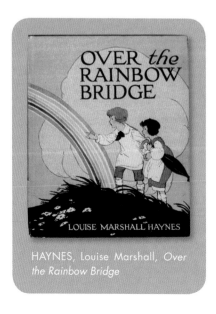

HAYNES, Louise Marshall, *Over the Rainbow Bridge*

HAYES, Geoffrey, see Series section, UNCLE TOOTH

HAYNES, Louise Marshall

Over the Rainbow Bridge, Volland, 1920, small hardcover, color illustrations by Carmen L. Brown, with original box: $150.00. Without box: $70.00

HAYS, Margaret

Kiddie Rhymes, Jacobs, 1911, oversize picture book, 29 pages, color plates and b/w illustrations by Grace Wiederseim (Grace Drayton): $60.00

HAYS, Wilma Pitchford

Christmas on the Mayflower, 1956, Coward-McCann, first edition, hardcover, illustrated by Roger Duvoisin: $35.00

Circus Girl Without a Name, Ives Washburn, 1970, illustrated by William Ferguson, first edition with dust jacket: $40.00

HAYWOOD, Carolyn (1898 – 1990),

author/illustrator, see also Series section, BETSY, EDDIE

Here Comes the Bus!, William Morrow, 1968, first edition with dust jacket: $60.00

When I Grow Up, Whitman, 1930, oversize, pictorial paper, full-color illustrations by author, author's first children's book: $80.00

HEARN, Michael Patrick, *Porcelain Cat*

HEARN, Michael Patrick

Porcelain Cat, Little Brown, 1987, oblong with gilt illustration, color illustrations throughout by Leo and Diane Dillon, first edition with dust jacket: $40.00

HEIDE, Florence Parry, see also Series section, TREEHORN

Mystery at Keyhole Carnival (A Spotlight Club Mystery), Albert Whitman, 1977, illustrated by Seymour Fleishman, green illustrated buckram boards, first edition: $100.00

Tales for the Perfect Child, Lothrop, Lee & Shepard, 1985, glazed picture cover, illustrated by Victoria Chess, first edition with dust jacket: $40.00

HEINLEIN, Robert, see Series section, HEINLEIN JUVENILES

HELM, Clementine

Cecily (Elf Goldihair), translated by Elisabeth Stork, 1924, J. B. Lippincott, cloth-over-board with gilt lettering and paste-on-illustration, 298 pages, illustrated endpapers, eight color plates by Gertrude Kay, first edition with dust jacket: $100.00

HELM, Clementine, illustration from *Cecily (Elf Goldihair)*

HELPS, Racey, author/illustrator

Guinea-Pig Podge, Medici Society, 1971, first edition with dust jacket: $80.00

Upside-down Medicine, Collins, London, 1946, pictorial boards, small, Barnaby Littlemouse story, color illustrations, first edition: $40.00

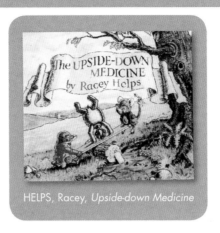
HELPS, Racey, *Upside-down Medicine*

HENDERSON, LeGrand, see Series section, AUGUSTUS

HENDRYX, James B. (pseudonym James Beardsley) see also Series section, CONNIE MORGAN

Courage of the North, Hammond, 1954, first edition with dust jacket: $50.00

HENRY, Marguerite, see also Series section, MISTY THE HORSE

Marguerite Henry called her long collaboration with artist Wesley Dennis "a joint venture" where Dennis had as much say in the development of the book as herself. Dennis and Henry often traveled together to locations, where Henry would conduct interviews while Dennis did location sketches. She would cut the text to make Dennis's many pictures fit, just as he would crop the paintings to accomodate her writing.

Album of Horses, Rand McNally, 1951, color and b/w illustrations by Wesley Dennis, first edition with dust jacket: $35.00

Black Gold, Rand McNally, 1957, black boards with gold text, illustrated endpapers, illustrated by Wesley Dennis, first edition with dust jacket: $35.00

Born to Trot, Rand McNally, 1950, oversize hardcover, illustrated by Wesley Dennis, first edition with dust jacket: $50.00

Brighty of the Grand Canyon, Rand McNally, 1953, oversize hardcover, illustrated by Dennis, first edition with dust jacket: $60.00

Cinnabar, the One O'Clock, Rand McNally, 1956, oversize hardcover, illustrated by Wesley Dennis, first edition with dust jacket: $50.00

Five O'Clock Charlie, Rand McNally, 1962, oversize hardcover, illustrated by Wesley Dennis, first edition with dust jacket: $40.00

Gaudenzia, Pride of the Palio, Rand McNally, 1960, red hardcover with gilt lettering, oversize, 237 pages, illustrated endpapers, b/w and color illustrations by Lynd Ward, first edition with dust jacket: $30.00

White Stallion of Lipizza, Rand McNally, 1964, illustrated by Wesley Dennis, first edition with dust jacket: $80.00

HENTY, G. A. (1832–1902)

Henty wrote historical and military adventure novels for boys. Like his American counterpart Horatio Alger, Henty was popular with young Victorians on both sides of the Atlantic. His primary publisher, Blackie & Son, estimated that more than 150,000 copies of his books were sold each year during the later half of the nineteenth century. Although not originally issued as a series, the Blackie/Scribner books were published in a uniform format. Both novels and magazine pieces were later collected into various boy and school reader formats.

Henty served in the Crimean War and later worked as a war correspondent from 1865 to 1876. He wrote a number of adult novels. His first juvenile appeared in 1872 and he also served as an editor for boys' magazines. Today, collectors seek early editions with their highly decorated covers. Firsts are difficult to identify because his publishers rarely identified reprints.

Henty books, Blackie/Scribner original editions, advertised as "the Famous Henty Books" by the 1890s: Early editions had cover illustrations printed on colored cloth-covered boards with gilt decoration on front and spine. All titles listed below were first published in England by Blackie & Son. In the US, they were originally imported by Scribner & Welford or by

Charles Scribner's Sons (referred to as Scribner in this listing). By the 1890s, Scribner was printing its own editions, still in the same format as the Blackie editions. Late printings of both publishers dropped the gilt decoration. By the 1920s, Scribner used paste-on illustrations and same-as-cover dust jackets. Illustrated with black-and-white illustrations, some books also included maps of battlefields or territory covered by the adventure. Reprints were done by various publishers, including Donahue and A. L. Burt.

Henty prices, Blackie, 1880s Blackie first editions: $300.00. 1890s Blackie first editions: $150.00. 1900s Blackie first editions: $100.00. Later editions with gilt and fully illustrated: $100.00. Plain editions with no gilt: $20.00

Henty prices, Scribner, Scribner & Welford first American editions or 1880s Scribner imported editions with Blackie also listed on copyright page: $250.00. 1880s Scribner first American editions: $150.00. 1890s – 1900s Scribner first American editions: $100.00. Later editions with gilt and illustrations: $75.00. Later editions with plain or paste-on covers: $20.00

(Henty reprints by Donahue, Hurst, and A. L. Burt, under $30.00)

Henty titles (a few of the many), and copyright dates of the first editions:

At Agincourt, Blackie, 1896, Scribner's, 12 illustrations by Wal Paget

Bonnie Prince Charlie, 1888, Blackie, 12 illustrations by Gordon Browne

Bravest of the Brave, 1887, Blackie, Scribner & Welford, eight illustrations by H. M. Paget

By Pike and Dyke, 1890, Blackie, Scribner & Welford, 10 full-page illustrations by Maynard Brown

By Right of Conquest, 1891, Blackie, 10 full-page illustrations by W. S. Stacey

By Sheer Pluck, 1884, Blackie, eight full-page illustrations by Gordon Browne

Dash for Khartoum, 1892, Blackie, 1891, Scribner, ten illustrations by Joseph Nash

Final Reckoning, 1887, Blackie, Scribner & Welford, eight full-page illustrations by W. B. Wollen

For Name and Fame, 1886, Blackie, eight full-page illustrations by Gordon Browne

No Surrender!, 1900, Blackie, 1899, Scribner, eight illustrations by Stanley L. Wood

One of the 28th, 1890, Blackie, Scribner & Welford, eight full-page illustrations and maps by W. H. Overend

On the Irrawaddy, 1897, Blackie, 1896, Scribner, eight full-page illustrations by W. H. Overend

Orange and Green, 1888, Blackie, Scribner, eight full-page illustrations by Gordon Browne

Redskin and Cowboy, 1892, Blackie, 1891, Scribner, 12 illustrations by Alfred Pearse

Soldier's Daughter, 1906, Blackie, cloth-covered boards with stamped-on illustrations of Afridi warrior carrying sword and shield and illustration of heroine dressed as boy on spine, no gilt, collection of three Henty stories including *Nita: A Tom-Boy Solider,* illustrated by Frances Ewan

St. George for England, 1885, Blackie, Scribner, eight full-page illustrations by Gordon Browne

Through the Sikh War, 1894, Blackie, 1893, Scribner, 12 illustrations by Hal Hurst and map

Through Three Campaigns, 1904, Blackie, 1903, Scribner, illustrated by Wal Paget

Tiger of Mysore, 1896, Blackie, 1895, Scribner, illustrations and map

To Herat and Cabul, 1902, Blackie, 1901, Scribner, eight illustrations by Charles Sheldon and map

When London Burned, 1895, Blackie, 1894, Scribner, 12 illustrations by J. Finnemore

With Kitchener in the Soudan, 1903 Blackie, 1902 Scribner, 10 illustrations by W. Rainey and maps

With Lee in Virginia, 1890, Blackie, Scribner, illustrated by Gordon Browne

Henty, Griffith & Farran editions, 1871 to 1883, earliest publisher of Henty's boys' books, these titles are similar in format to Blackie books. Cloth with printed illustrations and gilt decorations on cover and spine. Later editions issued by Blackie, Hurst, Copp Clarke, and others. First editions are rare. Early editions with gilt decorations: $200.00. Later editions with no gilt: $30.00

Henty, magazine annuals which reprinted Henty stories:

Nister's Holiday Annual, ca. 1902 – 1909, full pictorial paper-covered boards, Henty's short stories appeared in various volumes, each: $50.00

HERBEN, Beatrice Slayton, MD
Jack O'Health and Peg O'Joy, Scribner, 1921, cloth-over-board cover, 39 pages, color illustrations by Frederick Richardson: $65.00

HERGE, see Series section, TINTIN

HERRMANN, Frank
Giant Alexander, Methuen, 1964, tall, illustrations by George Him, first edition with dust jacket: $50.00

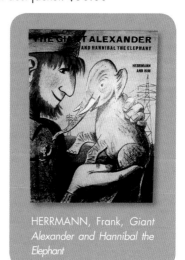

HERRMANN, Frank, *Giant Alexander and Hannibal the Elephant*

Giant Alexander and Hannibal the Elephant, McGraw-Hill, 1972, tall, pictorial boards, color illustrations by George Him, US first edition with dust jacket: $50.00

Giant Alexander and the Circus, McGraw-Hill, 1966, illustrated by George Him, first edition with dust jacket: $50.00

HEWARD, Constance, see also Series section, AMELIARANNE

Grandpa and the Tiger, Jacobs, 1924, cloth-over-board cover with paste-on-pictorial, small, 121 pages, illustrated endpapers, color and b/w illustrations by Lilian Govey: $35.00

Mr. Pickles and the Party, Frederick Warne, 1926, decorated boards, color illustrations by Anne Anderson, first edition: $90.00

Twins and Tabiffa, MacRae Smith, 1923, color plates and b/w illustrations by Susan Beatrice Pearse, early edition: $70.00

HEWETT, Anita
Elephant Big and Elephant Little and Other Stories, Bodley Head, London, 1959, tall, 64 pages, illustrated by Hough Charlott, first edition: $50.00

Hat for a Rhinoceros, and Other Stories, Bodley Head, 1959, illustrated by Margery Gill, first edition with dust jacket: $40.00

Mrs. Mopple's Washing Line, McGraw-Hill, 1966, US first edition with dust jacket: $100.00

Tale of the Turnip, Random House, 1975, first edition with dust jacket: $70.00

HEYLIGER, William, see Series section, JERRY HICKS, ST. MARY'S

HILL, Betsy Mabel, see Series section, APPLE MARKET STREET

HILL, Grace Brooks, see Series section, CORNER HOUSE GIRLS

HILL, Lorna, see Series section, SADLER'S WELLS

HILLIER, Caroline, *Winter's Tales for Children*

HILLIER, Caroline
Winter's Tales for Children, Macmillan, 1965, illustrated by Hugh Marshall, first edition with dust jacket: $150.00

HINTON, S. E.
Taking the Star Runner, Delacorte Press, 1988, first edition with dust jacket: $35.00

HIRSH, Marilyn, author/illustrator

Could Anything Be Worse, Holiday House, 1974, b/w and color illustrations, first edition with dust jacket: $80.00

Hannibal and His 37 Elephants, Holiday, 1977, first edition with dust jacket: $80.00

Joseph Who Loved the Sabbath, Viking Kestrel, 1986, glazed illustrated boards, Jewish folk tale, illustrated by Devis Grebu, first edition with dust jacket: $40.00

Leela and the Watermelon, Random House, 1971, co-author Maya Narayan, oversize illustrated cover: $40.00

Where Is Yonkela?, Crown, 1969, tall, classic Jewish children's storybook, early edition: $150.00

HITCHCOCK, Alfred, see Series section, ALFRED HITCHCOCK AND THE THREE INVESTIGATORS

HOBAN, Russell, see also Series section, FRANCES THE BADGER

Dinner at Alberta's, Crowell, 1975, illustrated by James Marshall, first edition with dust jacket: $30.00

Egg Thoughts and Other Frances Songs, Harper, 1972, illustrations by Lillian Hoban, first edition with dust jacket: $40.00

HOBAN, Russell, *Near Thing for Captain Najork*

Herman the Loser, Harper, 1961, 32 pages, illustrated by Lillian Hoban, first edition with dust jacket: $40.00

How Tom Beat Captain Najork and His Hired Sportsmen, Atheneum, 1974, oversize hardcover, color illustrations by Quentin Blake, first edition with dust jacket: $200.00

Near Thing for Captain Najork, Atheneum, 1976, oversize hardcover, color illustrations by Quentin Blake, first edition with dust jacket: $70.00

Pedalling Man and Other Poems, World's Work, 1969, 33 pages, illustrated by Lillian Hoban, first edition with dust jacket: $50.00

HODGES, Margaret
Avenger, Charles Scribner's Sons, 1982, map illustrated endpapers, Battle of Marathon background, first edition with dust jacket: $80.00

Gorgon's Head, a Myth from the Isles of Greece, Little, Brown, 1972, 31 pages, illustrated by Charles Mikolaycak, first edition with dust jacket: $50.00

Little Humpbacked Horse, a Russian Tale Retold, Farrar Straus Giroux, 1980, illustrated by Chris Conover, first edition with dust jacket: $40.00

Persephone and the Springtime, a Greek Myth, Little, Brown, 1973, illustrated by Arvis Stewart, first edition with dust jacket: $80.00

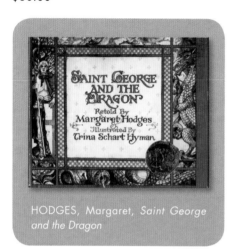

HODGES, Margaret, *Saint George and the Dragon*

Saint George and the Dragon, Little, Brown, 1984, color illustrations by Trina Schart Hyman, first edition with dust jacket: $70.00

Wave, Adapted from Lafcadio Hearn's Gleanings in Buddha-Fields, Houghton Mifflin, Boston, 1964, 45 pages, illustrated by Blair Lent (Caldecott Honor Book, 1965), first edition with dust jacket: $200.00

HOFF, Syd, author/illustrator

Although Hoff attended the National Academy of Design in New York, his early career centered on cartooning. A regular contributor to *New Yorker* magazine from the age of 18, he also created the syndicated strips "Tuffy" and "Laugh It Off." In the 1950s, he started illustrating the exploding genre of beginning readers.

Danny and the Dinosaur, Harper & Brothers, 1958, illustrated by Syd Hoff, first edition with dust jacket: $40.00

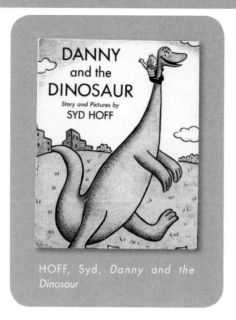

HOFF, Syd, *Danny and the Dinosaur*

Henrietta, Circus Star, Garrard, 1978, early edition: $30.00

Mahatma, Putnam, 1969, color illustrations by Syd Hoff, first edition with dust jacket: $50.00

Patty's Pet, Abelard-Schuman, 1955, early edition: $50.00

HOFF, Syd, *Sammy the Seal*

Sammy the Seal, Harper & Row, 1959, first edition with dust jacket: $30.00

HOFFMANN, Heinrich

Slovenly Peter, Winston, 1900 edition, oversize, hardcover with gilt, "illustrations colored by hand after the original style" printed on title page: $65.00

Slovenly Peter's Little Story Book, McLoughlin Bros., ca. 1890 edition, small, pictorial boards, color woodcut and b/w illustrations, an early edition of many editions of this title: $600.00

HOLBERG, Ruth (author) and Richard (illustrator)

Bells of Amsterdam, Crowell, 1940, blue cloth-over-board cover, color and b/w illustrations, first edition with dust jacket: $35.00

Mitty and Mr. Syrup, Doubleday, 1935, pictorial paper-over-board cover, illustrated endpapers, color and b/w illustrations: $30.00

Mitty on Mr. Syrup's Farm, Doubleday, 1936, color illustrated paper-on-board cover, illustrated endpapers, color and b/w illustrations: $30.00

Oh Susannah, 1939 Doubleday, cloth-over-board cover, first edition with dust jacket: $40.00

Wee Brigit O'Toole, 1938 Doubleday, color illustrated paper-over-board cover, illustrated endpapers, color and b/w illustrations, first edition with dust jacket: $30.00

HOLBERG, Ruth

Cubby Bear and the Book, E. P. Dutton, 1961, first edition with dust jacket: $50.00

Eager Beaver, E. P. Dutton, 1963, illustrated by author, first edition with dust jacket: $50.00

Koala Bear Twins, E. P. Dutton, 1955, first edition with dust jacket: $50.00

Littlest Satellite, E. P. Dutton, 1958, first edition with dust jacket: $50.00

HOGROGIAN, Nonny, author/illustrator

One Fine Day, Macmillan, 1971, 1972 Caldecott Award, illustrated by author, first edition with dust jacket: $40.00

One I Love, Two I Love, and Other Loving Mother Goose Rhymes, E. P. Dutton, 1972, illustrated by author, first edition with dust jacket: $30.00

Renowned History of Little Red Riding Hood, Crowell, 1967, 32 pages, color illustrations by author, first edition with dust jacket: $45.00

Rooster Brother, Macmillan, 1974, oblong hardcover, illustrated by author, first edition with dust jacket: $30.00

HOLL, Adelaide

ABC of Cars, Trucks and Machines, American Heritage Press, 1970, early edition: $40.00

HOLLAND, Isabelle

Man Without a Face, J. B. Lippincott, 1972, first edition with dust jacket: $40.00

HOLLAND, Marion

Big Ball of String, Random House, 1958, pictorial hardcover, illustrated by author, first edition with dust jacket: $80.00

HOLLAND, Marion, *Big Ball of String*

Billy Had a System, Albert A. Knopf, 1958, illustrated by author, first edition with dust jacket: $30.00

Billy's Clubhouse, Albert A. Knopf, 1955, first edition with dust jacket: $30.00

No Children, No Pets, Albert A. Knopf, hardcover, 1956, b/w illustrations by author, first edition with dust jacket: $50.00

No Room for a Dog, Random House, 1959, illustrated by Albert Orbaan, first edition with dust jacket: $30.00

Teddy's Camp-Out, Albert A. Knopf, 1963, illustrated by author, first edition with dust jacket: $30.00

HOLLAND, Rupert Sargent

Historic Boyhoods, George W. Jacobs & Co., 1909, gold pictorial cloth with green and red lettering and gilt, first edition: $50.00

Historic Railroads, Macrae-Smith, 1927, railway history for children, first edition with dust jacket: $100.00

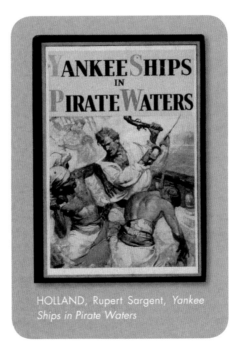

HOLLAND, Rupert Sargent, *Yankee Ships in Pirate Waters*

King Arthur and the Knights of the Round Table, George W. Jacobs, 1919, decorative cloth cover, retelling of Arthurian legend, color illustrations and b/w plates by Lancelot Speed, US first edition with dust jacket: $100.00

Race for a Fortune, J. B. Lippincott, 1931, color and b/w illustrations, first edition with dust jacket: $40.00

Splendid Buccaneer: A Tale of the Atlantic Coast in Pirate Days, J. B. Lippincott,

1928, illustrations by Stafford Good, first edition with dust jacket: $40.00

Yankee Ships in Pirate Waters, Garden City, 1931, front paste-on illustration, double spread title page and four color plates by Frank E. Schoonover, first edition: $75.00

HOLLAND, Vyvyan

Explosion of Limericks, Funk & Wagnalls, 1967, oversize hardcover, b/w illustrations by Sprod, first edition with dust jacket: $30.00

HOLLING, Holling Clancy (b. Holling Corners, Michigan, 1900 – 1973), and Lucille Webster Holling

Holling Clancy repeated his first name as his last name after he became a commercial artist. He graduated from the Chicago Art Institute, worked at the Field Museum in Chicago, worked briefly as an art instructor, and travelled around the United States with his artist wife, Lucille Webster Holling, scouting out story and illustration ideas for their children's books. The Hollings made their home in California.

Little Big Bye & Bye, P. F. Volland Company, 1926, a "Sunny Book," color illustrations: $100.00

Minn of the Mississippi, Houghton Mifflin, 1951, 86 pages, Newbery Honor book, illustrated by author, first edition with dust jacket: $65.00

Paddle-to-the-Sea, Houghton Mifflin, 1941, first edition with dust jacket: $300.00

Pagoo, Houghton Mifflin, 1957, oversize hardcover, 87 pages, color illustrations by author, first edition with dust jacket: $65.00

Road in Storyland, Platt & Munk Co, 1932, oversize, paste-on illustration, about 105 pages, full-page color illustrations by Lucille W. and H. C. Holling: $100.00

HOLLISTER, Warren, and Judith Pike

Moons of Meer, H. Z. Walck, 1969, illustrations by Richard Lebenson, first edition with dust jacket: $70.00

HOLMELUND, Else, see MINARIK, Else Holmelund

HOLMES, Oliver Wendell

Dorothy Q: Together with a Ballad of the Boston Tea Party and Grandmother's Story of Bunker Hill, Houghton Mifflin, 1893, gray cloth-over-board cover with silver gilt, 131 pages, illustrations and decorations by Howard Pyle: $50.00

Grandmother's Story of Bunker Hill Battle, Dodd, Mead, 1883, pictorial cream cloth, floral end papers, the first illustrated edition, full-page color illustrations throughout by H. W. McVicker, original russet printed dust jacket, first edition thus with dust jacket: $600.00

One-Hoss Shay: With Its Companion Poems, Houghton Mifflin, 1905, gilt stamped green cloth, color illustrations by Howard Pyle, early edition: $150.00

School Boy, Houghton Mifflin, 1879, cloth-over-board cover with gilt, illustrated endpapers, 79 pages, b/w illustrations: $45.00

HOOVER, H. M.

Children of Morrow, Four Winds Press, 1973, first edition with dust jacket: $50.00

Treasures of Morrow, Four Winds Press, 1976, first edition with dust jacket: $60.00

HORNIBROOK, Isabel, see Series section, SCOUT DRAKE

HOROWITZ, Anthony, see Series section, MARTIN HOPKINS

HOUSMAN, Laurence (1865 – 1959), author/illustrator

Although he wrote more than 80 books, some of Laurence Housman's most collectible works are the elaborate Art Noveau works that he prepared for other authors such as Christina Rossetti. Housman designed the cover as well as the highly detailed engravings for such titles as *Goblin Market.*

Princess Badoura, a Tale from the Arabian Nights, retold by Laurence Housman,

1913, Hodder & Stoughton, red morocco with gilt decoration, ten mounted color plates by Edmund Dulac, first trade edition: $800.00

Stories from the Arabian Nights, retold by Laurence Housman, 1907, Hodder & Stoughton, cloth-over-board with gilt, 133 pages, color frontispiece, 49 mounted color plates bound together at the end of the volume with tissue guards, illustrations by Edmund Dulac. First trade edition: $600.00

HOUSTON, Joan

Horse Show Hurdles, Crowell, 1957, illustrations by Paul Brown, first edition with dust jacket: $125.00

Jump-Shy, Crowell, 1959, illustrations by Paul Brown, first edition with dust jacket: $100.00

HOWARD, Joan

13th Is Magic!, Lothrop, Lee & Shepard, 1950, first edition with dust jacket: $300.00

HOWE, James, see Series section, BUNNICULA THE VAMPIRE BUNNY

HOWITT, Mary

English author Mary Howitt was one of the earliest translators of Hans Christian Andersen and produced numerous other books for children, including many translations of fairy tales.

The Fairy Gem, C. S. Francis & Co., New York, 1857, translations of French fairy tales with numerous illustrations: $175.00

HUCKE, Agnes, author/illustrator

Tale of Ten Little Toys, ca. 1900, Gabriel, color illustrated paper-over-board cover, 10 heavy cardboard pages with cut top, so that as each flips, there is one less toy across the top margin of book. Each page contains a poem explaining the loss of that toy. Color printing and illustrations throughout: $100.00

HUDSON, Gwynedd, artist

Hudson studied at the Brighton School of Art, and worked as both a poster artist

and a book illustrator in England. Her work appeared primarily in the 1920s and 1930s, and included a 1922 version of Carroll's *Alice in Wonderland* and a 1931 edition of Barrie's *Peter Pan* and Wendy.

HUDSON, Gwynedd, illustration

HUGHES, Langston (1902 – 1967)

Dream Keeper & Other Poems, Alfred A. Knopf, 1932, illustrations by Helen Sewell, first edition: $250.00. With dust jacket: $675.00

First Book of Rhythms, Franklin Watts, 1954, first edition with dust jacket: $100.00

Pictorial History of the Negro in America, Crown, 1956, first edition with dust jacket: $75.00

Popo and Fifina, Macmillan, 1932, six full-page illustrations by E. Simms Campbell, first edition: $250.00

HUGHES, Monica, see Series section, ISIS TRILOGY

HUGHES, Ted

Earth-Owl, Faber and Faber, 1963, author's third book for children, 23 poems, b/w illustrations by R.A. Brandt, first edition with dust jacket: $90.00

Meet My Folks, Faber and Faber, 1961, pictorial boards, poems, full-page b/w illustrations by George Adamson, first edition with dust jacket: $300.00

Nessie the Mannerless Monster, Faber, 1964, oblong oversize, paper covered boards illustrated in wraparound color illustrations, illustrated by Gerald Rose, first edition with dust jacket: $300.00

HUMPHREY, Maud, *Make-believe Men and Women*

HUMPHREY, Maud
Make-believe Men and Women, Frederick A. Stokes,1897, oversize paper-over-board illustrated cover, full-page color illustrations by Humphrey, line drawings by Elizabeth S. Tucker: $250.00

HUNT, Blanche Seale
Little Brown Koko stories are written in dialect.

Little Brown Koko Has Fun, 1945, American Colortype, oversize hardcover with paste-on-pictorial, 96 pages, illustrated by Dorothy Wagstaff, early edition with dust jacket: $80.00

Stories of Little Brown Koko, American Colortype, 1940, pictorial covers, oversize, 96 pages, illustrations by Dorothy Wagstaff, first edition with dust jacket: $130.00

HUNT, Clara Whitehill
About Harriet, Houghton Mifflin, 1916, 150 pages, color illustrated paste-on-pictorial cover, color illustrations throughout by Maginal Wright Enright: $60.00

HUNT, Irene
Across Five Aprils, Follett, 1964, first edition with dust jacket: $60.00

Trail of Apple Blossoms, Follett, 1968, illustrated by Don Bolognese, first edition with dust jacket: $40.00

Up a Road Slowly, Follett, 1966, jacket illustration by Don Bolognese, first edition with dust jacket: $60.00

HUNT, Mabel Leigh
Billy Button's Butter'd Biscuit, Frederick A. Stokes, 1941, cloth and paper-covered boards, illustrated by Katherine Milhous, first edition with dust jacket: $100.00

Lucinda: A Little Girl of 1860, Frederick A. Stokes, 1939, illustrated by Cameron Wright, first edition with dust jacket: $100.00

Michel's Island, Stokes, 1940, illustrated by Kate Seredy, first edition with dust jacket: $50.00

HURD, Edith Thatcher
Clement Hurd's wife wrote more than 75 children's books, starting in the 1930s.

It's Snowing, Sterling, 1957, first edition with dust jacket: $250.00

Mary's Scary House, Sterling or E. M. Hale (school library edition), 1956, illustrations by Clement Hurd, first edition: $250.00

Sky High, Lothrop Lee, 1941, illustrations by Clement Hurd, first edition with dust jacket: $125.00

Wreck of the Wild Wave (Being the True Account of the Wreck of the Clipper Ship Wild Wave of Boston), Oxford, 1942, first edition with dust jacket: $75.00

HURLIMANN, Ruth
Cat and Mouse Who Shared a House, Walck, 1973, boards with red borders and cat and mouse seen through a heart mousehole, US first edition with dust jacket: $50.00

Proud White Cat, William Morrow, 1977, first edition with dust jacket: $50.00

HUTCHINS, Pat, author/illustrator

Best Train Set Ever, Bodley Head Children's Books, 1979, UK first edition with dust jacket: $90.00

Changes, Changes, Simon & Schuster, 1971, first edition with dust jacket: $100.00

Good Night, Owl!, Simon & Schuster, 1972, first edition with dust jacket: $150.00

Happy Birthday, Sam, Greenwillow Books, 1978, first edition with dust jacket: $100.00

One-Eyed Jake, Greenwillow Books, 1979, pictorial cover, first edition: $70.00

HUTCHINS, Ross
Carpenter Bee, Addison-Wesley, 1972, color illustrations by Richard Cuffari, first edition with dust jacket: $40.00

Mayfly, Addison-Wesley, 1970, color illustrations by Jean Day Zallinger, first edition with dust jacket: $40.00

Paper Hornets, Addison-Wesley, 1973, color illustrations by Peter Zallinger, first edition with dust jacket: $40.00

Saga of Pelorus Jack, Rand McNally, 1971, oversize, 63 pages, illustrations by Jerome Connolly, first edition with dust jacket: $50.00

HYMAN, Trina Schart, illustrator

Hyman attended the Philadelphia Museum College of Art and the Museum School of Fine Arts in Boston, then continued her art education at the Swedish State Art School for Applied Arts in Stockholm. She started working in book illustration during the 1960s. In 1972, she began a seven-year stint as the art director for *Cricket* magazine, producing a number of magazine covers and illustrations for them. Although best known for her picture books of classic fairy tales such as Howard Pyle's *King Stork* (1973), she did dust jackets and interior illustrations for more than 100 books.

HYMAN, Trina Schart, *Little Red Riding Hood*

HYMAN, Trina Schart, *Self-Portrait*

How Six Found Christmas, 1969 Little, Brown, illustrated by author, first edition with dust jacket: $30.00

Little Red Riding Hood, Holiday House, 1983 (1984 Caldecott), square, color illustrations by author, first edition with dust jacket: $100.00

Self-Portrait, Addison Wesley, 1981, Hyman's life as an artist with full-color illustrations, illustrated by author, first edition with dust jacket: $130.00

■ ·········· **I** ·········· ■

IPCAR, Dahlov, author/illustrator

Bright Barnyard, Alfred A. Knopf, 1966, 34 pages, illustrations by author, first edition with dust jacket: $30.00

Brown Cow Farm, Doubleday, 1959, oblong oversize hardcover, illustrations by author, first edition with dust jacket: $40.00

Cat at Night, Doubleday, 1969, illustrations by author, first edition with dust jacket: $40.00

Cat Came Back, Alfred A. Knopf, 1971, purple oversize hardcover with gilt, color illustrations by author, first edition with dust jacket: $50.00

One Horse Farm, Doubleday,1950, oblong oversize hardcover, illustrations by author, first edition with dust jacket: $40.00

Whispering and Other Things, poetry, Knopf, 1967, oversize hardcover, illustrations by author, first edition with dust jacket: $30.00

Wonderful Egg, Doubleday, 1958, illustrations by author, first edition with dust jacket: $45.00

IRVING, Fannie Belle

Six Girls, Estes, 1884, elaborate color illustrated paper-on-board cover, illustrated endpapers, b/w engraving illustrations: $30.00

IRVING, Washington (1783 – 1859)

Although early editions of this American author's work were published for adults, many of his tales were later adapted for younger readers. Like many classics, the greatest difference in value comes from the illustrations.

Alhambra: Palace of Mystery and Splendor, Macmillan, 1926, 14 full-page illustrations by Warwick Goble, first edition: $40.00

Bold Dragoons and other Ghostly Tales, Alfred A. Knopf, 1930, illustrations by James Daugherty, first edition with dust jacket: $30.00

Legend of Sleepy Hollow, George Harrap, 1928, eight color plates by Arthur Rackham, first edition: $300.00

Rip Van Winkle, Heineman (UK) or Doubleday Page (US), 1905, 51 color plates by Arthur Rackham. Limited edition (250 copies numbered and signed by Rackham in 1905): $4,000.00. First edition: $500.00

Rip Van Winkle, David McKay, 1921, eight color plates by N.C. Wyeth, first edition: $200.00. With dust jacket: $750.00

IRWIN, Inez Hayes

Maida's Little Treasure Hunt, Grosset & Dunlap, 1955, first edition with dust jacket: $150.00

■ ·········· **J** ·········· ■

JACKSON, Charlotte

Sarah Deborah's Day, Dodd, 1941, illustrated paper-on-board cover, illustrated endpapers, b/w and three-color illustrations by Marc Simont, first edition with dust jacket: $50.00

JACKSON, Jesse

Tessie, Harper, 1968, 243 pages, pictures by Harold James, first edition with dust jacket: $35.00

JACKSON, Leroy

Animal Show and Other Peter Patter Rhymes, Rand McNally, 1965, oversize, glossy illustrated boards, illustrations by Dorothy Grider: $50.00

Billy-Be-Nimble, Rand McNally, 1920, pictorial boards and endpaper, color illustrations by Blanche Fisher Wright: $75.00

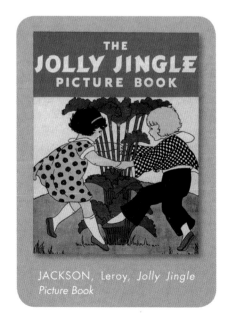

JACKSON, Leroy, *Jolly Jingle Picture Book*

Billy Bumpkins, Rand McNally, 1920, tall, full-page color illustrations by Blanche Fisher Wright: $70.00

Jolly Jingle Picture Book, Rand McNally, 1937 (new edition of the 1926 *Rimskittle Book),* oversize hardcover with paste-on-pictorial, color illustrations throughout by Ruth Caroline Eger: $80.00

Peter Patter Book, Rand McNally, 1918, oversize hardcover with paste-on pictorial, full-page color illustrations by Blanche Fisher Wright: $80.00

JACKSON, Shirley

Famous Sally, Harlin Quist,1966, hardcover with gilt, color illustrations by Charles B. Slackman, first edition with dust jacket: $50.00

9 Magic Wishes, Crowell-Collier, 1963, oversize, illustrated by Lorraine Fox, first edition: $200.00

JACOBS, Frank

Alvin Steadfast on Vernacular Island, 1965, Dial Press, yellow cloth hardcover, 64 pages, b/w illustrations by Edward Gorey, first edition with dust jacket: $60.00

JACOBS, Frank, *Alvin Steadfast on Vernacular Island*

JACOBS, Joseph (1854 – 1916)

A contemporary of Andrew Lang, Jacobs' collections introduced such tales as *Henny Penny* to the nursery. Numerous adaptations and picture books have been based on his original collections. Early David

Nutt (U.K) and G. P. Putnam (U.S.) editions often issued in the same year and format.

Celtic Fairy Tales, David Nutt, 1892, illustrations by John Batten, first edition in original cloth binding: $100.00

English Fairy Tales, David Nutt, 1890, first edition in original cloth binding: $75.00

Indian Fairy Tales, David Nutt (UK) or G.P. Putnam (U.S.), 1892, illustrations by John Batten, first edition in original cloth binding: $100.00

More Celtic Fairy Tales, David Nutt, 1894, illustrations by John Batten, first edition in original cloth binding: $100.00

More English Fairy Tales, David Nutt (UK) or G.P. Putnam (U.S.), 1894, illustrations by John Batten, first edition in original cloth binding: $75.00

JACOBS, Joseph, *Tales from Boccaccio*

Tales from Boccaccio, Ruskin House, UK, ca. 1890s, cloth-over-board cover with printed illustration and gilt, decorations and illustrations by B. Shaw, first edition thus: $200.00

JACOBS-BOND, Carrie

Tales of Little Dogs, Volland, 1921, small paper-over-board, color illustrations throughout by Katharine Sturges Dodge: $70.00

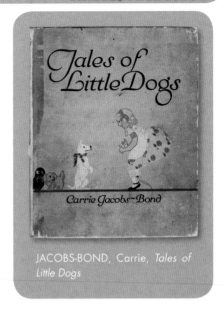

JACOBS-BOND, Carrie, *Tales of Little Dogs*

JACQUES, Brian, see Series section, REDWALL

JACQUES, Robin (b. London, 1920 – 1995)

Jacques received his education at the Royal Masonic School in Hertfordshire, but taught himself art. He worked in advertising and magazine illustration and was the art editor for *Strand* magazine. Although much of his work was for adults, he also illustrated children's books. His witty drawings built his reputation, and he was in demand as a teacher and lecturer at Harrow College of Art, London, and at Canterbury Art College and Wimbledon Art College. See also Series section, FREE TRADERS, MAGIC, WOLVES CHRONICLES.

JAMES, Frederick

JAMES, Frederick, *Cloud Hoppers*

Cloud Hoppers, Children's Press, Chicago, 1949, illustrated hardcover, color and b/w illustrations by Katherine Evans, first edition: $40.00

JAMES, Will, see also Series section, UNCLE BILL, WITH THE STARS AND STRIPES

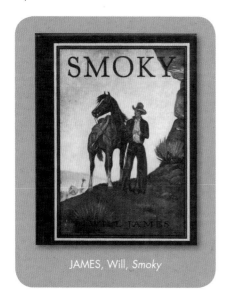

JAMES, Will, *Smoky*

Smoky, Scribner (1926), 1929 Classic edition, gilt lettering, paste-on pictorial, endpapers and color illustrations by author, this story first appeared in four installments in Scribner Magazine, with dust jacket: $1,000.00, without dust jacket: $100.00

JANSSON, Tove, see Series section, MOOMIN

JANVIER, Thomas A.
Aztec Treasure House, Harper, 1890, decorated cloth-over-board cover, small, illustrations by Frederic Remington: $100.00

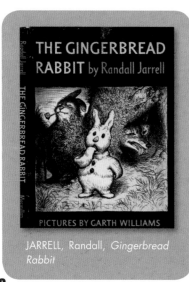

JARRELL, Randall, *Gingerbread Rabbit*

JARRELL, Randall (1914 – 1965)
Animal Family, Pantheon,1965, illustrations by Maurice Sendak, first edition with dust jacket: $70.00

Bat-Poet, Macmillan,1965, 43 pages, illustrations by Maurice Sendak, first edition with dust jacket: $45.00

Gingerbread Rabbit, Macmillan,1964, illustrations by Garth Williams, first edition with dust jacket: $150.00

JENKS, Albert Ernest
Childhood of Ji-Shib the Ojibwa, Mentzer Bush, 1900, pictorial cloth hardcover, 130 pages, illustrated by author: $40.00

JENKS, Tudor
Century World's Fair Book for Boys and Girls, Century, 1893, illustrated cloth-over-board cover, oversize, illustrations, maps, photos (reprinted in several sizes and editions), marked first edition: $110.00

Magician for One Day, Altemus, 1905, illustrated boards, small, 107 pages, illustrated endpapers, b/w illustrations by John Neill: $70.00

Magic Wand, Altemus, 1905, illustrated boards, small, 110 pages, illustrated endpapers, b/w illustrations by John Neill: $70.00

Prince and the Dragons, Altemus, 1905, illustrated boards, small, 101 pages, illustrated endpapers, b/w illustrations by John Neill: $70.00

Rescue Syndicate, Altemus, 1905, illustrated boards, small, 110 pages, illustrated endpapers, b/w illustrations by John Neill: $70.00

Timothy's Magical Afternoon, Altemus, 1905, illustrated boards, small, 98 pages, illustrated endpapers, b/w illustrations by John Neill: $70.00

JERROLD, Walter
Big Book of Fables, H. M. Caldwell, 1912, oversize, color plates, first edition with dust jacket: $500.00

Nonsense Nonsense!, undated, Frederick A. Stokes, ca. 1907, oversize, cloth-over-board cover with paste-on-pictorial, illustrated endpapers, color illustrations throughout by Charles Robinson: $250.00

JOHNS, Captain W. E., see also Series section, BIGGLES, GIMLET, KINGS OF SPACE, WORRALS

Worlds of Wonder, 1962, Hodder & Stoughton, first edition with dust jacket: $40.00

JOHNSON, Crockett (1906 – 1975), see also Series section, HAROLD AND THE PURPLE CRAYON

Ellen's Lion, Harper, 1959, illustrated hardcover, 62 pages, illustrations by author, first edition with dust jacket: $65.00

Lion's Own Story, Harper & Row, 1963, 63 pages, illustrations by author, first edition with dust jacket: $75.00

JOHNSON, Gerald W.
Pattern for Liberty, McGraw-Hill, 1952, oversize oblong hardcover with gilt lettering, 146 pages, 32 full-page color plates by artists: Frank Reilly, Simon Greco, James Bingham, first edition with dust jacket: $45.00

JOHNSON, Martha, see Series section, ANN BARTLETT

JOHNSON, Owen, see Series section, LAWRENCEVILLE SCHOOL

JOHNSTON, Annie Fellows, see also Series section, LITTLE COLONEL

Little Colonel, Burt, undated, ca. 1935, movie edition, blue hardcover with photo endpapers and illustrations from the Shirley Temple movie, in dust jacket: $70.00

Miss Santa Claus of the Pullman, 1913 Page, small, 172 pages, color frontispiece, eight b/w plates by Reginald Birch: $30.00

JOHNSTON, Isabel M.
Jeweled Toad, Bobbs-Merrill, 1907, illustrated cloth-over-board cover, 211 pages, color illustrations throughout by W. W. Denslow: $200.00

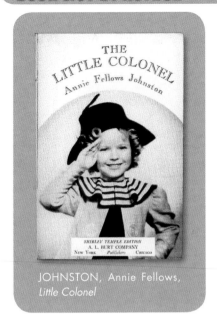

JOHNSTON, Annie Fellows, *Little Colonel*

JONES, Elizabeth Orton, *Big Susan*

JOHNSTON, Johanna

Great Gravity the Cat, Alfred A. Knopf, 1958, illustrations by Kurt Wiese, first edition with dust jacket: $50.00

JOHNSTON, Norma, see Series section, TISH STERLING

JONES, Diana Wynne, see also Series section, CHRESTOMANCI

Cart and Cwidder, Macmillan, 1975, first book in the *Dalemark* series, first UK edition, with dust jacket: $30.00

Ogre Downstairs, E. P. Dutton, 1975, US first edition with dust jacket: $30.00

JONES, DuPre

Adventures of Gremlin, J. B. Lippincott, 1966, illustrated by Edward Gorey, first edition with dust jacket: $150.00

JONES, Elizabeth Orton

Big Susan, Macmillan, 1947, dollhouse story, first edition with dust jacket: $200.00

Song of the Sun, St. Francis of Assisi, 1952, Macmillan, first edition, oversize hardcover, illustrations by author, first edition with dust jacket: $50.00

Twig, Macmillan, 1942, 152 pages, color illustrations by author, first edition with dust jacket: $200.00

JONES, Tom

Minnie the Mermaid, Oxford University Press, 1939, illustrated by Elizabeth Orton Jones, first edition: $800.00

JONES, Viola

Peter and Gretchen of Old Nuremberg, Albert Whitman, 1935, oversize, color and b/w illustrations by Helen Sewell, first edition with dust jacket: $40.00

JORDAN, David Starr

Starr was the first president of Stanford University, California.

Book of Knight and Barbara: Being a Series of Stories Told to Children, Corrected and Illustrated by the Children, Appleton, 1899, red cloth with b/w and yellow, 265 pages, b/w frontispiece and line drawings in the text: $100.00

Eric's Book of Beasts, Paul Elder, San Francisco, 1912, tan hardcover with red spine, deckle edges, 114 pages, watercolor illustrations by author: $90.00

Matka and Kotik: A Tale of the Mist-Islands, Whitaker & Ray, San Francisco (1897), 1903 edition, gray pictorial cloth with gilt, 79 pages, photos, in-text illustrations by Chloe F. Lesley $50.00

JOSLIN, Sesyle

Spy Lady and the Muffin Man, Harcourt Brace, Jovanovich, 1971, first edition with dust jacket: $80.00

What Do You Do, Dear?, Young Scott Books, 1961, illustrated by Maurice Sendak, first edition with dust jacket: $40.00

What Do You Say, Dear? A Book of Manners for All Occasions, 1958 Scott Young, first edition, small hardcover, illustrations by Maurice Sendak, first edition with dust jacket: $100.00

JUDD, Frances, see Series section, KAY TRACEY MYSTERY

JUDSON, Clara Ingram

Billy Robin and His Neighbors, Rand McNally, 1917, color plates, first edition with dust jacket: $70.00

Flower Fairies, Rand McNally, 1915, color illustrations by Maginel Wright Enright, first edition with dust jacket: $100.00

Foxy Squirrel in the Garden, Rand McNally, 1933, color throughout, first edition: $50.00

JUDSON, Clara Ingram, *Foxy Squirrel in the Garden*

JUSTER, Norton

Alberic the Wise and Other Journeys, Pantheon, 1965, first edition with dust jacket: $35.00

Dot and Line, Random House, 1963, first edition with dust jacket: $30.00

Phantom Tollbooth, Epstein and Carroll, 1961, illustrations by Jules Fieffer. First edition with dust jacket: $600.00. Without dust jacket: $200.00

JUSTUS, May, see also Series section, JERRY JAKE

At the Foot of Windy Low, Volland, 1930, green cloth-over-board cover with dark green print, full-color endpapers and illustrations by Carrie Dudley, first edition with dust jacket: $80.00

JUSTUS, May, illustration from
At the Foot of Windy Low

Fiddler's Fair, Whitman, 1945, 32-page picture book, color illustrated paper-on-board cover, color endpapers, color illustrations by Christine Chisholm: $30.00

Gabby Gaffer, Volland, 1929, green cover with gilt, 10 color plates by Carrie Dudley: $50.00

House in No-End Hollow, Doubleday, Doran, 1938, illustrations by Erick Berry, first edition with dust jacket: $50.00

Mr. Songcatcher and Company, Doubleday, Doran, 1940, first edition with dust jacket: $40.00

Peter Pocket, a Little Boy of the Cumberland Mountains, Doubleday, Page, 1927, illustrated by Mabel Pugh, first edition: $80.00

KAHN, Joan

Some Things Dark and Dangerous, 1971, Bodley Head or Harper & Row, first edition with dust jacket: $30.00

Some Things Fierce and Fatal: 14 Suspense Stories, Some Fact, Some Fiction, Harper & Row, 1971, first edition with dust jacket: $30.00

KASTNER, Erich (1899 – 1974)

German author Erich Kastner wrote the *Little Man* series as well as the 1949 novel, *Lisa and Lottie,* about twins separated by divorce, which inspired the 1961 Disney film, *The Parent Trap.* His *Emil* novels currently command the highest prices for the earliest English translations published by Cape and with intact dust jackets.

35th of May or *Conrad's Ride to the South Seas,* Jonathan Cape, illustrations by Walter Trier, first British edition with dust jacket: $175.00. Without dust jacket: $75.00

Emil and the Detectives, Jonathan Cape, 1931, illustrations by Walter Trier, first British edition with dust jacket: $175.00 Without dust jacket: $75.00

Emil and the Three Twins, Jonathan Cape, 1935, illustrations by Walter Trier, first British edition with dust jacket: $150.00. Without dust jacket: $75.00

Lisa and Lottie, Alfred A. Knopf, 1949, illustrated by Victoria de Larrea, first edition with dust jacket: $80.00

Emil, omnibus edition:

Emil, Jonathan Cape, 1949, illustrations by Walter Trier, an omnibus edition containing *Emil and the Detectives, Emil and the Three Twins,* and *35th of May.* First British edition with dust jacket: $100.00. Without dust jacket: $40.00

KAY, Gertrude Alice, author/illustrator

Adventures in Geography, Volland, 1930, oversize, orange cloth-over-board cover, illustrated endpapers, color illustrations by Kay, first edition with dust jacket: $100.00

Book of Seven Wishes, Moffat Yard, 1917, blue cloth cover with gilt, b/w illustrations by Kay: $50.00

Friends of Jimmy, Volland, 1926, hardcover,

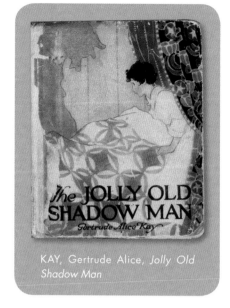

KAY, Gertrude Alice, *Jolly Old Shadow Man*

illustrated endpapers, color illustrations by Kay, with original Volland box: $200.00

Helping the Weatherman, Volland, 1920, illustrated endpapers, color illustrations by Kay, first edition: $100.00

Jolly Old Shadow Man, Volland Sunny Book, 1920, small, illustrated paper-over-board cover, illustrated endpapers, color illustrations throughout by author, first edition: $100.00

Peter, Patter and Pixie, McBride, 1931, hardcover, oversize, illustrations by the author: $80.00

Us Kids and the Circus, Volland, 1927, color illustrated paper-over-board cover, illustrated endpapers, color illustrations throughout: $70.00. With original box: $140.00

KEATS, Ezra Jack (1916 – 1983, b. Brooklyn, NY), author/illustrator

Keats' artwork includes portraits and landscape paintings, as well as magazine and book illustrations. His popular paintings for children's books are easily recognizable by the bold use of shape and clear colors. His best known book, *Snowy Day* (1962), began as a project to introduce a black child having an ordinary adventure into a mainstream picture book. Like so many illustrators, he attended the Art Students League, and also studied with Jean Charlot.

Goggles!, Macmillan, 1969, color illustrations by author, first edition with dust jacket: $50.00

Jennie's Hat, Harper, 1966, color illustrations by author, first edition with dust jacket: $40.00

John Henry, Pantheon, 1965, oversize hardcover, color illustrations by author, first edition with dust jacket: $100.00

Little Drummer Boy, Macmillan, 1968, oblong hardcover, words and music by Davis, Onorati, and Simeone, color illustrations by author, first edition with dust jacket: $50.00

Peter's Chair, Harper, 1967, illustrations by author, first edition with dust jacket: $90.00

Snowy Day, Viking Press, 1962 (1963 Caldecott Award), hardcover, color illustrations by author, first edition with dust jacket: $70.00

KEATS, Ezra Jack, *Whistle for Willie*

Whistle for Willie, Viking Press, 1964, color illustrations by author, first edition with dust jacket: $80.00

KEENE, Carolyn, see Series section, DANA GIRLS MYSTERY, NANCY DREW

KEEPING, Charles, (1924 – 1988, England) author/illustrator

After serving in the British navy, Keeping attended the Polytechnic School of Art in London. He began illustrating books for adults and children in the 1960s. For children, his work ranged from picture books to the historical novels of Rosemary Sutcliff or Leon Garfield. He received numerous international awards for his work, including the Kate Greenaway Medal.

Joseph's Yard, Oxford University Press, 1969, stiff pictorial boards, 32 pages, full-page color illustrations, first edition with dust jacket: $90.00

KEEPING, Charles, *Through the Window*

Through the Window, Oxford University Press, London, 1970, first edition with dust jacket: $70.00

Wasteground Circus, Oxford University Press, 1975, first edition with dust jacket: $60.00

KELLAND, Clarence, see Series section, MARK TIDD

KELLOGG COMPANY
Kellogg's Funny Jungleland, Kellogg Company, 1932, full color flip-strip "moving pictures" book, each page cut

KELLOGG COMPANY, *Kellogg's Funny Jungleland*

into three horizontal strips so that the reader can match or mismatch heads with bodies with legs of picture animals. Cereal advertisement on back: $60.00

KELLOGG, Steven
Kellogg studied art at the Rhode Island School of Design. The high point of his education, he once said, was an honors fellowship in his senior year which allowed him to study in Florence, Italy. Daily visits to the Uffizzi Museum allowed him to study the paintings and actually handle drawings of the masters. Later he worked as an instructor at American University in Washington, DC, and built his career as both an author and illustrator. He has also illustrated children's books by other authors.

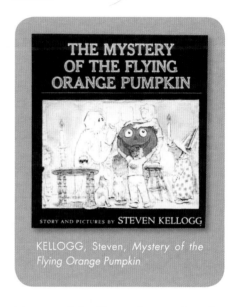

KELLOGG, Steven, *Mystery of the Flying Orange Pumpkin*

Mystery of the Flying Orange Pumpkin, Dial, 1980, first edition with dust jacket: $100.00

Orchard Cat, Dial Press, 1972, oblong, first edition with dust jacket: $40.00

Won't Somebody Play with Me?, Frederick Warne, 1972, oblong oversize, UK first edition: $40.00

KELLY, Eric P.
Amazing Journey of David Ingram, J. B. Lippincott, 1949, first edition with dust jacket: $50.00

Christmas Nightingale, Macmillan, 1932, b/w illustrations by Marguerite de Angeli, first edition with dust jacket: $50.00

In Clean Hay, Macmillan, 1953, color illustrations by Maud and Miska Petersham, first edition with dust jacket: $45.00

KELLY, Walt, see Series section, POGO

KELSEY, Vera
Maria Rosa, Doubleday, 1942, oversize picture book, color illustrations by Candido Portinari, first edition with dust jacket: $60.00

KENDALL, Carol
Gammage Cup, Harcourt Brace, 1959, oversize, Illustrated by Erik Blegvad, first edition with dust jacket: $200.00

KENDALL, Lace
Secret Lions, Coward-McCann,1962, illustrated by Douglas Howland, first edition with dust jacket: $70.00

KENDALL, Oswald
Missing Island, Houghton Mifflin, 1926, first edition with dust jacket: $150.00

Voyage of the Martin Connor (1916), Houghton Mifflin, 1931 edition, color paste-on-pictorial cover, illustrated by Donald Teague, with dust jacket: $50.00

KENNEDY, Jean
Nunga Punga & the Booch, Charles Scribner, 1975, illustrated endpapers, b/w drawings by Anne Burgess, first edition with dust jacket: $40.00

KENNEDY, Mary
Surprise to the Children, Doubleday, Doran, 1933, oversize, music by Deems Taylor, illustrated by J.H. Dowd, first edition with dust jacket: $50.00

KENNY, Kathryn, see Series section, TRIXIE BELDEN

KENT, Rockwell
American artist Rockwell Kent specialized in a "working man" style of illustration typical of the 1930s and 1940s. His publishers did a number of limited editions of his work, usually signed and numbered by the artist, which command the highest prices in today's market. Trade editions with his illustrations are easy to find, and price is dependent upon the collectibility of the author.

KENWARD, James
Market Train Mystery, James Nisbet, 1959, first edition with dust jacket: $50.00

Story of the Poor Author, James Nisbet, 1959, pictorial cover, illustrated: $40.00

Suburban Child, Oxford University Press, Cambridge, 1955, illustrations by Edward Ardizzone, first edition with dust jacket: $50.00

KERR, Judith
Mog, the Forgetful Cat, Parents' Magazine Press, 1972, illustrated boards, color illustrations by author, US first edition: $50.00

KERR, Judith, *Mog, the Forgetful Cat*

When Willy Went to the Wedding, Parents' Magazine Press, 1973, color illustrations by author: $30.00

KEY, Alexander
Bolts, a Robot Dog, Westminster Press, 1966, first edition with dust jacket: $150.00

Escape to Witch Mountain, 1963 Westminster Press, first edition with dust jacket: $200.00

Flight to the Lonesome Place, Westminster Press, 1971, first edition with dust jacket: $70.00

Forgotten Door, Westminster Press, 1965, first edition with dust jacket: $70.00

KEY, Alexander, *Bolts a Robot Dog*

Rivets and Sprockets, Westminster Press, 1964, first edition with dust jacket: $150.00

Sprockets, a Little Robot, Westminster Press,1963, first edition with dust jacket: $150.00

KEY, Ted
Biggest Dog in the World, E. P. Dutton, 1960, 72 pages, illustrations by author, first edition with dust jacket: $150.00

So'm I, E. P. Dutton, 1954, oversize, 70 pages, first edition with dust jacket: $100.00

KING, Alexander
Great Ker-Plunk, 1962, Simon & Schuster, illustrated by Robin Alexander, first edition with dust jacket: $35.00

KING, Frank
Skeezix and Uncle Walt, Reilly & Lee, 1924, paste-on-illustration on cloth hardcover, two-color illustrations by author, based on King's comic strip characters in *Gasoline Alley,* first edition: $50.00

KING, Marian
Kees, Harper, 1930, color paper-on-board cover, color illustrations by Elizabeth Enright: $50.00

Kees and Kleintje, Whitman, 1934, oversize picture book, 80 pages, color paper-

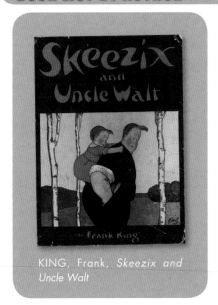

KING, Frank, *Skeezix and Uncle Walt*

on-board cover, color endpapers, color illustrations by Elizabeth Enright: $35.00

KING, Mona

Patsy Ann, Her Happy Times, Rand McNally, 1936, paper-over-board small hardcover, photos of Patsy Ann doll in various adventures, photos by G. Allan King, first edition: $60.00

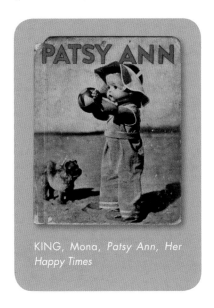

KING, Mona, *Patsy Ann, Her Happy Times*

KINGMAN, Lee

Flivver the Heroic Horse, Garden City, 1958, illustrations by Eric Blegvad, first edition with dust jacket: $35.00

Magic Christmas Tree, Ariel Books, 1956, illustrated endpapers, watercolor illustrations by Bettina, first edition with dust jacket: $40.00

Pierre Pidgeon, Houghton, 1943, brown cloth-over-board cover, oversize, 48 pages, lithograph illustrations by Arnold Edwin Bare: $45.00

KINGSLEY, Charles

Madam How and Lady Why, Macmillan, 1893, cloth-over-board cover with gilt illustration, small, 321 pages, b/w illustrations throughout: $30.00

Water Babies, Macmillan, UK and US, 1863, 350 pages, cloth with gilt, Noel Patton illustrations: $450.00

Water Babies, J. M. Dent & Sons Ltd., 1908 edition, green pictorial cloth, gilt top edge pages, blue pictorial endpapers, 12 color plates plus b/w chapter head illustrations by Margaret Tarrant: $300.00

Water Babies, Macmillan, 1909 edition, green cloth with title and decoration and edges in gilt, 34 color plates with captioned tissue guards by Warwick Goble: $900.00

Water Babies, undated, ca. 1900 – 1915 Raphael Tuck, UK, and David McKay, US, oversize, dark cover with gilt lettering, color plates plus b/w illustrations by Mabel Lucie Attwell: $150.00

Water Babies, Constable & Co. Ltd., 1915 edition, green cloth with gilt titles and decorations, eight color plates plus b/w illustrations by W. Heath Robinson: $350.00

Water Babies, Dodd, Mead, 1916 edition, green cloth, paste-on pictorial, gilt, color illustrations by Jessie Willcox Smith: $800.00

Water Babies, Nottingham, published by Hodder & Stoughton for Boots the Chemist edition, ca. 1920, green with gilt, oversize, 12 color plates by Jessie Willcox Smith, with captioned tissue guards plus decorations in the text, with dust wrapper: $400.00

Westward Ho!, Scribner, 1920, 14 color plates by N.C. Wyeth, first edition: $150.00

Westward Ho!, Scribner, 1940s edition, illustrations by N. C. Wyeth, with

dust jacket: $65.00. Without dust jacket: $40.00

KIPLING, Rudyard, see also Series section, JUST SO STORIES

Kipling's *Jungle Books* are two-volume collections of short stories, most of them about the boy Mowgli who was raised by wolves. Along with the *Just So Stories,* Kipling's tales quickly won popularity and have since been reproduced in hundreds of formats. As with any title with a large printing history, illustrator and condition determine the value.

A sampling of early editions of Kipling's children's books includes:

Captains Courageous: A Story of the Grand Banks, Macmillian, UK, 1897, gilt pictorial on blue cloth, 22 illustrations by I. W. Taber, first edition: $1,200.00

Captains Courageous, Century, 1897, cover stamped with gilt, New England coast fishing boat story, US first edition: $500.00

Jungle Book, Macmillan, 1894, blue cloth with decoration stamped in gilt on front cover and spine, dark green endpapers, all edges gilt, 212 pages, illustrations by J. L. Kipling, W. H. Drake, and P. Frenzeny, first edition starts at: $2,000.00

Kim, Macmillan, London, 1901, red cloth with gilt decoration of an elephant, b/w illustrations, first edition: $500.00

Land and Sea Tales For Scouts and Guides, Macmillan, 1923, Kipling book for Boy Scouts, first edition with dust jacket: $400.00

Puck of Pook's Hill, Macmillan, 1906, red cloth with gilt titles and gilt vignette, wood engravings by H.R. Millar, two children summon up the sprite, and journey through the past, first edition: $350.00

Puck of Pook's Hill, Doubleday, 1906, green with gilt cover, four color plates by Arthur Rackham, first US edition: $300.00

Second Jungle Book, Macmillan, 1895, illustrations by J. L. Kipling, 238 pages, first edition starts at: $2,000.00

Wee Willie Winkie and Other Child Stories, Allahabad, India, Indian Railway Library, 1888, gray-green pictorial wraps, No. 6 of the Indian Railway Library, 96 pages, first edition thus: $1,000.00

KIRKWOOD, Edith Brown

Animal Children, Volland, 1913, color illustrated paper-over-board cover, narrow, illustrated endpapers, color illustrations throughout by M. T. Ross, with original box: $150.00. Without box: $80.00

KJELGAARD, Jim

Fawn in the Forest, Dodd, Mead, 1962, first edition with dust jacket: $50.00

Furious Moose of the Wilderness, Dodd, Mead, 1965, illustrated by Mort Kunstler, first edition with dust jacket: $75.00

Nose for Trouble, Holiday House, 1949, illustrated by Kidder, first edition with dust jacket: $100.00

Ulysses and His Woodland Zoo, Dodd, Mead, 1960, first edition with dust jacket: $50.00

KLEIN, Norma (1938 – 1989)

Along with contemporary Judy Blume, Klein popularized the "problem" novel for older children and young adults in the 1970s. Most of her books received large printings and remain easy to find in good condition in the secondary marketing.

Girls Can Be Anything, E. P. Dutton, 1973, picture book illustrated by Roy Doty, first edition with dust jacket: $45.00

It's OK If You Don't Love Me, Dial Press, 1977, first edition with dust jacket: $100.00

KNIGHT, Eric

Lassie Come Home, John Winston, Philadelphia and Toronto, 1940, first American edition, illustrated by Marguerite Kirmse, with dust jacket: $50.00

KNIGHT, Forster M., see Series section, MR. TITTLEWIT

KNIGHT, Hilary, author/illustrator

Knight grew up in an artistic household. His mother, Katherine Sturges, and his father, Clayton Knight, were both commercial artists. Following service in the Navy during WWII, Hilary Knight studied with Reginald Marsh at the Art Students League in New York. During the 1940s, he entered the commercial art world through greeting cards and magazine illustrations. After a friend introduced him to Kay Thompson, suggesting his style complemented Thompson's breezy texts, Knight and Thompson collaborated closely on the Eloise picture books.

Circus Is Coming, Golden Press, 1978, glossy hardcover, oversize square, every page a full-page color illustration by Knight, first edition: $50.00

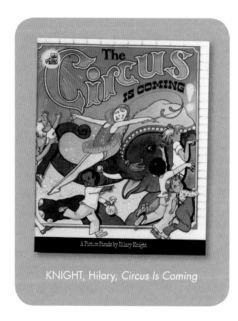

KNIGHT, Hilary, *Circus Is Coming*

Sylvia the Sloth, Harper & Row, 1969, a roundabout story, illustrations by author, first edition with dust jacket: $50.00

Where's Wallace?, Harper, 1964, oversize, illustrated paper-covered boards, 41 pages, story and panoramas by Knight, first edition with dust jacket: $80.00

KNIGHT, Marjorie, see also Series section, ALEXANDER

Doll House at World's End, E. P. Dutton, 1936, illustrated by Clinton Knight, first edition with dust jacket: $40.00

Humphrey the Pig, E. P. Dutton, 1937, oversize, illustrated by Clinton Knight, little pig has identity crisis, first edition with dust jacket: $40.00

KNOBEL, Elizabeth

When Little Thoughts Go Rhyming, Rand McNally, 1916, rose cloth-over-board cover with paste-on-pictorial, 96 pages, poetry, color and b/w illustrations by Maginel Wright Enright: $30.00

KNOBEL, Elizabeth, *When Little Thoughts Go Rhyming*

KONIGSBURG, E. L.

About the B'nai Bagels, Atheneum, 1969, oversize, illustrations by author, first edition with dust jacket: $60.00

Dragon in the Ghetto Caper, Atheneum, 1974, illustrations by author, first edition with dust jacket: $60.00

From the Mixed-Up Files of Mrs. Basil E. Frankweiler, Atheneum, 1967 (1968 Newbery Medal), 162 pages, illustrations by author, first edition with dust jacket: $200.00

KOS (Baroness Dombrowski)

Abdallah and the Donkey, 1928 Macmillan, green cloth-over-board cover, 155 pages, color plates by the author, first edition with dust jacket: $50.00

Boga the Elephant, Macmillan, 1928, pictorial boards, illustrations in b/w and two-tone color, first edition with dust jacket: $50.00

KOTZWINKLE, William

Day the Gang Got Rich, 1970, Viking Press, illustrated by Joe Servello, first edition with dust jacket: $75.00

Elephant Boy, 1970 Farrar, Straus, & Giroux, first edition, hardcover, illustrations by Joe Servello, first edition with dust jacket: $65.00

Return of Crazy Horse, Farrar, 1971, over-size hardcover, illustrations by Joe Servello, first edition with dust jacket: $75.00

Ship That Came Down the Gutter, Pantheon, 1970, illustrations by Joe Servello, first edition with dust jacket: $60.00

KRAHN, Fernando

April Fools, E. P. Dutton, 1974, small hardcover, illustrations by author, first edition with dust jacket: $30.00

Gustavus and Stop, E. P. Dutton, 1969, illustrations by author, first edition with dust jacket: $40.00

How Santa Claus Had a Long and Difficult Journey Delivering His Presents, Delacorte Press, 1970, wordless book with two-color illustrations, first edition with dust jacket: $70.00

Journeys of Sebastian, Delacorte Press, 1968, illustrations by author, first edition with dust jacket: $40.00

KRAKEMSIDES, Baron

Careless Chicken, undated, ca.1924, Warne, small, paper-over-board cover with paste-on-pictorial, illustrated endpapers, 48 pages, 16 color plates by Harry Neilson, first edition with dust jacket: $70.00

KRAUS, Robert

Amanda Remembers, Harper, 1965, illustrations, first edition with dust jacket: $45.00

Christmas Cookie Sprinkle Snitcher, Simon & Schuster, 1969, oversize, 32 pages, color illustrations by Virgil Franklin Partch, II (cartoonist VIP), hardcover: $300.00

Good Night Little ABC, E. P. Dutton, 1972, illustrated by Bodecker, first edition with dust jacket: $200.00

Milton, the Early Riser, Windmill Books, 1972, oversize hardcover, illustrations by Jose Aruego, first edition with dust jacket: $30.00

My Son the Mouse, Harper, 1966, first edition with dust jacket: $40.00

Tree That Stayed up Until Next Christmas, Windmill Books, 1972, 32 pages, illustrated by Edna Eicke, first edition: $70.00

Trouble with Spider, Harper, 1962, first edition with dust jacket: $55.00

KRAUSS, Ruth (1901 – 1993)

Carrot Seed, Harper, 1945, small picture book, color illustrated cover, brown/yellow illustrations by Crockett Johnson: $30.00

KRAUSS, Ruth, *Open House for Butterflies*

Charlotte and the White Horse, Harper & Brothers, 1955, illustrated by Maurice Sendak, first edition with dust jacket: $300.00

Hole Is to Dig, Harper, 1952, small hardcover, illustrated by Maurice Sendak, first edition with dust jacket: $250.00

I Want to Paint My Bathroom Blue, Harper & Row, 1956, illustrated by Maurice Sendak, first edition with dust jacket: $200.00

I'll Be You and You Be Me, Harper & Row, 1954, illustrated by Maurice Sendak, first edition with dust jacket: $200.00

Open House for Butterflies, Harper, 1960, small illustrated yellow hardcover with black spine, brown print, b/w illustrations by Maurice Sendak, first edition with dust jacket: $200.00

Very Special House, Harper & Brothers, 1953, illustrated by Maurice Sendak, first edition with dust jacket: $200.00

KREMENTZ, Jill

Sweet Pea, a Black Girl Growing Up in the Rural South, 1969, Harcourt Brace and World, oversize hardcover, 94 pages, photos, first edition with dust jacket: $40.00

KRUMGOLD, Joseph (1908 – 1980)

And Now Miguel, Crowell, 1953, color illustrated endpapers, illustrations by Jean Charlot (Newbery medal winner), first edition with dust jacket: $200.00

Henry 3, Atheneum, 1967, illustrations by Alvin Smith, first edition with dust jacket: $40.00

Onion John, 1959, Crowell, Newbery Award edition, b/w illustrations by Symeon Shimin, with dust jacket: $30.00

KRUSH, Beth (b. Washington, D.C.)
KRUSH, Joe (b. New Jersey)

Beth and Joe Krush met as students at the Philadelphia Museum of Art, then established their careers as illustrators, working on separate projects as well as joint assignments, including their light-hearted drawings for the *Borrowers* books. Beth Krush also taught art at the Moore College of Art, and Joe Krush taught at the Philadelphia Museum of Art. Beth believed that her childhood exposure to the Smithsonian and other Washington exhibits, including the federal buildings and the zoo, strongly influenced her career.

KUNHARDT, Dorothy, author/illustrator

Brave Mr. Buckingham, Harcourt Brace & World, 1935, pictorial hardcover, first edition: $200.00

Junket Is Nice, Harcourt Brace, 1933, oblong oversize, first edition with dust jacket: $200.00

Little Peewee, or, *Now Open the Box,* Little Golden Books, 1948 edition, color illustrations throughout by author: $30.00

Lucky Mrs. Ticklefeather, Golden Press, 1935, oversize picture book, illustrated cover, illustrations by author: $50.00

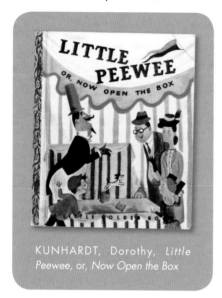

KUNHARDT, Dorothy, *Little Peewee,* or, *Now Open the Box*

Once There Was a Little Boy, Viking Press, 1946, illustrations by Helen Sewell: $50.00

Pat the Bunny, Simon & Schuster, 1940, 18 pages, illustrated boards, includes mirror and red squeak ball, early edition in original box: $300.00

Tiny Golden Library Set, including: Tiny Nonsense Stories and Tiny Animal Stories, 24 volume set, Golden Press, 1968, color illustrations by Garth Williams, housed in cardboard box that looks like a brick building, complete set: $300.00

KUSKIN, Karla
ABCDEFGHIJKLMNOPQRSTUVWXYZ, Harper & Row, 1963, first edition with dust jacket: $50.00

Rose on My Cake, Harper & Row, 1964, first edition with dust jacket: $50.00

Walk the Mouse Girls Took, Harper & Row, 1967, 32 pages, first edition with dust jacket: $60.00

Which Horse Is William?, Harper & Row, 1959, first edition with dust jacket: $50.00

■ ⋯⋯⋯⋯⋯⋯⋯ **L** ⋯⋯⋯⋯⋯⋯⋯ ■

LAMB, Charles and Mary
Tales From Shakespeare, E. P. Dutton (1807), 1909 edition, blue hardcover with gilt-stamped lettering and illustration, 12 color plates by Arthur Rackham: $120.00

Tales from Shakespeare (1807), Scribner, undated, ca. 1915 edition, gilt decorated cover, 324 pages, 20 color plates by Norman M. Price: $35.00

LAMBERT, Janet, see also Series section, CAMPBELL, CANDY KANE, CINDA HOLLISTER, DRIA MEREDITH, JORDAN, PARRI MacDONALD, PATTY AND GINGER, PENNY PARRISH AND TIPPY PARRISH

Janet Lambert wrote teen romances in the forties, fifties, and sixties. Her novels usually became series but in some cases, she only wrote one or two titles about a character. Her 50 titles were reprinted in various formats, sometimes under the name "Lambert Books."

Lambert books featuring Christie Drayton:

Grosset & Dunlap reprints: $35.00

Where the Heart Is, E. P. Dutton, 1948, first edition with dust jacket: $100.00

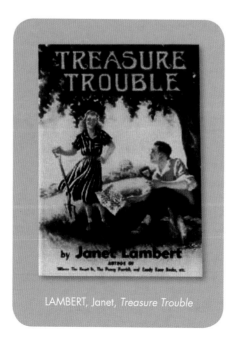

LAMBERT, Janet, *Treasure Trouble*

Treasure Trouble, E. P. Dutton, 1951, first edition with dust jacket: $100.00

Lambert books featuring Sugar Bradley:

Grosset & Dunlap reprints: $35.00

Hi, Neighbor, E. P. Dutton, 1968, first edition with dust jacket: $150.00

LAMBERT, Janet, *Sweet as Sugar*

Sweet as Sugar, 1967, E. P. Dutton, Lambert's fifitieth book, first edition with dust jacket: $150.00

LAMORISSE, Albert
Red Balloon, Doubleday, 1956, oversize hardcover, b/w and color photos from film, US first edition: $40.00

White Mane, E. P. Dutton, 1954, 44 pages, photo illustrations from film, US first edition with dust jacket: $40.00

LAMPMAN, Evelyn Sibley (1907–1980)
Bandit of Mok Hill, Doubleday, 1969, illustrated by Marvin Friedman, first edition with dust jacket: $50.00

City under the Back Steps, Doubleday, 1960, illustrated by Honore Valincourt, first edition with dust jacket: $100.00

Shy Stegosaurus at Indian Springs, Doubleday, 1962, illustrated by Paul Galdone, first edition with dust jacket: $70.00

Shy Stegosaurus of Cricket Creek, Doubleday, 1955, illustrations by Hubert Buel, first edition with dust jacket: $80.00

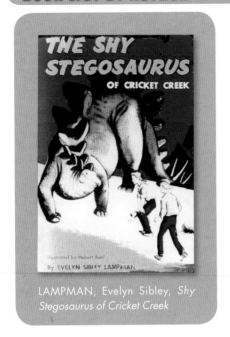

LAMPMAN, Evelyn Sibley, *Shy Stegosaurus of Cricket Creek*

Witch Doctor's Son, Doubleday, 1954, illustrations by Richard Bennet, first edition with dust jacket: $80.00

LAMPREY, L., *Children of Ancient Britain*

LAMPREY, L.

Children of Ancient Britain, Little, Brown, 1928, pictorial cover, illustrated by Maud and Miska Petersham, with dust jacket: $30.00

Children of Ancient Rome, Little, Brown, 1927, 262 pages, b/w drawings by Edna Hart-Hubon, first edition: $30.00

In the Days of the Guild, Frederick A. Stokes, 1918, 291 pages, color paste-on-illustration and gilt lettering on cover, four-color plates by Florence Gardiner, b/w drawings by Mabel Hart: $30.00

LANDECK, Beatrice

Echoes of Africa in Folk Songs of the Americas, David McKay, 1961, illustrations by Alexander Dobkin, first edition with dust jacket: $45.00

Wake Up and Sing! Folk Songs from America's Grassroots, Morrow, 1969, illustrations by Bob Blansky, first edition with dust jacket: $35.00

LANG, Andrew, see also Series section, LANG FAIRY TALES, PANTOUFLIA

Known best for his collections of fairy tales, Lang also compiled other books of stories and poetry for children. Their popularity guaranteed many editions. A few favorites include:

All Sorts of Stories Book, Longmans, Green, 1911, original crimson pictorial cloth, all edges gilt, illustrated by H. J. Ford: $250.00

Arabian Nights Entertainment, edited by Andrew Lang, 1898 Longmans, Green, UK, blue hardcover with gilt decoration of a flying mythical creature above a city skyline with minarets, b/w illustrations by H. J. Ford, first edition: $200.00

Gold of Fairnilee, Longmans, Green, 1888, green cloth, gilt lettering, illustrated in color by E.A. Lemann, first edition: $250.00

Old Friends among the Fairies, Puss in Boots and Other Stories, Longmans, Green, 1928, illustrated by H. J. Ford, and Lancelot Speed, mounted color plate on front panel of dust jacket, first edition with dust jacket: $270.00

Red Book of Animal Stories, Longmans, Green, 1899, red cloth with titles and pictorial decoration in gilt, illustrations by H. J. Ford, first edition with dust jacket: $250.00

LANGSTAFF, John

Frog Went a Courtin', Harcourt Brace, 1955 (1956 Caldecott Award), oversize hardcover, color illustrations by Feodor Rojankovsky, first edition with dust jacket: $30.00

LANGTON, Jane, see Series section, HALL FAMILY

LANIER, Sidney

Boy's King Arthur, Scribner, 1917 edition, 14 color plates by N. C. Wyeth, first edition: $125.00

Boy's King Arthur, Scribner, 1947 edition, nine color plates by N. C. Wyeth, with dust jacket: $70.00. Without dust jacket: $40.00

LANIER, Sterling

War for the Lot, a Tale of Fantasy and Terror, 1969, Follett, illustrations by Robert Baumgartner, first edition with dust jacket: $40.00

LARNED, Trowbridge

Fables in Rhyme for Little Folks, Volland, 1918, nine inches tall, color paper-over-board cover, illustrated endpapers, color illustrations throughout by John Rae: $50.00

LARNED, Trowbridge, *Reynard the Fox & Other Fables*

Fairy-Tales from France, Volland, 1920, nine inches tall, paper-over-board cover, illustrated endpapers, color illustrations throughout by John Rae: $50.00

Reynard the Fox & Other Fables, Volland, 1925, nine inches tall, color paper-over-board cover, illustrated endpapers, color illustrations throughout by John Rae: $50.00

LAROM, Henry V., see Series section, MOUNTAIN PONY

LARRABEITI, Michael, see Series section, BORRIBLES

LATHROP, Dorothy Pulis (1891 – 1980)
Angel in the Woods, Macmillan, 1947, illustrations by author, first edition with dust jacket: $100.00

Dog in the Tapestry Garden, Macmillan, 1962, 42 pages, illustrations by author, first edition with dust jacket: $10.00

Fairy Circus, Macmillan, 1931, orange cloth-covered boards, black/orange/gilt decorations on front board, 66 pages, color plates and b/w illustrations by author: $150.00

Lost Merry-go-round, Macmillan, 1934, color plates: $100.00

Presents for Lupe, Macmillan, 1934, oversize, cloth-over-board cover with paste-on-illustration, color illustrations by author: $100.00

LATTIMORE, Eleanor Frances (1904 – 1986), author/illustrator

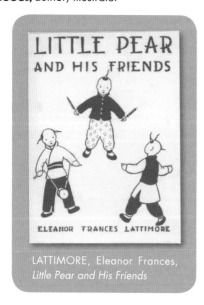

LATTIMORE, Eleanor Frances, *Little Pear and His Friends*

Deborah's White Winter, William Morrow, 1950, blue boards with illustra-

tion of girl skiing down hill, illustrated endpapers, first edition with dust jacket: $70.00

Indigo Hill, William Morrow, 1950, green cloth covered boards, illustrated endpapers, b/w illustrations by author, first edition with dust jacket: $50.00

Little Pear, Harcourt Brace, 1931, hardcover, illustrated by Lattimore, first edition: $80.00

Little Pear and His Friends, Harcourt Brace & World, 1934, b/w illustrations by Lattimore, first edition with dust jacket: $50.00

Little Pear and the Rabbits, Harcourt Brace & World, 1956, b/w illustrations by Lattimore, first edition with dust jacket: $30.00

LAURENCE, Margaret
Jason's Quest, Alfred A. Knopf, 1970 illustrations by Staffan Torell, first edition with dust jacket: $80.00

LAURITZEN, Jonreed
Ordeal of the Young Hunter, Little, Brown, 1954, illustrations by Hoke Denetsosie, first edition with dust jacket: $30.00

Treasure of the High Country, Little, Brown, 1959, illustrated by Eric Von Schmidt, first edition with dust jacket: $30.00

LAWSON, Marie
Dragon John, Viking Press, 1943, fairy tale, first edition with dust jacket: $50.00

Peter and Penny Plant a Garden, Frederick A. Stokes, 1936, illustrated by author, first edition with dust jacket: $50.00

Sea Is Blue, Viking Press, 1946, 126 pages, plates and drawings by author, first edition with dust jacket: $50.00

LAWSON, Robert (1892 – 1957), see also Series section, BEN AND ME

Lawson worked as an illustrator for *Vogue* and *Harper's Weekly*. In 1930 children's editor May Massee hired him to illustrate *Wee Men of Ballywooden* for Viking. This began his career illustrating for other

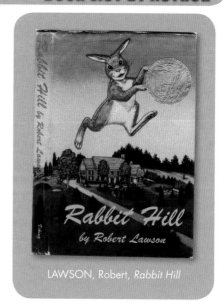

LAWSON, Robert, *Rabbit Hill*

writers and then writing and illustrating his own work. He won both the Caldecott and Newbery awards.

At That Time, Viking Press, 1947, oversize, 126 pages, illustrations by author, first edition with dust jacket: $60.00

Fabulous Flight, Little, Brown, 1949, cloth-over-board cover, illustrations by author, first edition with dust jacket: $70.00

Great Wheel, Viking Press, 1957, illustrations by author, first edition with dust jacket: $85.00

I Discover Columbus, Little, Brown, 1941, cloth-over-board cover, illustrations by author, first edition with dust jacket: $50.00

Mr. Twigg's Mistake, Little, Brown, 1947, illustrated endpapers, b/w illustrations by author, first edition with dust jacket: $40.00

Rabbit Hill, Viking Press, 1944 (Newbery Award), illustrated endpapers, illustrations by author, first edition with dust jacket: $250.00. First edition with Newbery sticker on dust jacket: $80.00

Robbut, a Tale of Tails, Viking Press, 1948, illustrated endpapers, illustrations by author, first edition with dust jacket: $70.00

Smeller Mart, Viking Press, 1950, illustrations by author, first edition with dust jacket: $60.00

LAWSON, Robert, *Robbut, a Tale of Tails*

Tough Winter, Viking Press, 1954, 128 pages, illustrated endpapers, illustrations by author, first edition with dust jacket: $60.00

LEAF, Munro (1905 – 1976)

Aesop's Fables, Heritage Press, 1941 edition, oversize, cloth-over-board cover with gilt lettering, illustrated by Robert Lawson, first edition with dust jacket: $100.00

Arithmetic Can Be Fun, J. B. Lippincott, 1949, oversize, 64 pages, Leaf cartoon illustrations throughout: $50.00

Boo Who Used to Be Scared of the Dark, Random House, 1948, illustrated by Frances Hunter, first edition with dust jacket: $70.00

LEAF, Munro, *Wee Gillis*

Ferdinand the Bull, Walt Disney edition, Whitman, 1938, 31 pages, oversize,

illustrated with stills from the Walt Disney production: $150.00

Gordon the Goat, J. B. Lippincott Company, 1944, illustrations by author, first edition with dust jacket: $200.00

Noodle, Stokes, 1937, illustrated tan cloth-over-board cover, oversize oblong, b/w/ brown illustrations by Ludwig Bemelmans, first edition with dust jacket: $70.00

Robert Francis Weatherbee, Frederick A. Stokes, 1935, small, blue cloth-over-board cover: $60.00

Story of Ferdinand, Hamish Hamilton, 1937, illustrations by Robert Lawson, first edition with dust jacket: $800.00

Story of Simpson and Sampson, Viking Press, 1941, illustrated by Robert Lawson, first edition with dust jacket: $150.00

Wee Gillis, Viking Press, 1938, tartan pattern paper-over-board cover, full-page b/w illustrations by Robert Lawson, first edition with dust jacket: $300.00

LEAR, Edward (1812 – 1888)

The "mad old Englishman," as he called himself, was an accomplished landscape artist, but his most famous works are his own illustrations of his nonsense verses. He was a good friend of Alfred Lord Tennyson and illustrated one volume of Tennyson's work.

Duck and the Kangaroo and Other Nonsense Rhymes, 1932 edition, Whitman, small, color illustrated paper-over-board cover, color illustrations throughout by Keith Ward: $40.00

Dong with a Luminous Nose, Young Scott, 1969, illustrations by Edward Gorey, first edition thus with dust jacket: $50.00

Jumblies, Young Scott, 1968, illustrations by Edward Gorey, first edition thus with dust jacket: $50.00

Laughable Lyrics: A Fourth Book of Nonsense Poems, Robert John Bush, UK, 1877, square, red cloth, pictorially stamped in gilt, red cloth slipcase: $1,000.00

LEAVITT, Ann H.

Three Little Indians, McNally, 1937, color illustrated boards, 36 pages, color and b/w illustrations by Lucille and Holling Clancy Holling, first edition: $80.00

LEE, Tanith, *Dragon Hoard*

LEE, Tanith

Dragon Hoard, Farrar, 1971, b/w illustrations by Graham Oakley, US first edition with dust jacket: $50.00

East of Midnight, Macmillan, London, 1977, first edition with dust jacket: $70.00

Prince on a White Horse, Macmillan, 1982, UK first edition with dust jacket: $60.00

Princess Hunchatti and Some Surprises, Macmillan, 1973, US first edition with dust jacket: $50.00

LEEK, Sybil

Jackdaw and the Witch, Prentice-Hall, 1966, b/w woodcut illustrations by Barbara Efting, US first edition with dust jacket: $50.00

Tree That Conquered the World, Prentice-Hall, 1969, illustrated by Barbara Efting, 135 pages, first edition with dust jacket: $50.00

LEET, Frank

Author Leet was the husband of artist Fern Bisel Peat and she illustrated many of his books (See PEAT, Fern Bisel).

LEET, Frank, illustration from *Purr and Miew Kitten Stories*

Animal Caravan, Saalfield, 1930, oversize, color llustrations by Fern Bisel Peat: $60.00

Christmas Carols, Saalfield, 1937, oversize, 70 pages, illustrated, first edition with dust jacket: $100.00

Hop, Skip and Jump, Three Little Kittens, Saalfield, 1936, oversize, color illustrated paper-over-board cover, color illustrations throughout by Fern Bisel Peat: $60.00

Purr and Miew Kitten Stories, Saalfield, 1931, oversize picture book, paper-over-board cover, 60 pages, color plates by Fern Bisel Peat: $60.00

Rag-Doll Jane, Her Story, Saalfield, 1930, oversize picture book, 59 pages, color plates by Peat: $55.00

LEFEVRE, Felicite

Cock, the Mouse and the Little Red Hen, Longman, 1907, small hardcover picture book, 24 color plates by Tony Sarg: $150.00

Soldier Boy, Greenberg, 1926, small, color and b/w illustrations by Tony Sarg: $50.00

LeGUIN, Ursula, see also Series section, EARTHSEA

Very Far Away from Anywhere Else, Atheneum, 1979, first edition with dust jacket: $50.00

LEIGHTON, Clare

Where Land Meets Sea, the Tide Line of Cape Cod, 1954 Rinehart, oversize hardcover, 202 pages, wood engraving illustrations, first edition with dust jacket: $50.00

LEMON, Mark

Fairy Tales, Bradbury, Evans, 1868, blue pictorial cloth with a gilt vignette, 50 illustrations by Richard Doyle and Charles H. Bennett, first edition: $500.00

Legends of Number Nip, Macmillan, 1864, cloth-over-board cover with gilt, small, 140 pages, six b/w illustrations: $40.00

L'ENGLE, Madeleine, see also Series section, O'KEEFE FAMILY CHRONICLES

And Both Were Young, Lothrop, Lee & Shepard 1949, author's first book for children (young adult market), first edition with dust jacket: $500.00

Camilla, Delacorte Press, 1965, first edition with dust jacket: $35.00

Circle of Quiet, Farrar, 1972, first edition with dust jacket: $50.00

Dance in the Desert, Farrar, 1969, illustrations by Symeon Shimin, first edition with dust jacket: $35.00

Wrinkle in Time, Constable, London, 1963, UK first edition with dust jacket: $800.00

LENSKI, Lois (1893 – 1974), author/illustrator, see also Series section, AMERICAN REGIONAL STORIES, LOIS LENSKI LITTLE BOOKS, ROUNDABOUT AMERICA

Alphabet People, Harper & Brothers, 1928, blue with pink title box, 104 pages, pictorial endpapers, each alphabet letter is illustrated in color and represents a different job, first edition with dust jacket: $400.00

Benny and the Penny, Alfred A. Knopf, 1931, oblong picture book, color illustrations throughout by author, first edition: $50.00

Blueberry Corners, J. B. Lippincott, 1940, cloth-over-board cover, illustrated endpapers, illustrations throughout by Lenski, first edition: $50.00

LENSKI, Lois, *Cowboy Small*

Cinderella, Platt & Munk, 1922 (undated but a book in the *Star Series 1050* for children), small, 16 pages, full-color and b/w illustrations, first edition: $100.00

Cowboy Small, Oxford University Press, 1949, small, color illustrations, first edition with dust jacket: $100.00

Flood Friday, 1956, J. B. Lippincott, first edition with dust jacket: $100.00

Papa Small, 1951, Walck, illustrations by author, first edition with dust jacket: $65.00

Skipping Village: A Town of Not So Very Long Ago, Frederick A. Stokes, 1927, cloth hardcover, 179 pages, b/w and color illustrations, first edition: $300.00

Susie Mariar, Oxford University Press, 1939, oblong cover with checkerboard pattern (classic American folk rhyme), full-page, two-color illustrations by Lenski, first edition with dust jacket: $400.00

LENTZ, Harold, artist and pop-up designer

Cinderella and Other Tales, Pop-Up Book, Blue Ribbon Books, 1933, illustrated cardboard cover, four stories, four pop-ups: $400.00

Jack the Giant Killer, Pop-Up Book, Blue Ribbon Books, 1932, cardboard cover with illustration of Jack the Giant Killer on front boards, dragon on rear boards, 96 pages, four stories, four pop-ups, with dust jacket: $1,000.00. Without dust jacket: $400.00

Little Orphan Annie and Jumbo the Circus Elephant, Pop-Up Book, by Harold Gray, 1935 Blue Ribbon Books, color illustrations: $400.00

Mother Goose, Pop-Up Book, Blue Ribbon Books, 1933, pictorial boards, 96 pages, four double-page, pop-up illustrations, with dust jacket: $450.00. Without dust jacket: $300.00

Pinocchio, Pop-Up Book, Blue Ribbon Books, 1932, book contains four stories with a pop-up for each, first edition with dust jacket: $1,000.00. Without dust jacket: $400.00

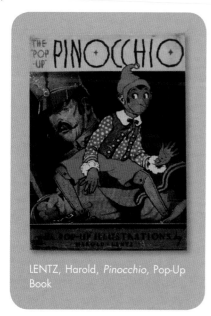

LENTZ, Harold, *Pinocchio,* Pop-Up Book

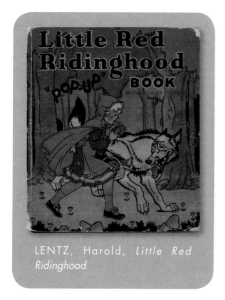

LENTZ, Harold, *Little Red Ridinghood*

Puss In-Boots, Pop-Up Book, Blue Ribbon Books, 1934, pictorial boards, color

throughout, three double-page pop-ups, first edition: $300.00

Little Red Ridinghood, Pop-Up Book, Blue Ribbon Books, 1934, pictorial boards, color throughout, three double-page pop-ups, first edition: $350.00

LEODHAS, Sorche Nic (1898 – 1969)
All in the Morning Early, Holt, Rinehart & Winston, 1963, illustrations by Evaline Ness, first edition with dust jacket: $70.00

Ghosts Go Haunting, Holt, 1965, first edition, blue hardcover, 128 pages, b/w illustrations by Nonny Hogrogian, first edition with dust jacket: $50.00

Kellyburn Braes, Holt, 1968, illustrations by Evaline Ness, first edition with dust jacket: $35.00

LeSIEG, Theo (Theodore Geisel), see also SEUSS, Dr.

Come Over to My House, Random House, 1966, illustrated by Richard Erdoes, first edition with dust jacket: $500.00

Hooper Humperdink...? Not Him!, Random House, 1976, oversize illustrated hardcover, illustrations by Charles E. Martin, first edition: $500.00

LeSIEG, Theo, (Theodore Geisel), Hooper Humperdink ...? Not Him!

I Can Write! A Book by Me, Myself, Random House, 1971, Bright and Early Books for Beginning Beginners series, first edition: $500.00

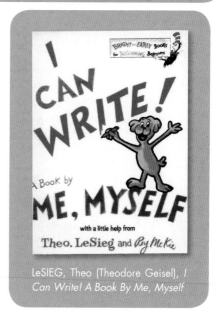

LeSIEG, Theo (Theodore Geisel), *I Can Write! A Book By Me, Myself*

Please Try to Remember the First of Octemter, Random House, 1977, Bright and Early Books, laminated paperback boards, full-color drawings, first edition: $500.00

LESSER, Milton
Stadium Beyond the Stars, Holt Rinehart Winston, 1960, first edition with dust jacket: $60.00

Star Seekers, Winston, 1953, first edition with dust jacket: $80.00

LEVINE, Rhoda
He Was There from the Day We Moved In, Harlin-Quist, 1968, color illustrations by Edward Gorey, first edition with dust jacket: $60.00

LEVINE, Rhoda, *He Was There from the Day We Moved In*

Herbert Situation, Harlin Quist, 1969, small, illustrations by Edward Gorey, first edition with dust jacket: $50.00

Three Ladies Beside the Sea, Atheneum, 1963, oblong, illustrations by Edward Gorey, first edition with dust jacket: $50.00

LEVOY, Myron
Penny Tunes and Princesses, 1972, Harper, oversize hardcover, color illustrations by Ezra Jack Keats, first edition with dust jacket: $35.00

Witch of Fourth Street and Other Stories, Harper & Row, 1972, pictorial hardcover, first edition with dust jacket: $30.00

LEWIS, C. S. (1898 – 1963), see Series section, CHRONICLES OF NARNIA

LEWIS, Janet
Keiko's Bubble, Doubleday, 1961, illustrations by Kazue Mizumura, first edition with dust jacket: $50.00

LEWIS, Shari
Folding Paper Puppets, Stein and Day, 1962, red boards w/taupe cloth, b/w illustrations by Dorothy Anderson, easy-to-follow instructions and illustrations for creating paper origami puppets and toys, first edition with dust jacket: $30.00

Tell It Make It Book, J. P. Tarcher, Inc, 1972, 113 pages, illustrated by Boze, first edition with dust jacket: $40.00

LEXAU, Joan M.
Archimedes Takes a Bath, Crowell, 1969, 56 pages, illustrated by Salvatore Murdocca, first edition with dust jacket: $40.00

Emily and the Klunky Baby and the Next-Door Dog, Dial Press, 1972, pictorial hardcover, color illustrations by Martha Alexander, first edition with dust jacket: $50.00

Homework Caper, Harper & Row, 1966, An I Can Read Mystery, 64 pages, Syd Hoff, first edition with dust jacket: $40.00

L'HOMMEDIEU, Dorothy K.
Leo the Little St. Bernard, J. B. Lippincott, 1948, illustrated boards, b/w and color illustrations throughout by Margaret Kirmse, first edition with dust jacket: $100.00

MacGregor the Little Black Scottie, J. B. Lippincott, 1941, illustrated boards, b/w and color illustrations throughout by Margaret Kirmse, first edition with dust jacket: $150.00

Nipper the Little Bull Pup, J. B. Lippincott, 1943, illustrated boards, b/w and color illustrations throughout by Kirmse, first edition with dust jacket: $180.00

Robbie the Brave Little Collie, J. B. Lippincott, 1936, illustrated boards, b/w and color illustrations throughout by Kirmse, first edition with dust jacket: $100.00

Rusty the Little Red Dachshund, Robert Hale Ltd., 1947, illustrated boards, 63 pages, b/w and color illustrations throughout by Margaret Kirmse, first edition with dust jacket: $80.00

Scampy the Little Black Cocker, J. B. Lippincott, 1939, illustrated boards, 63 pages, b/w and color illustrations throughout by Margaret Kirmse, first edition with dust jacket: $130.00

Skippy the Little Skye Terrier, Robert Hale Ltd., 1961, b/w and color illustrations throughout by Kirmse, first edition with dust jacket: $80.00

Tinker the Little Fox Terrier, J. B. Lippincott, illustrated boards, b/w and color illustrations throughout by Kirmse, first edition with dust jacket: $80.00

Topper and Madam Pig, Ariel Books, 1956, illustrated by Marie C. Nichols, first edition with dust jacket: $80.00

Tyke the Little Mutt, J. B. Lippincott, 1949, illustrated boards, b/w and color illustrations throughout by Kirmse, first edition with dust jacket: $80.00

LIFTON, Betty Jean
Cock and the Ghost Cat, Atheneum, 1965, illustrated by Fuku Akino, first edition with dust jacket: $70.00

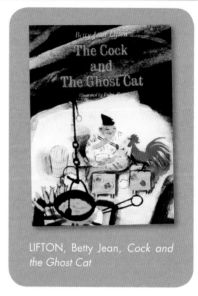

LIFTON, Betty Jean, *Cock and the Ghost Cat*

One-Legged Ghost, Atheneum, 1968, illustrated by Fuku Akino, first edition with dust jacket: $50.00

Rice-cake Rabbit, W. W. Norton, 1966, illustrated, first edition with dust jacket: $70.00

LILIUS, Irmelin, see Series section, HALTER CHILDREN

LINDGREN, Astrid, see also Series section, BILL BERGSON, EMIL, KARLSSON, NOISY VILLAGE, PIPPI

Brothers Lionheart, Viking Press, 1975, illustrated by J. K. Lambert, US first edition with dust jacket: $250.00

Children on Troublemaker Street, Macmillan, 1964, first edition with dust jacket: $100.00

Mio, My Son, Viking Press, 1956, illustrated by Ilon Wikland, US first edition with dust jacket: $70.00

Skrallan and the Pirates, Doubleday, 1967, 48 pages, illustrated with photos by Sven-Eric Deler and Stig Hallgren, US first edition with dust jacket: $70.00

LINDMAN, Maj, author/illustrator, see also Series section, FLICKA, RICKA, DICKA and SNIPP, SNAPP, SNURR

Dear Little Deer, Albert Whitman, 1953, first edition with dust jacket: $150.00

Fire Eye, Whitman, 1948, illustrated paper-over-board cover, 32 pages, color illustrations by author, first edition: $80.00

Sailboat Time, 1951, Albert Whitman, pictorial hardcover, color illustrations by author: $60.00

Snowboot, Son of Fire Eye, Whitman, 1950, first edition: $80.00

LINDOP, Audrey Erskine
Adventures of the Wuffle, McGraw-Hill, 1966, illustrations by William Stobbs, US first edition with dust jacket: $50.00

LINDQUIST, Jennie D.
Golden Name Day, Harper & Brothers, 1955, illustrations by Garth Williams, first edition with dust jacket: $80.00

LINDSAY, Maud (1874 – 1941)
Lindsay was the founder of the first free kindergarten in Alabama and a close friend of Helen Keller.

Jock Barefoot, Lothrop, Lee & Shepard, 1939, color illustrated cover, 177 pages, b/w illustrations by Jean Linton: $150.00

Little Missy, Lothrop, Lee & Shepard, 1922, full-page color illustrations by Florence Liley Young: $100.00

Posey and the Peddler, Lothrop, Lee & Shepard, 1938, illustrated by Ellis Credle, first edition with dust jacket: $100.00

Story Garden for Little Children, Lothrop, Lee & Shepard, 1913, illustrations by Florence Liley Young, first edition with dust jacket: $100.00

Toy Shop, Lothrop, Lee & Shepard, 1926, illustrations by Florence Liley Young, first edition with dust jacket: $100.00

LINES, Kathleen
Jack and the Beanstalk, a Book of Nursery Stories, Oxford University Press, 1960, illustrated throughout in color and b/w by Harold Jones, first edition with dust jacket: $100.00

Lavender's Blue, a Book of Nursery Rhymes, Oxford University Press, 1954, illustrated throughout in color and b/w by Harold Jones, first edition with dust jacket: $250.00

Ring of Tales, Franklin Watts, 1959, US first edition with dust jacket: $40.00

LIONNI, Leo, author/illustrator

Dutch-American illustrator Lionni earned a Ph.D. in economics before turning to graphic design. He headed the graphic arts department at the Parsons School of Design as well as working as an art director in the corporate world. Lionni started creating picture books in 1959 to entertain his grandchildren. Works like *Alexander and the Wind-Up Mouse* (1969) feature colorful paper collages. Four of his books, including *Alexander,* were named as Caldecott Honor books.

Alexander and the Windup Mouse, Random House, 1969, oversize hardcover, color illustrations by author, first edition with dust jacket: $300.00

LIONNI, Leo, *Swimmy*

Frederick, Pantheon Books, 1967, oversize, gray cloth, first edition with dust jacket: $80.00

Inch by Inch, Ivan Obolensky, 1960 (1961 Caldecott Medal Honor Book), illustrated by the author, first edition with dust jacket: $150.00

Little Blue and Little Yellow, Obolensky, 1959, oversize, Lionni's first book for children, first edition with dust jacket: $250.00

Swimmy, 1963, Pantheon, oversize hardcover, Caldecott Honor book, color illustrations by author, first edition with dust jacket: $50.00

LIPKIND, William
(Author name Will and Nicolas on books by William Lipkind and Nicolas Mordvinoff)

Boy with a Harpoon, Harcourt Brace, 1952, green cover, illustrations by Nicolas Mordvinoff, first edition with dust jacket: $100.00

Finders Keepers, Harcourt Brace, 1951 (1952 Caldecott Award), illustrated hardcover, illustrations by Nicolas Mordvinoff, first edition with dust jacket: $100.00

Magic Feather Duster, Harcourt, Brace & World, 1958, color illustrations by Nicolas Mordvinoff, first edition with dust jacket: $50.00

Nubber Bear, Harcourt Brace, 1966, illustrations by Roger Duvoisin, first edition with dust jacket: $80.00

Perry the Imp, Harcourt Brace, 1956, color illustrations by Nicolas Mordvinoff, first edition with dust jacket: $50.00

Professor Bull's Umbrella, Viking Press, 1954, oversize hardcover, illustrations by Georges Schreiber, first edition with dust jacket: $100.00

LIPMAN, Michael
Chatterlings, Volland, 1928, color illustrated paper-over-board cover: $50.00

Chatterlings in Wordland, 1935, Wise-Parslow revised edition, 96 pages, orange cover, full color Golden Hour Rainbow edition endpapers, color illustrations by author: $50.00

LIPPMAN, Peter, author/illustrator

New at the Zoo, Harper & Row, 1969, 32 pages, first edition with dust jacket: $30.00

Peter Lippman's Busy Trains, Random House, 1981, color illustrations by author, first edition with dust jacket: $30.00

Plunkety Plunk, Ariel, 1963, color illustrations, first edition with dust jacket: $30.00

LIPPMAN, Peter, *Busy Trains*

LITCHFIELD, Sarah
Hello Alaska, Whitman, 1951, oversize hardcover, 32 pages, map endpapers, color and b/w illustrations by Kurt Wiese, first edition with dust jacket: $40.00

LITTLE, Jean
Look Through My Window, Harper & Row, 1970, illustrations by Joan Sandin, first edition with dust jacket: $50.00

Mine for Keeps, Little, Brown, 1962, illustrated hardcover, first edition with dust jacket: $70.00

Take Wing, Little, Brown, 1968, first edition with dust jacket: $50.00

LIVELY, Penelope
Astercote, Heinemann, London, 1970, author's first novel, first edition with dust jacket: $150.00

Ghost of Thomas Kempe, E. P. Dutton, 1973, b/w illustrations by Antony Maitland, US first edition with dust jacket: $40.00

Whispering Knights, E. P. Dutton, 1971, US first edition with dust jacket: $30.00

LLOYD, Hugh, see Series section, HAL KEEN

LLOYD, John
Red Head, Dodd, Mead, 1903, decorated green cloth-over-board cover, decorated

text pages, b/w illustrations by Reginald Birch, first edition: $40.00

LOBEL, Anita, author/illustrator
Seamstress of Salzburg, Harper & Row, 1970, first edition with dust jacket: $50.00

LOBEL, Arnold (1933 – 1987), author/illustrator, see also Series section, FROG AND TOAD
Giant John, Harper, 1964, oversize hardcover, illustrations by author, first edition with dust jacket: $50.00

Holiday for Mister Muster, Harper & Row, 1963, oblong hardcover, illustrations by author, first edition with dust jacket: $60.00

Ice Cream Cone Coot and Other Rare Birds, Parents' Magazine Press, 1972, pictorial cover, first edition: $60.00

Mouse Tales, Harper, 1972, I Can Read Book, 64 pages, color illustrations by author, first edition with dust jacket: $50.00

On Market Street, Greenwillow Press, 1981, illustrations by Anita Lobel, first edition with dust jacket: $50.00

On the Day Peter Stuyvesant Sailed into Town, Harper, 1971, oblong hardcover, illustrations by author, first edition with dust jacket: $50.00

Zoo for Mister Muster, Harper, 1962, oblong hardcover, two-color illustrations by author, first edition with dust jacket: $30.00

LOCKRIDGE, Frances and Richard
Lucky Cat, J. B. Lippincott, 1953, illustrated by Zhenya Gay, first edition with dust jacket: $50.00

Nameless Cat, J. B. Lippincott, 1954, b/w drawings by Peggy Bacon, first edition with dust jacket: $50.00

Proud Cat, J. B. Lippincott, 1951, illustrated by Elinore Blaisdell, first edition with dust jacket: $50.00

LOFTING, Hugh (1886 – 1947), see Series section, DOCTOR DOLITTLE

LONDON, Jack (1876 – 1916)
Although London did not write for children, his two famous dog books, *White Fang* and *Call of the Wild,* and nautical adventures like *Sea-Wolf,* became known as classic boys' adventure stories.

Call of the Wild, Macmillan, 1903, illustrated by Philip R. Goodwin and Charles Livingston Bull, with decorations by Charles Edward Hooper, cloth pictorial boards stamped with gilt lettering, stamped with red, black and white, 11 color plate illustrations plus single-color decorations and chapter heads, first edition: $1,000.00. First edition with dust jacket starts at: $4,500.00. Later printings with all 11 color plates: $250.00

Call of the Wild, Macmillan, 1912, illustrated by Paul Bransom (American wildlife artist), decorated cloth binding with paste-down pictorial, color plates, early editions: $125.00

Call of the Wild, Grosset & Dunlap, 1920s, illustrated with b/w stills from 1923 Hal Roach movie, with dust jacket: $100.00. Without dust jacket: $50.00

Call of the Wild, Lynn, 1935, pictorial hardcover, illustrated with stills from Clark Gable movie: $50.00

Sea-Wolf, Grosset & Dunlap, 1920s, Photoplay edition, illustrated with b/w photographs from 1926 movie starring Ralph Ince: $75.00

Sea-Wolf, Grosset & Dunlap, 1940s, Photoplay edition, illustrated with pictures from 1941 film starring Edward G. Robinson, with dust jacket: $40.00

Sea-Wolf, Macmillan, 1904, possibly based on London's own experiences running off to be a sailor at the age of 17, cloth binding, stamped illustration on cover, gilt lettering on spine, illustrated by W. J. Aylward, first edition: $600.00. Later editions thus: $100.00

White Fang, Macmillan, 1906, cloth binding with title and illustration of White Fang stamped in b/w, eight color plates by Charles Livingston Bull, first edition: $1,000.00. Later Macmillan editions with Bull illustrations: $125.00. Grosset or Methuen editions thus: $40.00

White Fang and Other Stories, Dodd, Mead, 1963, Great Illustrated Classics edition, with dust jacket: $50.00

LONGFELLOW, Henry Wadsworth (b. Portland, Maine, 1807–1882)

Longfellow's poems were published in many editions, including illustrated editions meant to appeal to children. The following are some examples:

Children's Longfellow, Houghton Mifflin, 1908, illustrated cover with gilt lettering, color illustrations: $70.00

Courtship of Miles Standish, Bobbs-Merrill, 1903, blue cloth boards, gilt lettering, tissue guards, b/w and color illustrations by Howard Chandler Christy, first edition: $80.00

Courtship of Miles Standish, Houghton, Mifflin, 1920, illustrated by N. C. Wyeth, first edition: $85.00

Hiawatha, Reilly & Britton, Chicago, 1909, illustrated by John R. Neill, first edition: $150.00

Hiawatha's Childhood, Garden City, 1941, oversize with pictorial boards, 15 pages, color and b/w illustrations by Herbert Morton Stoops, first thus with dust jacket: $60.00

Story of Hiawatha, Put-Together Book, by Estelle M. Weingart, illustrations by Reginald P. Ward, Sam'l Gabriel Sons, 1930, oblong oversize, illustrated paper covered boards on red cloth spine, prose version of the poem, color illustrations of landscapes to use as background for cutout figures, with all cutouts present and uncut: $200.00

LONGSTRETH, T. Morris

Mounty in a Jeep, Macmillan, 1949, end-papers by George & Doris Hauman, US first edition with dust jacket: $50.00

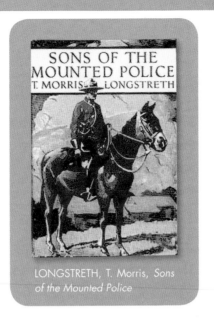

LONGSTRETH, T. Morris, *Sons of the Mounted Police*

Sons of the Mounted Police, Century, 1928, first edition with dust jacket: $100.00

LOVELACE, Maud Hart (1892 – 1980),

see also Series section, BETSY-TACY

Trees Kneel at Christmas, Crowell, 1951, illustrations by Gertrude Herrick Howe, first edition with dust jacket: $150.00

Valentine Box, Crowell, 1966, illustrated by Ingrid Fetz, first edition with dust jacket: $60.00

LOWNSBERY, Eloise

Boy Knight of Reims, Houghton Mifflin, 1927, blue cloth-over-board cover with gilt, b/w illustrations by Elizabeth Wolcott: $30.00

LUCAS, Marie Seymour

Granny's Story Box, undated, E. P. Dutton, ca. 1890s, color illustrated paper-over-board cover, 15 color plates, 100 b/w illustrations: $90.00

Told by the Fireside, J. B. Lippincott, ca.1890s, oversize, 88 pages, 16 color plates plus b/w illustrations in text, 16 stories by various writers: $100.00

LYNCH, Patricia, see Series section, BROGEEN THE LEPRECHAUN, TURF-CUTTER'S DONKEY

LYON, Elinor

Cathie Runs Wild, Follett, 1968, illustrated by Greta Elgaard, first edition with dust jacket: $50.00

House in Hiding, Coward-McCann, 1950, b/w map frontispiece, first edition with dust jacket: $50.00

Wishing Water-Gate, Hodder & Stoughton, London, 1949, first edition with dust jacket: $60.00

■ ·················· **M** ·················· ■

MacDONALD, Betty (1908 – 1958), see also Series section, MRS. PIGGLE-WIGGLE

MacDONALD, Betty, *Nancy and Plum*

Nancy and Plum, 1952, Lippincott, illustrations by Hildegarde Hopkins, first edition with dust jacket: $400.00

MacDONALD, George (1824 – 1905)

At the Back of the North Wind, Strahan and Co, London, 1871, blue cloth boards with gilt, gilt edges, illustrations by Arthur Hughes, first edition: $5,000.00

At the Back of the North Wind, David McKay, 1919, color paste-on pictorial, gilt-lettered spine, color illustrations by Jessie Willcox Smith, US first edition thus: $250.00

Dealings with the Fairies, Routledge and Sons, 1891 edition (first printed in UK 1867), blue cloth with gilt, beveled edges, illustrated by Leonard Leslie Brooke, five fairy tales: *Light Princess*, *Giant's Heart*, *Shadows*, *Cross Purposes*, and *Golden Key*, US first edition: $1,000.00

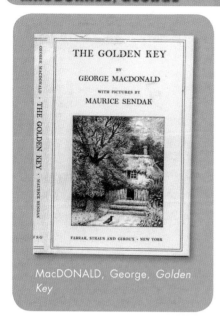

MacDONALD, George, *Golden Key*

Golden Key, Farrar, Straus, and Giroux, 1968, dark blue cloth with gilt design, illustrations throughout by Maurice Sendak, with dust jacket: $50.00

Light Princess and Other Fairy Tales, Putnam, New York and London, 1893, pictorial cloth, illustrated by Maud Humphrey, first edition thus: $500.00

Princess and Curdie, J. B. Lippincott, 1883, tan cloth illustrated in brown and gilt, illustrated by James Allen, US first edition: $800.00

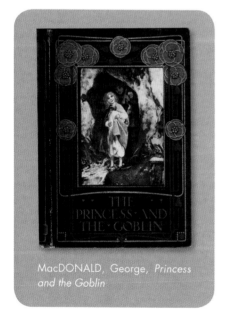

MacDONALD, George, *Princess and the Goblin*

Princess and Curdie, J. B. Lippincott, 1908, red hardcover with printed illustration

and gilt lettering, 12 color plates by Maria Kirk, 305 pages: $50.00

Princess and the Goblin, George Routledge and Sons, 1871, green cloth binding with pictorial decorations and gilt, edges gilt, 30 wood-engraved illustrations by Arthur Hughes, US first edition: $2,500.00

Princess and the Goblin, Blackie, UK, undated, ca. 1910, decorative blue cloth with color paste-on pictorial, 12 color plates plus b/w drawings: $40.00

Princess and the Goblin, David McKay, 1920, gray cloth with color paste-on pictorial, eight color plates by Jessie Willcox Smith: $130.00

Works of Fancy and Imagination, Strahan, London, 1871, small green hardcover with gilt lettering on spine, a ten-volume set of collected stories. Complete set of ten: $1,000.00

MacDONALD, Golden (pseudonym of Margaret Wise Brown)

Little Island, Doubleday, Doran, 1946, illustrated by Leonard Weisgard, first edition with dust jacket: $125.00

MacGREGOR, Ellen, see also Series section, MISS PICKERELL

Mr. Pingle and Mr. Buttonhouse, Whittlesey House, 1957, illustrations by Paul Galdone, first edition with dust jacket: $40.00

Theodore Turtle, Whittlesey House, 1955, oversize, first edition: $50.00

Tommy and the Telephone, Albert Whitman, 1947, cloth covered boards with pictorial paste-on, pictorial endpapers, color and b/w illustrations by Zabeth Selover, first edition: $50.00

MacKAYE, Arthur

Viking Prince, Page, 1928, green cloth-over-board cover with gilt, b/w illustrations by A. Thieme, first edition with dust jacket: $30.00

MacKINSTRY, Elizabeth (1879 – 1956)

MacKinstry was born in America but grew

up in France where she had the opportunity to study art under Rodin. Her first love was music, and she became a concert violinist, appearing in France and England. When health problems ended her concert career in the 1920s, MacKinstry turned to poetry and art, and built new careers in writing and illustration.

Fairy Alphabet as Used by Merlin, Viking Press, 1933, illustrated cloth-over-board cover, picture book, color plates and woodblock illustrations by author, first edition with dust jacket: $100.00

MacVICAR, Angus, see Series section, LOST PLANET

MAHY, Margaret

Dragon of an Ordinary Family, Heinemann, 1969, oblong glazed pictorial boards, illustrated in color by Helen Oxenbury, oblong quarto, first edition with dust jacket: $80.00

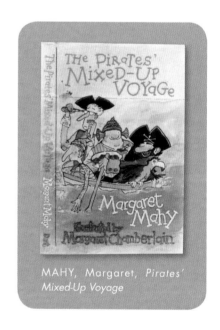

MAHY, Margaret, *Pirates' Mixed-Up Voyage*

Pirates' Mixed-Up Voyage, Dent, UK, 1983, illustrations by Margaret Chamberlain, first edition with dust jacket: $50.00

Ultra-Violet Catastrophe! or, The Unexpected Walk with Great Uncle Magnus Pringle, Parents' Press, 1975, illustrations by Brian Froud, first edition: $70.00

MAIDEN, Cecil

Speaking of Mrs. McCluskie, Vanguard Press, 1962, 43 pages, illustrations by

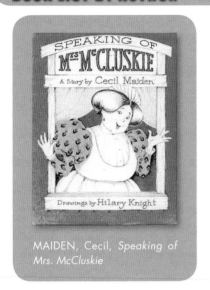

MAIDEN, Cecil, *Speaking of Mrs. McCluskie*

Hilary Knight, first edition with dust jacket: $60.00

MALCOLM, Anthony, see Series section, JENNINGS

MALCOLMSON, Anne
Song of Robin Hood, Houghton Mifflin, 1947, oversize, hardcover, 128 pages, illustrations by Virginia Burton (Caldecott Honor book for 1948), first edition with dust jacket: $200.00

Yankee Doodle's Cousins, Houghton Mifflin, 1941, cloth-over-board cover, 267 pages, illustrated by Robert McCloskey, first edition with dust jacket: $50.00

MALONE, (General) Paul, see Series section, WEST POINT

MALOT, Hector
Little Sister, Cupples & Leon, 1928, blue cloth-over-board cover with paste-on-illustration, 303 pages, illustrations by Thelma Gooch, first edition: $40.00

Nobody's Boy, Cupples & Leon, 1916, translated by Florence Crewe-Jones, color illustrations by Johnny Gruelle, US first edition with dust jacket: $100.00

Nobody's Girl, Cupples & Leon, 1922, 301 pages, color plate illustrations by Thelma Gooch: $50.00

MALVERN, Gladys
Dancing Girl, Macrae Smith, 1959, first edition with dust jacket: $90.00

Eric's Girls, Julian Messner, 1949, b/w illustrations by Corinne Malvern, first edition with dust jacket: $175.00

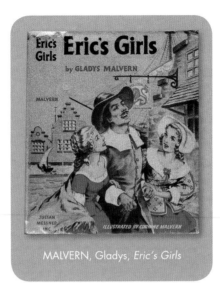

MALVERN, Gladys, *Eric's Girls*

Land of Surprise, McLoughlin Brothers, 1938, folio size, illustrated by Corinne Malvern, first edition with dust jacket: $80.00

Wilderness Island, Macrae Smith, 1961, first edition with dust jacket: $130.00

MANN, Arthur
Bob White: Farm Club Player, McKay, 1952, first edition with dust jacket: $40.00

Bob White: Spring Terror, David McKay, 1953, stories of organized baseball, first edition with dust jacket: $40.00

MANNING, Rosemary, see Series section, DRAGON

MANNING-SANDERS, Ruth
Animal Stories, Oxford University Press, 1967, illustrated by Joan Kiddell-Munroe, first edition with dust jacket: $60.00

Book of Giants, Pan Books, 1972, first edition with dust jacket: $100.00

Book of Magic Animals, E. P. Dutton, 1974 oversize hardcover, 127 pages, illustrations by Robin Jacques, US first edition with dust jacket: $100.00

Book of Marvels and Magic, Methuen, London, 1978, color illustrations by Robin

Jacques, first edition with dust jacket: $60.00

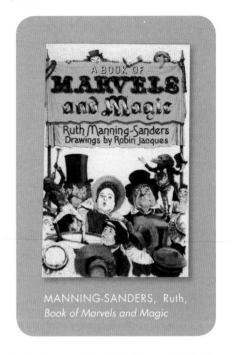

MANNING-SANDERS, Ruth, *Book of Marvels and Magic*

Book of Mermaids, E. P. Dutton, 1970, first edition with dust jacket: $100.00

Book of Monsters, Methuen, 1975, first edition with dust jacket: $60.00

Book of Wizards, E. P. Dutton, 1967, first edition with dust jacket: $70.00

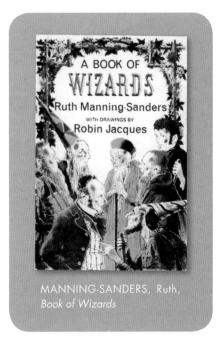

MANNING-SANDERS, Ruth, *Book of Wizards*

MANSO, Leo
Fire House, World Publishing, 1949, fold-out play book, includes unpunched pages

of punchouts, first edition with dust jacket: $100.00

Wild West, World, 1950, Rainbow Playbook, spiralbound pictorial hardcover, forms three scenes, includes unpunched pages of punchouts: $75.00

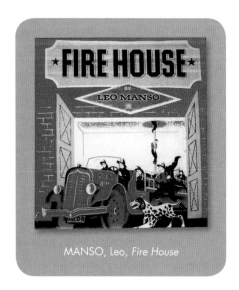

MANSO, Leo, *Fire House*

MARGE (Marjorie Henderson Buell),
see Series section, LITTLE LULU BOOKS

MARIANA, see Series section, MISS FLORA McFLIMSEY

MARINO, Josef
Hi! Ho! Pinocchio!, Reilly & Lee, 1940, sequel to the Collodi story, color frontispiece and b/w illustrations by William Donahey, first edition: $125.00

MARQUITH, Delmore, see Series section, SKYLARKING COMRADES

MARRYATT, Captain
Japhet in Search of a Father, Appleton, 1871, gold-stamped embossed dark green cloth, 421 pages, illustrated by J. C. Buttre: $30.00

Masterman Ready, Harper, 1928, paste-on-pictorial, b/w illustrations and color plates by John Rae: $40.00

MARSHALL, Archibald
Simple Stories for Children and Grown-ups, Harper & Brothers, 1927, small, miniature illustrations by George Morrow: $70.00

Peggy in Toyland, Dodd, Mead, 1920, illustrated by Helen M. Barton: $50.00

MARSHALL, Emma
Our Own Picture Book, Nisbet, 1888, blue pictorial cloth lettered in gilt, 304 pages, patterned endpapers, 152 engraved illustrations by 20+ artists, including Edmund Evans and J. W. Whymper: $50.00

Story of the Lost Emerald or, *Overcome Evil with Good*, Nelson, 1907, pictorial covers, gilt title, color frontispiece: $50.00

MARSHALL, James (1942 – 1992), see
Series section, GEORGE AND MARTHA

Marshall grew up in Texas, but left the Lone Star State to study the viola in Boston. A hand injury prevented a career in classical music but left him free to produce highly humorous picture books about such characters as the hippopotamus friends George and Martha. Marshall also taught at the Parsons School of Design in New York. Some of his books use the pseudonym Edward Marshall.

MARSHALL, James, illustration

Portly McSwine, Houghton Mifflin, 1979, square, oversize, illustrations by author, first edition with dust jacket: $60.00

Rapscallion Jones, Viking Press, 1983, illustrations by author, first edition with dust jacket: $50.00

Summer in the South, Houghton Mifflin, 1977, Marshall's first novel for children, illustrated by author, first edition with dust jacket: $100.00

What's the Matter with Carruthers?, Houghton, Mifflin, 1972, oversize, illustrations by author, first edition with dust jacket: $90.00

Yummers, Houghton Mifflin, 1973, illustrations by author, first edition with dust jacket: $60.00

MARTIN, George, with Fred Gwynne
Battle of the Frogs and the Mice, an Homeric Fable, Dodd, Mead, 1962, b/w illustrations by Fred Gwynne, first edition with dust jacket: $40.00

MARTIN, John
Fairy Tales, John Martin's House, 1944, pictorial boards, oversize, full-color illustrations by John Nielsen: $60.00

John Martin's Something-to-Do Book, John Martin's House, ca. 1920, a monthly publication in book form, hardcover, illustrations, advertised as "Things to do in infinite variety, to cut out, draw, paste, and color with scissors, crayons, paste and brush contained in the portfolio cover," with all pieces: $75.00

MARTIN, John Percival, see Series section, UNCLE CLEANS

MARTIN, Patricia Miles
Be Brave, Charlie, Putnam, 1972, oblong, illustrated cloth boards, double-page illustrated title, illustrated by Bonnie Johnson, first edition with dust jacket: $30.00

MARTIN, Patricia Miles, *Rice Bowl Pet*

Little Two and the Peach Tree, Atheneum, 1963, illustrated by Joan Berg: $50.00

Rice Bowl Pet, Crowell, 1962, illustrated by Ezra Jack Keats, first edition with dust jacket: $100.00

MARTINEK, Frank, see Series section, DON WINSLOW

MASCHLER, Fay
Child's Book of Manners, Jonathan Cape, 1978, hardcover, color illustrations by Helen Oxenbury: $40.00

MASCHLER, Fay, *Child's Book of Manners*

MASEFIELD, John (1878 – 1967)
British poet John Masefield wrote two fantasy novels for children: *Midnight Folk,* and its more popular sequel, *Box of Delights,* which was set at Christmas and inspired a TV adaptation.

Box of Delights, or *When Wolves Were Running,* William Heinemann, London, 1935, decorated endpapers, illustrated chapter heads and endings, first edition: $250.00. With dust jacket: $750.00

Midnight Folk, William Heinemann, London, 1927, first edition with dust jacket: $150.00

Midnight Folk, William Heinemann, London, 1931, first illustrated edition with six color plates by Rowland Hilder: $250.00

Reynard the Fox or *The Ghost Heath Run,* William Heinemann, London, 1920, blue cover with gilt: $50.00

MASHA, author/illustrator

Masha's Cats and Kittens, American Heritage Press, 1970, oversize hardcover, color illustrations by Masha, with dust jacket: $40.00

Masha's Stuffed Mother Goose, Garden City, 1946, oversize, 64 pages, color illustrations throughout by Masha, first edition with dust jacket: $100.00

MASON, Arthur
Fossil Fountain, Doubleday, Doran, 1928, 198 pages, illustrated by Jay Van Everen, first edition: $90.00

From the Horn of the Moon, Doubleday, Doran, 1931, blue cloth cover with pictorial paste-on, illustrated by Robert Lawson, first edition: $80.00

MASON, Arthur, *From the Horn of the Moon*

Wee Men of Ballywooden, Doubleday, Doran, 1930, b/w illustrations, first edition: $50.00

MASON, Miriam E.
Frances Willard, Girl Crusader, Bobbs Merrill, 1961, orange picture cover, illustrated by Leslie Goldstein, first edition with dust jacket: $50.00

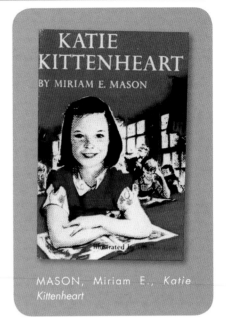

MASON, Miriam E., *Katie Kittenheart*

Katie Kittenheart, Macmillan, 1941, illustrations by Charles Geer, first edition with dust jacket: $30.00

Miss Posy Longlegs, Macmillan, 1955, illustrations by Maud & Miska Petersham, first edition with dust jacket: $50.00

Pony Called Lightning, Macmillan, 1949, illustrated by by C. W. Anderson, first edition with dust jacket: $80.00

Sara and the Winter Gift, Macmillan, 1968, first edition with dust jacket: $60.00

Susannah the Pioneer Cow, Macmillan, 1941, three-color illustrations throughout, first edition with dust jacket: $40.00

MASSIE, Diane Redfield
Birthday for Bird, Parents' Magazine Press, 1966, illustrated by author, first edition with dust jacket: $50.00

Tiny Pin, Harper, 1964, color illustrations by author, first edition with dust jacket: $40.00

Turtle and a Loon and Other Fables, 1965, Atheneum, illustrations by author, first edition with dust jacket: $40.00

MATHEWS, Joanna
Belle's Pink Boots, E. P. Dutton, 1881, blue cloth with decorative front cover with black and gold, illustrated by Ida Waugh: $70.00

Rudie's Goat, Frederick A. Stokes, 1873, green boards with filigree design, illustrated: $70.00

Toutou and Pussy Kitty and Lulu Books, Robert Carter and Brothers, 1872, hardcover, 243 pages: $40.00

MATTHEWS, Brander
American Patriotism, Scribner, 1922 edition, 14 color plates by N. C. Wyeth, first edition: $250.00

MATTHIESSEN, Peter
Great Auk Escape, Angus & Robertson, 1974, illustrated by William Pène du Bois, UK first edition: $200.00

Seal Pool, Doubleday, 1972, pictorial hardcover, illustrations by William Pène du Bois, first edition with dust jacket: $350.00

MAUGHAM, W. Somerset
Princess September and the Nightingale, Harcourt Brace, 1969 edition, oversize red hardcover, color illustrations by Richard C. Jones, first edition thus with dust jacket: $60.00

MAUGHAM, W. Somerset, *Princess September and the Nightingale*

MAUROIS, Andre
Fatapoufs and Thinifers, translated by R. Benet, Holt, 1940, oversize picture book, illustrated endpapers and color illustrations throughout by Jean Bruller, US first edition with dust jacket: $300.00

MAUZEY, Merritt (1897–1973)
Cotton Farm Boy, Henry Schuman, 1953, oversize hardcover, lithograph illustrations by Merritt Mauzey, first edition: $50.00

Rubber Boy, Abelard-Schuman, 1962, illustrated by author, first edition: $40.00

Texas Ranch Boy, Abelard-Schuman, 1955, oversize hardcover, 78 pages, illustrated by author: $40.00

MAXWELL, William
Heavenly Tenants, Harper, 1946, oversize, 57 pages, artwork by Ilonka Karasz, first edition with dust jacket: $150.00

MAXWELL, William, *Heavenly Tenants*

MAY, Robert
Rudolph the Red-Nosed Reindeer, Montgomery Ward, 1939, written by the company's ad salesman to be handed out in-store to children, paper cover, color illustrations by Denver Gillen, original paper giveaway first edition: $200.00

Rudolph the Red-Nosed Reindeer, Maxton Publishers, 1939, oversize glossy, first hardcover edition: $50.00

Rudolph the Red-Nosed Reindeer Pop-Up Book, 1950 pop-up edition, Maxton Publishing, oversize, cardboard cover, spiralbound, five pop-up illustrations plus color illustrations throughout by Marion Guild: $70.00

MAY, Robert, *Rudolph the Red-Nosed Reindeer*

MAYER, Herbert
Story of Little Ajax, 1949, Television Station WXEL, Cleveland, Channel 9, pictorial boards with black spine, drawings by Frances Mayer, TV station give-away, copyright 1949 by Empire Coil Co.: $30.00

MAYER, Mercer, see also Series section, FROG

Mayer studied at the Honolulu Academy of Arts and at the Art Students League. His earliest works were a series of wordless picture books for the pre-school set as well as simple books about childhood fears, such as *There's a Nightmare in My Closet* (1968). He also provided illustrations for other authors' works, including Fitzgerald's series, *Great Brain.* Occasionally, Mayer used the pseudonym "Professor Wormbog."

Great Cat Chase, 1974, Four Winds Press, small oblong hardcover, wordless book, illustrations by author, first edition with dust jacket: $30.00

Liza Lou and the Yeller Belly Swamp, Four Winds Press, 1976, glossy oversize pictorial hardcover, illustrated endpapers, color illustrations by author, first edition with dust jacket: $50.00

One Monster After Another, Golden Press, 1974, pictorial cover, first edition: $90.00

MAYER, Mercer, *Liza Lou and the Yeller Belly Swamp*

Professor Wormbog in Search for the Zipperump-a-Zoo, Golden Press, 1976, oversize glossy pictorial boards, 44 pages, pictorial endpapers, color illustrations, first edition: $60.00

There's a Nightmare in My Closet, Dial Press, 1968, oversize hardcover, color illustrations by Mayer, first edition with dust jacket: $90.00

What Do You Do with a Kangaroo?, Four Winds Press, 1973, illustrations by author, first edition with dust jacket: $80.00

MAYNE, William, see also Series section, EARTHFASTS TRILOGY

Blue Boat, Oxford University Press, 1957, illustrated by Geraldine Spence, first edition with dust jacket: $100.00

Game of Dark, Hamish Hamilton, 1971, first edition with dust jacket: $50.00

Patchwork Cat, Jonathan Cape, 1981, glazed illustrated boards, oversize, illustrations by Nicola Bayley, first edition: $60.00

MAZER, Norma Fox

I, Trissy, Delacorte Press, 1971, Mazer's first book for children. first edition with dust jacket: $40.00

Saturday, the Twelfth of October, Delacorte Press, 1975, first edition with dust jacket: $40.00

McCAFFERY, ANNE, see Series section, HARPER HALL

McCANDLISH, Edward, see also Series section, BUNNY TOTS

Little Miss Ducky-Daddles, Stoll and Edwards, 1926, illustrated paper-overboard cover, small easy-reader with full-page color illustrations by author: $30.00

Mother Goose Rhymes, Roycrofters, East Aurora, pictorial hardcover, illustrations by McCandlish: $700.00

McCAY, Winsor (1871–1934)
Best known for his "Little Nemo" character, Winsor McCay was also a profound influence on early animators Walt Disney and Walter Lanz.

Little Nemo in Slumberland, McCay Features Syndicate, 1945, softcover: $100.00. Rand McNally, pictorial boards: $75.00

McCLINTOCK, Theodore
Underwater Zoo, Vanguard, 1938, first edition: $100.00

McCLOSKEY, Robert, *Burt Dow, Deep-Water Man*

McCLOSKEY, Robert
Blueberries for Sal, Viking Press, 1948, oversize oblong illustrated hardcover, illustrated by McCloskey, first edition: $2,000.00

Burt Dow, Deep-Water Man, Viking Press, 1963, hardcover, illustrations by author, with dust jacket: $80.00

Homer Price, Viking Press, 1971, illustrated hardcover, illustrations by author, first edition with dust jacket: $1,000.00

Lentil, Viking Press, 1940, author's first book, oversize illustrated hardcover, illustrated by McCloskey, first edition with dust jacket: $1,500.00

Make Way For Ducklings, Viking Press, 1941, oversize illustrated hardcover, illustrated by McCloskey, first edition: $1,500.00

One Morning in Maine, 1952, Viking Press, oversize hardcover, 64 pages, illustrations by author, first edition with dust jacket: $400.00

McCORMICK, Wilfred, see also Series section, BRONC BURNETT, ROCKY McCUNE SPORTS STORIES

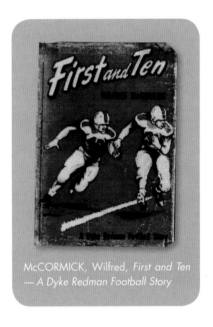

McCORMICK, Wilfred, *First and Ten — A Dyke Redman Football Story*

First and Ten — A Dyke Redman Football Story, G. P. Putnam's Sons, 1952, first edition with dust jacket: $100.00

McCRACKEN, Harold
God's Frozen Children, Doubleday, 1930, endpaper maps, 291 pages, photo plates: $50.00

Story of Alaska, Garden City, 1956, oversize, endpapers with maps, first edition with dust jacket: $40.00

Winning of the West, Garden City, 1955, illustrated cover, oversize, illustrated by Lee Ames, first edition with dust jacket: $50.00

McCREADY, T. L., Jr.

Adventures of a Beagle, Warne, London (1954), 1961 revised edition, illustrated by Tasha Tudor, 48 pages, first edition thus with dust jacket: $300.00

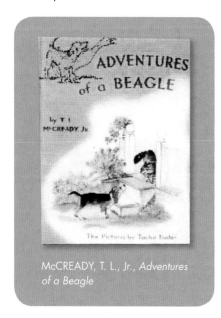

McCREADY, T. L., Jr., *Adventures of a Beagle*

Biggity Bantam, 1960 revised edition, Warne, beige hardcover, color and b/w illustrations by Tasha Tudor, UK first edition with dust jacket: $300.00

Increase Rabbit, Ariel Books, 1958, illustrated by Tasha Tudor, first edition with dust jacket: $150.00

Pekin White, Ariel Books, 1955, illustrated by Tasha Tudor, first edition with dust jacket: $150.00

McCULLERS, Carson

Sweet as a Pickle and Clean as a Pig, Houghton Mifflin, 1964, hardcover, illustrations by Rolf Gerard, first edition with dust jacket: $100.00

McDERMOTT, Gerald

Arrow to the Sun, Viking Press, 1974 (1975 Caldecott Award), first edition with dust jacket: $100.00

Papagayo, the Mischief Maker, Windmill/Wanderer, 1980, first edition with dust jacket: $30.00

Stonecutter, Viking Press, 1975, 31 pages, color illustrations by author, first edition with dust jacket: $50.00

McGINLEY, Phyllis

Boys Are Awful, Franklin Watts, 1961, first edition with dust jacket: $70.00

Horse Who Lived Upstairs, J. B. Lippincott, 1944, Weekly Reader Edition, illustrated by Helen Stone, hardcover: $90.00

Lucy McLocket, J. B. Lippincott, 1959, oversize hardcover, 48 pages, illustrations by Roberta McDonald, first edition with dust jacket: $40.00

Make Believe Twins, 1951 J. B. Lippincott, oversize hardcover, 48 pages, illustrations by Roberta McDonald, first edition with dust jacket: $40.00

McGINLEY, Phyllis, *Year Without a Santa Claus*

Merry Christmas, Happy New Year, Viking Press, 1958, illustrations by Ilonka Karasz, first edition with dust jacket: $40.00

Year Without a Santa Claus, J. B. Lippincott, 1957, oversize, color illustrations by Kurt Werth, first edition with dust jacket: $70.00

McGOVERN, Ann

If You Lived in Colonial Times, Scholastic, 1964, illustrated by Brinton Turkle, first edition with dust jacket: $50.00

Underwater World of the Coral Reef, Scholastic, 1976, first edition with dust jacket: $40.00

Zoo Where Are You?, Harper & Row, 1964, illustrated by Ezra Jack Keats, first edition with dust jacket: $50.00

McGOWEN, Tom

Sir MacHinery, Follett, 1970, illustrated by Trina Schart Hyman, first edition with dust jacket: $200.00

McGRAW, Eloise Jarvis

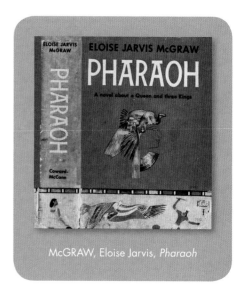

McGRAW, Eloise Jarvis, *Pharaoh*

Crown Fire, Coward-McCann, 1951, 254 pages, first edition with dust jacket: $30.00

Mara, Daughter of the Nile, Coward-McCann, 1953, first edition with dust jacket: $100.00

Master Cornhill, Atheneum, 1973, first edition with dust jacket: $40.00

Pharaoh, Coward-McCann, 1958, first edition with dust jacket: $400.00

Sawdust in His Shoes, Coward-McCann, 1950, first edition with dust jacket: $100.00

McHARGUE, Georges

Elidor and the Golden Ball, Dodd, Mead, 1973, illustrated by Emanuel Schongut, first edition with dust jacket: $40.00

Mermaid and the Whale, Holt, 1973, oversize hardcover, picture book, color illustrations by Robert Andrew Parker, first edition with dust jacket: $40.00

McINTYRE, John Thomas, see Series section, YOUNG CONTINENTALS

McKENNA, Dolores
Adventures of a Wee Mouse, Frederick A. Stokes, 1921, small, cloth-over-board cover with paste-on-pictorial, illustrated endpapers, six color plates by Ruth Bennett: $50.00

Adventures of Squirrel Fluffytail, Frederick A. Stokes, 1921, small, cloth-over-board cover with paste-on-pictorial, illustrated endpapers, color plates and b/w illustrations by Ruth Bennett: $50.00

Hootie the Owl, 1921, Saalfield, small, hardcover with paste-on-illustration, six color illustrations by Ruth Bennett: $30.00

McKILLIP, Patricia A., see also Series section, RIDDLE-MASTER OF HED TRILOGY

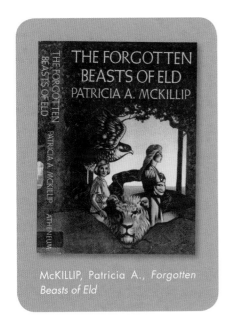

McKILLIP, Patricia A., *Forgotten Beasts of Eld*

Forgotten Beasts of Eld, Atheneum, 1974, first edition with dust jacket: $90.00

Throne of the Errill of Sherrill, Atheneum, 1973, first edition with dust jacket: $40.00

McKOWN, Robin
Boy Who Woke up in Madagascar, Putnam, 1967, illustrations by Robert Quakenbush, first edition with dust jacket: $30.00

McMAHON, Jo L. G.
In-and-out, Up-and-down, John Martin,

1922, oversize picture book with windows to cut out in pages, b/w/orange illustrations by author: $40.00

McNEER, May
Many of McNeer's books are illustrated by her husband, artist Lynd Ward.

Give Me Freedom, Abington, 1964, illustrations by Lynd Ward, first edition with dust jacket: $50.00

Golden Flash, Viking Press, 1947, illustrated endpapers, eight color plates by Lynd Ward, first edition with dust jacket: $60.00

My Friend Mac, Houghton Mifflin, 1960, illustrations by Lynd Ward, first edition with dust jacket: $50.00

Stop Tim! The Tale of a Car, Farrar and Rinehart, 1930, oblong, 39 pages, decorated paper-covered boards, illustrated by Lynd Ward: $150.00

Story of the Great Plains, Harper, 1943, oversize, color illustrated paper-over-board cover, illustrated endpapers with map, lithograph color and b/w illustrations throughout by C. H. DeWitt, first edition with dust jacket: $60.00

Story of the Southwest, Harper, 1948, oversize, color illustrated paper-over-board cover, illustrated endpapers with map, lithograph color and b/w illustrations throughout by C. H. DeWitt, about 30 pages, first edition with dust jacket: $60.00

Waif Maid, Macmillan, 1930, color frontispiece, b/w woodcut illustrations by Lynd Ward, first edition with dust jacket: $50.00

McNEIL, Marion L.
Children Across the Sea, Saalfield, 1931, oversize, color illustrations by Janet Laura Scott: $120.00

Jingleman Jack, Circusman, Saalfield, 1930, illustrated by Corinne Rinsel Bailey, first edition: $60.00

Little Green Cart, Saalfield, 1931, pictorial boards, oversize, color illustrations throughout by Francoise: $40.00

McNEIL, Marion L., *Round the Mulberry Bush*

Round the Mulberry Bush, Saalfield, 1933, oversize picture book, 36 pages, illustrated paper-over-board cover, eight full-page color illustrations by Fern Bisel Peat: $80.00

MEADER, Stephen W.
Behind the Ranges, Harcourt Brace, 1947, first edition with dust jacket: $100.00

Fish Hawk's Nest, Harcourt Brace, 1952, first edition with dust jacket: $100.00

Phantom of the Blockade, Harcourt Brace & World, 1962, illustrated by Victor Mays, first edition with dust jacket: $70.00

MEADER, Stephen W., *Fish Hawk's Nest*

Skippy's Family, Harcourt Brace, 1945, first edition with dust jacket: $350.00

T-Model Tommy (1938), 1940 edition, Harcourt Brace, illustrated by Edward Shenton: $150.00

Voyage of the Javelin, Harcourt Brace, 1959, first edition with dust jacket: $100.00

MEANS, Florence Crannell (1891–1980)

American author Florence Crannell Means often portrayed strong, independent girls from minority backgrounds, which has made her novels of particular interest to scholars and collectors looking for juvenile fiction sets outside the mainstream in the 1930s and 1940s. Means also wrote a number of nonfiction titles and historical novels.

Great Day in the Morning, Houghton Mifflin, 1946, illustrated by Helen Blair, first edition with dust jacket: $75.00

Moved-Outers, Houghton Mifflin, 1945, first juvenile novel about the Japanese internment and published during WWII, a Newbery Honor Book, illustrated by Helen Blair, first edition with dust jacket: $75.00

Tangled Waters: A Navajo Story, Houghton Mifflin, 1936, illustrated by Herbert Morton Stoops, first edition with dust jacket: $35.00

MEIGS, Cornelia (1884–1973)

Wonderful Locomotive, Macmillan, 1932, illustrated by Berta and Elmer Hader, first edition: $45.00. With dust jacket: $100.00

MENDOZA, George

Crack in the Wall, and Other Terribly Weird Tales, 1968, Dial Press, hardcover, b/w illustrations by Mercer Mayer, first edition with dust jacket: $50.00

Gillygoofang, Dial Press, 1968, square, illustrated by Mercer Mayer, first edition with dust jacket: $150.00

Herman's Hat, Doubleday, 1969, oblong hardcover, illustrations by Frank Bozzo, first edition with dust jacket: $30.00

Marcel Marceau Alphabet Book, Doubleday, 1970, color photographs by Milton H. Greene, first edition with dust jacket: $40.00

MERRIAM, Eve (1916–1992)

Don't Think About a White Bear, Putnam, 1965, color illustrations by Murray Tinkelman, first edition with dust jacket: $50.00

Epaminondas, Follett, 1968, based on the Sara Cone Bryant story, illustrated by Trina Schart Hyman, first edition with dust jacket: $150.00

MERRIAM, Eve, *Epaminondas*

MERRILL, Jean

Elephant Who Liked to Smash Small Cars, Pantheon, 1967, oversize hardcover, illustrations by Ronni Solbert, first edition with dust jacket: $100.00

Pushcart War, William Scott, 1964, illustrated hardcover, 223 pages, b/w illustrations by Ronni Solbert, first edition with dust jacket: $80.00

MERRYMAN, Mildred Plew

Daddy Domino, Volland/Buzza, 1929, small, illustrated paper boards, cloth spine, color illustrations throughout by Janet Laura Scott, first edition: $90.00

MILHOUS, Katherine

Appolonia's Valentine, Charles Scribner, 1954, oversize, color illustrations by author, first edition with dust jacket: $50.00

MERRYMAN, Mildred Plew, *Daddy Domino*

Egg Tree, Scribner, 1950 (1951 Caldecott Award), hardcover, color illustrations by author, first edition with dust jacket: $150.00

Patrick and the Golden Slippers, Scribner, 1951, red oversize hardcover, color illustrations by author, first edition with dust jacket: $50.00

Through These Arches, J. B. Lippincott, 1964, oblong hardcover, 96 pages, color illustrations by author, first edition with dust jacket: $35.00

With Bells On, Scribner, 1955, oversize hardcover, illustrations by author, first edition with dust jacket: $50.00

MILHOUS, Katherine, *With Bells On*

MILLER, Elizabeth
Pran of Albania, Doubleday, 1929, illustrations by Maud and Miska Petersham, first edition with dust jacket: $80.00

MILLER, Warren
Goings on at Little Wishful, Harcourt, 1959, oblong hardcover, illustrations by Edward Sorel, first edition with dust jacket: $100.00

King Carlo of Capri, Harcourt Brace, 1958, 32 pages, color illustrations by Edward Sorel, first edition with dust jacket: $50.00

MILLIGAN, Spike
Badjelly the Witch, Michael Joseph, 1973, illustrations by author, first edition with dust jacket: $200.00

Unspun Socks from a Chicken's Laundry and other Children's Verses, Michael Joseph, 1981, red cloth boards, first edition with dust jacket: $80.00

MILLS, G. R. and Zaida Nelson
Talking Dolls, Greenberg, 1930, oversize, hardcover, color illustrations throughout by Tony Sarg, first edition with dust jacket: $200.00

MILNE, A. A. (1882 – 1956), see also Series section, WINNIE-THE-POOH

Once on a Time. . ., Hodder & Stoughton, 1917, blue cloth with paste-on-pictorial, 316 pages, color frontispiece, four b/w plates, vignettes by Brock: $250.00

MILNE, A.A., *Once on a Time...*

Once on a Time..., Hodder & Stoughton, 1922, blue cloth hardcover with gilt, illustrations by Charles Robinson, first edition thus: $200.00

Once on a Time..., New York Graphic Society, 1962 edition, illustrated by Susan Perl, first edition thus with dust jacket: $60.00

Prince Rabbit and the Princess Who Could Not Laugh, E. P. Dutton, 1905, first US edition: $50.00

MINARIK, Else Holmelund
Cat and Dog, Harper, 1960, glossy cover, illustrated by Fritz Siebel, first edition with dust jacket: $80.00

MINARIK, Else Holmelund, *Cat and Dog*

Little Bear, Harper & Brothers, 1957, illustrated by Maurice Sendak, first edition with dust jacket: $300.00

Little Bear's Friend, Harper & Brothers, 1960, illustrated by Maurice Sendak, first edition with dust jacket: $150.00

Little Giant Girl and Elf Boy, Harper & Row, 1963, illustrations by Garth Williams, first edition with dust jacket: $100.00

No Fighting, No Biting!, Harper, 1958, 62 pages, illustrations by Maurice Sendak, first edition with dust jacket: $300.00

MITCHELL, Edith, *Otherside Book*

MITCHELL, Edith, author/illustrator
Betty, Bobby and Bubbles, Volland, 1921, small, about 20 pages, illustrated paper-over-board cover, color illustrations by Janet Laura Scott: $120.00

Otherside Book, Reilly Britton, 1915, oversize, paper-over-board cover, color illustrations throughout by author: $70.00

MITCHELL, J. A.
Romance of the Moon, Holt, 1886, cloth-over-board cover with gilt impressed illustration, small oblong picture book, green ink line drawings: $40.00

MIZUMURA, Kazue, author/illustrator
If I Built a Village, Crowell, 1971, first edition with dust jacket: $50.00

If I Were a Cricket..., Thomas Crowell, 1973, first edition with dust jacket: $30.00

MOESCHLIN, Elsa
Little Boy with the Big Apples, Coward-McCann, 1929, color illustrations and paper-over-board cover, oversize picture book, color illustrations by author: $120.00

Red Horse, Coward-McCann, 1929, pictorial paper-over-board cover, oversize picture book, color illustrations by author: $100.00

MOLESWORTH, Mrs.

Adventures of Herr Baby, Macmillan, 1881, red cloth with pictorial cover in gilt and black, b/w illustrations by Walter Crane, first edition: $100.00

Children of the Castle, Macmillan, 1880, illustrated orange cloth-over-board cover, plates by Walter Crane: $100.00

Christmas Posy, Macmillan, 1888, illustrated orange cloth-over-board cover, eight plates by Walter Crane: $50.00

Christmas-Tree Land, Macmillan, London, 1889, red decorated cloth with gilt, 228 pages, fantasy, illustrated by Walter Crane, eight b/w plates: $100.00

Four Winds Farm, Macmillan, 1887, wood engraved frontispiece, illustrated title-page, six plates by Walter Crane, first edition: $200.00

Mrs. Mouse and Her Boys, Macmillan, 1897, orange cloth-over-board cover, 198 pages, six plates by L. Leslie Brooke: $50.00

Rectory Children, Macmillan, 1889, cloth-over-board cover with gilt, small, 212 pages, b/w illustrations by Walter Crane: $50.00

Uncanny Tales, Hutchinson, 1896, "Hutchinson's Colonial Library," maroon cloth stamped in gold, 228 pages, collection of ghost stories, pictorial binding and title page designed by Fred Hyland: $600.00

MONJO, F. N. (1924 – 1978)

Me and Willie and Pa, Simon & Schuster, 1973, oversize hardcover, illustrations by David Gorsline, first edition with dust jacket: $30.00

Rudi and the Distelfink, E. P. Dutton, 1972, illustrations by George Kraus, first edition with dust jacket: $40.00

Secret of the Sachem's Tree, Coward-McCann, 1972, illustrations by Margot Tomes, first edition with dust jacket: $30.00

Vicksburg Veteran, Simon & Schuster, 1971, 62 pages, b/w illustrations, first edition with dust jacket: $30.00

MONTGOMERY, Frances, see Series section, BILLY WHISKERS THE GOAT

MONTGOMERY, L. M. (Lucy Maude, 1874 – 1942), see Series section, ANNE SHIRLEY

MONTGOMERY, Rutherford G., see Series section, GOLDEN STALLION, KENT BARSTOW

Capture of West Wind, Duell Sloan & Pearce, 1962, first edition with dust jacket: $50.00

McGonnigle's Lake, Doubleday, 1953, 219 pages, illustrations by Garry MacKenzie, first edition with dust jacket: $30.00

Walt Disney's Cougar, Golden Press, 1961, pictorial hardcover, illustrations by Robert Magnusen, first edition with dust jacket: $50.00

MOON, Grace and Carl

Illustrator Carl Moon travelled to the Southwest to build his career as a chronicler of Indian culture. His photographs, paintings, and writings earned him a reputation as an expert on Indian lore, and in 1906 he was invited by President Theodore Roosevelt to exhibit his paintings at the White House. Moon illustrated and co-authored numerous children's books with his wife, Grace Moon.

MOON, Grace and Carl, *Nadita*

Book of Nah-Wee, Doubleday, Doran, 1932, oversize, 59 pages, color illustrations, first edition with dust jacket: $200.00

Lost Indian Magic, Frederick A. Stokes, 1918, cloth-over-board cover with paste-on-illustration, 301 pages, color frontispiece, color plates by Carl Moon, first edition: $100.00

Nadita, Doubleday, 1927, color illustrations, first edition with dust jacket: $100.00

Shanty Ann, Frederick A. Stokes, 1935, color plates, first edition with dust jacket: $80.00

MOON, Sheila

Knee-Deep in Thunder, Atheneum, 1967, first edition with dust jacket: $30.00

MOORE, Beatrice T.

Swim for It, Bridget!, William Morrow, 1958, illustrations by E. Harper Johnson, first edition with dust jacket: $100.00

MOORE, Clement C. (1779 – 1863)

Professor Moore wrote a poem in 1822 for his children. It was first published in a Troy, New York, newspaper in 1823, picked up by other publications, and Moore's description of Santa quickly became a classic. The value of an edition usually depends on the availability and the popularity of the illustrator.

Sample titles:

Denslow's Night Before Christmas, G. W. Dillingham, 1902, oversize hardcover with paste-on-pictorial, color illustrations by W. W. Denslow: $250.00

Night Before Christmas, Houghton Mifflin, 1912, oversize oblong, orange cloth w/ white spine, color illustrations by Jessie Willcox Smith: $150.00

Night Before Christmas, E. P. Dutton, 1928, oversize, color illustrations by Elizabeth MacKinstry, with dust jacket: $300.00

Night Before Christmas, George G. Harrap & Co. Ltd., 1931, four color plates and 17 b/w illustrations by Arthur Rackham, first edition with dust jacket: $1,000.00

MOORE, Clement C., *Night Before Christmas*

Night Before Christmas, Harcourt Brace, 1937, illustrated by Reginald Birch, with dust jacket: $150.00

Night Before Christmas, Whitman, 1937, paper-over-board cover, oversize square, color illustrations throughout by Ruth E. Newton: $40.00

Night Before Christmas, Saalfield, 1937, oversize die-cut book, color illustrations throughout by Fern Bisel Peat, 12 pages: $100.00

Night Before Christmas, Worcester, 1962, miniature red leather hardcover with gilt edges, illustrations by Tasha Tudor, first edition with dust jacket: $200.00

MOORE, Clement C., *Night Before Christmas*

MOORE, Colleen
Colleen Moore's Doll House Cut-Outs, 1934, Ullman, oversize, 14 pages, cardboard cover with color photo illustration of the Colleen Moore doll castle, uncut: $90.00

MOORE, Marianne, poet

Puss in Boots, the Sleeping Beauty and Cinderella, Macmillan, 1963, pastel illustrations by Eugene Carlin, first edition with dust jacket: $60.00

MOORE, Nancy
Miss Harriet Hippopotamus and the Most Wonderful, Vanguard Press, 1963, oversize, 34 pages, paper covered boards, illustrations by Edward Leight, first edition with dust jacket: $70.00

Unhappy Hippopotamus, Vanguard Press, 1957, pictorial hardcover, illustrations by Edward Leight, first edition with dust jacket: $70.00

MOREY, Walt (1907 – 1992)
Gentle Ben, E. P. Dutton, 1965, illustrations by John Schoenherr, first edition with dust jacket: $40.00

Gloomy Gus, E. P. Dutton, 1973, first edition with dust jacket: $30.00

Kavik the Wolf Dog, E. P. Dutton, 1968, illustrations by Peter Parnell, first edition with dust jacket: $30.00

MORGENSTERN, Elizabeth
Little Gardeners, retold by L. Encking, 1935 edition, Whitman, cloth-over-board cover with paste-on pictorial, easy read picture book, color illustrations by Marigold Bantzer: $40.00

MORLEY, Christopher
Where the Blue Begins, J. B. Lippincott, 1922 edition, blue cloth-over-board cover, oversize, color and b/w illustrations by Arthur Rackham: $40.00

MORRISON, Mary Whitney
Stories True and Fancies New, Dana Estes, 1898, poetry, hardcover with wraparound printed illustration, 208 pages, color frontispiece, b/w illustrations by L. J. Bridgman: $50.00

MORRISON, Mary Whitney, *Stories True and Fancies New*

MORROW, Elizabeth
Painted Pig, Alfred A. Knopf, 1930, oversize picture book, illustrated endpapers, color frontispiece and color illustrations throughout by Rene D'Harnoncourt, with dust jacket: $100.00

Rabbit's Nest, Macmillan, 1914, pictorial boards, illustrated endpapers, small, 43 pages, b/w illustrations, first edition with dust jacket: $30.00

Shannon, Macmillan, 1941, small, 69 pages, b/w illustrations by Helen Torrey, first edition with dust jacket: $40.00

MOSES, Montrose, editor

Treasury of Plays for Children, Little, Brown, 1921, brown cloth-over-board cover, color frontispiece, b/w illustrations by Tony Sarg: $60.00

MOTHER GOOSE
Traditional rhymes have been collected under this name, and collections have been illustrated by many talented artists. For collectors who specialize in Mother Goose books, we've listed some of the best known editions. There are so many, we have undoubtedly missed some classics. Many of the following have been reprinted in a variety of later editions which are available at lower prices.

Mother Goose books in order by date of publication:

Mother Goose's Melodies, Porter & Coates, 1870, oversize, green cloth, bevelled edges, gilt, 16 pages with text, 15 large chromolithograph illustrations from original watercolors by Janette Ralson Chase (originally painted for a birthday gift to her father, U.S. Supreme Court member Salmon P. Chase): $400.00

Mother Goose or, the *Old Nursery Rhymes,* Routledge, London, 1881, small hardcover with cream boards and pink spine, title in brown surrounded by green latticework design, green endpapers, 48 pages, engraved and printed by Edmund Evans, full-page color illustrations by Kate Greenaway, was issued with an illustrated dust jacket: $1,500.00

Maud Humphrey's Mother Goose, Frederick A. Stokes, 1891, oversize, full color illustrations by Humphrey: $750.00

Mother Goose in Prose, classic poems turned into humorous stories by L. Frank Baum, Way & Williams, 1897, oversize, 12 illustrations by Maxfield Parrish, first edition: $4,000.00

Only True Mother Goose Melodies (first published by Munroe, 1833), ca. 1905, reproduction Lee & Shepard, small square glossy pictorial hardcover, introduction by Rev. Edward Everett Hale, includes a history of the Goose Family, woodcut illustrations throughout: $125.00

MOTHER GOOSE, *Mother Goose, Her Chimes*

Mother Goose, the Old Nursery Rhymes, Heinemann, London, 1913 trade edition, hardcover, color plates and b/w illustrations by Arthur Rackham, first edition: $500.00

Jessie Willcox Smith's Mother Goose, Dodd, Mead, 1914, oversize oblong with paste-on-pictorial, 12 full-color plates by Jessie Willcox Smith, first edition: $900.00

Mother Goose, Her Chimes, Saalfield, 1915, hardcover illustration and b/w illustrations by Buzz Ware, color plates mounted on brown paper pages by H. B. Matthews: $45.00

Real Mother Goose, Rand, 1916, oversized picture book, color paste-on picture on cover, illustrated endpapers and small and full-page color illustrations throughout by Blanche Fisher Wright, this is one of the best known Mother Goose books and is reprinted regularly in various sizes and formats. Early printing: $90.00. 1945 reprint with paste-on-pictorial: $50.00

Rhymes for Kindly Children, Modern Mother Goose Jingles, Volland, 1916, illustrated boards, color illustrations by Johnny Gruelle: $150.00

Mother Goose, edited by Eulalie Osgood Grover, Volland, 1917, illustrated cloth-over-board cover with printed illustration and gilt lettering, oversize, 108 lush color plates by Frederick Richardson: $250.00

Every Child's Mother Goose, introduction by Carolyn Wells, Macmillan, 1918, hardcover with paste-on-pictorial, photo illustrations of dolls by Edith Wilson, an unusual version: $150.00

Mother Goose, 1918, Donahue, oversize hardcover, numerous line drawings and 24 color plates by Ella Dolbear Lee, first edition in dust jacket: $150.00

Mother Goose or, *the Old Nursery Rhymes,* Warne, 1918 edition, Kate Greenaway illustrations, with dust jacket: $250.00

Mother Goose, Doubleday, 1924, oversize blue hardcover with orange lettering, 96 pages, color illustrations by C. B. Falls: $200.00

Mother Goose, Saalfield, 1929, hardcover, oversize, 60 pages, color illustrations by Fern Bisel Peat: $70.00

Berta and Elmer Hader's Picture Book of Mother Goose, Coward-McCann, 1930, illustrated endpapers, bright color illustrations by the Haders, early printing: $70.00

Mother Goose Rhymes, Platt & Munk, undated, ca. 1932, oversize red hardcover with paste-on-pictorial, full and partial page b/w and color illustrations by Eulalie and by Lois Lenski: $100.00

Mother Goose, Whitman, 1934, oversize, cloth cover, color illustrations by artist Ruth Newton who was also a doll and toy designer: $60.00

Mother Goose Parade: A Talking Book with Song, Sound and Color, lyrics by Carolyn Adams, music by Alice Remsen, Garden City Publishing, 1939, hardcover, illustrated by Charlotte Steiner, with record: $40.00

Tall Book of Mother Goose, Harper & Brothers, 1942, tall narrow hardcover, color illustrations by Feodor Rojankovsky, first edition with dust jacket: $100.00

Masha's Stuffed Mother Goose, Garden City, 1946, oversize pictorial hardcover, 64 pages, full-color and two-color illustrations of Mother Goose characters represented by stuffed animals or dolls: $40.00

Animated Mother Goose, Julian Wehr illustrations and animations, Duenewald, 1950, color illustrated hardcover with spiral spine, with animations in working condition: $60.00

Mother Goose Playhouse, J. S. Publications, 1953, illustrated cardboard playhouse box containing eight accordian-fold single page books with pop-ups of nursery rhymes: $125.00

Book of Nursery and Mother Goose Rhymes, Doubleday, 1954, graceful illustrations by Marguerite De Angeli, first edition with dust jacket: $85.00

Mother Goose Panorama, Grosset & Dunlap, 1957, oversize hardcover with color illustration, fold-out cardboard pages cut to illustration shapes, connected in a panorama, design and color illustrations by Julian Wehr who designed numerous animated books, first edition: $60.00

MOULTON, Louise

New Bed-Time Stories, Roberts, 1880, red cloth-over-board cover with gilt, small, 230 pages, b/w illustrations by Addie Ledyard: $30.00

MOWAT, Farley

Black Joke, McClelland, 1962, 177 pages, illustrations by D. Johnson, first edition with dust jacket: $60.00

Curse of the Viking Grave, McClelland, 1966, 243 pages, illustrations by Charles Greer, first edition with dust jacket: $50.00

Dog Who Wouldn't Be, Little, Brown, 1957, hardcover, 238 pages, illustrations by Paul Galdone, first edition with dust jacket: $50.00

Never Cry Wolf, McClelland, 1963, 243 pages, first edition with dust jacket: $50.00

Owls in the Family, McClelland, 1973, illustrated by Robert Frankenberg, first edition with dust jacket: $30.00

People of the Deer, Little, Brown, 1952, illustrated mapped endpapers, drawings by Samuel Bryant, first edition with dust jacket: $40.00

MULFORD, Clarence, see Series section, HOPALONG CASSIDY

MUNROE, Kirk

Flamingo Feather, Harper (1887), 1923 edition, oversize, cloth-over-board cover, 222 pages, 10 color plate illustrations by Frank Schoonover, first edition thus with dust jacket: $200.00

MURRAY, Gretchen Ostrander

Shoes for Sandy, Grosset & Dunlap, 1936, oversize picture book, illustrated paper-over-board cover, illustrated endpapers, full-page

color and b/w illustrations by author, first edition with dust jacket: $70.00

MUSSET, Paul de

Mr. Wind and Madam Rain, Harper & Brothers, 1864, black cloth with gilt illustration on cover, first edition: $200.00

Mr. Wind and Madam Rain, Putnam, undated, ca. 1905, cloth-over-board cover, 151 pages, b/w illustrations by Charles Bennett: $100.00

MYERS, Byrona

Turn Here for Strawberry Roan, Bobbs-Merrill, 1950, 134 pages, illustrations by Anne Marie Jauss, first edition with dust jacket: $90.00

Yo Ho for Strawberry Roan!, Bobbs-Merrill, 1951, illustrations by Anne Marie Jauss, first edition with dust jacket: $90.00

NASH, Ogden (1908 – 1971)

Adventures of Isabel, Little, Brown, 1963, first edition with dust jacket: $70.00

Animal Garden, M. Evans, 1965, illustrations by Hilary Knight, first edition with dust jacket: $50.00

Boy Is a Boy: The Fun of Being a Boy, Watts, 1960, oversize hardcover, first edition with dust jacket: $80.00

NASH, Ogden, *Adventures of Isabel*

NASH, Ogden, *Animal Garden*

Christmas That Almost Wasn't, Little, Brown, 1957, color illustrations by Linell Nash, first edition with dust jacket: $50.00

Custard the Dragon and the Wicked Knight, Little, Brown, 1961, color illustrations by Lynn Munsinger, first edition with dust jacket: $100.00

Girls Are Silly, Franklin Watts, 1962, orange hardcover, illustrations by Lawrence Beall Smith, first edition with dust jacket: $50.00

New Nutcracker Suite and Other Innocent Verses, Little, Brown, 1962, illustrations by Ivan Chermayeff, first edition with dust jacket: $120.00

Santa Go Home, Little, Brown, 1966, 56 pages, illustrated with 40 drawings by Robert Osborn, first edition with dust jacket: $40.00

Untold Adventures of Santa Claus, Little, Brown, 1964, illustrations by Walter Lorraine, first edition with dust jacket: $50.00

You Can't Get There from Here, Little, Brown, 1957, illustrated by Maurice Sendak, first edition with dust jacket: $180.00

NASH, Thomas (1840 – 1902)

As a political cartoonist in nineteenth century America, Thomas Nash created the Republican Elephant and the Democratic Donkey. For children, he drew a plump Santa Claus for *Harper's Weekly*. His illustrations for *The Night Before Christmas* created a view of Santa that would influence artists on both sides of the Atlantic.

NAYLOR, Phyllis Reynolds, see also
Series section, WITCH, YORK TRILOGY

Faces in the Water, Atheneum, 1981, first edition with dust jacket: $70.00

How Lazy Can You Get, Atheneum, 1970, first edition with dust jacket: $50.00

To Make a Wee Moon, Follett, 1969, 190 pages, illustrations by Beth and Joe Krush, first edition with dust jacket: $40.00

NEILL, John Rea (1876 – 1943), illustrator,
see also Series section, OZ BOOKS

Born in Philadelphia, Neill was only 26 when he took on a lifetime commitment, illustrating the Oz books. A prolific magazine and book illustrator, Neill was tapped by Reilly & Britton to replace W.W. Denslow. Denslow and L. Frank Baum (the author of the series) had a creative falling out after the successful publication of the the *Wonderful Wizard of Oz.* If Denslow was Arts & Crafts, then Neill was Art Nouveau. His ladies wore lovely, flowing gowns, reminiscent of Dana Gibson or Howard Christy's women, and even his most grotesque creatures had pretty touches. Dragons wore big silk bows, and the witches had lots of accessories. Neill illustrated the *Oz* series from 1904 to 1942, even writing three books towards the series' end. While doing the *Oz* series, Neill continued to do primarily pen-and-ink work for a variety of books and magazines stories. He often reworked drawings to fit other assignments, so you might find some distinctly Oz characters in his other books. His work is primarily sought by Oz collectors, although art collectors of the Edwardian era are beginning to recognize his talent.

Foolish Fox, Altemus, 1904, color illustrations: $70.00

Robber Kitten, Altemus, 1904, color pastedown on cover, color illustrations: $50.00

Three Little Pigs, Altemus, 1904, small, illustrated paper-over-board cover, full-color, full-page illustrations by Neill: $80.00

NELSEN, Donald

Sam and Emma, Parents' Magazine Press, 1971, oblong illustrated hardcover, 38 pages, color illustrations by Edward Gorey, first edition with dust jacket: $50.00

NELSEN, Donald, *Sam and Emma*

NESBIT, E. (Edith Bland, 1858 – 1924),
see also Series section, FIVE CHILDREN TRILOGY, TREASURE SEEKERS

Children's Shakespeare, Altemus, ca. 1900, illustrated and decorated cloth-over-board cover, full-page illustrations, US first edition with dust jacket: $400.00

Daphne in Fitzroy Street, Doubleday, 1909, cloth-over-board cover with paste-on-pictorial, color frontispiece by F. G. Coates: $90.00

Harding's Luck, Hodder & Stoughton, 1913, illustrations by H. R. Millar: $150.00

NESBIT, E., *Magic City*

Magic City, Macmillan, 1910, b/w illustrations by H. R. Millar, first edition: $400.00

Oswald Bastable and Others, Wells Gardner, 1905, red cloth-over-board cover with gilt, illustrations by Brock and H. Millar, first edition: $500.00

Story of the Amulet, E. P. Dutton, 1907, cloth-over-board cover, 374 pages, b/w illustrations by H. R. Millar, US first edition: $150.00

Story of Five Rebellious Dolls, ca. 1890s, Nister, London, or E. P. Dutton, New York, oversize oblong, 20 pages, illustrated cover and endpapers, eight color chromolithographs plus illustrations throughout by E. Stuart Hardy: $500.00

NESS, Evaline (1911 – 1986, b. Chicago)
After studying fine art at the Art Institute of Chicago and the Corcoran Gallery of Art, Ness continued her art education at the Art Students League and in Italy. She pursued a career in commercial art, including work for *Seventeen* magazine. In the 1960s, she began illustrating children's books, often writing her own charming stories such as *Sam, Bangs & Moonshine* (1967 Caldecott Medal). Ness used a variety of artistic techniques from ink and color wash to woodcuts, depending upon the mood of her tale.

Do You Have the Time, Lydia?, Dutton, 1971, first edition with dust jacket: $30.00

NESS, Evaline, *Sam, Bangs & Moonshine*

Mr. Miacca, Holt Rinehart, 1967, illustrated, first edition with dust jacket: $70.00

Sam, Bangs & Moonshine, Holt, 1966, (1967 Caldecott Medal), oversize, hardcover, illustrated endpapers, b/w/brown/green illustrations throughout by author, first edition with dust jacket: $300.00. Caldecott edition with dust jacket: $70.00

Tom, Tit, Tot, Scribner's, 1965, first edition with dust jacket: $60.00

Yeck Eck, E. P. Dutton, 1974, first edition with dust jacket: $50.00

NEWBERRY, Clare Turlay (1903 – 1970), author/illustrator

Ice Cream for Two, Harper & Brothers, 1953, first edition with dust jacket: $100.00

Kittens' ABC, HarperCollins, 1965, hardcover: $100.00

Mittens, Harper & Brothers, 1936, first edition with dust jacket: $130.00

Pandora, Harper, 1944, first edition with dust jacket: $100.00

T-Bone the Babysitter, Harper & Brothers, 1950, color illustrations by the author, first edition with dust jacket: $200.00

NEWBERRY, Clare Turlay, *Mittens*

NEWMAN, Isadora

Fairy Flowers, Oxford, 1929, oversize decorated boards, color illustrations by Willy Pogany: $100.00

NEWELL, Peter (1862 – 1929)

Peter Newell created a number of novelty books including the *Slant Book* that slanted and *Hole Book* with a hole in it. His *Topsys & Turvys* books were supposedly inspired by seeing one of his own children looking at a picture book upside down. Newell was also one of the earliest American illustrators to experiment in halftone washes that would print in black-and-white with single second color (a technique that helped minimize printing costs).

Topsys & Turvys, Century, 1893, illustrated by author, first edition: $300.00. Early Century reprints (pre-1900): $100.00

Topsys & Turvys Number 2, Century, 1894, illustrated by author, first edition: $300.00

Hole Book, Harper & Brothers, 1908, illustrated by author, first edition: $100.00

Slant Book, Harper & Brothers, 1910, cover and pages cut on slant, 23 color-tinted illustrations by author, first edition: $500.00

Rocket Book, Harper & Brothers, 1912, illustrations by author of rocket traveling through apartment house, first edition: $125.00

NEWTON, Ruth E., illustrator

Sometimes authorship of some of the following books is unclear, but illustrations are by Newton.

Animal Mother Goose, Whitman, 1942, oversize softcover, linen-texture paper, color illustrations throughout: $30.00

Baby Animals, Whitman, 1945, oversize softcover, color illustrations throughout: $30.00

Kittens and Puppies, Whitman, 1940, Linen Like line, softcover, oversize picture book, 12 pages, color illustrations throughout by Newton: $40.00

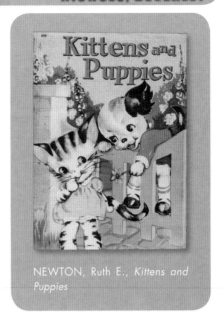

NEWTON, Ruth E., *Kittens and Puppies*

Let's Play Train, Whitman, 1936, square oversize, color illustrations by Newton: $100.00

Little Firemen, Whitman, 1936, oversize, 28 pages, color illustrations by Newton: $100.00

Peter Rabbit, Whitman, 1938, Giant Tell-A-Tale book, oversize glossy hardcover, color illustrations throughout by Newton: $70.00

NEWTON, Ruth E., *Peter Rabbit*

NICHOLS, Beverley

Book of Old Ballads, Hutchinson, London, 1934, color illustrations, first edition with dust jacket: $80.00

Mountain of Magic, Jonathan Cape, 1950, illustrated by Peggy Fortnum, first edition with dust jacket: $200.00

Stream That Stood Still, Jonathan Cape, 1948, illustrated endpapers, b/w line drawings throughout by Richard Kennedy, first edition with dust jacket: $60.00

NICHOLS, Ruth

Marrow of the World, Atheneum, 1972, illustrations by Trina Schart Hyman, first edition with dust jacket: $40.00

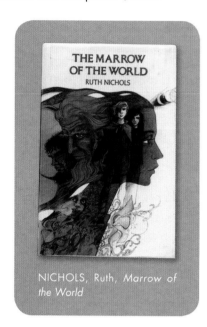

NICHOLS, Ruth, *Marrow of the World*

Walk Out of the World, 1969, Harcourt Brace, author's first book, illustrations by Trina Schart Hyman, first edition with dust jacket: $100.00

NICHOLS, Ruth Alexander (1893 – 1970)

American photographer Ruth Nichols launched a series of picture books for young readers with *Nancy* (1933). Nichols won her first camera in a magazine contest at the age of nine. Her first magazine spread in 1925 featured snapshots of her two-year-old daughter. Nichols freelanced for a variety of magazines and advertisers. Most of her photographs featured children.

Betty and Dolly, Bobbs-Merrill, 1935, small hardcover with photo illustrations by Nichols: $50.00

Nancy, Macmillan, 1933, small hardcover with photo illustrations by Nichols: $50.00

NICHOLS, Ruth Alexander, *Betty and Dolly*

NICHOLSON, William (1872 – 1949)

Sir William Nicholson illustrated a handful of picture books, including Margery William's *Velveteen Rabbit,* as well as designed the costumes and sets for the stage play, *Peter Pan,* in the 1920s. This British artist has been listed as an influence on such American illustrators as Wanda Gag and Maurice Sendak.

Clever Bill, Heinneman, UK, 1926, oblong format, woodcut illustrations by author. In 2007, one British dealer listed a fine first edition in dust jacket for: $5,600.00

Pirate Twins, Coward-McCann, US edition, 1929, illustrations by author, hardcover: $250.00

NICOLL, Helen, see Series section, MEG AND MOG

NIELSEN, Kay (1886 – 1957)

Following his first London art exhibition in 1912, Danish artist Kay Nielsen quickly received commissions from pubishers. Like his contemporaries Arthur Rackham and Edmund Dulac, Nielsen's fairytale books were issued in deluxe limited editions and regular trade editions on both sides of the Atlantic. In 1926, Nielsen moved to the United States and settled in Hollywood, where he worked as a set designer as well as a conceptual artist for the Walt Disney Studios. Prices for his Edwardian books began to climb in the 1980s, with the most collectible being early editions with numerous color plates.

NIELSEN, Martin

Brownie Numbers Combine Work and Fun (1934), 1935 edition, Farwest, oversize

picture book, illustrated cloth-over-board cover, b/w illustrations by Philip Sauve: $40.00

NORTH, Grace, see Series section, ADELE DORING

NORTH, Sterling

Rascal: A Memoir of a Better Era, E. P. Dutton, 1963, illustrations by John Schoenherr, first edition with dust jacket: $60.00

Wolfling, E. P. Dutton, 1969, hardcover, illustrated by John Schoenherr, first edition with dust jacket: $40.00

NORTON, Andre, see also Series section, GRYPHON, HIGH HALLACK, STAR KA'AT, WITCH WORLD

Forerunner Foray, Viking Press, 1973, dust jacket by Charles Mikolaycak, first edition with dust jacket: $100.00

Forerunner: The Second Venture, Tor, 1985, first edition with dust jacket: $50.00

NORTON, Andre, *Forerunner Foray*

Here Abide Monsters, Atheneum, 1974, first edition with dust jacket: $50.00

Huon of the Horn, Harcourt Brace, 1951, illustrations by Joe Krush, first edition stated on copyright page, with dust jacket: $125.00

Ice Crown, Viking Press, 1970, hardcover, 256 pages, with Laszlo Gal illustrated dust jacket: $30.00

Jargoon Pard (sequel to *Crystal Gryphon*), Atheneum, 1974, first edition with dust jacket: $50.00

Knave of Dreams, Viking Press, 1975, first edition with dust jacket: $35.00

Lavender-Green Magic, Crowell, 1974, 241 pages, illustrations by Judith Gwyn Brown, first edition with dust jacket: $50.00

Ordeal in Otherwhere, World, 1964, first edition with dust jacket: $100.00

Steel Magic, World, 1965, illustrations by Robin Jacques, first edition with dust jacket: $95.00

Storm Over Warlock, World, 1960, first edition with dust jacket: $100.00

Quest Crosstime, Viking Press, 1965, first edition with dust jacket: $30.00

NORTON, Mary (1903 – 1992), see also Series section, BORROWERS

Are All the Giants Dead?, Harcourt Brace, 1975, hardcover, b/w illustrations by Brian Froud, first US edition with dust jacket: $40.00

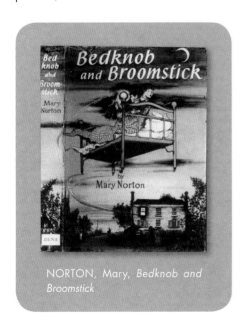

NORTON, Mary, *Bedknob and Broomstick*

Bedknob and Broomstick, J. M. Dent, UK, 1957, illustrations by Erik Blegvad, first edition with dust jacket: $140.00

Bonfires and Broomsticks, J. M. Dent, UK, 1947, illustrations by Mary Adshead, first edition with dust jacket: $100.00

Magic Bed-Knob or How to Become a Witch in Ten Easy Lessons, Hyperion Press, 1943, illustrated by Waldo Pierce, first edition with dust jacket: $500.00

NORWOOD, Edwin, see also Series section, DIGGELDY DAN

Circus Menagerie, Doubleday, 1929, yellow cloth-over-board cover, photo illustrations, first edition: $30.00

NOWLAN, Phil, see Series section, BUCK ROGERS

■ ························ **O** ························ ■

OAKLEY, Graham, see Series section, CHURCH MICE

O'BRIEN, Robert C. (1918 – 1973)
Mrs. Frisby and the Rats of NIMH, Atheneum, 1971, illustrated by Zena Bernstein, first edition with dust jacket: $150.00

O'CONNOR, Edwin
Benjy, a Ferocious Fairy Tale, Little, Brown, 1957, decorated hardcover, 143 pages, illustrated by Ati Forberg, first edition with dust jacket: $50.00

O'DELL, Scott (1898 – 1989)
Black Pearl, Houghton Mifflin, 1967, black hardcover with gilt, illustrated by Milton Johnson, first edition with dust jacket: $100.00

Island of the Blue Dolphins, Houghton Mifflin, 1960 (1961 Newbery Medal Award Winner), artwork by Evaline Ness, first edition with dust jacket: $400.00. 1961 edition with gold medal on dust jacket: $100.00

Journey to Jericho, Houghton Mifflin, 1969, hardcover, 41 pages, illustrated by Leonard Weisgard, first edition with dust jacket: $40.00

King's Fifth, Houghton Mifflin, 1966, illustrated by Samuel Bryant, first edition with dust jacket: $40.00

O'DONNELL, T. C.
Ladder of Rickety Rungs, Volland, 1923, color illustrated paper-over-board cover, color illustrations by Janet Scott: $100.00

O'FAOLAIN, Eileen, see also Series section, MISS PENNYFEATHER

Children of the Salmon, Little, Brown, 1965, Trina Schart Hyman illustrations, first edition with dust jacket: $50.00

King of the Cats, Dublin, Talbot Press, 1942, decorative cloth, Celtic fairy tale, illustrated by Nano Reid: $200.00

Shadowy Man, Longmans Green, London, 1949, square hardcover, illustrated by Phoebe Llewellyn Smith, first edition with dust jacket: $40.00

OFFIT, Sidney
Boy Who Made a Million, 1968, St. Martin's Press, illustrated hardcover, illustrated by Mercer Mayer: $40.00

Cadet Attack, St. Martin's Press, 1964, b/w illustrations by Peter Burchard, first edition with dust jacket: $70.00

Not All Girls Have Million Dollar Smiles and Other Tales from Sam Orlinski's Scene, Coward-McCann, 1971, first edition with dust jacket: $40.00

OGDEN, Ruth
Little Pierre and Big Peter, Frederick A. Stokes, 1915, cloth-over-board cover with paste-on-illustration, illustrated endpapers, color plates by Maria Kirk: $40.00

Little Queen of Hearts, Frederick A. Stokes, 1893, green cloth-over-board cover with gilt, 232 pages, b/w illustrations by H. A. Ogden, first edition: $60.00

Loyal Hearts and True, Frederick A. Stokes, ca. 1899, brown cloth-over-board cover, illustrations by H. A. Ogden: $40.00

Loyal Little Red-Coat, 1890, Frederick A. Stokes, cloth-over-board cover with gilt, b/w illustrations by H. A. Ogden: $40.00

O'HARA, David, see Series section, JIMMIE DRURY, CAMERA DETECTIVE

O'HARA, Mary (1885 – 1980)
Her most famous work started with *Flicka,* which began the three novels about the McLaughlin family, their son, Ken, and their horse ranch.

Early J. B. Lippincott editions with dust jackets: $45.00

Green Grass of Wyoming, J. B. Lippincott, 1946, first edition with dust jackets: $100.00

My Friend Flicka, J. B. Lippincott, New York, 1941, color frontispiece and b/w drawings by John Steuart Curry, first edition with dust jacket: $800.00

Thunderhead, J. B. Lippincott, 1943, first edition with dust jacket: $200.00

OLCOTT, Frances Jenkins
Adventures of Haroun Er Raschid and Other Tales from the Arabian Nights, Henry Holt, 1923, cloth with elaborate gilt, illustrated by Willy Pogany, with dust jacket: $200.00

OLCOTT, Frances Jenkins, *Story-Telling Ballads*

Book of Elves and Fairies, 1918, Houghton Mifflin, hardcover, color illustrations by Milo Winter: $90.00

Good Stories for Great Holidays, Houghton Mifflin, 1914, decorated hardcover, 248 pages, four-color plates: $50.00

Grimm's Fairy Tales, Hampton Publishing, 1922, cloth-over-board cover with paste-on-illustration, color plates by R. Cramer: $50.00

Jolly Book for Boys and Girls, Houghton Mifflin, 1915, red cloth-over-board cover, illustrated by Amy Sacker: $40.00

More Tales of the Arabian Nights, Holt, 1915, red cloth-over-board cover with gilt, 274 pages, 12 color plates by Willy Pogany, first edition: $100.00

Red Indian Fairy Book, Houghton Mifflin, 1917, color frontispiece and 18 b/w plates by Frederick Richardson: $150.00

Story-Telling Ballads, 1920, Houghton Mifflin, collection, green cloth-over-board cover with paste-on-illustration, four-color plates by Milo Winter: $40.00

OLCOTT, Virginia
Busy Billies, George W. Jacobs, Philadelphia, 1918, pictorial paste-down-cover, illustrated by Harriet M. Alcott: $50.00

O'LEARY, Michael
Great Automobile Club, Constable Young, UK, 1968, illustrated by John Haslam, first edition with dust jacket: $50.00

Penny to See the Piper, Constable Young, UK, 1967, oblong picture book, illustrated with two-color line drawings by John Haslam, first edition with dust jacket: $40.00

OLFERS, Sibylle
Butterfly Land, Frederick A. Stokes, 1931, color pictorial cover, oversize picture book, chromolithographic plates by author, printed in Germany: $200.00

Little Princess in the Wood, Frederick A. Stokes, 1931, oversize picture book, cloth-over-board cover with paste-on-illustration, illustrated endpapers, color frontispiece, color illustrated by author: $100.00

When the Root Children Wake Up, Frederick A. Stokes, 1930, oversize picture book, cloth-over-board cover with paste-on-illustration, illustrated endpapers, color frontispiece, color illustrated by author, first edition with dust jacket: $400.00

When the Root Children Wake Up, ca. 1940s, Lippincott reprinting of Stokes edition, oversize picture book, cloth-over-board cover with paste-on-illustration, illustrated endpapers, color frontispiece, color illustrated by author, first edition with dust jacket: $100.00

OLIVER, Marjorie Mary
A-Riding We Will Go, Lutterworth, London, 1951, b/w illustrations by Stanley Lloyd, first edition with dust jacket: $30.00

Ponies and Caravans, Country Life, 1941, with Eva Ducat, b/w photo illustrations, first edition with dust jacket: $30.00

Riddle of the Tired Pony, Children's Press, 1964, illustrated by Drake Brookshaw, first edition with dust jacket: $30.00

OLSON, Gene
Bonus Boy: The Story of a Southpaw Pitcher, Dodd, Mead, 1964, first edition with dust jacket: $30.00

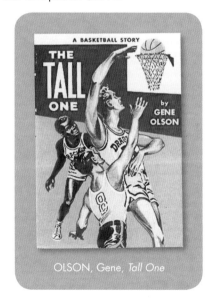

OLSON, Gene, *Tall One*

Tall One, a Basketball Story, Dodd, Mead, 1956, first edition with dust jacket: $80.00

O'NEILL, Mary
Hailstones and Halibut Bones, Doubleday, 1961, oversize hardcover, illustrated by Leonard Weisgard, first edition with dust jacket: $30.00

White Palace, Crowell, 1966, blue oversize hardcover, color and b/w illustrations by Nonny Hogrogian, first edition with dust jacket: $50.00

O'NEILL, Rose (1875 – 1944), see Series section, KEWPIE BOOKS

OPIE, Iona and Peter
Children's Games in Street and Playground, Oxford University Press, 1969, first edition: $100.00

Classic Fairy Tales, London, Oxford University Press, 1974, hardcover, illustrated, first edition with dust jacket: $50.00

Oxford University Nursery Rhyme Book, Oxford University Press, 1955, 400+ woodcuts from eighteenth and nineteenth century children's books, plus 150 illustrations by Joan Hassall, first edition with dust jacket: $100.00

OPTIC, Oliver (William Adams)
Under the pseudonym of Oliver Optic, Adams wrote dozens of juveniles, some as separate titles, some as series, and in later editions, some titles were mixed and matched to make up a new series or extend a series to a particular length for marketing purposes, so that there can be a confusing crossover of titles.

Oliver Optic's New Story Book, 1902 Hurst, pictorial boards, illustrated: $40.00

ORGEL, Doris
Sarah's Room, Harper & Row, 1963, pictorial cloth cover, illustrated by Maurice Sendak, first edition with dust jacket: $60.00

ORSKA, Krystyna and Miriam Peterson
Special Collection: Illustrated Poems for Children, Hubbard Press, 1973, oversize hardcover, half-bound in navy leatherette, white cloth boards, gilt lettering, color illustrations by Orska, first edition: $50.00

OUIDA (Louise De la Ramee)
Editions vary, and sometimes her pseudonym is used, sometimes her name, on the same stories.

Bimbi, Stories for Children, 1910 editon, J. B. Lippincott, red cloth-over-board cover, color illustrated by Maria Kirk: $50.00

Dog of Flanders, Nims and Knight, Troy, New York, 1892, small, cloth-over-board cover with gilt, gilt edges: $50.00

OUIDA (Louise De la Ramee), Dog of Flanders

Dog of Flanders, 1931 edition, Albert Whitman, illustrations by Harvey Fuller: $40.00

Moufflou and Other Stories, 1910 edition Lippincott, small, three-color plate illustrations by Maria Kirk, three b/w illustrations by Garrett: $30.00

Nurnberg Stove, 1916 edition, J. B. Lippincott, small, 96 pages, color plates by Maria Kirk: $40.00

OUSLEY, Odille and David H. Russell
Ousley and Russell wrote school reading books.

Around the Corner, Ginn, 1949, reader, pictorial hardcover, 240 pages, color illustrations: $50.00

Little White House, Ginn, 1948, hardcover, illustrations by Ellen Segner: $50.00

On Cherry Street, Ginn, 1948, hardcover, color illustrations: $50.00

Under the Apple Tree, Ginn, 1953: $40.00

OXENBURY, Helen (b. Suffolk, England), author/illustrator

Oxenbury attended the Ipswich School of Art and the Central School of Arts and Crafts, London. At art school, she met her husband, British illustrator John Burningham. Oxenbury pursued a career in theater design while Burningham concentrated on book illustration. After the birth of her first child, Oxenbury also began to design picture books so that she could work at home. She received two Kate Greenaway awards for her illustrations. In the 1980s, Oxenbury wrote and illustrated a series of board books for preschoolers.

Gran and Grandpa, Walker Books, London, 1984, pink illustrated glossy boards, 18 pages, first edition: $40.00

Helen Oxenbury's A B C of Things, 1971 Franklin Watts, first edition, with dust jacket: $40.00

Hunting of the Snark, Lewis Carroll poem, Heinemann, UK and Franklin Watts, US, 1970, first edition thus, pictorial oversize hardcover, illustrated by Oxenbury, with dust jacket: $35.00

Number of Things, 1967, Delacorte Press, oblong oversize hardcover, color illustrations, counting book, with dust jacket: $40.00

Nursery Story Book, Heinemann, London,1985, pictorial laminated boards, color illustrations throughout, first edition with dust jacket: $50.00

Pig Tale, Heinemann, UK, 1973, 32 pages, illustrated by author, first edition with dust jacket: $60.00

OXHAM, Elsie J., see Series section, ABBEY SCHOOL

■ ⋯⋯⋯⋯⋯⋯ **P** ⋯⋯⋯⋯⋯⋯ ■

PACKER, Eleanor
Packer wrote several books featuring Jane Withers, including a Whitman mystery and a Better Little Book.

Jane Withers, Her Life Story, Whitman, 1936, softcover with photo illustrations: $50.00

PAGE, Thomas Nelson
Captured Santa Claus, Scribner, 1902, illustrated: $60.00

PACKER, Eleanor, *Jane Withers*

Santa Claus's Partner, Charles Scribner's Sons, 1899, half-leather cover with gilt, marbled endpapers, 170+ pages, color title page vignette, seven color plates by W. Glackens: $100.00

Tommy Trot's Visit to Santa Claus, Charles Scribner's Sons, 1908, 94 pages, illustrated by Victor C. Anderson: $60.00

Two Little Confederates, Charles Scribner's Sons, 1888, Civil War story for children, oversize, pictorial gray cloth with gilt, frontis and seven plates: $150.00

PAINE, Albert Bigelow (1861 – 1937), see also Series section, HOLLOW TREE

Arkansaw Bear, a Tale of Fanciful Adventure, R. H. Russell, New York, 1898, oversize, decorated paper covered boards, cloth spine, 118 pages, illustrated by Frank Ver Beck: $80.00

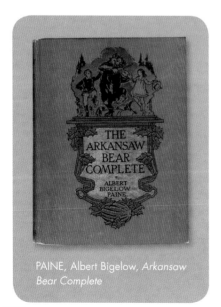

PAINE, Albert Bigelow, *Arkansaw Bear Complete*

Arkansaw Bear Complete, 1929 edition, Altemus, includes *Arkansaw Bear* and *Arkansaw Bear and Elsie*, red cloth-over-board cover with impressed decoration with gilt, illustrated endpapers, 297 pages, ten color plates plus b/w illustrations throughout by Frank Ver Beck: $50.00

Elsie and the Arkansaw Bear, Henry Altemus, 1909, cloth binding with stamped decoration, 31 color illustrations by Frank Ver Beck: $50.00

PAINE, Ralph D.

Blackbeard Buccaneer, Penn, 1922, illustrated paste-on, color frontispiece and b/w illustrations by Frank Schooner, first edition: $100.00

Head Coach, Scribner, 1910, cloth-over-board cover, six b/w illustrations by George Wright: $40.00

Privateers of '76, Penn, 1923, cloth-over-board cover with paste-on-illustration, color illustrated by Frank Schoonover: $50.00

PALAZZO, Tony, author/illustrator

Animal Babies, Garden City Books, 1960, oversize, pictorial covers, first edition: $60.00

Bianco and the New World, Viking Press, 1957, oversize, front paste-down, pictorial endpapers, 64 pages: $50.00

Tales of Don Quixote and His Friends, Garden City Books, 1958, oversize, story retold and illustrated by Tony Palazzo: $50.00

Giant Playtime Nursery Book, 1959 Garden City Books, first edition, hardcover, illustrated by author: $40.00

Great Othello: The Story of a Seal, Viking Press, 1952, first edition: $50.00

Let's Go to the Circus, Doubleday, 1961, first edition: $60.00

Susie the Cat, Viking Press, 1949, oversize, first edition with dust jacket: $60.00

PALMER, George Herbert

Odyssey of Homer, Houghton Mifflin, 1929, illustrated by N.C. Wyeth, first edition: $125.00

PALTENGHI, Madalena

Honey on a Raft, Garden City, 1941, illustrations by C. W. Anderson, first edition with dust jacket: $50.00

Honey the City Bear, Grosset & Dunlap, 1937, oversize, 31 pages, illustrated paper-over-board cover, illustrations by C. W. Anderson, first edition with dust jacket: $50.00

PALTOCK, Robert

Life and Adventures of Peter Wilkins, (1751), 1928 edition, Dent, London, oversize, 342 pages, blue cloth-over-board cover with gilt, illustrations by Edward Bawden: $50.00

PAPE, Eric (1870 – 1938)

An American illustrator for Macmillan, Eric Pape ran an art school in Boston and is often listed as a major influence by many of the children's book illustrators of the 1920s and 1930s.

PARDOE, M., see Series section, ARGLE TRILOGY

PARRISH, Anne

(Anne and Dillwyn Parrish were the children of artist Maxfield Parrish)

PARRISH, Anne, *Floating Island*

Dream Coach Fare: Forty Winks Coach Leaves Every Night for No One Knows Where... (Anne and Dillwyn), Macmillan,

New York, 1924, gold stamped star pattern on cover, illustrated by the author, first edition: $120.00

Floating Island, Harper & Row, 1930, paste-on-pictorial, illustrated throughout by author, first edition with dust jacket: $250.00. First edition without dust jacket: $120.00

Story of Appleby Capple, Harper & Brothers, 1950, oversize, 184 pages, first edition with dust jacket: $60.00

PARRISH, Maxfield (1870 – 1966), artist

Parrish was the son of a landscape painter, studied architecture in college, then art at the Pennsylvania Academy of Fine Arts. He also studied with Howard Pyle. His permanent home was in New

PARRISH, Maxfield, *Illustration from Arabian Nights*

PARRISH, Maxfield, *Illustration from Knave of Hearts.*

Hampshire. Time spent in Arizona for his health, and in Italy illustrating a garden book, influenced his work. He combined New Hampshire oaks, Arizona mountains and Italian sunshine, cypress and temples in his lush paintings. Books illustrated include *Hawthorne's Tanglewood Tales,* an edition of *Arabian Nights* edited by Nora Smith and Kate Douglas Wiggins, Baum's *Mother Goose in Prose,* and Louise Saunders's *Knave of Hearts.*

PARRY, Judge Edward Abbott

Butter-Scotia, or, *A Cheap Trip to Fairy Land,* London, David Nutt, 1896, pictorial cloth cover, illustrated by Archie MacGregor: $200.00

Don Quixote, retold by Parry, Blackie, 1900, oversize, pictorial cloth with picture of the Don mounted on Rosinante, color plates and b/w drawings by Walter Crane: $100.00

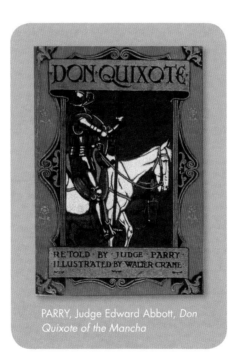

PARRY, Judge Edward Abbott, *Don Quixote of the Mancha*

PARTCH, Virgil, see VIP

PATCHETT, Mary Elwyn

Ajax: Golden Dog of the Australian Bush, Bobbs-Merrill, 1953, illustrated by Eric Tansley, first edition with dust jacket: $40.00

Tam the Untamed, Bobbs-Merrill, 1955, Gerald McCann illustrations, life on an

Australian cattle station, first edition with dust jacket: $70.00

PAULL, Grace (1898 – 1990)

New Yorker Paull began her art career as a greeting card designer, then moved into book illustration in the 1930s. At one point, Paull shared a studio with Helen Sewell, another popular illustrator of the time. Early works include Margery Bianco's *Street of Little Shops* (1932), and *Good Friends* (1934).

PAULL, Grace, *Come to the City*

Come to the City, Abelard, 1959, color illustrations, first edition: $40.00

Gloomy the Camel, Viking Press, 1938, pictorial hardcover, illustrated endpapers, color illustrations, first edition: $50.00

PAYNE, Joan Balfour

General Billycock's Pigs, Hastings House, 1961, blue hardcover, 64 pages, author illustrated, first edition with dust jacket: $30.00

Leprechaun of Bayou Luce, Hastings House, 1957, first edition with dust jacket: $50.00

Magnificent Milo, Hastings House, 1958, 64 pages, illustrated by author, adventures of a centaur, first edition with dust jacket: $40.00

PAYSON, Howard, see Series section, MOTOR CYCLE CHUMS

PEAKE, Mervyn, see Series section, GORMENGHAST

PEARCE, Philippa

Dog So Small, Constable, 1962, hardcover, illustrated by Antony Maitland, first edition with dust jacket: $30.00

PEARCE, Philippa, *Mrs. Cockle's Cat*

Mrs. Cockle's Cat, London, Constable, 1961, Kate Greenaway Medal for the b/w illustrations by Antony Maitland, first edition with dust jacket: $70.00

Squirrel Wife, Crowell, 1972, illustrated by Derek Collard, US first edition with dust jacket: $30.00

Tom's Midnight Garden, J. B. Lippincott, 1959, Carnegie medal winner, b/w illustrations by Susan Einzig, US first edition with dust jacket: $50.00

What the Neighbors Did and Other Stories, Longmans Young, 1972, green hardcover with gilt lettering on spine, 120 pages, b/w text illustrations by Faith Jaques, first edition with dust jacket: $30.00

PEARY, Josephine D.

Snow Baby, Frederick A. Stokes, 1901, oversize, impressed design and lettering on cloth-over-board cover with paste-on-pictorial photo, 84 pages, photo illustrations throughout: $150.00

PEARY, Josephine D., *Snow Baby*

PEARY, Marie Ahnighito (daughter of Josephine Peary)

Children of the Arctic, written by Snow Baby and her mother, Josephine Peary, Stokes, 1903, photo paste-on, illustrated with photographs, first edition: $150.00

Little Tooktoo, the Story of Santa Claus' Youngest Reindeer, William Morrow, 1930, red cloth with color pictorial paste-down, 62 pages, Christmas tale illustrated by Kurt Wiese with color plates and line illustrations: $100.00

Ootah and His Puppy, Heath, 1942, cloth-over-board cover with paste-on-illustration, small, 64 pages, map endpapers, color and b/w illustrations by Kurt Wiese: $50.00

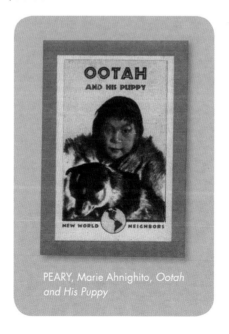

PEARY, Marie Ahnighito, *Ootah and His Puppy*

Red Caboose, Morrow, 1932, cloth-over-board cover, red/b/w illustrations by Horvath: $55.00

Snow Baby's Own Story, Frederick A. Stokes, 1934, cloth-over-board cover, first edition with dust jacket: $50.00

PEASE, Howard

Captain Binnacle, George G. Harrap, UK, 1939, illustrated by Charles E. Pont, first edition: $150.00

Dark Adventure, Doubleday, 1950, first edition with dust jacket: $75.00

Jinx Ship, Doubleday, Page, 1927, pictorial hardcover, illustrated endpapers depicting New York harbor by Mahlon Blaine, first edition with dust jacket: $200.00

Jungle River, Doubleday, Doran, 1938, pictorial leatherette binding, pictorial endpapers, illustrated by Armstrong Sperry, first edition: $100.00

Shipwreck, Doubleday, 1957, first edition with dust jacket: $100.00

Thunderbolt House, Doubleday, Doran, 1944, illustrated by Armstrong Sperry, first edition with dust jacket: $150.00

PEAT, Fern Bisel, artist

Calico Pets, Saalfield, 1931, oversize picture book, linen-like paper cover, full-page color illustrations throughout: $45.00

PEAT, Fern Bisel, illustration from *Calico Pets*

Cinderella, by Katharine Gibson, Harper, 1932, 48 pages, color plate illustrations: $55.00

Four Stories That Never Grow Old, 1943 Sandusky, oversize, 60 pages, color and b/w illustrations: $55.00

Gingerbread Man, 1941 edition, Whitman, oversize, 16 pages, color illustrations throughout: $50.00

PEAT, Fern Bisel, *Mother Goose*

Mother Goose, Saalfield, 1933, hardcover, oversize, color illustrated by Peat, with dust jacket: $65.00

Stories Children Like, Saalfield, 1933, oversize, color illustrated cover, color illustrations throughout: $65.00

Three Little Pigs, Saalfield, 1932, 20 pages, color and b/w illustrations: $50.00

Treasure Book of Best Stories, by Alta Taylor, Saalfield, 1939, oversize, color plate illustrations: $60.00

Ugly Duckling, adaptation of H. Anderson story, 1932, Saalfield, color illustrated paper-over-board cover, illustrations by Peat: $35.00

When Toys Could Talk, text by Jane Randall, Saalfield, 1939, full-page color illustrations, with dust jacket: $80.00

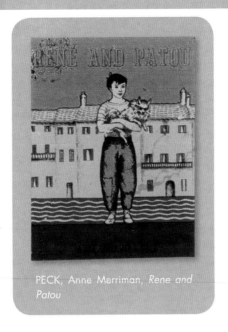

PECK, Anne Merriman, *Rene and Patou*

PECK, Anne Merriman, author/illustrator

Manoel and the Morning Star, Harper, 1943, oversize, 31 pages, color illustrated paper-over-board cover, illustrated endpapers, color plates and b/w illustrations by author: $30.00

René and Patou, Albert Whitman, 1938, illustrated by the author, first edition with dust jacket: $40.00

PECK, Richard, see also Series section, BLOSSOM CULP

Are You in the House Alone?, Viking Press, 1976, first edition with dust jacket: $40.00

Long Way from Chicago, Dial Press, 1978, first edition with dust jacket: $80.00

PEET, Bill, author/illustrator (Disney animator)

Peet began his career by studying at the John Herron Art Institute in Indianapolis. This was followed by 27 years with the Walt Disney Company, one of the few companies actively recruiting artists during the Depression years. While with Disney, Peet first worked on continuity drawings, telling the story of the movie through a series of pictures. This led to writing screenplays and, eventually, to illustrating his own books.

Countdown to Christmas, Golden Gate Junior Books, 1972, illustrated boards, first edition: $60.00

Ella, Houghton Mifflin, 1962, 48 pages, illustrated by author, first edition: $30.00

How Droofus the Dragon Lost His Head, Houghton Mifflin, 1971, oversize, first edition with dust jacket: $40.00

Hubert's Hair Raising Adventure, Houghton Mifflin, 1959, square, Peet's first children's book, first edition with dust jacket: $100.00

Jennifer and Josephine, Houghton Mifflin, 1967, first edition with dust jacket: $80.00

Spooky Tail of Prewitt Peacock, Houghton Mifflin,1972, full-color illustrations, first edition with dust jacket: $50.00

Whingdingdilly, Houghton Mifflin, 1970, oversize, 60 pages, first edition with dust jacket: $70.00

Wump World, Houghton Mifflin, 1970, illustrations by Peet, first edition with dust jacket: $40.00

PEET, Bill, *Wump World*

PENROSE, Margaret, see Series section, MOTOR GIRLS

PEPPE, Rodney

Mice Who Lived in a Shoe, Lothrop, Lee and Shepard Books, 1981, oversize pictorial cover, illustrated by author, US first edition: $30.00

PERRAULT, Charles (1628 – 1703, France)

Author Perrault collected traditional fairy tales from all over Europe. These have been printed both as collections of stories in single volumes and as picture books of a single story. A few of the many hundreds of collectible editions are listed. Single volume collections:

Bluebeard and Other Fairy Tales of Charles Perrault, introduction by Simone De Beauvoir, Macmillan, 1964, pictorial hardcover, illustrated by Saul Lambert: $30.00

Classic French Fairy Tales, Meredith Press, 1967, illustrated by Janusz Grabianski: $100.00

Fairy Garland, Being Fairy Tales from the Old French, Cassell, UK, 1928, and Scribner, US, 1929, hardcover, color plates by Edmund Dulac: $100.00

Fairy Tales of Perrault, Harrap, London, 1922, cloth-over-board hardcover with gilt, oversize, 160 pages, 24 color and b/w plates by Harry Clarke, limited first edition: $700.00. Later printings: $150.00

Old Friends Among the Fairies, Puss in Boots and Other Stories, retold by Andrew Lang, Longmans, Green, UK, 1926, green hardcover, decorated endpapers, 242 pages, color and b/w illustrations by G.P. Jacomb Hood, H. J. Ford, and Lancelot Speed: $50.00

Perrault, single title books:

Beauty and the Beast, McLoughlin, 1893, die-cut shape book resembles a theater, covers open to six fold-out scenes of the story in color, a McLoughlin book-toy: $180.00

Bluebeard, Routledge, London, 1875, oversize pictorial cover, eight color plates by Walter Crane, printed by Edmund Evans: $300.00

Cinderella, Heinemann, 1919, pictorial boards, 110 pages, mounted color plate, plus silhouette and three-tone illustrations

by Arthur Rackham, first trade edition: $300.00

How Cinderella Was Able to Go to the Ball, retold by Jessie King, G.T. Foulis & Co. Ltd., 1924, white pictorial paper-covered boards, ten mounted plates by Jessie M. King, a new take on the story, $700.00

Puss in Boots, Holiday House, 1936, pictorial paper-covered boards, small, wood-engraving illustrations by Fritz Eichenberg: $150.00

Puss in Boots, animation by Julian Wehr, Duenewald Printing, 1944, spiral binding, color illustrated boards, moveable parts, first edition with dust jacket: $300.00. Without dust jacket: $100.00

Puss in Boots, Charles Scribner's Sons, 1952, oversize yellow hardcover, color illustrations by Marcia Brown, first edition with dust jacket: $80.00

Story of Bluebeard, 1895, Stone & Kimball, Chicago, and Lawrence & Bullen, London, green decorated cloth, decorated title page, 61 pages, red/black print, engraved illustrations and decorative borders by Joseph Southall: $70.00

PERRY, Nora

Another Flock of Girls, Houghton Mifflin, 1890, cloth-over-board cover, eight b/w plates by Reginald Birch and Charles Copeland: $30.00

Flock of Girls, Houghton Mifflin, 1887, cloth-over-board cover with gilt illustration, eight b/w plates: $30.00

PETERSHAM, Maud (1889 – 1971) and Miska (1888 – 1960), authors/illustrators

Hungarian Miska emigrated to the United States in 1912 and met his future wife, Maud Fuller, while she was working at the International Art Service. At first they illustrated the works of other writers, but by 1929 they were writing and illustrating their own stories.

Box with Red Wheels, Macmillan, 1949, illustrated paper-over-board cover, oversize picture book, color illustrations by authors: $50.00

PETERSHAM, Maud and Miska, *Circus Baby*

Circus Baby, Macmillan, 1950, color illustrated paper-over-board cover, oversize picture book, 28 pages, color illustrations by authors, first edition with dust jacket: $60.00

Get-A-Way and Hary János, Viking Press, 1933, illustrated paper-over-board cover, oversize picture book, color illustrations by authors, first edition with dust jacket: $125.00

Off to Bed, Macmillan, 1954, first edition with dust jacket: $90.00

Peppernuts, Macmillan, 1958, small hardcover, first edition with dust jacket: $50.00

PETERSHAM, Maud and Miska, *Get-A-Way and Hary János*

Shepherd Psalm, Macmillan, 1962, over-size hardcover, first edition with dust jacket: $40.00

Silver Mace, a Story of Williamsburg, Macmillan, 1956, pictorial hardcover, first edition with dust jacket: $30.00

PETRY, Ann

Drugstore Cat, Crowell, 1949, red cloth boards, 87 pages, illustrated by Susanne Suba, first edition with dust jacket: $150.00

Tituba of Salem Village, Crowell, 1964, first edition with dust jacket: $80.00

PEYTON, K. M.

British author Kathleen Wendy Herald Peyton has written more than 50 books for young adults, including several early collaborations with her husband Michael (the "M" in the K. M.). Her *Flambards* trilogy was adapted for television and remains one of her most popular series.

Flambards, Oxford University Press, 1967, illustrated by Victor Ambrus, the first book about the Edwardian house and its occupants, first edition with dust jacket: $75.00

PHELPS, Elizabeth Stuart (1844 – 1911)

Supply at Saint Agatha's, 1899 edition Houghton Mifflin, green cloth-over-board cover with gilt, b/w plates by E. Boyd Smith and Marcia Woodbury: $50.00

Trotty's Wedding Tour, and Story-Book, James R. Osgood, 1874, hardcover, 224 pages, illustrated by Augustus Hoppin: $100.00

PHILLIPS, Ethel Calvert

Belinda and the Singing Clock, Houghton Mifflin, 1938, 112 pages, illustrated by Virginia Lee Burton: $100.00

Calico, Houghton Mifflin, 1937, color illustrated frontispiece, b/w illustrations by Maginal Wright Barney: $40.00

Little Rag Doll, Houghton Mifflin, 1930, cloth-over-board cover with paste-on-pictorial, 174 pages, illustrated endpapers, four-color plates by Lois Lenski: $100.00

Lively Adventures of Johnny Ping Wing, Houghton Mifflin, 1929, hardcover, illustrations by Jack Perkins: $30.00

Name for Obid, Houghton Mifflin, 1941, cloth-over-board cover, oversize, illustrated endpapers, b/w/blue illustrations by Lois Lenski, first edition with dust jacket: $100.00

Wee Ann, a Story for Little Girls, Houghton Mifflin, 1919, blue cloth-over-board cover, small, illustrated endpapers, four-color illustrations by Edith Butler: $40.00

PIATTI, Celestino

Happy Owls, Atheneum, 1964, oblong oversize hardcover, color illustrations by author, US first edition with dust jacket: $40.00

Nock Family Circus, Atheneum, 1968, oblong oversize hardcover, color illustrations by author, US first edition with dust jacket: $50.00

PIERCE, Meredith Ann, see also Series section, FIREBRINGER TRILOGY

Darkangel, Atlantic Monthly, 1982, dust jacket by Mark English, first edition with dust jacket: $70.00

PIERCE, Meredith Ann, *Darkangel*

PIERCE, Robert

Grin and Giggle Book, Golden Press, 1972, oversize, pictorial hardcover, first edition: $40.00

Terrible Beast from the Deep, Golden Press, 1967, laminated boards, first edition with dust jacket: $80.00

PIERCE, Tamora, see Series section, SONG OF THE LIONESS.

PIERSON, Clara Dillingham

Among the Pond People, E. P. Dutton, 1901, small, decorated cover with gilt, b/w illustrations by F. C. Gordon: $70.00

Dooryard Stories, E. P. Dutton, 1903, small, 10 full-page color illustrations by F. C. Gordon, nature stories, first edition: $70.00

Tales of a Poultry Farm, E. P. Dutton, 1904, pictorial hardcover with gilt, eight full-page b/w plates: $100.00

PINKWATER, Daniel Manus, author/illustrator, see also Series section, BLUE MOOSE, MAGIC MOSCOW

PINKWATER, Daniel Manus, *Big Orange Splot*

Although admired as much for his writing as his illustrations, Pinkwater's college career emphasized fine art. He studied sculpture at Bard College.

Big Orange Splot, Hastings House, 1977, first edition with dust jacket: $60.00

Blue Thing, Prentice-Hall, 1977, first edition with dust jacket: $100.00

Worms of Kukumlima, E. P. Dutton, 1981, first edition with dust jacket: $100.00

PIPER, Watty (editorial name created by Platt & Munk)

Bumper Book: A Collection of Stories and Verses for Children, Platt & Munk, 1946, oversize, full-size color paste-down on front board, illustrations by Eulalie: $100.00

Brimful Book, Platt & Munk, 1927, oversize, cloth-over-board cover with paste-on-pictorial, color and b/w illustrations by Eulalie, C. M. Burd, W. Gurney: $90.00

PIPER, Watty, *Brimful Book*

Fairy Tales That Never Grow Old, Platt & Munk, 1927, oversize, cloth-over-board cover with paste-on-pictorial, color and b/w illustrations by Eulalie, Lenski, and Colborne: $100.00

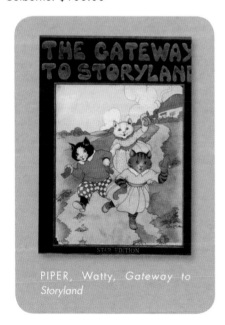

PIPER, Watty, *Gateway to Storyland*

Famous Fairy Tales, Platt, 1923, oversize, brown cloth-over-board cover with gilt let-

tering and paste-on-illustration, color illustrations throughout by Eulalie: $100.00

Gateway to Storyland, Platt & Munk, 1925, oversize, green cloth-over-board cover with gilt lettering and paste-on-illustration, color illustrations throughout by Eulalie: $100.00

Little Folks of Other Lands, Platt & Munk, 1929, oversize, blue cloth-over-board cover with paste-on illustration, color map endpapers, b/w and full-page color illustrations by Lucille W. and H. C. Holling: $100.00

Nursery Tales Children Love, Platt & Munk, 1925, oversize picture book, paste-on-pictorial cover, color illustrations throughout by Eulalie and others: $100.00

PIPER, Watty, *Nursery Tales Children Love*

PITZ, Henry (1895 – 1976)

American illustrator Henry Pitz worked for *St. Nicholas* and the *Saturday Evening Post* as well as illustrated more than 160 books. Pitz also wrote several books on illustration, including one on drawing for children's books.

PLATT, Kin

Ghost of Hellsfire Street, Delacorte Press 1980, another Steve and Sinbad adventure, first edition with dust jacket: $80.00

Mystery of the Witch Who Wouldn't, Chilton Books, 1969, first edition with dust jacket: $80.00

Sinbad and Me, Chilton Books, 1966, illustrated by Charles Geer, first edition with dust jacket: $250.00

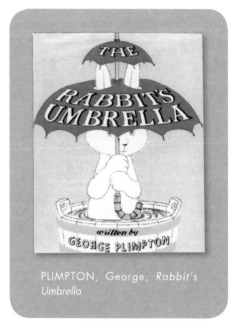

PLIMPTON, George, *Rabbit's Umbrella*

PLIMPTON, George

Rabbit's Umbrella, 1955, Viking Press, illustrated by William Pène du Bois, first edition with dust jacket: $100.00

POGANY, Nandor

Hungarian Fairy Book, Frederick A. Stokes, ca. 1915, illustrated by Willy Pogany, US first edition with dust jacket: $400.00

Magyar Fairy Tales, E. P. Dutton, 1930, green cloth-over-board cover with gilt, 268 pages, illustrations by Willy Pogany: $80.00

POGANY, Willy (1882 – 1955), illustrator

Hungarian artist Pogany emigrated to the United States in 1915 after working in England. Major influences on his work were Oriental artists and illuminated books. Besides illustration, he designed theatrical productions and worked as an art director in Hollywood. Children's books illustrated by Pogany include several of Padriac Colum's works and a 1929 edition of Carroll's *Alice in Wonderland.*

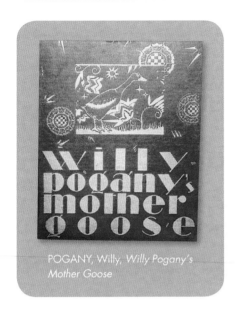

POGANY, Willy, *Willy Pogany's Mother Goose*

Willy Pogany's Mother Goose, Thomas Nelson, 1928, hardcover, color illustrations throughout by Pogany: $600.00

POHLMANN, Lillian
Myrtle Albertina's Song, Coward-McCann, 1958, b/w illustrations by Erik Blegvad, first edition with dust jacket: $40.00

POLITI, Leo (1908 – 1996), author/illustrator

Born in California, Politi moved to Italy with his parents when he was seven and studied art there at the National Art Institute of Monza. In 1931, he returned to the United States. Much of his work reflects his home city of Los Angeles and the lives of the immigrants who settled in Southern California.

Boat for Peppe, Scribner, 1950, illustrated by Politi, first edition with dust jacket: $100.00

Bunker Hill, Los Angeles, Reminiscences of Bygone Days, Dester-Southwest, 1964, color illustrations by Politi, first edition with dust jacket: $100.00

Butterflies Come, Scribner, 1957, oversize hardcover, 28 pages, illustrated by author, first edition with dust jacket: $50.00

Lito and the Clown, Scribner, 1964, pictorial hardcover, color illustrations by author, first edition with dust jacket: $100.00

Little Leo, Scribner, 1951, illustrated by author, first edition with dust jacket: $50.00

Mieko, Scott Foresman edition, 1969, oversize hardcover, illustrated by author, with dust jacket: $50.00

Mission Bell, Scribner, 1953, oversize hardcover, illustrated by author, first edition with dust jacket: $90.00

Nicest Gift, Scribner, 1973, illustrated by author, first edition with dust jacket: $80.00

Pedro, the Angel of Olvera Street, Scribner, 1946, cloth-over-board cover, color illustrations by author, first edition with dust jacket: $80.00

POLITI, Leo, *Song of the Swallows*

Song of the Swallows, Scribner, 1948, oversize picture book, paste-on illustrated cover, color illustrations by author, first edition: $80.00

POPE, Elizabeth M.
Perilous Gard, Houghton Mifflin, 1974, first edition with dust jacket: $65.00

Sherwood Ring, Houghton Mifflin, 1958, first edition with dust jacket: $50.00

PORTER, Eleanor, see Series section, GLAD BOOKS

PORTER, Jane
Scottish Chiefs, Scribner, 1921, 14 color plates and paste-on pictorial cover, illustrations by N. C. Wyeth, first edition: $125.00

POSTGATE, Oliver and Peter Firmin,
see Series section, IVOR THE ENGINE, NOGGIN

POTTER, Helen Beatrix (1866 – 1943)
author/illustrator

Peter Rabbit was originally conceived as a letter to amuse a sick child and the story was published by Potter herself in a small black-and-white edition. The book was then bought by the Frederick Warne company which published it in color. Potter preferred a small book designed to be held by small hands for most of her work but Warne did experiment with several different formats and sizes. From 1902 to 1909, Potter wrote and illustrated two books per year.

After her marriage to William Heelis, she slowed down her writing and concentrated on sheep breeding. Her home, Hilltop Farm, is now part of the National Trust. Her books were almost instantly best-sellers, with *Peter Rabbit* achieving sales of 50,000 books by 1903. However, firsts rarely survived their nursery days and are difficult to find in good condition. Warne also produced or licensed numerous toys, china, and other items based on the author's original artwork.

Tale of Peter Rabbit, privately printed by Potter with a flat back, 250 copies, December, 1901, followed by a second edition, round back, 200 copies, February, 1902: $50,000.00 range

Tailor of Gloucester, privately printed by Potter, 500 copies, 1902: $50,000.00 range

The Frederick Warne editions were printed with color illustrations and in the small format of the first book, except when noted.

First editions are hard to identify. Potter reference bibliographies can help with identification. The books have remained in print and old editions that are not firsts are available in many price ranges.

Potter, Warne, 1902 – 1908 first editions with original dust wrappers: $14,000.00 to $20,000.00

Potter, Warne, 1902 – 1908 first editions without wrappers: $8,000.00 to $12,000.00

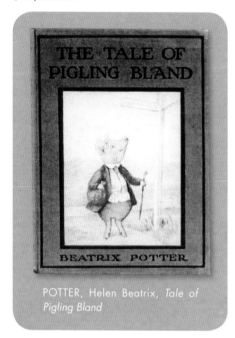

POTTER, Helen Beatrix, *Tale of Pigling Bland*

Tale of Peter Rabbit, 1902 (first edition points: page 51 text "wept big tears" was changed to "shed big tears" in later printings), gray-blue leaf pattern endpapers, both brown and blue paper boards reported for early editions

Tailor of Gloucester, 1903

Tale of Squirrel Nutkin, 1903

Tale of Benjamin Bunny, 1904

Tale of Two Bad Mice, 1904

Pie and the Patty-Pan, 1905, large format, 7⅛" by 5½", 51 pages

Tale of Mrs. Tiggy-Winkle, 1905

Tale of Mr. Jeremy Fisher, 1906

Tale of Tom Kitten, 1907

Roly-Poly Pudding, 1908, large format, later issued as *Tale of Samuel Whiskers*

Tale of Jemima Puddle-Duck, 1908

Potter, Warne, 1909 – 1913 first editions with original dust wrappers: $6,000.00 to $10,000.00

Potter, Warne, 1909 – 1913 first editions without wrappers: $800.00 to $5,000.00

Ginger and Pickles, 1909, large format, values start at $500.00 for this format

Tale of the Flopsy Bunnies, 1909

Tale of Mrs. Tittlemouse, 1910

Tale of Timmey Tiptoes, 1911

Tale of Mr. Tod, 1912

Tale of Pigling Bland, 1913

Potter, Warne, 1909 – 1918 first editions with original dust wrappers: $6,000.00 to $10,000.00

Potter, Warne, 1909 – 1918 first editions without wrappers: $1,000.00 to $5,000.00

Story of Miss Moppet, 1916 (first published in 1906 in the panoramic format)

Story of a Fierce Bad Rabbit, 1916 (first published in 1906 in the panoramic format)

Tale of Johnny Town-Mouse, 1918

Potter, Warne, from 1919 on:

Tale of Samuel Whiskers, 1926 (originally issued as *Roly-Poly Pudding*), first of 1926 editions: $900.00

Tale of Little Pig Robinson, 1930, first edition in dust jacket: $1,500.00

Potter, Warne, reprints: Since the majority of titles listed have stayed in print continuously, the value of later editions drops significantly. Generally, books reprinted within one year of the first edition date retail for half of the starting price of first editions. Much later reprints, such as those done in the 1960s, tend to sell in the same price range as new editions.

Tailor of Gloucester, Limited Edition Club, 1968, facsimile of Potter's original, 1,500 copies, with slipcase: $250.00

Potter, Warne, activity books, early editions: Warne continues to issue activity books for children based upon Potter's stories.

Activity books, depending on condition, $50.00 to $600.00:

Peter Rabbit's Painting Book, 1911

Tom Kitten's Painting Book, 1917

Jemima Puddle-Duck's Painting Book, 1925

Potter, Warne, *Nursery Rhymes*, first editions: $1,000.00

Appley Dapply's Nursery Rhymes, 1917

Cecily Parsley's Nursery Rhymes, 1922

POTTER, Helen Beatrix, *Story of a Fierce Bad Rabbit*

Potter, Warne, panoramic form, issued as a fold-out book where the whole story could be seen at once, this format was disliked by booksellers due to the fragile nature and was quickly withdrawn from the market. 14 illustrations and 14 pages of text were folded accordian style into a cloth wallet-style case. Cracks or breaks in folds reduce price significantly.

Story of Miss Moppet, 1906: $1,000.00

Story of a Fierce Bad Rabbit, 1906: $1,000.00

Potter, David McKay, first editions: In the late 1920s, Alexander McKay of David McKay, Philadelphia, met Potter and persuaded her to give him the right to publish three new books.

McKay first editions with dust jackets: $900.00

McKay first editions without jackets: $300.00

Fairy Caravan, 1929

Tale of Little Pig Robinson, 1930

Sister Anne, 1932

Potter, bibliographical references:

History of the Writings of Beatrix Potter, Leslie Linder, 1971, Warne, this is a full description of Potter's work and first editions by the collector who later donated his collection to the Victoria and Albert Museum.

Beatrix Potter: A Bibliographical Check List, Jane Quinby, 2001, Martino, reprint of a Potter reference originally published in 1954.

POTTER, Miriam Clark, see also Series section, MRS. GOOSE

Captain Sandman, E. P. Dutton, 1926, illustrated by Sophia T. Balcom: $90.00

Copperfield Summer, Follett, 1967, first edition with dust jacket: $50.00

Gigglebits, Volland, 1918, small, color illustrations by Tony Sarg: $100.00

Littlebits, J. B. Lippincott, 1951, b/w illustrations by Potter: $100.00

POULSSON, Emilie
Songs of a Little Child's Day, Milton Bradley, 1910, oversize, illustrated cover, 117 pages, color plates by Ruth E. Newton: $40.00

POWERS, Tom
Scotch Circus, the Story of Tammas who Rode the Dragon, Houghton Mifflin, 1934, 94 pages, frontispiece and three double-page color illustrations by Lois Lenski: $80.00

PRATCHETT, Terry
Carpet People, Colin Smythe, 1971, dark green hardcover, gilt title on spine, 195 pages, b/w illustrations by author, first edition with dust jacket: $400.00

PRATT, Anna
Friends from My Garden, Frederick A. Stokes, 1890, square, white enameled cover decorated with gilt and colors, 12 color plates by Laura Hill: $150.00

PRELUTSKY, Jack
Terrible Tiger, Macmillan, London, 1970, oversize illustrated hardcover, color illustrations by Arnold Lobel, first edition with dust jacket: $50.00

PREUSSLER, Otfried
Further Adventures of the Robber Hotzenplotz, Abelard-Schuman, London, 1970, illustrated by F.J. Tripp, first edition with dust jacket: $40.00

Little Ghost, Hodder & Stoughton, 1976, illustrated softcover, illustrations by F. J. Tripp: $30.00

Robber Hotzenplotz, Abelard-Schuman, London, 1965, hardcover, illustrated by F. J. Tripp, first edition with dust jacket: $40.00

Satanic Mill, Abelard-Schuman, UK, or Macmillan, US, 1973, first edition with dust jacket: $30.00

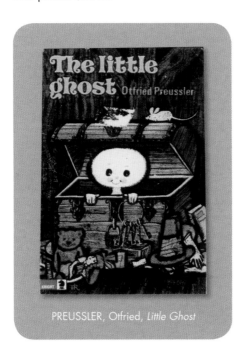

PREUSSLER, Otfried, *Little Ghost*

Wise Men of Schilda, Abelard-Shuman, 1962, hardcover: $40.00. With dust jacket: $60.00

PRICE, Margaret Evans, author/illustrator

Child's Book of Myths, Rand McNally, 1924, cloth-over-board cover with paste-on-pictorial, 111 pages, color illustrations by author: $90.00

PRICE, Margaret Evans, *Child's Book of Myths*

Enchantment Tales for Children, Child's Book of Myths, Rand McNally, 1926, cloth-over-board cover with paste-on-pictorial, color illustrations by author: $70.00

Legends of the Seven Seas, Harper, 1929, color frontispiece, b/w illustrations, first edition with dust jacket: $50.00

Mota and the Monkey Tree, Harper, 1935, illustrated by author, first edition with dust jacket: $90.00

PRICE, Olive
Donkey with Diamond Ears, Coward-McCann, 1962, illustrated by Mel Hunter, first edition with dust jacket: $50.00

PRICE, Willard, see Series section, HAL AND ROGER HUNT

PRIESTLEY, J. B.
Snoggle, Heinemann, UK, and Harcourt Brace, US, 1972, hardcover, first edition with dust jacket: $40.00

PRIESTLEY, J. B., *Snoggle*

PRISHVIN, M.

Treasure Trove of the Sun, Viking Press, 1952, oversize hardcover, illustrated by Feodor Rojankovsky, first edition with dust jacket: $50.00

PROCTOR, Beth

Little Sally Dutcher, Jordan, Chicago,1924, pictorial boards, color illustrated endpapers, color illustrations throughout by Fay Turpin, first edition: $50.00

Tale of a Lucky Dog, Albert Whitman, 1931, illustrated by Fay Turpin, first edition with dust jacket: $70.00

PROTTER, Eric

Monster Festival: Classic Tales of the Macabre, Vanguard, 1965, half-bound gilt-stamped hardcover, color and b/w illustrations by Edward Gorey, first edition with dust jacket: $60.00

PROUDFIT, Isabel, see Series section, FAMILY

PROVENSEN, Alice and Martin, authors/ illustrators

Animal Fair, Simon & Schuster, Giant Golden Book, 1953, oversize laminated cover, color illustrations by Martin and Alice Provensen, first edition with dust jacket: $70.00

Glorious Flight: Across the Channel with Louis Bleriot, Viking Press, 1983, oblong, 39 pages, first edition with dust jacket: $50.00

PROVENSEN, Alice and Martin, *Peaceable Kingdom: The Shaker Abecedarius*

Our Animal Friends at Maple Hill Farm, Random House, 1984, printed boards, first edition: $80.00

Peaceable Kingdom: The Shaker Abecedarius, Viking Press, 1978, New York Times Best Book of the Year winner, first edition with dust jacket: $80.00

PROVINES, Mary Virginia

Liz'beth Ann's Goat, Viking Press, 1947, oversize picture book, 40 pages, color illustrated paper-over-board cover, color illustrated by Grace Paull, first edition with dust jacket: $40.00

PROYSEN, Alf, see Series section, MRS. PEPPERPOT

PRUD'HOMMEAUX, Rene

Mystery of Marr's Hill, Macrae Smith, 1958, space adventure, first edition with dust jacket: $60.00

PUTNAM, Nina Wilcox, *Sunny Bunny*

PUTNAM, Nina Wilcox

Sunny Bunny, Volland, Chicago, 1918, small illustrated cover, color illustrations throughout by Johnny Gruelle, first edition: $100.00

PUZO, Mario

Runaway Summer of Davie Shaw, Platt & Munk, 1966, illustrated by Stewart Sherwood, first edition with dust jacket: $50.00

PYLE, Howard (1853 – 1911), artist/ author, see also Series section, KING ARTHUR

New Englander Pyle's Brandywine art school included many famous illustrators such as Maxfield Parrish, Jessie Willcox Smith, and N. C. Wyeth.

Garden Behind the Moon: A Real Story of the Moon Angel, Charles Scribner's Sons, 1895, cloth cover, 192 pages, b/w illustrations: $150.00

Howard Pyle's Book of Pirates, Harper & Bros., 1921, dark maroon, morocco leather cover, 36 plates, 12 in color: $1,000.00

PYLE, Howard, *King Stork*

King Stork, 1973 edition, Little, Brown, first edition thus, illustrated oversize hardcover, 48 pages, color illustrations by Trina Schart Hyman, with dust jacket: $50.00

Men of Iron, 1919, Harper & Bros., cloth-over-board cover, illustrations by author, first edition with dust jacket: $100.00

Merry Adventures of Robin Hood of Great Renown, in Nottinghamshire, Charles

PYLE, Howard, illustration from *Men of Iron*

Scribner's Sons, 1883, oversize, blue cloth lettered in gilt, b/w illustrations, first edition: $1,500.00

Otto of the Silver Hand, Charles Scribner's Sons, 1888, illustrated throughout: $500.00

Pepper and Salt or Seasoning for Young Folk, Harper & Brothers, 1886, decorated cloth cover, Pyle's first book, first edition: $200.00

Pepper and Salt or Seasoning for Young Folk, Harper & Brothers, 1913 edition, with dust jacket: $80.00

Ruby of Kishmoor, Harper & Brothers, 1908, pictorial cloth boards with gilt, ten color plates: $130.00

Stolen Treasure, Harper & Brothers, 1907, small, orange cloth boards, black lettering and decorative elements, color pictorial paper onlay, frontispiece with tissue guard, 254 pages, eight b/w illustrations by Pyle, four pirate stories: $130.00

Twilight Land, Harper & Brothers, 1895, decorated green boards backed with a light brown calf spine, titled in gilt with illustration, full-page and textual illustrations throughout by Howard Pyle, first edition: $250.00

Wonder Clock, Harper & Brothers, 1888, half leather cover, Pyle illustrations: $150.00

Yankee Doodle, an Old Friend in a New Dress, Dodd, Mead & Company, 1881, oversize, glazed pictorial boards, illustrations throughout by Pyle, first edition with slipcase: $1,500.00

PYLE, Howard, *Pepper and Salt or Seasoning for Young Folk*

PYLE, Katharine, author/illustrator

Black-Eyed Puppy (1923), 1931 edition, Dutton, green cloth-over-board cover with gilt lettering and paste-on-pictorial, 89 pages, 12 color plates by author: $30.00

Charlemagne and His Knights, J. B. Lippincott, 1932, red boards with gilt knights, color frontispiece, b/w illustrations, first edition with dust jacket: $70.00

Counterpane Fairy, E. P. Dutton, 1898, green cloth with gilt, 191 pages, b/w illustrations by Katharine Pyle, Pyle's first book, first edition: $400.00

Fairy Tales from India, J. B. Lippincott, 1926, cloth-over-board cover, 12 color plates by author: $125.00

Nancy Rutledge, Little, Brown, 1906, printed illustration on cloth-over-board cover, 206 pages, six b/w plates by author, first edition: $90.00

Rabbit Witch and Other Tales, E. P. Dutton, 1895, collection of nursery rhymes, first edition: $300.00

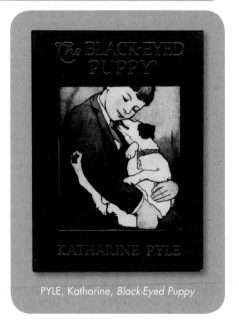

PYLE, Katharine, *Black-Eyed Puppy*

Tales of Folk and Fairies, Little, Brown, 1919, color illustrations by Pyle, first edition: $100.00

Tales of Two Bunnies, E. P. Dutton, 1923, hardcover, b/w illustrations: $50.00

PYRNELLE, Louise Clarke

Diddie, Dumps, and Tot, Harper, 1882, printed illustration on cloth-over-board cover, b/w illustrations, first edition: $150.00

■ ⋯⋯⋯⋯⋯ **Q** ⋯⋯⋯⋯⋯ ■

QUIGG, Jane

Betsy Goes A-Visiting, Oxford University Press, 1940, illustrated by Decie Merwin, first edition with dust jacket: $60.00

Jenny Jones and Skid, Oxford University Press, 1947, 99 pages, illustrated by Eloise Wilkin, first edition with dust jacket: $100.00

Jiggy Likes Nantucket, 1953, Oxford University Press, illustrated by Zhenya Gay: $80.00

Miss Brimble's Happy Birthday, Children's Reader, Oxford University Press, 1955, illustrated, first edition with dust jacket: $100.00

QUIRK, Leslie, see Series section, WELLWORTH COLLEGE

■ ·················· **R** ·················· ■

RACKHAM, Arthur (1867–1939), illustrator

Artist Rackham's illustrations for other authors' works are listed under the names of the authors. He was the most prolific of the Edwardian English illustrators, known best for his detailed pen-and-ink-drawings tinted with raw umber.

Arthur Rackham Fairy Book, George Harrap, 1933, trade edition with eight full-page illustrations, titled tissue guards, and 60 line drawings, cloth binding, first edition with pictorial dust jacket: $2,000.00. Without dust jacket: $500.00

Rackham, additional information:

Latimore, Sarah and Grace Haskell, *Arthur Rackham: A Bibliography,* Suttonhouse, 1936 (reprint: San Marco Bookstore, 1987)

Riall, Richard, *New Bibliography of Arthur Rackham,* Ross Press, 1994

RAE, John, author/illustrator

Granny Goose, Volland, 1926, oversize, pictorial boards, pictorial endpapers and color illustrations throughout: $100.00

RACKHAM, Arthur, illustration from *Peter Pan in Kensington Gardens*

Grasshopper Green and the Meadow-Mice, Algonquin, 1922 (originally published by Volland), illustrated boards, color illustrations throughout, first edition thus: $40.00

Lucy Locket, the Doll with the Pocket, Volland, 1928, pictorial boards, color and b/w illustrations by Rae, first edition: $150.00

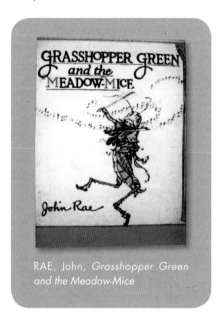

RAE, John, *Grasshopper Green and the Meadow-Mice*

New Adventure of "Alice," Volland, 1917, blue boards with oval onlay of Alice, gilt lettering, color plates and b/w illustrations, first edition: $150.00

RAINBOW, Elizabeth

Concha and the Silver Star, Duell, Sloan & Pearce, 1965, illustrated by George Wilson, first edition with dust jacket: $70.00

Mystery at Witchwood, Weybright & Talley, 1968, first edition with dust jacket: $100.00

RAND, Ann

Edward and the Horse, E. M. Hale, 1964, oversize, illustrated by Olle Eksell, first edition: $90.00

So Small, Harcourt Brace & World, 1962, illustrations by Feodor Rojanovsky, US first edition with dust jacket: $60.00

Umbrella, Hats and Wheels, Harcourt Brace, 1961, first edition, hardcover, illustrated by Jerome Snyder: $30.00

RAND, Ann and Paul

I Know a Lot of Things, Harcourt Brace, 1956, oversize green decorated cloth, color illustrations, first edition with dust jacket: $100.00

RANSOME, Arthur, illustration from *Aladdin and His Wonderful Lamp*

RANSOME, Arthur (1884 – 1967), see also Series section, SWALLOWS AND AMAZONS

Aladdin and His Wonderful Lamp, Ernest Nisbet, 1920, brown buckram, top edge gilt, b/w pictorial endpapers, in rhyme by Ransome, 12 color plates and b/w illustrations by Thomas Mackenzie, color plates mounted on black stock, with descriptive tissue guards, first trade edition: $900.00

Child's Book of Seasons, Anthony Treherne & Company, 1906: $1,500.00

Fool of the World and the Flying Ship, Farrar, Straus & Giroux, 1969, oblong, illustrated by Uri Shulevitz, winner of the 1969 Caldecott, first edition, no medal shown on dust jacket: $40.00

Fool of the World and the Flying Ship, Hamish Hamilton, 1970, oblong, illustrated by Uri Shulevitz, UK first edition: $250.00

Highways and Byways in Fairyland, Pinafore, 1906, blue cover with illustration of fairy and children, part of the Pinafore Library, starts at: $1,200.00

RANSOME, Arthur, *Fool of the World and the Flying Ship*

Hoofmarks of the Faun, Martin Secker, 1911: $500.00

Imp and the Elf and the Ogre, Nisbet, 1910, reprint of earlier Treherne titles: $800.00

Old Peter's Russian Tales, T C & E C Jack, 1916, illustrations by Dmitri Mitrokhin, first edition: $1,500.00

Old Peter's Russian Tales, early reprints by Jack (UK) or Stokes (US) with all color plates present: $100.00

Old Peter's Russian Tales, Nelson, 1971, illustrations by Faith Jacques, with dust jacket: $40.00

Old Peter's Russian Tales, Cape, 1984, illustrations by Faith Jacques, with dust jacket: $30.00

Pond and Stream, Treherne, 1906, ten color plate illustrations by Frances Craine, gray paper boards with paper inset illustrations of crane on cover: $1,500.00

Things in Our Garden or, *A Child's Book of the Garden*, Treherne, 1906, color illustrations by Frances Craine, green paper-covered boards with illustration of spider on cover: $1,500.00

RAPHAEL, Arthur M.

Great Jug, Reilly & Lee, 1936, cloth-over-board cover with impressed illustration, 136 pages, color frontispiece, b/w illustrations by Clifford Benton: $40.00

RASKIN, Ellen (1928 – 1984)

Raskin studied fine arts at the University of Wisconsin and then left the Midwest for New York and a career as a freelance commercial artist. She designed or illustrated more than 1,000 book jackets and advertisements, receiving many awards for her work. She started illustrating books with Dylan Thomas's *A Child Christmas in Wales* (1959). Her first venture into illustrating her own works, *Nothing Ever Happens on My Block* (1966), was named Best Picture Book of the Year by the *New York Herald Tribune*. Books for older children, such as the *Mysterious Disappearance of Leon, I Mean Noel*, (1971), used type to create both illustrations and puzzles for readers.

Figgs & Phantoms, E. P. Dutton, 1974, 154 pages, b/w illustrations by author, first edition with dust jacket: $30.00

Moose, Goose and Little Nobody, Parents' Magazine Press, 1974, oversize, illustrated hardcover, first edition: $40.00

Mysterious Disappearance of Leon, I Mean Noel, E. P. Dutton, 1971, first edition with dust jacket: $40.00

Silly Songs and Sad, Crowell, 1967, oblong yellow pictorial hardcover, illustrated by Ellen Raskin, first edition with dust jacket: $30.00

Tattooed Potato & Other Clues, E. P. Dutton, 1975, first edition with dust jacket: $50.00

Who, Said Sue, Said Whoo?, Atheneum, 1973, first edition with dust jacket: $40.00

World's Greatest Freak Show, Atheneum, 1971, color illustrations, first edition with dust jacket: $40.00

RASPE, Rudolf Erich (1737 – 1794)

Baron Munchausen Books were written by Rudolf Erich Raspe and others. Librarian and professional swindler Raspe found time between fleeing various countries to set down the adventures of Baron Munchausen. Although there was a real Baron, fond of recounting military adventures, the fictional Munchausen spawned numerous fantastic stories, including a trip to the moon. Throughout the nineteenth century, new tales of the Baron and lavishly illustrated volumes appeared. The first US edition was published in 1813 and the stories continued to inspire books and films including a 1989 movie by Terry Gilliam. A sampling of Munchausen titles includes:

Complete Original Edition of the Surprising Travels and Adventures of Baron Munchausen, in Russia, the Caspian Sea, Iceland, Turkey, Egypt, Gibraltar, up the Mediterranean, on the Atlantic Ocean, and through the Centre of Mount Aetna, into the South Sea. Also, An Account of a Voyage into the Moon and Dog Star. A Sequel, Containing His Expedition into Africa. Humbly dedicated to Mr. Bruce, London, R.S. Kirby, 1819, A New Edition, calf with gilt, preserved in marbled slipcase, frontispiece-portrait of Baron Munchausen, and 27 engraved plates, eight folding, all hand colored, first published in Oxford in 1786, this edition: $2,500.00

Adventures of Baron Munchausen, from the Best English and German editions, Warne, 1886, Dalziel Brothers, printer, red cloth cover, 104 pages, 18 chromolithograph plates, illustrated by A. Bichard: $400.00

Travels and Surprising Adventures of Baron Munchausen, Tegg, 1868, illustrated by George Cruikshank, hand-colored illustrations: $250.00

Surprising Travels and Adventures of Baron Munchausen, E. P. Dutton, 1903, illustrated by W. Heath Robinson: $150.00

RAWLINGS, Marjorie Kinnan (1896 – 1953)

Secret River, Scribner's, 1955, illustrations by Leonard Weisgard, first edition with dust jacket: $300.00

Yearling, Charles Scribner's Sons, 1938, illustrated by Edward Shenton, first edition with dust jacket: $300.00

Yearling, Charles Scribner's Sons, 1940, 400 pages, illustrated in full color by N. C. Wyeth, in its original pictorial box: $250.00

RAY, Anna Chapin, see Series section, NATHALIE

REDFORD, Polly

Christmas Bower, E. P. Dutton, 1967, 192 pages, illustrations by Edward Gorey, first edition with dust jacket: $70.00

REEDER, Red, see Series section, WEST POINT, CLINT LANE

REES, Ennis, *Brer Rabbit and His Tricks*

REES, Ennis

Brer Rabbit and His Tricks, Young Scott Books, 1967, color illustrations by Edward Gorey, first edition with dust jacket: $100.00

Lions and Lobsters and Foxes and Frogs, Young Scott Books, 1971, oblong hardcover, illustrated by Edward Gorey, first edition with dust jacket: $100.00

Little Greek Alphabet, Prentice-Hall, 1968, illustrated by George Salter, first edition with dust jacket: $30.00

More of Brer Rabbit's Tricks, Young Scott Books, 1968, oblong hardcover, color illustrations by Edward Gorey, first edition with dust jacket: $60.00

Pun Fun, Abelard-Schuman, 1965, illustrated by Quentin Blake, first edition with dust jacket: $50.00

REES, Leslie

Two-Thumbs: The Story of a Koala, John Sands, Sydney, 1950, hardcover, 44 pages, color illustrations by Margaret Senior, first edition with dust jacket: $80.00

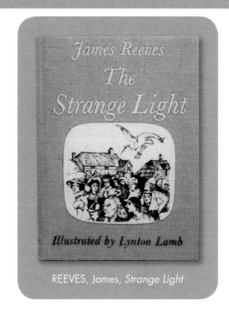

REEVES, James, *Strange Light*

REEVES, James

Angel and the Donkey, McGraw-Hill, 1970, oblong hardcover, 32 pages, illustrated by Edward Ardizzone, US first edition with dust jacket: $100.00

Blackbird in the Lilac, Oxford University Press, 1952, illustrations by Edward Ardizzone, first edition with dust jacket: $50.00

Exploits of Don Quixote, retold by Reeves, Blackie, 1959, illustrations by Edward Ardizzone, first edition with dust jacket: $70.00

How the Moon Began, Abelard-Schuman, 1971, oversize hardcover, illustrated by Edward Ardizzone, US first edition with dust jacket: $40.00

James Reeves Story Book, Heinemann, 1978, collected stories, illustrated by Edward Ardizzone, first edition with dust jacket: $60.00

Lion that Flew, Chatto & Windus, 1974, illustrated by Edward Ardizzone, first edition with dust jacket: $40.00

More Prefabulous Animals, Heinemann, 1975, green hardcover with gilt, illustrated by Edward Ardizzone, first edition with dust jacket: $40.00

Mr. Horrox and the Gratch, Abelard-Schuman, 1969, 32 pages, illustrations by Quentin Blake, first edition with dust jacket: $100.00

Prefabulous Animals, Heinemann, 1957, green hardcover with gilt, illustrated by Edward Ardizzone, first edition with dust jacket: $50.00

Story of Jackie Thimble, E. P. Dutton, 1964, small hardcover, 31 pages, b/w illustrations by Edward Ardizzone, first edition with dust jacket: $40.00

Strange Light, Heinemann, 1964, blue hardcover with gilt, illustrations by Lynton Lamb, first edition with dust jacket: $40.00

Titus in Trouble, Bodley Head, London, 1959, tall hardcover, illustrated by Edward Ardizzone, first edition with dust jacket: $50.00

RENICK, Marion

Champion Caddy, Charles Scribner's Sons, 1943, illustrated by John Fulton, first edition with dust jacket: $70.00

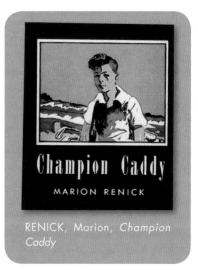

RENICK, Marion, *Champion Caddy*

Swimming Fever, Charles Scribner's Sons, 1947, illustrated by Dwight Logan, first edition with dust jacket: $30.00

Tommy Carries the Ball, Charles Scribner's Sons, 1940, illustrated by Frederick Machetanz, first edition with dust jacket: $40.00

REY, H. A. and Margaret, see also Series section, CURIOUS GEORGE

Pretzel, 1944, Harper, oversize, red cloth-over-board cover, first edition with dust jacket: $200.00

RICHARDS, Harvey, see Series section, SORAK

RICHARDS, Laura E., see also Series section, HILDEGARDE-MARGARET

Captain January, Estes & Lauriat, 1891, first edition: $200.00

Captain January, Page, 1924, Baby Peggy edition, hardcover with paste-on-illustration and gilt lettering, illustrated with photos from the film: $50.00

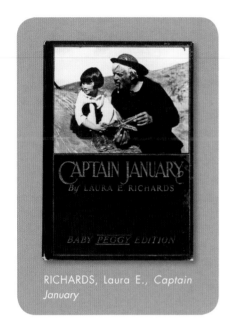

RICHARDS, Laura E., *Captain January*

Hildegarde's Home, Estes, 1892, red cloth-over-board cover: $50.00

Piccolo, Estes, 1906, cloth-over-board cover with illustration, illustrated endpapers, two-color illustrations throughout by Josephine Bruce and others: $50.00

Queen Hildegarde, Estes, 1889, red cloth-over-board cover: $30.00

RICHARDS, Mel
Peter Rabbit the Magician, Jewel Tea premium, 1942, spiralbound book in box with magic tricks and wand, color illustrations: $90.00

RICHARDSON, Frederick (b. Chicago, 1862 – 1937)

Richardson attended the St. Louis School of Fine Arts and the Academie Julien in Paris. He taught at the Chicago Art Institute for

a time as well as working for the *Chicago Daily News.* In 1903, he moved to New York. Richardson's first children's book was probably Queen Zixi of Ix by Oz author, L. Frank Baum. The story first appeared as a serialization in the *St. Nicholas* magazine in 1904, and most of Richardson's pictures were reproduced in the book edition published in 1905 by the Century Company. Richardson's most famous work was done for Volland, the Chicago publisher who specialized in full-color picture books. Richardson's elaborate *Mother Goose* was first published in 1915 and kept in print for more than 60 years by the M. A. Donahue company. He also illustrated a series of elementary school textbooks called the Winston Readers.

Frederick Richardson's Book for Children, Donohue, 1938, oversize oblong, cloth-over-board cover with paste-on-pictorial, 107 pages, illustrated endpapers, full-page color illustrations by author: $150.00

Mother Goose (edited by Eulalie Osgood Grover), Volland, 1917, illustrated cloth-over-board cover with printed illustration and gilt lettering, oversize, 108 color plates by Richardson: $250.00

Mother Goose, Volland Popular Edition, 1921, oversize, cloth-over-board cover with paste-on-pictorial, color illustrations by Richardson: $100.00

Mother Goose, Donohue, ca. 1937 edition, illustrated cloth-over-board cover, oversize, 128 pages, with full-page, full-color illustrations throughout by Richardson: $150.00

RICHARDSON, Frederick, *Frederick Richardson's Book for Children*

Old Old Tales Retold, Donohue, ca. 1936, oversize oblong, cloth-over-board cover with paste-on-pictorial, 108 pages, full-page, full-color illustrations by author: $150.00

RIDDLE BOOKS, James Riddell, Riddle Books, London, novelty books with clever illustrations and themes to amuse children and adults.

Animal Lore and Disorder, undated, pictorial oblong hardcover, split pages with animal illustrations can be matched or mismatched to create numerous creatures: $100.00

Farce of Fashion, 1946, oversize hardcover with picture of man and woman dressed in reverse clothing, pages split horizontally to be flipped in numerous combinations, showing a variety of outfits from various ages, illustrations by John Berry: $100.00

Hit or Myth, More Animal Lore and Disorder, undated, pictorial oblong hardcover, split pages with animal illustrations can be matched or mismatched to create numerous creatures: $80.00

Very Wild Life, an Unnatural History Book for First and Second Childhood, 1948, hardcover, blue boards, b/w text illustrations by James Riddell: $40.00

RILEY, James Whitcomb (1849 – 1916)
Defective Santa Claus, Bobbs-Merrill, 1904, cloth-over-board cover with gilt and decoration, 78 pages, b/w illustrations by Relyea and W. Vawter: $30.00

Riley Fairy Tales, Bobbs-Merrill, 1923 edition, blue cloth-over-board cover with paste-on-illustration, oversize, 96 pages, color illustrated by Will Vawter: $30.00

RINEHART, Susan
Something Old, Something New, Harper, 1961, 32 pages, illustrated by Arnold Lobel, first edition with dust jacket: $50.00

RIPPEY, Sarah Cory
Goody-Naughty Book, Rand McNally, 1913, cloth with paste-on pictorials, turn book over to read from opposite direction, stories of good children and naughty

RIPPEY, Sarah Cory, *Goody-Naughty Book*

children, color and b/w illustrations by Blanche Fisher Wright: $50.00

ROBB, Esther Chapman
There's Something about a River, Duell, Sloan and Pearce, 1961, first edition with dust jacket: $50.00

ROBERTSON, Keith (1914 – 1991), see also Series section, HENRY REED

Missing Brother, Viking Press, 1950, red illustrated hardcover, illustrated by Rafaello Busoni, first edition with dust jacket: $60.00

ROBINSON, Charles, Thomas Heath, William Heath, illustrators

The three Robinson brothers were sons of Thomas Robinson, a chief staff artist for the *Penny Illustrated Paper,* London. The brothers sometimes worked on art projects together, especially the fairy tales of Hans C. Andersen. Thomas, the oldest (b. 1869) did a few children's books but was better known for his illustrations for adult novels, including an edition of Hawthorne's *Scarlet Letter.* Charles (1870 – 1937) illustrated editions of Burnett's *Secret Garden,* and Field's *Lullaby-Land,* as well as other children's books. The works of William (1872 – 1944) include DeLaMare's *Peacock Pie* and Kingsley's *Water Babies.* William also wrote and illustrated the *Uncle Lubin* stories.

Adventures of Uncle Lubin, by W. Heath Robinson, Grant Richards, 1902, illustrations by author, green cloth with white, red and light green decorative boards, color frontispiece, decorative endpapers, line drawing on every page: $6,000.00

Bill the Minder, by W. Heath Robinson, Henry Holt, 1912, green cloth, 15 mounted color plates by author, with illustrated dust jacket: $2,000.00

ROBINSON, Tom
Buttons, Viking Press, 1938, oversize, 64 pages, illustrations by Peggy Bacon, first edition with dust jacket: $80.00

Greylock and the Robins, Viking Press, 1956, oversize, 31 pages, color illustrations by Robert Lawson, first edition with dust jacket: $80.00

In and Out, Viking Press, 1943, poetry, cloth-over-board cover, illustrations by Marguerite de Angeli, first edition with dust jacket: $40.00

Trigger, John's Son, Viking Press, 1961, illustrations by Robert McCloskey, first edition with dust jacket: $50.00

ROCKWELL, Anne
Gypsy Girl's Best Shoes, Parents' Magazine Press, 1966, first edition with dust jacket: $40.00

I Like the Library, E. P. Dutton, 1977, pictorial hardcover, first edition with dust jacket: $50.00

ROCKWELL, Carey, see Series section TOM CORBETT SPACE CADET

ROCKWELL, Norman (1894 – 1978)
Famous for his more than 300 *Saturday Evening Post* covers, American arist Norman Rockwell also did a number of illustrations for early boys' books such as the sports books of Ralph Henry Barbour (circa 1915 – 1916, $100 to $500 for titles with four full-color Rockwell plates). His name on any illustration, especially those published before the height of his fame, adds to the value of a book.

ROCKWOOD, Roy, see Series section, BOMBA, DEEP SEA, GREAT MARVEL

RODGERS, Mary, see also Series section, FREAKY FRIDAY

Rotten Book, Harper & Row, 1969, illustrated by Steven Kellogg, first edition with dust jacket: $60.00

ROLLESTON, C. W.
Parsifal, Crowell, undated, ca. 1912, oversize art book, 194 pages, suede cover with gilt design, 16 tipped in color plates plus full-page lithos and text illustrations by Willy Pogany: $275.00

ROLLINS, Philip
Jinglebob: A Story of a True Cowboy, Scribner, 1930, illustrations by N.C. Wyeth, first edition: $150.00

ROLT-WHEELER, Francis, see Series section, UNITED STATES SERVICE

ROOSE-EVANS, James, see Series section, ODD AND ELSEWHERE

ROSELLI, Auro
Cats of the Eiffel Tower, Delacorte Press, 1967, illustrated by Laurent DeBrunhoff, first edition with dust jacket: $70.00

ROSMAN, Alice Grant
Jock the Scot, Cassell, 1951 edition, blue cloth-over-board cover with paste-on-pictorial, 204 pages, color plates by Joan Esley: $80.00

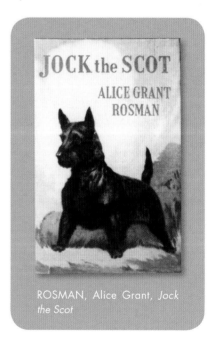

ROSMAN, Alice Grant, *Jock the Scot*

ROSS, Diana, see also Series section, LITTLE RED ENGINE

Old Perisher, Faber and Faber, London, 1965, oversize hardcover, color and b/w illustrations by Edward Ardizzone, first edition with dust jacket: $100.00

ROSS, M. T., illustrator (1881 – 1937, b. Illinois)

Marion Thomas "Penny" Ross was a graduate of the Chicago Art School and an art instructor at the Lewis Institute. He began his career at the *Chicago Tribune* where he illustrated the comic strip *Mama's Angel Child*, using the pen name Penny Ross. His work included children's book illustration, interior and home decoration, ads for Marshall Field's department store, Chicago, art work for the Chicago World's Fair ca. 1933, postcard design, and various art assignments for RKO Studios. Of most interest to children's book collectors are his watercolor illustrations for many books published by Volland including several books in the Nature Children series. The delightful photo of Ross at his drawing board working in a tie and cuff-linked white shirt was provided by his daughter. Note his large paint palette, and the wind-up phonograph in the background.

ROSS, M. T., illustrator

ROSSETTI, Christina (1830 – 1894)

Younger sister of Dante Gabriel Rossetti, Christina Rossetti had published her first volume of poetry by the time that she was 17. She wrote three books specifically for children and many of her poems were later adapted into picture books.

Goblin Market, Macmillan, 1893, 12 full-page and in-text illustrations by Laurence Housman, elaborate gilt decoration on cover, first edition: $500.00

Goblin Market, George Harrap, 1933, illustrated by Arthur Rackham. Harrap offered several editions including limited editions bound with original

Rackham watercolors (less than ten made): $50,0000.00. Limited edition signed by Rackham but no original drawing (approximately 410 made), with original vellum cover: $1,500.00. First trade edition with four color plates: $250.00

Goblin Market, J. B. Lippincott, 1933, four color plates by Arthur Rackham, paste-on pictorial cover, first American edition: $150.00

Goblin Market, E. P. Dutton, 1970, illustrated by Ellen Raskin, hardcover with dust jacket: $30.00

Maude: A Story for Girls, James Bowden, 1897, a limited edition published by Rossetti's brother William Michael after her death, in original cloth with gilt decoration: $225.00

Maude: A Story for Girls, Archon Books, 1976, hardcover with dust jacket: $35.00

Sing-Song: Nursery Rhyme Book, George Routledge, 1872, with 121 illustrations by Arthur Hughes, engraved by the Dalziel Brothers, first edition: $350.00

Sing-Song: Nursery Rhyme Book, Macmillan, 1926, with illustrations by Marguerite Davis, first edition thus: $40.00

Speaking Likeness, Macmillan, 1874, illustrations by Arthur Hughes, gilt decoration on cover, first edition: $300.00

Speaking Likeness, Robert Bros., 1875, illustrations by Arthur Hughes, first American edition: $200.00

ROUNDS, Glenn (b. 1906, South Dakota), see also Series section, MR. YOWDER, WHITEY

Rounds was raised on a horse ranch, a childhood that shaped his career as an illustrator. He studied art at the Art Institute in Kansas City and the Art Students League in New York. A born storyteller, he combined his tales of life in the West with his drawings and colorful paintings of horses, ranch life, and children.

Hunted Horses, Holiday House, 1951, small, full-page illustrations by author, first edition with dust jacket: $40.00

ROY, Lillian Elizabeth, see Series section, GIRL SCOUTS, WOODCRAFT

RUDSTROM, Lennart

Home, Putnam, 1974, watercolor illustrations by Carl Larsson, US first edition with dust jacket: $30.00

RUGH, Belle Dorman

Crystal Mountain, Houghton Mifflin, 1955, illustrated by E. H. Shepard, first edition with dust jacket: $50.00

RUSKIN, John

Dame Wiggins of Lee and Her Seven Wonderful Cats, Macmillan, 1925 edition, small, cloth-over-board cover, illustrated endpapers, 76 pages, color illustrations throughout by Roy Meldrum: $40.00

RYAN, Cheli Duran

Hildilid's Night, Macmillan, 1971, oblong hardcover, illustrated by Arnold Lobel, first edition with dust jacket: $40.00

Paz, Macmillan, 1971, square blue hardcover, 39 pages, color illustrations by Nonny Hogrogian, first edition with dust jacket: $40.00

■ ⋯⋯⋯⋯⋯ **S** ⋯⋯⋯⋯⋯ ■

SABOLY, Nicholas

Bring a Torch, Jeannette, Isabella, Scribner, 1963, illustrated by Adrienne Adams, first edition with dust jacket: $60.00

SAGE, Juniper (pseudonym of Margaret Wise Brown)

Man in the Manhole and the Fix-It Men, William R. Scott, Inc. and E. M. Hale, 1946, orange cloth binding: $30.00

SAINSBURY, Noel, see Series section, GREAT ACE

SAINT-EXUPERY, Antoine de (1900 – 1944)

Little Prince, Reynal & Hitchcock, 1943, illustrated by author, limited edition of

525 copies signed by Saint-Exupery on a tipped-in page, in original binding: $15,000.00

Little Prince, Reynal & Hitchcock, 1943, illustrated by author. A first edition dust jacket should show a $2.00 price at top of front flap and "386 Fourth Avenue, New York" address below the publisher's name at the bottom of the front flap, among other points. First edition with dust jacket: $1,500.00 Reynal hardcover without dust jacket: $50.00

SALINGER, J. D.

Catcher in the Rye, Little & Brown, 1951, first edition with first edition dust jacket showing elusive author's photo on back: $4,500.00. Book of the Month Club reprint with facsimile first edition jacket with author's photo: $100.00

SALISBURY, KENT

Ookpik Visits the USA, Golden Press, 1963, orange pictorial hardcover, includes magnetic Ookpik in his auto, illustrated by Beverly Edwards, first edition with dust jacket: $70.00

SALTEN, Felix (1869 – 1945)

Bambi, Collins, 1945, book came with four detachable pictures "suitable for framing" based on the Walt Disney movie, with all pictures intact: $150.00

Bambi: A Life in the Woods, Simon & Schuster, 1928, translated from German by Whittaker Chambers, illustrations by Kurt Wiese, first American edition: $30.00. With dust jacket: $300.00

Hound of Florence, Simon & Schuster, 1930, illustrations by Kurt Wiese, a fantasy novel that inspired Disney's *Shaggy Dog* movies. First American edition: $30.00

SAMSON, Anne S.

Lines, Spines and Porcupines, Doubleday, 1969, illustrated by author, first edition with dust jacket: $40.00

SAMUELS, Adelaide

Father Gander's Melodies for Mother Goose's Grandchildren, Roberts, 1894, green cloth-over-board cover with gilt lettering and illustration, 121 pages, illustrated: $60.00

SANDBURG, Carl (1878 – 1967)

Potato Face, Harcourt Brace, 1930, small hardcover, 96 pages, first edition with dust jacket: $150.00

Rootabaga Pigeons, Harcourt Brace, 1923, color frontispiece, b/w illustrations by Maude and Misha Petersham, first edition with dust jacket: $300.00

Rootabaga Stories, Harcourt Brace, 1922, illustrations by Maude and Misha Petersham, first edition with dust jacket: $250.00

SANDERS, Martha

Alexander and the Magic Mouse, American Heritage Press, 1969, illustrated hardcover, 44 pages, illustrated by Philippe Fix, first edition with dust jacket: $90.00

SANDOZ, Mari

Winter Thunder, Westminster Press, 1954, based on a true story of school children lost in a blizzard, first edition with dust jacket: $50.00

SARG, Tony (1880 – 1942), author/illustrator

Born in Guatamala and educated in Germany, Sarg moved to America in 1915 and worked in window display and magazine illustration. A favorite hobby and pastime of designing marionettes spread into the writing of plays as well as books about marionette theater. Sarg wrote and illustrated a number of oversize color illustrated paper-over-board hardcovers,

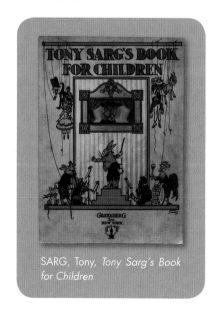
SARG, Tony, *Tony Sarg's Book for Children*

color illustrations throughout, usually with activity features. Sarg also designed some of the first balloons for the annual Macy's Thanksgiving Day Parade in New York City.

His books include:

Tony Sarg's Book for Children, Greenberg Publishers Inc., 1924, first edition, oversize, paper-over-board cover with cut-out theater, lifting curtain and turning wheel mounted on inside of front cover to show scenes from Red Riding Hood, color illustrated endpapers, color illustrations throughout: $90.00

SARG, Tony, *Tony Sarg's Savings Book*

Tony Sarg's Book of Animals, Greenberg Publishers Inc., 1925, oversize, paper-over-board hardcover, color illustrations: $75.00

Tony Sarg's Book of Marionette Plays, Greenberg Publishers Inc., 1927, title page and chapter heading illustrations, first edition with dust jacket: $120.00

Tony Sarg's Magic Movie Book, B. F. Jay, 1943, oversize, cloth-over-board cover, complete with magic lenses: $200.00

Tony Sarg's New York, Greenberg Publishers Inc., 1927, 24 full-page color illustrations: $300.00

Tony Sarg's Savings Book, World, 1946, oblong, hardcover, spiral binding, color illustrations, bank envelope attached to inside cover: $90.00

Tony Sarg's Surprise Book, B. F. Jay, 1941, oversize, color pictorial boards, spiral binding, color illustrations, moveable and textured parts, with box: $200.00. Without box: $100.00

SARG, Tony, *Tony Sarg's Surprise Book*

Tony Sarg's Treasure Book, B. F. Jay, 1942, pictorial hardcover, full color, includes six pages with moveable features, with box: $200.00

Who's Who in Tony Sarg's Zoo, McLoughlin, 1937, color illustrations: $75.00

SASEK, Miroslav, see Series section, SASEK

SAUNDERS, F. Wenderoth

Building Brooklyn Bridge, Little, Brown, 1965, illustrated, first edition with dust jacket: $40.00

SAUNDERS, Louise

Knave of Hearts, Artists & Writers Guild (Racine, Wisconsin), 1925, full-page color illustrations by Maxfield Parrish, spiral binding: $850.00 to $1,000.00

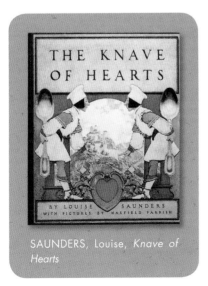

SAUNDERS, Louise, *Knave of Hearts*

Knave of Hearts, Scribner, 1925, illustrated by Maxfield Parrish, full-color plate on black cloth cover, pictorial endpapers, 14 color plates, tissue guard over frontis, and nine in-text color illustrations. (This is considered the most desirable of all Parrish books for its lavish oversized illustrations.) Without presentation box or glassine jacket, first edition thus: $3,000.00 to $4,000.00

SAVAGE, Blake, see Series section, RICK BRANT ELECTRONIC ADVENTURE

SAWYER, Ruth (1880 – 1970)

Christmas Anna Angel, Viking Press, 1944, small, 48 pages, double-page color illustrations by Kate Seredy, first edition with dust jacket: $60.00

Enchanted Schoolhouse, Viking Press, 1956, illustrated by Hugh Troy, first edition with dust jacket: $100.00

Maggie Rose, Her Birthday Christmas, Harper & Brothers, 1952, illustrated by Maurice Sendak, first edition with dust jacket: $40.00

Roller Skates, Viking Press, 1936 (1937 Newbery Medal winner), illustrations by Valenti Angelo, first edition with dust jacket: $80.00

Tale of the Enchanted Bunnies, Harper & Brothers, 1923, illustrated by author, first edition with dust jacket: $100.00

This Way to Christmas, Harper & Brothers, 1924, illustrated by Maginal Wright Barney, with dust jacket: $150.00

Year of the Christmas Dragon, Viking Press, 1960, illustrated by Hugh Troy, first edition with dust jacket: $40.00

SCARRY, Patricia M.

Jeremy Mouse Book, American Heritage Press, 1969, illustrated hardcover, illustrated by Hilary Knight: $70.00

SCARRY, Richard (1919 – 1994), author/illustrator, see also Series section, TINKER AND TANKER

Scarry received his art education at the Boston Museum School. Like many other young men graduating in 1941, he served for five years in the army before embarking on a career as a commercial artist. His first illustration jobs were for Golden Press. By the 1960s, he was creating his own books, such as *Richard Scarry's Best Word Book Ever* (1963). Scarry wrote or illustrated more than 100 books during his long career.

SCARRY, Richard, illustration

I Am a Bunny, Golden Sturdy Book, 1963, narrow glossy hardcover, stiff pages, color illustrations by author: $50.00

Richard Scarry's ABC Word Book, Random House, 1971, illustrated hardcover, 61 pages, color illustrations by author: $50.00

Richard Scarry's Best Mother Goose Ever, Golden Book/Western, 1970, pictorial oversize hardcover, color illustrations by Scarry: $60.00

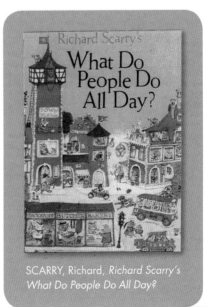

SCARRY, Richard, *Richard Scarry's What Do People Do All Day?*

Richard Scarry's Best Story Book Ever, Golden Book/Western, 1967, pictorial oversize hardcover, color illustrations by Scarry: $80.00

Richard Scarry's Busy, Busy World, Golden Press, 1965, pictorial oversize hardcover, color illustrations by Scarry: $100.00

Richard Scarry's Please and Thank You Book, Norcross, 1973, square hardcover, illustrated by author: $30.00

Richard Scarry's What Do People Do All Day?, Random House, 1968, oversize hardcover, illustrated by author: $80.00

SCHAEFER, Jack
Stubby Pringle's Christmas, Houghton Mifflin, 1964, illustrated by Lorence Bjorkland, first edition with dust jacket: $200.00

SCHAEFFER, Mead (1898 – 1980)
A friend of Norman Rockwell, American artist Mead Schaeffer began illustrating a series of classics for Dodd Mead while still in his twenties. He also painted numerous covers for the *Saturday Evening Post,* including a famous series depicting the various branches of the military during WWII.

SCHAFFNER, Val
Algonquin Cat, Delacorte Press, 1980, illustrations by Hilary Knight, first edition with dust jacket: $50.00

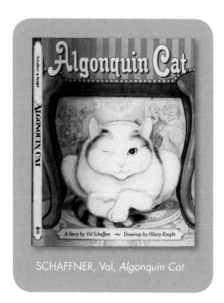

SCHAFFNER, Val, *Algonquin Cat*

SCHEALER, John M.
Zip-Zip and the Red Planet, E. P. Dutton, 1961, illustrated by Robert MacLean, first edition with dust jacket: $80.00

Zip-Zip Goes to Venus, E. P. Dutton, 1958, 125 pages, science fiction, first edition with dust jacket: $150.00

SCHEER, Julian
Rain Makes Applesauce, Holiday House, 1964, oversize hardcover, illustrated by Marvin Bileck (1965 Caldecott Honor winner), first edition with dust jacket: $100.00

SCHOONOVER, Frank (1877 – 1972)
illustrator

Another American illustrator trained by Pyle at the Brandywine School, Schoonover did illustrations for books and magazines and designed stained glass windows. He followed Pyle's advice to immerse himself in the subject, travelling to Hudson Bay country when commissioned to illustrate a series on frontier life. His double-page title page illustrations and brilliant color plates were popular for adventure stories.

SCHOONOVER, Frank, double-page title page illustrations

SCHULKERS, Robert, see Series section, SECKATARY HAWKINS

SCHWETZKY, Prof. Otto H. L.
Peter Teeter Stories, Thompson, 1904, oversize oblong, illustrated paper-over-board cover, illustrated endpapers, color illustrations throughout by Raymond H. Garman: $75.00

SCHWETZKY, Prof. Otto H. L., *Peter Teeter Stories*

SEARLE, Ronald
Dick Deadeye, Jonathan Cape, 1975, oblong oversize hardcover, Searle interpretation of Gilbert & Sullivan opera, illustrated by Searle, UK first edition with dust jacket: $40.00

SEARLE, Ronald, *Dick Deadeye*

Terror of St. Trinian's or, Angela's Prince Charming, with Timothy Shy, Max Parrish, 1952, 128 pages, illustrated by Searle: $30.00

Those Magnificent Men in Their Flying Machines, with Bill Richardson and Allen Andrews, Norton, 1965, illustrated by Ronald Searle, first edition with dust jacket: $40.00

SELDEN, George (1929 – 1989), see also Series section, CHESTER CRICKET

Garden Under the Sea, Viking Press, 1957, illustrations by Garry MacKenzie, first edition with dust jacket: $60.00

Sparrow Socks, Harper & Row, 1965, illustrated by Peter Lippman, first edition with dust jacket: $50.00

SEMPE, Jean-Jacques

Young Nicolas, Bobbs-Merrill, 1962, square hardcover, decorative green boards, 121 pages, first edition with dust jacket: $50.00

SEMPLE, Daisy

Tommy and Jane and the Birds, Saalfield, 1929, oversize, 94 pages, color and b/w illustrations by Fern Bisel Peat, with dust jacket: $70.00

SENDAK, Jack

Happy Rain, Harper & Brothers, 1956, illustrations by Maurice Sendak, first edition with dust jacket: $200.00

SENDAK, Jack, *King of the Hermits and Other Stories*

King of the Hermits and Other Stories, Farrar, Straus, 1966, illustrated by Margot Zemach: $50.00

Martze, Farrar, Straus & Giroux, 1968, line drawings by Mitchell Miller, first edition with dust jacket: $40.00

SENDAK, Maurice, author/illustrator

Caldecott winner Sendak illustrated a number of books for other authors including his first assignment, *A Hole Is to Dig,* by Ruth Krauss (1952), and the *Little Bear* series by Else Holmelund Minarik, before writing his own stories. His education included time at the Art Students League, New York. *The Art of Maurice Sendak,* by Thelma G. Lanes, documents the enormous scope of his work. Today first editions and out-of-print works continue to escalate in value.

Hector Protector and As I Went over the Water, Harper & Row, 1965, oblong hardcover, illustrated and written by Sendak, first edition with dust jacket: $70.00

Higglety Pigglety Pop! or There Must Be More to Life, Harper & Row, 1967, 69 pages, dust jacket price $4.95, first edition with dust jacket: $80.00

In the Night Kitchen, Harper Row, 1970, illustrated white oversize hardcover, color illustrations by Sendak (some dust jacket indications of first: $4.95 price, "1070" on bottom inside flap, title list ending with *Higglety Pigglety Pop,* no Caldecott sticker), first edition with dust jacket: $400.00

Juniper Tree, and Other Tales from Grimm, Farrar, 1973, b/w illustrations by Maurice Sendak, 2 volume boxed set, first edition with dust jackets and box: $200.00

Kenny's Window, Harper & Row, 1956, Sendak's first book, hardcover, illustrated by author, first edition with dust jacket: $500.00

Lullabies and Night Songs, Harper & Row, 1965, oversize hardcover, music by Alec Wilder, illustrated by Sendak, first edition with dust jacket: $90.00

Seven Little Monsters, Harper & Row, 1975, oblong pictorial hardcover, first edition with dust jacket: $100.00

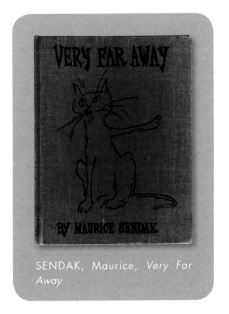

SENDAK, Maurice, *Very Far Away*

Sign on Rosie's Door, Harper & Row, 1960, illustrated by author, first edition with dust jacket: $200.00

Very Far Away, Harper & Row, 1957, small hardcover, 53 pages, pink/b/w illustrations by author, first edition with dust jacket: $100.00

Where the Wild Things Are, Harper & Row, 1963 (1964 Caldecott Medal winner), pre-Caldecott announcement first printing without Caldecott seal, color illustrations throughout, first edition with dust jacket, starts at: $5,000.00

SENN, Steve, see Series section, SPACEBREAD

SEREDY, Kate (b. Hungary, 1896 – 1975)

Seredy studied at the Academy of Art in Hungary, then moved to New York in 1922 where she began her art career as an illustrator of greeting cards. She also worked in the fashion design illustration field as well as magazine illustration, then gained recognition as an illustrator of children's books.

SEREDY, Kate, *Singing Tree*

Chestry Oak, Viking Press, 1948, illustrated by author, first edition with dust jacket: $60.00

Open Gate, Viking Press, 1943, farm story, illustrated by author, first edition with dust jacket: $90.00

Philomena, Viking Press, 1955, illustrated by author, first edition with dust jacket: $70.00

Singing Tree, George G. Harrap, 1940, illustrated by author, first edition with dust jacket: $60.00

Tenement Tree, Viking Press, 1959, illustrated by author, first edition with dust jacket: $50.00

White Stag, Viking Press, 1937 (1938 Newbery Medal), red cloth with design of stag on front cover, Hungarian legends illustrated by author, first edition with dust jacket: $150.00

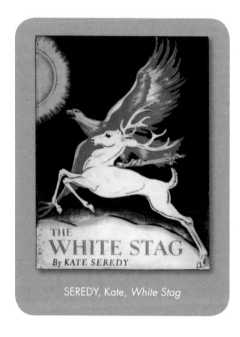

SEREDY, Kate, *White Stag*

SERRAILLIER, Ian

Captain Bounsaboard and the Pirates, Jonathan Cape, London, 1949, illustrations by Arline V. Braybrooke and Michael Bartlett, first edition with dust jacket: $100.00

Challenge of the Green Knight, Walck, 1967, illustrated by Victor Ambrus, US first edition with dust jacket: $30.00

Enchanted Island Stories from Shakespeare, Walck, 1964, hardcover, color and b/w illustrations by Peter Farmer, US first edition with dust jacket: $30.00

Gorgon's Head, Walck, 1962, US first edition with dust jacket: $40.00

Suppose You Met a Witch, Little, Brown, 1973, 34 pages, illustrated by Ed Emberley, first edition thus with dust jacket: $50.00

Tale of Three Landlubbers, Coward-McCann, 1970, illustrated by Raymond Briggs, US first edition with dust jacket: $30.00

SETON, Ernest Thompson (1860 – 1946)

Canadian artist and naturalist Ernest Thompson Seton was best known during his lifetime for his "animal biographies" and his works were reprinted regularly. Highest prices are paid for most heavily illustrated editions and for books connected with the Boy Scouts. A sampling of collectible titles includes:

Boy Scouts of America, Doubleday Page, 1910, text incorporates General Sir Robert Baden-Powell's "Scouting For Boys," hardcover: $3,500.00

Rolf in the Woods: The Adventures of a Boy Scout with Indian Quonad and Little Dog Skookum, Doubleday Page, 1911, 12 full-page b/w plates by author, first edition: $30.00

Wild Animals That I Have Known, Charles Scribner, 1898, 28 full-page b/w plates by author, first edition: $60.00

SEUSS, Dr. (Theodor Geisel, 1904 – 1991), see also LeSIEG, Theo

Theodor Geisel took his pen name from his middle name of Seuss. Seuss studied at Oxford and the Sorbonne and was a well-established illustrator by the 1930s. In the 1950s and 1960s he created the beginning reader series for Random House. Beginner Books had color illustrated oversize hardcovers, color illustrations throughout, and most important, limited vocabulary. Seuss used a number of pseudonyms for books that he wrote but did not illustrate, including the name LeSieg. All books using the Dr. Seuss pseudonym were written and illustrated by Geisel. Dr. Seuss books were so popular, the early printings were large; later printings were usually of equal quality, and are available for under $30.00. First editions are often

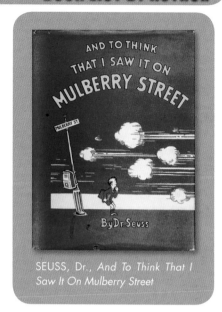

SEUSS, Dr., *And To Think That I Saw It On Mulberry Street*

hard to identify. His most popular books include:

500 Hats of Bartholomew Cubbins, Vanguard, 1938, author's second book, first edition with dust jacket: wide range from $800.00 to $6,000.00

And to Think That I Saw It on Mulberry Street, Vanguard, 1937, oversize, color illustrations by author, his first picture book, first edition with dust jacket: $8,000.00 up

Cat in the Hat, Random House, 1957, oversize hardcover, color illustrations by author, first edition with dust jacket: $7,000.00

Cat in the Hat Comes Back, Random House, 1958, Beginner Books, hardcover, glossy pictorial boards, color illustrations by author, first edition with dust jacket: $500.00

Cat in the Hat Songbook, Collins, London, 1968, hardcover: $40.00

Dr. Seuss's Sleep Book, Random House, 1962, glossy oversize hardcover, 54 pages, color illustrations by author, first edition with dust jacket: $500.00

Green Eggs and Ham, Random House, 1960, Beginner Books, first edition with dust jacket: $4,000.00

Happy Birthday to You!, Random House, 1959, illustrated endpapers, full-color illustrations, first edition with dust jacket: $350.00

Horton Hears a Who!, Random House, 1954, oversize hardcover, illustrated endpapers, color illustrations by author, first edition with dust jacket: $600.00

How the Grinch Stole Christmas!, Random House, 1957, illustrated by author, first edition with dust jacket: $2,000.00

I Had Trouble in Getting to Solla Sollew, Random House, 1965, oversize hardcover, illustrated endpapers, color illustrations by author, first edition with dust jacket: $500.00

If I Ran the Circus, Random House, 1956, first edition with dust jacket: $700.00

If I Ran the Zoo, Random House, 1950, oversize hardcover, color illustrations by author, first edition with dust jacket: $1,500.00

On beyond Zebra, Random House, 1955, oversize hardcover, illustrated by author, first edition with dust jacket: $600.00

One Fish Two Fish Red Fish Blue Fish, Random House, Beginner Book, 1960, first edition with dust jacket: $700.00

Sneetches and Other Stories, Random House, 1961, first edition with dust jacket: $400.00

Yertle the Turtle, Random House, 1958, oversize hardcover, green glossy pictorial boards, color illustrations by author, first edition with dust jacket: $700.00

Seuss reference book:

First Editions of Dr. Seuss Books: A Guide to Identification, Helen and Marc Younger and Dan Hirsch, Saco, ME, Custom Communications, 2002, issued without dustwrapper, a complete guide to identifying the first editions of Dr. Seuss, illustrated in color, limited printing of 1,000 copies.

SEWELL, Anna (1820 – 1878)
Since the publication of *Black Beauty* in 1877, Anna Sewell's horse novel was reprinted so many times that some Victorians speculated only the Bible had more editions. Highest prices are paid today for well-illustrated volumes or for the earliest editions of historical significance such as the 1890 American Humane Society's edition.

Black Beauty, J.M. Dent, UK, or E.P. Dutton, US, 1915, 24 color plates by Lucy Kemp-Welch, first edition: $40.00

Black Beauty, Jarrolds, ca. 1920, 18 color plates by Cecil Aldin, green pictorial boards, first edition: $60.00. Later editions with eight color plates by Aldin: $30.00

SEWELL, Helen (b. California, 1896 – 1957)

Sewell's childhood years included residence in New York and then in Guam, where her father served as a governor. She studied at Packer Institute, the Pratt art school and Archipenko's art school, and spent most of her adult years in New York State. She illustrated her own writing, but is also widely known for the large volume of her work for other authors, including the first editions of the Laura Ingalls Wilder books.

SEWELL, Helen, *Ming and Mehitable*

ABC for Everybody, Macmillan, 1930, oversize, paper-covered boards, first edition: $100.00

Blue Barns, Macmillan, 1933, b/w illustrations by author, first edition with dust jacket: $80.00

Ming and Mehitable, Macmillan, 1936, small, yellow boards, yellow/pink pictorial jacket, color illustrations throughout, based on the author's own childhood and her dog, first edition with dust jacket: $60.00

SHANKLAND, F.
Friends of the Forest, written by F. Shankland, 1932, Saalfield, pictorial paper-over-board cover, 12 color plates by Fern Bisel Peat: $60.00

SHARP, Margery (1905 – 1991), see also Series section, RESCUERS

Melisande, Little, Brown, 1960, illustrated by Roy McKie, first edition with dust jacket: $50.00

SHEPARD, Ernest (1879 – 1976), artist

Shepard illustrated Milne's *Winnie-the-Pooh* books, Grahame's *Wind in the Willows*, other books, calendars, and advertisements.

Betsy and Joe, E. P. Dutton, 1967, illustrated by author, first edition with dust jacket: $30.00

SHEPARD, Mary Elinor (daughter of E.H. Shepherd)

Mary Elinor Shepard began her career by illustrating the tales of Mary Poppins, and continued to illustrate books into the 1980s.

SHEPPARD, W. Crispin, see Series section, RAMBLER CLUB

SHERMAN, Harold, see Series section, GRIDIRON, TAHARA ADVENTURE

SHERRILL, Dorothy, author/illustrator

Story of Sleepy Sally, Greenberg Publishers, Inc., 1933, small, green cloth covered boards with color illustrated pastedown, first edition: $150.00

Little White Teddy Bear Who Didn't Want to Go to Bed, Farrar & Rinehart, 1931, pictorial label on cloth, small, first edition: $150.00

Story of Roly and Poly the Santa Claus Bears, Crowell, 1952, yellow cloth, first edition: $100.00

SHIPPEN, Katherine
Bridle for Pegasus, Viking Press,1951, illustrated by C. B. Falls, first edition with dust jacket: $40.00

SHULEVITZ, Uri, author/illustrator

Dawn, Farrar, Straus, 1974, illustrated by author, first edition with dust jacket: $30.00

Magician, Macmillan, 1973, b/w illustrations by Shulevitz, first edition with dust jacket: $80.00

SHURA, Mary Francis
Garret of Greta McGraw, Alfred A. Knopf, 1961, illustrated by Leslie Goldstein, first edition with dust jacket: $40.00

Pornada, Atheneum, 1968, illustrated by Erwin Schachner, first edition with dust jacket: $100.00

SIDNEY, Margaret (1844 – 1924)
Margaret Sidney's novel about the Pepper family became an instant hit and led to 11 sequels. Like many books with a wide circulation, highest prices are paid for the earliest editions. In 2007, one dealer offered a set of ten Pepper novels, all early Lothrop editions in good condition, for $650.00.

Five Little Peppers and How They Grew, Lothrop, 1880, heavily decorated with gilt on cover, first edition: $150.00

SILVERSTEIN, Shel (b. Chicago, 1932 – 1999)

Silverstein was considered a Renaissance man by his friends, with talents ranging from art to music to writing, and he even did some acting in films. As a cartoonist, Silverstein's art appeared in *Pacific Stars and Stripes* as well as *Playboy* magazine. As a songwriter, his lyrics include such hits as "A Boy Named Sue."

Giving Tree, Harper, 1964, illustrated by author, first edition with dust jacket: $100.00

SILVERSTEIN, Shel, *Lafcadio: The Lion Who Shot Back*

Lafcadio: The Lion Who Shot Back, 1963 Harper, hardcover, illustrated by author, first edition with dust jacket: $70.00

Light in the Attic, HarperCollins, 1981, collection of poems and drawings, first edition with dust jacket: $150.00

Uncle Shelby's Zoo, Don't Bump the Glump, W. H. White, 1964, black boards, imaginary menagerie of zany animals, full-color illustrations, first edition with dust jacket: $200.00

Where the Sidewalk Ends, 1974, Harper, hardcover, b/w illustrations by author, first edition with dust jacket: $40.00

SILVERSTEIN, Shel, *Light in the Attic*

SIMONT, Marc (b. Paris)

Simont's father worked as a draftsman for the French magazine, *L'Illustration.* Simont trained in France at the Academie Julien as well as attended the National Academy of Design in New York. He began illustrating children's books in 1939 and even shared an apartment with Robert McCloskey and a bunch of ducklings. Simont received a Caldecott Honor in 1950 for *Happy Day* by Ruth Krauss, and won the Caldecott Medal in 1955 for *A Tree Is Nice* by Janice May Udry. Also in the 1950s, he provided stylized color illustrations for James Thurber's two classic tales, the *Thirteen Clocks* (1951) and *The Wonderful O* (1957). Simont continued to illustrate through the 1980s including new illustrations for an earlier Thurber tale, *Many Moons* (1990 edition, originally illustrated by Slobodkin in 1943).

Opera Soufflé, Henry Schuman, 1950, decorated endpapers, illustrated by author, first edition with dust jacket: $50.00

SIMONT, Marc, *Opera Soufflé*

Polly's Oats, Harper, 1951, illustrated by author, first edition with dust jacket: $30.00

SINDELAR, Joseph, see Series section, NIXIE BUNNY

SINGER, Isaac Bashevis (1904 – 1991)
Alone in the Wild Forest, Farrar, 1971, 80 pages, illustrations by Margot Zemech, first edition with dust jacket: $40.00

Elijah the Slave, Farrar, Straus and Giroux, 1970, oversize hardcover, illustrated by Antonio Frasconi, first edition with dust jacket: $60.00

Fearsome Inn, Scribner's, 1967, illustrated by Nonny Hogrogrian, first edition with dust jacket: $50.00

Joseph and Koza, Farrar, 1970, illustrated by Symeon Shimin, first edition with dust jacket: $50.00

Zlateh the Goat and Other Stories, ca. 1966, Harper, 90 pages, illustrated by Maurice Sendak, first edition with dust jacket: $50.00

SKELTON, Red

Skelton was best known as an actor, but was also an artist.

Gertrude & Heathcliffe, Charles Scribner, 1974, 60 pages, b/w and color illustrations by author, first edition with dust jacket: $150.00

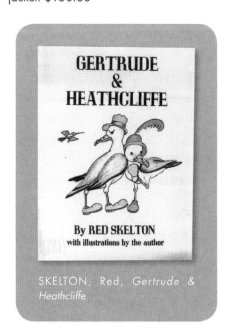

SKELTON, Red, *Gertrude & Heathcliffe*

SKINNER, Ada M. and Eleanor M.

Child's Book of Modern Stories, Duffield, 1920, dark blue cloth-over-board cover with paste-on-illustration and gilt, 341 pages, eight color plates by Jessie Willcox Smith: $100.00

SLEATOR, William

Among the Dolls, E. P. Dutton, 1975, illustrations by Trina Schart Hyman, first edition with dust jacket: $50.00

SLEIGH, Barbara, see also Series section, CARBONEL THE CAT

Jessamy, Collins, 1967, first edition with dust jacket: $150.00

No One Must Know, Bobbs-Merrill, 1962, illustrations by Jillian Willett, US first edition: $40.00

North of Nowhere, Coward-McCann, 1966, b/w illustrations, first US edition with dust jacket: $90.00

Seven Days, Meredith Press, 1968, illustrations by Joan Schwartzberg, US first edition: $50.00

Stirabout Stories, 1972, Bobbs-Merrill, US first edition: $30.00

West of Widdershins, Collins, 1971, collection of fairy stories, b/w illustrations by Victor Ambrus, first edition with dust jacket: $50.00

SLOANE, Eric

Cracker Barrel, 1967, Funk, oversize hardcover, 109 pages, illustrated by author, first edition: $40.00

Eric Sloane's Book of Storms, Duell, Sloan and Pearce, 1956, first edition with dust jacket: $100.00

Our Vanishing Landscape, Funk, 1955, oversize hardcover, 107 pages, illustrated by author, first edition: $40.00

SLOBODKIN, Louis (1903 – 1975), see also Series section, SPACE SHIP

The son of immigrants from the Ukraine, New York-born Slobodkin brought much of that colorful background to his later art work. He studied at Beaux Arts Institute of Design in New York and then built his career as a sculptor. In the 1940s he was commissioned to illustrate *The Moffats,* and began another phase of his art career. Four years later he won the Caldecott Medal for his illustrations for Thurber's *Many Moons.*

Bixxy and the Secret Message, Macmillan, 1949, first edition with dust jacket: $60.00

Colette and the Princess, E. P. Dutton, 1965, first edition, hardcover, illustrated by author: $25.00

SLOBODKIN, Louis, *Melvin the Moose Child*

Excuse Me! Certainly, Vanguard, 1959, oblong hardcover, illustrated by author: $30.00

Gogo, the French Sea Gull, Macmillan, 1960, oversize hardcover, illustrated by author, first edition with dust jacket: $60.00

Late Cuckoo, Vanguard, 1962, oversize hardcover, color illustrations by author, first edition with dust jacket: $40.00

Luigi and the Long-Nosed Soldier, 1963, Macmillan, first edition, hardcover, illustrated by author: $30.00

Melvin the Moose Child, Macmillan, 1957, color illustrations by author, first edition with dust jacket: $40.00

One Is Good but Two Are Better, Vanguard, 1956, oversize hardcover, illustrated by author, first edition with dust jacket: $40.00

Space Ship in the Park, Macmillan, 1972, hardcover, 168 pages, illustrated by author, first edition with dust jacket: $30.00

Thank You, You're Welcome, Vanguard, 1957, oblong hardcover, color illustrations by author: $30.00

Trick or Treat, Macmillan, 1959, color illustrations by author, first edition with dust jacket: $40.00

Up High and down Low, Macmillan, 1960, hardcover, illustrated by author, first edition with dust jacket: $30.00

Wilbur and the Warrior, Vanguard, 1972, hardcover, 40 pages, illustrated by author, first edition with dust jacket: $30.00

SLOBODKINA, Esphya
Caps for Sale, HarperCollins, 1947, illustrated by author, first edition with dust jacket: $50.00

Flame, the Breeze, and the Shadow, Rand McNally, 1969, oversize orange decorated hardcover, first edition with dust jacket: $70.00

Pezzo the Pedlar and the Thirteen Silly Thieves, Ebelard-Schuman, 1970, oversize, first edition with dust jacket: $40.00

SMITH, Dodie
Hundred and One Dalmatians, Viking Press, 1957, green hardcover, illustrations by Janet and Anne Grahame-Johnstone, US first edition with dust jacket: $300.00

Starlight Barking, Simon & Schuster, 1967, hardcover, illustrated by Janet and Anne Grahame-Johnstone, US first edition with dust jacket: $200.00

SMITH, Dorothy Hall
Tall Book of Christmas, Harper, 1954, tall hardcover, color illustrations by Gertrude Elliott Espenscheid: $75.00

SMITH, E. Boyd (b. Canada, 1860 – 1943), author/illustrator

Aesop's Fables, Century, 1911, b/w illustrations by author: $80.00

Early Life of Mr. Man, Houghton Mifflin, 1914, illustrated: $90.00

Farm Book: Bob and Betty Visit Uncle John, Houghton Mifflin, 1910, oblong oversize, pictorial boards, illustrated endpapers, 12 color plates: $70.00

Lions 'n' Elephants 'n' Everything, Putnam, 1929, oblong oversize, hardcover, 12 color plates: $70.00

My Village, Scribner, 1896, vignettes throughout text by author: $80.00

Railroad Book, Bob and Betty's Summer on the Railroad, Houghton Mifflin, 1913, oblong oversize, pictorial boards, illustrated endpapers, 12 color plates: $70.00

Seashore Book: Bob and Betty's Summer with Captain Hawes, Houghton Mifflin, 1912, oblong oversize, pictorial boards, illustrated endpapers, 12 color plates: $70.00

Story of Noah's Ark, Houghton Mifflin, 1905, hardcover, color plates by author: $70.00

SMITH, Emma
Emily, Thomas Nelson Ltd., 1959, red hardcover, illustrated endpapers, eight color plates plus b/w illustrations by Katherine Wigglesworth, first edition with dust jacket: $50.00

SMITH, Jessie Willcox (1863 – 1936)
American illustrator Jessie Willcox Smith studied illustration with Howard Pyle at the Brandywine School, and illustrated children's books as well as stories and articles and covers for *McClures* and *Good Housekeeping* magazines.

Baby's Red Letter Day, Just Food's Company, 1901, baby book for new parents, unmarked in original glasscine wrapper: $250.00

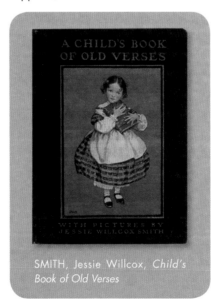

SMITH, Jessie Willcox, *Child's Book of Old Verses*

Child's Book of Old Verses, 1910, E. P. Dutton, navy cloth-over-board cover with

gilt lettering and paste-on-illustration with gilt background, color plates by author: $250.00

Dickens's Children, Charles Scribner, 1912, paste-on pictorial cover, stories taken from the works of Charles Dickens, color illustrations by Smith, first edition: $75.00

SMITH, Kate
Kate Smith Stories of Annabelle, Tell-Well Press, 1951, hardcover, illustrations by Bill and Bernard Martin, based on the original Annabelle stories by Jane Gale: $40.00

SMITH, Laura Rountree
Candy Shop Cotton-Tails, Flanagan, Chicago, 1920, small cloth-over-board cover with printed illustration, map endpapers, 128 pages, two-color illustrations throughout by Fred Stearns: $40.00

Fifty Funny Animal Tales, Albert Whitman, 1953, illustrated by Sue Seeley and J. J. Mora: $80.00

SMITH, Laura Rountree, *Candy Shop Cotton-Tails*

Jolly Polly and Curly Tail, Albert Whitman, 1925, green cloth with color paste-on illustration, illustrated by Mae H. Scannell: $100.00

Happy Mannikin in Manners Town, 1925, Whitman, small, color and b/w illustrations by Mildred Lyon, first edition with dust jacket: $40.00

Party Twins and Their Forty Parties, Plays and Games, 1924, Whitman, paste-on-illustration, small, 128 pages, illustrations by Helen Lyon: $40.00

Seventeen Little Bears, Flanagan, 1909, small, illustrated by Dorothy Reilly and Helen Hodge: $70.00

Snubby Nose and Tippy Toes, Flanagan, 1922, illustrated by Fred Stearns, first edition with dust jacket: $60.00

Tiddly Winks Primer, Whitman, 1926, small, black hardcover with paste-on-illustration, easy reader, illustrated, first edition with dust jacket: $40.00

Treasure Twins, ca. 1920s, Whitman, Just Right Books, hardcover with paste-on-pictorial, easy-read print, two-color and b/w illustrations throughout by Marguerite Jones: $40.00

Twinkle Toes and His Magic Mittens, Whitman, 1919, pictorial cover, full-page color plates by F. R. Morgan, first edition with dust jacket: $100.00

SMITH, William Jay
Laughing Time, 1955, Little, Brown, first edition, hardcover, color illustrations by Juliet Kepes: $40.00

Mr. Smith & Other Nonsense, Delacorte Press, 1968, illustrations by Don Bolognese, first edition with dust jacket: $100.00

Puptents and Pebbles, a Nonsense ABC, Atlantic Monthly, 1959, oversize hardcover, 32 pages, color illustrations by Juliet Kepes, first edition with dust jacket: $30.00

Typewriter Town, E. P. Dutton, 1960, oversize hardcover, 32 pages, b/w and color illustrations, first edition with dust jacket: $40.00

SNELL, Roy J., see Series section, MYSTERY STORIES FOR BOYS, MYSTERY STORIES FOR GIRLS

SNYDER, Zilpha Keatley, see also Series section, GREEN SKY TRILOGY

Black and Blue Magic, Atheneum, 1966, illustrated by Gene Holtan, first edition with dust jacket: $80.00

Egypt Game, Atheneum, 1967, illustrated hardcover, b/w illustrations by Alton Raible, first edition with dust jacket: $150.00

Truth About Stone Hollow, Atheneum, 1974, first edition with dust jacket: $80.00

Velvet Room, Atheneum, 1965, 183 pages, illustrated by Alton Raible, first edition with dust jacket: $100.00

Witches of Worm, Atheneum, 1972 (1973 Newbery Honor book), 183 pages, illustrated by Alton Raible, first edition with dust jacket: $90.00

SOGLOW, O.
Little King, John Martin's House, 1945 edition, paper-over-board cover, 30 pages, color illustrations throughout by Soglow, with dust jacket: $130.00. Without dust jacket: $40.00

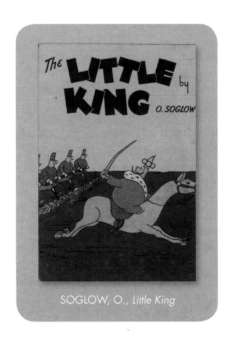

SOGLOW, O., *Little King*

SOPER, Eileen
Dormouse Awake, Macmillan, UK, 1948, glossy boards with color illustrations, color plate illustrations by author, first edition with dust jacket: $300.00

Happy Rabbit, Macmillan, 1947, color illustrations by Eileen A. Soper: $70.00

SORENSEN, Virginia
Curious Missie, Harcourt Brace, 1953, illustrated by Marilyn Miller, first edition with dust jacket: $40.00

Miracles on Maple Hill, Harcourt Brace, 1956 (1957 Newbery Award winner), illustrated by Beth and Joe Krush, first edition with dust jacket: $70.00

SOWERBY, J. G.
Afternoon Tea, Rhymes for Children, Rhodes and Washburn, 1881, decorated hardcover, 64 pages, illustrated: $80.00

SPAETH, Sigmund
Maxims to Music, McBride, 1939, oversize, color illustrations by Tony Sarg, first edition: $200.00

SPARK, Muriel
Very Fine Clock, Alfred A. Knopf, 1968, illustrated by Edward Gorey, first edition with dust jacket: $100.00

SPEARE, Elizabeth George
Witch of Black Bird Pond, Houghton Mifflin, 1958, Newbery Medal book, first edition with dust jacket: $40.00

SPIER, Peter, author/illustrator

And So My Garden Grows, World's Work, UK, 1969 (Mother Goose Library), oblong, unpaginated, nursery rhymes, color illustrations of two nineteenth-century children with background of Italian gardens and architecture, first edition with dust jacket: $70.00

Erie Canal, Doubleday, 1970, first edition: $80.00

Fox Went out on a Chilly Night, Doubleday, 1961, color illustrations, first edition: $40.00

SPILKA, Arnold
And the Frog Went Blah, Charles Scribner, 1972, illustrated by author, first edition with dust jacket: $30.00

SPYRI, Johanna, *Heidi*

SPYRI, Johanna (1827 – 1901)

Spyri's original novel, *Heidi,* inspired numerous editions, many illustrated by well-known artists. Shortened versions were featured in picture books for younger children. A very young Shirley Temple starred as Heidi in a film adaptation. Two sequels by another author continued Heidi's story. A sampling of the many editions include:

Heidi 1. Her Years of Wandering and Learning & 2. How She Used What She Learned: Stories for Children and Those Who Love Children, translation by Louise Brooks, Cupples, Upham & Company, Boston, 1885, two volumes bound in one, first American edition: $2,000.00. Later editions thus: $500.00

SPYRI, Johanna, *Mäzli*

Heidi, Rand McNally, 1921, Windermere edition, black with silver trim and paste-on illustration, color illustrations by Maginal Wright Barney: $50.00

Heidi, David McKay, 1922 edition, pictorial cover, color plates by Jessie Willcox Smith, first thus: $100.00

Heidi's Children, Grosset & Dunlap, 1939 edition, hardcover, color and b/w illustations by Pelagie Doane: $40.00

Mäzli, J. B. Lippincott, 1921, red hardcover with gilt, eight color plates by Maria Kirk: $40.00

STAHL, Ben

Blackbeard's Ghost, Houghton Mifflin, 1965, illustrations by author, first edition with dust jacket: $50.00

Secret of Red Skull (sequel to *Blackbeard's Ghost*), Houghton Mifflin, 1971, first edition with dust jacket: $40.00

STAPP, Emilie Blackmore, see Series section, ISABELLA THE GOOSE

STEIG, William (1907 – 2003), author/illustrator

Steig attended City College in New York, then continued his art education at the National Academy of Design. He was awarded both the Caldecott for art and the Newbery for writing. Steig's work included *New Yorker* illustrations as well as numerous children's books, including the 1990 book, *Shrek,* the basis of the films.

Abel's Island, Farrar, 1976 (Newbery Medal winner), illustrated by author, first edition with dust jacket: $100.00

Agony in the Kindergarten, Duell, Sloan & Pearce, 1950, oversize hardcover, illustrated by author: $50.00

Amos & Boris, Farrar, Straus, Giroux, 1971, author's second children's book, first edition with dust jacket: $200.00

Bad Island, Windmill Books/Simon & Schuster, 1969, illustrations in psychadelic colors by author, first edition with dust jacket: $500.00

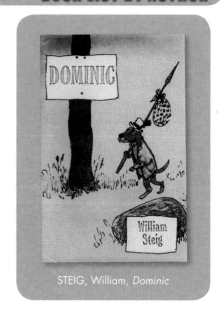

STEIG, William, *Dominic*

Bad Speller, Simon & Schuster, 1970, illustrated by author, first edition with dust jacket: $70.00

Dominic, Farrar, 1972, illustrated by author, first edition with dust jacket: $100.00

Farmer Palmer's Wagon Ride, Farrar, 1974, oversize hardcover, illustrated by author: $50.00

Real Thief, Farrar, 1973, 58 pages, b/w illustrations by author: $60.00

STEINER, Charlotte, author/illustrator

Charlotte Steiner's ABC, Franklin Watts, 1946, first edition with dust jacket: $70.00

Listen to My Seashell, Alfred A. Knopf, 1959, pictorial boards: $50.00

STEINER, Charlotte, *Listen to My Seashell*

Red Ridinghood Goes Sledding, Macmillan, 1962, oversize hardcover, 27 pages, first edition with dust jacket: $70.00

Red Ridinghood's Little Lamb, Knopf 1964, illustrated by the author, first edition with dust jacket: $70.00

STEPHENS, Mary Jo
Witch of the Cumberlands, Houghton Mifflin, 1974, 243 pages, illustrated by Arvis Stewart, first edition with dust jacket: $30.00

Zoe's Zodiac, Houghton Mifflin, 1971, illustrated by Leonard Shortall, first edition with dust jacket: $50.00

STEPTOE, John (1950 – 1989)
Stevie, Harper, 1969, pictorial hardcover, color illustrations by author, first edition with dust jacket: $130.00

Train Ride, Harper, 1971, first edition with dust jacket: $80.00

Uptown, Harper, 1970, pictorial paper-covered hardcover, first edition with dust jacket: $80.00

STERNE, Emma Gelders
All About Little Boy Blue, Cupples & Leon, 1924, blue paper over boards with small color plate paste-on, 48 pages, b/w and eight color plates by Thelma Gooch, first edition: $30.00

Drums of Monmouth, Dodd, Mead & Company, 1935, illustrated by Robert Lawson, first edition with dust jacket: $60.00

Miranda Is a Princess, 1937, Dodd, cloth-over-board cover, illustrated endpapers, 221 pages, b/w illustrations by Robert Lawson: $80.00

STEVENSON, James, author/illustrator

Here Comes Herb's Hurricane!, Harper, 1973, first edition, small hardcover, b/w illustrations by author, first edition with dust jacket: $40.00

STEVENSON, Robert Louis (1850 – 1894)
Black Arrow, Charles Scribner's Sons,

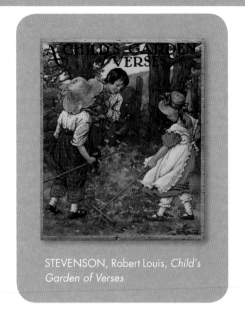

STEVENSON, Robert Louis, *Child's Garden of Verses*

1916, black cloth with pasted color plate, gilt lettering on spine, gilt top leaves, 328 pages, 14 color plates plus color title page by N.C. Wyeth, first edition thus: $600.00

Child's Garden of Verses, Charles Scribner's Sons, 1885, small blue cloth over green paper boards, blue-stamped front board, gilt-stamped spine, first US edition: $900.00

Child's Garden of Verses, Saalfield, 1930 edition, oversize, black cloth-over-board cover with paste-on-pictorial and gilt trim, flowered endpapers, 60 pages, 13 color plate illustrations by Clara Burd: $85.00

Child's Garden of Verses, by Robert Louis Stevenson, 1940, Saalfield color-throughout, oversize picture book, 89 pages, illustrations by Fern Bisel Peat, with dust jacket: $120.00. Without dust jacket: $60.00

Child's Garden of Verses, John Martin's House, 1942 edition, oversize hardcover with illustrated endpapers and color illustrations by Pelagie Doane: $35.00

David Balfour, Scribner's, 1893, decorative cloth, sequel to *Kidnapped,* US first edition: $300.00

Kidnapped: Being Memoirs of the Adventures of David Balfour in the Year 1751, Cassell, 1886, red cloth, gilt-lettered spine, black endpapers, contains the map, UK first edition: $1,700.00

Kidnapped, Charles Scribner's Sons, 1913, top edges gilt, 14 tissue guarded color plates by N.C. Wyeth, fold-out map, first edition thus: $700.00

Travels with a Donkey, Roberts Brothers, 1879, gilt-decorated green cloth, first American edition: $500.00

Treasure Island, Cassell, 1883, green cloth (serial publication by *Young Folks* magazine, was anonymous, by "Captain George North"), first edition consisted of 2,000 copies, has ads curiously dated October or December 1883: $9,000.00

Treasure Island, Roberts Brothers, 1884, Boston, cloth with pictorial, decorated endpapers, first American printing and first illustrated edition, with four full-page plates by T. T. Merrill, two-color map frontispiece with tissue guard, US first edition: $1,200.00

Treasure Island, Scribner's, 1911, cloth cover with paste-on illustration, top gilt edges, 14 color plates by N.C. Wyeth, first edition thus: $400.00

STEWART, Grace Bliss
Good Fairy, Reilly & Lee, 1930, green cloth-over-board cover with gilt illustration, 128 pages, color and b/w illustrations by P. B. Adams: $60.00

In and out of the Jungle, D. C. Heath & Co., Boston, 1922, small, illustrated cloth cover, full-page b/w illustrations, 165 pages: $60.00

STOCKTON, Frank Richard (1834 – 1902)
Bee-Man of Orn, 1964, Holt, Rinehart and Winston, first edition thus, hardcover, color illustrations by Maurice Sendak, first edition with dust jacket: $70.00

Casting Away of Mrs. Lecks and Mrs. Aleshine (1886), 1933 edition, Appleton, hardcover, 290 pages, illustrations by George Richards: $80.00

Griffin and the Minor Canon, Holt, 1963, first edition thus, hardcover, illustrated by Maurice Sendak, with dust jacket: $100.00

Queen's Museum and Other Fanciful Tales, Charles Scribner's Sons, 1906, black cloth with gilt, 10 color plates by Frederick Richardson: $80.00

Ting-a-Ling, Hurd & Houghton, 1870, decorated green cloth, collection of stories for children about the fairy Ting-A-Ling and his adventures, first edition: $400.00

What Might Have Been Expected, Routledge, 1875, green pictorial cloth with gilt, 12 plates, UK first edition: $140.00

STOLZ, Mary, see also Series section, ASA AND RAMBO

Emmett's Pig, Harper & Brothers, 1959, 63 pages, illustrated by Garth Williams, first edition with dust jacket: $40.00

STONG, Phil

High Water, Dodd, Mead & Company, 1937, illustrated by Kurt Wiese, first edition with dust jacket: $50.00

Honk the Moose, Dodd, Mead & Company, 1935, oversize, black cloth spine, color pictorial paper boards, 80 pages, color pictorial endpapers, frontispiece, illustrated by Kurt Wiese: $60.00

Horses and Americans, Frederick A. Stokes, 1939, oversize, illustrated by Kurt Wiese: $60.00

Prince and the Porker, Dodd, Mead & Company, 1950, hardcover, illustrated by Kurt Wiese, first edition with dust jacket: $70.00

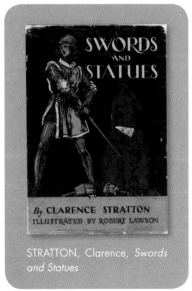

STRATTON, Clarence, *Swords and Statues*

STRATTON, Clarence (1880 – 1951)

Swords and Statues, Literary Guild, 1937, orange cloth-over-board cover, color frontispiece, b/w illustrations by Robert Lawson, with dust jacket: $45.00

STREATFEILD, Noel (1897 – 1986), see also Series section, SHOES

Growing Summer, Collins, 1966, hardcover, illustrated by Edward Ardizzone: $40.00

Thursday's Child, Random House, 1970, illustrations by Peggy Fortnum, first American edition with dust jacket: $50.00

STRIKER, Fran, see Series section, LONE RANGER, TOM QUEST

STUART, Ruth McEnery

Daddy Do-Funny's Wisdom Jingles, Century, 1916, yellow cloth-covered boards with green decoration and lettering, 95 pages, illustrated by G. H. Clements: $70.00

George Washington Jones, a Christmas That Went A-Begging, Henry Altemus, 1903, decorative cloth, small, illustrations by Edward Potthast: $100.00

Gobolinks or Shadow Pictures for Young and Old, Century, 1896, pictorial boards, oblong, illustrated by Albert Bigelow Paine: $150.00

Napoleon Jackson, Century, 1902, cloth-over-board cover with gilt, small, 132 pages, b/w illustrations by Edward Potthast: $40.00

River's Children, Century, 1904, green cloth with gilt, first edition with dust jacket: $600.00

SUTCLIFF, Rosemary (1920 – 1992), see also Series section, KING ARTHUR TRILOGY

Brother Dusty Feet, Oxford, 1952, b/w illustrations by Walter Hodges, first edition with dust jacket: $80.00

Dawn Wind, Oxford, 1961, b/w illustrations by Charles Keeping, first edition with dust jacket: $60.00

SUTCLIFF, Rosemary, *Shield and the Ring*

Knight's Fee, Oxford, 1960, illustrated by Charles Keeping, first edition with dust jacket: $60.00

Mark of the Horse Lord, 1965, Oxford, first edition, hardcover: $40.00

Shield Ring, Oxford, 1956, first edition with dust jacket: $100.00

Sword at Sunset, Hodder & Stoughton, 1963, map endpapers, dust jacket by Brian O'Hanlon, first edition with dust jacket: $100.00

Sword at Sunset, Coward-McCann, 1963, map endpapers, US first edition with dust jacket: $50.00

Tristan and Iseult, Bodley Head, 1971, illustrated by Victor Ambrus, UK first edition with dust jacket: $50.00

Witch's Brat, Oxford, 1970, first edition with dust jacket: $50.00

SUTTON, Margaret, see Series section, JUDY BOLTON MYSTERY

SYMONDS, John

Elfrida and the Pig, Franklin Watts, 1959, oversize hardcover, illustrated by Edward Ardizzone: $30.00

Magic Currant Bun, J. B. Lippincott, 1952, pictorial cover, illustrated by Andre Francois, with dust jacket: $30.00

Tom & Tabby, 1964, laminated pictorial boards, oversize, illustrated with drawings by Andre Francois, US first edtion: $70.00

SZYK, Arthur (1894 – 1951)
Polish-born Szyk studied art in Poland and Paris, then exhibited his paintings in Europe and the United States, including a series of paintings titled "George Washington and His Times." After WWII, Szyk and his wife remained in the States. He continued his career in fine art, magazine illustration, and children's books illustration. Examples of his detailed style are found in his 1945 edition of *Andersen's Fairy Tales.* In 1946 the Limited Edition Club published several books with Szyk illustrations, including Mary Chase's *Book of Ruth* and Chaucer's *Canterbury Tales.*

T

TAMBURINE, Jean
Almost Big Enough, Abingdon Press, 1963, red cloth, illustrated by author, first edition with dust jacket: $30.00

How Now Brown Cow, Abingdon Press, 1967, first edition, hardcover, author illustrated: $35.00

TANDY, Russell H. (1893 – 1961)
Tandy was a New York commercial artist, already recognized for his work in catalog and fashion illustration, when he

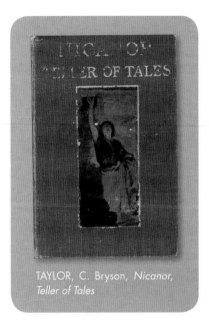

TANDY, Russell H., *Nancy Drew* books

was hired to design a cover for the new *Nancy Drew* series in 1930. Tandy was a graduate of the Art Students' League in New York City. Tandy based Nancy's face on fashion model Grace Horton. As well as painting the dust jacket designs and interior illustrations for 25 *Nancy Drew* books, he hand-lettered the dust jacket titles. He also did covers for other series, including *Hardy Boys* and Howard Garis's *Buddy* series.

TARKINGTON, Booth (1869 – 1946), see also Series section, PENROD

TARRANT, Margaret (1888 – 1959)
Daughter of English artist Percy Tarrant (d. 1930), Margaret Tarrant's long-legged children appeared in postcards, greeting cards, birthday books, and a variety of gift books published by the Medici Society in the 1920s. She also illustrated editions of Kingsley's *Water Babies* (one of her first commissions) and Carroll's *Alice in Wonderland.*

Picture Birthday-Book for Boys and Girls, Harrap, 1916, cloth boards decorated with roses and gilt title, one color picture per month: $150.00

TARRY, Ellen
Hezekiah Horton, Viking Press, 1955, illustrated by Oliver Harrington, first edition with dust jacket: $90.00

Janie Belle, Garden City, 1940, color pictorial paper-coverd boards with cloth spine, brown and white full-page illustrations throughout by Myrtle Sheldon, first edition with dust jacket: $100.00

My Dog Rinty, Viking Press, 1964, illustrated by Marie Hall Ets, first edition with dust jacket: $100.00

TASHJIAN, Virginia
Once There Was and Was Not, Armenian Tales Retold, Little, Brown, 1966, illustrated by Nonny Hogrogian, first edition with dust jacket: $50.00

Three Apples Fell from Heaven, Armenian Tales Retold, 1971, Little, Brown, illustrated by Nonny Hogrogian, first edition with dust jacket: $30.00

TATHAM, Julie Campbell, see Series section, CHERRY AMES, NURSE SERIES, TRIXIE BELDEN, VICKI BARR FLIGHT STEWARDESS

TAYLOR, C. Bryson
Nicanor, Teller of Tales, a story of Roman Britain, McClurg, 1906, paste-on-illustration, five mounted color plates by Troy and Margaret West Kinney: $50.00

TAYLOR, C. Bryson, *Nicanor, Teller of Tales*

TAYLOR, Sidney Bremer (1904 – 1978), see Series section, ALL-OF-A-KIND FAMILY

TAZEWELL, Charles
I'm a Fridgit!, Holton House, 1963, color illustrations by Joyce Langelier, first edition with dust jacket: $40.00

Littlest Angel, Chicago, Children's Press, 1946, Tazewell wrote the story for radio, illustrated endpapers and illustrations by Katherine Evans, first edition with dust jacket: $250.00

Small One: Story for Those Who Like Christmas and Small Donkeys, Franklin Limited Edition, 1958, gilt decorated paper-over-board hardcover, 26 pages, designed by Donald E. Cooke, illustrated by Marian Ebert, first edition with dust jacket: $100.00

TEMPLE, Shirley, see also Series section, SHIRLEY TEMPLE EDITION BOOKS

Shirley Temple Treasury, 1959, Random House, first edition, oversize hardcover, illustrated by Robert Patterson drawings and photographs from films featuring Shirley Temple, including *Heidi, Little Colonel, Rebecca of Sunnybrook Farm,* and *Captain January:* $50.00

TENGGREN, Gustaf (b. Sweden, 1896 – 1970)

Tenggren grew up in Sweden, studied at an art school in Gothenburg, and began his career illustrating Scandanavian fairy tales. When he was 24, he moved to America. He illustrated Lowrey's bestselling *Poky Little Puppy,* Little Golden Books, 1942.

TENGGREN, Gustaf, illustration for Lowrey's *Poky Little Puppy*

New Illustrated Book of Favorite Hymns, Garden City, 1941, pictorial boards, color illustrations throughout: $30.00

Tenggren's Story Book, Simon & Schuster, 1944, oversize pictorial boards, color illustrations by author, 90 pages, first edition with dust jacket: $100.00

Tenggren Tell-It-Again Book, Little, Brown, 1942, oversize, 199 pages, illustrations by Tenggren: $50.00

THAYER, Jane, see also Series section, GUS THE GHOST

Little Dog Called Kitty, William Morrow, 1961, pictorial gold cover, illustrated by Seymour Fleishman: $40.00

Popcorn Dragon, Morrow, 1953, hardcover picture book, illustrated by Jay Hyde Barnum, first edition with dust jacket: $50.00

THEISS, Lewis, see Series section, MAIL PILOT, PEE WEE DEWIRE

THELWELL, Norman (1923 – 2004)

English cartoonist Norman Thelwell created more than 20 books under the name "Thelwell" as well as contributing cartoons and illustrations to popular British magazines.

Angels on Horseback, E. P. Dutton, 1958, first American edition of Thelwell's first book, b/w illustrations by author, with dust jacket: $75.00

Thelwell Country, Methuen, 1959, first edition, oversize hardcover picture book, b/w illustrations by author: $35.00

Thelwell's Horse Box: Angels on Horseback and Elsewhere; A Leg at Each Corner; Thelwell's Gymkhana; Thelwell's Riding Academy, Methuen, London, four of the horse books in reprint edition in matching box: $70.00

Thelwell's Horse Sense, Methuen, London, 1980, laminated pictorial board, color illustrations that first appeared in a set of prints, first edition in book form: $40.00

THOMPSON, Blanche Jennings

Bible Children, Dodd, Mead, 1937, illustrated by Kate Seredy, first edition: $50.00

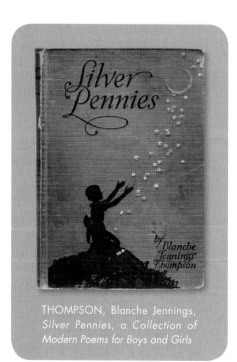

THOMPSON, Blanche Jennings, *Silver Pennies, a Collection of Modern Poems for Boys and Girls*

Golden Trumpets, Macmillan, 1927, small, 163 pages, cloth-over-board cover with gilt, orange/b/w illustrations by Helen Torrey: $30.00

More Silver Pennies, Macmillan, 1928, cloth with illustration in silver, small, b/w illustrations, first edition with dust jacket: $70.00

Silver Pennies, a Collection of Modern Poems for Boys and Girls, Macmillan, 1925, cloth with illustration in silver, small, b/w illustrations, first edition with dust jacket: $80.00

THOMPSON, Kay, see also Series section, ELOISE

Miss Pooky Peckinpaugh, Harper, 1970, first edition in dust jacket: $100.00

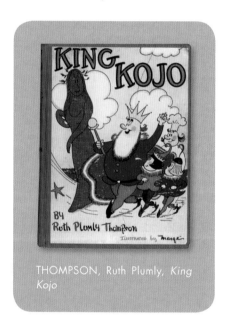

THOMPSON, Ruth Plumly, *King Kojo*

THOMPSON, Ruth Plumly, see also Series section, OZ

King Kojo, David McKay, 1938, pasteon-pictorial, 239 pages, b/w and color illustrations by Marge (Little Lulu creator), first edition: $200.00

Perhappsy Chaps, Volland, 1918, color illustrated paper-over-board cover, color illustrations by Arthur Henderson: $200.00

Princess of Cozytown, Volland, 1922, color illustrated paper-over-board cover, color illustrations by Janet Laura Scott: $100.00. In original box: $500.00

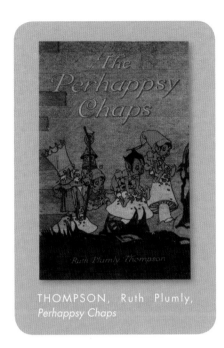

THOMPSON, Ruth Plumly, *Perhappsy Chaps*

THOMPSON, Ruth Plumly, *Wonder Book*

Wonder Book, Reilly & Lee, 1929, brown cloth-over-board cover with paste-on-pictorial, color plate illustrations by William Donahey, b/w illustrations by other artists: $300.00

THOMPSON, William

Wigwam Wonder Tales, Scribner, 1919, cloth-over-board cover with decoration, small, 156 pages, b/w illustrations by Carle Michel Boog: $40.00

THOREAU, Henry David

Men of Concord, Houghton Mifflin, 1936, illustrated by N.C. Wyeth, hardcover: $75.00. With original box: $500.00

THORNDYKE, Helen Louise, see Series section, HONEY BUNCH

THORNE-THOMSEN, Gudrun

Birch and the Star, Row Peterson, 1915, cloth-over-board cover with paste-on-illustration, illustrated endpapers, small, 129 pages, six color plates by Frederick Poole: $30.00

East o' the Sun and West o' the Moon, Peterson, 1912, tan cloth-over-board cover, color plates by Frederick Richardson: $40.00

THURBER, James (1894 – 1961)

13 Clocks, Simon & Schuster, 1957, blue/b/w illustrations by Marc Simont, first edition with dust jacket: $100.00

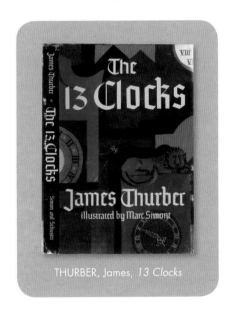

THURBER, James, *13 Clocks*

Wonderful O, Simon & Schuster, 1957, blue/b/w illustrations by Marc Simont, first edition with dust jacket: $65.00

TIMLIN, William M.

Ship That Sailed to Mars, Fredrick A. Stokes, New York, or George Harrap, London, 1923, oversize, 48 mounted color plates, original half-vellum binding with gilt decoration: $4,000.00

Ship That Sailed to Mars, Stonewall Publications, 1993, reproduction of 1923 original, with dust jacket: $150.00

TIMLIN, William M., *Ship That Sailed to Mars*

TITUS, Eve, see Series section, ANATOLE, BASIL OF BAKER STREET

TODD, Ruthven, see also Series section, SPACE CAT

First Animal Book, Peter Lunn, London, 1946, illustrated by Bewick, collection of verses, first edition with dust jacket: $50.00

TOLKIEN, J. R. R. (1892 – 1973), see also Series section, LORD OF THE RINGS

Farmer Giles of Ham, Houghton Mifflin, 1950 edition, first American edition thus, hardcover, 80 pages, color frontispiece, illustrated by Pauline Baynes, first edition with dust jacket: $100.00

Road Goes Ever On, George Allen & Unwin Ltd., 1968, first edition, oversize white hardcover, 67 pages, songs: $50.00

TOLMAN, Albert, see Series section, JIM SPURLING

TOMPKINS, Walker A., see also Series section, TOMMY ROCKFORD HAM RADIO MYSTERY

CQ Ghost Ship!, 1960, Macrae Smith, first edition with dust jacket: $150.00

TOUSEY, Sanford

Jerry and the Pony Express, Doubleday, 1936, oblong, illustrated paper-over-board

169

cover, illustrated endpapers, color illustrated throughout by author: $40.00

Steamboat Billy, Doubleday, 1935, oblong, illustrated paper-over-board cover, illustrated endpapers, color illustrated throughout by author: $40.00

TOURTEL, Mary (1897 – 1940), see Series section, RUPERT LITTLE BEAR

TOWLE, Faith
Magic Cooking Pot, Houghton Mifflin, 1975, oblong hardcover, batik illustrations by author, first edition with dust jacket: $80.00

TOWNSEND, John Rowe
Gumble's Yard, Hutchinson, 1961 (this title was also released as *Trouble in the Jungle* in the U.S.), first edition with dust jacket: $75.00

TRAVERS, P. L., see also Series section, MARY POPPINS

Friend Monkey, Harcourt Brace, 1971, 284 pages, illustrated by Charles Keeping, US first edition with dust jacket: $30.00

I Go by Sea, I Go by Land, Harper, 1941, cloth-over-board cover, illustrations by Gertrude Hermes, first edition with dust jacket: $30.00

TREASE, Geoffrey (1909 – 1997)
British author Geoffrey Trease wrote more than 100 novels, including many mystery and historical novels for children. Some of his titles issued in the 1930s were revised and reissued in the 1960s. Highest prices are paid for early works with well-preserved dust jackets.

Bows against the Barons, Martin Lawrence, 1934, first edition with dust jacket: $50.00

Black Night, Red Morning, Martin Lawrence, 1944, first edition with dust jacket: $125.00

Mystery on the Moors, Black, 1937, hardcover: $50.00

TREECE, Henry (1911 – 1966)
British poet Henry Treece wrote several

novels for children, including the following trilogy about Vikings:

Road to Miklagard, Bodley Head, 1957, first British edition with dust jacket: $50.00

Viking's Dawn, Criterion, 1956, first US edition with dust jacket: $30.00

Viking's Sunset, Criterion, 1961, first US edition with dust jacket: $35.00

TRESSELT, Alvin
Autumn Harvest, Lothrop, 1951, oversize hardcover, illustrated by Roger Duvoisin, first edition with dust jacket: $50.00

TREVOR, Elleston, see Series section, DEEP WOOD

TUDOR, Tasha, author/illustrator

1 Is One, Oxford, 1956, pink oblong oversize hardcover, illustrated by Tudor, first edition with dust jacket: $200.00

A Is for Anna Belle, Oxford, 1954, oblong hardcover, illustrated by Tasha Tudor, first edition with dust jacket: $200.00

Around the Year, Oxford, 1957, yellow hardcover, illustrated by Tasha Tudor, first edition with dust jacket: $100.00

Becky's Christmas, Viking Press, 1961, color illustrations, first edition with dust jacket: $150.00

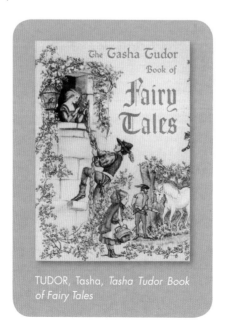

TUDOR, Tasha, *Tasha Tudor Book of Fairy Tales*

Corgiville Fair, Crowell, 1971, probable first edition, oblong hardcover with gilt animal illustration and lettering, color illustrations by author, first edition with dust jacket: $200.00

Country Fair, Walck (1940), 1968 enlarged first edition thus, color illustrations by author, first edition with dust jacket: $100.00

Doll's Christmas, Oxford, 1950, square red hardcover with paste-on-pictorial, illustrated by author, first edition with dust jacket: $200.00

First Delights, Platt & Monk, 1966, color illustrations by Tudor, first edition with dust jacket: $75.00

First Graces, Oxford, 1955, small hardcover, color illustrations by author, first edition with dust jacket: $100.00

First Poems of Childhood, Platt & Munk, 1967, Tudor illustrations, first edition with dust jacket: $170.00

First Prayers, Oxford, 1952, small blue-gray hardcover, illustrated endpapers, 48 pages, color illustrations by author, first edition with dust jacket: $125.00

Linsey Woolsey, Oxford, 1946, color illustrations by Tudor, first edition with dust jacket: $220.00

Pumpkin Moonshine, Henry Z. Walck, 1962, enlarged edition, 6" x 7", color illustrations throughout, first edition thus with dust jacket: $120.00

Take Joy!, World, 1966, oblong oversize hardcover, color illustrations by author, first edition with dust jacket: $100.00

Tasha Tudor Book of Fairy Tales, Platt & Munk, 1961, oversize, pictorial cover, first edition with dust jacket: $150.00

Tasha Tudor's Favorite Stories, J. B. Lippincott, 1965, oversize hardcover, green cloth spine, pictorial boards, first edition with dust jacket: $125.00

Snow Before Christmas, Oxford, 1941, first edition with dust jacket: $295.00

Wings from the Wind, J. B. Lippincott, 1964, illustrated by Tudor, first edition with dust jacket: $100.00

TUNIS, John R., see also Series section, KID FROM TOMKINVILLE

Buddy and the Old Pro, Morrow,1955, illustrated by Jay Hyde, first edition with dust jacket: $200.00

TURKLE, Brinton

Adventures of Obadiah, Viking Press, 1972, color illustrations by author, first edition with dust jacket: $60.00

Fiddler of High Lonesome, Viking Press, 1968, first edition with dust jacket: $70.00

Magic of Millicent Musgrave, Viking Press, 1967, first edition with dust jacket: $50.00

TURNER, Nancy Byrd

Magpie Lane, Harcourt Brace, 1927, cloth-over-board cover, silhouette illustrations by Decie Merwin: $30.00

Ray Coon to the Rescue, Rand McNally, 1931, pictorial endpapers, 80 pages, illustrated by Keith Ward, first edition with dust jacket: $60.00

Sycamore Silver, Dodd, Mead, 1942, illustrated by Victor J. Dowling, first edition with dust jacket: $50.00

Zodiac Town, Atlantic Monthly Press, 1921, b/w illustrations by Winifred Bromhall, first edition with dust jacket: $50.00

TWAIN, Mark (Samuel Clemens, 1835 – 1910)

Twain's American classics are reprinted regularly by a variety of publishers and in various formats, and are easily available. Tom Sawyer's adventures begin in Hannibal, Missouri, a small river town where Twain once lived, and include Tom's best friends, Becky Thatcher and Huckleberry Finn.

Tom Sawyer books, sample listing of early editions and values:

Adventures of Huckleberry Finn, Charles L. Webster and Company, NY, 1885, green pictorial cloth with gilt, title leaf shows copyright dated 1884, first edition: $17,000.00

Adventures of Huckleberry Finn, Webster, 1885, pictorial green hardcover with gilt, illustrated by Edward Kemble: $3,000.00

Adventures of Huckleberry Finn, Harper & Bros., ca. 1940, paste-on-pictorial hardcover, b/w plates by Worth Brehm, with dust jacket: $45.00

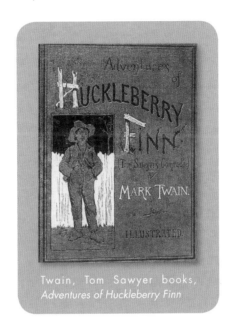

Twain, Tom Sawyer books, *Adventures of Huckleberry Finn*

Adventures of Tom Sawyer, American Publishing Company, 1880, original blue cloth with gilt, frontispiece plus 150 or more vignettes in text: $2,500.00

Adventures of Tom Sawyer, Harper & Bros., ca. 1930s, black hardcover with paste-on-pictorial, color frontispiece, 15 b/w plates by Worth Brehm, with dust jacket: $45.00

Tom Sawyer, Whitman, 1931, pictorial boards, color photograph illustrations from the Paramount movie starring Jackie Coogan as Tom and Junior Durkin as Huck, with movie text on facing pages: $50.00

Tom Sawyer Abroad, Chatto & Windus, London, 1894, red hardcover with black decoration, illustrations by Dan Beard, first UK edition: $450.00

Tom Sawyer Abroad: Tom Sawyer, Detective and Other Stories, Charles L. Webster, ca. 1894, light hardcover with a decoration depicting a lion chasing Tom and Huck, probable first edition: $1,000.00

Tom Sawyer Abroad: Tom Sawyer, Detective and Other Stories, Webster, ca. 1896, illustrated by Arthur Frost: $150.00

Twain, other:

Mysterious Stranger, Harper, 1916, illustrated by N. C. Wyeth, hardcover: $75.00

Prince and the Pauper, Osgood, Boston, 1882, square, 411 pages, gilt decorated cover, 192 illustrations: $400.00

Tragedy of Pudd'nhead Wilson and the Comedy of Those Extraordinary Twins, American Publishing Company, Hartford, Connecticut, 1894, cloth hardcover: $2,000.00

■ ⋯⋯⋯⋯⋯⋯ **U** ⋯⋯⋯⋯⋯⋯ ■

UCHIDA, Yoshiko

New Friends for Susan, Scribner's, 1951, illustrations by Henry Sugimoto, first edition with dust jacket: $50.00

Rokubei and the Thousand Rice Bowls, Scribner's, 1962, illustrations by Kazue Mizumura, first edition with dust jacket: $50.00

Sumi's Prize, Scribner's, 1964, oversize, illustrations by Kazue Mizumura, first edition with dust jacket: $40.00

UDRY, Janice May

Let's Be Enemies, Harper, 1968, illustrated by Maurice Sendak, first edition with dust jacket: $80.00

Mary Ann's Mud Day, Harper & Row, 1967, square, paper-covered boards, 29 pages, color illustrations by Martha Alexander, first edition with dust jacket: $100.00

Mean Mouse and Other Mean Stories, Harper, 1962, pictorial hardcover, color illustrations by Ed Young: $50.00

Moon Jumpers, Harper & Row, 1959, pictorial hardcover, color illustrations by Maurice Sendak, first edition with dust jacket: $80.00

UNDERWOOD, Betty
Tamarack Tree, Houghton Mifflin, 1971, 230 pages, b/w illustrations by Bea Holmes, first edition with dust jacket: $70.00

UNGERER, Tomi, author/illustrator, see also Series section, MELLOPS

A rare adult work by Tomi Ungerer, *A Childhood Under the Nazis* (1998), chronicles his early years in Strasbourg, France. His childhood experiences triggered much of Ungerer's interest in art. Drawing became a way to both comment about and escape from the chaos that surrounded him. Following a brief time at the Ecole des Arts Decoratifs in Strasbourg, France, Ungerer spent many years wandering Europe and working in odd jobs as an illustrator. In 1956, he immigrated to the United States and worked for a time in magazine illustration. His first book, *Mellops Go Flying* (1957), led to a prolific career in writing and illustrating picture books for children, including a series of titles about the Mellops.

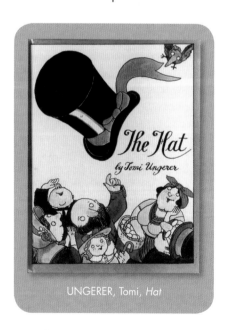

UNGERER, Tomi, *Hat*

Adelaide, Harper & Row, 1959, 40 pages, illustrated by author, first edition with dust jacket: $150.00

Ask Me a Question, Harper & Row, 1968, first edition, hardcover, 32 pages, illustrated by author: $50.00

Beast of Monsieur Racine, Farrar, 1971, first edition, hardcover, illustrated by author: $40.00

Crictor, Harper & Brothers, 1958, pictorial boards, picture-book, story of a pet boa constrictor, first edition: $100.00

Hat, Parents' Magazine Press, 1970, oversize, illustrated hardcover, color illustrations throughout by author, first edition: $40.00

I Am Papa Snap and These Are My Favorite No Such Stories, Harper & Row, 1971, illustrated oversize hardcover, illustrated by author, first edition: $40.00

Rufus, Harper & Row, 1961, first edition, hardcover, color illustrations by author: $50.00

UNWIN, Nora S.
Doughnuts for Lin, Aladdin Books, 1950, illustrated by author, first edition with dust jacket: $100.00

UPDIKE, John
Magic Flute, Alfred A. Knopf, 1962, illustrated by Warren Chappell, first edition with dust jacket: $700.00

Bottom's Dream, Alfred A. Knopf, 1969, illustrated by Warren Chappell, first edition with dust jacket: $200.00

UPTON, Bertha, see Series section, GOLLIWOGG AND DUTCH DOLLS

URBAN, Joseph
Sinbad the Sailor: His Adventures with Beauty and the Peacock Lady in the Castle of the Forty Thieves, 1917, Houghton Mifflin, hardcover with paste-on-pictorial, 146 pages, title page and decorations by Joseph Urban, first edition: $100.00

UTTLEY, Alison, see Series section, LITTLE BROWN MOUSE, LITTLE RED FOX, SAM PIG, SNUG AND SERENA

■·····················■ V ·····················■

VANCE, Eleanor Graham
Everything Book, Golden Book, 1974, oversize, color illustrated paper-over-board cover, 140+ pages, color and b/w illustrations throughout by Trina Schart Hyman: $50.00

VANCE, Jack
Vandals of the Void, Winston, 1953, jacket and endpaper design by Alex Schombeurg, Vance's first hardcover, science fiction, first edition with dust jacket: $200.00

Van DYNE, see BAUM, L. Frank

Van LOON, Hendrik
Story of Mankind, Boni and Liveright, 1921, recipient of the first Newbery Award, first edition: $50.00

VARNEY, Joyce
Half-Time Gypsy, Bobbs-Merrill, 1966, illustrated by Trina Schart Hyman, first edition with dust jacket: $40.00

VENTURA, Piero
Book of Cities, Random House, 1975, oversize hardcover picture book, illustrated by author: $30.00

VerBECK, Frank (William Francis, 1858 – 1933)

This Ohio artist specialized in comic drawings, often featuring animals mimicking

VerBECK, Frank, illustration from *Arkansas Bear* stories

human behavior. Early books included *A New Wonderland,* 1900 (reprinted as *Magical Monarch of Mo*), by L. Frank Baum, as well as contributions to *Told by Uncle Remus* by Joel Chandler Harris. Baum told family members that he preferred VerBeck's illustrations to those of any of the other artists he had worked with, quite a compliment considering that Baum's earlier books had been illustrated by Maxfield Parrish and W. W. Denslow. One of the most popular VerBeck projects was Paine's *Arkansas Bear* stories.

VERNE, Jules, see Series section, EXTRAORDINARY JOURNEYS

VERRILL, A. Hyatt, see Series section, DEEP SEA HUNTERS

VIMAR, A.

Curly Haired Hen, Fitzgerald, 1914, first edition, oversize picture book, 95 pages, paste-on-pictorial cover, b/w illustrations by Nora Hill: $50.00

VIORST, Judith

Alexander and the Terrible, Horrible, No Good, Very Bad Day, Atheneum, 1972, oversize hardcover, drawings by Ray Cruz, first edition with dust jacket: $50.00

Rosie and Michael, Simon & Schuster, 1974, first edition: $40.00

Sunday Morning, Harper, 1968, hardcover, illustrations by Hilary Knight, first edition with dust jacket: $40.00

VIP (Virgil Partch)

Christmas Cookie Sprinkle Snitcher, Windmill Books/Simon & Schuster, 1969, oversize, color illustrations by author, first edition with dust jacket: $500.00

VIP's Mistake Book, Windmill, 1970, pictorial orange hardcover, illustrated by author's cartoons, first edition with dust jacket: $30.00

VonHIPPEL, Ursula, author/illustrator

Craziest Halloween, Coward-McCann, 1957, first edition with dust jacket: $60.00

Story of the Snails Who Traded Houses, Coward-McCann, 1961, first edition with dust jacket: $40.00

■ ·················· **W** ·················· ■

WABER, Bernard

Animals traipse through a number of Waber's whimsical stories such as *Lyle, Lyle, Crocodile* (1965). Following army service in World War II, Waber enrolled in the Philadelphia College of Art and went to work after college at Conde Nast, the publisher of such fashion magazines as *Vogue.* Lyle first appeared in 1962 as part of *House on East 88th Street.* Another series character is Arthur, the anteater.

Anteater Named Arthur, 1967, Houghton Mifflin, first edition, oversize hardcover, two-color illustrations by author: $30.00

But Names Will Never Hurt Me, Houghton Mifflin, 1976, decorative cloth, first edition with dust jacket: $100.00

I Was All Thumbs, Houghton Mifflin, 1975, first edition with dust jacket: $60.00

Rich Cat, Poor Cat, Houghton Mifflin, 1963, oversize, 48 pages, first edition with dust jacket: $50.00

Torchy, Houghton Mifflin, 1970, oversize, first edition with dust jacket: $60.00

WADSWORTH, Wallace

Jack Found His Fortune and Other Stories, Rand McNally, 1935, color and b/w illustrations by Margaret Evans Price, first edition: $90.00

Real Story Book, Rand McNally, 1927, oversize with paste-on pictorial, color and b/w illustrations by Margaret Evans Price, first edition: $90.00

WAHL, Jan

Cabbage Moon, Holt, Rinehart and Winston, 1965, 32 pages, illustrations by Adrienne Adams, first edition with dust jacket: $150.00

Cobweb Castle, Holt, 1968, small, 32 pages, color illustrations by Edward Gorey, first edition with dust jacket: $100.00

Crabapple Night, Holt, Rinehart and Winston, 1971, illustrated by Steven Kellogg, first edition with dust jacket: $100.00

Cristobal and the Witch, Putnam, 1972, oversize, illustrated by Janet McCaffery, first edition with dust jacket: $60.00

Pleasant Fieldmouse, Harper, 1964, first of a series of books about this character, illustrations by Maurice Sendak, first edition with dust jacket: $100.00

WALLACE, Ivy, see Series section, POOKIE

WALSH, John

Truants, Rand McNally, 1968, illustrated by Edward Ardizzone, US first edition with dust jacket: $50.00

WALTERS, Hugh, see Series section, CHRIS GODFREY

WARD, Lynd (1905 – 1985)

Ward began his art career in 1929 when he produced a graphic novel, *God's Man,* illustrated with woodcuts. The son of a Methodist minister who worked in the Boston settlements, Ward identified with the problems of the working class. Ward illustrated two Newbery Medal winners, Coatsworth's *Cat Who Went to Heaven,* 1930, and Forbes's *Johnny Tremain,* 1944. From 1937 through 1938 Ward directed the graphic arts division of the Federal Writers Project in New York City.

WARD, Lynd, *Biggest Bear*

Biggest Bear, Houghton Mifflin, 1952 (1953 Caldecott Award), illustrated by author, first edition with dust jacket: $50.00

Silver Pony, Houghton Mifflin, 1973, illustrated endpapers, b/w illustrations, first edition with dust jacket: $100.00

WARD, Marion B.
Boat Children of Canton, McKay, 1944, tan cloth-over-board cover, illustrated endpapers, color and b/w illustrations by Helen Sewell, first edition with dust jacket: $50.00

WARD, Nanda
Hi, Tom, Hastings House, 1962, illustrated by Lynd Ward, first edition with dust jacket: $40.00

Mister Mergatroid, Hastings House, 1960, illustrated by Bob Haynes, first edition with dust jacket: $30.00

WARNER, Lucy
Five Little Finger Stories, Lothrop, 1893, oversize, cloth-over-board cover with gilt, 126 pages, b/w illustrations by Carida: $50.00

WASHBURNE, Heluiz, see Series section, LITTLE ELEPHANT

WASHBURNE, Marion Foster
Old Fashioned Fairy Tales (1909), 1928 edition, Rand McNally, green hardcover with paste-on-illustration, illustrated endpapers, 104 pages, two-color illustrations by Margaret Ely Webb: $60.00

WASSERMAN, Selma and Jack
Bill and Nancy, Liveright Publishing, New York, 1940, illustrated by Gertrude Howe, first edition with dust jacket: $50.00

Nancy Sails, Harper & Brothers, 1936, illustrations by Erick Berry, first edition with dust jacket: $50.00

WATKINS-PITCHFORD, Denys, author/illustrator

B.B.'s Fairy Book, Wind in the Wood, Hollis & Carter, UK, 1952, illustrated by author, first edition with dust jacket: $400.00

Bill Badger's Voyage to World's End, Kaye, Ward, 1969, pictorial paper boards, illustrated by author, first edition with dust jacket: $800.00

Tide's End, Hollis & Carter, 1950, gray cloth with gilt lettering and decoration, full-page color illustrations plus b/w by author, first edition with dust jacket: $450.00

WATSON, Jane Werner
Golden History of the World, Simon & Schuster, 1955, color illustrations by Cornelius De Witt, Giant Golden book: $50.00

How to Tell Time, 1957, Little Golden Books, first edition, small hardcover, clock face: Gruen Precision, metal clock hands: $30.00

Mike and Melissa and Their Magic Mumbo-jumbo: A Story Book with Paper Dolls to Cut Out and Dress, Golden Press, 1959, color drawings by Adriana Mazza Saviozzi, uncut: $150.00

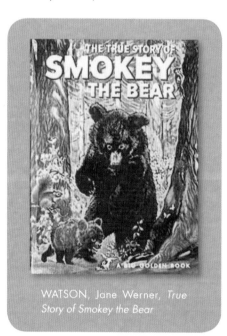

WATSON, Jane Werner, *True Story of Smokey the Bear*

True Story of Smokey the Bear, Big Golden Book, 1955, hardcover, color illustrations by Feodor Rojankovsky: $40.00

WATSON, Sally
Boy Who Listened to Everyone, Parents' Magazine Press, 1963, illustrated endpapers, color illustrations by Ervine Metzl, first edition with dust jacket: $50.00

WATSON, Sally, *Highland Rebel*

Highland Rebel, Henry Holt, 1954, illustrated by Scott Maclain, first edition with dust jacket: $300.00

Lark, Holt, Rinehart and Winston, 1964, first edition with dust jacket: $70.00

Magic at Wychwood, Alfred A. Knopf, 1970, pictorial boards, illustrated by Frank Bozzo, Arthurian spoof, first edition with dust jacket: $250.00

Mistress Malapert, Henry Holt, 1955, first edition with dust jacket: $400.00

Poor Felicity, Doubleday, 1961, first edition with dust jacket: $200.00

Witch of the Glens, Viking Press, 1962, illustrated by Barbara Werner, first edition with dust jacket: $200.00

WEATHERLY, Fred E.
Holly Boughs, E. P. Dutton, undated, ca. 1885, cloth spine, pictorial boards, eight chromolithograph plates: $45.00

Needles and Pins, Hildesheimer, ca. 1880, oversize, 29 pages, paper-over-board cover with color and gilt illustration, chromos and brown/white illustrations by Helena Maguire: $55.00

WEBER, Lenora Mattingly, see Series section, BEANY MALONE, KATIE ROSE, STACY BELFORD

WEBSTER, Jean (1876 – 1916)
Jean Webster's *Daddy-Long-Legs,* about an orphan girl sent to college, became an instant hit and has inspired numerous play

WEBSTER, Jean, *Daddy-Long-Legs*

and film adaptations. Webster wrote a sequel, *Dear Enemy*, and both novels have been continuously reprinted since their first appearance.

Daddy-Long-Legs, Century, 1912, illustrations by author, first edition: $90.00

Daddy-Long-Legs, Grosset Photo-Play, 1912, green hardcover, photos from film starring Mary Pickford plus drawing by author, with dust jacket: $50.00

Dear Enemy, Century, 1915, hardcover: $30.00. With dust jacket: $125.00

Four Pools Mystery, Century, 1908, first edition: $75.00. With dust jacket: $125.00

Jerry Junior, Century, 1907, first editon: $75.00

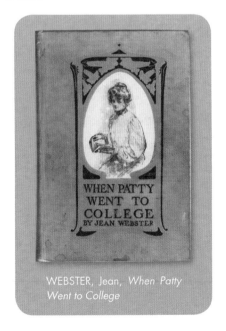

WEBSTER, Jean, *When Patty Went to College*

Just Patty, Century, 1911, hardcover with medallion portrait of Patty on cover: $75.00

Just Patty, Grosset & Dunlap, early reprint in same format as 1911 Century: $50.00

Much Ado About Peter, Doubleday Page, 1909, first edition: $100.00

Wheat Princess, Hodder & Stoughton, circa 1920s, reprint of a 1905 title, hardcover: $100.00

When Patty Went to College, Century, 1903, six b/w plates, first edition: $100.00

When Patty Went to College, Grosset & Dunlap, 1912, medallion illustration on cover, six b/w plates: $30.00

WEHR, Julian

Julian Wehr's highly collectible Play Books have heavy board covers and spiral bindings, and inside the color illustrations have animation features designed by Wehr. As this type of book is fragile, very good condition is required for top values.

WEHR, Julian, *Night Before Christmas, Animated*

Animated Antics in Playland, Saalfield, 1946, illustrated paper-over-board cover with red spiral spine, color illustrated and animated by Julian Wehr: $200.00

Animated Picture Book of Alice in Wonderland, Grosset, 1945, oblong picture book, red plastic, spiralbound, paper-over-board cover, color illustrations and animations by Julian Wehr: $200.00

Animated Mother Goose, Grosset & Dunlap, New York, 1942, first edition with dust jacket: $300.00

Exciting Adventures of Finnie the Fiddler, Cupples & Leon, 1942, first edition: $200.00

Cock, the Mouse, and the Little Red Hen, E. P. Dutton, 1946, oblong, oversize, spiral binding, first edition: $100.00

Gingerbread Boy, E. P. Dutton, 1943, first edition: $150.00

Jack & the Beanstalk, Duenewald, 1944, animated by Wehr, 20 pages, color illustrations: $110.00

WEHR, Julian, *Toyland*

Night Before Christmas, Animated, by Clement Moore, Duenewald, 1949, red plastic, spiralbound, paper-over-board cover, animated by Wehr, color illustrations: $150.00

Toyland, stories by Martha Paulsen, Saalfield, 1944, red plastic, spiralbound, paper-over-board cover, color illustrations and animations, first edition: $100.00

Wizard of Oz, adaptation of L. Frank Baum story, Saalfield, 1944, first edition with dust jacket: $300.00

WEIL, Lisl, author/illustrator

Jacoble Tells the Truth, Houghton Mifflin, 1946, red cloth with black lettering, color illustrations, first edition with dust jacket: $60.00

King Midas' Secret and Other Follies, McGraw-Hill, 1969, first edition with dust jacket: $50.00

WEIR, Rosemary, see Series section, ALBERT THE DRAGON

WEISGARD, Leonard, illustrator

Weisgard trained at the Pratt Institute and worked in New York as a commercial artist and illustrator. He illustrated the *Noisy Book* series, 1939 – 1951, and numerous other children's books. He won the Caldecott medal in 1947 for his illustrations for *Little Island* by Margaret Wise Brown.

Cinderella, Garden City, New York, 1938, pictorial cover, first edition with dust jacket: $150.00

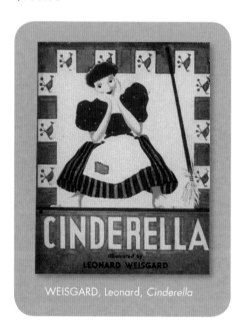

WEISGARD, Leonard, *Cinderella*

Mr. Peaceable Paints, Scribner, 1956, oblong oversize pictorial hardcover, illustrated by author, first edition with dust jacket: $90.00

Treasures to See, a Museum Picture Book, Harcourt Brace, 1956, oversize, introduction to museums, full-color illustrations, first edition with dust jacket: $100.00

Who Dreams of Cheese?, Scribner, 1950, oversize, illustrated in color and brown tones, first edition with dust jacket: $100.00

WELLMAN, Manly Wade

To Unknown Lands, Holiday House, 1956, illustrated by Leonard Everett Fisher, first edition with dust jacket: $70.00

Rifles at Ramsour's Mill, 1961, Ives Washburn, first edition with dust jacket: $150.00

WELLS, Carolyn, wrote several series that were popular in her time, including *Dick and Dolly,* and *Two Little Women.*

Folly for the Wise, Bobbs-Merrill, 1904, small, 170 pages, cloth-over-board cover with gilt, b/w illustrations by Cory, Herford, Shinn, and Verbee: $40.00

Merry-Go-Round, Russell, 1901, cloth-over-board cover with Newell design and gilt, small, 152 pages, b/w illustrations by Peter Newell: $60.00

WELLS, Carveth

Jungle Man and His Animals, McBride, 1925, oversize, full color paper-over-board cover, 68 pages, 12 color plates plus b/w illustrations by Tony Sarg: $200.00

WELLS, Helen, see Series section, CHERRY AMES, NURSE, VICKI BARR FLIGHT STEWARDESS

WELLS, Rosemary

Illustrator Rosemary Wells started out doing traditional picture books in the late 1960s, but became a household name with the preschool set for the creation of board books about Max the rabbit. Wells began her art training at the Museum School in Boston, but left there to work in publishing. She was an art editor at Allyn and Bacon. She later became an art director for Macmillan, which published her first book, *A Song to Sing, O!,* in 1968. Max first appeared in 1977, inspired by the relationship between Wells' own children.

Benjamin and Tulip, Dial Press, 1973, first edition with dust jacket: $100.00

Don't Spill It Again, James, Dial Press, 1977, paper-covered boards, first edition with dust jacket: $70.00

Noisy Nora, 1974, Dial Press, illustrated hardcover: $35.00

WELTY, Eudora

Shoe Bird, Harcourt Brace, 1964, illustrated by Beth Krush, first edition with dust jacket: $200.00

WERSBA, Barbara

Brave Balloon of Benjamin Buckley, Atheneum, 1963, first edition, oversize hardcover, b/w illustrations by Tomes: $30.00

Do Tigers Ever Bite Kings?, Atheneum, 1966, colored wood engravings, rhyming text, first edition with dust jacket: $40.00

Land of Forgotten Beasts, Atheneum, first edition with dust jacket: $40.00

Let Me Fall Before I Fly, Atheneum, 1971, illustrated by Mercer Mayer, first edition with dust jacket: $30.00

Run Softly, Go Fast, Atheneum, 1970, first edition with dust jacket: $50.00

Song for Clowns, Victor Gollancz Ltd., 1966, red with gilt, drawings by Mario Rivoli, first edition with dust jacket: $70.00

WESSELHOEFT, Lily

Madam Mary of the Zoo, Little, Brown, 1899, small, cloth-over-board cover with gilt, b/w illustrations by Lowell and Verbeek: $80.00

WEST, Marvin, see Series section, MOTOR RANGERS

WEST, Paul

Pearl and the Pumpkin, G. W. Dillingham, 1904, cloth hardcover with paste-on-pictorial, illustrated endpapers and color illustrations throughout by W. W. Denslow, first edition: $300.00

WHEELER, Marguerite and Willard

Dotty Dolly's Tea Party, Rand McNally, 1914, cloth-over-board cover with paste-on-pictorial, full-color illustrations by author: $40.00

WHITE, Anne H.

Adventures of Winnie and Bly, Little, Brown, 1947, illustrated by Ursula Koering, first edition with dust jacket: $70.00

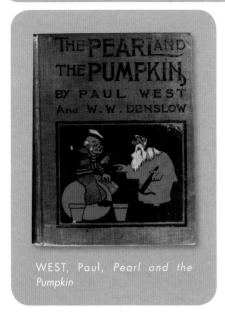

WEST, Paul, *Pearl and the Pumpkin*

Junket, Viking Press,1955, illustrated endpapers, illustrated by Robert McCloskey, first edition with dust jacket: $70.00

WHITE, Bessie F.

Bear Named Grumms, Houghton Mifflin, 1953, b/w illustrations by Sari, 82 pages, illustrated by Sari, first edition with dust jacket: $80.00

WHITE, Billy and Betty

Land of Whatsit, Macaulay, 1935, cloth-over-board cover, 333 pages, cartoon illustrations by Joe Banks: $30.00

WHITE, E. B. (1899 – 1985)

Charlotte's Web, Harper, 1952, b/w illustrations by Garth Williams, first American edition with dust jacket: $450.00

WHITE, E. B., *Stuart Little*

Stuart Little, Harper, 1945, White's first children's book, illustrated endpapers, 87 b/w illustrations by Garth Williams, first edition with dust jacket: $1,800.00

Trumpet of the Swan, Harper, 1970, 210 pages, b/w illustrations by Edward Frascino, first edition with dust jacket: $65.00

WHITE, Eliza Orne

Where is Adelaide?, Houghton Mifflin, 1933, orange cloth-over-board cover, 155 pages, b/w illustrations by Helen Sewell, first edition with dust jacket: $70.00

WHITE, Roma

Brownies and Rose-Leaves, Innes, 1892, cloth-over-board cover, small, 200 pages, b/w illustrations by L. L. Brooke: $45.00

WHITE, T. H. (1906 – 1964), see Series section, ONCE AND FUTURE KING

WHITING, Helen Adele

Negro Folk Tales, Associated Publishers, 1938, cloth-over-board cover, b/w illustrations by Lois M. Jones: $60.00

WIEDERSEIM, Grace, see DRAYTON, Grace Gibbie Wiederseim

WIGGIN, Kate Douglas (1856 – 1923), see also Series section, PENELOPE

Bird's Christmas Carol , Houghton Mifflin, 1888, small, blue with stamped title, 69 pages, early edition: $40.00

WIGGIN, Kate Douglas, *New Chronicles of Rebecca*

New Chronicles of Rebecca, 1903 Riverside, cloth hardcover, color plate illustrations: $75.00

WIGGIN, Kate Douglas and Nora A. Smith

Arabian Nights, Their Best-Known Tales, Kate Douglas Wiggin and Nora A. Smith, editors, 1909, Charles Scribner's Sons, oversize black hardcover with paste-on pictorial, 339 pages with gilt top edges, illustrated endpapers, 12 color plates with tissue overlays by Maxfield Parrish: $100.00

WIGGIN, Kate Douglas and Nora A. Smith, *Arabian Nights, Their Best-Known Tales*

WILDER, Cherry, see Series section, TORIN TRILOGY

WILDER, Laura Ingalls, see Series section, LITTLE HOUSE

WILDSMITH, Brian, author/illustrator

Brian Wildsmith's Mother Goose, Watts, 1965, oversize pictorial hardcover, illustrated by author, first edition with dust jacket: $60.00

Owl and the Woodpecker, Oxford, 1971, oversize hardcover, illustrated by Wildsmith, first edition with dust jacket: $60.00

WILKIN, Eloise, illustrator

Baby's Mother Goose, Golden Press, 1958, oversize glossy hardcover, color illustrations by Wilkin: $50.00

WILLARD, Barbara
Sprig of Broom, E. P. Dutton, 1971, hardcover, first edition with dust jacket: $50.00

WILLARD, Nancy, see Series section, ANATOLE TRILOGY

WILLIAMS, Garth, author/illustrator

American-born Williams spent his childhood in Canada and England. Returning to the US in the 1940s, he did illustrations for *New Yorker,* then expanded to children's book illustration with his drawings for Margery Sharpe's *Rescuer* series as well as the reissue of the Laura Ingalls Wilder books. He also authored and illustrated his own popular children's books.

Adventures of Benjamin Pink, Harper, 1951, b/w illustrations by author, first edition with dust jacket: $75.00

WILLIAMS, Garth, *Baby Animals*

Baby Animals, 1952, Simon & Schuster, Golden Book, hardcover with glossy cardboard weight pages for very small children, large color illustrations by Williams: $30.00

Rabbits' Wedding, Harper & Row, 1958, oversize hardcover, color illustrations by author, first edition with dust jacket: $80.00

WILLIAMS, Jay, see also Series section, DANNY DUNN

Everyone Knows What a Dragon Looks Like, Four Winds Press, 1976, illustrated by Mercer Mayer, first edition with dust jacket: $120.00

Hero From Otherwhere, Walck, 1972, first edition with dust jacket: $200.00

Practical Princess, Parents' Magazine Press, 1969, pictorial hardcover, illustrations by Frisco Henstra, first edition with dust jacket: $100.00

WILLIAMS, Ursula Moray
Adventures of the Little Wooden Horse, J. B. Lippincott, 1939, green cloth boards with wooden horse, illustrated by Brisley, first edition with dust jacket: $80.00

Nine Lives of Island Mackenzie, Chatto & Windus, London, 1959, oversize hardcover, 128 pages, color illustrated endpapers, b/w illustrations by Edward Ardizzone, first edition with dust jacket: $100.00

WILLIAMSON, Hamilton
Lion Cub, a Jungle Tale, Doubleday, 1931, pictorial boards, color illustrations by Berta and Elmer Hader, first edition with dust jacket: $80.00

Little Elephant, 1930, Doubleday, small picture book, cloth-over-board cover, color and b/w illustrations by Berta and Elmer Hader: $40.00

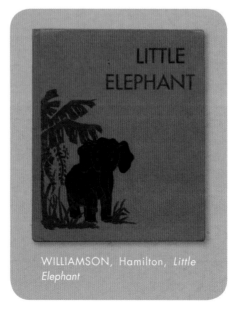
WILLIAMSON, Hamilton, *Little Elephant*

Monkey Tale, Doubleday, Doran, 1929, illustrated by Berta and Elmer Hader, first edition with dust jacket: $100.00

WILLSON, Dixie
Honey Bear, Volland, 1923, cloth spine, paper covered boards, color illustrations by Maginal Wright Barney, first edition in original box: $350.00. Without box: $150.00

WILLSON, Dixie, *Honey Bear*

Pinky Pup and the Empty Elephant, Volland, 1928, illustrated boards with black cloth spine, color illustrations by Erick Berry: $100.00

Tuffy Good Luck, Volland, 1927, small, cloth spine, illustrated paper-covered boards, illustrations by Ilona de Karekjarto: $80.00

Where the World Folds up at Night, 1932, Appleton, first edition, red cloth-over-board cover with gilt lettering, 209 pages, photo illustrations: $50.00

WILSON, Gahan
Bang Bang Family, Charles Scribner, 1974, hardcover, illustrated by author, first edition with dust jacket: $50.00

Harry and the Sea Serpent, Scribner, 1976, first edition with dust jacket: $70.00

WILSON, Hazel, see Series section, HERBERT YADON

WINDSOR, Mary

About Things, Grosset & Dunlap, 1935, color illustrated boards, oversize, color and b/w illustrations by Charlotte Stone: $50.00

Flip-Flap Book, Garden City, 1950, boards with spiral binding, 48 pages, color illustrations by Harriet Hentschel, novelty book where pages fold in and out to reveal next pages: $80.00

Soap and Bubbles, Whitman, 1935, oversize, illustrated cover, 14 pages, color illustrations throughout by Ruth Newton: $50.00

WINFIELD, Arthur M., see Series section, ROVER BOYS

WINSOR, Frederick

Space Child's Mother Goose, Simon & Schuster, 1958, b/w illustrations by Marian Parry, first edition with dust jacket: $200.00

WINSOR, Frederick, *Space Child's Mother Goose*

WINTER, Milo (1888 – 1956), illustrator

Midwest artist Winter trained at the Art Institute of Chicago. He illustrated numerous books with color plates and drawings, including several of the novels in the *Windemere* series. His favorite subjects were fantasy and fairy tale scenes, his style both colorful and whimsical.

Billy Popgun, Houghton Mifflin, 1912, gilt stamped brown paper covered boards, 61

pages, eight full-page color plates, b/w illustrations by Winter, small limited edition of 350 copies: $600.00

Wonderful ABC Book, 1946, Reuben Lilja Co., Chicago, oversize picture book, paper cover, 12 pages, verses and color illustrations by Winter: $40.00

WINTERFIELD, Henry

Star Girl, Harcourt Brace, 1957, illustrated by Fritz Wegner, first edition with dust jacket: $200.00

WIRT, Mildred A. (Mildred Wirt Benson) (pseudonyms included Joan Clark), see Series section, GIRL SCOUTS, PENNY NICHOLS, PENNY PARKER MYSTERY, RUTH DARROW FLYING STORIES

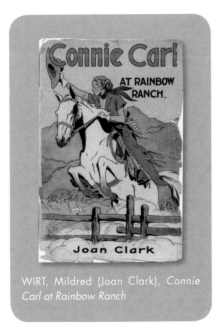

WIRT, Mildred (Joan Clark), *Connie Carl at Rainbow Ranch*

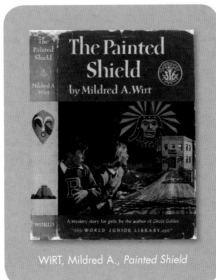

WIRT, Mildred A., *Painted Shield*

Wirt also wrote many of the early *Nancy Drew* mysteries.

Connie Carl at Rainbow Ranch, by Joan Clark, Goldsmith, 1939, with dust jacket: $30.00

Painted Shield, World, 1939, first edition with dust jacket: $50.00

Quarry Ghost, Dodd, Mead & Company, 1959, first edition with dust jacket: $100.00

WISTER, Owen

Journey in Search of Christmas, 1904, Harper, decorated cloth-over-board cover, 93 pages, illustrations by Frederic Remington: $200.00

WOLLHEIM, Donald, see also Series section, MIKE MARS

Secret of Saturn's Rings, John C. Winston, 1954, illustrated by Alex Schomberg, sci-fi novel, first edition with dust jacket: $170.00

WOOD, Lorna, see Series section, HAG DOWSABEL THE WITCH

WOOD, Nancy

Little Wrangler, 1966, Doubleday, hardcover, illustrated by Myron Wood, photos, first edition: $40.00

WOODWARD, Alice Bolingbroke (1862 – 1951)

English illustrator Alice Woodward contributed delicate watercolor pictures to numerous children's books between 1895 and 1930, including Gilbert's *Pinafore Picture Book.* Although charming, her works have not reached the price levels of the major Edwardian illustrators.

WPA, Federal Writers' Project

Who's Who in the Zoo, Whitman, 1938, oversize, cloth-over-board cover, illustrated endpapers, 204 pages, b/w illustrations, maps, photos, first edition: $60.00

WRIGHT, Dare, see Series section, EDITH THE LONELY DOLL

WRIGHT, Henrietta Christian

Little Folk in Green, White & Stokes, 1883, small, 92 pages, cloth-over-board cover with gilt decoration, color illustrations by Lydia Emmet: $40.00

WRIGHT, Mabel Osgood

Dream Fox Story Book, Macmillan, ca. 1900, decorated cloth-over-board cover, illustrated by Oliver Herford, early editions: $30.00 to $50.00

Gray Lady and the Birds, Macmillan, 1907, hardcover, illustrated: $30.00

Wabeno the Magician, Macmillan, 1899, green cloth-over-board cover with gilt decoration, small, 346 pages, b/w illustrations by Joseph Gleeson: $30.00

WRIGHT, Maginel (1881–1966), illustrator

Frank Lloyd Wright's younger sister began her career illustrating the stories of Laura Bancroft, an L. Frank Baum pseudonym. Her use of dramatic color and elegant style made her a favorite of the Volland illustrators. She illustrated Willson's *Honey Bear* and Gordon's *Billy Bunny's Fortune.* Her work also appears under the names Maginel Wright Enright and Maginal Wright Barney.

WRIGHT, Maginel, illustration

WRIGHTSON, Patricia, see Series section, WIRRUN TRILOGY

WUORIO, Eva-Lis

Land of Right Up and Down, World, 1964, color and b/w illustrations by Edward Ardizzone, first edition with dust jacket: $50.00

WYCKOFF, Capwell, see Series section, MYSTERY HUNTERS

WYETH, N. C. (1881–1945)

Pirates, Indians, battling heroes, Wyeth painted them all for action-packed illustrations. He illustrated more than 100 books, including 25 of the Scribner classics series, and his paintings stand alone as art, often making up shows at art galleries. He studied with Pyle at the Brandywine school. His talent ran in the family, and both his son and grandson became famous artists. Wyeth's illustrated titles are listed under the author's name.

Wyeth, reference:

Allen, Douglas, N. C. Wyeth: *The Collected Paintings, Illustrations and Murals,* Grammercy, 1996

WYSS, Johann (1743–1818)

Inspired by Defoe's *Robinson Crusoe,* Johann Wyss wrote *Swiss Family Robinson* about a shipwrecked family. The novel has inspired multiple adaptations, including a Disney movie.

Swiss Family Robinson, C. Arthur Pearson, 1904, illustrations by H. M. Brock, hardcover: $30.00

Swiss Family Robinson, Henry Frowde, ca. 1920s, 20 color illustrations mounted on card stock, illustrations by T. H. Robinson, cover with gilt decorations: $175.00

Swiss Family Robinson, John Winston, ca. 1920s, four-color plates by Frank Godwin, hardcover: $30.00

■ ········· **Y** ········· ■

YALE, Catharine Brooks

Nim and Cum, and the Wonderhead Stories, Way & Williams, 1895, small, 126 pages, cloth-over-board cover with gilt, b/w chapter headings: $30.00

YEAGER, Dorr, see Series section, BOB FLAME

YLLA, author/illustrator

Little Bears, Harper, 1954, oversize hardcover, 30 pages, illustrated by Ylla: $40.00

YOLEN, Jane, see also Series section, PIT DRAGONS TRILOGY

Bird of Time, Crowell, 1971, illustrated by Mercer Mayer, first edition with dust jacket: $40.00

Boy Who Had Wings, Crowell, 1974, first edition, oversize hardcover, illustrated by Helga Aichinger: $50.00

YOLEN, Jane, *Girl Who Cried Flowers and Other Tales*

Emperor and the Kite, World, 1967, Caldecott Honor book, oblong hardcover, illustrated by Ed Young: $30.00

Girl Who Cried Flowers and Other Tales, Crowell, 1974, color illustrations by David Palladini, first edition with dust jacket: $80.00

Invitation to the Butterfly Ball: A Counting Rhyme, Parents' Magazine Press, 1976, color illustrations by Jane Breskin Zalben, first edition with dust jacket: $60.00

Rainbow Rider, Crowell, 1974, blue hardcover with gilt, illustrated by Michael Foreman, first edition with dust jacket: $60.00

Ring Out! A Book of Bells, Clarion, 1974, b/w illustrations by Richard Cuffari, first edition with dust jacket: $30.00

YONGE, Charlotte

Dove in the Eagle's Nest, Macmillan, 1926 edition, impressed design on cloth-over-board cover, illustrated endpapers, three-color plates and b/w illustrations by Marguerite de Angeli: $40.00

Heartsease, or the Brother's Wife, Macmillan, 1882 edition, cloth-over-board cover with gilt, 548 pages, illustrations by Kate Greenaway: $50.00

YORK, SUSANNAH

In Search of Unicorns, Hodder & Stoughton, 1973, oversize brown buckram hardcover with gilt, pictorial endpapers, color and b/w illustrations by Wendy Hall, first edition with dust jacket: $70.00

YOUNG, Ella, endpages for *Unicorn with Silver Shoes*

YOUNG, Ella

Tangle-Coated Horse, Longmans, 1929, illustrated by Vera Bock, first edition: $100.00

Unicorn with Silver Shoes, Longmans, 1932, cloth-over-board cover with impressed silver design, illustrated endpapers, b/w illustrations by Robert Lawson, first edition: $300.00

YOUNG, Martha

Behind the Dark Pines, D. Appleton, 1912, illustrations by J. M. Conde: $50.00

Bessie Bell, Scott-Thaw, 1904, small hardcover, 116 pages, illustrations by Ida Dougherty: $50.00

When We Were Wee, 1912 edition, Macmillan, Everychild's Series, cloth-over-

board cover with impressed illustration, small, b/w photos plus drawings by Sophie Schneider: $40.00

YOUNG, Percy

Ding Dong Bell, a First Book of Nursery Rhymes, co-authored with Edward Ardizzone, Dennis Dobson, London, 1957, decorated hardcover, 143 pages, illustrated, first edition with dust jacket: $50.00

■ ·················· **Z** ·················· ■

ZEMACH, Harve

Duffy and the Devil, Farrar, 1973 (1974 Caldecott Award), hardcover, illustrated by Margot Zemach, first edition with dust jacket: $60.00

Mommy, Buy Me a China Doll, Follett, 1966, hardcover, adaptation of old Ozarks song, color illustrations by Margot Zemach, first edition with dust jacket: $70.00

Penny a Look, an Old Story, Farrar, 1973, color illustrations by Margot Zemach, first edition with dust jacket: $40.00

Princess and Froggie, with Kaethe Zemach, Farrar, 1975, blue hardcover, illustrated by Margot Zemach, first edition with dust jacket: $40.00

Small Boy Is Listening, Houghton Mifflin, 1959, small hardcover, 30 pages, b/w illustrations by Margot Zemach, first book by Zemachs, first edition with dust jacket: $60.00

Too Much Nose: An Italian Tale, Holt, 1967, first edition, hardcover, first edition with dust jacket: $40.00

ZHENYA, see GAY, Zhenya

ZIEGLER, Ursina

Squaps the Moonling, Atheneum, 1969, pictorial hardcover, color illustrations by Sita Jucker, US first edition with dust jacket: $60.00

ZINDEL, Paul

Confessions of a Teenage Baboon, HarperCollins, 1977, first edition with dust jacket: $80.00

ZINDEL, Paul, *Pardon Me, You're Stepping on My Eyeball!*

Pardon Me, You're Stepping on My Eyeball!, 1976, Harper & Row, first edition with dust jacket: $40.00

Pigman, Harper & Row, 1968, first edition with dust jacket: $90.00

ZION, Gene, see Series section, HARRY THE DOG

ZOLOTOW, Charlotte

Mr. Rabbit and the Lovely Present, Harper, 1962, oblong pictorial boards, pictures by Maurice Sendak, first edition: $100.00

Park Book, Harper, 1944, oblong picture book, color illustrations cloth-over-board cover, easy read, color illustrations by H. A. Rey: $40.00

Quarreling Book, Harper, 1963, illustrated by Arnold Lobel, first edition with dust jacket: $40.00

Rose, a Bridge, and a Wild Black Horse, Harper & Row, 1964, illustrated by Uri Shulevitz, first edition with dust jacket: $40.00

Sky Was Blue, Harper & Row, 1963, illustrations by Garth Williams, first edition with dust jacket: $70.00

Storm Book, Harper, 1952, oversize pictorial hardcover, color illustrations by Margaret Bloy Graham: $30.00

Unfriendly Book, Harper & Row, 1975, small with pictorial hardcover, b/w illustrations by William Pène du Bois, first edition with dust jacket: $80.00

Series are listed alphabetically by series name, but book titles within each series are listed by date of publication, rather than alphabetically, because many series contain progressing stories.

■ ···················· **A** ···················· ■

ABBEY SCHOOL SERIES, Elsie J. Oxenham, 1920s through 1960s, Collins, London, hardcover with frontispiece. First edition dates are shown with the titles; however, this series was constantly reprinted, and printing dates are often difficult to identify. First edition values are generally higher in England, and with a good dust jacket: $100.00

Abbey Girls, 1920

Abbey Girls Go Back to School, 1922

New Abbey Girls, 1923

Abbey Girls in Town, 1926

Queen of the Abbey Girls, 1926

Jen of the Abbey School, 1927

Abbey Girls Win Through, 1928

Abbey School, 1928

Abbey Girls at Home, 1930

Abbey Girls Play Up, 1930

Abbey Girls on Trial, 1931

Biddy's Secret, 1932

Rosamund's Victory, 1933

Call of the Abbey School, 1934

Maidlin to the Rescue, 1934

ABBEY SCHOOL SERIES, Elsie J. Oxenham, *Dancer from the Abbey*

Joy's New Adventure, 1935

Rosamund's Tuckshop, 1936

Maidlin Bears the Torch, 1937

Schooldays at the Abbey, 1938

Rosamund's Castle, 1938

Secrets of the Abbey, 1939

Two Joans at the Abbey, 1945

An Abbey Champion, 1946

Abbey Girls at Home, 1947

Fiddler for the Abbey, 1948

Guardians of the Abbey, 1950

Schoolgirl Jen at the Abbey, 1950

Stowaways at the Abbey, 1951

Dancer from the Abbey, 1953

Rachel in the Abbey, 1954

Strangers at the Abbey, 1960

Abbey Girls in Town, 1967

ADELE DORING SERIES, Grace North, 1919 –1923, Lothrop, Lee & Shepard, illustrated with color plates by Florence Liley Young: $30.00

Adele Doring of the Sunnyside Club, 1919

Adele Doring on a Ranch, 1920

Adele Doring at Boarding-school, 1921

Adele Doring in Camp, 1922

Adele Doring at Vineyard Valley, 1923

ADVENTURE SERIES, Enid Blyton, ca. 1944 – 1955, Macmillan, UK, hardcover, illustrated by Stuart Tresilian, featuring four children and Kiki the parrot. Early British editions featured hardcover with contrasting picture stamped on cover, and colorful wraparound dust jacket illustration by Tresilian. First editions with dust jacket: $100.00

Island of Adventure, 1944

Castle of Adventure, 1946

Valley of Adventure, 1947

ADVENTURE SERIES, Enid Blyton, *River of Adventure*

Sea of Adventure, 1948

Mountain of Adventure, 1949

Ship of Adventure, 1950

Circus of Adventure, 1952

River of Adventure, 1955

ADVENTURE GIRLS SERIES, Clair Blank, 1920, Burt, three titles, hardcover, first edition with dust jacket: $30.00

Adventure Girls at K-Bar-O

Adventure Girls in the Air

Adventure Girls at Happiness House

ADVENTURES IN THE UNKNOWN SERIES, Carl H. Claudy (1879 – 1957), Grosset & Dunlap, cloth-over-board cover, illustrated endpapers with scenes from the story, frontispiece illustration by A. C. Valentine, adventure novels that were rewritten and expanded from original short stories done for *American Boy* magazine, science fiction adventures. With dust jacket: $80.00 to $150.00

Land of No Shadow, 1933

Mystery Men of Mars, 1933

Thousand Years a Minute, 1933

Blue Grotto Terror, 1934

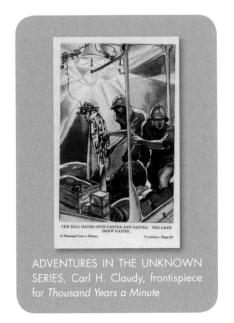

ADVENTURES IN THE UNKNOWN SERIES, Carl H. Claudy, frontispiece for *Thousand Years a Minute*

Adventures in the Unknown, related title:

Year after Tomorrow, anthology edited by DelRey, Matschaat and Carmer, 1954, Winston, illustrated by Mel Hunter, contains two of the stories in their original magazine version, first edition with dust jacket: $50.00

AGATON SAX SERIES, Nils-Olof Franzen, Andre Deutsch, London, translated from Swedish, hardcover, illustrated endpapers, humorous b/w drawings throughout by Quentin Blake, adventures of Swedish "arch-enemy of the criminal" Agaton Sax, master of disguises and numerous other weird and wonderful skills. Deutsch first edition with dust jacket: $40.00 to $70.00

AGATON SAX SERIES, Nils-Olof Franzen, *Agaton Sax and the Scotland Yard Mystery*

Agaton Sax and the Diamond Thieves, 1967

Agaton Sax and the Scotland Yard Mystery, 1969

Agaton Sax and the Incredible Max Brothers, 1970

Agaton Sax and the Criminal Doubles, 1971

Agaton Sax and the Colossus of Rhodes, 1972

Agaton Sax and the London Computer Plot, 1973

Agaton Sax and the League of Silent Exploders, 1974

Agaton Sax and the Haunted House, 1975

Agaton Sax and the Lispington's Grandfather Clock, 1978

Agaton Sax and the Big Rig, 1981

AIRPLANE BOYS SERIES, Edith Janice Craine, 1932, World, hardcover, also called SKY BUDDIES, five titles, first edition with dust jacket: $30.00

AIRPLANE GIRL SERIES, Harrison Bardwell and Edith Craine, ca. 1930, World Syndicate, hardcover, four titles, first edition with dust jacket: $30.00

ALBERT THE DRAGON SERIES, Rosemary Weir, 1960s, Abelard-Schuman, London, hardcover, illustrated by Quentin Blake, first edition with dust jacket: $40.00

Albert the Dragon, 1961

Further Adventures of Albert the Dragon, 1964

Albert the Dragon and the Centaur, 1968

Albert and the Dragonettes, 1977

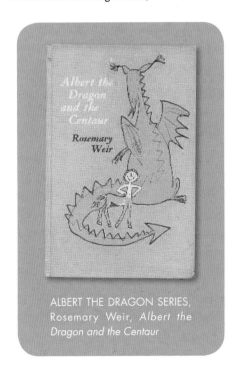

ALBERT THE DRAGON SERIES, Rosemary Weir, *Albert the Dragon and the Centaur*

ALEXANDER SERIES, Marjorie Knight, E. P. Dutton, b/w and color illustrations by Howard Simon, first edition with dust jacket: $40.00 to $70.00

Alexander's Christmas Eve, 1938

Alexander's Birthday, 1940

Alexander's Vacation, 1943

ALFRED HITCHCOCK AND THE THREE INVESTIGATORS SERIES, Random House, color illustrated paper-over-board covers, graveyard illustration endpapers, b/w full-page illustrations, about 150 pages, series titles listed on back cover. Robert Arthur (1909 – 1969), wrote ten of the early titles in the 43 book series. Later titles are the most difficult to find, due to the limited number of printings. First editions generally list to self.

After 1979 the series name changed to *Three Investigators* and reprints of earlier stories had the titles revised, dropping the Hitchcock reference.

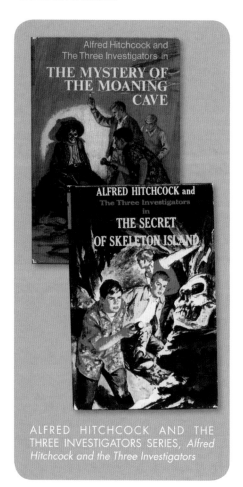

ALFRED HITCHCOCK AND THE THREE INVESTIGATORS SERIES, *Alfred Hitchcock and the Three Investigators*

Alfred Hitchcock and the Three Investigators, 43 titles, probable firsts: $40.00

ALGER BOOKS, Horatio Alger, Jr. (1834 – 1899)

Alger's first published work appeared in 1856 and new titles continued to appear after his death, authored by others but using his name. Many of the titles originally published between 1900 and 1908 were written by Edward Stratemeyer, who later created his own profitable syndicate of boys and girls series books. Alger wrote both series and individual titles. The value varies depending on the presentation of the book. The more elaborate the binding and illustrations, the greater the appeal to many collectors. First printings can command double to triple the price of early editions. Value is also affected by the rarity of the title. Nineteenth century wrappers (dust jackets) also add considerably to the desirablity of the book.

Loring of Boston published many of Alger's earliest titles, 1860s through 1870s, with other publishers printing his books after 1880. Points for first editions are discussed in *First Printings of American Authors,* Vol. 5 (Gale Research, 1987), edited by Philip Eppard, and in specialized bibliographies written by Bob Bennett and Ralph Gardner. Additional bibliographies are available through the Alger Society's website. Prices range from $5.00 to $1,000.00, depending on rarity of edition, so that each title and edition needs to be checked individually. A sampling of one of Alger's most famous titles, Ragged Dick, shows the wide range of material available:

Ragged Dick or, *Life in the Street with the Bootblacks,* 1868, Loring, cloth decorated with gilt on front and spine, frontispiece with tissue guard and three inserted plates, first edition should have no books advertised for series past *Fame and Fortune* for December, first edition thus: $1,500.00. Later Loring printings, still before 1870: $400.00.

Ragged Dick, 1895, Henry T. Coates, pictorial cover: $30.00

Ragged Dick Series, 1898, John C Winston, six volumes in matched bindings, each book with frontispiece with tissue guard and one plate, price for set: $200.00

Ragged Dick, 1993, Heritage Press, illustrated by J. Kinnsley, fine edition in original slipcase: $30.00

ALICE IN WONDERLAND, related titles:

Lewis Carroll's popular *Alice in Wonderland* and *Alice through the Looking Glass* inspired numerous spinoffs. (See Booklist by Author section for information on the original books.)

Examples of other books using the Alice character by other authors:

New Alice in the Old Wonderland, Anna M. Richards, 1895, Lippincott, red cover with gilt trim, b/w illustrations by Anna M. Richards: $100.00

Emblemland Alice, John Kendrick Bangs, 1902, Russell, hardcover, illustrated by C. R. Macauley, a parody of Alice: $70.00

Alice in Blunderland, John Kendrick Bangs, 1907, Doubleday, cloth-over-board hardcover, illustrated by Albert Levering, political parody: $100.00

Uncle Wiggily and Alice in Wonderland, by Howard R. Garis, 1918, Donohue, blue hardcover with gilt lettering, 177 pages, illustrated endpapers, color plate illustrations by Edward Bloomfield: $100.00

Alice in Wonderland Printed in Gregg Shorthand, undated, Gregg Publishing, small hardcover, translation to shorthand by Georgie Gregg, chapter headings in English, text in typical double columns with a few b/w Tenniel-style illustrations: $200.00

Alice in the Delighted States, by Edward Hope, ca. 1928, George Routledge, London, political satire, b/w political cartoon-style illustrations by Rea Irwin, with dust jacket: $200.00

Malice in Kulturland, by Horace Wyatt, 1927, E. P. Dutton, small hardcover with

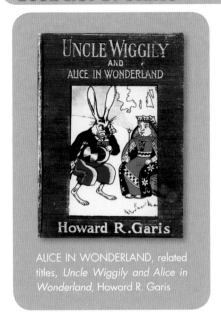

ALICE IN WONDERLAND, related titles, *Uncle Wiggily and Alice in Wonderland*, Howard R. Garis

paste-on-pictorial, a political satire parody of Alice with humorous illustrations, with dust jacket: $80.00

ALL ABOUT SERIES, Johnny Gruelle, author of the Raggedy Ann books, hardcover, color illustrations by Gruelle, re-tellings of classic tales.

Cupples & Leon, ca. 1916, small size, color illustrations, paste-on pictorial, hardcover with dust jacket: $300.00. Without dust jacket: $50.00

Cupples & Leon, 1920s reprints: $40.00

All About Cinderella, 1916

All About Little Red Riding Hood, 1916

ALL ABOUT SERIES, Johnny Gruelle, *All About Little Black Sambo*

All About Mother Goose, 1916

All About the Little Small Red Hen, 1917

All About Hansel and Gretel, 1917

All About Little Black Sambo (retelling of Bannerman story), 1917

Related title:

All About Story Book, includes *Little Black Sambo, Miss Fluffy Chick, Mickie Long Tale,* and *Kitty Cat,* by Thelma Gooch with Gruelle illustrations for *Sambo* story, Cupples & Leon, 1929, oversize orange hardcover, color illustrations with dust jacket: $100.00. Without dust jacket: $50.00

ALL-OF-A-KIND FAMILY SERIES, Sydney Bremer Taylor, various publishers and illustrators. First edition with dust jacket: $30.00 to $75.00

ALL-OF-A-KIND FAMILY SERIES, Sydney Bremer Taylor, *All-of-a-Kind Family Uptown*

All-of-a-Kind Family, 1951, Wilcox and Follett, illustrated by Helen John

More All-of-a-Kind Family, 1954, Wilcox, illustrated by Mary E. Stevens

All-of-a-Kind Family Uptown, 1958, Wilcox, illustrated by Mary E. Stevens

All-of-a-Kind Family Downtown, 1972, b/w illustrations by Beth and Joe Krush,

oversize, 187 pages, wraparound illustration dust jacket

Ella of All-of-a-Kind Family, 1978, E. P. Dutton, illustrated by Gail Owens

AMELIARANNE SERIES, originated by Constance Heward and illustrator Susan Beatrice Pearce, 1920 – 1940 McKay, London and US, small hardcover, color illustrations throughout, with dust jacket: $85.00

AMELIARANNE SERIES, Constance Heward, *Ameliaranne Keeps School*

Ameliaranne and the Green Umbrella, 1920

Ameliaranne Keeps Shop, 1928

Ameliaranne, Cinema Star, 1929

Ameliaranne at the Circus, by Margaret Gilmour, 1931, McKay

Ameliaranne at the Farm, 1937

Ameliaranne Gives a Christmas Party, 1938

Ameliaranne Camps Out, 1939

Ameliaranne Keeps School, 1940

AMERICAN REGIONAL STORIES SERIES, Lois Lenski, Frederick A. Stokes and J. B. Lippincott, hardcover, illustrated endpapers, b/w illustrations by author.

First edition with dust jacket: $200.00

185

Later printings with dust jacket: $40.00

Bayou Suzette, 1943

Strawberry Girl, 1945

Blue Ridge Billy, 1946

Judy's Journey, 1947

Boom Town Boy, 1948

Cotton in My Sack, 1949

Texas Tomboy, 1950

Prairie School, 1951

Mama Hattie's Girl, 1953

Corn-Farm Boy, 1954

San Francisco Boy, 1955

Houseboat Girl, 1957

Coal Camp Girl, 1959

Shoo-Fly Girl, 1963

To Be a Logger, 1967

Deer Valley Girl, 1968

AMERICAN REGIONAL STORIES SERIES,
Lois Lenski, *Deer Valley Girl*, *Shoo-Fly Girl*,
Prairie School

ANATOLE THE MOUSE SERIES, Eve Titus, Bodley Head, UK, McGraw-Hill, small hardcover, 32 pages, b/w illustrations by Paul Galdone. The first title is a Caldecott Honor book, early printings with dust jacket: $30.00

Oversize editions with color illustrations, 32 pages: $60.00

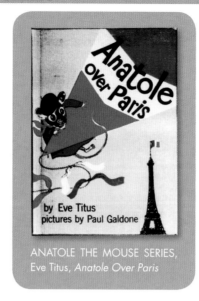

ANATOLE THE MOUSE SERIES,
Eve Titus, *Anatole Over Paris*

Anatole, 1956

Anatole and the Cat, 1957

Anatole and the Robot, 1960

Anatole Over Paris, 1961

Anatole and the Poodle, 1965

Anatole and the Piano, 1966

Anatole and the Thirty Thieves, 1969

Anatole and the Toyshop, 1970

Anatole in Italy, 1973

Anatole and the Pied Piper, 1979

ANATOLE TRILOGY, Nancy Willard, Harcourt Brace, trilogy, tales of boy's fantastical journeys, illustrated by David McPhail, first edition with dust jacket: $30.00

Sailing to Cythera, and Other Anatole Stories, 1974

Island of the Grass King: Further Adventures of Anatole, 1979

Uncle Terrible: More Adventures of Anatole, 1982

ANDY BLAKE SERIES, Leo Edwards, ca. 1928 – 1930, Grosset & Dunlap, illustrated by Bert Salg, four titles, with dust jacket, start at: $200.00

Without dust jacket: $40.00

Andy Blake, 1928

Andy Blake's Comet Coaster, 1928

Andy Blake's Secret Service, 1929

Andy Blake and the Pot of Gold, 1930

ANDY LANE FLIGHT SERIES, Eustace L. Adams, 1928 – 1932, Grosset & Dunlap, early air adventure series, with dust jacket: $35.00

Fifteen Days in the Air

Over the Polar Ice

Racing Around the World

Runaway Airship

Pirates of the Air

On the Wings of Flame

Mysterious Monoplane

Flying Windmill

Plane Without a Pilot

Wings of Adventure

Across the Top of the World

Prisoners of the Clouds

ANDY LANE FLIGHT SERIES,
Eustace L. Adams, *Over the
Polar Ice*

ANGUS THE DOG SERIES, Marjorie Flack (1897 – 1958), Doubleday, 32 pages, color illustrations by author, first edition with dust jacket: $40.00

Angus and the Ducks, 1930

Angus and the Cat, 1931

Angus Lost, 1932

ANGUS THE DOG SERIES, Marjorie Flack, *Angus Lost*

ANN BARTLETT SERIES, Martha Johnson, ca. 1940s, Crowell, hardcover, first edition with dust jacket: $150.00. Without dust jacket: $70.00

ANNE SHIRLEY SERIES, L. M. Montgomery, originally published in U. S. by L. C. Page, Boston, hardcover, paste-on pictorial, gilt lettering on some titles, illustrators include Geoge Gibbs and Maria Kirk.

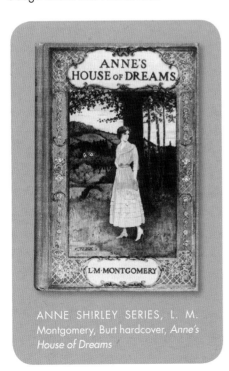

ANNE SHIRLEY SERIES, L. M. Montgomery, Burt hardcover, *Anne's House of Dreams*

McClelland and Stewart, Toronto first editions with dust jacket: $300.00

Page first editions: $250.00

Burt hardcover with paste-on-pictorial early reprints: $50.00

Anne of Green Gables, 1908

Anne of Avonlea, 1909

Chronicles of Avonlea, 1912

Anne of the Island, 1915

Anne's House of Dreams, 1917

Further Chronicles of Avonlea, 1920

Anne of Windy Poplars, 1936

Anne of Ingleside, 1939

ANT AND BEE SERIES, Angela Banner, Edmund Ward, London, UK, Franklin Watts, US, illustrated by Bryan Ward, an ant and a bee lead pre-schoolers through lessons with humorous stories and funny pictures, small hardcovers.

ANT AND BEE SERIES, Angela Banner, Kaye and Ward edition, *Ant and Bee and the Doctor*

Ward, first UK edition with dust jacket: $200.00

Ant and Bee and the Doctor, Kaye and Ward edition, illustrated hardcover: $150.00

Franklin Watts, first US edition with dust jacket: $150.00

First editions without dust jackets: $50.00 to $100.00

Ant and Bee, 1951

More Ant and Bee, 1958

Around the World with Ant and Bee, 1960

More and More Ant and Bee, 1961

Ant and Bee and the Rainbow, 1962

Happy Birthday, Ant and Bee, 1964

Ant and Bee and the ABC, 1966

One, Two, Three with Ant and Bee, 1968

Ant and Bee and the Kind Dog, 1968

Ant and Bee Time, 1969

Ant and Bee and the Secret, 1970

Ant and Bee Big Bag Buy, 1971

Ant and Bee Go Shopping, 1972

Ant and Bee and the Doctor, 1978

ANTHONY MONDAY SERIES, John Bellairs, Harcourt Brace, hardcover, fantasy and mystery combined in stories of a teenager.

Treasure of Alpheus Winterborn, 1978, b/w illustrations and color dust jacket by Judith Gwyn Brown, first edition with dust jacket: $100.00

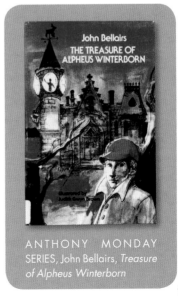

ANTHONY MONDAY SERIES, John Bellairs, *Treasure of Alpheus Winterborn*

187

Dark Secret of Weatherend, 1984, b/w illustrations and color dust jacket by Edward Gorey, first edition with dust jacket: $100.00

Lamp from the Warlock's Tomb, 1988, b/w illustrations and color dust jacket by Edward Gorey, first edition with dust jacket: $100.00

Mansion in the Mist, 1992, b/w illustrations and color dust jacket by Edward Gorey, first edition with dust jacket: $50.00

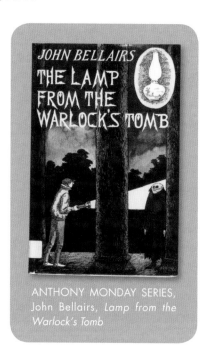

ANTHONY MONDAY SERIES, John Bellairs, *Lamp from the Warlock's Tomb*

APPLE MARKET STREET SERIES, Betsy Mabel Hill, author/illustrator, 1934 – 1943, Frederick A. Stokes and J. B. Lippincott, featuring protagonist Judy Jo, b/w and color illustrations by author, first edition with dust jacket: $70.00

Early printings with paste-on-pictorial: $30.00

Down along Apple Market Street, 1934

Surprise for Judy-Jo, 1939

Along Comes Judy-Jo, 1943

Judy Jo's Winter in Ducklight Cove, 1951

Snowed in Family, 1951

Judy Jo's Magic Island, 1953

ARABEL SERIES, Joan Aiken, Doubleday and Harper, also BBC/Jonathan Cape, hardcover, comical b/w illustrations by Quentin Blake, young Arabel Jones finds her life constantly complicated by her pet raven, Mortimer, first edition with dust jacket: $100.00

ARABEL SERIES, Joan Aiken, *Arabel and Mortimer*

Arabel's Raven, 1974

Arabel and Mortimer, 1981

Mortimer's Cross, 1984

Mortimer Says Nothing, 1985

ARGLE TRILOGY, M. Pardoe, published 1956 – 1959, Routledge, UK, illustrations by Audrey Fawley. Three children travel back in time to Celtic Britain. The first book appeared as a stand-alone novel in the United States under a different title. First edition with dust jacket: $60.00

Argle's Mist, 1956

Argle's Causeway, 1957

Argle's Oracle, 1959

ASA AND RAMBO MOUSE SERIES, Mary Stolz, Harper, adventures of mice versus housecat Siri, illustrated by Beni Montresor, first edition with dust jacket: $30.00

Belling the Tiger, 1961, Newbery Medal Honor Book

Great Rebellion, 1961

Siri the Conquistador, 1963

Maxmillian's World, 1966

ASH STAFF TRILOGY, Paul R. Fisher, ca. 1980, Atheneum, hardcover with gilt lettering on spine, magic, lost kingdoms, orphans raised in a mountain cave, this fantasy trilogy draws on Welsh legends, wraparound illustration dust jackets by David K. Stone, first edition with dust jacket: $30.00

ASH STAFF TRILOGY, Paul R. Fisher, *Hawks of Fellheath*

Ash Staff

Hawks of Fellheath

Princess and the Thorn

ASH STAFF TRILOGY, Paul R. Fisher, *Princess and the Thorn*

ASTÉRIX SERIES, Rene Goscinny and Albert Uderzo, comic strip character, originally produced in French. Astérix the warrior bumbles through fantasy adventures that spoof ancient history.

Astérix Légionionnaire, une Aventure d'Astérix, Goscinny, 1967, Dargaud, France, oversize glossy pictorial cover, story told in color comics, original French version: $30.00

Astérix, English translations for Hodder and Brockhampton, UK, translations by Anthea Bell and Derek Hockridge, oversize laminated hardcovers, 48 or 64 pages, first editions with dust jackets: $50.00

ASTÉRIX SERIES, Rene Goscinny and Albert Uderzo, *Astérix Légionionnaire, une Aventure d'Astérix*

AUGUSTUS SERIES, LeGrand Henderson, 1940s, Bobbs-Merrill, oversize, about 130 pages, pictorial endpapers, three-color illustrations by author, first edition with dust jacket: $35.00

Augustus and the River, 1939, through *Augustus and the Desert,* 1948

AUNT JANE'S NIECES, Edith Van Dyne (L. Frank Baum), created as a series for Reilly, Chicago, and Copp Clark, Canada, cloth covers, impressed and color paste-on cover illustration, illustrations by E. A. Nelson. Firsts are usually identified by list-to-self method, with book being the last title listed on advertising page.

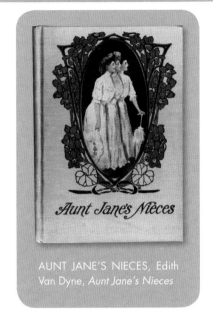

AUNT JANE'S NIECES, Edith Van Dyne, *Aunt Jane's Nieces*

Firsts with dust jacket: $300.00 up

Firsts without dust jacket: $100.00

Impressed illustration hardcover without dust jacket, later printings: $40.00

Aunt Jane's Nieces, 1906

Aunt Jane's Nieces Abroad, 1906

Aunt Jane's Nieces at Millville, 1908

Aunt Jane's Nieces at Work, 1909

Aunt Jane's Nieces in Society, 1910

Aunt Jane's Nieces and Uncle John, 1911

Aunt Jane's Nieces on Vacation, 1912

Aunt Jane's Nieces on the Ranch, 1913

Aunt Jane's Nieces Out West, 1914

Aunt Jane's Nieces in the Red Cross, 1915

AUSTIN CHRONICLES, see O'KEEFE FAMILY CHRONICLES

AUTOMOBILE GIRLS SERIES, Laura Crane, 1910, Altemus, six books, first edition with dust jacket: $30.00

AZOR BOOKS, Maude Crowley, Oxford and Walck, small hardcover, about 70 pages, b/w illustrations by Helen Sewell.

First edition with dust jacket: $50.00

Azor, 1948

Azor and the Haddock, 1949

Azor and the Blue Eyed Cow, 1951

Tor and Azor, 1955, illustrated by Veronica Reed

■ ···················· **B** ···················· ■

BABAR SERIES, created by Jean de Brunhoff (1899 – 1937), continued and revised by Laurent de Brunhoff, see also SERAFINA THE GIRAFFE, color illustrations by authors, first published in French. These popular books about the elephant, Babar, and his family and kingdom, enjoy large printings and constant reprintings. Random House editions are usually issued in illustrated oversize hardcover, with matching dust jacket. Some price exceptions on first editions and editions by other publishers are noted below.

Histoire de Babar, le Petit Elephant, 1931, Jardin Des Modes, Conde Nast Publications, Paris, oversize red boards with blue cloth spine, color illustrations throughout, 47 pages, French language, first edition: $800.00

Babar, Jean de Brunhoff books, English translations, published by Metheun, UK and Random House, US first edition with dust jacket: $200.00 to $500.00

BABAR SERIES, created by Jean de Brunhoff, *Babar and Father Christmas* and *Babar's Concert*

Story of Babar, 1933

Travels of Babar, 1934

Babar the King, 1935

Babar's ABC, 1936

Babar's Friend Zephyr, 1937

Babar and His Children, 1938

Babar and Father Christmas, 1940

Babar Series, continued by Laurent de Brunhoff, son of Jean de Brunhoff, Random House, 1947 – 1970, first editions with dust jacket: $100.00

Picnic at Babar's, 1950

Babar's Visit to Birdland, 1952

Babar and Zephyr, 1957

Babar and the Professor, 1958

Babar's Castle, 1962

Babar's French Lessons, 1965

Babar Comes to America, 1965

Babar's Spanish Lessons, 1965

Babar Loses His Crown, 1967

Babar, Random House, 1970s, first editions with dust jacket: $50.00

Babar's Birthday Surprise, 1970

Babar Visits Another Planet, 1972

Meet Babar and His Family, 1973

Babar and the Wully-Wully, 1975

Babar Saves the Day, 1975

Babar Learns to Cook, 1978

Babar's Trunk, 1969, Random House, four books, each approximately 4" x 4½", hardcover, color illustrations, packaged together in a color illustrated cardboard slipcase that looks like a trunk. Complete package: $40.00

Babar's Bookmobile, 1974, Random House, four books, each approximately 4" x 4½", oblong, paper-over-board illustrated hardcover, 16 pages, color illustrations, packaged together in a color illustrated cardboard slipcase, titles include: *Babar to the Rescue, Babar's Concert, Babar Bakes a Cake, Babar's Christmas Tree*; complete package: $40.00

Babar, related Pop-Up Books: pictorial hardcover, color illustrations, pop-ups and pull tab animations, pop-up book prices require pop-up and mechanicals all to be in very good working condition:

Pop-Up Babar's Games, 1968, Random House: $40.00

Babar's Moon Trip, 1969, Random House: $40.00

BAGTHORPES SERIES, Helen Cresswell, 1977 – 1993, Macmillan, hardcover, humorous tales of an eccentric family with an "ordinary" son, first edition with dust jacket by Trina Schart Hyman: $40.00

Ordinary Jack, 1977

Absolute Zero, 1978

Bagthorpes Unlimited, 1978

Bagthorpes Vs. the World, 1979

Bagthorpes Abroad, 1984

Bagthorpes Haunted, 1985

Bagthorpes Liberated, 1989

Bagthorpes Triangle, 1993

BASEBALL JOE SERIES, Lester Chadwick (pseudonym of Edward Stratemeyer), Cupples & Leon, gray hardcover with red/black printed illustration and lettering, four b/w plates.

Early editions, titles through *Home Run King*, with dust jacket: $65.00

Early editions, titles after *Home Run King*, with dust jacket: $150.00

Later editions, with dust jacket: $50.00

Baseball Joe of the Silver Stars, 1912

Baseball Joe on the School Nine, 1912

Baseball Joe at Yale, 1913

Baseball Joe in the Central League, 1914

Baseball Joe in the Big League, 1915

Baseball Joe on the Giants, 1916

Baseball Joe in the World Series, 1917

Baseball Joe around the World, 1918

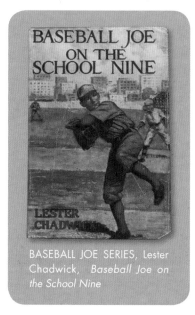

BASEBALL JOE SERIES, Lester Chadwick, *Baseball Joe on the School Nine*

Baseball Joe: Home Run King, 1922

Baseball Joe: Saving the League, 1923

Baseball Joe: Captain of the Team, 1924

Baseball Joe, Champion of the League, 1925

Baseball Joe, Club Owner, 1926

Baseball Joe: Pitching Wizard, 1928

BASIL OF BAKER STREET SERIES, Eve Titus (see ANATOLE THE MOUSE), Whittlesey House, hardcover, about 96 pages, b/w illustrations by Paul Galdone, Basil the mouse imitates the methods of Sherlock Holmes. First edition with dust jacket: $30.00

Basil of Baker Street, 1958

Basil and the Lost Colony, 1964

Basil and the Pigmy Cats, 1971

Basil in Mexico, 1975

Basil in the Wild West, 1982

BASIL OF BAKER STREET SERIES, Eve Titus, *Basil of Baker Street*

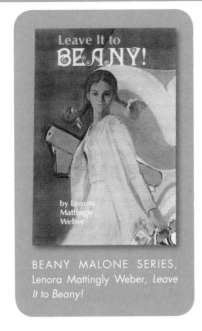

BEANY MALONE SERIES, Lenora Mattingly Weber, *Leave It to Beany!*

BEANY MALONE SERIES, Lenora Mattingly Weber, Crowell, hardcover. These books are favorites of those who read them as teenagers in the 1950s. First edition with dust jacket: $200.00 to $300.00

Later printings with dust jacket: $50.00

Meet the Malones, 1943

Beany Malone, 1948

Leave It to Beany!, 1950

Beany and the Beckoning Road, 1952

Beany Has a Secret Life, 1955

Make a Wish for Me, 1956

Happy Birthday, Dear Beany, 1957

More the Merrier, 1958

Bright Star Falls, 1959

Welcome Stranger, 1960

Pick a New Dream, 1961

Tarry Awhile, 1962

Something Borrowed, Something Blue, 1963

Come Back, Wherever You Are, 1969

Related title:

Beany Malone Cookbook, 1972

BEARS BOOKS, Margaret J. Baker, Farrar, hardcover, illustrated by Leslie Wood or Daphne Rowles, with dust jacket: $30.00

Shoeshop Bears, 1963, illustrated by C. Walter Hodges

BEARS BOOKS, Margaret J. Baker, *Hi-jinks Joins the Bears*

Hannibal and the Bears, 1966, illustrated by Hodges

Bears Back in Business, 1967, illustrated by Daphne Rowles

Hi-jinks Joins the Bears, 1969, illustrated by Daphne Rowles

Teabag and the Bears, 1970, illustrated by Leslie Wood

Boots and the Ginger Bears, 1972, illustrated by Leslie Wood

BEDTIME STORY-BOOKS SERIES, Thornton W. Burgess, originally published ca. 1917, Little, Brown, this series has seen several reprints, Harrison Cady illustrations, first edition with dust jacket: $30.00

BEDTIME STORY-BOOKS SERIES, Thornton W. Burgess, *Adventures of Mr. Mocker*

BEN AND ME BOOKS, Robert Lawson, Little, Brown, illustrated by author. Although never issued as a series, Lawson did the following four books (with very long titles!) that recounted the lives of famous people from the perspective of an animal friend, and many collectors consider them a set:

Ben and Me: A New and Astonishing Life of Benjamin Franklin As Written by His Good Mouse, Amos: Lately Discovered, 1939, First edition with dust jacket: $200.00

I Discover Columbus: A True Chronicle of the Great Admiral and His Finding of the

New World, narrated by the Venerable Parrot Aurelio, Who Shared in the Glorious Venture, 1941, first edition with dust jacket: $100.00

Mr. Revere and I: Being an Account of Certain Episodes in the Career of Paul Revere, Esq., as Recently Revealed by His Horse, Scheherazade, Late Pride of His Royal Majesty's 14th Regiment of Foot, 1953, first edition with dust jacket: $50.00

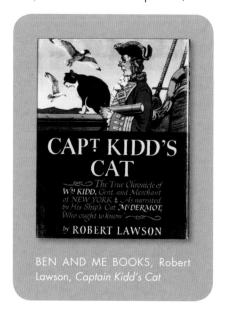

BEN AND ME BOOKS, Robert Lawson, *Captain Kidd's Cat*

Captain Kidd's Cat: Being the True and Dolorous Chronicle of Wm. Kidd, Gentleman and Merchant of New York; Late Captain of the Adventure Galley; of the Vicissitudes Attending His Unfortunate Cruise in the Eastern Waters, of His Unjust Trial and Execution, as Narrated by His Faithful Cat, McDermot, Who Ought to Know, 1956, map endpapers, first edition with dust jacket: $50.00

BENJY THE DOG SERIES, Margaret Bloy Graham (b. 1920, Canada)

Raised in Toronto, Graham moved to New York to work as a commerical artist. There she met her husband and collaborator, Gene Zion. Together, they created the *Harry the Dog* series. When the marriage ended in 1968, Graham went on to illustrate and write her own books including the *Benjy* stories.

Harper & Row, oversize hardcover, illustrated by author, first edition with dust jacket: $30.00

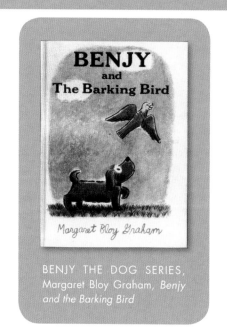

BENJY THE DOG SERIES, Margaret Bloy Graham, *Benjy and the Barking Bird*

Benjy and the Barking Bird, 1971

Benjy's Dog House, 1973

Benjy's Boat Trip, 1977

Benjy and His Friend Fifi, 1988

BERENSTAIN BEARS BOOKS, Stan and Jan Berenstain

Berenstain, Jan (b. 1923, American)

Berenstain, Stan (b. 1923, American)

When Theodor Geisel (Dr. Seuss), saw the Berenstains' proposal for a beginning reader about a family of bears, he advised them against it. "Do this," said Geisel,

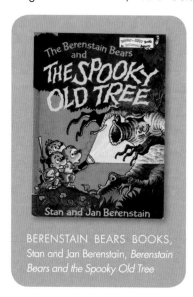

BERENSTAIN BEARS BOOKS, Stan and Jan Berenstain, *Berenstain Bears and the Spooky Old Tree*

"and you'll be stuck with bears forever." The *Berenstain Bears* books now number in the triple digits. The married couple met at the Philadelphia College of Art and began their careers as magazine cartoonists — a style that still shows in the Bear family's pictorial adventures. Reprints are easy to find, some in hardcover, some in paper covers, large printings keep values low. Titles include:

Berenstain Bears, firsts, sample list of a few favorites, first edition with dust jacket: $30.00

Bike Lesson, Another Adventure of the Berenstain Bears, 1964

Bears' Picnic, 1966

Bears in the Night, 1968

Berenstain Bears' Vacation, 1968

Bears on Wheels, 1968

Berenstain Bears and the Spooky Old Tree, 1978

BERT WILSON SERIES, J. W. Duffield, ca. 1910 – 1915, Sully & Kleintech, boys' adventure series, hardcover with gilt, four b/w plates: $35.00

Ca. 1924 Western Printing reprints with dust jacket: $30.00

BERTRAM SERIES, Paul Gilbert, small books, color illustrated endpapers, each about 125 pages long, illustrated with b/w line drawings, a very normal looking little boy and his family and friends live in

BERTRAM SERIES, Paul Gilbert, *Bertram and His Funny Animals*

a pleasant small town where Bertram's fantastic adventures begin. Plain hardcovers without dust jackets sell in the $30.00 range. First edition with dust jacket: $150.00

Bertram and His Funny Animals, 1934, Rand McNally, illustrations by Minnie Rousseff

Bertram and His Fabulous Animals, 1937, Rand McNally, illustrations by Minnie Rousseff

With Bertram in Africa, 1939, Rand McNally, illustrations by Anne Stossel

Bertram's Trip to the North Pole, 1940, Rand McNally, illustrations by Anne Stossel

Bertram and His Marvelous Adventures, 1951, Dodd, Mead & Company, 175 pages

Bertram and the Camel, edited by Frances Cavanaugh, 1968, Prentice Hall, illustrated by Maurice Brevannes

Bertram, related books:

BERTRAM SERIES, Paul Gilbert, *Bertram and the Ticklish Rhinoceros*

Bertram and the Ticklish Rhinoceros, 1948, Rand McNally Elf Book, small color illustrated hardcover, illustrations by Ruth Van Tellingham: $50.00

BETSY SERIES, Carolyn Haywood, Harcourt Brace, cloth-over-board oversize

cover, illustrated endpapers, b/w illustrations by author. There are crossover stories with the EDDIE series. First editions with dust jacket: $40.00 to $70.00

"B" is for Betsy, 1939

Betsy and Billy, 1941

Back to School with Betsy, 1943

Betsy and the Boys, 1945

Betsy and the Circus, 1954

Snowbound with Betsy, 1962

Betsy and Mr. Kilpatrick, 1967

Merry Christmas from Betsy, 1970

Betsy's Play School, 1977

BETSY-TACY SERIES, Maud Hart Lovelace, Crowell, cloth-over-board hardcover, b/w illustrations by Lois Lenski, becoming highly collectible. Dust jackets triple the price.

First editions with dust jacket: $150.00

Early printings with dust jacket: $60.00

Betsy-Tacy, 1941

Betsy-Tacy and Tib, 1941

Betsy and Tacy Go over the Big Hill, 1942

BETSY-TACY SERIES, Maud Hart Lovelace, *Betsy and Tacy Go over the Big Hill*

Betsy and Tacy Go down Town, 1943

Heaven to Betsy, 1945

Betsy in Spite of Herself, 1946

Betsy Was a Junior, 1947

Betsy and Joe, 1948

Betsy-Tacy, 1950 – 1955 first editions with dust jackets start at: $300.00

Emily of Deep Valley, 1950

Betsy and the Great World, 1952, Crowell, hardcover, b/w illustrations by Vera Neville

Winona's Pony Cart, 1953, b/w illustrations by Vera Neville

Betsy's Wedding, 1955, Crowell, illustrations by Vera Neville

BETTER LITTLE BOOKS, see BIG LITTLE BOOKS AND BETTER LITTLE BOOKS

BEVERLY GRAY COLLEGE MYSTERY SERIES, Clair Blank, girl sleuth series, first eight books were published by Burt, hardcover with illustrated endpapers and frontispiece. *World's Fair* was published only by Burt; the others were reprinted by Grosset.

1934 – 1937 Burt editions, except *World's Fair,* with dust jacket: $50.00

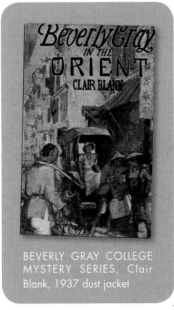

BEVERLY GRAY COLLEGE MYSTERY SERIES, Clair Blank, 1937 dust jacket

1935, Burt, *Beverly Gray at the World's Fair,* with dust jacket: $200.00

1940s, Grosset & Dunlap, hardcover, new titles with dust jacket: $30.00

1950 – 1954, Grosset & Dunlap, hardcover, new titles with dust jacket: $40.00

BIFF BREWSTER SERIES, Andy Adams (Walter B. Gibson/Maxwell Grant), Grosset & Dunlap, blue-gray hardcover. First editions are not clearly marked, but are usually judged by title being the last on the title list.

1961 pictorial glossy hardcover, first edition: $30.00

Brazilian Gold Mine Mystery, 1961

Mystery of the Chinese Ring, 1961

Hawaiian Sea Hunt Mystery, 1961

African Ivory Mystery, 1962, first edition with dust jacket: $50.00

Mystery of the Ambush in India, 1962, first edition with dust jacket: $75.00

Mystery of the Tibetan Caravan, 1963, first edition with dust jacket: $65.00

Egyptian Scarab Mystery, 1963, first edition with dust jacket: $65.00

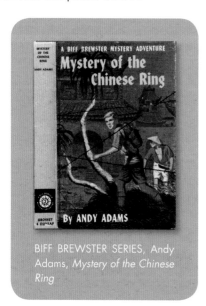

BIFF BREWSTER SERIES, Andy Adams, *Mystery of the Chinese Ring*

BIG LEAGUE SERIES, Burt L. Standish, ca. 1920s, Barse, features Lefty Locke, cloth-over-board cover with logo of baseball and player's face on front, logo of baseball on spine, b/w frontispiece. Barse edition with dust jacket: $50.00

BIG LITTLE BOOKS and BETTER LITTLE BOOKS, Whitman, series introduced in 1933, approximately 4½" high x 3½" wide x 1½" thick, color illustrated paper-over-cardboard covers, b/w illustrations facing each page of text, stories generally based on newspaper comic strips. Most are priced in the $20.00 to $40.00 range.

BETTER LITTLE BOOKS, Whitman

Generally, greatest demand is for science fiction characters such as *Flash Gordon,* and for specific collector favorites such as *Tarzan, Dick Tracy, Popeye,* etc. See series characters under their series name. Condition affects value dramatically, and so does changing popularity with collectors of specific characters or titles. Low-end price is about $25.00, with prices ranging up to $200.00 for hard-to-find titles.

BIGGLES SERIES, Captain W. E. Johns (1893 – 1968), published 1938 – 1970, 96 titles. Johns was one of the best-selling authors of children's series in Great Britain, with some 167 books credited to him. His longest and most popular series was *Biggles,* based originally on the author's aviation exploits in WWI. As the series continued, Biggles moved forward in time, fighting in WWII and later running his own air company or solving aviation mysteries.

Biggles books were issued by various publishers, including Hodder & Stoughton, Oxford, Brockhampton, Dean, Thames, or Marks and Spencer. First editions were rarely identified as such. Collectors rely on such clues as the publishers' advertisements to identify probable publication dates.

BIGGLES SERIES, Captain W. E. Johns, Dean & Sons edition

Probable first edition with dust jacket: $50.00

Dean laminated pictorial hardcovers, probable first editions of later 1960s titles: $35.00

There are over 90 titles, from *Camels Are Coming,* 1932, to *Biggles Sees Too Much,* 1970

Biggles, related books, nonfiction:

Biggles Book of Heroes, 1959, Max Parrish, with dust jacket: $85.00

Biggles Book of Treasure Hunting, 1962, Max Parrish, with dust jacket: $150.00

BILL BERGSON SERIES, Astrid Lindgren, 1952 – 1965, Viking Press, hardcover, illustrations by Don Freeman, first edition with dust jacket: $50.00

Bill Bergson, Master Detective, 1952

Bill Bergson Lives Dangerously, 1954

Bill Bergson and the White Rose, 1965

BILL BRUCE AVIATOR SERIES, Maj. Henry H. Arnold "of the U.S. Army Air Corps," ca. 1928, Burt, hardcover with print illustration, "for boys 12 to 16 years," first edition with dust jacket: $60.00

Bill Bruce and the Pioneer Aviators

Bill Bruce, the Flying Cadet

Bill Bruce Becomes an Ace

Bill Bruce on Border Patrol

Bill Bruce in the Trans-Continental Race

Bill Bruce on Forest Patrol

BILLY BUNNY SERIES, David Cory, ca. 1920s, Cupples & Leon, small size, b/w/ orange illustrations by H. Hasting, first edition with dust jacket: $40.00

Billy Bunny and the Friendly Elephant, 1920

Billy Bunny and Daddy Fox, 1920

Billy Bunny and Uncle Bull Frog, 1920

Billy Bunny and Uncle Lucky Lefthindfoot, 1920

Billy Bunny and Robbie Redbreast, 1921

Billy Bunny and Timmie Chipmunk, 1921

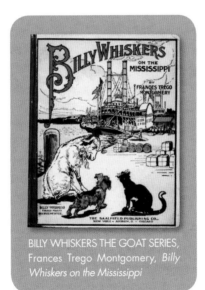

BILLY BUNNY SERIES, David Cory, *Billy Bunny and Uncle Bull Frog*

BILLY TO-MORROW SERIES, Sarah Pratt Carr, ca. 1910, A. C. McClurg, four titles, hardcover, b/w plates by Charles Relyea: $30.00

BILLY WHISKERS THE GOAT SERIES, Frances Trego Montgomery, Saalfield, cloth cover with imprint, or white paper-over-board with color illustration and cloth spine, oversize, color plates plus detailed b/w illustrations, illustrators include Constance White, Paul Hawthorne, and Frank Murch. The first titles apparently were not issued with illustrated dust jackets, though they may have had plain or tissue wrappers, but later titles did have color illustrated jackets. Dust jacket prices are for illustrated jackets.

Early editions with dust jackets: $75.00

Early editions without dust jackets: $40.00

Billy Whiskers, 1902

Billy Whiskers Kids, 1903

Billy Whiskers Vacation, 1908

Billy Whiskers in an Aeroplane, 1912

Billy Whiskers at the Fair, 1909

Billy Whiskers Grandchildren, 1909

Billy Whiskers Twins, 1911

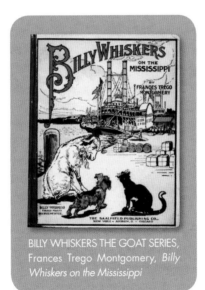

BILLY WHISKERS THE GOAT SERIES, Frances Trego Montgomery, *Billy Whiskers on the Mississippi*

Billy Whiskers on the Mississippi, 1915

Billy Whiskers Adventures, 1920

Billy Whiskers in the Movies, 1921

Billy Whiskers Pranks, 1925

Billy Whiskers in Mischief, 1926

Billy Whiskers Treasure Hunt, 1928

Billy Whiskers, Tourist, 1929

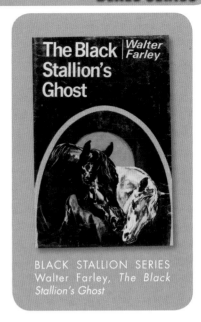

BLACK STALLION SERIES Walter Farley, *The Black Stallion's Ghost*

BLACK STALLION SERIES and ISLAND STALLION SERIES, Walter Farley, ca. 1941 – 1971, Random House, hardcover, 18 titles. 1950s first edition hardcover with dust jacket: $30.00

Black Stallion, related books, Farley, Random House, I Can Read Beginner Books, color endpapers and full-color illustrations by James Schucker, with dust jacket: $50.00 to $95.00

Little Black, a Pony, 1961

Little Black Goes to the Circus, 1963

BLAZE SERIES, Clarence W. Anderson (1891 – 1971), Macmillan, oversize

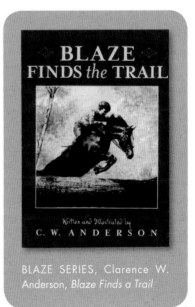

BLAZE SERIES, Clarence W. Anderson, *Blaze Finds a Trail*

hardcover, horse stories, full-page b/w illustrations by author. Early editions with dust jacket: $35.00

Billy and Blaze, 1936

Blaze and the Gypsies, 1937

Blaze and the Forest Fire, 1938

Blaze Finds a Trail, 1950

Blaze and Thunderbolt, 1955

Blaze and the Gray Spotted Pony, 1968

Blaze Shows the Way, 1969

Blaze Finds Forgotten Roads, 1970

BLOSSOM CULP SERIES, Richard Peck, hardcover, humorous tales of teenage Alexander Armsworth, his feisty neighbor, Blossom Culp, and their unwanted psychic abilities. First edition with dust jacket: $30.00

Ghost Belonged to Me, 1975, Viking Press

Ghosts I Have Been, 1977, Viking Press

Dreadful Future of Blossom Culp, 1983, Delacorte Press

Blossom Culp and the Sleep of Death, 1986, Delacorte Press

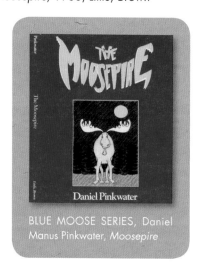

BLOSSOM CULP SERIES, Richard Peck, *Ghost Belonged to Me*

BLUE DOMERS SERIES, Jean Finley, ca. 1920s, Burt, pictorial boards, small, color illustrated endpapers, color illustrations, with paste-on pictorial: $30.00

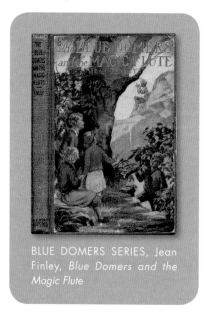

BLUE DOMERS SERIES, Jean Finley, *Blue Domers and the Magic Flute*

BLUE MOOSE SERIES, Daniel Manus Pinkwater (see also MAGIC MOSCOW), adventures of a talking moose by a writer described on a dust jacket as "an expert in zane." Hardcover, b/w illustrations by author. First edition with dust jacket: $40.00

Blue Moose, 1975, Dodd, Mead & Company

Return of the Moose, 1979, Dodd, Mead & Company

Moosepire, 1986, Little, Brown

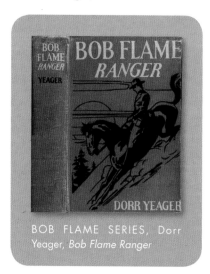

BLUE MOOSE SERIES, Daniel Manus Pinkwater, *Moosepire*

BOB AND BETTY SERIES, Boyd E. Smith (b. Canada, 1860 – 1943), author/illustrator,

pictorial paper-over-board hardcover with cloth spine, oblong oversize, illustrated endpapers, 12 full-page watercolor illustrations by the author: $65.00

Farm Book: Bob and Betty Visit Uncle John, 1910

Railroad Book, Bob and Betty's Summer on the Railroad, 1912

Seashore Book: Bob and Betty's Summer with Captain Hawes, 1913

BOBBSEY TWINS, Laura Lee Hope (Stratemeyer Syndicate pseudonym), Chatterton-Peck and Mershon b/w illustrations. Series was created in 1904 by the Stratemeyer Syndicate. Grosset first editions appeared after 1913. By 1950 Grosset began re-issuing the earlier books, sometimes with text revisions, often with title revisions to appeal to the contemporary market.

Chatterton-Peck and Mershon hardcovers, list-to-self first editions with dust jackets: $35.00

BOB DEXTER SERIES, Willard F. Baker, 1925 – 1932, Cupples & Leon, boys' mystery series, hardcover, first edition with dust jacket: $40.00

BOB FLAME SERIES, Dorr Yeager, 1934 – 1937, Dodd, cloth-over-board cover, photo plate illustrations, first edition with dust jacket: $200.00. Without dust jacket: $40.00

Bob Flame Ranger, 1934

BOB FLAME SERIES, Dorr Yeager, *Bob Flame Ranger*

Bob Flame Rocky Mountain Ranger, 1935

Bob Flame in Death Valley, 1937

BOB STEELE SERIES, also called MOTOR POWER SERIES, Donald Grayson (pseudonym), 1909, McKay, yellow-beige pictorial hardcover, with wheel-shaped logo inscribed "Motor Power Series," frontispiece by George Avison: $50.00

BOMBA SERIES, Roy Rockwood (Stratemeyer pseudonym), ca. 1926 – 1938, Cupples & Leon, then Grosset. First editions are difficult to identify, but if jacket lists to self, this is used as determiner. First edition with dust jacket: $70.00. Later editions below: $30.00

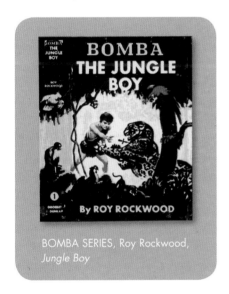

BOMBA SERIES, Roy Rockwood, *Jungle Boy*

BONNIE AND DEBBIE SERIES, Rebecca Caudill, 1950 – 1960, Winston, small hardcover, b/w illustrations by Decie Merwin, first edition with dust jacket: $40.00

Happy Little Family, 1947

Schoolhouse in the Woods, 1949

Up and Down the River, 1951

Schoolroom in the Parlor, 1959

BORRIBLES SERIES, Michael de Larrabeiti, Macmillan and Bodley, hardcover, tales of fantasy street gangs.

Borribles, 1976, first edition with dust jacket: $75.00

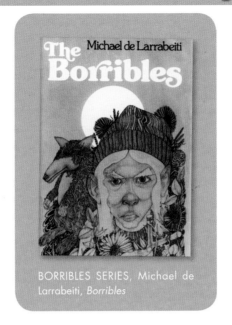

BORRIBLES SERIES, Michael de Larrabeiti, *Borribles*

Borribles: Across the Dark Metropolis, 1978, first edition with dust jacket: $30.00

Borribles Go for Broke, 1981, first edition with dust jacket: $30.00

BORROWERS SERIES, Mary Norton, Harcourt Brace, hardcover, b/w illustrations by Beth and Joe Krush, the Borrowers are miniature people existing in small hiding places. First editions with dust jacket: $50.00

Borrowers, 1953

Borrowers Afield, 1955

Borrowers Afloat, 1959

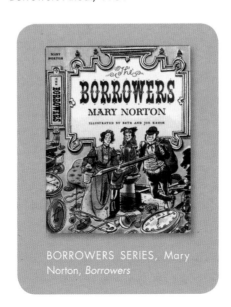

BORROWERS SERIES, Mary Norton, *Borrowers*

Borrowers Aloft, 1961

Borrowers Avenged, 1982

Related books:

Borrowers Omnibus, 1966, Dent & Sons, UK, hardcover, b/w illustrations by Diana Stanley, contains first four titles. First edition with dust jacket: $75.00

Complete Adventures of the Borrowers, 1967, Harcourt Brace & World, first edition, hardcover, includes the four books of the *Borrowers* in one volume: *Borrowers, Borrowers Afloat, Borrowers Afield,* and *Borrowers Aloft,* with dust jacket: $60.00

Poor Stainless, 1971, Dent & Sons, UK, hardcover, b/w illustrations by Diana Stanley, first edition with dust jacket: $75.00

Poor Stainless: A New Story About the Borrowers, Harcourt Brace, 1971, illustrations by Joe and Beth Krush, US first edition with dust jacket: $40.00

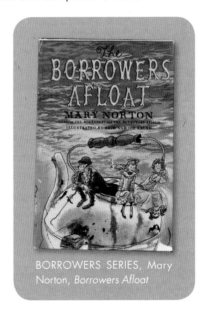

BORROWERS SERIES, Mary Norton, *Borrowers Afloat*

BOY ALLIES WITH THE ARMY SERIES, Clair W. Hayes, ca. 1915 – 1919, A. L. Burt, adventures of two American boys stranded in Europe during WWI, illustrated cloth-over-board cover, frontispiece illustration, first edition with dust jacket: $40.00

BOY FORTUNE HUNTERS SERIES, Floyd Akers (L. Frank Baum), ca. 1908, Reilly

BOY ALLIES WITH THE ARMY SERIES, Clair W. Hayes, *Boy Allies in the Trenches*

and Britton, hardcover. Publisher launched the *Boy Fortune Hunter* series in 1908, using the two Sam Steele books under new titles.

Sam Steele titles, by Capt. Hugh Fitzgerald (L. Frank Baum):

Sam Steele's Adventures on Land and Sea, 1906, Reilly, first edition, color plates, and gilt cover lettering: $700.00

Sam Steele's Adventures in Panama, 1907, Reilly, color plates, cloth, gilt lettering: $700.00

Boy Fortune Hunter titles, brown cloth covers with printed illustrations. Due to small printings for this highly collectible author, first edition values range from: $400.00 to $2,000.00

BOY FORTUNE HUNTERS SERIES, Floyd Akers, *Boy Fortune Hunters in China*

Boy Fortune Hunters in Alaska (first titled *Sam Steele's Adventures on Land and Sea*), 1908

Boy Fortune Hunters in Panama (first titled: *Sam Steele's Adventures in Panama*), 1908

Boy Fortune Hunters in Egypt, 1908

Boy Fortune Hunters in China, 1909

Boy Fortune Hunters in the Yucatan, 1910

Boy Fortune Hunters in the South Seas, 1911

BROGEEN THE LEPRECHAUN SERIES, Patricia Lynch, 1952 – 1975, Burke, UK, illustrated by Ralph Pinto or H. B. Vestal or Martin Gale or Beryl Sanders, first UK editions with dust jacket: $30.00

BROGEEN THE LEPRECHAUN SERIES, Patricia Lynch, *Brogeen and the Bronze Lizard*

BROKEN CITADEL TRILOGY, Joyce Ballou Gregorian, hardcover, story of a door into a fantasy world, with map, b/w illustrations and dust jacket by author, first edition with dust jacket: $30.00

Broken Citadel, 1975, Atheneum

Castledown, 1977, Atheneum

Great Wheel, 1987, TOR

BRONC BURNETT SERIES, Wilfred McCormick, late 1948 – 1960s, Grosset & Dunlap (some by Putnam), tweed hardcover, high school sports stories centered around sixteen-year-old Bronc, first edition with dust jacket: $80.00

BROKEN CITADEL TRILOGY, Joyce Ballou Gregorian, *Castledown*

Three-Two Pitch, 1948

Legion Tourney, 1948

Fielder's Choice, 1949

Flying Tackle, 1949

Bases Loaded, 1950

Rambling Halfback, 1950

Grand Slam Homer, 1951

Quick Kick, 1951

Eagle Scout, 1952

Stranger in the Backfield, 1960

Go-Ahead Runner, 1965

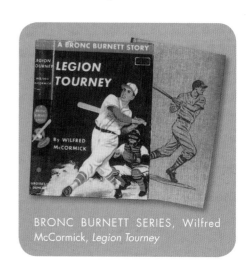

BRONC BURNETT SERIES, Wilfred McCormick, *Legion Tourney*

Big Ninth, 1958

Last Put-Out, 1960

One O'Clock Hitter, 1960

No Place for Heroes, 1966

Tall at the Plate, 1966

One Bounce Too Many, 1967

Incomplete Pitcher, 1967

BROWNIES SERIES, Palmer Cox, 1840 – 1924, author/illustrator, oversize color pictorial hardcover, characters originated for stories for *St. Nicholas* magazine and probably inspired by Scottish fairy tales. Illustrations throughout by author.

Brownies: Their Book, 1887, Century, pictorial green boards, 144 pages: $400.00

Another Brownie Book, 1890, Century, oversize, paper-over-board illustrated cover, first edition: $350.00. Later printings, ca. 1920, Century: $90.00

Brownies at Home, 1893, Century: $150.00

Brownies Round the World, 1894, Unwin: $300.00

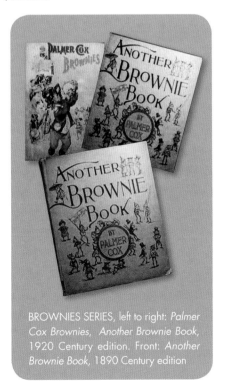
BROWNIES SERIES, left to right: *Palmer Cox Brownies, Another Brownie Book,* 1920 Century edition. Front: *Another Brownie Book,* 1890 Century edition

Brownies Around the World, 1894, Century, first edition, oversize, glazed color illustrated cover: $300.00

Brownie Year Book, 1895, Century: $100.00

Brownies Through the Union, ca. 1895, Century, oversize pictorial boards, 144 pages, color illustrations plus drawings: $150.00

Brownies Primer Together with Queerie Queers, 1901, Hill, oversize pictorial boards, 12 full-page color illustrations of alphabet letters, plus nonsense rhymes: $300.00

Brownies in the Philippines, 1904, Century, glazed pictorial boards: $300.00

Palmer Cox Brownies, ca. 1906, Century, illustrated oversize boards, cloth spine: $150.00

Brownies Latest Adventures, 1910, Century, oversize pictorial boards, 144 pages: $150.00

Brownies and Prince Florimel, 1918, Century, pictorial boards, 246 pages, b/w illustrations: $150.00

Palmer Cox Brownie Primer, 1924, Century, pictorial boards, 108 pages, two-color illustrations: $100.00

Brownies related books: *Palmer Cox Primers,* illustrated by Palmer Cox, 1897, small eight-page pamphlets, done as a giveaway to insert in packages of Jersey Coffee, complete set of six: $250.00

BUBBLE BOOK SERIES, "Books That Sing," ca. 1918, Harper, small, color illustrated paper-over-board cover, two-color illustrations by Rhoda Chase, book contains three 78 rpm one-sided records in envelope-shaped pages, records include songs to augment the stories and games in the book.

With all records in good condition: $100.00

Without records: $45.00

BUBBLE BOOK SERIES, *Third Bubble Book*

BUCK ROGERS SERIES, Phil Nowlan, illustrated by Lt. Dick Calkins. Buck Rogers first appeared in an 1928 *Amazing Stories* magazine story, titled "Armegeddon 2419 AD" by Nowlan. In 1929 the idea became a comic strip, drawn by Calkins and several other artists, and continued until 1967. Nowlan wrote the stories until his death in 1940. Radio show began in 1932. Titles include:

Story of Buck Rogers on the Planetoid Eros, 1934, Whitman Big Big Book, pictorial boards, 317 pages, 150 illustrations suitable for coloring: $100.00

Buck Rogers, Whitman Big Little Books, pictorial pasteboard cover, b/w illustrations: $60.00. Titles include:

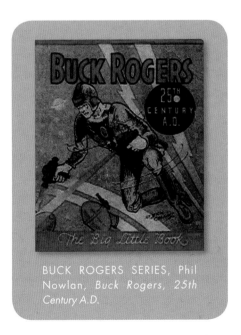
BUCK ROGERS SERIES, Phil Nowlan, *Buck Rogers, 25th Century A.D.*

Buck Rogers, 25th Century A.D., the first Buck Rogers book, 1933

Buck Rogers in the City Below the Sea, 1934

Buck Rogers on the Moons of Saturn, 1934

Buck Rogers and the Doom Comet, 1935

Buck Rogers and the Depth Men of Jupiter, 1935

Buck Rogers and the Planetoid Plot, 1936

Buck Rogers, Whitman Better Little Books, pictorial pasteboard cover, b/w illustrations: $60.00. Titles include:

Buck Rogers, 25th Century A.D., in a War with the Planet Venus, 1938

Buck Rogers 25th Century A.D. Vs. the Fiend of Space, 1940

Buck Rogers and the Overturned World, 1941

Buck Rogers, pop-up:

Buck Rogers, Pleasure Books, 1934, color illustrations: $600.00

Buck Rogers 25th Century Featuring Buddy and Allura in "Strange Adventures in the Spider Ship," 1935, Blue Ribbon, color Illustrated hardcover, three double spread pop-ups: $400.00

Buck Rogers, related:

Armegeddon 2419 AD, Nowlan, story collection, 1962, Avalon, blue hardcover with black lettering, science fiction, first edition with dust jacket: $50.00

Collected Works of Buck Rogers in the 25th Century, 1969, Chelsea House, oversize hardcover, b/w and color illustrations, edited by Robert C. Dille, first edition with dust jacket: $50.00

Buck Rogers, 1979 film: movie related books and posters issued at that time are highly collectible, but were issued in extremely large quantities and so are usually easily available and reasonably priced.

BUNNICULA, THE VAMPIRE BUNNY SERIES, James Howe, Atheneum, hardcover, b/w illustrations by Lynn Munsinger. Harold, the dog, and Chester, the cat, try to expose the crimes of a vampire bunny.

Bunnicula, a Rabbit Tale of Mystery, 1979, first edition with dust jacket: $45.00

Later titles were issued in quantity, therefore used copies sell at less than cover price.

Howliday Inn, 1982, through *Bunnicula Escapes,* 1994

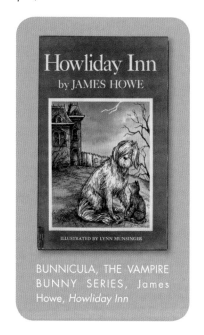

BUNNICULA, THE VAMPIRE BUNNY SERIES, James Howe, *Howliday Inn*

BUNNY TOTS SERIES, Edward McCandlish, ca. 1915, Burt, paste-on-pictorial hardcover, color frontispiece, b/w illustrations by author, picture books for pre-schoolers: $65.00

1920s reprints, hardcover with dust jacket: $40.00

BUSTER BROWN SERIES, R. F. Outcault, oversize, color and b/w illustrations by author, ca. 1900, London, and Frederick A. Stokes, New York. Buster Brown, a saucy lad with a clever dog, became a logo for children's shoes.

Buster Brown, His Dog Tige and Their Troubles, 1900, London, color illustrations: $85.00

BUNNY TOTS SERIES, Edward McCandlish, *Bunny Tots' Snow Book*

Buster Brown Abroad, 1904, Frederick A. Stokes, oversize dark blue hardcover: $80.00. Chambers, London edition: $200.00

Buster Brown, My Resolutions, 1906, Stokes, small red hardcover with white lettering: $85.00

Buster Brown Nugget Series, R. F. Outcault, ca. 1905 Cupples & Leon, small paper-over-board hardcovers, 36 pages, full-color full-page illustrations by author: $75.00

Buster Brown Goes Fishing

Buster Brown Goes Swimming

Buster Brown Plays Indian

BUSTER BROWN SERIES, R. F. Outcault, *Buster Brown Abroad*

BUSTER BROWN SERIES, R. F. Outcault, *Buster Brown Goes Swimming*

Buster Brown Goes Shooting

Buster Brown Plays Cowboy

Buster Brown on Uncle Jack's Farm

Buster Brown, Tige and the Bull

Buster Brown and Uncle Buster

Buster Brown, related items:

Buster Brown Playing Cards, 1904, U.S. Play Card Co., deck of 52 cards with a different picture on each card telling a story of Buster and Tige, in a leather and fur case: $250.00

Buster Brown's Painting Book, 1916, Cupples & Leon, color and b/w illustrations: $50.00

BYE-LO BOOKS, ca. 1910 – 1915, Rand McNally, small size, color illustration on cover, approximately 60 pages with b/w/

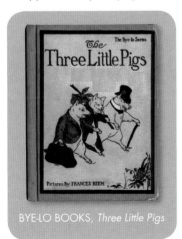

BYE-LO BOOKS, *Three Little Pigs*

orange illustrations, various authors, re-tellings of popular stories: $45.00

CAMPBELL SERIES, Janet Lambert, ca. 1958 – 1960, E. P. Dutton, hardcover, popular teen romance novels, with dust jacket: $150.00. Without dust jacket: $30.00

Grosset & Dunlap reprints with dust jacket: $30.00

Precious Days, 1957

For Each Other, 1959

Forever and Ever, 1961

Five's a Crowd, 1963

First of All, 1966

CANDY KANE SERIES, Janet Lambert, E. P. Dutton, hardcover, first edition with dust jacket: $150.00

Grosset & Dunlap reprints with dust jacket: $35.00

Candy Kane, 1943

Whoa, Matilda, 1944

One for the Money, 1946

CANDY KANE SERIES, Janet Lambert, *One for the Money*

CAPTAIN MIDNIGHT SERIES, stories feature brave flyers and fantastic adversaries

in mysterious locations, began as a popular World War II radio show.

Joyce of the Secret Squadron, a Captain Midnight Adventure, 1942, Whitman, plain hardcover, Russ Winterbotham, first edition with dust jacket: $35.00

Captain Midnight, ca. 1945, Whitman Better Little Books, pictorial cardboard cover, b/w illustrations: $100.00

Captain Midnight and Shiek Jornan Khan, Book #1402

Captain Midnight and the Moon Woman, Book #1452

Captain Midnight Vs. Terror of the Orient, Book #1458

CARBONEL THE CAT SERIES, Barbara Sleigh

CARBONEL THE CAT SERIES, Barbara Sleigh, *Carbonel: the King of the Cats*

Dust jacket doubles price with this series.

Carbonel: the King of the Cats, British title: Carbonel, published by M. Parrish, 1955, ca. 1957, Bobbs-Merrill, illustrated by V. H. Drummond, US first edition with dust jacket: $200.00

Carbonel: the King of the Cats, 1966, E. M. Hale & Co, illustrated by V. H. Drummond, with dust jacket: $125.00

Kingdom of Carbonel, 1960 edition, Clarke Irwin, Canada, also Bobbs-Merrill, US, hardcover, illustrations by D.M.

Leonard & Stephen P. Haas, first edition with dust jacket: $150.00

Carbonel and Calidor, 1982, Puffin paperback, illustrated by Charles Front: $35.00

CASTLEMON BOOKS, Harry Castlemon (pseudonym of Charles A. Fosdick, 1842 – 1915). Fosdick wrote 58 adventure novels, usually as a three or four book series, and many of his stories were based on his service in the US Navy during the Civil War. Like other Victorian series, advertisements in back of editions tend to be a better indicator of age than copyright dates, which were not updated for later printings. Reprints by houses such as Winston generally fall in the $10.00 to $20.00 range as do later reprints by publishers listed below. Individual titles are clearly identified (on cover or title page) as part of a series and are not listed below.

Castlemon Series, value per volume in series:

Afloat and Ashore Series, Henry T. Coates, 1897 – 1898, cover illustrations printed on cloth in yellow, orange, and gold with gilt lettering on spine, frontispiece and three plates, early editions: $30.00

Boy Trapper Series, Porter & Coates, 1877 – 1879, cloth binding with printed decorative type and title, spine decorated in gilt with small illustrations, frontispiece and three full-page plates. Porter & Coates editions not listing series past 1879: $40.00

Castlemon's War Series, Porter & Coates, 1889 – 1893, three-color plus gilt cover illustration printed on light brown cloth shows two cadets struggling for American flag, same cover illustration used for all titles, spine also decorated, illustrations by George G. White, early editions: $35.00

Forest and Stream Series, Porter & Coates, 1886 – 1888, cloth binding stamped in black and gold, frontispiece and three plates, early editions: $35.00

Frank Nelson Series, Porter & Coates, 1876 – 1877, original copyright held by R. W. Carroll but first editions issued by Porter & Coates. Both Porter and Carroll's names appear in earliest editions: $45.00

CASTLEMON BOOKS, Harry Castlemon, *Frank Nelson Series*

Frank Nelson Series, ca. 1910, Burt editions, paste-on pictorial: $30.00

Gun-Boat Series, also listed as the Gunboat series with no hyphen by publishers. R. W. Carroll, 1865 – 1868. The first series written by Castlemon and first issued by R. W. Carroll & Co of Ohio. Later reprinted under the series name *Frank and Archie.* R. W. Carroll editions start at: $35.00

House-Boat Series, Henry T. Coates, 1895 – 1896, front cover two-color illustrations printed on cloth with gilt type on spine, frontispiece and three full-page illustrations, early editions: $35.00

Hunter Series, Porter & Coates, 1892, cover illustrations printed in black, gray, and gold, illustrated with frontispiece and three full-page plates, early editions: $30.00

Lucky Tom Series, Porter & Coates or Henry T. Coates (publisher name changed during series run), 1887 – 1895, early editions: $30.00

Pony Express Series, Henry T. Coates, 1898 – 1900, cloth binding stamped in black and gilt, frontispiece and three plates, early editions: $30.00

Rocky Mountain Series, R. W. Carroll, 1871, continuing adventures of the heroes of the *Gun-Boat* series, earliest Carroll editions issued with pebbled cloth binding, blind-stamped on front, spine heavily decorated in gilt, decorative title page and

two full-page illustrations on coated paper. Starting in 1872, reissued by Porter & Coates under the joint imprint of "R. W. Carroll & Company/Porter & Coates." Carroll first editions start at: $75.00. Porter & Coates early editions: $35.00

Rod and Gun Series, Porter & Coates, 1883 – 1885, continues adventures of Don Gordon, first introduced in *Boy Trapper* series, cloth binding stamped black and gilt or brown and gilt, early editions: $45.00

Rolling-Stone Series (also called "Go-Ahead" after 1872), R. W. Carroll, 1869 – 1871. Earliest editions issued with pebbled cloth binding and blind-stamped on front, spine heavily decorated in gilt, frontispiece, decorative title page and two full-page illustrations on coated paper. Starting in 1872, reissued by Porter & Coates under a joint imprint of "R. W. Carroll & Company/Porter & Coates." Carroll imprint pre-1872 starts at: $100.00, Porter & Coates early editions: $30.00

Roughing It Series, Porter & Coates, 1879 – 1882, continuing adventures of George Ackerman introduced in the *Boy Trapper* series, cloth binding with printed decorative type and title, spine decorated in gilt with small illustrations, frontispiece and three full-page plates, early editions: $30.00

Sportsman Club Series, 1873 – 1874, Porter & Coates (original copyright held by R. W. Carroll but first editions issued by Porter & Coates). Both Porter and Carroll's names appear in earliest editions, cloth binding with spine heavily decorated in gilt, four plates including frontispiece. See also "Frank Nelson." Porter early editions: $35.00

CAT CLUB SERIES, Esther Averill, Harper, pictorial hardcover, illustrations by author, a series of stories that increase in reading difficulty levels, tales of city cats, featuring Jenny Linsky, a small black cat, and other cats in the cat club in New York.

Cat Club, 1944 – 1959, first edition with dust jacket: $200.00

CAT CLUB SERIES, Esther Averill, *Jenny's Birthday Book*

Cat Club or, *the Life and Times of Jenny Linsky*, 1944

School for Cats, 1947

Jenny's First Party, 1948

Jenny's Moonlight Adventure, 1949

How the Brothers Joined the Cat Club, 1953

When Jenny Lost Her Scarf, 1951

Jenny's Birthday Book, 1954

Jenny Goes to Sea, 1957

Jenny's Bedside Book, 1959

Cat Club, 1970s, first edition with dust jacket: $100.00

Hotel Cat, 1969

Captain of the City Streets, 1972

Jenny and the Cat Club, 1973

CHALET SCHOOL, Elinor M. Brent-Dyer (1894 – 1969), W. R. Chambers, UK, hardcover. Original dust jacket illustrations from 1925 through 1950 drawn by Nina K. Brisley, dust jackets in the 1950s through the 1970s illustrated by Walter Spence and later by D. Brooks. Both artists also did revised dust jacket illustrations for earlier titles. Later paperback reprints were often abridged or adapted from the earlier books. Books command highest prices from British and Canadian collectors.

CHALET SCHOOL, Elinor M. Brent-Dyer, 1940s – 1960s first edition with dust jacket

1920s and 1930s first editions, hardcovers with gilt: $400.00

1940s – 1960s first editions with dust jackets: $150.00

1950s – 1960s reprints with dust jackets: $100.00

Chalet School, related titles: Chalet Books, Chambers, UK. Three collections of short stories or novellas, some stories later released as individual paperback titles. Also reprinted in the 1970s as part of the *My Treasure Hour* annuals. Hardback with dust jacket: $150.00. Without dust jacket: $50.00

Chalet Book for Girls, 1947

Second Chalet Book for Girls, 1948

Third Chalet Book for Girls, 1949

Chalet School, nonfiction title:

Chalet Girls' Cookbook, 1953, Chambers, hardback with dust jacket: $200.00

CHANGES TRILOGY, Peter Dickinson, English science fiction trilogy, hardcover. American editions sell at cover price.

Weathermonger, 1968 Gollancz, UK, first edition with dust jacket: $100.00

CHANGES TRILOGY, Peter Dickinson, *Weathermonger*

Heartsease, 1969, Gollancz, UK, first edition with dust jacket: $75.00

Devil's Children, 1970, Gollancz, UK, first edition with dust jacket: $25.00

CHARLIE SERIES, Helen Hill and Violet Maxwell, 1920s, Macmillan, small cloth-over-board cover with impressed illustration, illustrated endpapers, color illustrations by authors, early edition with dust jacket: $65.00

Charlie and His Kitten Topsy, 1922

Charlie and His Coast Guards, 1925

Charlie and His Surprise House, 1926

Charlie and His Friends, 1927

Charlie and His Puppy Bingo, 1929

CHARLIE SERIES, Helen Hill and Violet Maxwell, *Charlie and His Coast Guards*

CHERRY AMES, NURSE SERIES, Helen Wells or Julie Campbell Tatham, Grosset & Dunlap. There were 27 books written between 1943 and 1968. A planned 28th book was not published. A few of the later books had small printings which makes them more difficult to find and raises the value.

Plain hardcover with dust jacket: $30.00

Student Nurse, 1943

Senior Nurse, 1944

Army Nurse, 1944

Chief Nurse, 1944

Flight Nurse, 1945

Veterans' Nurse, 1946

Private Duty Nurse, 1946

Visiting Nurse, 1947

Cruise Nurse, 1948

At Spencer, 1949

Night Supervisor, 1950

Mountaineer Nurse, 1951

Clinic Nurse, 1952

Dude Ranch Nurse, 1953

Rest Home Nurse, 1954

Country Doctor's Nurse, 1955

Boarding School Nurse, 1955

CHERRY AMES, NURSE SERIES,
Helen Wells, *Rural Nurse*

Department Store Nurse, 1956

Camp Nurse, 1957

At Hilton Hospital, 1959

Island Nurse, 1960

Rural Nurse, 1961

Staff Nurse, 1962

Companion Nurse, 1964

Jungle Nurse, 1965

Hard-to-find titles:

Book of First Aid & Home Nursing, 1959, gray tweed hardcover, first edition with dust jacket: $150.00

Mystery in the Doctor's Office, 1966, illustrated hardcover: $50.00

Ski Nurse Mystery, 1968, illustrated hardcover: $50.00

CHESTER CRICKET SERIES, George Selden, an odd assortment of creatures meet under difficult conditions and become friends.

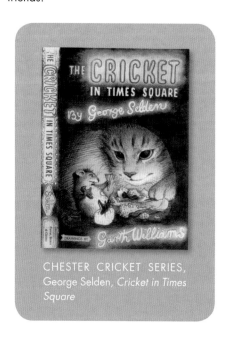

CHESTER CRICKET SERIES,
George Selden, *Cricket in Times Square*

Cricket in Times Square, 1960, Farrar, hardcover, first edition, b/w illustrations by Garth Williams, first edition with dust jacket: $50.00

Tucker's Countryside, 1969, Farrar, 165 pages, b/w illustrations by Garth Williams, first edition with dust jacket: $40.00

Harry Cat's Pet Puppy, 1973, Farrar, illustrations by Garth Williams, first edition with dust jacket: $50.00

CHILDREN'S RED BOOKS SERIES, ca. 1915, Reilly & Britton, and CHILDREN'S OWN BOOKS SERIES, ca. 1918, Reilly & Britton which lists the same 12 books as the RED BOOKS SERIES plus volumes 13 and 14. Small size, two stories in each book, color covers, illustrations and endpapers, many by *Oz* book illustrator John R. Neill: $45.00

CHILDREN'S RED BOOKS
SERIES, *Black Beauty*

CHIP HILTON SPORTS SERIES, Clair Bee, Grosset & Dunlap, red tweed hardcover, sport design endpapers, b/w illustrations, probable first edition with dust jacket: $40.00 to $75.00

Touchdown Pass, 1948

Championship Ball, 1948

Strike Three, 1949

Clutch Hitter!, 1949

Hoop Crazy, 1950

Pitchers' Duel, 1950

Pass and a Prayer, 1951

Dugout Jinx, 1952

CHIP HILTON SPORTS SERIES,
Clair Bee, *Clutch Hitter!*

Freshman Quarterback, 1952

Backboard Fever, 1953

Fence Busters, 1953

Ten Seconds to Play, 1955

Fourth Down Showdown, 1956

Tournament Crisis, 1957

Hardcourt Upset, 1957

Pay-Off Pitch, 1958

No-Hitter, 1959

Triple-Threat Trouble, 1960

Backboard Ace, 1961

Buzzer Basket, 1962

Comeback Cagers, 1963

Home Run Feud, 1964

Hungry Hurler, 1966

CHRESTOMANCI SERIES, Diana Wynne
Jones, 1978 – 1988, various publishers, a
loosely related series of books in which
the magician Chrestomanci pops up to
put right what went wrong in several magical worlds, first edition with dust jacket:
$30.00

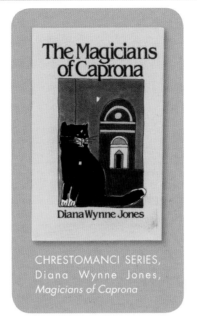

CHRESTOMANCI SERIES,
Diana Wynne Jones,
Magicians of Caprona

Charmed Life, 1977, Greenwillow

Magicians of Caprona, 1980, Greenwillow

Witch Week, 1982, Greenwillow

Lives of Christopher Chant, 1988,
Greenwillow, a prequel to the early books
that explains how Chrestomanci acquired
his powers

Chrestomanci Quartet, 2000, Science
Fiction Book Club, contains the above four
titles

CHRIS GODFREY SERIES, Hugh Walters,
1960s – 1980s, Faber & Faber, UK. Chris
grows up and advances his career in
the UNEXA, United Nations Exploration
Agency. Some of the books were reprinted
by Criterion, US, and Thomas Nelson, US,
hardcover, sometimes with title variations.

Faber, 1960s titles, first edition with dust
jacket: $200.00

Faber, 1970s and 1980s titles, first edition
with dust jacket: $100.00

Chris Godfrey, UK titles include:

Blast Off at Woornera, 1957

Domes of Pico, 1958

Operation Columbus, 1960

Moon Base One, 1962

Expedition Venus, 1963

Destination Mars, 1963

Terror By Satellite, 1964

Mission to Mercury, 1965

Journey to Jupiter, 1966

Spaceship to Saturn, 1967

Mohole Mystery, 1968

Nearly Neptune, 1969

First Contact?, 1971

Passage to Pluto, 1973

Tony Hale, Space Detective, 1973

Murder on Mars, 1975

Boy Astronaut, 1977

Caves of Drach, 1977

Last Disaster, 1978

Blue Aura, 1979

First Family on the Moon, 1979

Dark Triangle, 1981

School on the Moon, 1981

CHRIS GODFREY SERIES, Hugh
Walters, *Outpost on the Moon*

Chris Godfrey, US editions, Criterion and Nelson, first edition with dust jacket: $50.00

First four titles:

Blast Off at 0300, 1958

Menace from the Moon, 1959

First on the Moon, 1960

Outpost on the Moon, 1962

CHRISTMAS STOCKING SERIES, 1905, Reilly & Britton, hardcover, color illustrations by John R. Neill, six volumes in a box illustrated to resemble a wardrobe trunk, first edition, complete set with box: $2,000.00. Each volume: $100.00

Cinderella and the Sleeping Beauty

Fairy Tales from Andersen

Fairy Tales from Grimm

Little Black Sambo

Night Before Christmas

Story of Peter Rabbit

CHRONICLES OF NARNIA SERIES, C. S. Lewis, ca. 1950s, Macmillan editions, hardcover, b/w illustrations by Pauline Baynes, dust jacket illustration by Roger Hane. Reprints are plentiful.

Lion, the Witch and the Wardrobe, 1950, first edition with dust jacket: $1,000.00

Prince Caspian, 1951, first edition with dust jacket: $300.00

Voyage of the Dawn Treader, 1952, oversize hardcover, first edition with dust jacket: $500.00

Silver Chair, 1953, first edition with dust jacket: $250.00

Horse and His Boy, 1954, first edition with dust jacket: $250.00

Magician's Nephew, 1954, first edition with dust jacket: $200.00

Silver Chair, later edition with Roger Hane dust jacket

Magician's Nephew, 1955, Bodley Head, London, oversize green hardcover with silver lettering, first UK edition thus, with dust jacket: $800.00

Last Battle, 1956, first edition with dust jacket: $200.00

Last Battle, 1956, Geoffrey Bles, London, first UK edition thus, light blue hardcover with silver gilt lettering, first edition with dust jacket: $600.00

CHUDLEIGH HOLD SERIES, Elinor M. Brent-Dyer, W.R. Chambers, UK, hardcover, early edition with dust jacket: $100.00

Chudleigh Hold, 1954

CHUDLEIGH HOLD SERIES, Elinor Brent-Dyer, *Susannah Adventure*

Condor Crags Adventure, 1954

Top Secret, 1955

Chudleigh related titles, some of the same characters also appear in:

Fardingales, 1950

Susannah Adventure, 1953

CHUNKY BOOKS, ca. 1920s, McLoughlin Bros., oversize, hardcover, shape books with color illustrations start at: $100.00. Titles include:

Chunky Cottage

Chunky Scouts

Chunky Store

Good Ship Chunky

CHUNKY BOOKS, McLoughlin Bros., *Chunky Cottage*

CHURCH MICE SERIES, Graham Oakley, Macmillan, UK, and Atheneum, US, over-size oblong hardcover, highly detailed full-page color illustrations by author.

Oakley studied art at Warrington Art School. His career includes writing, book illustration, as well as set design for both opera, film, and TV productions. Oakley likes to see authors illustrate their own work, believing that this creates the best opportunity to interpret an idea.

CHURCH MICE SERIES, Graham Oakley, *Church Cat Abroad* illustration

The church cat and a community of mice relate their version of their adventures, while the clever illustrations often show a different viewpoint.

Pre-1995 first edition with dust wrapper: $75.00

Church Mouse, 1972

Church Cat Abroad, 1973

Church Mice and the Moon, 1974

Church Mice Spread Their Wings, 1975

Church Mice Adrift, 1977

Church Mice at Bay, 1979

Church Mice at Christmas, 1980

Church Mice in Action, 1982

Diary of a Church Mouse, 1987

CHURCH MICE SERIES, Graham Oakley, *Church Mice Spread Their Wings*

Church Mice and the Ring, 1992

Humphrey Hits the Jackpot, 1999

Church Mice Take a Break, 2000

CHURCHMOUSE SERIES, Margot Austin, E. P. Dutton, oversize hardcover, full-page b/w illustrations by author, first edition with dust jacket: $60.00

Peter Churchmouse, 1941

Gabriel Churchkitten, 1942

Trumpet Churchdog, 1948

Gabriel Churchkitten and the Moths, 1948

Churchmouse Stories, 1956, E. P. Dutton, hardcover, illustrated by author, with dust jacket: $30.00

CINDA HOLLISTER SERIES, Janet Lambert, E. P. Dutton, hardcover with dust jacket: $150.00

CINDA HOLLISTER SERIES, Janet Lambert, *Love to Spare*

Grosset & Dunlap tweed hardcover reprint with dust jacket: $50.00

Cinda, 1954

Fly Away Cinda, 1956

Big Deal, 1958

Triple Trouble, 1965

Love to Spare, 1967

CITIES IN FLIGHT SERIES, James Blish, Faber and Faber, UK, and Putnam, US, hardcover, science fiction.

They Shall Have Stars, 1956, first edition with dust jacket: $150.00

Life for the Stars, 1962, first edition with dust jacket: $60.00

Earthman, Come Home, 1965, first edition with dust jacket: $100.00

Triumph of Time, 1968, Avon paperback: $10.00

CLONAR SERIES, see WINSTON SCIENCE FICTION CLASSICS

COLLEGE SPORTS SERIES, Lester Chadwick, ca. 1925, Cupples & Leon, hardcover, b/w plates, with dust jacket: $35.00

Rival Pitchers

Quarterback's Pluck

Batting to Win

Winning Touchdown

For the Honor of Randall

Eight-Oared Victors

CONNIE BLAIR MYSTERY SERIES, Betsy Allen, ca. 1940s, Grosset & Dunlap, cloth-over-board cover, advertised as "Connie is a career girl with a job in an advertising agency ...you can identify a Connie Blair Mystery at a glance because a color is always in the title."

Connie Blair, Clue in Blue, through *Peril in Pink*, first edition (list-to-self) with dust jacket: $80.00. Later editions with dust jacket: $40.00

Clue in Blue

Riddle in Red

Puzzle in Purple

Secret of Black Cat Gulch

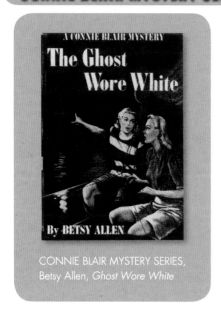

CONNIE BLAIR MYSTERY SERIES,
Betsy Allen, *Ghost Wore White*

Green Island Mystery

Ghost Wore White

Yellow Warning

Gray Menace

Brown Satchel Mystery

Peril in Pink

Connie Blair, last two titles:

Silver Secret, 1956, with dust jacket: $120.00

Mystery of the Ruby Queens, 1958, with dust jacket: $150.00

CONNIE MORGAN SERIES, James B. Hendryx (pseudonym, James Beardsley, 1880 – 1963), Putnam and Doubleday, hardcover with paste-on pictorial, b/w illustrations by W. W. Clarke, first edition: $100.00

Connie Morgan in Alaska, 1916

Connie Morgan with the Mounted, 1918

Connie Morgan in the Lumber Camps, 1919

Connie Morgan in the Fur Country, 1921

Connie Morgan in the Cattle Country, 1923, illustrations by Frank E. Schoonover

Connie Morgan with the Forest Rangers, 1925

Connie Morgan Hits the Trail, 1929

Connie Morgan in the Arctic, ca. 1936

CONQUEST OF THE UNITED STATES SERIES, H. Irving Hancock, 1916, Altemus, hardcover, a four-part adventure drawing on Hancock's real world series, *Dick Prescott,* which sell in the $35.00 range with dust jacket. This science fiction series pits the Gridley High School Cadets against an invading German army in a fictional future war set in 1920. Illustrated hardcover with dust jacket: $300.00. Without dust jacket: $120.00

Invasion of the United States, or, *Uncle Sam's Boys at the Capture of Boston*

CONQUEST OF THE UNITED STATES SERIES, H. Irving Hancock, *Invasion of the United States*

In the Battle for New York, or, *Uncle Sam's Boys in the Desperate Struggle for the Metropolis*

At the Defense of Pittsburgh, or, *the Struggle to Save America's Fighting Steel Supply*

Making the Stand for Old Glory, or, *Uncle Sam's Boys in the Last Frantic Drive*

CORNER HOUSE GIRLS SERIES, Grace Brooks Hill, 1915 – 1926, Barse, illustrated cloth-over-board cover, illustrated endpapers, four b/w illustrations by

Emmett Owen, with dust jacket: $30.00

CURIOUS GEORGE SERIES, H. A. Rey and Margret Rey, Houghton Mifflin, oversize hardcover, bright color illustrations by authors.

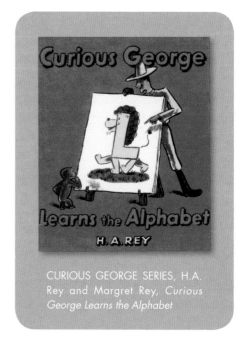

CURIOUS GEORGE SERIES, H.A. Rey and Margret Rey, *Curious George Learns the Alphabet*

Rey, H. A. (1898 – 1977)

Rey, Margret (1906 – 1996)

Hans Augusto Rey and Margret Waldstein were both born in Germany. He served in the German army, then went to Brazil to work in a company owned by his family. There he met Margret Waldstein, who had studied art in Dusseldorf and Berlin. Rey was a self-taught artist. The couple married and returned to Paris. In 1940 they fled the Nazi invasion on bicycles, carrying manuscripts, including Rey's ideas for *Curious George.* When they reached the U. S. and were able to pursue their writing and art careers, they worked on a number of projects, but the *Curious George* stories made them famous.

The series features a playful monkey and the Man with the Yellow Hat. Margret Rey continued the *Curious George* books after her husband's death. This popular series is constantly reprinted, including new stories, collections, and activity books featuring Curious George.

Dust jackets triple the value of early first editions. Collectors also rely on dust jackets to help identify first editions (looking at listing of additional titles in series, prices, etc., for dating is generally more reliable than copyright information on earliest editions).

Curious George, original series, Houghton Mifflin, values start at:

Curious George, 1941, first edition with dust jacket: $2,000.00 to $10,000.00

Curious George Takes a Job, 1947, first edition with dust jacket: $1,500.00

Curious George Rides a Bike, 1952, first edition with dust jacket: $800.00

Curious George Gets a Medal, 1957, first edition with dust jacket: $800.00

Curious George Flies a Kite, 1958, first edition with dust jacket: $800.00

Curious George Learns the Alphabet, 1963, first edition with dust jacket: $300.00

Curious George Goes to the Hospital, 1966, first edition with dust jacket: $300.00

Curious George, other:

Cecily G and the Nine Monkeys, Houghton Mifflin, 1942, first children's book by H. A. Rey about a lonely giraffe and a group of monkeys including one named Curious George. Originally published in France as *Rafi et les 9 Singes* (the George character was named Fifi in this version) in 1939. First edition: $500.00

Raffy and the Nine Monkeys, Chatto and Windus, 1939, first British edition, published same year as the French edition: $200.00. 1960s reprint of *Raffy:* $100.00

Curious George, a Pop-Up Book, 1976, hardcover: $40.00

Curious George, later titles edited by Margret Rey and Alan J. Shalleck (1980s) or "New Adventures" illustrated by Viph

Interactive (1990s), sell at or below cover price in the used market.

CURLYTOPS SERIES, Howard R. Garis, ca. 1920s, Cupples & Leon, paste-on pictorial, hardcover, b/w illustrations by Julia Greene, first edition with dust jacket: $30.00

CURLYTOPS SERIES, Howard R. Garis, *Curlytops at Silver Lake*

■ ·················· D ·················· ■

DANA GIRLS MYSTERY SERIES, Carolyn Keene (Stratemeyer Syndicate pseudonym), ca. 1934 – 1968, Grosset & Dunlap, hardcover, various illustrators.

First edition with dust jacket: $35.00

DANA GIRLS MYSTERY SERIES, Carolyn Keene, *Secret at the Hermitage*

DANNY DUNN SERIES, Jay Williams and Raymond Abrashki, school boys engage in science fiction and fantasy adventures.

1956 – 1970s, McGraw-Hill Children's Book Club, first edition with dust jacket: $60.00

Danny Dunn and the Anti-Gravity Paint, 1957, illustrated by Ezra Jack Keats

Danny Dunn on a Desert Island, 1957, illustrated by Ezra Jack Keats

Danny Dunn and the Homework Machine, 1959, illustrated by Ezra Jack Keats

Danny Dunn and the Weather Machine, 1959, illustrated by Ezra Jack Keats

Danny Dunn on the Ocean Floor, 1960, illustrated by Brinton Turkle

Danny Dunn and the Fossil Cave, 1961, illustrated by Brinton Turkle

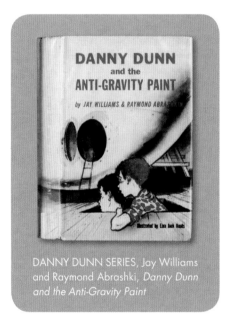

DANNY DUNN SERIES, Jay Williams and Raymond Abrashki, *Danny Dunn and the Anti-Gravity Paint*

Danny Dunn and the Heat Ray, 1962, illustrated by Owen Kampen

Danny Dunn, Time Traveler, 1963, illustrated by Owen Kampen

Danny Dunn and the Automatic House, 1965, illustrated by Owen Kampen

Danny Dunn and the Voice from Space, 1967, illustrated by Leo Summers

Danny Dunn and the Smallifying Machine, 1969, illustrated by Paul Sagsoorian

Danny Dunn and the Swamp Monster, 1971, illustrated by Paul Sagsoorian

Danny Dunn, Invisible Boy, 1974, illustrated by Paul Sagsoorian

Danny Dunn, Scientific Detective, 1976, illustrated by Paul Sagsoorian

Danny Dunn and the Universal Glue, 1977, illustrated by Paul Sagsoorian

DANNY ONE, ROBOT SERIES, Alfred Slote, Lippincott, hardcover, stories of a robot and his owner, Jack, b/w llustrations throughout by James Watts, first edition with dust jacket: $30.00

My Robot Buddy, 1975

My Trip to Alpha 1, 1978

C.O.L.A.R., 1981

Omega Station, 1983

Trouble on Janus, 1985

DANNY ONE, ROBOT SERIES, Alfred Slote, *My Robot Buddy*

DARK IS RISING SERIES, Susan Cooper, 1966 – 1977, Atheneum, including *Over Sea, under Stone.* Although *Over Sea, under Stone,* was written several years before the other books, most collectors count it as the first of the series because it features the same characters.

Over Sea, under Stone, 1966, Harcourt Brace, hardcover, illustrated by Margery Gil, first edition with dust jacket: $175.00

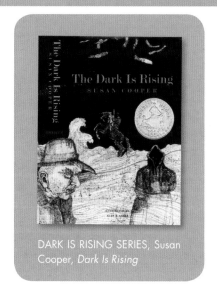

DARK IS RISING SERIES, Susan Cooper, *Dark Is Rising*

Dark Is Rising, 1973, first edition with dust jacket: $75.00

Greenwitch, 1974, first edition with dust jacket: $75.00

Grey King, 1975, first edition with dust jacket: $65.00

Grey King, 1975, first edition with Newbery Medal winner seal on dust jacket: $50.00

Silver on the Tree, 1977, first edition with dust jacket: $50.00

DAVID BLAIZE SERIES, E. F. Benson (Edward Frederic). The second book of this series sends David on some distinctly "Alice in Wonderland" adventures, although the rest of the series stays anchored in the real world. Benson is best known today for his popular *Mapp and Lucia* series, but he wrote a number of supernatural novels and ghost stories.

DAVID BLAIZE SERIES, E. F. Benson, *David Blaize and the Blue Door*

David Blaize, 1916, Hodder & Stoughton, hardcover, first edition: $150.00

David Blaize and the Blue Door, undated, ca.1918, Hodder & Stoughton, blue pictorial hardcover shows figure flying above a blue door, 228 pages, illustrated by H.J. Ford, first edition: $100.00

David Blaize and the Blue Door, ca. 1919, Doubleday, US, includes the b/w Ford illustrations plus a color frontispiece by Thomas Fogarty: $60.00

David Blaize of Kings (also published as *David of Kings*), 1924, George H. Doran, hardcover, 306 pages, first edition with dust jacket: $100.00

DEEP SEA SERIES, Roy Rockwood (Stratemeyer Syndicate pseudonym), 1905 – 1908, Stitt, also published by Chatterton-Peck, Mershon, and Grosset & Dunlap, adventure novels. The first three titles were reprinted as Dave Fearless Series in 1918 by Sully, and ten years later Garden City picked up the Dave Fearless name and continued the series in paperback.

Hardcover with dust jacket: $40.00

Rival Ocean Divers, or, *After a Sunken Treasure,* 1905

Cruise of the Treasure Ship, or, *Castaways of Floating Island,* 1906

Adrift on the Pacific, or, *Secret of the Island Cave,* 1908

Jack North's Treasure Hunt, or, *Daring Adventures in South America,* 1907

DEEP SEA HUNTERS SERIES, A. Hyatt Verrill, 1922 – 1924, Appleton, red or blue hardcover with clipper ship design, frontispiece: $60.00

Deep Sea Hunters Adventures on a Whaler, 1922

Deep Sea Hunters in the Frozen Seas, 1923

Deep Sea Hunters in the South Seas, 1924

DEEP WOOD SERIES, Elleston Trevor, hardcover, b/w illustrations throughout by Leslie Atkinson, tales of the animals of Deep Wood, Falcon Press Ltd, UK, color illustrated endpapers, b/w illustrations, first edition with dust jacket: $60.00

Heinemann and Criterion editions with dust jacket: $40.00

Badger's Beech, 1948

Badger's Moon, 1949

Mole's Castle, 1950

Badger's Wood, 1959

Sweethallow Valley, 1970

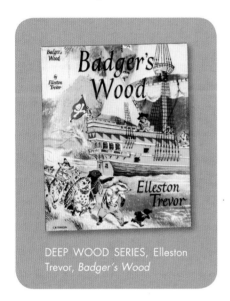

DEEP WOOD SERIES, Elleston Trevor, *Badger's Wood*

DICK AND JANE BOOKS, William Gray and others, 1927 – 1970, Scott, Foresman and Company. The first grade primers featuring Dick and Jane were updated every five years to reflect changes in clothing, automobiles, and American lifestyles. Last update occurred in 1965. Original illustrations of early books are by Eleanor Campbell. Prices given show the date of publication of that particular book, not its original date of copyright. "Ex-school copies" are the most commonly available types, stamped with school names, room numbers, and so forth.

Because these first grade readers are almost always ex-schoolroom books, prices vary widely, depending on condition. Condition varies from a neatly written room number to heavy stamping and

wear. Prices given are for clean copies with few marks and need to be discounted for condition.

Dick and Jane paperbound hardcover pre-primers, 1950s and 1960s editions: $50.00 to $100.00

Dick and Jane clothbound hardcovers, 1950s and 1960s editions: $30.00 to $65.00

John and Jean hardcover readers:

Fun with John and Jean, 1951, same story as *Fun with Dick and Jane,* but revised for Catholic schools and labeled "New Cathedral Basic Reader," light green hardcover, 159 pages, illustrated by Eleanor Campbell: $50.00

Dick and Jane hardcover readers, 1950s – 1960s, first printing: $60.00 to $100.00

Dick and Jane workbooks, 1950s – 1960s, workbook unused: $100.00

Dick and Jane "Before We Read" Picture Books, oversize oblong hardcover, also softcover workbook edition, b/w and color illustrations, no words: $40.00 to $100.00

Dick and Jane teacher's edition, 1940s:

Guidebook to Our New Friends, 1946 – 1947: $125.00

Guidebook to Fun with Dick and Jane, 1946 – 1947: $125.00

Dick and Jane teacher's editions, 1950s and 1960s:

New Guess Who, 1962, teacher's edition, hardcover, guide to pre-primers: $85.00

We Read Pictures, 1963, Cathedral Basic Reader, teacher's edition, oblong oversize hardcover, 48 pages, with instructions to teacher to use John, Jean, and Judy names: $60.00

We Read More Pictures, 1951, teacher's edition, oblong oversize hardcover, 48 pages: $75.00

We Read More Pictures, 1962, teacher's edition, oblong oversize softcover, 78-page "teacher notes" section precedes 48 story pages: $75.00

Dick and Jane related books:

White House Murder Case and Dick and Jane, Jules Feiffer, 1970, Grove, hardcover, illustrated by Feiffer, first edition with dust jacket: $40.00

DICK HAMILTON SERIES, Howard R. Garis, 1909 – 1914, Grosset & Dunlap, brown hardcover with color illustration, frontispiece and three plates, with dust jacket: $30.00

Fortune, or, *Stirring Doings of a Millionaire's Son,* 1909

Cadet Days, or, *Handicap of a Millionaire's Son,* 1910

Steam Yacht, or, *Young Millionaire and the Kidnappers,* 1911

Football Team, or, *Young Millionaire on the Gridiron,* 1912

Dick Hamilton's Touring Car, or, *Young Millionaire's Race for a Fortune,* 1913

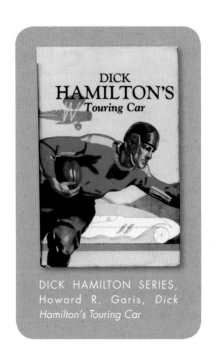

DICK HAMILTON SERIES, Howard R. Garis, *Dick Hamilton's Touring Car*

Airship, or, *Young Millionaire in the Clouds*

DICK PRESCOTT SERIES, H. Irving Hancock, a continuing saga in which Dick Prescott and/or his friends, including Greg Holmes, Dave Darrin, Dan Dalzell, Harry Hazeling and Tom Reade, expand their adventures. The series takes these characters from grammar school through college, war service, and careers. Published by Altemus, also Donohue, hardcover, black and white line drawing illustrations in many of these books attributed to John R. Neill, with dust jacket: $35.00

DICK TRACY SERIES, Chester Gould, based on the *Tribune-News Syndicate* newspaper comic strip, first published in 1931, the detective character inspired numerous books. Titles include:

Dick Tracy, 1940s – 1950s, Whitman Authorized Editions, plain hardcover, line drawing illustrations, with dust jacket: $50.00

Dick Tracy, Ace Detective, 1943

Dick Tracy Meets the Night Crawler, 1945

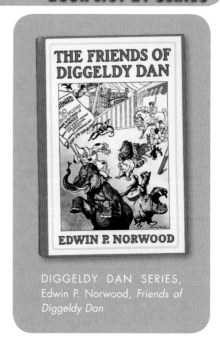

DICK TRACY SERIES, Chester Gould, *Dick Tracy Meets the Night Crawler*

Dick Tracy, Big Little Books and Better Little Books, small color illustrated cardboard covers with b/w illustration on every other page facing text page:

Dick Tracy and the Racketeer Gang, 1936: $80.00

Dick Tracy and His G-Men, 1941: $40.00

Dick Tracy the Super-Detective, ca. 1939: $40.00

Dick Tracy and the Wreath Kidnapping Case, ca. 1944: $40.00

Dick Tracy on Voodoo Island, ca. 1944: $40.00

Dick Tracy, pop-ups:

Dick Tracy and the Capture of Boris Arson, 1935, Pleasure Books, Chicago, pictorial hardcover, three-color pop-ups: $700.00

Pop-Up Dick Tracy, 1935, Blue Ribbon, pictorial hardcover, three-color pop-ups: $400.00

Dick Tracy, other:

Adventures of Dick Tracy, Gould, 1934, Whitman Big Big Book, pictorial hardcover, 316 pages, b/w illustrations: $150.00

Celebrated Cases of Dick Tracy, 1965, Bonanza, oversize hardcover coffee table book, edited by Herb Galewitz and with introduction by Ellery Queen, with dust jacket: $75.00

Dick Tracy and the Thirties, Tommy Guns and Hard Times, 1978, Chelsea House, oblong blue hardcover, b/w comic strips, with dust jacket: $35.00

DIGGELDY DAN SERIES, Edwin P. Norwood, circus adventures, Little, Brown, paste-on-pictorial hardcover, 240 pages, eight color plate illustrations by A. Conway Peyton: $40.00

Adventures of Diggeldy Dan, 1922

In the Land of Diggeldy Dan, 1923

Friends of Diggeldy Dan, 1924

DIMSIE SERIES, Dorita Fairlie Bruce, 1921 – 1927, Oxford University Press, pictorial hardcover with gilt, illustrated by Gertrude Hammond (*Dimsie Carries On,* last book in the series, added in the 1940s). There have been several

DIGGELDY DAN SERIES, Edwin P. Norwood, *Friends of Diggeldy Dan*

reprintings, and occasionally titles are changed. First edition: $60.00

Dimsie Carries On, Oxford University Press, Australian edition, 1946, first edition thus, with dust jacket: $50.00

DIMSIE SERIES, Dorita Fairlie Bruce, *Dimsie Carries On*

DINNY GORDON SERIES, Anne Emery, 1959 – 1967, MacRae, hardcover, beginning with *Dinny Gordon, Freshman,* and continuing through the four school years, first edition with dust jacket: $65.00

DOC SAVAGE SERIES, Kenneth Robeson, Doc Savage originally appeared in Street & Smith pulps. Books were issued with pictorial paper hardboards, 25 cent price printed on cover. Some were reprints of stories that first were published in the *Doc Savage Magazine*. There were also more than 80 titles in a reprint paperback series. Titles include:

Doc Savage, Man of Bronze, 1933, Street & Smith: $200.00

Doc Savage, Land of Terror, 1933, Street & Smith: $150.00

Doc Savage, Quest of the Spider, 1933, Street & Smith: $125.00

Doc Savage, 1975, Golden Press, color illustrated hardcover, illustrated endpapers, b/w illustrations, re-issues of old titles: $30.00

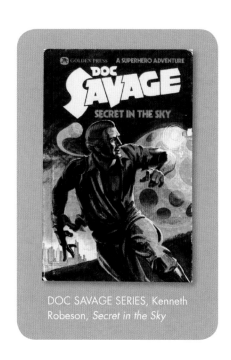

DOC SAVAGE SERIES, Kenneth Robeson, *Secret in the Sky*

Man of Bronze

Death in Silver

Ghost Legion

Quest of Qui

Sargasso Ogre

Secret in the Sky

DOCTOR DOLITTLE SERIES, Hugh Lofting, 1886 – 1947, hardcover with paste-on-pictorial, color illustrated endpapers, color frontispiece with tissue guard, b/w illustrations by author, classic stories of the English doctor who "talked to the animals."

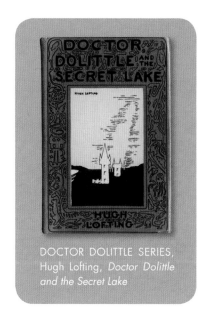

DOCTOR DOLITTLE SERIES, Hugh Lofting, *Doctor Dolittle and the Secret Lake*

Early printings of 1920s and 1930s titles, Stokes: $175.00

1940s and 1950s J. B. Lippincott hardcover with dust jacket: $100.00

Story of Doctor Dolittle, 1920

Voyages of Doctor Dolittle, 1922

Doctor Dolittle's Post Office, 1923

Doctor Dolittle's Circus, 1924

Doctor Dolittle's Zoo, 1925

Doctor Dolittle's Caravan, 1926

Doctor Dolittle's Garden, 1927

Doctor Dolittle in the Moon, 1928

Gub Gub's Book, 1932

Doctor Dolittle's Return, 1933

Doctor Dolittle, 1940s – 1950s:

Doctor Dolittle and the Secret Lake, 1948, Lippincott, orange hardcover with paste-

on illustration, 366 pages, illustrations by author, with dust jacket: $150.00

Doctor Dolittle and the Green Canary, 1950, Lippincott, stories written for *Herald Tribune Syndicate* by Lofting, gathered and completed for book publication by sister-in-law Olga Michael after Lofting's death, yellow hardcover, color frontispiece, illustrations by Lofting. With dust jacket: $80.00

Doctor Dolittle's Puddleby Adventures, 1952, Lippincott, lavender hardcover, collection of Lofting stories, illustrations by author, with dust jacket: $80.00

Doctor Dolittle, related books:

Adventures of Doctor Dolittle, a Pop-Up Book, 1967, Random House, illustrated boards, pop-ups and moveables, color illustrations by Brehm, Edwards, and Harvey: $45.00

DOGTOWN SERIES, Frank Bonham, E. P. Dutton, hardcover, first edition with dust jacket: $30.00

Mystery of the Fat Cat, 1968

Nitty-Gritty, 1968

Vivi Chicano, 1970

Cool Cat, 1971

Hey, Big Spender, 1972

DOLLY AND MOLLY SERIES, Elizabeth Gordon, 1914, Rand McNally, small hardcover, 60 pages, illustrations by Frances Beem: $75.00

1930s reprints, pictorial hardcover, illustrations: $40.00

Dolly and Molly at the Circus

Dolly and Molly at the Seashore

Dolly and Molly and the Farmer Man

DON WINSLOW SERIES, Frank Martinek, based on the comic strip character Don Winslow of the Navy, frontispiece by Warren. This character was also featured in a radio series and later, on TV.

1940 – 1941, Grosset & Dunlap, four titles, blue hardcover with yellow lettering, with dust jacket: $30.00

Don Winslow of the Navy

Don Winslow Face to Face with the Scorpion

Don Winslow Breaks the Spy Net

Don Winslow Saves the Secret Formula

1946 Whitman Authorized Edition, hardcover with dust jacket: $30.00

Don Winslow and the Scorpion's Stronghold

Don Winslow, Whitman Big Little Books, ca. 1938 – 1940: $45.00

Don Winslow of the Navy Versus the Scorpion Gang

Don Winslow of the Navy and the Great War Plot

Don Winslow, Navy Intelligence Ace

Don Winslow of the Navy and the Secret Enemy Base

DOROTHY DAINTY SERIES,

Amy Brooks, author/illustrator, 1902 – 1923, Lothrop-Lee, small hardcovers with illustrations by Brooks, 22 titles. Early edition hardcovers, with dust jackets, up to: $100.00

DORRIE THE LITTLE WITCH SERIES,

Patricia Coombs, Lothrop, Lee & Shepard Company, Inc., oversize hardcover, full-page b/w and color illustrations by author, a well-meaning child witch cannot always control her magic. Newer Dorrie books have values closer to cover price.

Coombs graduated from the University of Washington, Seattle, in 1950 with a degree in English literature. She is the author-illustrator of these stories that began as entertainment for her small daughters, then grew into a series of oversized picture books.

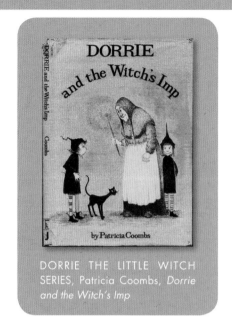

DORRIE THE LITTLE WITCH SERIES, Patricia Coombs, *Dorrie and the Witch's Imp*

Dorrie, 1970s titles, first edition with dust jacket: $75.00

Dorrie and the Weather-Box, 1967

Dorrie and the Witch Doctor, 1967

Dorrie and the Wizard's Spell, 1968

Dorrie and the Haunted House, 1970

Dorrie and the Birthday Eggs, 1971

Dorrie and the Blue Witch, 1971

Dorrie and the Goblin, 1972

Dorrie and the Fortune Teller, 1973

Dorrie and the Witch's Imp, 1975

Dorrie and the Halloween Plot, 1976

Dorrie and the Dreamyard Monsters, 1977

Dorrie and the Screebit Ghost, 1979

DOT AND DASH SERIES,

Dorothy West (pseudonym of Mildred Wirt), 1938 – 1940, Cupples & Leon, hardback, with dust jacket: $60.00

Dot and Dash at the Sugar Maple Camp, 1938

Dot and Dash at Happy Hollow, 1938

Dot and Dash in the North Woods, 1938

Dot and Dash at the Seashore, 1940

DRAGON SERIES,

Ruth Stiles Gannett, Random House, hardcover, b/w illustrations by Ruth Chrisman Gannett, stories feature Elmer Elevator's curious travels in the land of dragons.

Ruth Chrisman Gannett (1896 – 1979, American) studied at the University of California at Berkeley, later attending the Art Students League. During the 1930s, she began illustrating adult novels as well as children's books. In the 1950s, she provided the illustrations for her stepdaughter's series.

My Father's Dragon, 1948, first edition with dust jacket: $50.00

Elmer and the Dragon, 1950, first edition with dust jacket: $40.00

Dragons of Blueland, 1951, first edition with dust jacket: $80.00

DRAGON SERIES,

Rosemary Manning, tribulations of a small green dragon.

Green Smoke, 1957, Doubleday, illustrated by Constance Marshall, first edition with dust jacket: $50.00

Dragon in Danger, 1959, Doubleday, illustrated by Constance Marshall, first edition with dust jacket: $50.00

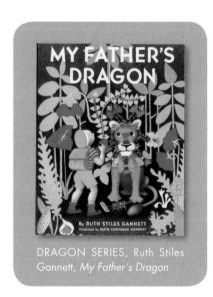

DRAGON SERIES, Ruth Stiles Gannett, *My Father's Dragon*

Dragon in the Harbour, 1980, Kestrel, illustrated by Peter Rush, first edition with dust jacket: $20.00

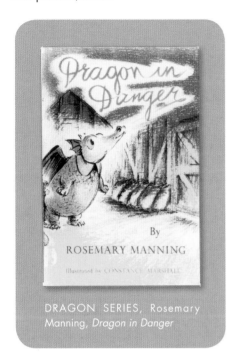

DRAGON SERIES, Rosemary Manning, *Dragon in Danger*

DRAGONFALL 5 SPACE SERIES, Brian Earnshaw, illustrated by Simon Stern, Methuen, ca. early 1970s, UK, and Lothrop, Lee & Shephard, US, adventures of a spaceship, first edition with dust jacket: $30.00. Titles include:

Dragonfall 5 and the Space Cowboys, 1972

Dragonfall 5 and the Empty Planet, 1973

Dragonfall 5 and the Hijackers, 1974

Dragonfall 5 and the Royal Beast, 1975

DRIA MEREDITH SERIES, Janet Lambert, ca.1952, E. P. Dutton, hardcover, with dust jacket: $75.00

1950s Grosset & Dunlap reprints, with dust jackets: $40.00

Star Dream

Summer for Seven

High Hurdles

DR. MERLIN SERIES, Scott Corbett, 1970s Little, Brown.

DRAGONFALL 5 SPACE SERIES, Brian Earnshaw, *Dragonfall 5 and the Empty Planet*

Dr. Merlin's Magic Shop, 1973, illustrations by Joe Mathieu, first edition with dust jacket: $80.00

Great Custard Pie Panic, 1974, illustrations by Joe Mathieu, first edition with dust jacket: $30.00

Foolish Dinosaur Fiasco, 1978, illustrations by Jon McIntosh, first edition with dust jacket: $30.00

DRIA MEREDITH SERIES, Janet Lambert, *Star Dream*

DUNGEONS & DRAGONS SERIES, Gary Gygax, TSR Games, Wisconsin. In 1974, Gygax and friends created a fantasy role playing game that spawned a vast number of rule books, encyclopedias, and soft-cover books with prewritten adventures for

players. Novels and other fiction for the fans appeared in the 1980s. Earliest editions of the game books refer to characters called hobbits, and later printings change these terms to "halflings" to avoid copyright conflicts. In the 1990s, the firm was bought out by the Northwest company, Wizards of the Coast, creators of the popular Magic card game. While D&D was not the first or the only fantasy role playing game, it has remained the most popular. Collectors pay the highest prices for first editions of manuals, out-of-print campaigns, and other ephemera. Condition makes enormous impact on price as early books tended to be treated casually by young owners. Truly rare campaigns have approached the $1,000.00 mark in eBay auctions but prices are volatile. Wizards of the Coast has re-released some previously unavailable material and makes others downloadable from its website. A sampling of collectible hardcover books and complete boxed game systems are listed below.

Dungeons & Dragons, boxed set:

Dungeons & Dragons, Gary Gygax and Dave Arneson, 1974, TSR, one 40-page booklet, two 36-page booklets, tables, and charts, simulated wood grain box with white label, starts at: $250.00

Dungeons & Dragons, Gary Gyrax and Dave Arneson, 1976, TSR, one 40-page booklet, two 36-page booklets, tables, and charts, in all-white box with dice: $200.00

10th Anniversary Dungeons & Dragons Collector's Set, Gyrax and others, 1984, TSR, 12 booklets, 3-D Dragon Tiles, D&D Combat Shield, dice, complete in box, sold by mail order only, starts at $75.00.

Advanced Dungeons & Dragons (AD&D), introduced in 1978 as a modification of D&D. New books continue to appear under the Wizards of the Coast name. Some collectible titles:

Advanced Dungeons & Dragons, Dieties & Demigods, James Ward and Robert Kuntz, 1980, TSR, 144 pages, hardbound, first edition contains references to Michael Moorcock's Elric series and H.P. Lovecraft's Cthulhu, first edition starts at: $50.00

Advanced Dungeons & Dragons Dungeon Masters Guide, Gygax, 1979, TSR, hardcover, 232 pages, illustrated, first printing: $30.00

Advanced Dungeons & Dragons Monster Manual, 1977, TSR, hardcover, first printing: $30.00

Encyclopedia Magica — Advanced Dungeons & Dragons, Dale Slade Henson, 1994 – 1995, TSR, oversize hardcover in decorative simulated leather bindings, attached cloth page marker, four volumes, each 416 pages, each volume: $40.00

■ ···················· **E** ····················· ■

EARTHFASTS TRILOGY, William Mayne, theft of a candle from King Arthur's tomb transports a teenager to modern times and adventures.

Earthfasts, 1966, Hamish Hamilton, hardcover, UK first edition with dust jacket: $75.00

Earthfasts, 1967, E. P. Dutton, hardcover, US first edition with dust jacket by David Knight: $40.00

Cradlefasts, 1995, Hodder Childrens' Books, hardcover, UK first edition with dust jacket: $40.00

Candlefasts, 2000, Hodder Childrens' Books, hardcover, UK first edition with dust jacket: $40.00

EARTHFASTS TRILOGY, William Mayne, *Earthfasts*

EARTHSEA SERIES, Ursula K. Le Guin, hardcover, a series based on the education and destiny of a young wizard.

Wizard of Earthsea, 1968, Parnassus, illustrated by Ruth Robbins, first edition with dust jacket: $225.00

Wizard of Earthsea, 1971, Gollancz, first UK edition with dust jacket: $100.00

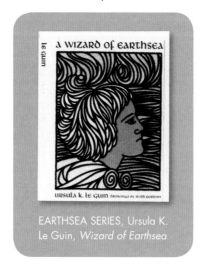

EARTHSEA SERIES, Ursula K. Le Guin, *Wizard of Earthsea*

Tombs of Atuan, 1971, Atheneum, illustrated by Gail Garrity, first edition with dust jacket: $125.00

Farthest Shore, 1972, Atheneum, illustrated by Gail Garrity, first edition with dust jacket: $125.00

Tehanu, the Last Book of Earthsea, 1990, Atheneum, and *Tales from Earthsea*, 2001, Harcourt Brace, are later additions to the series, available used at less than cover price.

EDDIE SERIES, see also BETSY SERIES, similar artwork and crossover of characters. Carolyn Haywood, author/illustrator, 1947 – 1991, Morrow, hardcover, b/w illustrations throughout by author.

Pre-1960 first editions with dust jackets: $40.00

1970s first editions with dust jackets: $30.00

Little Eddie, 1947

Eddie and the Fire Engine, 1949

Eddie and Gardenia, 1951

Eddie's Pay Dirt, 1953

Eddie and His Big Deals, 1955

Eddie Makes Music, 1957

Eddie and Louella, 1959

Annie Pat and Eddie, 1960

Eddie's Green Thumb, 1964

Eddie the Dog Holder, 1966

Ever-Ready Eddie, 1968

Eddie's Happenings, 1971

Eddie's Valuable Property, 1975

Eddie's Menagerie, 1978

Merry Christmas from Eddie, 1986

Eddie's Friend Boodles, 1991

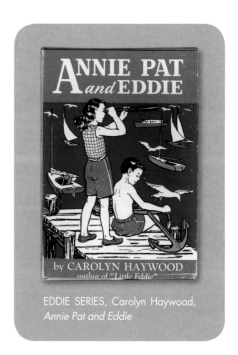

EDDIE SERIES, Carolyn Haywood, *Annie Pat and Eddie*

EDITH THE LONELY DOLL SERIES, Dare Wright, Doubleday, oversize pictorial hardcover with photo illustrations and checkered border, b/w photo illustrations throughout feature a doll and her bear friends, first edition with dust jacket: $250.00. Without dust jacket: $100.00

Lonely Doll, 1957

Holiday for Edith and the Bears, 1958

Doll and the Kitten, 1960

Lonely Doll Learns a Lesson, 1961

Edith and Mr. Bear, 1964

Gift from Lonely Doll, 1966

Edith and Big Bad Bill, 1968

Edith and Little Bear Lend a Hand, 1972

Edith and Midnight, 1978

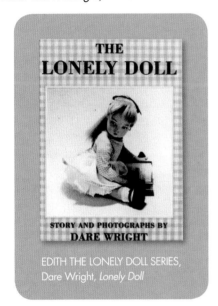

EDITH THE LONELY DOLL SERIES,
Dare Wright, *Lonely Doll*

ELLERY QUEEN, JR. MYSTERY SERIES,

Ellery Queen, Jr. (pseudonym for Frederick Dannay, and Manfred B. Lee), 1940 titles first published by Lippincott, some by Stokes, titles added in the 1950s by Little, Brown, complete series reprinted in hardcover by Grosset & Dunlap. Most are priced under $30.00.

Other Ellery Queen, Jr. collectible editions:

Black Dog Mystery, Frederick A. Stokes, 1941, Djuna and his Scottie dog, Champ, solve a local mystery. (Author may be Samuel Duff McCoy), b/w chapter head drawings by William Sanderson, UK first edition with dust jacket: $400.00

Green Turtle Mystery, Collins, 1945, green hardcover, 268 pages, illustrations by E. A.

Watson, features junior sleuth Djuna, UK first edition thus with dust jacket: $40.00

White Elephant Mystery, Little, Brown, 1950, first edition with dust jacket: $150.00

Yellow Cat Mystery, Little, Brown, 1952, first edition with dust jacket: $600.00

Blue Herring Mystery, Little, Brown, 1954, first edition with dust jacket: $150.00

Purple Bird Mystery, Putnam, 1965, purple cover, Djuna and Jimmy solve a golf mystery, first edition with dust jacket: $180.00

ELOISE SERIES,

Kay Thompson (1909 – 1998, b. St. Louis, Missouri, famous musical performer and voice coach), Simon & Schuster, oversize hardcover, illustrations by Hilary Knight. The first book was reprinted continually, but the others had limited printings. New editions for all titles issued in 1999 and 2000.

Eloise, 1955, first edition with dust jacket: $300.00

Eloise in Paris, 1957, first edition with dust jacket: $700.00

Eloise at Christmastime, 1958, first edition with dust jacket: $800.00

Eloise in Moscow, 1959, first edition with dust jacket: $800.00

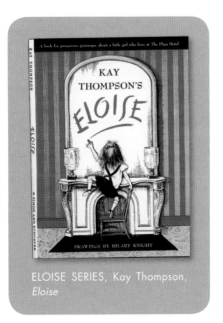

ELOISE SERIES, Kay Thompson,
Eloise

ELSIE DINSMORE SERIES,

Martha Finley, 1867 – 1905, Dodd, 28 titles, 1880s printings: $40.00

ELSIE DINSMORE SERIES, Martha
Finley, *Elsie's Motherhood*

EMIL SERIES,

Astrid Lindgren, 1960s, hardcover, illustrations by Bjorn Berg. Emil is a small Scandanavian boy whose pranks turn into disasters for everyone else.

Brockhampton English translations, first editions with dust jackets: $70.00

Emil in the Soup Tureen, 1963

Emil's Pranks, 1971

Emil and the Piggy Beast, 1973

That Emil, 1973

Emil and His Clever Pig, 1974

EMIL SERIES, Astrid Lindgren,
Emil's Pranks

EMILY SERIES, L. M. Montgomery (1874 – 1942), 1920s, Frederick A. Stokes, hardcover, less famous than the author's *Anne of Green Gables* series, this series is thought to be closer to the author's own life story.

McClelland and Stewart, hardcover with paste-on-illustration by M. L. Kirk, color frontispiece, first edition Canada, with dust jacket: $75.00

Frederick A. Stokes, hardcover with paste-on-illustration by M. L. Kirk, color frontispiece, US first edition with dust jacket, starts at: $100.00

Ca. 1930 Grosset & Dunlap reprints with dust jackets: $30.00

Emily of New Moon, 1923

Emily Climbs, 1925

Emily's Quest, 1927, Frederick A. Stokes

EXILES TRILOGY, Ben Bova, juvenile series by well-known writer of adult science fiction.

Exiled from Earth, 1971, E. P. Dutton, first edition with dust jacket: $50.00

Flight of Exiles, 1972, E. P. Dutton, first edition with dust jacket: $50.00

End of Exile, 1975, first edition with dust jacket: $30.00

EXILES TRILOGY, Ben Bova, *Flight of Exiles*

Exiles, related title:

Year After Tomorrow, anthology edited by Lester DelRay, 1954, Winston, contains two of the stories in their original magazine version, first edition with dust jacket: $45.00

EXTRAORDINARY JOURNEYS BOOKS, (Voyage Extraordinaire), Jules Verne (1828 – 1905), more than 60 titles originally published in French.

Verne's adventure novels relied on possible or probable technology as a major plot point and inspired a number of juvenile series imitators. From the beginning, Verne's friend and French publisher, Jules Hetzel, published the novels under the series title *Voyage Extraordinaire,* with uniform bindings and illustrations. English translations appeared in more varied forms, sometimes using the Hetzel format, sometimes substituting new illustrations. Because English translations were primarily published for the juvenile market, Verne's stories were often abridged from the original French text and/or titles might be changed to appeal to a younger audience. This has led to debate among Verne collectors over which were the true first printings in English (see bibliographies listed below for further information). Prices on the Verne books have been especially volatile in the last few years, given Verne's reputation as the father of science fiction, with a number of auction records set for highly desirable copies of titles such as *Twenty Thousand Leagues under the Sea.*

Extraordinary Journeys, first American editions, hardcover, gilt on cloth, b/w illustrations unless otherwise noted:

EXTRAORDINARY JOURNEYS BOOKS *(Voyage Extraordinaire),* Jules Verne, a sample of bindings from the 1870s to the 1930s

Adrift in the Pacific, Bromfield, New York, 1889: $2,000.00

Antarctic Mystery, J. B. Lippincott, Philadelphia, 1898: $2,000.00

Archipelago on Fire, Sampson Low, Marston, Searle and Rivington, London, 1886 (see also George Munro Seaside Library): $2,500.00

Around the World in 80 Days, see *Tour of the World in 80 Days*

Begum's Fortune; with an Account of the Mutineers of the Bounty, J. B. Lippincott, Philadelphia, 1879: $1,200.00

Caesar Cascabel, Cassell, New York, 1890: $1,000.00

Castaways of the Flag, G. Howard Watt, New York, 1924, second part of Verne's sequel to *Swiss Family Robinson* (first part published as *Their Island Home*). Color pictorial pastedown on cloth cover, full-color frontispiece by H. C. Murphy: $50.00. With dust jacket: $1,000.00

Demon of Cawnpore, Scribner, New York, 1881, see *Tigers and Traitors* on page 219: $500.00

Dick Sand or A Captain at Fifteen, George Munro, 1878: $1,000.00

Doctor Ox, and Other Stories, James R Osgood, Boston, 1874: $650.00

Facing the Flag, F. Tennyson Neely, New York, 1897 (published as *For the Flag* in Great Britain): $700.00

Five Weeks in a Balloon, D. Appleton, New York, 1869, six illustrations and plain cover: $4,500.00

Five Weeks in a Balloon, Osgood, 1873 edition, 48 illustrations (the first French edition had 80), first edition thus with gilt on cloth cover: $1,200.00

Floating City, and the Blockade Runners, Scribner Armstrong, New York, 1874: $750.00

From the Earth to the Moon, Scribner Armstrong, New York, 1874, with its cover illustration of a rocket ship bound for the moon, one of the more desirable early Verne works for science fiction collectors: $1,200.00

Hector Servadac or the Career of a Comet, Scribner Armstrong, New York, 1878 (parts of this novel were published as *Off on a Comet or To the Sun?*, in English). Cover shows a comet heading towards Earth: $1,000.00

In Search of the Castaways, J. B. Lippincott Philadelphia, 1873: $500.00

Journey to the Centre of the Earth, Scribner Armstrong, New York, 1873, popular edition 305 pages, 20 full-page illustrations: $850.00. Deluxe subscription edition, 1873 or 1874, 384 pages, 52 illustrations: $2,500.00

Master of the World, a Tale of Mystery and Marvel, J. B. Lippincott, Philadelphia, 1915, rare, mid-twentieth century reprints of this title start at: $50.00

Meridiana: Adventures of Three Englishmen and Three Russians in South Africa, 1873, Scribner Welford Armstrong, New York: $1,000.00

Michael Strogoff, the Courier of the Czar, Scribner Armstrong, New York, 1877: $750.00

Michael Strogoff, an earlier, paper-cover edition was published by Frank Leslie in 1876 as *Michael Strogoff, from Moscow to Irkoutsk*, and this fragile and difficult to find pirated edition starts at: $1,000.00

Mistress Branican, Cassell, New York, 1891: $600.00

Mysterious Island, Wrecked in the Air, Scribner Armstrong, New York, 1875: $500.00

Mysterious Island, The Abandoned, Scribner Armstrong, New York, 1875: $500.00

Mysterious Island, The Secret of the Island, Scribner Armstrong, New York, 1876: $500.00

North Against South, see *Texar's Revenge* and Seaside Library.

Steam House, see *Tigers and Traitors*.

Texar's Revenge, Rand McNally & Company, Chicago, 1888. This tale of the American Civil War was published as *North Against South* by Sampson in Great Britain and as *Texar's Vengeance* by George Munro in US. Rand McNally edition: $6,000.00

Texar's Revenge, Worthington Company edition, also with copyright 1888: $500.00

Their Island Home, Later Adventures of the Swiss Family Robinson, G. Howard Watt, 1924: $85.00

Tigers and Traitors, Scribner, New York, 1881: $500.00

Tigers and Traitors and *Demon of Cawnpore*, were later issued under the original Verne title, *The Steam House*, Scribner, 1886: $250.00

Topsy Turvey, J. S. Ogilvie, New York, 1890 (also published as *Purchase of the North Pole*, 1890, Sampson Low, London, and later Scribner editions): $1,500.00

Tour of the World in 80 Days (Later title: *Around the World in 80 Days*), 1873, James R. Osgood, Boston, smaller unillustrated edition: $500.00. After Osgood came out with a small volume, probably the first edition in English, an illustrated British edition was published in late 1873, and Osgood used the illustrations from that for its next edition in 1873. Illustrated Osgood edition with 1873 or 1874 copyright starts at: $2,700.00

Tribulations of a Chinese in China, Lee & Shepard, Boston, 1880: $800.00

Twenty Thousand Leagues under the Sea, James R. Osgood, Boston, 1873, the most sought-after and well-known Verne first edition, with jellyfish as the front cover vignette, auction prices start at: $16,000.00 to $20,000.00

Twenty Thousand Leagues under the Sea, Geo. M. Smith, Boston, 1873, shows Captain Nemo on the front cover: $2,500.00

Voyages and Adventures of Captain Hatteras, James R. Osgood, Boston, 1875: $500.00

Wreck of the Chancellor, James R. Osgood, Boston, 1875: $500.00

Extraordinary Journeys, later US editions:

Burt, Donahue, Hurst, and other reprints, 1880s – 1920s. Verne's works were extraordinarily popular and cheaper reprints appeared as soon as a first English translation was published. Well-decorated bindings or unusual illustrations add to appeal and the price: $30.00 to $150.00

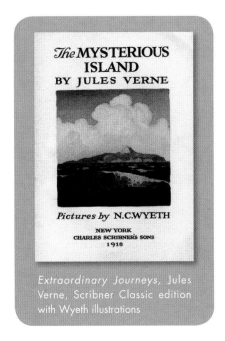

Extraordinary Journeys, Jules Verne, Scribner Classic edition with Wyeth illustrations

Extraordinary Journeys, George Munro Seaside Library editions, 1877 – 1889, pulp magazine, first American editions of several titles such as *Archipelago of Fire* and *North Against South*, hard to find in good or any condition. Early editions from the 1870s or 1880s start at: $300.00

George Munro pulp novel version, such as *Victor Series of Paper Novels*, starts at: $35.00

Extraordinary Journeys, James R. Osgood editions, circa 1870s: Decorated hardcovers with illustrations. Osgood had various production and financial problems, and auctioned off his Verne stock in 1876, including plates and unbound pages, and his books were later reproduced by Porter & Coates, Lee & Shepard, and others. Osgood reprint values depend on rarity of title, number of illustrations, and quality and amount of gilt on cover (see also first edition prices listed above), and start at: $300.00

Extraordinary Journeys, Scribner, Welford and Armstrong, reprint editions, circa 1870s. Started as an import house, this publisher bought British editions of Sampson Lowe, slapped its own name on the binding or title sheets, and published this as the American edition. Early Scribner and Sampson Lowe editions sell for similar values, although the latter are harder to find in the American market. "Welford" was dropped by 1875 and the firm eventually became a part of Scribner & Sons. Reprints of earlier titles begin at: $500.00

Extraordinary Journeys, Scribner, reprint editions, circa 1880s, reprints of earlier titles: $200.00

Extraordinary Journeys, Scribner, reprint editions, circa 1890s – 1900, reprints of earlier titles: $100.00

Extraordinary Journeys, Scribner Classic editions with Wyeth illustrations, 1910 – 1930. Scribner began to reissue many of the Verne titles in its catalog as part of the Scribner Classic series with new full-color N. C. Wyeth illustrations. First editions thus start at: $125.00. Later reprints: $35.00

Extraordinary Journeys, some of the illustrators:

Bayard, Emile-Antoine (1837 – 1891, French). A popular portrait painter and magazine illustrator, Bayard collaborated

with De Neuville on Jules Verne's *Around the Moon.*

Benett, Leon (1839 – 1917, French). After an early government job which required travel to the French colonies of IndoChina, Martinque, New Caledonia, and Algeria, Benett returned to France and began his career as an illustrator for French publisher Hetzel. From the early 1870s until his death, he illustrated numerous novels of adventure, fantasy and science fiction, including 25 volumes of Jules Verne's work. He is considered the most influential and prolific of all Verne's illustrators, creating nearly 2,000 illustrations for *Extraordinary Voyages.*

De Montaut, Henri (French). De Montaut worked primarily as a cartoonist and caricaturist for French magazines of the late nineteenth century. In 1872, he drew 43 illustrations for Jules Verne's *From the Earth to the Moon.* His pictures of the rocket ship influenced many other science fiction artists as his work was reprinted in numerous editions of the Verne novel.

De Neuville, Alphonse Marie (1835 – 1885, French). A pupil of French painter Eugue Delacroix, De Neuville illustrated major French histories, won awards for his military paintings, and contributed drawings for Jules Verne's novels *From the Earth to the Moon* (1872), *Around the World in 80 Days* (1874), and *Twenty Thousand Leagues under the Sea* (1873).

Riou, Edouard (1833 – 1900, French). Although he was best known to his contemporaries for his landscape paintings and commerations of historic events such as the opening of the Suez canal, Riou also worked for French publisher Hetzel and contributed numerous drawings for 13 of Jules Verne's novels. In 1869, Verne sat for Riou and served as his model for Professor Pierre Aronnax.

Roux, Georges (d. 1929, French). From 1890 on, Roux was one of the most prolific illustrators of Jules Verne's novels. The French painter and illustrator would draw as many as 85 illustrations for a single novel.

Extraordinary Journeys, bibliographies:

Myers, Edward and Judith, *Jules Verne: A Collector's Bibliography of First Editions & Printings in English.* Clock & Rose Press, Harwich Port, 2004 Revised Edition. Information about how to identify true first editions and other valuable early English translations.

Gallagher, E. J., *Jules Verne: A Primary and Secondary Bibliography.* G.K. Hall, 1980. Parts A, B, and C list published fiction and nonfiction by Verne, while parts D and E provide annotated lists of English language and French language criticism. Out-of-print.

Taves, Brian and Stephen Michaluk. *The Jules Verne Encyclopedia.* Scarecrow Press, Lanham, Maryland, 1996. Includes biographical information, contemporary newspaper interviews with Verne, a reprint of Verne's *The Humbug,* and bibliography listing thousands of different editions, retitlings, translations, and abridgments.

■ ⋯⋯⋯⋯⋯ **F** ⋯⋯⋯⋯⋯ ■

FAIRVIEW BOYS SERIES, Frederick Gordon (Stratemeyer Syndicate), ca. 1914, Graham and Matlock, hardcover, illustrated. There are cross-over titles with Stratemeyer's *Up and Doing* series. With dust jacket: $30.00

FAIRY LIBRARY, ca. 1850s, Routledge, London, small, printed covers, 30 to 40 pages each, b/w etching illustrations by George Cruikshank, first edition of four volumes with slipcase: $3,000.00

First edition individual titles: $300.00

Cinderella and the Glass Slipper

History of Jack and the Bean-Stalk

Hop o' My Thumb and the Seven League Boots

Puss in Boots

FAMILY SERIES, Isabel Proudfit, David McKay Publishers, pictorial hardcover, picture books featuring fanciful stories about household items. Dust jackets double price.

Bottle Family, 1938, illustrations by Caroline Whitehead, early edition with dust jacket: $75.00

Broom Closet Family, 1938, illustrations by Caroline Whitehead, early edition with dust jacket: $75.00

FAMILY SERIES, Isabel Proudfit, *Broom Closet Family*

Sewing Box Family, 1942, illustrations by Caroline Whitehead, early edition with dust jacket: $50.00

Pantry Family, 1942, illustrations by Caroline Whitehead, early edition with dust jacket: $50.00

Pencil Box Family, 1945, illustrations by Carolyn Matson: $20.00

Ice Box Family, 1945, illustrations by Carolyn Matson: $20.00

FAMOUS FIVE SERIES, Enid Blyton, 1942 – 1970s, Hodder & Stoughton, hardcover, illustrated, this series was reprinted regularly in paperback.

Pre-1950 early hardcover editions with dust jacket: $65.00

1950 – 1960s first edition with dust jacket: $55.00

Famous Five, 1960s, Reilly & Lee editions, hardcover, b/w illustrations by Frank Aloise, with dust jacket: $30.00

Five on a Treasure Island

Five Go Adventuring Again

Five Run Away Together

Five Go to Smuggler's Top

Five Go Off in a Caravan

Five on Kirrin Island Again

Five Go Off to Camp

Five Get into Trouble

Five Fall into Adventure

Five on a Hike Together

Five Have a Wonderful Time

Five Go down to the Sea

Five Go to Mystery Moor

Five Have Plenty of Fun

Five on a Secret Trail

Five Go to Billycock Hill

Five Get into a Fix

Five on Finniston Farm

Five Go to Demon's Rocks

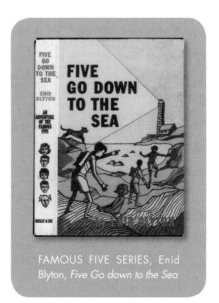

FAMOUS FIVE SERIES, Enid Blyton, *Five Go down to the Sea*

Five Have a Mystery to Solve

Five Are Together Again

FATHER TUCK'S NURSERY SERIES, ca. 1900, Raphael Tuck, London, cardboard cover with chromolithographic illustrations on linen-like pages, for small children: $100.00 to $200.00

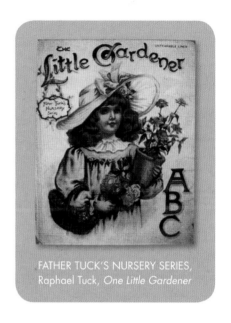

FATHER TUCK'S NURSERY SERIES, Raphael Tuck, *One Little Gardener*

FELIX THE CAT BOOKS were based on the cartoon character, originally written and illustrated by Pat Sullivan.

Felix, Wonder Books, illustrated glossy hardcover, color illustrations by Joe Oriolo, first edition: $30.00

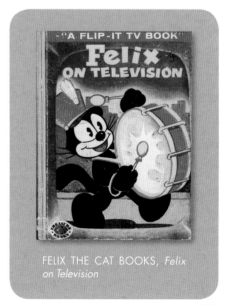

FELIX THE CAT BOOKS, *Felix on Television*

221

Felix the Cat, 1953

Felix on Television, 1956

Surprise for Felix, 1959

Felix, other:

Felix the Cat All Pictures Comics, 1944 Whitman Big Little Book # 1465, color paper-over-board cover: $30.00

Felix on Television, flip-it book, 1956 Treasure Books, pictorial cover, color illustrations: $30.00

FIREBALL SERIES, John Christopher (see also SWORD OF SPIRITS TRILOGY, TRIPODS), a fireball carries Simon and Brad into parellel worlds, E. P. Dutton first edition with dust jacket: $35.00

Fireball, 1981

New Found Land, 1983

Dragon Dance, 1986

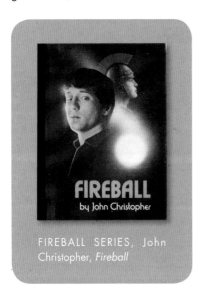

FIREBALL SERIES, John Christopher, *Fireball*

FIREBRINGER TRILOGY, Meredith Ann Pierce, fantasy of magic and adventure, first edition with dust jacket: $250.00

Birth of the Firebringer, 1985, Four Winds Press

Dark Moon, 1992, Little, Brown

Son of Summer Stars, 1996, Little, Brown

FIVE CHILDREN TRILOGY, Edith Nesbit, fantasy by a prolific English author of children's books.

1930s reprint editions, Ernest Benn, hardcover, with H. R. Millar illustrations: $30.00

Early editions:

Five Children and It, 1902, Fisher Unwin, hardcover, gilt lettering, b/w illustrations by H. R. Millar: $500.00

Five Children and It, 1905 edition, Dodd, Mead & Company, hardcover with paste-on-pictorial by H. R. Millar, b/w illustrations: $80.00

Phoenix and the Carpet, 1904, Newnes, UK, blue hardcover with stamped decoration and gilt, color frontispiece and numerous line drawings by H. R. Millar, UK first edition: $400.00

Phoenix and the Carpet, 1904, Macmillan, hardcover, eight b/w plates by H. R. Millar, US first edition: $400.00

Story of the Amulet, 1906, Fisher Unwin, London, red hardcover with gilt pictorial, H. R. Millar illustrations, first edition: $300.00

FIVE DOLLS SERIES, Helen Clare and Pauline Clarke, Bodley Head, London, illustrated hardcover, illustrations by Cecil Leslie: $50.00

Prentice-Hall 1960s editions with illustrations by Aliki, with dust jackets: $75.00 to $100.00

Five Dolls in a House, 1953, fold-out frontispiece with a color diagram of the doll house

Five Dolls and the Monkey, 1956

Five Dolls in the Snow, 1957

Five Dolls and Their Friends, 1959

Five Dolls and the Duke, 1963

FIVE FIND-OUTERS SERIES, Enid Blyton, ca. 1950, Methuen, gray hardcover, 170+ pages, b/w illustrations by Treyer Evans, with dust jacket: $40.00

Mystery of the Burnt Cottage

Mystery of the Disappearing Cat

Mystery of the Secret Room

Mystery of the Hidden House

Mystery of the Spiteful Letters

Mystery of the Pantomime Cat

Mystery of the Missing Necklace

Mystery of the Invisible Thief

Mystery of the Vanished Prince

Mystery of the Strange Bundle

Mystery of Holly Lane

Mystery of the Strange Messages

Mystery of Tally-Ho Cottage

Mystery of the Missing Man

FIVE LITTLE PEPPERS SERIES, Margaret Sidney (Harriet Lothrop, 1880 – 1916), Lothrop, hardcover with gilt trim, b/w plates, numerous reprints, price range for Lothrop first editions: $60.00 to $200.00

FLASH GORDON SERIES, *Flash Gordon*

FLASH GORDON SERIES, books were based on the 1934 King Features Syndicate comic strip character created by Alex Raymond, continued in 1944 by Austin Briggs, and in 1984 by Mac

Raboy. The character was also featured in film and television productions and in a paperback series.

Flash Gordon in the Caverns of Mongo, 1937, Grosset & Dunlap, hardcover with dust jacket: $75.00

Flash Gordon, Whitman Big Little and Better Little titles, pictorial cover, b/w illustrations:

Flash Gordon and the Monsters of Mongo, ca. 1935: $50.00

Flash Gordon and the Tournament of Mongo, Alex Raymond, ca. 1935: $50.00

Flash Gordon and the Perils of Mongo, 1940: $50.00

Flash Gordon and the Ice World of Mongo, 1942: $50.00

Flash Gordon and the Pioneer Men of Mongo, 1943: $50.00

Flash Gordon and the Red Sword Invaders, Alex Raymond, 1945: $70.00

Flash Gordon, other:

Flash Gordon, 1956, Treasure Books, pictorial hardcover with glued-on-glitter highlights, small book similar to Wonder Books format, 24 pages, color illustrations throughout by Alex Burger: $40.00

FLICKA, RICKA AND DICKA SERIES,

written and illustrated by Maj Lindman, Whitman, oversize hardcover books with bright cover illustrations, color illustrations throughout, first edition with dust jacket: $175.00. Without dust jacket: $100.00

Flicka, Ricka and Dicka and the New Dotted Dresses, 1939

Flicka, Ricka and Dicka and the Girl Next Door, 1940

Flicka, Ricka and Dicka and the Three Kittens, 1941

Flicka, Ricka and Dicka and Their New Friend, 1942

Flicka, Ricka and Dicka and the Strawberries, 1944

Flicka, Ricka and Dicka and Their New Skates, 1950

Flicka, Ricka and Dicka Bake a Cake, 1955

Flicka, Ricka and Dicka Go to Market, 1958

Flicka, Ricka and Dicka and the Big Red Hen, 1960

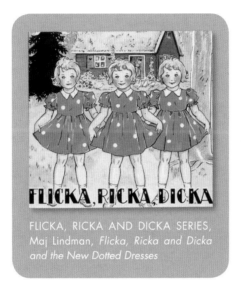

FLICKA, RICKA AND DICKA SERIES, Maj Lindman, *Flicka, Ricka and Dicka and the New Dotted Dresses*

FLIP SERIES, Wesley Dennis, Viking, hardcover, 63 pages, illustrations by author, first edition with dust jacket: $35.00

Flip, 1941

FLIP SERIES, Wesley Dennis, *Flip and the Morning*

Flip and the Cows, 1942

Flip and the Morning, 1951

FLOWER FAIRIES SERIES, Cicely Mary Barker, undated, Blackie, London, small, color illustrations throughout by author, first issued in the mid-1920s and apparently went through several printings through the 1930s. (Warne re-issued the six titles in various formats in the 1990s.) Blackie, 1920s edition: $500.00

1930s editions *Blackie* with dust jacket: $150.00. Without dust jacket: $100.00

1970s re-issue *Blackie,* undated with dust jacket: $40.00

FLOWER FAIRIES SERIES, Cicely Mary Barker, *Flower Fairies of the Spring*

Flower Fairies of the Garden

Flower Fairies of the Trees

Flower Fairies of the Spring

Flower Fairies of the Autumn

Flower Fairies of the Wayside

Flower Fairies of the Summer

Flower Fairies, related song books by Cicely Mary Barker, ca. 1920s, undated Blackie, oversize, music by Olive Linnell, tipped-in color plates, with dust jacket: $250.00. Without dust jacket: $90.00

Autumn Songs with Music from "Flower Fairies of the Autumn"

Spring Songs with Music from "Flower Fairies of the Spring"

Summer Songs with Music from "Flower Fairies of the Summer"

FLYING FISH SERIES, Harry Collingwood (pseudonym of William Joseph C. Lancaster), adventures of a flying submarine named the Flying Fish, commanded by Sir Reginald Elphinstone, and later books feature his children. Undated Burt reprints: $30.00

Log of the Flying Fish, a Story of Peril and Adventure, undated, ca. 1887, Blackie, UK, and 1889, Scribner, US, about 380 pages, illustrated by Gordon Browne, early edition: $80.00

With Airship and Submarine, a Tale of Adventure, 1907, Blackie, UK, pictorial cloth hardcover: $80.00

Cruise of the Flying Fish, the Airship-Submarine, undated, ca. 1924, Sampson Lowe, Marston, UK, orange cloth hardcover, color frontispiece: $40.00

FOOTBALL ELEVEN SERIES, Ralph Henry Barbour, 1914 – 1925, Dodd, Mead & Company, hardcover, 11 titles, with dust jacket: $50.00

Reprints by Grosset & Dunlap with dust jackets: $35.00

Left End Edwards, 1914

Left Tackle Thayer, 1915

Left Guard Gilbert, 1916

Center Rush Rowland, 1917

Full-Back Foster, 1918

Quarter-Back Bates, 1920

Left Half Harmon, 1921

Right End Emerson, 1922

Right Guard Grant, 1923

Right Tackle Todd, 1924

Right Half Hollins, 1925

FOUR LITTLE BLOSSOMS SERIES, Mabel C. Hawley, 1920 – 1930, Cupples & Leon, small, cloth hardcover with color imprint, with dust jacket: $40.00

FOURS CROSSING TRILOGY, Nancy Garden, Farrar, Straus, Giroux, hardcover, young teen meets supernatural, dust jacket by Frances Kuehn.

Fours Crossing, 1981, first edition with dust jacket: $70.00

Watersmeet, 1983, first edition with dust jacket: $70.00

Door Between, 1987, first edition with dust jacket: $50.00

FOURS CROSSING TRILOGY, Nancy Garden, *Fours Crossing*

FRANCES THE BADGER SERIES, Russell Hoban, illustrated by Garth Williams, then Lillian Hoban. Artist Lillian Hoban studied at the Philadelphia Museum School of Art, but worked as a dance instructor prior to launching a career in illustration.

Bedtime for Frances, 1960, Harper, illustrated hardcover, b/w/green illustrations by Garth Williams, first edition with dust jacket: $100.00

Egg Thoughts and Other Frances Songs, 1972, Harper, hardcover, illustrations by

Lillian Hoban, first edition with dust jacket: $75.00

Frances, other titles, first edition with dust jacket: $30.00

Bread and Jam for Frances, 1964

Baby Sister for Frances, 1964

Birthday for Frances, 1968

Bargain for Frances, 1970

FRANCES THE BADGER SERIES, Russell Hoban, *Bedtime for Frances*

FRANK READE LIBRARY SERIES, author listed as "Noname." Published 1892 – 1898 by Frank Tousey Publisher, New York, 191 dime novels, put out weekly or bi-weekly, later repackaged in hardcover format. Science fiction adventures of boy inventor Frank Reade originally appeared in *The Boys of New York* magazine in 1876. Author Harry Enton created Frank Reade based on a suggestion from Tousey. The series was taken over by Luis Philip Senarens, who shifted the focus from the original hero to the hero's son, Frank Reade, Jr. The popularity of the boy inventor's adventures prompted Tousey to launch the Frank Reade Library with "a complete story in every issue" in September of 1892. The "Library" both continued the series and reprinted earlier stories. Frank Reade Library, early editions, hard to find in good condition.

Tousey, black-and-white cover, about 28 pages, each: $50.00. Titles include:

Frank Reade Jr.'s Electric Cyclone, 1893

Young Frank Reade and His Electric Air Ship, 1899

Frank Reade Jr. and His Clean Clipper of the Clouds, 1899

Frank Reade, circa 1902, Tousey, colored front illustration, about 28 pages. Tousey reissued stories from the series with a colored front illustration in attempt to gain new readers, each: $50.00 to $75.00

Frank Reade, Aldine Romance of Invention, Travel, & Adventure Library editions:

Frank Reade, Junior, with His New Steam Horse in the Great American Desert, or, *Sandy Trail to Death,* ca. 1900, Aldine Publishing, London, in a color illustrated wrapper, 32 pages, pages printed in double column: $40.00

Frank Reade Among the Esquimaux, or, *Frozen Ship,* ca. 1900, Aldine Publishing, London, in a color illustrated wrapper, 32 pages, pages printed in double column: $40.00

Frank Reade, Dime Novel Club, circa 1940s, facsimile reprints of the Frank Reade and related Jack Wright stories, tabloid newsprint, stapled, black-and-white: $30.00

Frank Reade, other:

FRANK READE LIBRARY SERIES, the Garland facsimile of the original newsprints

Frank Reade Library, 1979 – 1986, Garland Publishing, New York, reprints, edited by E. F. Blieler, omnibus editions, oversize dark green hardcover, gilt lettering on spine, facsimile reproductions of the original issues, approximately 15 issues per book, 10 volumes. Per volume: $100.00

FREAKY FRIDAY SERIES, Mary Rodgers, Harper, hardcover, first title is the basis of the popular movie in which weird things happen to otherwise average people, dust jackets by Edward Gorey, first edition with dust jacket: $45.00

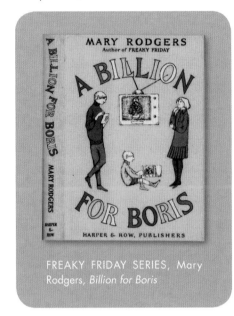

FREAKY FRIDAY SERIES, Mary Rodgers, *Billion for Boris*

Freaky Friday, 1972

Billion for Boris, 1974

Summer Switch, 1982

FRED FENTON SERIES, Allen Chapman (Stratemeyer pseudonym), ca. 1920s, Cupples & Leon, sports stories for boys beginning with Fred Fenton, the Pitcher, small hardcover with dust jacket: $30.00

FREDDY THE PIG SERIES, Walter R. Brooks (1886 – 1958). Published 1930s – 1950s Knopf, hardcover, illustrated endpapers, b/w illustrations by Kurt Wiese, funny adventures of a clever pig.

First editions with dust jackets, up to: $400.00

Freddy Goes to Florida, ca. 1930

Freddy Goes to the North Pole, ca. 1930

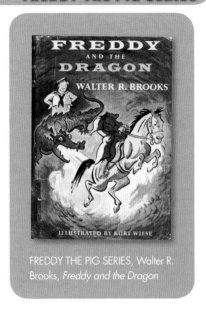

FREDDY THE PIG SERIES, Walter R. Brooks, *Freddy and the Dragon*

Freddy the Detective, 1932

Freddy the Politician, 1938

Freddy's Cousin Weedly, 1940

Freddy and the Ignormus, 1941

Freddy and the Perilous Adventure, 1942

Freddy and the Bean Home News, 1943

Freddy and Mr. Camphor, 1944

Freddy and the Popinjay, 1945

Freddy the Pied Piper, 1946

Freddy the Magician, 1947

Freddy Goes Camping, 1948

Freddy Plays Football, 1949

Freddy the Cowboy, 1950

Freddy Rides Again, 1951

Freddy the Pilot, 1952

Freddy and the Space Ship, 1953

Freddy and the Men from Mars, 1954

Freddy and the Baseball Team from Mars, 1955

Freddy and Simon the Dictator, 1956

Freddy and the Flying Saucer Plans, 1957

Freddy and the Dragon, 1958

Freddy's Poetry Book: Collected Poems of Freddy the Pig, 1953 Knopf, Kurt Wiese illustrations, 81 pages, with dust jacket: $250.00. Without dust jacket: $50.00

Freddy, reprints: Puffin paperbacks and Overlook Press hardcover editions with dust jackets are widely available.

FREE TRADERS SERIES, André Norton, four titles. This science fiction series is also called "Moon Magic" or "Moon Singer" by collectors.

Moon of Three Rings, 1966, Viking Press, dust jacket by Robin Jacques, first edition with dust jacket: $100.00

Exiles of the Stars, 1971, Viking Press, first edition with dust jacket: $100.00

Flight in Yiktor, 1986, Tor, first edition with dust jacket by Victoria Poyser: $30.00

Dare to Go A-Hunting, 1990, Tor, first edition with dust jacket: $30.00

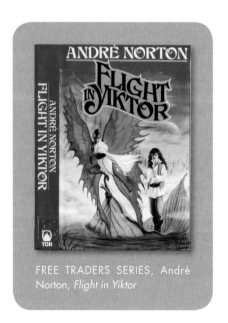

FREE TRADERS SERIES, André Norton, *Flight in Yiktor*

FRENCH AND INDIAN WAR SERIES, Joseph Altsheler, North American frontier stories set in 1755 – 1763, ca. 1916 – 1919, Appleton, hardcover with pictorial paste-on, four b/w plates, this popular series

of six adventure books was reissued in similar format several times. Probable first edition: $75.00

Hunter of the Hills, 1916

Shadow of the North, 1917

Rulers of the Lake, 1917

Masters of the Peaks, 1918

Lords of the Wild, 1919

Sun of Quebec, 1919

FRIENDS SERIES, Blackie, UK, ca. 1902 – 1910, picture books with illustrations by Frank Adams, Cecil Aldin, Arthur Rackham, and others. Price given is typical for that found in American bookstores. In the UK these titles are usually priced much higher. Individual titles in good condition: $150.00

Faithful Friends, 1902, color plates by Cecil Aldin and Arthur Rackham, additional pictures by Louis Wain, Gunning King, and others

Farm Friends for Little Folks, 1908, illustrations by Cecil Aldin, Arthur Rackham, and others

My Book of Doggies: Stories & Pictures for Little Folk, 1910, illustrations by Cecil Aldin, Arthur Rackham, and others

FROG AND TOAD SERIES, Arnold Lobel, Harper, hardcover, 64 pages, illustrations by author, first edition with dust jacket: $40.00

Frog and Toad Are Friends, 1970

Frog and Toad Together, 1972

Frog and Toad All Year, 1976

Days with Frog and Toad, 1979

Frog and Toad Pop-Up-Book, 1986

FROG SERIES, Mercer Mayer and Mariana Mayer, Dial, hardcover, short picture books without words, illustrations in brown ink.

FROG AND TOAD SERIES, Arnold Lobel, Harper, *Frog and Toad Together*

First editions with dust jackets: $35.00

Boy, a Dog, and a Frog, 1967

Frog, Where Are You?, 1969

Boy, a Dog, a Frog and a Friend, 1971

Frog on His Own, 1973

Frog Goes to Dinner, 1974

One Frog Too Many, 1975

FROG SERIES, Mercer Mayer and Mariana Mayer, *Four Frogs in a Box*

Four Frogs in a Box, undated, early 1970s Dial, 3¼" x 4⅛" box, covered with illustrated paper, contains four books in miniature size, illustrated paper-over-board covers plus dust jackets, first four titles. Complete set: $65.00

Individual miniature books with dust jackets: $10.00

FRONTIER GIRL SERIES, Alice Turner Curtis, 1929 – 1942, Penn, hardcover with paste-on-pictorial, illustrators include R. Pallen Coleman, and Hattie Longstreet Price, with dust jacket: $60.00

Without dust jacket: $30.00

Frontier Girl of Virginia, 1929, through *Frontier Girl of Pennsylvania,* 1942

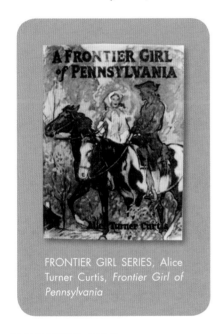

FRONTIER GIRL SERIES, Alice Turner Curtis, *Frontier Girl of Pennsylvania*

FUZZY WUZZY BOOKS, Whitman, oversize, cardboard cover, eight page picture book, short verses and color illustrations with flocking (velvet texturing) on the picture of one character throughout book: $40.00

Woofus the Woolly Dog, Jane Curry, 1944

Miss Sniff, Jane Curry, illustrations by Florence Winship, 1946

Fuzzy Wuzzy Waddles, 1945

Fuzzy Wuzzy Kitten, No. 940, 1947

Patchy, Fuzzy Wuzzy Pony, Clarence Biers, 1946

Fuzzy Wuzzy Bear, 1947

FUZZY WUZZY BOOKS, Louise W. Myers, *Santa Claus and the Little Lost Kitten*

Sir Gruff, by Nan Gilbert, illustrations by Florence Winship, 1947

Santa Claus and the Little Lost Kitten, Louise W. Myers, 1947

Fuzzy Wuzzy Puppy, Clarence Biers, 1949

Tommy and Timmy, Alice Sankey, 1951

Fuzzy Duckling, Sharon Banigan, 1951

Snow Ball, Betty Wright, 1952

Good Night, Elisabeth Burrowes, 1954

Mr. Moggs' Dogs, Revena, 1954

Pitty Pat the Fuzzy Cat, Gladys Horn, 1954

Fuzzy Wuzzy Puppy, Florence Winship, 1955

Fuzzy Pet, Alice Hanson, 1959

Cinnamon Bear, Alice Hanson, 1961

■·····················**G**·····················■

GALAXY GANG SERIES, Milton and Gloria Dank, Delacorte Press, hardcover, about 85 to 110 pages, first edition in dust jacket: $35.00

UFO Has Landed, 1983

Computer Caper, 1983

3-D Traitor, 1984

Treasure Code, 1985

Computer Game Murder, 1985

GEORGE AND MARTHA SERIES, James Marshall, Houghton Mifflin, hardcover picture books, color illustrations by author, adventures of two hippo friends.

George and Martha, 1972, first edition with dust jacket: $50.00

Later titles, first editions with dust jackets: $30.00

George and Martha Encore, 1973

George and Martha Rise and Shine, 1976

George and Martha One Fine Day, 1978

George and Martha, Tons of Fun, 1980

George and Martha Back in Town, 1984

George and Martha 'Round and 'Round, 1988

GEORGE AND MARTHA SERIES, James Marshall, *George and Martha*

GEORGIE THE GHOST SERIES, Robert Bright, Doubleday, oversize oblong hardcover picture book, illustrations by author, child ghost seeks companionship.

227

Robert Bright, author/illustrator, attended Phillips Academy and Princeton University. Much of Bright's childhood was spent in Europe. Besides his children's books, Bright's career included work as a journalist, art and music critic, and teacher. His inspirations for many of his children's stories, he once said, were his own children and later, his grandchildren.

Georgie, 1944, first edition with dust jacket: $75.00

Georgie to the Rescue, 1956, first edition with dust jacket: $50.00

Georgie's Halloween, 1958, first edition with dust jacket: $30.00

Georgie and the Robbers, 1963, first edition with dust jacket: $30.00

Georgie and the Magician, 1966, first edition with dust jacket: $30.00

Georgie, continuing titles, first edition with dust jacket, usually available for less than cover price.

GIMLET SERIES, Captain W. E. Johns (1893 – 1968), Capt. Corrington King, better known as Gimlet, leads his crack commando squad through a series of thrilling WWII adventures. Like Johns' popular *Biggles* books, this series went through a number of reprintings and changes in publishers.

1940s Oxford University Press first editions with dust jackets: $200.00 to $2,000.00

1950s Brockhampton editions with dust jackets: $50.00

King of the Commandos, 1943

Gimlet Goes Again, 1944

Gimlet Comes Home, 1946

Gimlet Mops Up, 1947

Gimlet's Oriental Quest, 1948

Gimlet Lends a Hand, 1949

Gimlet Bores In, 1950

Gimlet Off the Map, 1951

Gimlet Gets an Answer, 1952

Gimlet Takes a Job, 1954

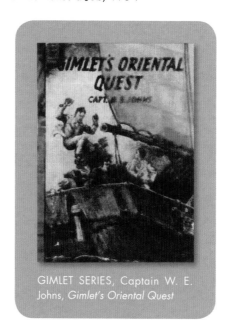

GIMLET SERIES, Captain W. E. Johns, *Gimlet's Oriental Quest*

GIRL AVIATORS SERIES, Margaret Burnham, 1911 – 1912, Hurst, illustrated cloth hardcover, frontispiece, air adventures of Peggy and Jess, with dust jacket: $30.00

Girl Aviators and the Phantom Airship

Girl Aviators on Golden Wings

Girl Aviators' Sky Cruise

Girl Aviators' Motor Butterfly

GIRL SCOUT SERIES, Katherine Galt, 1921, Saalfield, hardcover, with dust jacket: $35.00

Girl Scouts at Home

Girl Scouts Rally

Girl Scout's Triumph

GIRL SCOUTS SERIES, Edith Lavell, 1922 – 1925, Burt, 10 books, brown hardcover with printed illustration and gilt lettering, with dust jacket: $35.00

GIRL SCOUTS SERIES, Lillian Elizabeth Roy, ca. 1915, Grosset & Dunlap, advertised as

"The heroines of these pleasant stories are Girl Scouts and woven through the adventures and fun you will find the principles of Scouting carried out." Hardcover: $35.00

Girl Scouts at Dandelion Camp through *Little Woodcrafter's Fun on the Farm*

GIRL SCOUTS SERIES, Mildred Wirt, ca. 1950, Cupples & Leon, hardcover, with dust jacket: $30.00

Girl Scouts at Penguin Pass

Girl Scouts at Singing Sands

Girl Scouts at Mystery Mansion

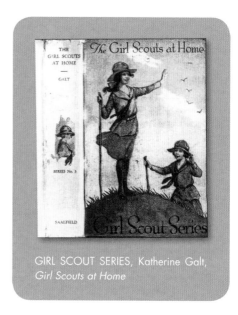

GIRL SCOUT SERIES, Katherine Galt, *Girl Scouts at Home*

GLAD BOOKS (Pollyanna) SERIES, Eleanor Porter, continued by authors Harriet Lummis Smith, Elizabeth Borten, Margaret Piper Chalmers, and Virginia May Moffit, 1913 – 1949, Page Publications, hardcover with paste-on-pictorial, six b/w plates: $50.00

Eleanor Porter titles:

Pollyanna, 1913

Pollyanna Grows Up, 1915

Harriet Lummis Smith titles:

Pollyanna of the Orange Blossoms, 1924

Pollyanna's Jewels, 1925

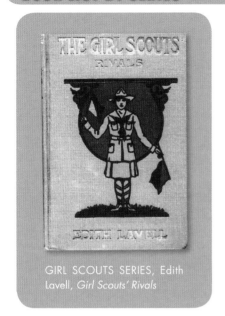

GIRL SCOUTS SERIES, Edith Lavell, *Girl Scouts' Rivals*

Pollyanna's Debt of Honor, 1927

Pollyanna's Western Adventure, 1929

Elizabeth Borten titles:

Pollyanna in Hollywood, 1931

Pollyanna's Castle in Mexico, 1933

Pollyanna's Door to Happiness,1936

Pollyanna's Golden Horseshoe, 1939

Margaret Piper Chalmers titles:

Pollyanna's Protegee, 1944

GLAD BOOKS (Pollyanna) SERIES, Eleanor Porter, *Pollyanna's Jewels*

Pollyanna at Six Star Ranch, 1948

Virginia May Moffit title:

Pollyanna of Magic Valley, 1949

GLOWING EYE BOOKS, Marjorie Barrows, color illustrated paper-over-board hardcover picture books with a round hole cut-out on the cover and in the pages. The main character's face is painted on a raised circle form attached to the inside back cover and visible through all the pages and the front cover. Instructions on JoJo read "hold JoJo close to a lightbulb...take into darkened room...JoJo's eyes shine!" Actually, his whole round face shines, and it still works on our 1944 book! First editions: $70.00

Ezra the Elephant, 1936, Grosset & Dunlap, illustrated endpapers, color and b/w illustrations by Nell Smock

Fraidy Cat, a Glowing-Eye Book, 1942, Rand McNally, 22 pages, illustrations by Barbara Maynard

JoJo, a Glowing-Eye Book, 1944, Rand McNally, b/w/brown/blue illustrations by Clarence Biers

Lancelot, a Glowing-Eye Book, 1946, Rand McNally, color illustrations by Sue Simons

Pudgy the Little Black Bear, 1948, Rand Mcnally, illustrated by Clarence Biers

Scamper, a Glowing-Eye Book, 1949, Rand McNally, color illustrations by Clarence Biers

Timothy Tiger, a Glowing-Eye Book, 1944, Rand McNally, color illustrations by Keith Ward

Waggles, Glow-in-Dark book, 1945, Rand McNally, color illustrations by Clarence Biers

Glowing Eye, related book:

Bright-Eye Book, Barrows, 1941, Ruben H. Lilja, oversize pictorial hardcover, collection of verses illustrated by Milo Winter, features a wiggle-eye novelty on cover: $30.00

GLOWING EYE BOOKS, Marjorie Barrows, *Bright-Eye Book*

G-MEN SERIES, William Engle, Grosset & Dunlap, hardcover, pictorial endpapers.

First edition with dust jacket: $85.00

Later printings with dust jackets: $35.00

G-Men Smash the "Professor's" Gang, 1939

G-Men in Jeopardy, 1938

G-Men Trap the Spy Ring, 1939

G-MEN SERIES, William Engle, *G-Men Smash the "Professor's" Gang*

GOLDEN STALLION SERIES, Rutherford G. Montgomery, Little, Brown, some titles reissued by Grosset & Dunlap as part of the FAMOUS HORSE STORIES. British editions issued by Hodder or White Lion.

Little, Brown first editions with dust jackets: $35.00

Capture of the Golden Stallion, 1951

Golden Stallion's Revenge, 1953

Golden Stallion to the Rescue, 1954

Golden Stallion's Victory, 1956

Golden Stallion and the Wolf Dog, 1958

Golden Stallion's Adventure at Redstone, 1959

Golden Stallion and the Mysterious Feud, 1967

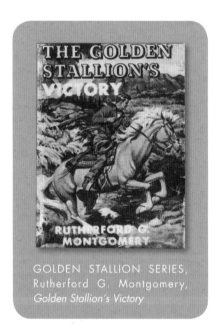

GOLDEN STALLION SERIES, Rutherford G. Montgomery, *Golden Stallion's Victory*

GOLDEN WEST BOYS SERIES, William S. Hart, ca. 1920, Houghton Mifflin, illustrated cloth-over-board cover, with dust jacket: $45.00

Injun and Whitey

Injun and Whitey to the Rescue

Injun and Whitey Strike out for Themselves

GOLLIWOGG AND DUTCH DOLLS SERIES,
Bertha Upton (1849 – 1912), Longmans, UK, color illustrations by author's daughter, Florence Upton. These books created a new demand for old-style peg wooden dolls plus an enormous market for stuffed cloth Golliwogg dolls. Format was over-

GOLLIWOGG AND DUTCH DOLLS SERIES, Bertha Upton, *Adventures of Two Dutch Dolls*

sized paper-over-board cover with printed color illustration and cloth spine, interior color illustrations.

Later printings, 1900 – 1915: $200.00

Later printings, 1920s: $40.00

Golliwogg, early editions:

Golliwogg's Bicycle Club, 1893, first edition: $1,000.00

Adventures of Two Dutch Dolls, 1895, first edition: $800.00

Golliwogg at the Sea-Side, 1898, first edition: $1,000.00

Golliwogg in War, 1899, first edition: $1,000.00

Golliwogg's Polar Adventures, 1900, first edition: $700.00

Golliwogg's Auto-Go-Cart, 1901, first edition: $700.00

Golliwogg's Airship, 1902, first edition: $600.00

Golliwogg's Circus, 1903, first edition: $600.00

Golliwogg in Holland, 1904, first edition: $400.00

Golliwogg's Fox Hunt, 1905, first edition: $400.00

Golliwogg's Desert Island, 1906, first edition: $400.00

Golliwogg's Christmas, 1907, first edition: $400.00

Golliwogg in the African Jungle, 1909, first edition: $400.00

GOOP SERIES, Gelett Burgess (1866 – 1951), usually oversize hardcover, b/w line drawings by author, nonsense characters presenting educational messages.

Later editions: $30.00

Goop, early editions:

Goop Directory of Juvenile Offenders, 1913 Stokes, oversize, illustrations, first edition: $200.00

Goops and How to Be Them, 1900, Stokes, oversize, illustrations, first edition: $200.00

Goop Encyclopedia, 1916, Frederick A. Stokes, hardcover, first edition: $100.00

Goops and How to Be Them, 1928 edition, J. B. Lippincott, oversize: $40.00

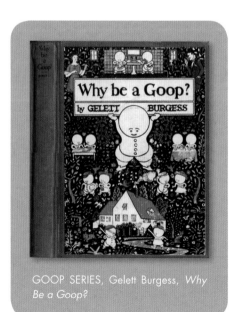

GOOP SERIES, Gelett Burgess, *Why Be a Goop?*

More Goops and How Not to Be Them, 1903, Frederick A. Stokes, oversize, illustrations, first edition: $200.00

Goop Tales Alphabetically Told, 1904, Frederick A. Stokes, oversize, illustrations, first edition: $200.00

Why Be a Goop?, 1924, Frederick A. Stokes, standard size hardcover with paste-on-pictorial, b/w illustrations, first edition: $100.00

GORMENGHAST SERIES, Mervyn Peake, Eyre and Spottiswoode Publishers, London, UK, first edition with dust jacket: $300.00

Reynal & Hitchcock, US, first edition with dust jacket: $100.00

Reprints with dust jackets: $30.00

Gormenghast, 1950

Titus Groan, 1946

Titus Alone, 1959

GRACE HARLOWE SERIES, Jessie Graham Flower, printed illustration on hardcover, advertised as the "college girls series."

Altemus editions with dust jackets: $40.00

Grace Harlowe High School Girls Series, ca. 1915

Grace Harlowe College Girls Series, ca. 1915 – 1925

GRACE HARLOWE SERIES, Jessie Graham Flower, *Grace Harlowe College Girls Series, Golden Summer*

Grace Harlowe Overland Riders Series, ca.1920

Grace Harlowe Overseas Series, ca. 1920s

GRAFTON SCHOOL SERIES, Ralph Henry Barbour, Appleton, hardcover, four plates, sports stories, especially collectible for the three well-known artists who did the illustrations, with same-as-cover dust jacket: $50.00

Rivals for the Team, 1916, ilustrations by Charles Relyea

Winning His Game, 1917, ilustrations by Walter Louderback

Hitting the Line, 1917, ilustrations by Norman Rockwell

GREAT ACE SERIES, Noel Sainsbury, Cupples & Leon, hardcover with printed illustration of biplane, illustrated endpapers and frontispiece, adventures of Billy Smith, with dust jacket: $40.00

Billy Smith, Exploring Ace, or, By Airplane to New Guinea, 1928 (first published by McBride)

Billy Smith, Exploring Ace, or, By Airplane to New Guinea, 1928

Billy Smith, Secret Service Ace, or, Airplane Adventures in Arabia, 1932

Billy Smith, Mystery Ace, or, Airplane Discoveries in South America, 1932

Billy Smith, Trail Eater Ace, or, Into the Wilds of Northern Alaska by Airplane, 1933

Billy Smith, Shanghaied Ace, or, Malay Pirates and Solomon Island Cannibals, 1934

GREAT BRAIN SERIES, John D. Fitzgerald, Dial, hardcover, b/w illustrations by Mercer Mayer.

First editions with dust jackets: $30.00 to $50.00

Great Brain, 1967

GREAT BRAIN SERIES, John D. Fitzgerald, *Great Brain Does It Again*

More Adventures of the Great Brain, 1969

Me and My Little Brain, 1972

Great Brain at the Academy, 1972

Great Brain Reforms, 1973

Return of the Great Brain, 1974

Great Brain Does It Again, 1975

GREAT MARVEL SERIES, Roy Rockwood (Stratemeyer pseudonym), first eight titles were probably written by Howard Garis, ca. 1906 – 1930s, Cupples & Leon. Stratemeyer Syndicate's first science fiction series was modeled upon the stories

GREAT MARVEL SERIES, Roy Rockwood, *Lost on the Moon*

of Jules Verne. Stories feature Mark, Jack, Professor Henderson, and several other adventurers.

Great Marvel, Cupples & Leon, Charles Nuttall illustrations, pictorial hardcover, early printings had four b/w plates, with dust jacket: $100.00

Later printings have frontispiece only, with dust jacket: $80.00

Through the Air to the North Pole, 1906

Under the Ocean to the South Pole, 1907

Five Thousand Miles Underground, 1908

Great Marvel, four b/w plates, Cupples & Leon, pictorial hardcover, various illustrators, early printings had four b/w plates, with dust jacket: $100.00

Later printings have frontispiece only, with dust jacket: $80.00

Through Space to Mars, 1910, illustrated by G. M. Kizer

Lost on the Moon, 1911, illustrator unknown

On a Torn-Away World, 1913, illustrator unknown

City beyond the Clouds, 1925, illustrated by Ernest Townsend

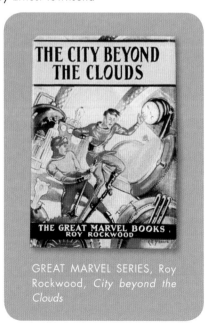

GREAT MARVEL SERIES, Roy Rockwood, *City beyond the Clouds*

GREAT MARVEL SERIES, Roy Rockwood, new dust jacket, *By Air Express to Venus*

By Air Express to Venus, 1929, illustrated by Ed Whittemore

Great Marvel, frontispiece only, Cupples & Leon, pictorial hardcover with dust jacket: $50.00

By Space Ship to Saturn, 1935, illustrated by C.R. Schaare

Great Marvel, other:

Mystery and Adventure Stories for Boys, Cupples & Leon, circa 1930s. Contains text for *Through the Air to the North Pole* as well as three other unrelated novels for boys, with dust jacket: $30.00

Great Marvel, Whitman editions, printed illustration on hardcover, four b/w plates, with dust jacket: $35.00

Whitman Publishing Company, reprinted books 3, *Five Thousand Miles*, through 9, *By Space Ship*, as plain hardcovers with new dust jackets and no interior illustrations in the 1930s and 1940s.

Through Space to Mars, 1940 edition, Whitman, blue hardcover, 248 pages, with dust jacket by J. Chambers: $30.00

Great Marvel, related series: Deep Sea Series, Roy Rockwood, Stitt, also published by Chatterton-Peck, Mershon, and Grosset & Dunlap, hardcover, the second

through fourth titles were reprinted as Dave Fearless Series in 1918 by Sully, and ten years later Garden City picked up the Dave Fearless name and continued the series in paperback.

First edition hardcover by Stitt or Sully: $30.00

Wizard of the Sea, or, *Trip Under the Ocean*, 1900

Rival Ocean Divers, or, *After a Sunken Treasure*, 1905

Cruise of the Treasure Ship, or, *Castaways of Floating Island*, 1906

Jack North's Treasure Hunt, or, *Daring Adventures in South America*, 1907

Adrift on the Pacific, or, *Secret of the Island Cave*, 1908

GREAT WEST SERIES, Edward Legrand Sabin, 1916 – 1919, Thomas Y. Crowell, protagonist is Terry, pictorial hardcover, four-color plates, 300+ pages: $30.00

Boy Settler, or, *Terry in the New West*

Great Pike's Peak Rush, or, *Terry in the New Gold Fields*

On the Overland Stage, or, *Terry as a King Whip Cub*

Opening the Iron Trail, or, *Terry as a "U Pay" Man*

GREEN FOREST SERIES, Thornton W. Burgess, *Buster Bear's Twins*

GREEN FOREST SERIES, Thornton W. Burgess, ca. 1920s, Little, Brown, dark cloth-over-board cover with paste-on-pictorial, 200+ pages, eight color plates by Harrison Cady, hardcover with dust jacket: $50.00

Buster Bear's Twins, 1921

Lightfoot the Deer, 1921

Blacky the Crow, 1922

Whitefoot the Mouse, 1922

GREEN HORNET BOOKS, based on the comic book character, titles include:

Green Hornet Strikes, 1941, Better Little Book #1453: $75.00

Green Hornet Returns, 1941, Better Little Book #1496, flip-action corner on pages: $75.00

Green Hornet Cracks Down, 1942, Better Little Book #1480: $75.00

Case of the Disappearing Doctor, Brandon Keith, 1966, Whitman Authorized Edition, glossy pictorial hardcover, 212 pages, illustrated endpapers, illustrations by Larry Pelini: $35.00

Green Hornet Annual, 1967, Manchester, World Distributors, pictorial hardcover, oversize: $40.00

Green Hornet Lunchbox, Shirley Gordon, 1970, Houghton Mifflin, hardcover picture book, illustrated by Margaret Bloy Graham, with dust jacket: $30.00

Green Hornet, other:

Green Hornet Fights Crime, 1948, Harvey Publications comic book, 52 pages: $80.00

Green Hornet: Collector's Edition, Van Williams, 1990, Bonus Books, Chicago, oversize black hardcover with silver, green endpapers, reprints of comic books, first edition with dust jacket: $40.00

GREEN KNOWE SERIES, L. M. Boston, Harcourt or Atheneum, US editions, and Faber, UK editions, hardcover, illustrated by Peter Boston. This series was based on the author's own house.

Early UK editions with dust jackets: $50.00

First US editions with dust jackets: $70.00

Children of Green Knowe, 1955

Treasure of Green Knowe, 1958 (British title: *Chimneys of Green Knowe*)

River at Green Knowe, 1959

Stranger at Green Knowe, 1961

Enemy at Green Knowe, 1964

Guardians of the House, 1974

Stones of Green Knowe, 1976

Green Knowe, related book:

Memory In a House, 1973, Bodley Head, non-fiction hardcover relating author's experience restoring her house, first edition with dust jacket: $40.00

GREEN MEADOW SERIES, Thornton W. Burgess, published ca. 1919, Little, Brown, hardcover, color illustrations by Harrison Cady.

Early editions, Little, Brown, with dust jackets: $100.00

Happy Jack

GREEN MEADOW SERIES, Thornton W. Burgess, *Old Granny Fox*

Mrs. Peter Rabbit

Bowser the Hound

Old Granny Fox

On the Green Meadow

GREEN SKY TRILOGY, Zilpha Keatley Snyder, Atheneum. Trilogy features the Erdlings and the Kindar who live in different sections of the trees of their world, illustrated by Alton Raible. First edition with dust jacket: $100.00

Below the Root, 1975

And All Between, 1976

Until the Celebration, 1977

GRIDIRON SERIES, Harold M. Sherman, 1926 – 1930, Grosset & Dunlap, school football stories, with dust jacket: $45.00

Fight 'em, Big Three, 1926

Touchdown! 1927

Block That Kick! 1928

Hold That Line! 1930

Number 44, and Other Football Stories, 1930

Goal to Go!

GREEN HORNET BOOKS, *Case of the Disappearing Doctor*

Crashing Through

One Minute to Play (novelization of the photoplay by Byron Morgan, illustrated with photographs from film which starred Red Grange, "the Galloping Ghost," himself), 1929, first edition with dust jacket: $90.00

GRIDIRON SERIES, Harold M. Sherman, *One Minute to Play*

GRYPHON SERIES, Andre Norton, a subseries of Norton's larger Witch World series, these books focus specifically on the adventures of Kerovan and Josian and their descendants. See also HIGH HALLECK and WITCH WORLD.

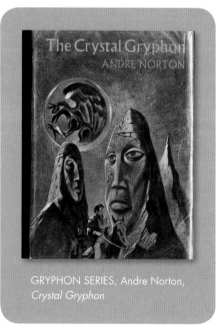

GRYPHON SERIES, Andre Norton, *Crystal Gryphon*

Crystal Gryphon, 1972 Atheneum, hardcover, dust jacket by Jack Gaughan, first printing listed on copyright page, first edition with dust jacket: $150.00

Gryphon in Glory, 1981, Atheneum, first edition with dust jacket: $40.00

Gryphon's Erie, 1985, Tor, with A.C. Crispin, first edition with dust jacket: $25.00

GUS THE GHOST SERIES, Jane Thayer, William Morrow, hardcover, color illustrations by Seymour Fleishman, the first title gives the theme of this series, first edition with dust jacket: $30.00

Gus Was a Friendly Ghost, 1962

Gus Was a Christmas Ghost, 1969

Gus and the Baby Ghost, 1972

Gus Was a Mexican Ghost, 1974

What's a Ghost Going to Do?, 1974

Gus Was a Gorgeous Ghost, 1978

Gus Was a Real Dumb Ghost, 1982

Gus Goes to School, 1982

Gus Loved his Happy Home, 1989

GUS THE GHOST SERIES, Jane Thayer, *Gus Was a Friendly Ghost*

HAG DOWSABEL THE WITCH SERIES, Lorna Wood (author of *Ameliaranne Series*), Dent, UK, hardcover, color and b/w illustrations by Joan Kiddell-Monroe, sensible English children befriend a magical witch in the garden and often have to solve the problems she creates.

People in the Garden, 1954, first edition with dust jacket: $70.00

Rescue by Broomstick, 1956, first edition with dust jacket: $50.00

Hag Calls for Help, 1957, first edition with dust jacket: $40.00

Holiday on Hot Bricks, 1958, first edition with dust jacket: $30.00

Seven League Ballet Shoes, 1959, first edition with dust jacket: $30.00

Hags on Holiday, 1960, first edition with dust jacket: $30.00

Hag in the Castle, 1963, first edition with dust jacket: $30.00

Hags by Starlight, 1970, first edition with dust jacket: $20.00

HAL AND ROGER HUNT SERIES, Willard Price, Jonathan Cape, London, hardcover, color frontispiece, illustratons by Pat Marriot, early printing, with dust jacket: $50.00

John Day edition, map endpapers, illustrations by Peter Burchard, with dust jacket: $45.00

Amazon Adventure, 1949

South Sea Adventure, 1952

Underwater Adventure, 1954

Volcano Adventure, 1956

Whale Adventure, 1960

African Adventure, 1963

HAL AND ROGER HUNT SERIES,
Willard Price, *Cannibal Adventure*

Elephant Adventure, 1964

Safari Adventure, 1966

Lion Adventure, 1967

Gorilla Adventure, 1969

Diving Adventure, 1970

Cannibal Adventure, 1972

Tiger Adventure, 1980

Arctic Adventure, 1983

HAL KEEN SERIES, Hugh Lloyd, 1931 –
1934, Grosset & Dunlap, illustrations by
Bert Salg, with dust jacket, start at: $60.00

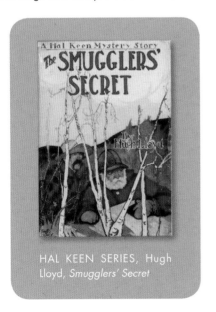

HAL KEEN SERIES, Hugh
Lloyd, *Smugglers' Secret*

Hermit of Gordon's Creek

Kidnapped in the Jungle

Copperhead Trail Mystery

Smugglers' Secret

Mysterious Arab

Lonesome Swamp Mystery

Clue at Skeleton Rocks

Doom of Stark House

Lost Mine of the Amazon

Mystery at Dark Star Ranch

HALF MAGIC SERIES, Edward Eager,
Harcourt Brace, illustrated by N.M.
Bodecker. Loosely connected plots and
characters deal with the children who
appear in the first book or with their children. First edition with dust jacket: $60.00

Later Harcourt editions with dust jackets:
$35.00

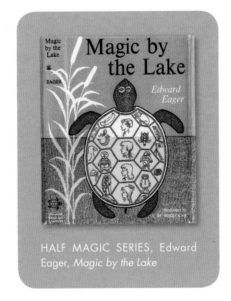

HALF MAGIC SERIES, Edward
Eager, *Magic by the Lake*

Half Magic, 1954

Knight's Castle, 1956

Magic by the Lake, 1957

Time Garden, 1958

Seven Day Magic, 1962

HALL FAMILY SERIES, Jane Langton,
Harper & Row, pictorial hardcover, magical adventures of Edward and Eleanor.

First edition with dust jacket: $50.00

Diamond in the Window, 1962

Swing in the Summer House, 1967

Astonishing Stereoscope, 1971, b/w illustrations by Erik Blegvad

Fledgling, 1980

Fragile Flag, 1984

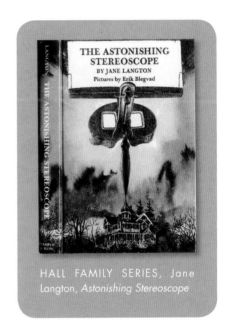

HALL FAMILY SERIES, Jane
Langton, *Astonishing Stereoscope*

HALTER CHILDREN SERIES, Irmelin Lilius,
Finland, English translation, Delacorte,
hardcover, illustrations by Ionicus, first US
edition with dust jacket: $30.00

Gold Crown Lane, 1969

Goldmaker's House, 1970

Horse of the Night, 1971

HAPPY CHILDREN BOOKS, ca. 1915
– 1925, Volland Publishing, Chicago.
Advertised with the same slogan as the
SUNNY BOOKS, but the added line, "That
is why they are called Books for Good
Children." As far as we know, Volland
never did books for bad children, probably because its publishing philosophy ran

along the lines of believing all children were good. This larger format included the early Raggedy Ann books. (See also RAGGEDY ANN) Somewhat fragile books with paper-over-board covers, beautiful color endpapers and illustrations. Volland hired students of the Chicago Art Institute as well as other artists. Although styles vary, the clear watercolor tones are consistent in Volland illustrations. Titles cross over and turn up in other Volland series, as well as in other publishers' editions. Volland books were often packaged in cardboard boxes with box lids matching the book cover. See listings under author's name. Values vary based on collectibility of the author or artist. Average values for these books, with a good condition box: $200.00. Without box: $100.00

HAPPY HOME SERIES, Howard R. Garis (see also Booklist by Author section, GARIS, Howard R.), ca. 1925, Grosset & Dunlap, small, about 160 pages, plain red covers with black lettering, color illustrated endpapers, b/w frontispiece by Lang Campbell, with dust jacket: $40.00

Adventures of the Galloping Gas Stove

Adventures of the Runaway Rocking Chair

Adventures of the Traveling Table

Adventures of the Sliding Foot Stool

Adventures of the Sailing Sofa

Adventures of the Prancing Piano

HAPPY HOME SERIES, Howard R. Garis, *Adventures of the Prancing Piano*

HAPPY LION SERIES, Louise Fatio, Whittlesey House, color illustrations by

Roger Duvoisin, the happy lion enjoys the friendship of a French village.

Happy Lion, 1954, first edition with dust jacket: $150.00

Happy Lion, continuing titles, 1955 – 1980, first edition with dust jacket: $45.00

Happy Lion in Africa, 1955

Happy Lion Roars, 1957

Three Happy Lions, 1959

Happy Lion's Present, 1961

Happy Lion's Quest, 1961

Happy Lion and the Bear, 1964

Happy Lion's Holiday, 1967

Happy Lion's Treasure, 1970

Happy Lion's Rabbits, 1974

Happy Lioness, 1980

HAPPY LION SERIES, Louise Fatio, *Happy Lion*

HARDY BOYS SERIES, Franklin W. Dixon (pseudonym for Stratemeyer Syndicate authors), Grosset & Dunlap, 124 volumes published between 1927 – 1994. Canadian Leslie McFarlane wrote many titles in the series between 1927 and 1947. Starting in 1959, the Stratemeyer Syndicate began revising all books published earlier. In 1979, Simon & Schuster

bought out the Stratemeyer Syndicate and published new *Hardy Boys* titles under the "Wanderer Books" imprint. Grosset & Dunlap retained publication rights to older titles. Like other Grosset & Dunlap series, first editions are not marked, and dating books can be tricky. Most collectors identify "firsts" as books that do not list past their own title on the title list. Numerous reprints keep later editions' prices low.

Hardy Boys, 1927 – 1932, first three books (*Tower Treasure, House on the Cliff,* and *Secret of the Old Mill*) released in 1927 with red cloth imprinted with a black shield, blank endpapers, and dustjackets with white spine. Probable firsts with dust jackets: $50.00

Tower Treasure

House on the Cliff

Secret of the Old Mill

Missing Chums

Hunting for Hidden Gold

Shore Road Mystery

Secret of the Caves

Mystery of Cabin Island

Great Airport Mystery

What Happened at Midnight

While the Clock Ticked

Hardy Boys, 1932 – 1941, blank endpapers are replaced with brown or orange endpapers showing one of the Hardys peering across a river with a pair of binoculars. Brown cloth binding, dust jackets switch from white spine to yellow spine in 1934, volumes 1 – 12 still reprinted with white spine into 1940s. Editions printed during WWII, 1943 – 1948, use thinner paper and pages tend to brown. Probable firsts with dust jacket: $35.00

Footprints under the Window

Mark on the Door

Hidden Harbor Mystery

Sinister Sign Post

Figure in Hiding

Secret Warning

Twisted Claw

Disappearing Floor

Mystery of the Flying Express

Clue of the Broken Blade

Flickering Torch Mystery

Melted Coins

Short-Wave Mystery

Hardy Boys, 1945 – 1950, wraparound scene on dust jackets, brown cloth cover, new cover art created for many of the older titles. Probable first with dust jacket: $30.00

Secret Panel

Phantom Freighter

Secret of Skull Mountain

Sign of the Crooked Arrow

Secret of the Lost Tunnel

Wailing Siren Mystery

Hardy Boys, 1960s on, new titles and new editions of old titles continue to be printed, with large printings and easy availability.

HAROLD AND THE PURPLE CRAYON SERIES,

Crockett Johnson (David Johnson Leisk), Harper, small hardcover, two color illustrations by author, picture stories about a small boy whose imagination takes him on simple adventures, for the pre-school set.

Johnson studied art as part of his curriculum at New York University. Like many creative people, his career took numerous turns, including an advertising job at Macy's Department Store. He gained fame through his humorous cartoons for *Collier's* magazine, as well as his *Barnaby* comic

HAROLD AND THE PURPLE CRAYON SERIES, Crockett Johnson, *Harold and the Purple Crayon*

strip, then used those skills in his fanciful *Harold* stories.

First edition with dust jacket starts at: $700.00

Harold and the Purple Crayon, 1955

Harold's Fairy Tale, 1956

Harold's Trip to the Sky, 1957

Harold at the North Pole, 1958

Harold's Circus, 1959

Picture for Harold's Room, 1960

Harold's ABC, 1963

HARPER HALL SERIES,

Anne McCaffrey, based in the same world of dragon riders as her bestselling *Pern* series for adults. Dust jacket by Fred Marcellino.

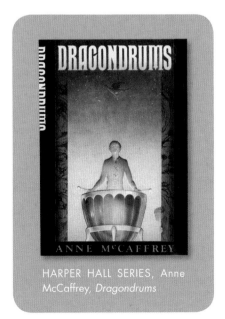

HARPER HALL SERIES, Anne McCaffrey, *Dragondrums*

Atheneum, first editions with dust jackets:

Dragonsong, 1976: $175.00

Dragonsinger, 1977: $100.00

Dragondrums, 1979: $100.00

HARRIET THE SPY SERIES,
Louise Fitzhugh, Harper, hardcover.

Harriet the Spy, 1964, Harper, first edition with dust jacket: $100.00

Long Secret, 1965, Harper, first edition with dust jacket: $60.00

Sport, 1979, Delacorte Press, first edition with dust jacket by Robert Kinyon: $85.00

HARRIET THE SPY SERIES, Louise Fitzhugh, *Harriet the Spy*

HARRY POTTER,
J. K. Rowling, Bloomsbury (UK) or Scholastic (US), 1997 – 2007, seven books, collectors consider the UK editions to be the "true firsts" of the series through book 3; after that books were issued simultaneously in Great Britain and the US in print runs exceeding four million. As the popularity of the books grew, both Bloomsbury and Scholastic returned to earlier titles to issued limited editions with new artwork, signed by artists or author, and other decorations. Prices on these limited editions have been extremely volatile over the past five years and should be checked at the time of sale.

Harry Potter and the Philosopher's Stone (US title changed to *"and the Sorcerer's Stone"*), July 1997, Bloomsbury, pictorial boards by Thomas Taylor, copyright page shows author as Joanne Rowling and has a reverse number line ending in 1, original print run under 1,000 books, auction estimates for hardcover first edition thus begin at: $10,000.00

Harry Potter and the Chamber of Secrets, July 1998, Bloomsbury, pictorial boards with dust jacket illustrated by Cliff Wright, number line on copyright page ends in 1, estimated print run approximately 10,000 copies, first trade edition with fine dust jacket starts at: $1,000.00

Harry Potter and the Prisoner of Azkaban, July 1999, Bloomsbury, dust jacket illustrated by Cliff Wright, copyright page shows author as Joanne Rowling (probable first state of book) or J.K. Rowling (probable second state of book) and has a number line ending in 1, estimated print run approximately 10,000 copies, first trade edition with fine dust jacket starts at: $1,000.00

HARRY THE DOG SERIES, Gene Zion, Harper, illustrated oversize hardcover, simple text, funny stories, color illustrations by Margaret Bloy Graham.

First editions with dust jackets: $40.00

Harry the Dirty Dog, 1956

No Roses for Harry!, 1958

Harry and the Lady Next Door, 1960

Harry by the Sea, 1965

HARRY THE DOG SERIES, Gene Zion, *No Roses for Harry!, Harry by the Sea*

Harry, other:

Harry the Dirty Dog, the First Talking Storybook, 1956, with 33¹/₃ RPM record: $50.00

HAUNTED SERIES, Barbara Byfield, Doubleday, oblong hardcover, illustrated by author, with dust jacket: $30.00

Haunted Spy, 1969

Haunted Churchbell, 1971

Haunted Ghost, 1973

Haunted Tower, 1976

HEINLEIN JUVENILES, Robert A. Heinlein, Scribner's, individual novels published in hardcover in matching format, illustrators include Thomas Voter and Clifford Geary. First printings usually have a letter "A" on the copyright page with the Scribner seal. UK editions by Gollancz.

HEINLEIN JUVENILES, Robert A. Heinlein, *Rocket Ship Galileo*

Heinlein, Scribner's editions:

Rocket Ship Galileo, 1947, illustrated by Thomas Voter, first edition with dust jacket: $900.00

Space Cadet, 1948, hardcover, illustrated by Clifford Geary, first edition with dust jacket: $500.00

Heinlein, Scribner's, 1949 – 1958, first edition with dust jacket: $250.00

Red Planet: A Colonial Boy on Mars, 1949

Farmer in the Sky, 1950

Between Planets, 1951

Rolling Stones, 1952 (UK title: *Space Family Stone,* 1969)

Starman Jones, 1953

Star Beast, 1954

Tunnel in the Sky, 1955

Time for the Stars, 1956

Citizen of the Galaxy, 1957

Have Space Suit, Will Travel, 1958

Heinlein Juvenile, Putnam:

Podkayne of Mars: Her Life and Times, 1963, Putnam, first edition with dust jacket: $200.00

HENRY HUGGINS SERIES, Beverly Cleary, Morrow, hardcover, b/w illustrations by Louis Darling, dust jackets by Alan Tiegreen, first edition with dust jacket:

Henry Huggins, 1950: $300.00

Henry and Beezus, 1952: $300.00

Henry and Ribsy, 1954: $200.00

HENRY HUGGINS SERIES, Beverly Cleary, *Henry and the Paper Route*

Henry and the Paper Route, 1957: $100.00

Henry and the Clubhouse, 1962: $100.00

Ribsy, 1964: $80.00

HENRY REED SERIES, Keith Robertson, Viking, hardcover, b/w illustrations by Robert McCloskey, first edition with dust jacket:

Henry Reed, Inc., 1958: $200.00

Henry Reed's Journey, 1963: $200.00

Henry Reed's Babysitting Service, 1966: $100.00

Henry Reed's Big Show, 1970: $100.00

Henry Reed's Think Tank, 1986: $60.00

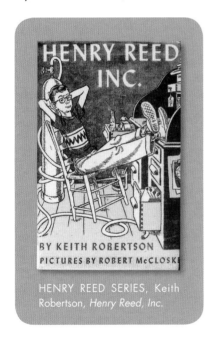

HENRY REED SERIES, Keith Robertson, *Henry Reed, Inc.*

HERBERT YADON SERIES, Hazel Wilson, Knopf, hardcover, Herbert is an ordinary schoolboy but somehow he finds himself doing strange things, including landing on Mars and saving a planet. Pictorial hardcover, b/w illustrations, with dust jacket: $40.00

Herbert, 1950, illustrations by John Barron

More Fun with Herbert, 1954, illustrations by John Barron

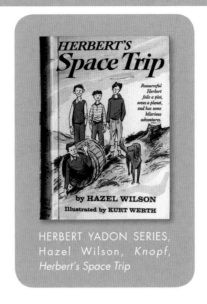

HERBERT YADON SERIES, Hazel Wilson, *Knopf, Herbert's Space Trip*

Herbert's Homework, 1960, illustrations by Kurt Werth

Herbert's Space Trip, 1965, illustrations by Kurt Werth

Herbert Again, 1966, illustrations by Kurt Werth

Herbert's Stilts, 1972, illustrations by Kurt Werth

HIGH HALLECK SERIES, Andre Norton, part of Norton's larger *Witch World* series, these books focus specifically on the adventures taking place in the country of High Halleck. Some characters and events crossover to the *Gryphon* series. See also WITCH WORLD.

HIGH HALLECK SERIES, Andre Norton, *Jargoon Pard*

Year of the Unicorn (first published as 1965 Ace paperback), 1977 edition,

Gregg, hardcover with dust jacket: $100.00

Spell of the Witch World (1972, Ace), Gregg edition, hardcover with dust jacket: $100.00

Jargoon Pard, 1974, Atheneum, first edition with dust jacket by Jack Gaughan: $80.00

Zarsthor's Bane, 1978, Ace, paperback only, first edition: $10.00

Horn Crown, 1981, Daw, hardcover, first edition with dust jacket: $20.00

HILDEGARDE-MARGARET SERIES, Laura Richards, ca. 1890s, Estes & Lauriat, Boston, small, decorated hardcover, 350+ pages, full-page tipped-in illustrations, first edition: $80.00

HILLSFIELD SERIES, Ralph Henry Barbour, 1931 – 1934, Appleton, hardcover, like most Barbour books, reappear in several formats. Good printings of Neill illustrations can increase price, with dust jacket: $30.00

Fumbled Pass

Hero of the Camp

Cub Battery

Goal to Go

Beaton Runs the Mile

Southworth Scores

HILTON SERIES, Ralph Henry Barbour, Appleton, hardcover, more school sports from this prolific writer, six b/w plates plus maps: $45.00

Halfback, 1899

For the Honor of the School, 1900

Captain of the Crew, 1901

HOLLOW TREE SERIES, Albert Biglelow Paine (1861 – 1937), 1898 – 1917, Harper & Bros., illustrated by J.M. Conde. Series of stories about the animals of the

Deep Woods. *Hollow Tree* books were issued both as individual titles in small hardcover editions, and in omnibus editions. They were also published under other series names.

Harper first editions, small cloth hardcovers with gilt, paste-on-pictorials, b/w plates: $60.00

1930s Harper printings, plain covers with dust jackets: $30.00

Hollow Tree, 1898

In the Deep Woods, 1899

How Mr. Dog Got Even, 1900

Mr. Rabbit's Big Dinner, 1901

Hollow Tree Snowed-In Book, 1910

How Mr. Rabbit Lost His Tail, 1910

Making up with Mr. Dog, 1915

Hollow Tree Nights and Days, 1916

Mr. Possum's Great Balloon Trip, 1915

Mr. Crow and the Whitewash, 1917

Mr. Rabbit's Wedding, 1917

Mr. Turtle's Flying Adventure, 1917

When Jack Rabbit Was a Little Boy, 1915

Hollow Tree Collection:

Hollow Tree and Deepwoods Book, 1937, oversize, 272 pages: $50.00

HONEY BUNCH SERIES, Helen Louise Thorndyke (pseudonym, Stratemeyer Syndicate), many by Josephine Lawrence or Mildred Wirt Benson, ca. 1920 – on, Grosset & Dunlap, 30+ books, hardcover with paste-on-pictorial, b/w plates, illustrators include Walter S. Rogers, Marie Schubert, and Corinne Dillon, advertised as "pleasing series of stories for little girls from four to eight years old."

Ca. 1957 this series became the *Honey Bunch and Norman* series, featuring Honey

HONEY BUNCH SERIES, Helen Louise Thorndyke, *Honey Bunch: Just a Little Girl*

Bunch Morton and her friend, Norman Clark, who appeared in earlier titles and was very popular with readers. Reprints of earlier titles (sometimes titles were altered) are included with new titles in the later series.

Honey Bunch: Just a Little Girl, first edition with paste-on-pictorial and dust jacket: $80.00

Honey Bunch, first edition with paste-on-pictorial, no dust jacket: $40.00

Honey Bunch, plain hardcover with dust jacket: $35.00

HOPALONG CASSIDY SERIES, Clarence E. Mulford

Hopalong Cassidy, 1910, A. C. McClurg, full-color plates by Maynard Dixon, illustrated cover with cowboy on horse: $200.00

Buck Peters, the Story of What Happened When Buck Peters, Hopalong Cassidy and Their Bar-20 Associates Went to Montana, 1912, A. C. McClurg, Chicago, four-color illustrations by Maynard Dixon, brown hardcover with gilt lettering, first edition: $100.00

Hopalong Cassidy and the Square Dance Holdup, 1919, Capitol Records, Hollywood, includes two records and a booklet of movie stills, hardcover, first edition: $100.00

Hopalong Cassidy Returns, 1924, Doubleday, Page, first edition with dust jacket: $200.00

Hopalong Cassidy's Protege, 1926, Doubleday, first edition with dust jacket: $200.00

Hopalong Cassidy, ca. 1950s, Grosset & Dunlap, hardcover with dust jacket: $30.00

Hopalong Cassidy

Coming of Hopalong Cassidy

Hopalong Cassidy Sees Red

Hopalong Cassidy's Private War

Hopalong Cassidy's Rustler Round-Up

HOPALONG CASSIDY SERIES, Clarence E. Mulford, *Hopalong Cassidy's Rustler Round-Up*

IN WORDS OF ONE SYLLABLE, Mary Godolphin, written and published in the late 1800s, these are simplified re-writes of the classics and have been published in many editions.

Following are a sampling of editions, titles listed alphabetically:

Pilgrim's Progress in Words of One Syllable, 1884, McLoughlin Bros., hardcover, six full-page color illustrations: $65.00

Pilgrim's Progress in Words of One Syllable, 1939 edition, Lippincott, hardcover, b/w illustrations by Robert Lawson: $75.00

Robinson Crusoe in Words of One Syllable, 1882, McLoughlin, decorated hardcover, six full-page color illustrations: $55.00

Sanford and Merton in Words of One Syllable, undated, ca. 1900, hardcover: $35.00

Swiss Family Robinson in Words of One Syllable, undated, ca. 1913 edition, McKay, 96 pages, brown cloth-over-board cover with illustration, illustrated with engravings: $35.00

IN WORDS OF ONE SYLLABLE, Mary Godolphin, *Robinson Crusoe in Words of One Syllable*

INDIAN IN THE CUPBOARD SERIES, Lynne Reid Banks. A magic cupboard allows Patrick and Omri's toys to come to life as well as travel back in time.

Indian in the Cupboard, 1981, Doubleday, illustrated by Brock Cole (British copyright 1980), first edition with dust jacket: $80.00

Return of the Indian, 1986, Doubleday, first edition with dust jacket: $40.00

Secret of the Indian, 1989, Doubleday, illustrated by Ted Lewin, first edition with dust jacket: $40.00

Mystery of the Cupboard, 1993, Morrow, illustrated by Tom Newsom, first edition with dust jacket: $30.00

Key to the Indian, 1998, Avon Camelot, blue hardcover with gilt, illustrated by James Watling, first edition, no dust jacket issued: $30.00

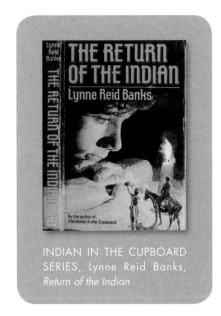

INDIAN IN THE CUPBOARD SERIES, Lynne Reid Banks, *Return of the Indian*

INVISIBLE SCARLET O'NEIL SERIES, this character was featured in a newspaper comic strip and comic books.

Invisible Scarlet O'Neil, Russell Stamm, 1943, Whitman, hardcover, illustrated endpapers, b/w illustrations, with dust jacket: $40.00

Invisible Scarlet O'Neil, Big Little Books, ca. 1940s, small, pictorial cardboard cover, b/w illustrations: $30.00

INVISIBLE SCARLET O'NEIL SERIES, Russell Stamm, *Invisible Scarlet O'Neil*

Invisible Scarlet O'Neil, All Pictures Comics, #1403

Invisible Scarlet O'Neil vs. the King of the Slums, #1406

ISABEL CARLETON SERIES, Margaret Ashmun, ca. 1915, Macmillan, cloth-over-board cover with paste-on-pictorial and gilt lettering, three b/w plates. Early editions with dust jacket: $60.00

Isabel Carleton's Year

Heart of Isabel Carleton

Isabel Carleton's Friends

Isabel Carleton in the West

Isabel Carleton at Home

ISABELLA THE GOOSE SERIES, Emilie Blackmore Stapp, Winslow Press, hardcover with paste-on-pictorial, illustrated endpapers, two-color illustrations by Forrest Orr or George Rock, with dust jacket: $40.00.

Isabella the Wise Goose, 1940

Isabella's Big Secret, 1946

Isabella the Bride, 1947

Isabella Queen of Gooseland, 1948

Isabella's Goose Village, 1950

Isabella's New Friend, 1952

ISIS TRILOGY, Monica Hughes, hardcover, haunting fantasy of a teenager and robot alone on a far planet.

Atheneum, US, and Hamish Hamilton, UK, first edition with dust jacket: $50.00

Keeper of the Isis Light, 1980

Guardian of Isis, 1982, dust jacket by Andrew Rhodes

Isis Pedlar, 1982

IVOR THE ENGINE SERIES, Oliver Postgate, illustrations by Peter Firmin. Firmin attended

Colchester Art School, Central School of Art. His talents include cartoon art, illustration, writing, and puppet making. He created the hand puppet, *Basil Brush*, best known in Britain as the star of a children's TV show. In this series, Ivor is a railway engine in Wales. Titles include:

Ivor the Engine, 1962, Picture Lions, pictorial hardcover: $50.00

Ivor's Outing, 1967, Picture Lions, pictorial hardcover: $40.00

Ivor the Engine Annual, 1978, Pemberton, glazed pictorial hardcover, 63 pages, color illustrations: $40.00

Ivor the Engine Story Book, 1982, Collins, London, glazed pictorial hardcover, contains four stories, color illustrations: $40.00

Ivor the Engine Red Story Book, 1986 Guild Publishing, Glasgow, glazed pictorial hardcover, contains two stories, color illustrations: $40.00

■ ·················· **J** ·················· ■

JACK ARMSTRONG SERIES, based on the radio program and featuring the All-American boy. Premiums offered by the radio show are popular with collectors and include an explorer telescope, sun watch, hike-o-meter, etc.

Jack Armstrong hardcover titles include:

Jack Armstrong's Mystery Eye, Stanley Wallace, 1936, Cupples & Leon, tan hardcover, 206 pages, with dust jacket: $100.00

Jack Armstrong's Mystery Crystal, 1936, Cupples & Leon, tan hardcover with dust jacket: $100.00

Jack Armstrong and the Ivory Treasure, Leslie Daniels, Jr., 1937, Big Little Book, color illustrated cardboard cover, b/w illustrations: $30.00

Jack Armstrong and the Mystery of the Iron Key, 1939, Better Little Book, color

JACK ARMSTRONG SERIES, Leslie Daniels Jr., *Jack Armstrong and the Ivory Treasure*

illustrated cardboard cover, b/w illustrations: $30.00

JACK SERIES, George Bird Grinnell, 1899 – 1913, Stokes, pictorial hardcover, numerous b/w illustrations by Edward Demming.

First edition with dust jacket: $200.00

Other early editions with dust jackets: $60.00

Jack, the Young Ranchman, or, A Boy's Adventures in the Rockies

Jack among the Indians, or, A Boy's Summer on the Buffalo Plains

Jack in the Rockies, or, A Boy's Adventures with a Pack Train

Jack, the Young Canoeman, or, An Eastern Boy's Voyage in a Chinook Canoe

Jack, the Young Trapper, or, An Eastern Boy's Fur Hunting in the Rocky Mountains

Jack, the Young Explorer, or, A Boy's Experiences in the Unknown Northwest

Jack, the Young Cowboy, or, An Eastern Boy's Experiences on a Western Roundup

JACK RANGER SERIES, Clarence Young, Stratemeyer Syndicate pseudonym, ca. 1910s, Cupples & Leon, red hardcover, eight b/w plates by Charles Nuttell, with dust jacket: $100.00

Hardcover without dust jacket: $30.00

Jack Ranger's School Days

Jack Ranger's Western Trip

Jack Ranger's School Victories

Jack Ranger's Ocean Cruise

Jack Ranger's Gun Club

Jack Ranger's Treasure Box

JANE ALLEN COLLEGE SERIES, Edith Bancroft, ca. 1920, Cupples & Leon, advertised as "a series recognized as an authoritative account of the life of a college girl," hardcover with paste-on-illustration, b/w illustrations, with dust jacket: $50.00

Jane Allen of the Sub Team

Jane Allen: Right Guard

Jane Allen: Center

Jane Allen: Junior

JANE ALLEN COLLEGE SERIES, Edith Bancroft, *Jane Allen of the Sub Team*

JENNINGS SERIES, Anthony Malcolm Buckeridge, 1950 – 1977, Collins, hardcover, 22 titles. This English series began as radio plays in 1948, telling the adventures of Jennings and his friend, Darbishire, at the Linbury Court School. In the 1990s, Collins issued two final titles: *Jennings Again!* and *That's Jennings*. Like the

William Brown books, prices in England tend to be higher than in the USA. First edition with dust jacket: $40.00

Jennings Goes to School, 1950

Jennings Follows a Clue, 1951

Jennings' Little Hut, 1951

Jennings and Darbishire, 1952

Jennings' Diary, 1953

According to Jennings, 1954

Our Friend Jennings, 1955

Thanks to Jennings, 1957

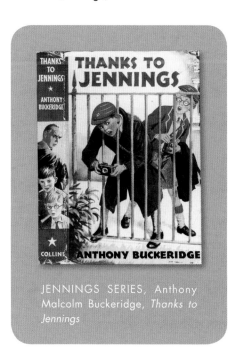

JENNINGS SERIES, Anthony Malcolm Buckeridge, *Thanks to Jennings*

Take Jennings, for Instance, 1958

Jennings, As Usual, 1959

Trouble with Jennings, 1960

Just Like Jennings, 1961

Leave It to Jennings, 1963

Jennings, of Course!, 1964

Especially Jennings!, 1965

Bookfull of Jennings, 1966

Jennings Abounding, 1967

Jennings in Particular, 1968

Trust Jennings! 1969

Jennings Report, 1970

Typically Jennings!, 1971

Speaking of Jennings!, 1973

Jennings at Large, 1977

JERRY FORD WONDER SERIES, Fenworth Moore (Stratemeyer Syndicate pseudonym), ca. 1930s, Cupples & Leon, red hardcover, frontispiece, illustrations by Russell Tandy, with dust jacket: $40.00

Wrecked on Cannibal Island

Lost in the Caves of Gold

Castaway in the Land of Snow

Prisoners on the Pirate Ship

Thrilling Stories for Boys, 1937, large volume containing the above four novels

JERRY HICKS SERIES, William Heyliger, 1920s, Grosset & Dunlap, green hardcover, four b/w plates by Bert Salg, with dust jacket: $100.00

Yours Truly, Jerry Hicks

Jerry Hicks, Ghost Hunter

Jerry Hicks and His Gang

Jerry Hicks, Explorer

JERRY JAKE SERIES, May Justus, 1942 – 1945, Albert Whitman, adventures of a Tennessee mountain boy, books include Tennessee songs, hardcover with paste-on-pictorial, decorated endpapers, illustrations by Christine Chisholm, with dust jacket: $50.00

Stepalong and Jerry Jake, 1942

Jerry Jake Carries On, 1943

Hurrah for Jerry Jake, 1945

JERRY JAKE SERIES, May Justus, *Hurrah for Jerry Jake*

JERRY TODD SERIES, Leo Edwards, 1923 – 1938, Grosset & Dunlap, red hardcover, illustrated or map endpapers, four b/w plate illustrations by Bert Salg, through Buffalo Bill Bathtub. Advertised as "Detective stories for boys! Jerry Todd and his trusty pals solve many a baffling mystery in their home town." First editions with dust jackets are priced to: $100.00

Later editions with dust jackets: $40.00

Jerry Todd, illustrations by Bert Salg:

Jerry Todd and the Whispering Mummy, 1924

Jerry Todd and the Rose-Colored Cat, 1924

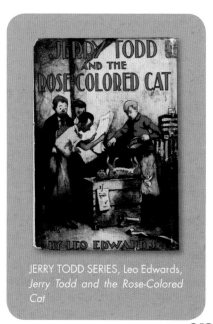

JERRY TODD SERIES, Leo Edwards, *Jerry Todd and the Rose-Colored Cat*

Jerry Todd and the Oak Island Treasure

Jerry Todd and the Waltzing Hen, 1925

Jerry Todd and the Talking Frog, 1925

Jerry Todd and the Purring Egg,1926

Jerry Todd and the Whispering Cave,1927

Jerry Todd and the Pirate, 1928

Jerry Todd and the Bob-Tailed Elephant,1929

Jerry Todd and the Editor-in-Grief, 1930

Jerry Todd and the Caveman, 1932

Jerry Todd and the Flying Flapdoodle, 1934

Jerry Todd and the Buffalo Bill Bathtub, 1936

Jerry Todd, other illustrators:

Jerry Todd and the Up-the-Ladder Club, illustrated by Myrtle Sheldon, 1937

Jerry Todd and the Poodle Parlor, illustrated by Myrtle Sheldon, 1938

Jerry Todd and the Cuckoo Camp, illustrated by Herman Bachrach, 1938

JIM SPURLING SERIES, Albert Tolman, 1918 – 1927, Harper, pictorial hardcover, frontispiece and b/w plates, first edition with dust jacket: $100.00

Jim Spurling, Fisherman, or, Making Good, illustrated by Bert Salg

Jim Spurling, Millman

Jim Spurling, Leader, or, Ocean Camp

Jim Spurling, Trawler, or, Fishing with Cap'n Tom

JIM STANLEY SERIES, see WINSTON SCIENCE FICTION CLASSICS

JIMMIE DRURY, CAMERA DETECTIVE SERIES, David O'Hara, 1938 – 1941, Grosset & Dunlap, orange hardcover, illustrated endpapers and frontispiece, mysteries, with dust jacket: $35.00

Jimmie Drury: Candid Camera Detective

What the Dark Room Revealed

Caught by the Camera

By Bursting Flash Bulbs

JOAN FOSTER SERIES, Alice Ross Colver, Dodd Mead, hardcover, first edition with dust jacket: $70.00 to $100.00

Joan Foster, Freshman, 1942

Joan Foster, Sophomore, 1948

Joan Foster, Junior, 1950

Joan Foster, Senior, 1950

Joan Foster in Europe, 1951

Joan Foster, Bride, 1952

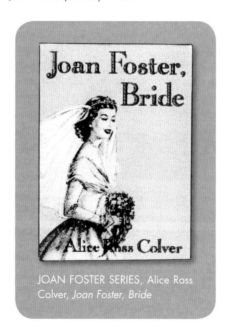

JOAN FOSTER SERIES, Alice Ross Colver, *Joan Foster, Bride*

JOHNNY CROW SERIES, L. Leslie Brooke (1862 – 1940), hardcover, often with paste-on pictorial, color illustrations by author. These books have been reprinted many times and value depends on edition. Like most Warne books, editions can be hard to identify because they are not always dated.

Johnny Crow's Garden, 1903, Warne: $70.00

Johnny Crow's Garden, 1932 edition, Warne, with dust jacket: $40.00

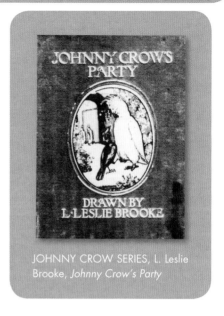

JOHNNY CROW SERIES, L. Leslie Brooke, *Johnny Crow's Party*

Johnny Crow's Party, 1907, Warne, with dust jacket: $65.00

Johnny Crow's Party, 1928 edition, Warne, illustrated paper-over-board cover: $40.00

Johnny Crow's New Garden, 1935, Warne, hardcover with paste-on-pictorial, eight color plates plus b/w illustrations by author, with dust jacket: $100.00

Johnny Crow, related book:

Leslie Brooke and Johnny Crow, Henry Brooke, 1982, Warne, London, oversize hardcover with gilt lettering, biography of Brooke includes color and b/w illustrations plus photos, first edition with dust jacket: $40.00

JOHNNY DIXON SERIES, John Bellairs and Brad Strickland, 1983 – 1999, Dial Books, Johnny solves mysteries with his friend, Professor Childermass. The series was created by Bellairs. After his death in 1991, Strickland completed *Drum, the Doll and the Zombie,* and then continued the series. Frontispiece and dust jacket by Edward Gorey.

First editions with dust jackets: $50.00

Curse of the Blue Figurine, 1983

Mummy, the Will, and the Crypt, 1983

Spell of the Sorcerer's Skull, 1984

Revenge of the Wizard's Ghost, 1985

Eyes of the Killer Robot, 1986

Trolley to Yesterday,1989

Chessmen of Doom, 1989

Secret of the Underground Room, 1990

Drum, the Doll and the Zombie, written with Brad Strickland, 1994

Bell, the Book and the Spellbinder, by Brad Strickland, 1997

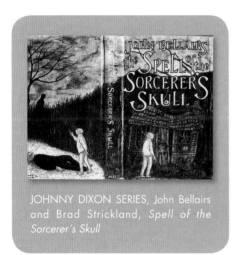

JOHNNY DIXON SERIES, John Bellairs and Brad Strickland, *Spell of the Sorcerer's Skull*

JOLLY GOOD TIMES SERIES, Mary P. Wells Smith (1840 – 1930), ca. 1870s – 1990s Roberts, eight titles, small decorated hardcover, 275+ pages, frontispiece, early editions by Roberts: $30.00

JOLLY JUMP-UPS POP-UP SERIES, Geraldine Clyne, author/illustrator, McLoughlin Publishing, oversize pop-up books with color illustrated paper-over-board hardcovers, six pop-ups, color illustrations. This popular series features bright primary colors and pop-ups that are both detailed and sturdy. Condition is the most important factor in pricing pop-ups. Price range: $60.00 to $150.00

Jolly Jump-Ups and Their New House, 1939

Jolly Jump-Ups on the Farm, 1940

Jolly Jump-Ups Favorite Nursery Stories, ca. 1942

JOLLY JUMP-UPS POP-UP SERIES, Geraldine Clyne, *Jolly Jump-Ups ABC*

Jolly Jump-Ups on Vacation Trip, 1942

Jolly Jump-Ups See the Circus, ca. 1944

Jolly Jump-Ups Mother Goose Book, ca. 1944

Jolly Jump-Ups, Stevenson's Child's Garden of Verse, 1946

Jolly Jump-Ups at the Zoo, 1946

Jolly Jump-Ups ABC, ca. 1948

Jolly Jump-Ups Number Book, 1950

JORDAN SERIES, Janet Lambert, 1945 – 1950s, E. P. Dutton, first edition with dust jacket: $100.00

Grosset & Dunlap reprint with dust jacket: $40.00

Just Jennifer

JORDAN SERIES, Janet Lambert, *Confusion By Cupid*

Friday's Child

Confusion by Cupid

Dream for Susan

Love Taps Gently

Myself and I

Stars Hang High

Wedding Bells

Bright Tomorrow

JOURNEYS THROUGH BOOKLAND SET, edited by Charles Sylvester, ten-volume collection of stories and poetry, 1909, Bellows-Reeve, Chicago, gold-stamped brown cloth-over-board hardcover, about 500 pages, color and b/w illustrations.

First edition set of ten volumes and index: $300.00

1922 edition, black hardcover, set: $200.00

1939 edition, red hardcover, set: $150.00

JUDY BOLTON MYSTERY SERIES, Margaret Sutton, ca. 1930s, Grosset & Dunlap, cover and endpaper illustrations by Pelagie Doane. Girl sleuth solves crimes with the aid of friends. Collectors of girl sleuths consider Judy one of the brightest and most believable. Sutton confined Judy to a small town setting and realistic crimes.

Pelagie Doane's high fashion dust jackets (1932 through 1948) are another plus. Originally the books contained four plates, but after 1939 there is only a frontispiece. Some of the war year prints, ca. late 1940s, dropped the frontispiece. Titles from 1964 on *(Hidden Clue)* were issued in illustrated hardcover without a dust jacket.

Judy Bolton, 1930s titles, early printings with Doane dust jacket: $75.00

Vanishing Shadow, 1932

Haunted Attic, 1932

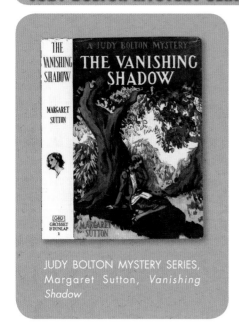

JUDY BOLTON MYSTERY SERIES,
Margaret Sutton, *Vanishing Shadow*

Invisible Chimes, 1932

Seven Strange Clues, 1932

Ghost Parade, 1933

Yellow Phantom, 1933

Mystic Ball, 1934

Voice in the Suitcase, 1935

Mysterious Half Cat, 1936

Riddle of the Double Ring, 1937

Unfinished House, 1938

Midnight Visitor, 1939

Judy Bolton, 1940s titles, early printings with Doane dust jackets: $50.00

Name on the Bracelet, 1940

Clue in the Patchwork Quilt, 1941

Mark on the Mirror, 1942

Secret of the Barred Window, 1943

Rainbow Riddle, 1946

Living Portrait, 1947

Secret of the Musical Tree, 1948

Judy Bolton, 1949 – 1956, early printings with dust jackets: $35.00

Warning on the Window, 1949

Clue of the Stone Lantern, 1950

Spirit of Fog Island, 1951

Black Cat's Clue, 1952

Forbidden Chest, 1953

Haunted Road, 1954

Clue in the Ruined Castle, 1955

Trail of the Green Doll, 1956

Judy Bolton, 1957 – 1963, early printings with dust jackets: $75.00

Haunted Fountain, 1957

Clue of the Broken Wing, 1958

Phantom Friend, 1959

Discovery at Dragon's Mouth, 1960

Whispered Watchword, 1961

Secret Quest, 1962

Puzzle in the Pond, 1963

Judy Bolton, 1964 – 1968 titles published in pictorial hardcover only:

Hidden Clue, 1964: $100.00

Pledge of the Twin Knights, 1965: $100.00

Search for the Glowing Hand, 1966: $120.00

Secret of the Sand Castle, 1967: $200.00

JULIA REDFERN SERIES, Eleanor Cameron, Dutton, hardcover, full-page b/w illustrations by Gail Owens. Irrepressible Julia plunges from one disaster to another, in a series that moves backwards in time, first edition with dust jacket: $80.00

Room Made of Windows, 1971

JULIA REDFERN SERIES, Eleanor
Cameron, *Julia's Magic*

Julia and the Hand of God, 1977

That Julia Redfern, 1982

Julia's Magic, 1984

Private World of Julia Redfern, 1988

JUST SO STORIES, Rudyard Kipling, a collection of read-aloud fables originally released as one volume in 1902 but later broken up into several series of picture books.

Just So, early editions:

Just So Stories for Little Children, London, Macmillan, 1902, red cloth hardcover with stamped illustration, illustrated by the author, 12 stories and 12 poems, small, 249 pages, 11 of the stories had appeared in periodicals between 1897 and 1902, first edition: $2,500.00

Just So Stories, 1902, Macmillan, second printing: $100.00. Post-1920 edition: $40.00

Just So Song Book, 1903, Doubleday, words by Kipling, music by German, green cloth hardcover: $75.00

Just So Stories, 1913, Macmillan, 12 color plates by J. M. Gleeson: $95.00

Just So Stories Series, 1942 – 1947, Garden City, illustrated in full-color by Feodor Rojansky, pictorial hardcover with dust jacket: $30.00

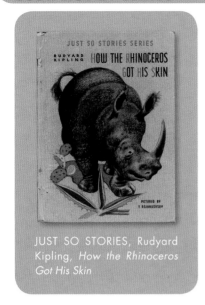

JUST SO STORIES, Rudyard Kipling, *How the Rhinoceros Got His Skin*

KARLSSON SERIES, Astrid Lindgren, *Karlsson-on-the-Roof*

Hans und Fritz, 1917, Saalfield, oversize illustrated cardboard cover, oblong, 36 pages, b/w illustrations by Rudolph Dirks, first edition: $100.00

Katzenjammer Kids in the Mountains, 1934, Saalfield, hardcover, b/w illustrations, adapted from the comic strip: $100.00

Katzenjammer Kids Story Book, 1937, Whitman, oversize color pictorial hardcover, b/w illustrations, 46 pages: $100.00

Katzenjammer Kids, 1945, John Martin's House, small pictorial hardcover with metal spiral rings, an Animated Novelty book, color illustrations, four animated pages include: the Captain's bath, Captain and the alligator, double page pop-up of Captain in tree, and animation of Captain Rollo and kids: $85.00

Butterfly That Stamped

Cat That Walked by Himself

Elephant's Child

How the Camel Got His Hump

How the Leopard Got His Spots

How the Rhinoceros Got His Skin

Just So, 1973 – 1974, Walker, illustrated by Leonard Weisgard with dust jacket: $45.00

Elephant's Child

How the Leopard Got His Spots

How the Rhinoceros Got His Skin

Just So, individual picture books:

How the Elephant Got His Trunk, 1912, Country Life, illustrated by John Gleeson: $90.00

Cat That Walked by Himself, 1970, Hawthorn, illustrated by Rosemary Wells, with dust jacket: $30.00

■ ·················· **K** ·················· ■

KARLSSON SERIES, Astrid Lindgren, various publishers. By the author of the *Pippi Longstocking* series, Karlsson is a little

flying man who lives on Erik's roof. The spelling of their names seems to vary by translator.

Erik and Karlson on-the-Roof, UK title for *Karlsson-on-the-Roof*, 1958, Oxford, UK, illustrations by Richard Kennedy, with same-as-cover dust jacket: $150.00

Karlsson-on-the-Roof, 1971, Viking Press, first American edition, illustrated by Jan Pyk, with dust jacket: $150.00

Karlsson Flies Again, 1977, Methuen, UK, illustrations by Ilon Wikland, with dust jacket: $100.00

World's Best Karlsson, 1980, Methuen, UK, with dust jacket: $300.00

KATIE ROSE SERIES, Lenora Mattingly Weber, Crowell, hardcover.

First edition with dust jacket: $150.00

Don't Call Me Katie Rose, 1964

Winds of March, 1965

New and Different Summer, 1966

I Met a Boy I Used to Know, 1967

Angel in Heavy Shoes, 1968, dust jacket by Muriel Wood

KATRINKA SERIES, Helen Haskell, 1915 – 1939, E. P. Dutton, five books, with dust jacket: $50.00

KATZENJAMMER KIDS SERIES, hardcover books based on the famous King Features Syndicate comic strip by H. H. Knerr.

KATZENJAMMER KIDS SERIES, *Katzenjammer Kids*

Katzenjammer Kids, related books:

All the Funny Folks, 1926, World, oversize hardcover, 120 pages, includes King Features characters Krazy Kat, Barney Google, Jiggs and Maggie, Little Nemo, the Katzenjammer Kids, and others: $100.00

Comics, an Illustrated History from the Katzenjammer Kids to the Sad Sack, Coulton Waugh, 1947, hardcover, first edition with dust jacket: $100.00

KAY TRACEY MYSTERY SERIES, Frances K. Judd (pseudonym of Stratemeyer Syndicate), 1934 – 1942, Cupples & Leon, yellow hardcover, frontispiece. Dust jacket features a design of an open book, and a black bar under the title with the words "Kay Tracey Mystery Stories," first edition with dust jacket: $50.00

Secret of the Red Scarf, 1934

Strange Echo, 1934

Mystery of the Swaying Curtains, 1935

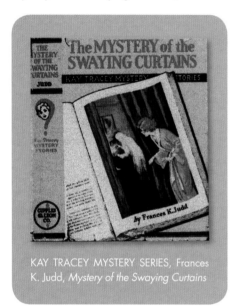

KAY TRACEY MYSTERY SERIES, Frances K. Judd, *Mystery of the Swaying Curtains*

Shadow on the Door, 1935

Six Fingered Glove Mystery, 1936

Green Cameo Mystery, 1936

Secret at the Windmill, 1937

Beneath the Crimson Brier Bush, 1937

Message in the Sand Dunes, 1938

Murmuring Portrait, 1938

When the Key Turned, 1939

In the Sunken Garden, 1939

Forbidden Tower, 1940

Sacred Feather, 1940

Lone Footprint, 1941

Double Disguise, 1941

Mansion of Secrets, 1942

Mysterious Neighbors, 1942

KEMLO SERIES, E. C. Eliott (Reginald Alec Martin), 1954 – 1963, Thomas Nelson, UK, illustrated boards, color frontispiece, b/w illustrations, tales of first generation teenagers born in a space station, and featuring Kemlo, Captain of the Space Scouts, and Krillie, 15 titles, illustrators include R. J. Jobson, A. Bruce Cornwell, George Craig.

First edition, with dust jacket: $70.00

Kemlo and the Crazy Planet, 1954

Kemlo and the Zones of Silence, 1954

Kemlo and the Sky Horse, 1954

Kemlo and the Martian Ghosts, 1954

Kemlo and the Star Men, 1955

Kemlo and the Space Lanes, 1955

Kemlo and the Craters of the Moon, 1955

Kemlo and the End of Time, 1957

Kemlo and the Purple Dawn, 1961

Kemlo and the Gravity Rays, 1959

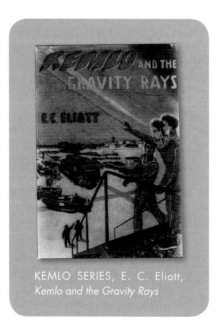

KEMLO SERIES, E. C. Eliott, *Kemlo and the Gravity Rays*

Kemlo and the Zombie Men, 1958

Kemlo and the Space Men, 1959

Kemlo and the Satellite Builders, 1960

Kemlo and the Space Invaders, 1961

Kemlo and the Masters of Space, 1963

Kemlo, related books: Eliott, Thomas Nelson, UK, hardcover, with dust jacket: $30.00

Tas and the Space Machine, 1955

Tas and the Postal Rocket, 1955

KEN HOLT MYSTERY SERIES, Bruce Campbell (pseudonym of Samuel and Beryl Epstein), 1949 – 1963, Grosset & Dunlap, hardcover, 18 titles. Each came with a white dust jacket with different color illustration for each book. Spine shows head of Ken Holt in a shield-shaped panel. Uncredited illustrations. Illustrated endpapers signed "James M. Will" or "Wills." Firsts, list-to-self: $50.00 to $100.00

Later editions with dust jackets: $30.00

Secret of Skeleton Island, 1949

Riddle of the Stone Elephant, 1949

Black Thumb Mystery, 1950

Clue of the Marked Claw, 1950

Clue of the Coiled Cobra, 1951

Secret of Hangman's Inn, 1951

Mystery of the Iron Box, 1952

Clue of the Phantom Car, 1953

Mystery of the Galloping Horse, 1954

Mystery of the Green Flame, 1955

Mystery of the Grinning Tiger, 1956

Mystery of the Vanishing Magician, 1956

Mystery of the Shattered Glass, 1958

Mystery of the Invisible Enemy, 1959

Mystery of Gallows Cliff, 1960

Clue of the Silver Scorpion, 1961

Mystery of the Plumed Serpent, 1962

Mystery of the Sultan's Scimitar, 1963

KEN HOLT MYSTERY SERIES, Bruce Campbell, *Mystery of Gallows Cliff*

KENT BARSTOW SERIES, Rutherford Montgomery, Duell Sloan & Pearce

Kent Barstow Aboard the Dyna Soar, 1964, first edition with dust jacket: $150.00

KENT BARSTOW SERIES, Rutherford Montgomery, *Kent Barstow on a B-70 Mission*

Kent Barstow and the Commando Flight, 1963, first edition with dust jacket: $100.00

Kent Barstow, Space Man, 1962, first edition with dust jacket: $100.00

Kent Barstow Special Agent, 1961, first edition with dust jacket: $100.00

Kent Barstow on a B-70 Mission, 1964, first edition with dust jacket: $150.00

KEWPIE BOOKS, Rose O'Neill, artist/author. The Kewpies were elfish babies, first created by O'Neill for a magazine feature for *Ladies' Home Journal* in 1909. They gained wide popularity and eventually appeared in other magazines, both in features and in advertisements for Jell-O and other products, and in newspaper columns, including a syndicated page for *Hearst* Sunday papers, ca. 1917. O'Neill had already established her reputation as an illustrator. The Kewpies gave her an entrance into humor. They inspired many toys, including the popular Scootles doll.

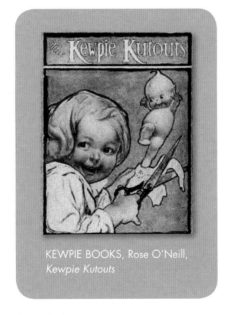

KEWPIE BOOKS, Rose O'Neill, *Kewpie Kutouts*

Titles include:

Kewpie Primer, gray hardcover with Kewpie illustration, illustrations by O'Neill, text and music by Elisabeth V. Quinn: $100.00

Kewpies, Their Book, 1913, Frederick A. Stokes, author illustrations: $100.00

Kewpie Kutouts, 1914, Frederick A. Stokes, hardcover with color paste-on illustration, 48 pages, includes paper dolls and eight stories, illustrated endpapers, red/black ink drawings by O'Neill: $700.00

KID FROM TOMKINVILLE SERIES, John R. Tunis, Morrow, hardcover, baseball stories, first edition with dust jacket: $50.00

Kid from Tomkinville, 1940

Keystone Kids, 1943

Rookie of the Year, 1944

Kid Comes Back, 1946

KING ARTHUR SERIES, Howard Pyle, author/illustrator. The four books cover a full retelling of the Arthurian legends.

King Arthur Series editions:

Scribner, US first edition, large pictorial brown cloth hardcover decorated in red, black, and gilt, gilt lettering on spine, 340+ pages, b/w illustrations by author, first edition: $150.00 to $350.00

Scribner reprints, ca. 1915 – 1920s: $40.00

George Newnes, UK first edition, oversize hardcover, full-page b/w illustrations: $175.00

Ca. 1933 Brandywine anniversary edition, red hardcover with gilt, color frontispiece with tissue overlay, b/w illustrations, with dust jacket: $80.00

Story of King Arthur and His Knights, 1903

Story of the Champions of the Round Table, 1905

Story of Sir Lancelot and His Companions, 1907

Story of the Grail and the Passing of Arthur, 1910

King Arthur Series, related:

King Arthur and the Magic Sword, pop-up

book, 1990, Dial, illustrated hardcover, adapted from the Pyle book, designed by Keith Moseley, illustrated by John James: $30.00

KING ARTHUR TRILOGY, Rosemary Sutcliff, 1980 – 1981, E. P. Dutton, trilogy based on Malory's *La Morte D'Arthur,* plus careful historical research.

E. P. Dutton, US, first edition with dust jacket: $30.00

Bodley Head, UK, first edition with dust jacket: $50.00

Sword and the Circle, wraparound illustration on dust jacket by Shirley Felts

Light Beyond the Forest

Road to Camlann

KINGS OF SPACE SERIES, Captain W. E. Johns, Hodder & Stoughton, science fiction series by the prolific author of the Biggles books. Prof. Brane and Rex Clinton explore alien planets. Color illustrations by Stead.

Kings of Space, 1954, first edition with dust jacket: $70.00

Kings of Space, continuing titles, 1955 – 1963, first edition with dust jacket: $40.00

Return to Mars, 1955

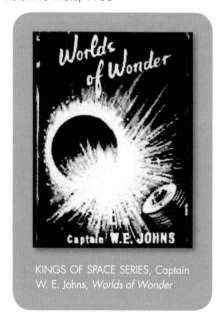

KINGS OF SPACE SERIES, Captain W. E. Johns, *Worlds of Wonder*

Now to the Stars, 1956

To Outer Space, 1957

Edge of Beyond, 1958

Death Rays of Ardilla, 1959

To Worlds Unknown, 1960

Quest for the Perfect Planet, 1961

Worlds of Wonder, 1962

Man Who Vanished into Space, 1963

KNOCKABOUT CLUB SERIES, authors as listed, 1880s, Estes, Boston, dark cloth hardcover with gilt lettering and design, plain endpapers: $60.00

KNOCKABOUT CLUB SERIES, F. A. Ober, *Knockabout Club in the Everglades*

1890s, Estes, color illustrated paper-over-board cover, illustrated endpapers, b/w illustrations: $30.00

Knockabout Club in the Woods, C. A. Stephens

Knockabout Club Alongshore, Stephens

Knockabout Club in the Tropics, Stephens

Knockabout Club in the Everglades, F. A. Ober

Knockabout Club in the Antilles, Ober

■ ·················· **L** ·················· ■

LANG FAIRY TALES, 12 in series, Andrew Lang (1844 – 1912), collections of traditional fairy tales from around the world.

Lang Fairy Tales, first editions, Longmans Green, London, illustrated primarily by Henry Justice Ford:

Blue Fairy Book, 1889, blue cloth hardcover with gilt decoration, 390 pages plus 16 advertising pages, gilt edged pages, tissue guarded frontispiece, eight plates plus b/w drawings by Ford and G. P. J. Hood: $1,200.00

Red Fairy Book, 1890, red cloth hardcover with gilt decoration, plum endpapers, 367 pages plus 16 advertising pages, gilt edged pages, illustrations by Ford and Lancelot Speed: $1,200.00

Green Fairy Book, 1892, green cloth hardcover with gilt decoration, black endpapers, 366 pages plus two advertising pages, gilt edged pages, illustrations by Ford: $600.00

Yellow Fairy Book, 1894, yellow cloth hardcover with gilt decoration, 321 pages, gilt edged pages, tissue guarded frontispiece, b/w illustrations by Ford: $400.00

Pink Fairy Book, 1897, pink cloth hardcover with gilt decoration, gilt edged pages, tissue guarded frontispiece, b/w illustrations by Ford: $400.00

Grey Fairy Book, 1900, yellow cloth hardcover with gilt decoration, black endpapers, 387 pages, gilt edged pages, tissue guarded frontispiece, b/w illustrations by Ford: $400.00

Violet Fairy Book, 1901, purple cloth hardcover with gilt decoration, 388 pages, gilt edged pages, tissue guarded frontispiece, eight color plates plus b/w illustrations by Ford: $800.00

Crimson Fairy Book, 1903, crimson cloth hardcover with gilt decoration, 371 pages, gilt edged pages, eight color plates plus b/w illustrations by Ford: $400.00

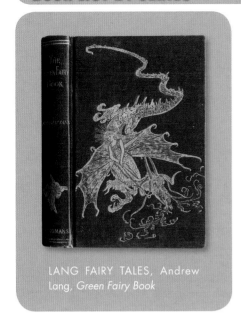

LANG FAIRY TALES, Andrew Lang, *Green Fairy Book*

Brown Fairy Book, 1904, brown cloth hardcover with gilt decoration, brown endpapers with silver fairy decoration, 350 pages, gilt edged pages, eight color plates plus b/w illustrations by Ford: $400.00

Orange Fairy Book, 1906, orange cloth hardcover with gilt decoration, 336 pages, gilt edged pages, eight color plates plus b/w illustrations by Ford: $500.00

Olive Fairy Book, 1907, olive green cloth hardcover with gilt decoration, green pictorial endpapers, 358 pages, gilt edged pages, eight color plates plus b/w illustrations by Ford: $500.00

Lilac Fairy Book, 1910, lavendar cloth hardcover with gilt decoration, 369 pages, gilt edged pages, six color plates plus b/w illustrations by Ford: $300.00

Lang Fairy Tales, reprint descriptions, each title:

Ca. 1890s to 1900, Longmans, similar to first edition: $150.00

Ca. 1924, David McKay, oversize red hardcover with paste-on-pictorial, eight color plates by Gustaf Tenggren: $100.00

Ca. 1929, Longmans Green Crown Edition, gilt lettering and design on cloth cover, four to eight color plate illustrations plus b/w illustrations by Ford and Lancelot Speed: $45.00

Ca. 1930s editions, McKay, color paste-on pictorial on cloth cover, four color plate illustrations by Jennie Harbor: $35.00

Ca. 1949, Longmans Green edition, pictorial cloth hardcover, color and b/w plates by Ben Kutcher, Vera Bock, Marc Simont, Anne Vaughn, Dorothy Lake Gregory, or Christine Price, with dust jacket: $35.00

Lang Fairy Tales, related:

Strange Story Book, Mrs. Lang, 1913, Longmans Green, red hardcover with gilt, 312 pages, 12 color plates and b/w illustrations by H. J. Ford, first edition: $100.00

LANSING SPORTS SERIES, Hawley Williams (William Heyliger), 1912 – 1917, Appleton, illustration on hardcover, four plates by George Avison, early editions: $200.00 to $300.00

Titles are:

Quarterback Reckless

Batter Up

Five Yards to Go

Winning Hit

Johnson of Lansing

Fair Play

Straight Ahead

LA ROCHELLE SERIES, Elinor Brent-Dyer, W.R. Chambers, UK, hardcover. Several early dust jackets illustrated by Percy Tarrant but re-issued later with dust jackets by Nina K. Brisley. 1920s editions: $300.00

1950s reprints with dust jackets: $90.00

Gerry Goes to School, 1922

Head Girl's Difficulties, 1923

Maids of La Rochelle, 1924

Seven Scamps, 1927

Heather Leaves School, 1929

Janie of La Rochelle, 1932

Janie Steps In, 1953

LARRY DEXTER SERIES, labeled "Newspaper Series" on cover, Howard R. Garis, 1907 – 1915, Grosset & Dunlap, hardcover, b/w plates, with dust jacket: $40.00

From Office Boy to Reporter

Larry Dexter, Young Reporter

Larry Dexter in Belgium

LAWRENCEVILLE SCHOOL SERIES, Owen Johnson, these popular novels were also serialized in magazines and used for PBS TV productions.

Lawrenceville, 1909 – 1922, Dodd, Mead & Company, hardcover, 10 b/w plates: $100.00

Lawrenceville, 1909 – 1922, Little, Brown reprint, hardcover, 10 b/w plates: $50.00

Lawrenceville, 1910 – 1922, Baker & Taylor edition, first thus, pictorial hardcover (dust jackets are rare), halftone frontispiece and plates by Frederic. R. Gruger, hardcover without dust jacket: $100.00

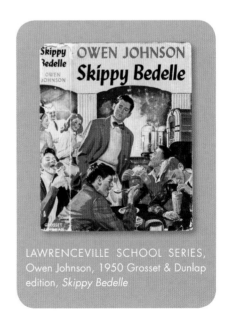

LAWRENCEVILLE SCHOOL SERIES, Owen Johnson, 1950 Grosset & Dunlap edition, *Skippy Bedelle*

Lawrenceville, ca. 1950, Grosset & Dunlap, with dust jacket: $30.00

Eternal Boy (Baker & Taylor title: *Prodigious Hickey*)

Hummingbird

Varmint: A Lawrenceville Story

Tennessee Shad

Skippy Bedelle

Related book:

Stover at Yale, 1912, Frederick A. Stokes, hardcover: $30.00

LEWIS BARNAVELT AND UNCLE JONATHAN SERIES, John Bellairs, Dial, hardcover, b/w illustrations, illustrators include Edward Gorey and Richard Egielski. Spooky adventures of an orphan, his wizard uncle, a witch neighbor, and a young friend named Rosa Rita.

First edition with dust jacket: $100.00

House with the Clock in Its Walls, 1973

Figure in the Shadows, 1975

Letter, the Witch, and the Ring, 1976

Lewis Barnavelt series, after the death of Bellairs in 1991, the series was continued by Brad Strickland. Used copies of continuing titles sell at or below sticker price.

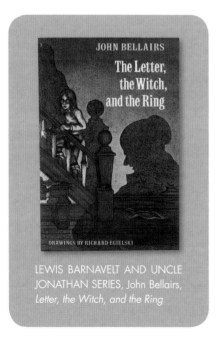

LEWIS BARNAVELT AND UNCLE JONATHAN SERIES, John Bellairs, *Letter, the Witch, and the Ring*

LIMITED EDITION CLUB BOOKS, New York, featured new editions of classics, sometimes with new illustrations, signed by the author or the illustrator or, in the case of *Alice*, signed by Alice Hargreaves, the original Alice. The club published numerous titles, most of them adult novels. Below are listed some of their children's titles. Reprints without the signatures, with slipcases: $40.00

Travels of Baron Munchausen, 1929, limited edition of 1,500, calfskin spine, gilt lettering, illustrated and signed by John Held, Jr., with slipcase: $200.00

Alice's Adventures in Wonderland, 1932, limited edition of 500 signed by Alice Hargreaves, with slipcase: $700.00

Alice's Adventures in Wonderland, 1932, limited edition of 1,500, red leather bound hardcover with gilt design and edges, signed by the binder, Frederick Warde, with slipcase: $350.00

Pinocchio, Carlo Collodi, 1937, limited edition of 1,500, illustrated and signed by illustrator Richard Floethe, with orange slipcase: $150.00

Wind in the Willows, Kenneth Grahame, 1940, limited edition of 2,200, 16 color plates of Rackham illustrations, signed by Bruce Rogers, edition designer, with slipcase: $550.00

Voyage to Brobdingnap and Voyage to Lilliput made by Lemuel Gulliver in the Year MDCCII, Jonathan Swift, 1950 limited edition of 1,500, oversize 18+ x 13+ inches, map frontispiece, a unique presentation by Aldus Printers, with gilt and red decorations, a two-volume set designed and initialed by Bruce Rogers, in slipcase with ribbons: $400.00

LITTLE BLACK CHILDREN BOOKS, Helen Bannerman (1863 – 1946), hardcover, various publishers, variety of sizes, usually with color illustrations.

These stories were written in India to send to the author's children at school in Scotland, and originally illustrated by the author with simple line drawings. 1990s reprints of some of the titles with the

Bannerman illustrations are available. The stories were reprinted numerous times and illustrated by other artists. Value depends on the edition and illustrator and scarcity. First editions are generally sold through auctions, with wide ranges in price.

Little Black Children, early editions with author illustrations:

Story of Little Black Sambo, 1899, Richards, small size, author illustrations in color, first edition: $14,000.00. Second printing: $600.00

Story of Little Black Sambo, 1901, edition Stokes, pictorial boards, color illustrations, pages printed on one side only, author illustrated: $400.00

Story of Little Black Sambo, 1905, Chicago edition with introduction by L. Frank Baum: $125.00

Story of Little Black Mingo, 1901, John Nisbit, London, second edition, decorated cloth hardcover, small, 144 pages printed on one side only, 36 full-page color illustrations: $400.00

Story of Little Black Quibba, ca. 1902, James Nisbet, London, small size, cloth with paste-on-illustration, 143 pages, color illustrations, text and illustrations printed on facing pages on one side of paper only: $600.00

Little Black Quasha, 1908, Frederick A. Stokes, first thus, red hardcover, small, color illustrations: $300.00

Story of Little Black Bobtail, ca. 1909, James Nisbet, small paper-over-board cover with paste-on-illustration, 122 pages, 30 color plates by author: $300.00

Little Black Children, other illustrators:

Little Black Sambo, 1925 edition, Platt & Munk, illustrated hardcover, color illustrations by Eulalie: $75.00

Little Black Sambo, ca. 1932, Saalfield, color and b/w illustrations by Fern Bisel Peat: $150.00

LITTLE BLACK CHILDREN BOOKS, Helen Bannerman, reprint with Bannerman illustration

LITTLE BROWN BEAR SERIES, Elizabeth Upham, *Little Brown Bear*

Mary Ware: The Little Colonel's Chum, 1908

Mary Ware in Texas, 1910

Mary Ware's Promised Land, 1912

Little Colonel Good Time Book, (unknown)

Little Colonel Stories, 1919, b/w plates, 192 pages

Little Colonel Stories, Second Series, 1931, illustrated by Harold Cue

Little Colonel, related titles by Johnston, published by Page:

Story of the Red Cross As Told to the Little Colonel, illustrated by John Goss, 1918, an excerpted story from *Little Colonel's Hero,* hardcover with oval paste-on-illustration: $70.00

Land of the Little Colonel, reminiscence and autobiography, illustrated from original photographs, 1929, Page, pictorial cover with gilt in slipcase: $90.00

Little Black Sambo Story Book, 1935, Platt & Munk, first thus, blue hardcover, illustrations by Frank Ver Beck: $150.00

New Little Black Sambo, 1939, Whitman, oversize, color illustrations by Juanita Bennett: $30.00

Little Black Sambo, Julian Wehr animations, 1943 edition, Duenewald, New York, spiral bound hardcover with six pages of animated illustrations, all in good working condition, first thus: $300.00

Little Black Sambo, 1948, Little Golden Books, small pictorial hardcover, 42 pages, color illustrations by Gustaf Tenggren: $30.00

Little Black Children Books, reference:

Sambo Sahib, the Story of Little Black Sambo and Helen Bannerman, by Elizabeth Hay, 1981, Paul Harris, Edinburgh, 195 pages, 47 illustrations, with dust jacket: $50.00

LITTLE BROWN BEAR SERIES, Elizabeth Upham, short stories that first appeared in *Children's Activities* magazine, illustrated by Guy J. Brown. Hardcover collections of stories, Platt & Munk, illustrations by Marjorie Hartwell: $40.00

Little Brown Bear, 1942

Little Brown Monkey, 1949

Little Brown Bear and His Friends, 1952

Merry Adventures of Little Brown Bear, 1966

LITTLE BROWN MOUSE SERIES, Alison Uttley, Heinemann Publishers, Melbourne, small hardcover, color illustrations by Katherine Wigglesworth, with dust jacket: $50.00

Going to the Fair, 1951

Toad's Castle, 1951

Christmas at the Rose and Crown, 1952

LITTLE COLONEL SERIES, Annie Fellows Johnston, 1894 – 1914, Page, 17 books, beige hardcover with printed color illustration, b/w plates, first edition list-to-self on title or advertising page: $50.00

Little Colonel, 1895

Little Colonel's House Party, 1900

Little Colonel's Holidays, 1901

Little Colonel's Hero, 1902

Little Colonel at Boarding School, 1903

Little Colonel in Arizona, 1904

Little Colonel's Christmas Vacation, 1906

Little Colonel: Maid of Honor, 1907

Little Colonel's Knight Comes Riding, 1907

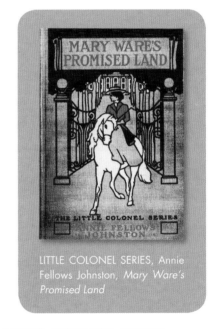

LITTLE COLONEL SERIES, Annie Fellows Johnston, *Mary Ware's Promised Land*

LITTLE ELEPHANT SERIES, Heluiz Washburne, Whitman, pictorial hardcover, illustrated endpapers, color illustrations by Jean McConnell, 32 pages: $40.00

Little Elephant Catches a Cold, 1937

Little Elephant's Christmas, 1938

253

LITTLE ELEPHANT SERIES, Heluiz Washburne, *Little Elephant's Christmas*

Little Elephant Visits the Farm, 1941

Little Elephant's Picnic, 1944

LITTLE GIRL SERIES, Amanda Douglas, 1896 – 1909, Dodd, hardcover, each novel about a girl in a different historical or geographic location: $30.00

LITTLE GREY RABBIT SERIES, Alison Uttley, published 1930s – 1970s, Collins & World, illustrated by Margaret Mary Tempest or Katherine Wigglesworth. Small books, similar in format to Beatrix Potter books, with soft color illustrations and simple text. These books have been re-printed often, and dating is sometimes confusing or non-existent in book. For clues to age, look at the cover materials and type of paper and compare to other books of the era.

LITTLE GREY RABBIT SERIES, Alison Uttley, *Fuzzypeg Goes to School*

Little Grey Rabbit titles, undated, from *Fuzzypeg Goes to School*, 1938, through *Little Grey Rabbit's Washing Day*, 1942, pre-1960 editions with dust jackets: $50.00

Little Grey Rabbit, related book:

Little Grey Rabbit's Third Painting Book, 1953, Collins, oversize hardcover, six color plates by Margaret Tempest, eight illustrations to color, with dust jacket: $75.00. Without dust jacket: $45.00

LITTLE HOUSE SERIES, Laura Ingalls Wilder, Harper Brothers, cloth hardcover with a small single-color illustration printed on the cloth, color decoration endpapers, b/w illustrations by Helen Sewell. Some of the books had color frontispieces, some had two-color illustrations. This classic series is a fictionalized biography based on the author's childhood. The length, vocabulary, and plot complication increases throughout the books as Laura grows from the four-year-old in *Little House in the Big Woods,* to a young wife in *These Happy Golden Years.* The books were sold with a plain protective tissue overwrap which adds about $20.00 to the value. Early printings: $75.00

LITTLE HOUSE SERIES, Laura Ingalls Wilder, *Little House in the Big Woods*

Little House in the Big Woods, 1932

Farmer Boy, 1933

Little House on the Prairie, 1935

LITTLE HOUSE SERIES, Laura Ingalls Wilder, *Farmer Boy* illustration

On the Banks of Plum Creek, 1937

On the Shores of Silver Lake, 1939

Long Winter, 1940

Little Town on the Prairie, 1941

These Happy Golden Years, 1943

Little House Series, same text with new b/w illustrations by Garth Williams, 1953 editions, Harper, hardcover. Williams travelled to many of the story locations and filled his illustrations with authentic historical detail.

First edition thus, with dust jacket: $50.00

LITTLE JACK RABBIT SERIES, David Cory, illustration

LITTLE JACK RABBIT SERIES, David Cory, 1915 – 1921, Grosset & Dunlap, hardcover, glossy frontispiece, decorated endpapers, color plates by H. S. Barbour, with dust jacket: $40.00

LITTLE JOURNEYS TO HAPPYLAND SERIES,

David Cory, published ca. 1922 – 1927, Grosset & Dunlap, small, paste-on-pictorial covers, color illustrated endpapers, b/w illustrations by H. Barbour, with dust jacket: $30.00

Cruise of Noah's Ark, 1922

Wind Wagon, 1923

Iceberg Express, 1922

Magic Soap Bubble, 1922

Magic Umbrella, 1923

LITTLE LULU BOOKS, created and drawn
by Marge (Marjorie Henderson Buell), Little Lulu and her friends appeared in comic strips, comic books, individual magazine cartoons, and in numerous hardcover books, usually with brightly illustrated paper-over board hardcovers. Titles include:

Little Lulu, 1935, Curtis, collection of previously published b/w cartoons: $50.00

Little Lulu, 1937, Rand McNally, small hardcover: $50.00

Little Lulu and Her Pals, 1939, McKay, oversize, illustrated hardcover, color illustrations, with dust jacket: $100.00

Little Lulu on Parade, 1941, David McKay, b/w/red illustrations, with same-as-cover dust jacket: $100.00

Laughs with Little Lulu, 1943, McKay, hardcover, two-color cartoons from *Saturday Evening Post*: $50.00

Oh, Little Lulu!, 1943, McKay, oversize, illustrated hardcover, color illustrations, with dust jacket: $75.00

Fun with Little Lulu, 1944, David McKay, small hardcover with dust jacket: $75.00

Little Lulu at the Circus, 1946, McLoughlin Bros., cardboard cover, color and b/w illustrations: $40.00

Little Lulu at Grandma's Farm, 1946, McLoughlin Bros., cardboard cover, color and b/w illustrations: $40.00

Little Lulu at the Seashore, 1946, McLoughlin Bros., cardboard cover, color and b/w illustrations, with dust jacket: $80.00

Little Lulu and Her Magic Tricks, 1954, Little Golden Books, #203 with Kleenex package still containing Kleenex: $75.00. Without Kleenex: $30.00

This is Little Lulu, 1956, Dell paperback, collection of comic strips: $80.00

LITTLE ORPHAN ANNIE BOOKS, Harold
Gray, ca. 1930s, Cupples & Leon, illustrated cardboard cover, numbered volumes, 84+ pages of *Chicago Tribune* comics per book: $60.00

Little Orphan Annie, 1926

Little Orphan Annie in the Circus, 1927

Little Orphan Annie Bucking the World, 1929

Little Orphan Annie Shipwrecked, 1931

Little Orphan Annie and Uncle Dan, 1933

Little Orphan Annie, Whitman Big Little Books, cardboard covers, b/w illustrations:

Little Orphan Annie and the $1,000,000 Formula, 1936: $55.00

Little Orphan Annie in the Movies, 1941: $55.00

Little Orphan Annie with the Circus, 1941: $35.00

Little Orphan Annie, other:

Little Orphan Annie and Jumbo, the Circus Elephant, 1935, Pleasure Books, a pop-up book with three full-color pop-ups: $150.00

Little Orphan Annie and the Haunted Mansion, 1941, Whitman Better Little Book, cardboard covers, 425 pages, a Flip It book: $40.00

Arf! The Life and Hard Times of Little Orphan Annie: 1935 – 1945, 1970, Arlington House, hardcover, collection of daily strips, with dust jacket: $40.00

LITTLE PEOPLE BOOKS, Ernest Nister pub-
lisher, full-color chromolithographs, illustrated covers, oversize, many titles, some credit authors, many do not, some list both Nister and E. P. Dutton as the publisher. Sample titles:

Little Stories for Little People, ca. 1900, illustrated paper covered boards, illustrators include Edith Taylor and E. A. Cubitt, three pages of advertisments: $200.00

Little People's Animal Book, Alfred J. Fuller, 1905, printed in Bavaria, pictorial boards with red cloth spine, about 64 pages,

16 pages in color, plus b/w illustrations: $180.00

Little People's Book of Airships, circa 1906, oblong, hardcover, varnished pictorial chromolithographic cover: $1,800.00

Jingles and Rhymes for Little People, 1915, ¼ bound brown cloth with bright illustrated color paper boards, collection of rhymes, 12 color plates plus b/w illustrations: $150.00

Little People's Scrap Book, ca. 1900, pictorial hardcover, printed in Bavaria, cover illustration of Little Bo Peep, decorative endpapers, 16 full-page lithographs plus half-page to three-quarter-page lithographs: $150.00

LITTLE RED ENGINE SERIES, Diana Ross, oversize, oblong pictorial boards, color and b/w illustrations by Leslie Wood except for the first title, which was illustrated by Lewitt-Him.

LITTLE RED ENGINE SERIES, Diana Ross, *Little Red Engine Goes Travelling*

Little Red Engine, 1959, Faber and Faber, 1942 – 1958, first edition with dust jacket: $100.00. Without dust jacket: $40.00

Little Red Engine Gets a Name, 1942, illustrated by Lewitt-Him

Story of the Little Red Engine, 1945, through *Little Red Engine Goes Home*, 1958

Little Red Engine Goes Travelling, 1959, Faber and Faber, pictorial hardcover: $50.00

Little Red Engine, Faber and Faber, 1968 – 1971 first edition with dust jacket: $60.00. Without dust jacket: $30.00

Little Red Engine and the Taddlecombe Outing, 1968

Little Red Engine Goes Carolling, 1971

LITTLE RED FOX SERIES, Alison Uttley, Heinemann, UK, and Bobbs-Merrill, US, hardcover, 62 pages, 12 color plates and b/w illustrations, little fox is raised by a badger.

Little Red Fox, illustrated by Katherine Wigglesworth, with dust jacket: $75.00:

Little Red Fox and the Wicked Uncle, 1954

Little Red Fox and Cinderella, 1956

Little Red Fox and the Magic Moon, 1958

Little Red Fox Book, 1962

Little Red Fox and the Unicorn, 1962

Little Red Fox, illustrated by Jennie Corbett:

Little Red Fox and the Big Big Tree, 1968, small pictorial hardcover: $25.00

LITTLE TOOT SERIES, Hardie Gramatky, G. P. Putnam's Sons, pictorial hardcover, picture book stories of a tug boat, illustrated in color by the author, six titles.

Little Toot, 1939, first edition with dust jacket: $50.00

Little Toot, continuing titles, first edition with dust jacket: $30.00

Little Toot on the Thames, 1964

Little Toot and the Grand Canal, 1968

Little Toot on the Mississippi, 1973

Little Toot Through the Golden Gate, 1975

Little Toot and the Loch Ness Monster, 1989

LITTLE WOMEN SERIES, Louisa May Alcott (1832 – 1888), the continuing tales of the March family, these books have been reprinted continuously in various formats and illustrated by numerous illustrators. Prices of first editions vary widely depending on condition.

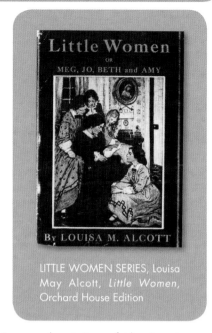

LITTLE WOMEN SERIES, Louisa May Alcott, *Little Women*, Orchard House Edition

Some early printings of Alcott's series:

Little Women, 1868, Roberts Brothers, Boston, wine hardcover with gilt lettering, illustrated by May Alcott. Frontispiece with tissue protective sheet shows Meg, Jo, Beth, Amy, and Marmee, includes six pages of ads, first edition: $8,000.00

Little Women, 1871, Roberts Brothers, Boston, cloth hardcover with gilt lettering, advertising pages, b/w illustrations: $700.00

Little Women, 1926, John C. Winston edition, hardcover with paste-on-pictorial, illustrated endpapers, four color plates plus b/w illustrations by Clara Burd: $40.00

Little Men, Life at Plumfield with Jo's Boys, 1871, Roberts Brothers, frontispiece and illustrations, hardcover with gilt lettering, first edition: $1,000.00

Aunt Jo's Scrap-Bag, 1872, Roberts Brothers, early edition in green hardcover, 215 pages, illustrated: $125.00

Eight Cousins, 1875, Roberts Brothers, dark blue hardcover with gilt, 291 pages, frontispiece with tissue, first edition: $500.00

Rose in Bloom (1876 copyright), sequel to *Eight Cousins*, Roberts Brothers, 1891 publishing date, tan cloth with black lettering: $500.00

Jo's Boys, and How They Turned Out, 1886, Roberts Brothers, first edition: $700.00

Little Women, Orchard House Edition, ca. 1936, Little, Brown, advertised as "The complete story of the Little Women is told in Little Women, Little Men, and Jo's Boys.... The Orchard House edition has been published to answer the need for an attractive, popular-priced, uniform edition of all three books." Hardcover with endpaper photograph of Alcott home, Orchard House, at Concord, Massachusetts, with dust jacket: $35.00

LIVE DOLLS SERIES, Josephine Scribner Gates, 1901 – 1912, Bobbs-Merrill, hardcover, paste-on-pictorials, color illustrations.

First edition: $100.00

Early editions, pre-1920: $50.00 to $75.00

Bobbs-Merrill, paper-over-board covers, 1920s – 1930s editions: $40.00

Donohue reprints, 1920s – 1930s, with dust jackets: $40.00

Live Dolls titles include:

Story of Live Dolls, 1901, b/w plates by Mabel Rogers

More about Live Dolls, 1903, illustrations by Virginia Keep

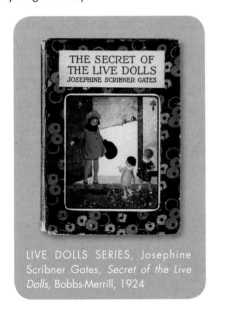

LIVE DOLLS SERIES, Josephine Scribner Gates, *Secret of the Live Dolls*, Bobbs-Merrill, 1924

Secret of the Live Dolls, 1904, illustrations by Keep

Live Dolls House Party, 1906, illustrations by Keep

Live Dolls' Busy Days, 1907, illustrations by Keep

Live Dolls Play Days, 1908, illustrations by Keep

Live Dolls in Wonderland, 1912, illustrations by Keep

Live Dolls, omnibus:

Book of Live Dolls, an Omnibus, 1931, orange hardcover, illustrations, contains the first three books, 150 pages, with dust jacket: $50.00

LOIS LENSKI LITTLE BOOKS SERIES, written and illustrated by Lenski, Oxford, illustrated cloth-over-board hardcover, square shape, b/w/contrasting color illustrations, illustrated endpapers, easy readers, first edition with dust jacket: $50.00 to $100.00

Little Auto, 1934

Little Sail Boat, 1937

Little Airplane, 1938

Little Farm, 1942

Little Fire Engine, 1946

LONE RANGER SERIES, Fran Striker, Grosset & Dunlap, brown, tan, or gray hardcover with red lettering, pictorial endpapers, frontispiece, novels based on the radio and comic strip stories, early edition with dust jacket: $50.00

Lone Ranger, 1937

Lone Ranger and the Mystery Ranch, 1938

Lone Ranger and the Gold Robbery, 1939

Lone Ranger and the Outlaw Stronghold, 1939

Lone Ranger and Tonto, 1940

LONE RANGER SERIES, Fran Striker, *Lone Ranger Traps the Smugglers*

Lone Ranger at the Haunted Gulch, 1941

Lone Ranger Traps the Smugglers, 1941

Lone Ranger Rides Again, 1943

Lone Ranger Rides North, 1946

Lone Ranger and the Silver Bullet, 1948

Lone Ranger on Powder Horn Trail, 1949

Lone Ranger in Wild Horse Canyon, 1950

Lone Ranger and the War Horse, 1951

Lone Ranger West of Maverick Pass, 1951

Lone Ranger on Gunsight Mesa, 1952

Lone Ranger and the Bitter Spring Feud, 1953

Lone Ranger and the Code of the West, 1954

Lone Ranger: Trouble on the Santa Fe, 1955

Lone Ranger on Red Butte Trail, 1956

Lone Ranger, coloring books, prices are for clean, uncolored books:

Hi-Yo Silver!, the Lone Ranger Paint Book, 1938, Whitman, illustrated by Ted Horn: $50.00

Lone Ranger Coloring Book, 1951, Whitman: $35.00

257

Lone Ranger Coloring Book, 1953, Whitman: $30.00

Tonto Coloring Book, 1957, Whitman: $35.00

Lone Ranger, other:

Lone Ranger Adventure Stories, adapted by Arthur Groom for the Warner film, 1957 Western, oversize pictorial hardcover, 77 pages, photo illustrations: $30.00

LORAINE SERIES, Elizabeth Gordon (1866 – 1922), Rand McNally, small, color illustrated paper-over-cover or cloth hardcover with paste-on-pictorial, color and b/w illustrations, Loraine meets fairies in her garden and elsewhere.

Loraine and the Little People, 1915, illustrations by M. T. Ross, first edition: $200.00

Loraine and the Little People of Spring, 1918, illustrations by Ella Dolbear Lee, first edition: $60.00

Loraine and the Little People of Summer, 1920, illustrations by James McCracken, first edition: $40.00

Loraine and the Little People of the Ocean, 1922, illustrations by James McCracken, first edition: $40.00

LORAINE SERIES, Elizabeth Gordon, *Loraine and the Little People of Spring*

LORD OF THE RINGS SERIES, J.R.R. Tolkien, *Hobbit*

LORD OF THE RINGS SERIES, J.R.R. Tolkien, originally published by George Allen & Unwin, London, and Houghton Mifflin, Boston. *The Hobbit* was written in the 1930s as a single novel. In the 1950s, the *Lord of the Rings* trilogy was published, continuing the adventures of the *Hobbit* characters. With the advent of the film series, first edition prices escalated and continue to change.

Lord of the Rings, Hobbit novel:

Hobbit, 1937, Unwin, first edition, 1,500 copies printed with dust jacket, has been auctioned in the $20,000.00 range.

Hobbit, 1938, Houghton Mifflin, first American edition, and also the first illustrated edition, about 5,000 copies. With good dust jacket, this is an auction item and price varies widely, usually in the thousands.

Hobbit, 1966 – 1967, Houghton Mifflin, US, and Unwin, UK, revised edition (also called second or third editions) containing a new foreword, first printing stated on copyright page, with dust jacket: $200.00. Later printings with dust jacket: $35.00

Hobbit, 1977, Harry Abrams, color illustrations taken from the Rankin/Bass animated film. With painted acetate dust jacket: $75.00

Lord of the Rings, trilogy:

Fellowship of the Ring, volume 1, 1953, George Allen & Unwin, red cloth, first edition with dust jacket: $14,000.00

Fellowship of the Ring, 1967, Houghton Mifflin, US, and George Allen & Unwin,

UK, revised second edition, black cloth hardcover, first printing stated on copyright page, pull-out map intact, with dust jacket: $200.00. Without dust jacket: $50.00

Two Towers, volume 2, 1954, George Allen & Unwin, red cloth, dust jacket: $14,000.00

Two Towers, 1967, Houghton Mifflin, US, and George Allen & Unwin, UK, revised second edition, first printing stated on copyright page, with dust jacket: $200.00

Return of the King, volume 3, 1955, George Allen & Unwin, red cloth: $12,000.00

Return of the King, 1967, Houghton Mifflin, US, and George Allen & Unwin, UK, revised second edition, first printing stated on copyright page, with dust jacket: $200.00

Lord of the Rings, complete set, volume 1 through 3, 1953 – 1955, George Allen & Unwin, red cloth, gilt lettering on covers, folding maps, first edition thus with dust jackets: $60,000.00

Lord of the Rings, complete set, volumes 1 through 3, 1967, Houghton Mifflin, US, and George Allen & Unwin, UK, revised second edition, first printing clearly stated on copyright page, with dust jackets: $700.00

Lord of the Rings complete set, volumes 1 through 3, 1967, Houghton Mifflin, book club editions, three volumes in slipcase: $75.00

Lord of the Rings, related books:

Adventures of Tom Bombadil and Other Verses from the Red Book, 1963, Riverside Press, Cambridge, first English edition with dust jacket: $150.00

Simarillion, 1977, George Allen & Unwin, hardcover, first edition with dust jacket: $40.00

Lord of the Rings, other:

Tolkien Bestiary, David Day, 1979, Mitchell Beazley, London, hardcover, 287 pages, hundreds of color and b/w illustrations by numerous illustrators, a fun encyclopedia of beasts and monsters found in Middle Earth, with dust jacket: $30.00

LOST PLANET SERIES, Angus MacVicar, published 1953-1964 by Burke. In this British science fiction series, teenager Jeremy Grant eventually works his way up to becoming a space agent. Like many series, the later titles seem to be the hardest to find and may command higher prices, first edition with dust jacket: $40.00

Lost Planet

Return to the Lost Planet

Secret of the Lost Planet

Red Fire on the Lost Planet

Peril on the Lost Planet

Space Agent from the Lost Planet

Space Agent and the Isles of Fire

Space Agent and the Ancient Peril

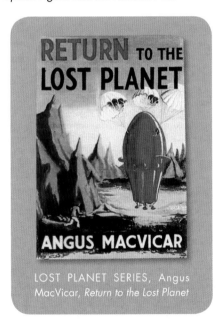

LOST PLANET SERIES, Angus MacVicar, *Return to the Lost Planet*

LUCKY STARR SERIES, Paul French (pseudonym of Isaac Asimov), Doubleday, hardcover, first edition listing appears on copyright page. Adventures of space ranger David "Lucky" Starr. Reissued in hardcover by Twayne in 1970s, later issued in paperback format by Signet, Fawcett, Ballantine, and Bantam Books double volumes under Asimov's name.

LUCKY STARR SERIES, Paul French, *Lucky Starr and the Rings of Saturn*

Doubleday hardcovers with dust jackets: $150.00

Twayne hardcovers with dust jackets: $35.00

Lucky Starr titles:

David Starr, Space Ranger, 1952

Lucky Starr and the Pirates of the Asteroids, 1953

Lucky Starr and the Oceans of Venus, 1954

Lucky Starr and the Big Sun of Mercury, 1956

Lucky Starr and the Moons of Jupiter, 1957

Lucky Starr and the Rings of Saturn, 1958

MADELINE SERIES, Ludwig Bemelmans, oversize picture books with color illustrated hardcovers and endpapers, and color illustrations throughout by author. The first book was published in 1939.

These books are constantly reprinted, usually in full-size reproductions of the originals, including same-as-cover dust jackets and used copies are usually available below cover price.

MADELINE SERIES, Ludwig Bemelmans, *Madeline in London*

Madeline, 1939, Simon & Schuster, first state, first edition shows 12 little girls in the picture illustrating "They went home and broke their bread." The author/illustrator corrected this to 11 little girls in later editions as Madeline is in the hospital at this point in the story. First edition, first state, with dust jacket: $800.00

Madeline, 1939, Simon & Schuster, 46 pages, with illustration corrected to 11 little girls illustrating the line "They went home and broke their bread," first edition thus with dust jacket: $300.00

Madeline's Rescue, 1953, Viking Press, first American edition with dust jacket: $400.00

Madeline and the Bad Hat, 1957, Viking Press, first American edition with dust jacket: $400.00

Madeline and the Gypsies, 1959, Andre Deutsch, UK first edition with dust jacket: $75.00

Madeline in London, 1961, Viking Press, first US edition, and 1962, Andre Deutsch, first UK edition, with dust jacket: $75.00

Madeline's Christmas, first published as a special Christmas insert, 1956, *McCall's Magazine* Christmas edition, issued with envelope, 24 pages, insert without envelope: $350.00

Madeline's Christmas, 1985, Viking Press, first edition with dust jacket: $50.00

MAGIC MOSCOW SERIES, Daniel Manus Pinkwater, ca. 1980, Four Winds Press, humorous science fiction by the author of the *Blue Moose Series.* The Magic Moscow restaurant is "transported through space to compete in an intergalactic junk food cooking contest." Hardcover, under 100 pages, for young readers, dust jacket art by the author.

Magic Moscow, 1980, first edition with dust jacket: $50.00

Attila the Pun, 1981, first edition with dust jacket: $50.00

Slaves of Spiegel, 1982, first edition with dust jacket: $30.00

MAGIC MOSCOW SERIES, Daniel Manus Pinkwater, *Slaves of Spiegel*

MAGIC SERIES, Ruth Chew, author/illustrator, dust jacket and b/w illustrations by author. The series has continued in Scholastic's paperback line.

First edition hardcover with dust jacket: $75.00

Later edition hardcover with dust jacket: $40.00

Trouble with Magic, 1976, Scholastic

Summer Magic, 1977, Scholastic

Magic Cave, 1978, Hastings House, originally published as *Hidden Cave*, 1973, Scholastic

Earthstar Magic, 1979, Hastings House

Secondhand Magic, 1981, Holiday House

Mostly Magic, 1982, Holiday House

Do-It-Youself Magic, 1987, Hastings House

MAGIC SERIES, Andre Norton, six titles. Time travel fantasies where the children discover an object to send them into the past or into adventures inspired by mythology. Used reprints available below cover price.

Steel Magic, 1965, World (also published as *Gray Magic,* paperback, Scholastic), first edition stated on copyright page, first edition with dust jacket: $150.00

Octagon Magic, 1967, World, illustrated by Mac Conner, first has no other printings listed on copyright page, first edition with dust jacket: $100.00

Fur Magic, 1968, World, illustrated by John Kaufmann, first has no other printings listed on copyright page, first edition with dust jacket: $100.00

Dragon Magic, 1972, Crowell, illustrated by Robin Jacques, first has number code "1" on copyright page, first edition with dust jacket: $100.00

Lavender Green Magic, 1974, Crowell, illustrated by Judith G. Brown, first has number code "1" on copyright page, first edition with dust jacket: $100.00

Red Hart Magic, 1976, Crowell, illustrated by Donna Diamond, first has number code "1" on copyright page, first edition with dust jacket: $100.00

MAGIC SERIES, Andre Norton, *Dragon Magic*

MAIL PILOT SERIES, Lewis E. Theiss, Wilde, Boston, gray hardcover with photo illustrations, see PEE WEE DEWIRE for overlapping characters, with stories of the WWII volunteer civil air patrol, with dust jacket: $100.00

Flying the US Mail to South America, 1934

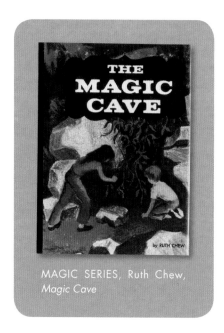

MAGIC SERIES, Ruth Chew, *Magic Cave*

MAIL PILOT SERIES, Lewis E. Theiss, *Flood Mappers Aloft*

Mail Pilot of the Caribbean, 1935

Flying Explorer, 1936

From Coast to Coast with the US Mail, 1936

Flood Mappers Aloft, 1937

Wings Over the Andes, 1939

MALORY TOWERS SERIES, Enid Blyton, ca. 1945 – 1950s, Metheun, small hardcover, b/w illustrations by Stanley Lloyd, map and illustration of the school and grounds on the endpapers. It's off to boarding school for young Darrell Rivers. First edition with dust jacket: $100.00

First Term at Malory Towers

Second Form at Malory Towers

Third Year at Malory Towers

Upper Fourth at Malory Towers

In the Fifth at Malory Towers

Last Term at Malory Towers

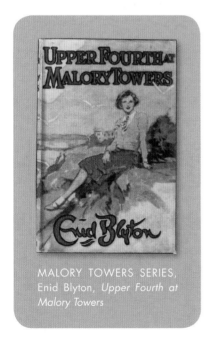

MALORY TOWERS SERIES, Enid Blyton, *Upper Fourth at Malory Towers*

MANDRAKE THE MAGICIAN SERIES, Lee Falk, author, Phil Davis, illustrator, based on the long-running newspaper comic strip featuring a stage magician who uses real magic to catch criminals.

Mandrake titles, Better Little Books:

Mandrake the Magician, ca. 1939, Whitman #1167: $50.00

Mandrake the Magician, Mightly Solver of Mysteries, ca. 1940s, Whitman #1454: $50.00

Mandrake the Magician and the Midnight Monster, ca. 1940s, Whitman #1431: $50.00

Mandrake the Magician and the Flame Pearls, 1946 Whitman, #1418: $50.00

MARCY RHODES SERIES, Rosamund DuJardin (1902 – 1963), 1950s, Lippincott, hardcover, first edition with dust jacket: $35.00

Wait for Marcy, 1950

Marcy Catches Up, 1952

Man for Marcy, 1954

Senior Prom, 1957

MARK TIDD SERIES, Clarence Kelland, 1913 – 1928, Harper & Brothers, pictorial hardcover, illustrated endpapers in some, b/w illustrations. In each book the protagonist explains, "My name is Marcus Aurelius Fortunatus Tidd. My f-f-friends call me Mark Tidd." Early printing with dust jacket: $125.00. Without dust jacket: $65.00

Grosset, orange hardcover, pictorial endpapers, frontispiece, with dust jacket: $75.00

MARLOWS SERIES, Antonia Forest, 1948 – 1976, Faber and Faber, London. Although the author never meant to write a series, new accounts of the eight Marlow children appeared regularly. Editions are not always clearly marked. Prices in England tend to be double that of American prices.

First editions with dust jackets start at: $100.00

Later editions with dust jackets: $35.00

MARLOWS SERIES, Antonia Forest, *Thuggery Affair*

Autumn Term, 1948

Marlows and the Traitor, 1953

Falconer's Lure: Story of a Summer Holiday, 1957

End of Term, 1959

Peter's Room, 1961

Thuggery Affair, 1965

Ready-Made Family, 1967

Cricket Term, 1974

Attic Term, 1976

Marlows, related books:

Player's Boy, 1970, Faber, first edition with dust jacket: $50.00

Players and the Rebels, 1971, Faber, first with dust jacket: $50.00

MARS SERIES, Edgar Rice Burroughs, author of the *Tarzan* books.

First editions of the *Mars* books are scarce and prices for first editions with their original dust jackets often run into the thousands. The earlier books were reprinted often but slight variations can help the collector identify exact printings. For collectors dealing in rare books price ranges, more detailed descriptions than can be given

MARS SERIES, Edgar Rice Burroughs, *Thuvia, Maid of Mars*, 1920s

here will be required, and can be found in publications dedicated to Burroughs' work and to rare book collections.

The *Mars* books were written for adults, usually appearing as stories and serials in magazines such as *All-Story, Argosy, Blue Book,* and *Amazing Stories,* before appearing in hardbound novel form. Like the *Tarzan* books, their fast-paced, action-packed stories soon became favorites of young readers.

The following is a list of the titles, dates, and publishers of the ten *Mars* books written by the creator of *Tarzan.*

Except when stated otherwise:

Grosset & Dunlap reprints without dust jackets: $15.00 to $30.00.

Edgar Rice Burroughs reprints without dust jackets: $20.00 to $45.00.

Mars, book 1:

Princess of Mars, 1917, McClurg, brown cloth-over-board cover with red lettering, five sepia plates by Frank Schoonover, dust jacket: $5,000.00. Without dust jacket: $400.00.

Princess of Mars, 1918 – 1940, Grosset & Dunlap editions, cloth-over-board cover, b/w plates by Frank Schoonover. Redesign of dust jacket by Schoonover, using orig-

inal illustration but changing the placement of lettering, with dust jacket: $60.00

Princess of Mars, 1940, Grosset & Dunlap edition, blue cloth-over-board cover, no illustrations, with Schoonover dust jacket: $50.00

Princess of Mars, 1948, Edgar Rice Burroughs edition, tan cloth-over-board cover, frontispiece by Schoonover, with dust jacket: $75.00

Mars, book 2:

Gods of Mars, 1918, McClurg, dark red cloth-over-board cover, black lettering, sepia frontispiece by Schoonover, with dust jacket: $5,000.00. Without dust jacket: $150.00

Gods of Mars, 1920s – 1930s, Grosset & Dunlap editions, cloth-over-board cover, frontispiece by Schoonover, with dust jacket: $60.00

Gods of Mars, 1940, Grosset & Dunlap edition, green cloth-over-board cover, no frontispiece, Schoonover dust jacket: $35.00

Gods of Mars, 1948, Edgar Rice Burroughs edition, tan cloth-over-board cover, frontispiece by Schoonover, with dust jacket: $50.00

Mars, book 3:

Warlord of Mars, 1919, McClurg, red cloth-over-board cover with gold lettering, sepia frontispiece and dust jacket by J. Allen St. John, with dust jacket: $4,000.00. Without dust jacket: $175.00

Warlord of Mars, 1920, Methuen, UK, hardcover: $45.00

Warlord of Mars, 1920s – 1930s, Grosset & Dunlap editions, cloth-over-board cover, frontispiece by J. Allen St. John, with dust jacket: $50.00

Warlord of Mars, 1940, Grosset & Dunlap edition, cloth-over-board cover, no frontispiece, with dust jacket: $35.00

Warlord of Mars, 1948, Edgar Rice Burroughs, tan cloth-over-board cover, fron-

tispiece by J. Allen St. John, with dust jacket: $75.00

Mars, book 4:

Thuvia, Maid of Mars, 1920, McClurg, yellow-green cloth-over-board cover with black lettering, ten sepia plates by J. Allen St. John, dust jacket by P. J. Monahan, with dust jacket: $4,000.00. Without dust jacket: $120.00.

Thuvia, Maid of Mars, 1920s – 1930s, Grosset & Dunlap editions, cloth-over-board cover, four b/w plates by J. Allen St. John, variations of the Monahan dust jacket, with dust jacket: $50.00

Thuvia, Maid of Mars, 1940, Grosset & Dunlap edition, red cloth-over-board cover, no plates, with dust jacket: $35.00

Thuvia, Maid of Mars, 1948, Edgar Rice Burroughs, tan cloth-over-board cover, frontispiece by J. Allen St. John, with dust jacket: $100.00

Mars, book 5:

Chessmen of Mars, 1922, McClurg, red cloth-over-board cover with black lettering, eight sepia plates by J. Allen St. John. Dust jacket by J. Allen St. John, with dust jacket: $4,000.00. Without dust jacket: $75.00

Chessmen of Mars, 1923, Methuen UK first edition, hardcover with St. John illustrations, with dust jacket: $1,200.00. Without dust jacket: $75.00

Chessmen of Mars, 1920s – 1930s, Grosset & Dunlap editions, cloth-over-board cover, four b/w plates by J. Allen St. John, dust jacket by J. Allen St. John, with dust jacket: $55.00

Chessmen of Mars, 1940, Grosset & Dunlap edition, red cloth-over-board cover, with dust jacket by J. Allen St. John: $35.00

Chessmen of Mars, 1948, Edgar Rice Burroughs, tan cloth-over-board cover, frontispiece by J. Allen St. John, with dust jacket: $75.00

Mars, book 6:

Master Mind of Mars, 1928, McClurg, orange cloth-over-board cover with black lettering, b/w drawings on title page, five b/w illustrations with yellow background by J. Allen St. John, dust jacket by St. John (Robert Zeuschner states that only 5,000 copies of this edition were printed), with dust jacket: $4,000.00. Without dust jacket: $250.00

Master Mind of Mars, 1920s – 1930s, Grosset & Dunlap editions, cloth-over-board cover, five b/w illustrations by J. Allen St. John, with dust jacket: $65.00

Master Mind of Mars, 1948, Edgar Rice Burroughs, tan cloth-over-board cover, title page illustration by J. Allen St. John, with dust jacket: $75.00

Mars, book 7:

Fighting Man of Mars, 1931, Metropolitan, textured red cloth-over-board cover with green lettering, b/w frontispiece by Hugh Hutton, dust jacket by Hutton: $4,000.00. Without dust jacket: $250.00

Fighting Man of Mars, 1932, John Lane, UK first edition, hardcover: $60.00

Fighting Man of Mars, 1932, Grosset & Dunlap edition, labeled "Grosset" on dust jacket and hardcover, retains Metropolitan title page, red cloth-over-board cover, frontispiece and dust jacket design from first edition: $100.00

MARS SERIES, Edgar Rice Burroughs, *Fighting Man of Mars*

Fighting Man of Mars, 1948, Edgar Rice Burroughs, tan cloth-over-board cover, frontispiece and dust jacket from first edition: $75.00

Mars, book 8:

Swords of Mars, 1936, Edgar Rice Burroughs, blue cloth with orange lettering, five b/w plates by J. Allen St. John, wraparound dust jacket illustration by J. Allen St. John, with dust jacket: $2,000.00. Without dust jacket: $60.00

Swords of Mars, 1937, Grosset & Dunlap edition, red cloth-over-board cover, five b/w plates by J. Allen St. John, with wraparound dust jacket illustration by St. John: $150.00

Swords of Mars, 1938, Grosset & Dunlap edition, red cloth-over-board cover, two illustrations by J. Allen St. John, wraparound dust jacket illustration by St. John, with dust jacket: $100.00

Swords of Mars, 1948, Edgar Rice Burroughs edition, tan cloth-over-board cover, wraparound dust jacket illustration by St. John with slight variation, with dust jacket: $85.00

Mars, book 9:

Synthetic Men of Mars, 1940, Edgar Rice Burroughs, blue cloth-over-board cover with orange lettering, five b/w plates by John Coleman Burroughs, with dust jacket by J. C. Burroughs: $600.00. Without dust jacket: $60.00

Synthetic Men of Mars, 1948, Edgar Rice Burroughs edition, tan cloth-over-board cover, frontispiece by John Coleman Burroughs, with dust jacket by Burroughs: $90.00

Mars, book 10:

Llana of Gathol, 1948, Edgar Rice Burroughs, blue cloth-over-board cover with red lettering, five b/w plates by John Coleman Burroughs, with dust jacket by Burroughs: $200.00. Without dust jacket: $75.00

Mars, other:

John Carter of Mars, ca. 1940s, Whitman Better Little Books #1431, color pictorial cardboard cover, small, b/w illustrations: $100.00

Mars, Canaveral reprints:

1960s, hardcover reissues of many then out-of-print Burroughs novels, often with new dust jacket and interior illustration art, with dust jacket: $55.00

Mars, 1970s, book club editions, Doubleday Science Fiction Book Club, plain hardcover, dust jacket illustrated by Frank Frazetta, with dust jacket: under $30.00

Mars, reference:

Edgar Rice Burroughs, the Exhaustive Scholar's and Collector's Descriptive Bibliography, Robert B. Zeuschner, 1996, McFarland & Co., hardcover, 237 pages, b/w photos of book covers, complete explanations of editions: $70.00

Edgar Rice Burroughs Library of Illustration, Russ Cochran, publisher and editor, 1976 – 1985. Three volumes, limited edition of 2,000 copies, books reproduced original artwork that appeared in the *Tarzan* and *Mars* series as drawn from Burroughs' private collection. Hardcover, folio, slipcase. Set of three volumes: $800.00

MARTIN HOPKINS SERIES, also called *Power of Five* Series, Anthony Horowitz, Putnam Pacer, US, and Methuen, UK, hardcover. Thirteen-year-old Martin draws on the power of a Druidic stone circle to defeat the black magic of his guardian.

MARTIN HOPKINS SERIES, Anthony Horowitz, *Night of the Scorpion*

Methuen, UK, first edition with dust jacket: $40.00

Devil's Door-Bell, 1983

Night of the Scorpion, 1984

Silver Citadel, 1987

MARY FRANCES SERIES, Jane Eayre Fryer, Winston, cloth-over-board cover with paste-on-pictorial, illustrated endpapers, color illustrations throughout. The *Mary Frances* books are now being reprinted.

Mary Frances Garden Book, or, *Adventures among the Garden People*, 1916, color illustrations by William Zwirner, early editions with dust jacket: $200.00. Without dust jacket: $100.00

Mary Frances Housekeeper Book, or, *Adventures among the Doll People*, 250 pages, early editions with dust jacket: $250.00. Without dust jacket: $150.00

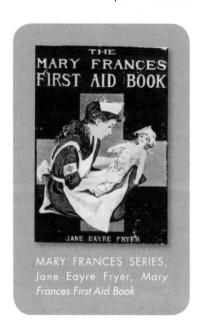

MARY FRANCES SERIES, Jane Eayre Fryer, *Mary Frances First Aid Book*

Mary Frances Sewing Book, 1913, Winston, color illustrations by Jane Allen Boyer, early editions with dust jacket: $200.00. Without dust jacket: $100.00

Mary Frances Cook Book, or, *Adventures among the Kitchen People*, 170 pages, illustrations by Margaret Hayes and Jane Allen Boyer, early editions with dust jacket: $200.00. Without dust jacket: $100.00

Mary Frances First Aid Book, 1916, color frontispiece, blue type, blue/red line drawings by Jane Allen Boyer, early editions with dust jacket: $300.00. Without dust jacket: $200.00

Mary Frances Storybook, 1921, illustrated by Edwin Prittie, early editions with dust jacket: $100.00. Without dust jacket: $50.00

MARY LOUISE SERIES, Edith Van Dyne, (pseudonym of L. Frank Baum who began the series, titles after 1919 were written by Emma Sampson), Reilly, Chicago, first edition: $70.00

Mary Louise, 1916

Mary Louise in the Country, 1916

Mary Louise Solves a Mystery, 1917

Mary Louise and the Liberty Girls, 1918

Mary Louise Adopts a Soldier, 1919

Mary Louise Stands the Test, 1919

Mary Louise at Dorfield, 1920

MARY POPPINS SERIES, P. L. Travers, illustrated by Mary Shepard, magical Mary Poppins is probably the most famous English nanny in children's literature, and has inspired the Disney film and many toys.

Numerous reprints available, most use the original dust jacket designs.

Some first edition prices:

MARY POPPINS SERIES, P. L. Travers, *Mary Poppins Comes Back*

Mary Poppins, 1934, Gerald Howe, London, yellow cloth with illustration on front cover, gray and yellow dust jacket, first edition with dust jacket: $4,000.00

Mary Poppins, 1934, Reynal & Hitchcock, New York, blue hardcover, pictorial endpapers, full-page and small b/w drawings throughout, first US edition, with dust jacket: $500.00

Mary Poppins Comes Back, 1935, Lovat Dickson & Thompson, first UK edition, with dust jacket: $500.00

Mary Poppins Comes Back, 1935, Reynal & Hitchcock, New York, first US edition, with dust jacket: $200.00

Mary Poppins and *Mary Poppins Comes Back*, 1937, Reynal & Hitchcock, New York, oversize, illustrations in color, first edition, with dust jacket: $75.00

Mary Poppins Opens the Door, 1943 Reynal & Hitchcock, New York, gray hardcover, pictorial endpapers, illustrated by Shepard and Agnes Sims, US first edition with dust jacket: $300.00

Mary Poppins in the Park, 1952, Peter Davies, London, embossed hardcover, illustrated endpapers, yellow dust jacket, UK first edition with dust jacket: $150.00

Mary Poppins in the Park, 1952, Harcourt Brace, light blue-gray cloth hardcover, pink endpapers, 235 pages, pink and black dust jacket, first US edition, with dust jacket: $250.00

Mary Poppins from A to Z, 1962, Collins, pink hardcover, UK first edition with dust jacket: $150.00

Mary Poppins from A to Z, 1962, Harcourt, yellow hardcover, blue pictorial endpapers, blue dust jacket, US first edition with dust jacket: $300.00

Mary Poppins in the Kitchen, a Cookery Book with a Story, 1975, Harcourt Brace, pink and white cloth hardcover, 122 pages, first edition with dust jacket: $75.00. Without dust jacket: $30.00

Mary Poppins in the Cherry Tree, 1982, Delacorte Press, glossy pictorial hardcover, oversize, 90 pages, first edition with dust jacket: $40.00

Mary Poppins and the House Next Door, 1988, HarperCollins, UK, and 1989, Delacorte Press, US, pictorial hardcover, Mary Shepard illustrations, first edition with dust jacket: $80.00. Without dust jacket: $40.00

MATTHEW LOONEY SERIES, Jerome Beatty, Jr., 1960s, William R. Scott, Matthew and his uncle, Lockhard, travel from their home on the moon to explore Earth, b/w drawings throughout by Gahan Wilson, first edition with dust jacket: $60.00

Matthew Looney's Voyage to Earth, 1961

Matthew Looney's Invasion of the Earth, 1965

Matthew Looney and the Space Pirates, 1972

MATTHEW LOONEY SERIES, Jerome Beatty, Jr., *Matthew Looney's Invasion of the Earth*

MEG AND MOG SERIES, Helen Nicoll, Heinemann, UK, Atheneum, US, comic illustrations by Jan Pienkowski of an unskilled witch and her cat, pictorial hardcover, five titles: $60.00

Meg and Mog, 1972

Meg's Eggs, 1972

Meg at Sea, 1973

Meg on the Moon, 1973

Meg's Castle, 1975

MEL MARTIN BASEBALL SERIES, John Cooper (Stratemeyer Syndicate pseudonym), 1947 – 1953, Cupples & Leon, hardcover, six titles. Baseball-related mystery stories. Reprints by Garden City or Books Inc., Cupples & Leon editions with dust jacket: $30.00

MELENDY FAMILY SERIES, Elizabeth Enright, Holt, Rinehart, hardcover, illustrated by author, early edition with dust jacket: $100.00

Saturdays, 1941

Four Story Mistake, 1942

Then There Were Five, 1944

Spiderweb for Two, 1951

MELLOPS SERIES, Tomi Ungerer, Harper, oversize hardcovers, color illustrations by author, adventures of a pig family, first edition with dust jacket: $80.00

Mellops Go Diving for Treasure, 1957

Mellops Go Flying, 1957

Mellops Strike Oil, 1958

Christmas Eve at the Mellops', 1960

Mellops Go Spelunking, 1963

MELODY LANE MYSTERY SERIES, Lilian Garis, ca. 1930s, Grosset & Dunlap, eight titles, with dust jacket: $50.00

Ghost of Melody Lane

Forbidden Trail

Tower Secret

Wild Warning

Terror at Moaning Cliff

Drogon of the Hills

Mystery of Stingyman's Alley

Secret of the Kashmir Shawl

MIKE MARS SERIES, Donald A. Wollheim, Doubleday, hardcover, color illustrated endpapers, b/w illustrations by Albert Orbaan, first editions identified on copyright page. Astronaut adventures. Later paperbacks published by Paperback Library update, Cape Canaveral to Cape Kennedy.

Doubleday first edition with dust jacket: $40.00

Mike Mars, Astronaut, 1961

Mike Mars Flies the X-15, 1961

Mike Mars at Cape Canaveral, 1961

Mike Mars in Orbit, 1961

Mike Mars Flies the Dyna-soar, 1962

Mike Mars, South Pole Spaceman, 1962

Mike Mars and the Mystery Satellite, 1963

Mike Mars Around the Moon, 1964

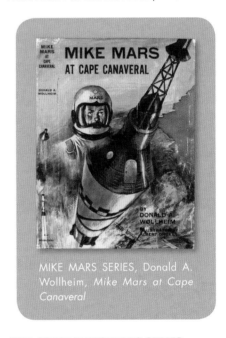

MIKE MARS SERIES, Donald A. Wollheim, *Mike Mars at Cape Canaveral*

MILL CREEK IRREGULARS SERIES, August Derleth, first eight titles published by Duell Sloan and Pearce, first edition with dust jacket: $60.00

Moon Tenders, 1958

Mill Creek Irregulars, Special Detectives, 1959

MILL CREEK IRREGULARS SERIES, August Derleth, *Moon Tenders*

Pinkertons Ride Again, 1960

Ghost of Black Hawk Island, 1961

Tent Show Summer, 1963

Irregulars Strike Again, 1964

House by the River, 1965

Watcher on the Heights, 1966

Mill Creek, additional titles:

Prince Goes West, 1968, Meredith Press

Three Straw Men, 1968, Candlelight Press

MILLERS SERIES, Alberta Constant, Crowell, hardcover, first edition with dust jacket: $40.00

Those Miller Girls, 1965

Motoring Millers, 1969

Does Anybody Care About Lou Emma Miller?, 1979

MILLY-MOLLY-MANDY SERIES, Joyce Lankester Brisley, author/artist, studied art in London and, with her two artist sisters, had paintings hung at the Royal Academy. She wrote and illustrated many single titles, as well as this popular series.

Harrap, London, small hardcover with color frontispiece and b/w illustrations

by author, early editions with dust jacket: $70.00

McKay and Australian reprints with dust jacket: $30.00

Milly-Molly-Mandy Stories, 1928, through *Milly-Molly-Mandy and Billy Blunt*, 1967

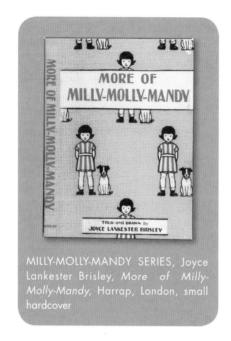

MILLY-MOLLY-MANDY SERIES, Joyce Lankester Brisley, *More of Milly-Molly-Mandy*, Harrap, London, small hardcover

MISS FLORA MCFLIMSEY SERIES, Mariana (Foster), Lothrop, Lee & Shepard, small square hardcover, watercolor illustrations, stories of an old attic doll.

First editions of 1940s and 1950s titles, with dust jackets: $100.00

First editions of 1960s and 1970s titles, with dust jackets: $70.00

Miss Flora McFlimsey's Christmas Eve, 1949

Miss Flora McFlimsey's Easter Bonnet, 1951

Miss Flora McFlimsey and the Baby New Year, 1951

Miss Flora McFlimsey's Birthday, 1952

Miss Flora McFlimsey and Little Laughing Water, 1954

Miss Flora McFlimsey and the Little Red Schoolhouse, 1957

MISS FLORA MCFLIMSEY SERIES, Mariana (Foster), *Miss Flora McFlimsey and the Little Red Schoolhouse*, and *Miss Flora McFlimsey and Little Laughing Water*

Miss Flora McFlimsey's Valentine, 1962

Miss Flora McFlimsey's May Day, 1969

Miss Flora McFlimsey's Halloween, 1972

MISS MINERVA SERIES, created by Frances Boyd Calhoun (1867 – 1909, b. Virginia), who wrote the first title, but died the year of its publication. Emma Speed Sampson continued the series through the 1920s. Reilly & Lee, red hardcover with black lettering and illustration, b/w drawings thoughout. Illustrator for the Sampson titles was Wiliam Donahey, 12 titles plus a cookbook.

First edition with dust jacket: $200.00

Early printings with dust jackets: $70.00

Miss Minerva and William Green Hill, 1909, illustrated by Angus MacDonall

Billy and the Major, 1919

Miss Minerva's Baby, 1920

Miss Minerva and the Old Plantation, 1923

Miss Minerva Broadcasts Billy, 1925

Miss Minerva's Scallywags, 1927

Miss Minerva's Neighbors, 1929

Miss Minerva Goin' Places, 1931

Miss Minerva's Cookbook, 1931

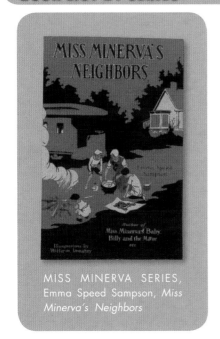

MISS MINERVA SERIES, Emma Speed Sampson, *Miss Minerva's Neighbors*

Miss Minerva's Mystery, 1933

Miss Minerva's Problem, 1936

Miss Minerva's Vacation, 1939

MISS PENNYFEATHER SERIES, Eileen O'Faolain, young Garrett has a number of magical adventures based on traditional Irish fairy tales.

Little Black Hen, 1940, Random House, illustrated by Aldren Watson, first edition with dust jacket: $50.00

Little Black Hen, 1943, Oxford University Press, UK, illustrated boards, color and b/w illustrations by Trefor Jones: $50.00

King of Cats, 1942, Morrow, b/w illustrations by Vera Bock, first edition with dust jacket: $150.00

Miss Pennyfeather and the Pooka, 1946, Random House, two-color illustrations by Aldren Watson, first edition with dust jacket: $50.00

MISS PICKERELL SERIES, Ellen MacGregor and Dora Pantell, Whittlesey House and McGraw-Hill, hardcover with b/w illustrations, with dust jacket: $35.00

Miss Pickerell books, illustrated by Paul Galdone:

Miss Pickerell Goes to Mars, 1951

Miss Pickerell and the Geiger Counter, 1953

Miss Pickerell Goes Undersea, 1953

Miss Pickerell Goes to the Arctic, 1954

Miss Pickerell books, illustrated by Charles Geer:

Miss Pickerell on the Moon, 1965

Miss Pickerell Goes on a Dig, 1966

Miss Pickerell Harvests the Sea, 1968

Miss Pickerell and the Weather Satellite, 1971

Miss Pickerell Meets Mr. H.U.M., 1974

Miss Pickerell Takes the Bull by the Horns, 1976

Miss Pickerell to the Earthquake Rescue, 1977

Miss Pickerell and the Super Tanker, 1978

Miss Pickerell Tackles the Energy Crisis, 1980

Miss Pickerell on the Trail, 1982

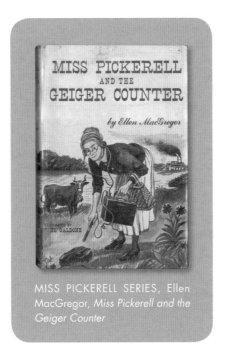

MISS PICKERELL SERIES, Ellen MacGregor, *Miss Pickerell and the Geiger Counter*

Miss Pickerell and the Blue Whales, 1983

Miss Pickerell and the War of the Computers, Dora Pantell, 1985

MISTER PENNY, Marie Ets, Viking Press, illustrated by author, picture book series for young children. Mr. Penny works at the safety pin factory in Waddles.

Mister Penny, 1935, Viking Press, cover is pictorial paper on boards with cloth spine, woodcut illustrations. This is Ets' first children's book, first edition: $60.00

Mister Penny's Race Horse, 1956, Viking Press, first edition, hardcover, illustrated endpapers, illustrations by author, first edition with dust jacket: $50.00

Mister Penny's Circus, 1961, Viking Press, hardcover, illustrations by author, first edition with dust jacket: $40.00

MISTY THE HORSE SERIES, Marguerite Henry, Rand McNally and Macmillan, hardcover, color and b/w illustrations by Wesley Dennis, early edition prices shown with titles.

MISTY THE HORSE SERIES, Marguerite Henry, *Misty of Chincoteague*

Misty of Chincoteague, 1947 (Newbery winner), first edition with dust jacket: $200.00

Sea Star, 1949, first edition with dust jacket: $80.00

Stormy, Misty's Foal, 1963, first edition with dust jacket: $50.00

Misty, related book:

Pictorial Life Story of Misty, 1976, Rand McNally, pictorial hardcover, b/w and color photos and Wesley Dennis illustrations, a "true story" of the pony that inspired the original *Misty* book, first edition: $60.00

MOOMIN SERIES, Tove Jansson, Finland, English translations, light-hearted tales of fantasy folk in snow country, with b/w line drawing illustrations by the author. The daughter of a sculptor and a known artist in her own right, Jansson is most often recognized for her deceptively simple black-and-white drawings of moomins. These friendly trolls populate Jansson's series of books based in part upon her childhood in the Finnish archipelago. There was also a foreign cartoon series and some softcover reading and math workbooks in Japanese in recent years featuring the moomins.

Walck, US, first editions with dust jackets: $50.00

Benn, London, UK, first editions with dust jackets: $60.00

Finn Family Moomintroll, 1950

Comet in Moominland, 1951

Exploits of Moominpappa, 1952

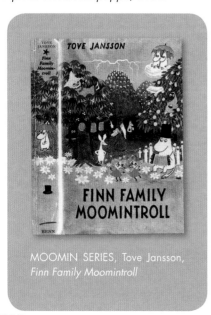

MOOMIN SERIES, Tove Jansson, *Finn Family Moomintroll*

MOOMIN SERIES, Tove Jansson, illustration from *Who Will Comfort Toffle?*

Moominland in Midwinter, 1958

Moominsummer Madness, 1961

Tales from Moominvalley, 1963

Moominpappa at Sea, 1966

Moominvalley in November, 1971

Moomin, related book:

Book about Moomin, Mymble and Little My, 1953, Benn, London, ovesize hardcover, first English edition, cut-outs and color illustrations throughout, text in script, first edition: $300.00, 1996 Blue Lantern reprint edition: $40.00

Who Will Comfort Toffle?, 1960, Benn, London, oversize hardcover, picture book features the search of a small Moomin for a friend, with dust jacket: $300.00

MOON QUEEN BOOKS, T. Benjamin Faucett, ca. 1924, A. L. Burt Publishers, illustrations by author, paper-over-board hardcover, odd tales from the garden: $100.00

Folksy Fruits: Amusing Adventures in Opal Orchard

Brainy Berries: A Night in Crystal Cave

Frolicsome Flowers: They See the Wonderful "Rajah" Rug

Venturous Vegetables at the "Frolic Grounds"

MOON QUEEN BOOKS, T. Benjamin Faucett, *Venturous Vegetables at the "Frolic Grounds"*

MOTHER WEST WIND SERIES, Thornton W. Burgess, ca. 1910 – 1918, Little, Brown, illustrated hardcover, color plates by Harrison Cady, first edition: $100.00

Old Mother West Wind

Mother West Wind's Children

Mother West Wind's Animal Friends

Mother West Wind's Neighbors

Mother West Wind "Why" Stories

Mother West Wind "How" Stories

Mother West Wind "When" Stories

Mother West Wind "Where" Stories

Mother West Wind, 1940s editions with dust jackets: $40.00

Mother West Wind, other:

Old Mother West Wind, 1990, Holt, oversize, color illustrations by Michael Hague, first edition thus, with dust jacket: $50.00

MOTION PICTURE COMRADES SERIES, Elmer Barnes, 1917, New York Book, pictorial hardcover, frontispiece by Lester, with dust jacket: $50.00

Motion Picture Comrades' Great Venture, or, On the Road with the Big Round-Top

Motion Picture Comrades in African Jungles, or, Camera Boys in Wild Animal Land

Motion Picture Comrades along the Orinoco, or, Facing Perils in the Tropics

Motion Picture Comrades aboard a Submarine, or, Searching for Treasure under the Sea

Motion Picture Comrades Producing a Success, or, Featuring a Sensation

MOTOR BOAT BOYS SERIES, Louis Arundel, 1912 – 1915, Donohue, hardcover with *Motor Boat Boys* in white lettering on front and spine, pictorial endpapers, frontispiece, with dust jacket: $30.00

MOTOR BOAT CLUB SERIES, H. Irving Hancock, 1909 – 1912, Altemus, hardcover with printed illustration, b/w frontispiece, with dust jacket: $40.00

MOTOR BOYS SERIES, Clarence Young (Stratemeyer Syndicate pseudonym), ca. 1906 – 1920s, Cupples & Leon, hardcover with printed illustration, four b/w plates, early editions with dust jackets: $75.00

Motor Boys

Motor Boys Overland

Motor Boys in Mexico

Motor Boys Across the Plains

Motor Boys Afloat

Motor Boys on the Atlantic

Motor Boys in Strange Waters

Motor Boys in on the Pacific

Motor Boys in the Clouds

Motor Boys over the Rockies

Motor Boys over the Ocean

Motor Boys on the Wing

Motor Boys After a Fortune

Motor Boys on the Border

Motor Boys under the Sea

Motor Boys on Road and River

Motor Boys at Boxwood Hall

Motor Boys on a Ranch

Motor Boys in the Army

Motor Boys on the Firing Line

Motor Boys Bound for Home

Motor Boys on Thunder Mountain

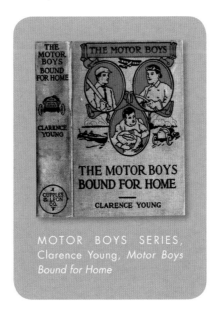

MOTOR BOYS SERIES, Clarence Young, *Motor Boys Bound for Home*

Motor Boys, Second Series, by Clarence Young, ca. 1920, Cupples & Leon, pictorial hardcover, frontispiece, early editions with dust jackets: $75.00

Ned, Bob and Jerry at Boxwood Hall

Ned, Bob and Jerry on the Ranch

Ned, Bob and Jerry in the Army

Ned, Bob and Jerry on the Firing Line

Ned, Bob and Jerry Bound for Home

MOTORCYCLE CHUMS SERIES, Andrew Carey Lincoln, 1912 – 1914, Donohue, khaki pictorial hardcover, pictorial endpa-

MOTORCYCLE CHUMS SERIES, Andrew Carey Lincoln, *Motorcycle Chums on the Santa Fe Trail*

pers, frontispiece by C. H. Lawrence, first edition with dust jacket: $150.00

Motorcycle Chums, first edition without dust jacket: $80.00

Motorcycle Chums in New England

Motorcycle Chums in the Land of the Sky

Motorcycle Chums on the Santa Fe Trail

Motorcycle Chums in Yellowstone Park

Motorcycle Chums in the Adirondacks

Motorcycle Chums Stormbound

MOTOR CYCLE CHUMS SERIES, Lieutenant Howard Payson, 1912, Hurst, pictorial hardcover, four plates by Charles Wrenn, first edition with dust jacket: $250.00

Motor Cycle Chums, without dust jacket: $30.00

Motor Cycle Chums around the World

Motor Cycle Chums of the Northwest Patrol

Motor Cycle Chums in the Goldfields

Motor Cycle Chums Whirlwind Tour

Motor Cycle Chums South of the Equator

MOTOR CYCLE CHUMS SERIES, Lieutenant Howard Payson, *Motor Cycle Chums of the Northwest Patrol*

Motor Cycle Chums through Historic America

MOTOR GIRLS SERIES, Margaret Penrose (Stratemeyer Syndicate pseudonym), ca. 1920s, Cupples & Leon, small size, cloth covers, illustrations, advertised as "No one is better equipped to furnish these tales than Mrs. Penrose who, besides being an able writer, is an expert automobilist," with dust jacket: $40.00

MOTOR MAIDS SERIES, Katherine Stokes, ca. 1911 – 1912, Donohue, blue cloth-over-board cover with impressed illustration, illustrations by Charles Wrenn, four travelers, a chaperone, and a little red car tour the world: $30.00

Hurst edition with pictorial boards has same-design dust jacket: $30.00

MOTOR RANGERS SERIES, Marvin West, 1911 – 1914, Hurst, illustrated cloth-over-board cover, illustrations by Charles Wrenn, with dust jacket: $50.00

MOUNTAIN PONY SERIES, Henry V. Larom, 1946 – 1950, Whittsley, hardcover, with dust jacket: $30.00

MOVING PICTURE BOYS SERIES, Victor Appleton (Stratemeyer Syndicate pseudonym), ca. 1913 – 1920s, Grosset & Dunlap, with dust jacket: $35.00

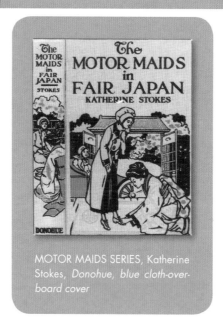

MOTOR MAIDS SERIES, Katherine Stokes, *Donohue, blue cloth-over-board cover*

MR. TITTLEWIT SERIES, Forster M. Knight, mouse adventures in Fern Woods, US and UK first editions with dust jackets: $45.00

Mr. Tittlewit's Holiday, 1940, Lippincott, red pictorial hardcover, illustrated endpapers, color frontispiece, b/w illustrations throughout by author.

Return of Sandypaws, 1942, Lippincott, red hardcover, 151 pages, color frontispiece, illustrated endpapers, b/w illustrations throughout by author.

Mr. Tittlewit's Zoo, undated, ca. 1942, Country Life Ltd, hardcover, illustrated endpapers, color frontispiece, b/w illustrations throughout by author.

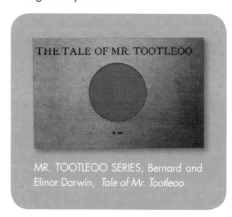

MR. TOOTLEOO SERIES, Bernard and Elinor Darwin, *Tale of Mr. Tootleoo*

MR. TOOTLEOO SERIES, Bernard and Elinor Darwin, fanciful tales of a sailor, illustrations by authors, Nonesuch Press, UK, Harper, US, illustrated oblong over-size hardcover, blue/red color plates.

Nonesuch first edition with dust jacket start at: $400.00

Tale of Mr. Tootleoo, 1925

Tootleoo Two, 1927

Mr. Tootleoo One and Two, 1932

Mr. Tootleoo and Company, 1935

MR. TWIDDLE SERIES, Enid Blyton, ca. 1950s, George Newnes, London, hardcover, illustrated by Hilda McGavin, with dust jacket: $35.00

Hello, Mr. Twiddle!

Well, Really, Mr. Twiddle!

Don't Be Silly, Mr. Twiddle!

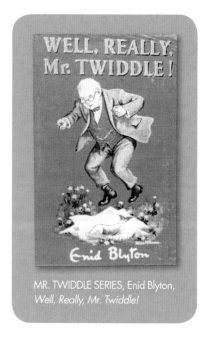

MR. TWIDDLE SERIES, Enid Blyton, *Well, Really, Mr. Twiddle!*

MR. WICKER SERIES, Carley Dawson, 1952 – 1955, three titles. An antique shop sends a young man back in time to the Revolutionary War in the first title of this series.

Mr. Wicker's Window, 1952, Houghton Mifflin, illustrated by Lynd Ward, first edition with dust jacket: $150.00

Sign of the Seven Seas, 1954, Houghton Mifflin, illustrated by Lynd Ward, first edition with dust jacket: $60.00

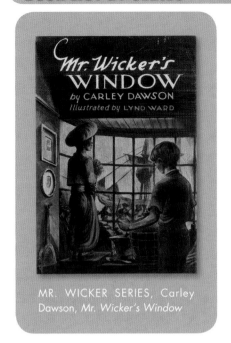

MR. WICKER SERIES, Carley Dawson, Mr. Wicker's Window

Dragon Run, 1955, Houghton Mifflin, illustrated by Lynd Ward, first edition with dust jacket: $50.00

MR. YOWDER SERIES, Glen Rounds, Holiday House, oblong or standard hardcover, b/w illustrations by author, tall tales about Xenon Zebulon Yowder, a sign painter, first edition with dust jacket: $35.00

Mr. Yowder and the Lion Roar Capsules, 1976

Mr. Yowder and the Steamboat, 1977

Mr. Yowder and the Giant Bull Snake, 1978

MR. YOWDER SERIES, Glen Rounds, Mr. Yowder and the Train Robbers

Mr. Yowder and the Train Robbers, 1981

Mr. Yowder and the Windwagon, 1983

MRS. EASTER SERIES, written and illustrated by V. H. Drummond, magical adventures of a proper lady and her young friends.

Faber and Faber, London, oversize, pictorial boards, color illustrations, Kate Greenaway medal winner, first edition with dust jacket: $40.00

A. S. Barnes, US, editions, pictorial paper-over-board hardcover, color illustrations by author: under $30.00

Mrs. Easter's Parasol, 1944

Mrs. Easter and the Storks, 1957

Mrs. Easter and the Golden Bounder, 1970

Mrs. Easter's Christmas Flight, 1972

MRS. EASTER SERIES, V. H. Drummond, Mrs. Easter and the Storks

MRS. GOOSE SERIES, Miriam Clark Potter, hardcover, b/w illustrations by author, funny stories for young readers about Animaltown's residents.

Potter (1886 – 1965) graduated from the University of Minnesota, then began her career in New York City. She wrote and illustrated a daily feature titled Pinafore Pocket for the *New York Evening Post*

MRS. GOOSE SERIES, Miriam Clark Potter, *Mrs. Goose and Three-Ducks*

from 1919 to 1921 and was syndicated in 65 papers. At Lippincott she moved into children's books, writing and illustrating many including her famous *Mrs. Goose* series. Potter drew the pictures and her artist husband, Zenas Potter, inked them for her. He was fond of joking "thinked by you, inked by me!" The Potters freelanced and were able to live in Mexico, Europe, and India, studying the art and culture, and later lived in Carmel, California.

Later reprints with dust jackets: $30.00

Mrs. Goose and Three-Ducks, 1936, Stokes, first edition with dust jacket: $100.00

Mrs. Goose of Animal Town, 1939, Frederick A. Stokes, first edition with dust jacket: $100.00

Hello, Mrs. Goose, 1947, J. B. Lippincott, first edition with dust jacket: $80.00

Here Comes Mrs. Goose, ca. 1951, J. B. Lippincott, illustrated by Miriam and Zenas Potter, first edition with dust jacket: $80.00

Our Friend Mrs. Goose, 1956, J. B. Lippincott, green hardcover, embossed design of Mrs. Goose on front cover, 125 pages, illustrated by Miriam and Zenas Potter, first edition with dust jacket: $80.00

Just Mrs. Goose, 1957, J. B. Lippincott, illustrated by Miriam and Zenas Potter, first edition with dust jacket: $80.00

Queer, Dear Mrs. Goose, 1959, J. B. Lippincott, illustrated by Miriam and Zenas Potter, first edition with dust jacket: $50.00

Goodness, Mrs. Goose!, 1960, J. B. Lippincott, illustrated by Miriam and Zenas Potter, first edition with dust jacket: $50.00

No, No, Mrs. Goose, 1962, J. B. Lippincott, illustrated by Miriam Potter, first edition with dust jacket: $40.00

Goofy Mrs. Goose, 1963, J. B. Lippincott, illustrations by Miriam Potter, first edition with dust jacket: $40.00

Mrs. Goose and Her Funny Friends, 1964, J. B. Lippincott, illustrations by Miriam Potter, first edition with dust jacket: $40.00

MRS. PEPPERPOT SERIES, Alf Proysen, translated from Norwegian by Marianne Helwig, hardcover, b/w illustrations by Bjorn Berg, Sweden, Mrs. Pepperpot has an odd problem with size. Reprints, with dust jacket: $35.00. Titles include:

Little Old Mrs. Pepperpot, 1960, Obolensky, US first edition with dust jacket: $50.00

Mrs. Pepperpot Again, 1961, Obolensky, US first edition with dust jacket: $50.00

Mrs. Pepperpot to the Rescue, 1964, Pantheon, US first edition with dust jacket: $40.00

Mrs. Pepperpot in the Magic Wood, 1968, Pantheon, US first edition with dust jacket: $40.00

Mrs. Pepperpot's Outing, 1971, Pantheon, US first edition with dust jacket: $40.00

Mrs. Pepperpot's Year, 1973, Pantheon, US first edition with dust jacket: $40.00

MRS. PEPPERPOT SERIES, Alf Proysen, *Mrs. Pepperpot in the Magic Wood*, *Mrs. Pepperpot Again*, and *Mrs. Pepperpot to the Rescue*

MRS. PIGGLE-WIGGLE SERIES, Betty MacDonald, Lippincott, and HarperCollins, small, hardcover, about 220 pages, b/w illustrations. Perennial favorite, this series has been reprinted often. Kind Mrs. Piggle-Wiggle, whose husband is away at sea, has odd flashes of magic in her dealings with the neighbor children.

First edition with dust jacket: $200.00

1950s later printings with dust jackets: $40.00

Mrs. Piggle-Wiggle, 1947, hardcover, b/w illustrations by Hilary Knight

Mrs. Piggle-Wiggle's Magic, 1949, b/w illustrations by Hilary Knight

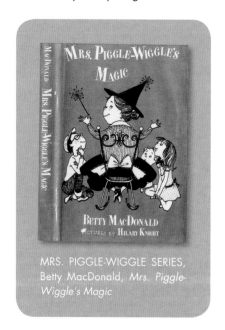

MRS. PIGGLE-WIGGLE SERIES, Betty MacDonald, *Mrs. Piggle-Wiggle's Magic*

Mrs. Piggle-Wiggle's Farm, 1954, green hardcover, b/w illustrations by Maurice Sendak

Hello, Mrs. Piggle-Wiggle, 1957, b/w illustrations by Hilary Knight

MUSHROOM PLANET SERIES, Eleanor Cameron, Little, Brown, hardcover, b/w illustrations, first edition with dust jacket: $200.00

Later printings with dust jackets: $30.00

Wonderful Flight to the Mushroom Planet, 1954, illustrations by Robert Henneberger

Stowaway to the Mushroom Planet, 1956, illustrations by Robert Henneberger

Mr. Bass's Planetoid, 1958, illustrations by Louis Darling

Mystery for Mr. Bass, 1960, illustrations by Leonard Shortall

Time and Mr. Bass, 1967, illustrations by Fred Miese

MUSHROOM PLANET SERIES, Eleanor Cameron, *Mystery for Mr. Bass*

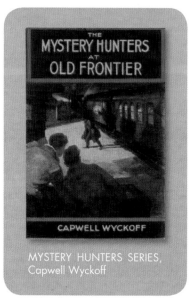

MYSTERY HUNTERS SERIES, Capwell Wyckoff

MY BOOK HOUSE SET, edited by Olive Beaupre Miller, collections of stories, poems, articles for children, ca. 1920, Book House for Children, Chicago, and reprinted periodically with color paste-on-pictorials on covers, color illustrations throughout matched sets:

Early edition set of first six: $200.00. Matched set of twelve volumes: $400.00

Later editions, set of six: $75.00. Set of 12: $195.00

MYSTERY HUNTERS SERIES, Capwell Wyckoff, 1934 – 1936, Burt, dark green hardcover with yellow lettering, pictorial endpapers, frontispiece, with dust jacket: $40.00

MYSTERY STORIES FOR BOYS BOOKS, Roy J. Snell, 1920 – 1939, Reilly & Lee, hardcover, frontispiece by Garrett Price, with dust jacket: $50.00 Triple Spies

Lost in the Air

Panther Eye

Crimson Flash

White Fire

Black Schooner

Hidden Trail

Firebug

Red Lure

Forbidden Cargoes

Johnny Longbow

Rope of Gold

Arrow of Fire

Gray Shadow

Riddle of the Storm

Galloping Ghost

Whispers at Dawn

Mystery Wings

Red Dynamite

Seal of Secrecy

Shadow Passes

Sign of the Green Arrow

MYSTERY STORIES FOR GIRLS BOOKS, Roy J. Snell, 1920 – 1939, Reilly & Lee, hardcover, about 185 pages, with dust jacket: $80.00

Blue Envelope

Cruise of the O'Moo

Secret Mark

Purple Flame

Crimson Thread

Hour of Enchantment

Witches Cove

Gypsy Shawl

Green Eyes

Golden Circle

Magic Curtain

Phantom Violin

Gypsy Flight

Crystal Ball

MYSTERY STORIES FOR GIRLS BOOKS, Roy J. Snell, *Crystal Ball*

MYSTERY STORIES FOR GIRLS BOOKS, ca. 1936, Cupples & Leon, various authors, hardcover with dust jacket: $75.00

Titles include:

Clue at Crooked Lane, Mildred A. Wirt

Hollow Wall Mystery, Mildred A. Wirt

Shadow Stone, Mildred A. Wirt

Wooden Shoe Mystery, Mildred A. Wirt

Through the Moon-Gate Door, Mildred A. Wirt

Secret Stair, Pemberton Ginther

Thirteenth Spoon, Pemberton Ginther

■ ···················· **N** ···················· ■

NANCY AND SLUGGO BOOKS, based on the comic strip characters created by Ernie Bushmiller, sturdy children in real world adventures with zany twists.

Nancy and Sluggo All Picture Comics, Bushmiller, 1946, Whitman Better Little Book #1400, small pictorial hardcover, illustrated: $75.00

Nancy and Sluggo, a Pop-Up Book, 1981, Random House, color illustrations by George Wildman, paper engineering

NANCY AND SLUGGO BOOKS, Nancy paper doll

by Penick, 16 pages, pop-ups and animations: $35.00

Nancy and Sluggo paper dolls:

Nancy Paper Doll, 1971, Whitman, over-size cardboard cover, one doll, six pages of clothes: $40.00

Nancy and Sluggo Paper Dolls, 1974, Whitman, oversize cardboard cover, seven pages of cut-outs: $40.00

NANCY DREW SERIES, Carolyn Keene, pseudonym, 1930 – 1979, Grosset & Dunlap, Edward Stratemeyer syndicated books, early plot outlines by Stratemeyer, plot outlines after 1930 were created by his daughter Harriet S. Adams. Girl sleuth lives with her widowed father who is an attorney, and a motherly house-keeper, and drives around in her own car. See *Penny Nichols* series and *Penny Parker Mystery* series for similar heroines created by Mildred Wirt.

Nancy Drew Scrapbook, by Karen Plunkett Powell, states that the first seven books, and several later books, were written by Mildred Wirt Benson, others were written by Walter Karig, Harriet Adams, Margaret Sherf Beebe, Iris Vinton, possibly Lilian Garis, and other writers, all working from Stratemeyer or Adams outlines. 1930 – 1950, b/w illustrations and color dust jackets by Russell Tandy.

Later illustrators include Bill Gillies and Rudy Nappi. Gillies began a new series of dust jackets in the 1950s and Rudy Nappi did new dust jacket designs in the 1960s. Books issued from 1950 – 1953, had only a frontispiece illustration, books printed after 1954 had six black-and-white illustrations.

In 1962, Grosset & Dunlap dropped the hardcover format with dust jacket and began issuing all titles in the yellow spine picture-cover hardcovers. In 1979, Simon & Schuster began publishing new Drew titles under their Minstrel or Wanderer imprints. Collectors identify "firsts" as books that do not list beyond their own title in the book or dust jacket advertisements.

NANCY DREW SERIES, Carolyn Keene, *Clue in the Diary,* Russell Tandy 1930s dust jacket

For non-firsts, the last title on the dust jacket list helps identify printing date.

Nancy Drew, 1930 – 1950:

Blue hardcovers with dust jackets, first editions: $60.00 to $300.00

Later edition blue hardcovers with dust jackets: $40.00 to $100.00

Nancy Drew, 1950 – 1962, new titles published by Grosset & Dunlap after 1950, unrevised versions have 24 or 25 chapters:

1950 – 1953 blue hardcover, frontispiece illustrations, with dust jackets: $30.00 to $60.00

1952 – 1962 blue tweed hardcovers, six illustrations, with dust jacket: $40.00

Tweed hardcover, 1959 – 1961, text shortened to 20 chapters, with dust jacket: $30.00

Yellow spine pictorial hardcovers beginning in 1962: $15.00

Nancy Drew Cameo Editions, 1959 – 1960, Grosset & Dunlap, book club hard-covers with "cameo locket" picture of Nancy on endpapers, color dust jackets by Polly Bolian, nine illustrations per volume, with dust jacket: $30.00

Nancy Drew titles:

Secret of the Old Clock, 1930

Hidden Staircase, 1930

Bungalow Mystery, 1930

Mystery of Lilac Inn, 1930

Secret of Shadow Ranch, 1931

Secret of Red Gate Farm, 1931

Clue in the Diary, 1932

Nancy's Mysterious Letter, 1932

Sign of the Twisted Candles, 1933

Password to Larkspur Lane, 1933

Clue of the Broken Locket, 1934

Message in the Hollow Oak, 1935

Mystery of the Ivory Charm, 1936

Whispering Statue, 1937

Haunted Bridge, 1937

Clue of the Tapping Heels, 1939

Mystery of the Brass Bound Trunk, 1940

Mystery at the Moss Covered Mansion, 1941

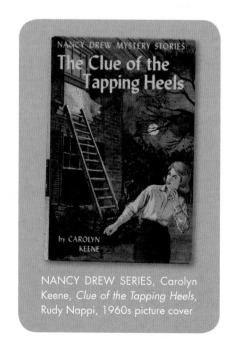

NANCY DREW SERIES, Carolyn Keene, *Clue of the Tapping Heels,* Rudy Nappi, 1960s picture cover

NANCY DREW SERIES, Carolyn Keene, *Mystery of the Tolling Bell,* Russell Tandy, 1940s dust jacket

Quest of the Missing Map, 1942

Clue in the Jewel Box, 1943

Secret in the Old Attic, 1944

Clue in the Crumbling Wall, 1945

Mystery of the Tolling Bell, 1946

Clue in the Old Album, 1947

Ghost of Blackwood Hall, 1948

Clue of the Leaning Chimney, 1949

Secret of the Wooden Lady, 1950

Clue of the Black Keys, 1951

Mystery at the Ski Jump, 1952

Clue of the Velvet Mask, 1953

Ringmaster's Secret, 1953

Scarlet Slipper Mystery, 1954

Witch Tree Symbol, 1955

Hidden Mystery, 1956

Haunted Showboat, 1957

Secret of the Golden Pavilion, 1959

Clue in the Old Stagecoach, 1960

Mystery of the Fire Dragon, 1961

Clue of the Dancing Puppet, 1962

Moonstone Castle Mystery, 1963

Clue of the Whistling Bagpipes, 1964

Phantom of Pine Hill, 1965

Mystery of the 99 Steps, 1966

Clue in the Crossword Cipher, 1967

Spider Sapphire Mystery, 1968

Invisible Intruder, 1969

Mysterious Mannequin, 1970

Crooked Bannister, 1971

Secret of Mirror Bay, 1972

Double Jinx Mystery, 1973

Mystery of the Glowing Eye, 1974

Secret of the Forgotten City, 1975

Sky Phantom, 1976

Strange Message in the Parchment, 1977

Mystery of Crocodile Island, 1978

Thirteenth Pearl, 1979

NANCY DREW SERIES, Carolyn Keene, *Clue of the Black Keys,* Bill Gillies, 1950s dust jacket

Nancy Drew, other:

Nancy Drew Cookbook: Clues to Good Cooking, 1973, Grosset & Dunlap, yellow illustrated hardcover, red endpapers, first printing 1973, on copyright page, no other dates: $40.00

NAN SHERWOOD SERIES, Annie Rowe Carr (Stratemeyer Syndicate pseudonym), 1916 – 1937, Saalfield, also World, hardcover, frontispiece illustration, with dust jacket: $30.00

NATHALIE SERIES, Anna Chapin Ray, ca. 1905, Little, Brown, cloth hardcover with print illustration and gilt lettering, color frontispiece and b/w plates by Alice Barber Stephens: $30.00

Nathalie's Chum

Ursula's Freshman

Nathalie's Sister

NATHALIE SERIES, Anna Chapin Ray, *Nathalie's Sister*

NAT RIDLEY, Nat Ridley, Jr. (pseudonym), ca. 1926, Garden City Publishing, hardcover. The Nat Ridley character appeared in magazine and dime novel editions, also. Hardcover: $30.00

Crime on the Limited or, Nat Ridley in the Follies

Guilty or Not Guilty? or, Nat Ridley's Great Race Track Case

In the Nick of Time or, *Nat Ridley Saving a Life*

Scream in the Dark or, *Nat Ridley's Crimson Clue*

Tracked to the West or, *Nat Ridley at the Magnet Mine*

NATURE STORIES BOOKS, Thornton W. Burgess, 1946, Little, Brown, cloth-over-board cover with silhouette illustration, about 184 pages, two-color and b/w illustrations by Harrison Cady, first edition with dust jacket: $30.00

Crooked Little Path

Dear Old Briar-Patch

At Paddy the Beaver's Pond

Along Laughing Brook

NATURE STORIES BOOKS, Thornton W. Burgess, *Crooked Little Path*

NAVY BOYS SERIES, Halsey Davidson, *Navy Boys at the Big Surrender*

NAVY BOYS SERIES, Halsey Davidson, 1918 – 1920, Sully, gray pictorial hardcover, frontispiece by R. G. Herbert, World War I stories for boys: $30.00

NIXIE BUNNY SERIES, Joseph Sindelar, ca. 1915, Beckley-Cardy, hardcover, illustrated endpapers, b/w/green or red three-color illustrations throughout by Helen Geraldine Hodge, music by Alys Bentley. First editions: $60.00

NODDY SERIES, Enid Blyton (1897 – 1968, b. London). Noddy has been printed in 40 languages and sales have reached 200 million copies. Noddy, a little wooden boy who lives in Toyland, was created in 1949 by Blyton. Noddy progressed from a storybook bestseller to an animated TV series, and then to a live action TV program. These are simple stories about a small fellow who drives a taxi in toyland.

NODDY SERIES, Enid Blyton, *Noddy Goes to Toyland*

Sampson Low Marston, London, 1949 – 1962, small pictorial hardcover, 60 pages, color illustrations by Beek. Reprints numerous.

First editions, with dust jackets: $150.00. Without dust jackets: $30.00.

NOGGIN SERIES, Oliver Postgate, illustrations by Peter Firmin, British TV series set in a Viking-like land of snow, adventures of Noggin, the king of the Nogs. Tie-in books followed as a beginning reader series.

NOGGIN SERIES, Oliver Postgate, Kaye and Ward, Noggin and the Dragon

David White, US first editions with dust jackets: $75.00

Collins, UK, 1965 – 1977, first editions with dust jackets: $75.00

Kaye and Ward, UK, first editions, glazed pictorial boards: $30.00

Holiday House reprints with dust jackets: $35.00

NOISY VILLAGE SERIES, Astrid Lindgren, Viking, hardcover, b/w illustrations by Ilon Wikland, first edition with dust jacket: $50.00

Children of Noisy Village, 1962

Happy Times in Noisy Village, 1963

Christmas in Noisy Village, 1964

Springtime in Noisy Village, 1966

NORBY CHRONICLES, Janet and Isaac Asimov, Walker, hardcover with dust jacket. Adventures of a mixed-up robot who travels through history as well as space. Isaac wrote literally hundreds of other books and Janet also wrote standalone children's science fiction novels under her maiden name of J. O. Jeppson.

Walker first edition with dust jacket:

Norby, the Mixed-Up Robot, 1983: $50.00

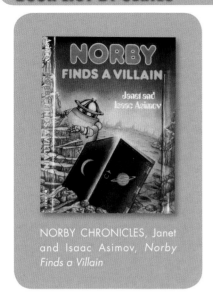

NORBY CHRONICLES, Janet and Isaac Asimov, *Norby Finds a Villain*

Norby's Other Secret, 1984: $40.00

Norby and the Lost Princess, 1985: $40.00

Norby and the Invaders, 1985: $40.00

Norby and the Queen's Necklace, 1986: $30.00

Norby Finds a Villain, 1987: $30.00

Norby titles continued through 1997.

NORTH POLE SERIES, Edwin James Houston (1847 – 1914), 1907, Winston, green pictorial hardcover, four plates by Louis Dougherty, map, 370+ pages: $60.00

Search for the North Pole, 1907

Discovery of the North Pole, 1907

Cast Away at the North Pole, 1907

NUTSHELL LIBRARY, Harper & Row, four cloth hardcover books, each with illustrated paper dust jacket, 2½" x 4" high, with color illustrations throughout, packaged in an illustrated paper-covered slipcase.

Bunny's Nutshell Library, Robert Kraus, 1965, includes *Silver Dandelion, First Robin, Juniper,* and *Springfellow's Parade.* Complete first edition set with dust jackets and box: $150.00

NUTSHELL LIBRARY, *Christmas Nutshell Library*

Christmas Nutshell Library, Hilary Knight, 1963, includes *Angels and Berries and Candy Canes, Firefly in a Fir Tree, Christmas Stocking Story,* and *Night Before Christmas,* all illustrated by Knight. Complete first edition set: $150.00. Later sets: $50.00

Complete Nutshell Library, Maurice Sendak, 1962, includes *Alligators All Around, Chicken Soup, One Was Johnny,* and *Pierre.* Complete first edition set: $300.00. Later complete sets: $45.00

NUTSHELL LIBRARY, *Complete Nutshell Library*

See FROG series, *Four Frogs in a Box,* for similar set by Dial.

OAKDALE ACADEMY SERIES, Morgan Scott, 1911 – 1913, Hurst, impressed illustration on hardcover, four b/w plates by Martin Lewis, 300+ pages: $30.00

Burt edition, hardcover, with dust jacket: $40.00

OBADIAH SERIES, Brinton Turkle, ca. 1970s, E. P. Dutton, oblong hardcover, color illustrations by author, first edition with dust jacket: $75.00. Later printings and book club edition with dust jacket: $35.00

Obadiah the Bold, 1965

Thy Friend, Obadiah, 1969

Adventures of Obadiah, 1972

Rachel and Obadiah, 1978

ODD & ELSEWHERE SERIES, James Roose-Evans, *Secret of Tippity Witchit*

ODD & ELSEWHERE SERIES, James Roose-Evans, Andre Deutsch, UK, b/w illustrations by Brian Robb, a toy clown and toy bear team up in light-hearted adventures, first edition with dust jacket: $50.00

Adventures of Odd & Elsewhere, 1971

Secret of the Seven Bright Shiners, 1972

Odd and the Great Bear, 1973

Elsewhere and the Gathering of the Clowns, 1974

Return of the Great Bear, 1975

Secret of Tippity Witchit, 1975

Lost Treasure of Wales, 1977

O'KEEFE FAMILY CHRONICLES, Madeleine L'Engle, fantasy, Farrar, first edition with dust jacket:

Wrinkle in Time, 1962: $100.00

Wind in the Door, 1973: $75.00

Swiftly Tilting Planet, 1978: $40.00

Many Waters, 1986: $40.00

O'Keefe, related novels:

Arm and the Starfish, 1965: $50.00

Dragons in the Water, 1976: $40.00

House Like a Lotus, 1984: $40.00

O'Keefe, related series: *Austin Chronicles,* crossover characters appear in the *O'Keefe* and *Austin Chronicles,* hardcover novels that fall between real world adventures and fantasy. The first Austin title was published by Vanguard. The other titles were first published by Farrar, and all have been reprinted by Farrar.

Meet the Austins, 1960, Vanguard, first edition with dust jacket: $50.00

Farrar, first edition with dust jacket:

Moon by Night, 1963: $100.00

Twenty-Four Days Before Christmas, 1964, red hardcover, color illustrations by Inge: $100.00

Young Unicorns, 1968: $50.00

Ring of Endless Night, 1980: $50.00

OLGA DA POLGA SERIES, Michael Bond, stories of Olga the guinea pig, various publishers in the UK and US. Bond is the author of the *Paddington Bear* books.

Hardcover, b/w illustrations by Hans Helwig, nine titles, first editions with dust jackets: $100.00

Tales of Olga da Polga, 1971

Olga Meets Her Match, 1975

Olga Carries On, 1977

Olga's New Home, 1977

Olga's Second House, 1977

Olga's Special Day, 1977

Olga Takes a Bite, 1977

Olga Takes Charge, 1982

Complete Adventures of Olga da Polga, 1983

OLIVER OPTIC SERIES, William T. Adams, 1822 – 1897. Adams was a prolific writer of adventure novels for young readers. His numerous titles cross-over in series and appear under other series names. His series dealing with Civil War themes are the most popular.

OLIVER OPTIC SERIES, William T. Adams, *In School and Out*

Early editions with Civil War themes, gilt-decorated or gilt lettered hardcovers: $35.00 to $50.00

Early editions with non-Civil War themes, gilt-decorated or gilt lettered hardcovers: $20.00 to $40.00

Boat Club, or, *Bunkers of Rippleton, 1855,* may have been the first *Optic* title for children, printed as an individual title, but in later editions it was included in various series.

ONCE AND FUTURE KING, T. H. White, various publishers. One of those difficult series, like the LORD OF THE RINGS, where the first book was quickly adopted for and marketed to children, while the later books were clearly written for adults but read by children anyway. Also, like *Lord of the Rings,* this Arthurian series was re-written by White at various times to fit into new formats such as the omnibus edition. These books inspired the musical *Camelot* and the Disney movie *The Sword in the Stone.*

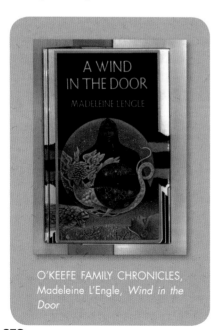

O'KEEFE FAMILY CHRONICLES, Madeleine L'Engle, *Wind in the Door*

OLGA DA POLGA SERIES, Michael Bond, *Tales of Olga da Polga*

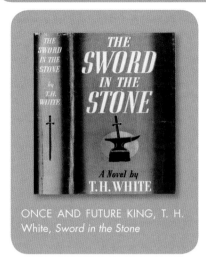

ONCE AND FUTURE KING, T. H. White, *Sword in the Stone*

Sword in the Stone, 1938, Collins, black hardcover, 339 pages, first edition with dust jacket: $600.00

Sword in the Stone, 1939, Putnam, dark hardcover with gilt lettering, US first edition with dust jacket: $250.00

Witch in the Wood, 1939, Putnam, US, and 1940, Collins, UK, first edition with dust jacket: $250.00

Ill-Made Knight, 1940, Putnam, blue hardcover, first edition with dust jacket: $500.00

Ill-Made Knight, 1941, Collins, brown hardcover, UK first edition with dust jacket: $200.00

Once and Future King, omnibus edition:

Once and Future King, 1958, Collins, contains the first three books as well as the story *Candle in the Wind,* UK first edition with dust jacket: $400.00

Once and Future King, 1958, Putnam, contains the first three books with considerable rewriting in parts as well as the story *Candle in the Wind,* US first edition with dust jacket: $200.00

Once and Future King, related title:

Book of Merlyn, 1977, University of Texas, originally written in 1941 for *Once and Future King,* but never published in that format, no price printed on dust jacket, first edition with dust jacket: $125.00

ONE END STREET SERIES, Eve Garnett, ca. 1940s, Vanguard, hardcover, b/w drawings by author, first edition with dust jacket: $100.00

Later printings with dust jackets: $30.00

Family from One End Street

Further Adventures of Family from One End Street

Holiday at Dewdrop Inn

ORLANDO THE CAT SERIES, Kathleen Hale, Country Life, London, oversize hardcover, color and b/w illustrations by author, tales of a marmalade cat.

1940s first editions with dust jackets: $300.00. Without dust jackets: $100.00

1950s and 1960s first editions with dust jackets: $200.00. Without dust jackets: $60.00

Reprints with dust jackets: $30.00

ORLANDO THE CAT SERIES, Kathleen Hale, *Orlando the Marmalade Cat*

Jonathon Cape, glossy pictorial hardcover: $35.00

Orlando the Marmalade Cat, 1938

Orlando Buys a Farm, 1941

Orlando's Evening Out, 1941

Orlando's Home Life, 1942

Orlando, His Silver Wedding, 1944

Orlando Becomes a Doctor, 1944

Orlando Keeps a Dog, 1949

Orlando the Judge, 1950

Orlando the Marmalade Cat, a Seaside Holiday, 1952

Orlando Buys a Cottage, 1963

Orlando and the Three Graces, 1966

Orlando and the Water Cats, 1972

ORPHELINES SERIES, Natalie Savage Carlson, 1957 – 1964, Harper, oversize, illustrated hardcover, charming b/w illustrations by Fermin Rocker or Garth Williams, girls in a French orphanage create their own family through a number of funny adventures. Five titles. First edition with dust jacket: $30.00

ORPHELINES SERIES, Natalie Savage Carlson, *Happy Orpheline*

Happy Orpheline, 1957

Brother for the Orphelines, 1959

Pet for the Orphelines, 1962

Orphelines in the Enchanted Castle, 1964

Grandmother for the Orphelines, 1964

OTTO THE GIANT DOG SERIES, William Pène du Bois, Viking Press, oversize hardcover, color illustrations by author, first edition with dust jacket:

Giant Otto, 1936: $200.00

Otto at Sea, 1936: $100.00

Otto in Texas, 1959: $50.00

Otto in Africa, 1961: $30.00

Otto and the Magic Potatoes, 1970: $30.00

OTTO THE GIANT DOG SERIES, William Pène du Bois, *Otto and the Magic Potatoes*

OUR YOUNG AEROPLANE SCOUTS SERIES, Horace Porter, *In the Balkans*

OUR YOUNG AEROPLANE SCOUTS SERIES, Horace Porter, 1914 – 1917, Burt, printed illustration on cloth-over-board cover, b/w frontispiece, with dust jacket: $35.00

OUTBOARD BOYS SERIES, Roger Garis, 1933 – 1934, Burt, cloth-over-board cover, frontispiece by Warre, mysteries for boys, with dust jacket: $50.00

OUTDOOR GIRLS SERIES, Laura Lee Hope (Stratemeyer Syndicate pseudonym), 1913 – 1933, Grosset & Dunlap, hardcover, b/w illustrations, with dust jacket: $30.00

OUTDOOR GIRLS SERIES, Laura Lee Hope, *Outdoor Girls at Cedar Ridge*

OZ BOOKS SERIES, L. Frank Baum, all first edition Oz novels from 1900 to 1935 are the same size and have a color-stamped cloth cover or color pictorial paste-on, tipped-in full-page color illustrations facing text except in *Ozma of Oz, Road to Oz,* and *Patchwork Girl of Oz,* and have illustrated endpapers. After 1935 the size and format remained the same but the illustrations were all b/w. In 1919, the Reilly & Britton publisher's name changed to Reilly & Lee. The books were issued with dust jackets, but these are difficult to find on the Baum titles and bring a wide range of prices at auctions.

Generally books must be dated by the advertisement lists (also check gift inscriptions), as the printed copyright information was not changed. In the mid-1920s, blue captions were often added to the color plate illustrations. These later printings fall in the $100.00 range.

Baum created a fairyland of four distinct and different colored countries surrounded by a poisonous desert, and in the center was the Emerald City, where the ruler of all Oz resided in an emerald castle. Additional lands developed as the stories continued. Involved in the fairyland adventures are several American children and their pets, including Dorothy and her little dog, Toto.

Oz illustrators: *Wonderful Wizard of Oz* was illustrated by W. W. Denslow. *Marvelous Land of Oz* and all remaining Baum *Oz* books through *Glinda of Oz* were illustrated by John R. Neill.

The *Oz* novels followed a series progression, but because of their popularity other collections of stories and novelty books appeared. The *Oz* novels are listed here in order of copyright date, followed by additional story collections and novelty items.

Oz titles by L. Frank Baum, first editions thus:

Wonderful Wizard of Oz, 1900, Hill, 24 color plate illustrations by Denslow: $30,000.00

New Wizard of Oz, 1903 edition, Bobbs-Merrill, used Hill plates with new title

OZ BOOKS SERIES, L. Frank Baum

and cover, 16 color plate illustrations by Denslow: $200.00

New Wizard of Oz, 1913 edition, Donohue, same plates as Bobbs-Merrill, 2nd edition: $100.00

Marvelous Land of Oz, 1904, Reilly & Britton, 16 color plate illustrations by Neill: $300.00

Land of Oz, 1904, Reilly & Britton, short-ened title: $200.00

Land of Oz, 1917, variant reduced to 12 color plate illustrations: $150.00

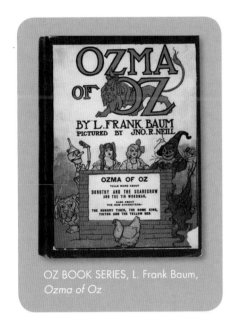

OZ BOOK SERIES, L. Frank Baum, *Ozma of Oz*

Ozma of Oz, 1907, Reilly & Britton, color throughout text illustrations, no inserted color plates, illustration by Neill: $300.00

Dorothy and the Wizard in Oz, 1908, Reilly & Britton, 16 color plate illustrations by Neill: $200.00

Road to Oz, text printed on tinted stock in solid colors (easily faded), line drawings throughout but no color plates, illustrations by Neill: $200.00

Emerald City of Oz, 1910, Reilly & Britton, 16 color plate Neill illustrations embel-lished with metallic green ink: $300.00

Emerald City of Oz, 1917, Reilly & Britton, 12 color plate Neill illustrations omitting metallic ink: $150.00

Patchwork Girl of Oz, 1913, Reilly & Britton, colored text illustrations throughout book by Neill, no color plates: $300.00

Tik-Tok of Oz, 1914, Reilly & Britton, col-ored endpapers are maps of Oz, 12 color plates by Neill: $200.00

Tik-Tok of Oz, 1920, Reilly & Lee edition, maps omitted: $60.00

Scarecrow of Oz, 1915, Reilly & Britton, 12 color plate illustrations by Neill: $250.00

Rinkitink in Oz, 1916, Reilly & Britton, 12 color plate illustrations by Neill: $250.00

Lost Princess of Oz, 1917, Reilly & Britton, 12 color plate illustrations by Neill: $250.00

Tin Woodman of Oz, 1918, Reilly & Britton, 12 color plates by Neill: $200.00

Magic of Oz, 1919, Reilly & Lee, 12 color plates by Neill, in first edition publisher's ad page lists to Tin Woodman: $200.00

Glinda of Oz, 1920, Reilly & Lee, 12 color plates by Neill, in first edition pub-lisher's ad page lists to Glinda: $200.00

Oz Books, Ruth Plumly Thompson, color plates. After Baum's death, children's author Ruth Plumly Thompson was hired to continue the series. For sales purposes, Baum's name was used alone on the cover of the first Thompson book, *Royal Book of Oz.* Thereafter, Thompson is credited.

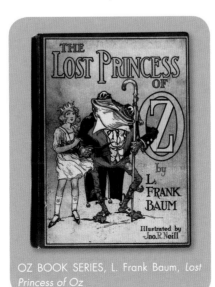

OZ BOOK SERIES, L. Frank Baum, *Lost Princess of Oz*

OZ BOOK SERIES, Ruth Plumly Thompson, *Ojo in Oz*

Reilly & Lee first editions were illustrated by John R. Neill, same size and format as Baum books. Cloth covers with color pictorial paste-on, 12 full-color tipped-in pages, b/w pictorial endpapers, except in *Wishing Horse of Oz.*

Oz Books, Ruth Plumly Thompson, Reilly & Lee, with color plates and with dust jackets: $300.00. Without dust jackets: $175.00

Reprints, 1935 – 1950s, b/w illustrations only: $50.00

Royal Book of Oz, 1921

Kabumpo in Oz, 1922

Cowardly Lion of Oz, 1923

Grampa in Oz, 1924

Lost King of Oz, 1925

Hungry Tiger of Oz, 1926

Gnome King of Oz, 1927

Giant Horse of Oz, 1928

Jack Pumpkinhead of Oz, 1929

Yellow Knight of Oz, 1930

Pirates in Oz, 1931

Purple Prince of Oz, 1932

OZ BOOKS SERIES, Ruth Plumly Thompson, *Ozoplaning with the Wizard of Oz*

Ojo in Oz, 1933

Speedy in Oz, 1934

Wishing Horse of Oz, 1935, blank endpapers

Oz books, Thompson, b/w illustrations only. After 1935 the color plates were discontinued. Reilly & Lee, first editions, cloth covers with color pictorial paste-on, b/w illustrations only, b/w pictorial endpapers, illustrations by John Neill, with dust jackets: $150.00. Without dust jackets: $100.00

Captain Salt in Oz, 1936

Handy Mandy in Oz, 1937

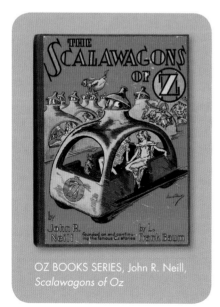

OZ BOOKS SERIES, John R. Neill, *Scalawagons of Oz*

Silver Princess in Oz, 1938

Ozoplaning with the Wizard of Oz, 1939

Oz books continued by John R. Neill. When Thompson retired, artist Neill authored and illustrated three books. Same size and format, cloth covers w/ pictorial color paste-ons, b/w illustrations, pictorial b/w endpapers, with dust jacket: $150.00. Without dust jacket: $100.00

OZ BOOKS SERIES, Jack Snow, *Shaggy Man*

Wonder City of Oz, 1940

Scalawagons of Oz, 1941

Lucky Bucky in Oz, 1942

Oz books continued by Jack Snow. Same size and format, cloth covers w/pictorial color paste-ons, b/w illustrations by Frank Kramer, with dust jacket: $150.00. Without dust jacket: $100.00

Magical Mimics in Oz, 1946, pictorial green print on yellow endpapers:

Shaggy Man of Oz, 1949, b/w endpapers

Oz books, related stories, L. Frank Baum, books featuring characters that appear in the Oz series:

Sea Fairies, 1911, similar format as *Oz* books, with color plate illustrations by Neill, features Cap'n Bill and Trot in an undersea adventure: $250.00

Sea Fairies, 1928 edition, similar format as *Oz* books, b/w illustrations with color frontispiece: $150.00

Sky Island, 1912, similar format as *Oz* books, with color illustrations by Neill, features Cap'n Bill and Trot in a cloud world adventure: $250.00

Oz, Little Wizard Series, L. Frank Baum, 1913, Reilly, six volumes, small size, 29 pages, full-color illustrations by Neill: $45.00

Cowardly Lion and the Hungry Tiger

Little Dorothy and Toto

Tiktok and the Nome King

Ozma and the Little Wizard

Jack Pumpkinhead and the Sawhorse

Scarecrow and the Tin Woodman

Oz, other *Little Wizard* Books, L. Frank Baum:

Little Wizard Stories of Oz, 1914, Reilly & Britton, 196 pages, contains all six stories in the series, color illustrations from the series: $500.00

Oz, Little Wizard Set, 1939 edition, Rand McNally, three volumes, each containing two

OZ BOOKS SERIES, *Sea Fairies*

of the original *Little Wizard* stories in abridged form, small size, about 62 pages: $30.00

Oz, Little Wizard Jell-O Series: 1932, Reilly, four volumes, small size, 29 pages, revised editions of original Baum stories with Jell-O advertisements and recipes added, each: $130.00

Tiktok and the Nome King

Ozma and the Little Wizard

Jack Pumpkinhead and the Sawhorse

Scarecrow and the Tin Woodman

Oz books, Denslow picture books:

W. W. Denslow, illustrator of the first *Oz* book, later wrote and illustrated some *Oz* related stories of his own.

Denslow's Scarecrow and the Tin-Man, 1904, Dillingham, softcover, oversize, 12 pages, color illustrations, ad on back cover for a Denslow picture book series: $500,00

Denslow's Scarecrow and the Tin-Man and Other Stories, 1904, Dillingham, original story plus others written and illustrated by Denslow, cloth hardcover, 74 pages, color illustrations. $1,500.00

Denslow's Scarecrow and the Tin-Man and Other Stories, 1913, Donohue, reprint of the Dillingham book, color variations on cover and illustrations: $230.00

Five Favorite Stories, 1943, American Crayon, a Mary Perks book, oversize, illustrated hardcover, includes the *Scarecrow and Tin-Man* story with some of the Denslow illustrations, plus four other stories: $50.00

Scarecrow and Tin-Man, Perks Publishing, 1943, oversize, illustrated softcover, includes the Scarecrow and Tin-Man story plus four other stories: $30.00

Oz book, Frank Joslyn Baum, L. Frank Baum's son:

Laughing Dragon of Oz, 1935, Whitman Big Little Book, color illustrated hardcover, illustrations by Milt Youngren: $300.00

Oz books, Junior Editions, 1939, Rand McNally, small, pictorial hardcovers, 62 pages, color illustrations based on original illustrations, shortened adaptations of Baum books, each: $30.00 to $50.00

Land of Oz

Road to Oz

Emerald City of Oz

Patchwork Girl of Oz

Rinkitink of Oz

Lost Princess of Oz

Oz books, *Oz-Man Tales*, 1917, Reilly & Lee, small color illustrated paper-overboard hardcovers, 62 pages, four color plates, each: $75.00

Little Bun Rabbit

Once Upon a Time

Yellow Hen

Magic Cloak

Jack Pumpkinhead

Gingerbread Man

Oz books, additional titles from Reilly & Lee:

OZ BOOKS SERIES, *Scarecrow and Tin-Man*

Hidden Valley of Oz, Rachel Cosgrove, 1951, Reilly & Lee, first edition, blue

hardcover with paste-on-pictorial, 313 pages, illustrated endpapers, b/w illustrations by Dirk Gringhuis with dust jacket: $325.00. Without dust jacket: $150.00

Hidden Valley of Oz, later printings, hardcover without paste-on-pictorial: $50.00

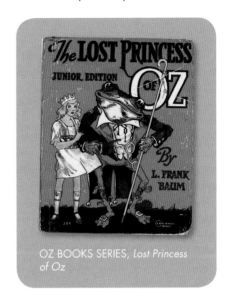

OZ BOOKS SERIES, *Lost Princess of Oz*

Merry Go Round in Oz, Eloise Jarvis McGraw and Lauren McGraw Wagner, 1963, Reilly & Lee, first edition, white hardcover with printed illustration, b/w illustrations by Dick Martin, with dust jacket: $150.00. Without dust jacket: $50.00

OZ BOOKS SERIES, *Visitors from Oz*

Visitors from Oz, Jean Kellogg, re-telling of a selection of Baum short stories, 1960, Reilly & Lee, green background color illustration printed on oversize hardcover, 60 pages, b/w and color illustrations by Dick

Martin, with dust jacket: $250.00. Without dust jacket: $100.00

Who's Who in Oz, Jack Snow, 1954 Reilly & Lee, tan hardcover with gilt lettering, 277 pages, Oz map endpaper, illustrated with artwork from the earlier books, a bibliography of Oz characters, with dust jacket: $150.00. Without dust jacket: $50.00

Oz, Roycraft cover editions, ca. 1959, Reilly & Lee, hardcovers, issued with new dust jackets signed "Roycraft," with dust jacket: $75.00

Roycroft titles include: *Wizard of Oz, Land of Oz, Ozma of Oz, Dorothy and the Wizard in Oz, Road to Oz, Scarecrow of Oz, Lost Princess of Oz, Tin Woodman of Oz, Hungry Tiger of Oz, Pirates in Oz,* and *Speedy in Oz*

Oz books, Dick Martin cover editions, ca. 1960, Reilly & Lee, hardcovers, issued with new dust jackets by Dick Martin, same book format as the "Roycraft" editions with dust jackets: $75.00

Dick Martin covers include: *Wizard of Oz, Patchwork Girl of Oz, Rinkitink in Oz, Magic of Oz, Glinda of Oz, Kabumpo in Oz, Cowardly Lion of Oz, Purple Prince of Oz, Captain Salt in Oz, Shaggy Man of Oz*

Oz books, Kellogg and Martin editions, 1961, Reilly & Lee, oversize, color illustrated laminated hardcover, 60 pages, rewritten by Jean Kellogg, color and b/w illustrations by Dick Martin, with dust jacket: $75.00. Without dust jacket: $35.00

Kellogg editions include: *Wizard of Oz, Land of Oz, Ozma of Oz, Dorothy and the Wizard of Oz*

Oz books, "White Cover" editions, 1964, Reilly & Lee, white cloth-over-board hardcovers with printed illustration on front, back and spine, a re-issue of the original Baum texts, original illustrations by Denslow and Neill adapted to b/w illustrations by Dick Martin. The cover designs were also adapted by Martin from Denslow and Neill illustrations. No dust jackets issued: $35.00

OZ BOOKS SERIES, *Wizard of Oz Waddle Book*

Wizard of Oz, 1964 edition, full-color wraparound design printed on hardcover. (Although this is the first of the "white cover" editions, its cover is blue/green.)

1964 white covers include: *Emerald City of Oz, Patchwork Girl of Oz, Tik-Tok of Oz, Scarecrow of Oz, Lost Princess of Oz*

Oz books, 1965 white cover editons: $30.00

Wizard of Oz, 1965 edition, design printed on white background on hardcover, to match the rest of the white covers.

1965 white covers include *Land of Oz* through *Glinda of Oz*.

Oz book, novelty book:

Woggle-Bug Book, 1905, Reilly & Britton, 15" x 11"+, 48 pages, board cover, illustrated by Ike Morgan and produced to coincide with the opening in Chicago of Baum's play *The Woggle-Bug,* described as a musical extravaganza, stapled gatherings, full-color illustrations, text printed in dark blue: $30,000.00

Wizard of Oz Waddle Book, 1934, Blue Ribbon Books, same size as original *Oz* books, cloth hardcover with paste-on-pictorial, original story, Denslow color plates, six waddles, which are cardboard cut-out figures of *Oz* characters, on pages added to back of book. With waddles: $3,000.00. Without waddles: $200.00

Wizard of Oz, adaptation of L. Frank Baum story, Saalfield, 1944, red plastic spiralbound paper-over-board cover, animated by Julian Wehr, color illustrations, first edition with dust jacket: $300.00

Oz, reference book:

Bibliographia Oziana, compiled by Douglas Greene and Peter Hanff, published by the International Wizard of Oz Club, revised and updated since its first publication in 1976. For information on ordering new copies, check the Club's website, www.ozclub.org

■ ⋯⋯⋯⋯⋯⋯ P ⋯⋯⋯⋯⋯⋯ ■

PADDINGTON BEAR SERIES, Michael Bond, Collins, London, pictorial boards, and Houghton Mifflin, Boston, cloth-over-board hardcover, b/w illustrations by Peggy Fortnum. A few *Paddington* books had other illustrators, as noted. Paddington is a toy bear named after the London train station, and the popularity of the books inspired numerous toys, especially stuffed bears.

1960s, Collins, first edition with dust jacket: $100.00

1970s, Collins, first edition with dust jacket: $50.00

1960s – 1970s, Houghton Mifflin, US first edition with dust jacket: $50.00

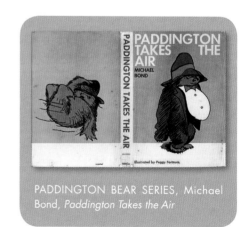

PADDINGTON BEAR SERIES, Michael Bond, *Paddington Takes the Air*

Paddington titles include:

Bear Called Paddington, 1960

More About Paddington, ca. 1960

Paddington Helps Out, 1960

Paddington Abroad, 1961

Paddington at Large, 1962

Paddington Marches On, 1964

Paddington at Work, 1966

Paddington Goes to Town, 1968

Paddington Takes the Air, 1970

Paddington Abroad, 1972

Paddington Goes Shopping, 1973

Paddington's Garden, 1973

Five Paddingtons at the Circus, 1973

Paddington on Top, 1974

Paddington Takes to TV, 1974, illustrated by Ivor Wood

Paddington's Lucky Day, 1974

Paddington on Stage, 1974

Paddington on Top, 1974

Paddington at the Sea-Side, 1975

Paddington on Stage, 1977, plays for children

Paddington Takes the Test, 1979

Paddington on Screen, 1982

PAM AND PENNY SERIES, Rosamund DuJardin (1902 – 1963), see also MARCY RHODES and TOBY HEYDON.

Lippincott first edition with dust jacket: $150.00

Double Date, 1952

Double Feature, 1953

Showboat Summer, 1955

Double Wedding, 1958

PAN-AMERICAN SERIES, Edward Stratemeyer, 1902 – 1911, Lothrop, Lee and Shepard, pictorial hardcover, gilt lettering on spine, some Charles Nuttall illustrations, first edition, wide price variation: $35.00 to $100.00

Lost on the Orinoco, or, American Boys in Venezuela

Young Volcano Explorers, or, American Boys in the West Indies

Young Explorers of the Isthmus, or, American Boys in Central America

Young Explorers of the Amazon, or, American Boys in Brazil

Treasure Seekers of the Andes, or, American Boys in Peru

Chased Across the Pampas, or, American Boys in Argentina

PANTOUFLIA SERIES, Andrew Lang, three titles, original adventures in a fairy court by Lang, who is best known for his collections of world fairy tales, see also LANG FAIRY TALES.

Prince Prigio, 1889, Arrowsmith & Simpkin Marshall, brown hardcover with gilt, 144 pages, b/w illustrations by Gordon Browne: $300.00

Prince Prigio, 1942 edition, Little, Brown, square green pictorial hardcover, blue/white endpapers, b/w illustrations by Robert Lawson, first edition with dust jacket: $75.00

Prince Ricardo of Pantouflia, 1893, Arrowsmith & Simpkin Marshall, small green hardcover with gilt, 204 pages, b/w illustrations by Gordon Browne: $50.00

My Own Fairy Book, 1895, Longmans Green, UK, hardcover with silver gilt, b/w illustrations by Gordon Browne, T. Scott, and E. A. Lemann: $300.00

PARRI MacDONALD SERIES, Janet Lambert, E. P. Dutton, first edition with dust jacket: $175.00

Introducing Parri, 1962

That's My Girl, 1964

Stagestruck Parri, 1966

PARRI MacDONALD SERIES, Janet Lambert, *Stagestruck Parri*

PATTY AND GINGER SERIES, Janet Lambert, 1950s

Dutton Book Club edition with dust jacket: $35.00

PATTY AND GINGER SERIES, Janet Lambert, *Summer Madness*

Dutton first edition with dust jacket:

We're Going Steady: $150.00

Boy Wanted: $75.00

Spring Fever: $75.00

Summer Madness: $100.00

Extra Special: $75.00

On Her Own: $150.00

PEANUTS BOOKS, Charles M. Schulz, books featuring Charlie Brown, Snoopy, Lucy, and all the other characters from the popular *Peanuts* comic strip.

Peanuts, a Holt, Rinehart series:

Holt Rinehart, small hardcover, illustrations by author, one illustration and one or two sentences per page for young readers.

First editions of the 1960s and early 1970s titles with dust jackets: $80.00

Early titles include:

Snoopy and the Red Baron, 1966

Snoopy and His Sopwith Camel, 1969

Snoopy's Grand Slam, 1972

Peanuts Books, other publishers, a few examples, listed alphabetically:

Charlie Brown Christmas, 1965, World, adapted from the Bill Melendez production, first edition: $40.00

Charlie Brown's All-Stars, 1966, World, hardcover, illustrated by author, first edition: $35.00

Happiness Is a Warm Puppy, 1962, Determined Productions, small square hardcover, brown and black pictorial paper over boards, 62 pages on heavy stock in a variety of colors, illustrated by author, first edition with dust jacket: $40.00

Love Is Walking Hand in Hand, 1965, San Francisco Determined Productions, illustrated by author, first edition with dust jacket: $30.00

PEANUTS BOOKS, Charles M. Schulz, *Charlie Brown Christmas*

It's the Great Pumpkin, Charlie Brown, 1967, World, oblong pictorial hardcover, illustrated in color, first edition: $30.00

You're a Good Man, Charlie Brown, 1967, Random House, hardcover, music, lyrics, and adaptation by Clark Gesner, illustrated with photos from the stage play which starred Gary Burghoff as Charlie Brown, with dust jacket: $50.00

You're in Love, Charlie Brown, 1968, World, square illustrated hardcover, illustrated by author, first edition: $40.00

Peanuts, related books:

Numerous collections of the beloved cartoon strips are available in small and oversize formats, in both hard and softcover. Most are intended for the general market rather than the children's market.

PEEPSHOW BOOKS, ca. 1950, Houghton Mifflin, small, carousel books produced by Folding Books Ltd., color illustrated paper-over-board cover, book opens to form a circle with six double-page cut-out three-layered scenes, with six or seven lines of print on bottoms of pages. Ribbon ties hold book closed. Price drops dramatically for any missing pieces, each: $150.00

Cinderella, illustrated by Roland Pym

Ali Baba and the Forty Thieves, illustrated by Ionicus

Puss-in Boots, illustrated by Kathleen Hale

Sleeping Beauty, illustrated by Roland Pym

PEE WEE DEWIRE SERIES, Lewis Theiss, World War II adventures of Pee Wee Dewire and Colvin Criswell. See also MAIL PILOT SERIES.

Wilde, b/w illustrations, first edition with dust jacket: $50.00 to $100.00

Flying with the CAA: How Two of Uncle Sam's Youngest Airmen Saved a Great Defense Plant, 1941

Flying for Uncle Sam: A Story of Civilian Pilot Training, 1942

Flying with the Coastal Patrol, 1943

PEE-WEE HARRIS SERIES, Percy Keese Fitzhugh, comic version of Boy Scout adventures.

Grosset & Dunlap, four b/w plates by Barbour, early edition with dust jacket: $40.00

Pee-Wee Harris, 1922

Pee-Wee Harris on the Trail, 1922

Pee-Wee Harris in Camp, 1922

Pee-Wee Harris in Luck, 1922

Pee-Wee Harris Adrift, 1922

Pee-Wee Harris, F O B Bridgeboro, 1923

Pee-Wee Harris: Fixer, 1924

PEE-WEE HARRIS SERIES, Percy Keese Fitzhugh, *Pee-Wee Harris on the Trail*

Pee-Wee Harris as Good as His Word, 1925

Pee-Wee Harris: Mayor for a Day, 1926

Pee-Wee Harris and the Sunken Treasure, 1927

Pee-Wee Harris on the Briny Deep, 1928

Pee-Wee Harris in Darkest Africa, 1929

Pee-Wee Harris Turns Detective, 1930

PENELOPE SERIES, Kate Douglas Wiggin, ca. 1910 – 1915, Houghton Mifflin, hardcover, frontispiece. Also published by Gay & Bird, London, with Charles Brock illustrations, first edition with dust jacket: $40.00

Penelope's Experiences

Penelope's Irish Experiences

Penelope's Progress

Penelope's Postscripts

PENNY NICHOLS SERIES, Joan Clark (Mildred Wirt), 1936 – 1939, Goldsmith, red cloth-over-board cover, Penny's dad runs the Nichols Detective Agency, and somehow Penny is constantly the center of a mystery. Penny is a cute blonde teenager who roars around in her own roadster, and lives with her widowed father and motherly housekeeper. The author penned the majority of the *Nancy*

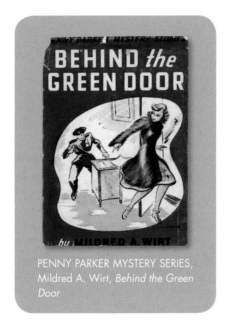

PENNY NICHOLS SERIES, Joan Clark, *Penny Nichols and the Black Imp*

Drew books and also wrote the *Penny Parker* books. The three series are fun to compare, first edition with dust jacket: $30.00

Penny Nichols Finds a Clue, 1936

Penny Nichols and the Black Imp, 1936

Penny Nichols and the Mystery of the Lost Key, 1936

Penny Nichols and the Knob Hill Mystery, 1939

PENNY PARKER MYSTERY SERIES, Mildred A. Wirt, blonde girl sleuth lives with her widowed father and kindly housekeeper, drives her own car (see PENNY NICHOLS series and NANCY DREW series), but is much sassier and more independent than Nichols or Drew. She is also an extremely careless driver.

PENNY PARKER MYSTERY SERIES, Mildred A. Wirt, *Behind the Green Door*

Cupples & Leon, cloth-over-board cover, frontispiece illustration, dust jacket illustrated by K. S. Woerner, first edition with dust jacket: $70.00

Tale of the Witch Doll, 1939

Vanishing Houseboat, 1939

Danger at the Drawbridge, 1940

Behind the Green Door, 1940

Clue of the Silken Ladder, 1941

Secret Pact, 1941

Clock Strikes Thirteen, 1942

Wishing Well, 1942

Saboteurs on the River, 1943

Ghost Beyond the Gate, 1943

Hoofbeats on the Turnpike, 1944

Voice from the Cave, 1944

Guilt of the Brass Thieves, 1945

Signal in the Dark, 1946

Whispering Walls, 1946

Swamp Island, 1947

Cry at Midnight, 1947

PENNY PARRISH AND TIPPY PARRISH SERIES, Janet Lambert

E. P. Dutton, first edition hardcover with dust jacket: $80.00

Grosset & Dunlap reprints with dust jackets: $40.00

Star Spangled Summer, 1941

Dreams of Glory, 1942

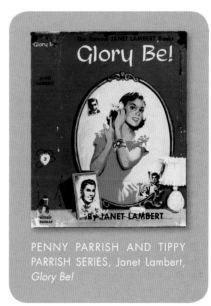

PENNY PARRISH AND TIPPY PARRISH SERIES, Janet Lambert, *Glory Be!*

Glory Be!, 1943

Up Goes the Curtain, 1946

Practically Perfect, 1947

Reluctant Heart, 1950

Miss Tippy, 1948

Little Miss Atlas, 1949

Miss America, 1951

Don't Cry, Little Girl, 1952

Penny Parrish, last three titles, E. P. Dutton first editions with dust jackets: $100.00

Rainbow After Rain, 1953

Welcome Home, Mrs. Jordan, 1953

Song in Their Hearts, 1956

PENROD SERIES, Booth Tarkington, Doubleday, hardcover, re-issued continually, Gordon Grant drawings illustrate the first and last titles, illustrations by Brehm Worth in the second title. First editions with dust jacket start at: $50.00

Penrod, 1914

Penrod and Sam, 1916

Penrod Jashber, 1929

PETER RABBIT SERIES, (see also POTTER, Helen Beatrix, in the Book List by Author section) books by other authors based on the Beatrix Potter character first introduced in 1900 in *Tale of Peter Rabbit.*

Peter Rabbit, by Linda Almond, Altemus, also Platt, small pictorial or paste-on-pictorial hardcovers, with color illustrations throughout signed "J. L. G.," many titles published by Altemus in the 1920s, then re-issued by Platt as Platt Wee Books in 1935.

Altemus 1920s editions: $45.00

Platt 1935 editions with dust jackets: $50.00. Without dust jackets: $35.00

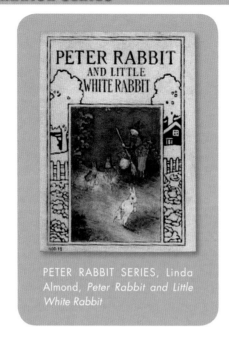

PETER RABBIT SERIES, Linda Almond, *Peter Rabbit and Little White Rabbit*

Peter Rabbit's Easter, 1921

Peter Rabbit's Birthday, 1921

Peter Rabbit Goes A-Visiting, 1921

When Peter Rabbit Went to School, 1921

Peter Rabbit and Jack-the-Jumper, 1922

Peter Rabbit, Jack-the-Jumper and the Old Witch Woman, 1923

When Peter Rabbit Went A-Fishing, 1923

Peter Rabbit and Little White Rabbit, 1923

Peter Rabbit and the Little Boy, 1935

Peter Rabbit and the Little Girl, ca. 1935, illustrated by Bessie Goe Willis

Peter Rabbit and the Tiny Bits, 1935

Peter Rabbit's Holiday, 1935

Peter Rabbit, more Linda Almond books, Saalfield Publishers:

Peter Rabbit and His Pa, 1916, Saalfield, small, color illustrated paper-over-board cover, illustrated endpapers, color illustrations by Virginia Albert: $35.00

Peter Rabbit and His Ma, 1927, Saalfield, small, color illustrated paper-over-board

cover, illustrated endpapers, full-page color illustrations by Virginia Albert: $35.00

Peter Rabbit, by other authors, based on the Beatrix Potter character:

Mrs. Peter Rabbit, Thornton Burgess, 1919, Little, Brown, hardcover, illustrations by Harrison Cady, first edition with dust jacket: $100.00

New Story of Peter Rabbit, Samuel Lowe, 1926, Whitman, small size, color illustrations by Allan Wright: $35.00

Tale of Peter Rabbit, 1943, Merrill, Chicago, oversize picture book, linen-textured paper, paper cover, 12 pages, full-color illustrations by Milo Winter: $30.00

PETUNIA THE GOOSE SERIES, Roger Duvoisin (see also VERONICA SERIES), Knopf, oversize picture books, pictorial hardcovers, illustrated endpapers, color illustrations throughout, adventures of a large white goose.

First edition with dust jacket: $75.00

Later printings with dust jackets: $35.00

Petunia, 1950

Petunia and the Song, 1951

Petunia's Christmas, 1952

Petunia Takes a Trip, 1953

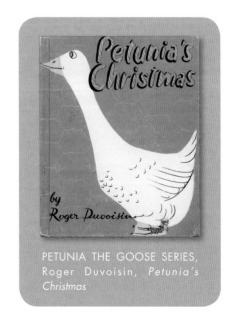

PETUNIA THE GOOSE SERIES, Roger Duvoisin, *Petunia's Christmas*

Petunia, Beware!, 1958

Petunia's Treasure, 1975

Petunia the Silly Goose Stories, 1987

Petunia, other:

Petunia, I Love You, 1965, Bodley Head, UK edition, with dust jacket: $40.00

PHANTOM SERIES, Lee Falk, books based on the newpaper comic strip character, Phantom, who lives on a secret island and defeats wrong-doers through a combination of wits and strength.

Son of the Phantom, 1946, Whitman, hardcover, dust jacket illustration shows Phantom on his throne with his son next to him, with dust jacket: $50.00

Phantom, ca. 1940s, Whitman Better Little Books: $50.00

Phantom and the Sky Pirates, #1468

Phantom and Desert Justice, #1421

Phantom and the Girl of Mystery, #1416

Return of the Phantom, #1489

Phantom and the Sign of the Skull, #1474

![PHANTOM SERIES cover]

PHANTOM SERIES, Lee Falk, *Son of the Phantom*

PINOCCHIO ONCE-UPON-A-TIME SERIES, the original story and continuing adventures of the Italian wooden toy written by different authors.

Pinocchio, Adventures of a Marionette, Walter Cramp translation of the original Collodi story, 1904, Ginn, gray hardcover, illustrations by Charles Copeland: $50.00

Pinocchio in Africa, Angelo Patri, 1911, Ginn, small blue hardcover, b/w illustrations by Charles Copeland: $50.00

Pinocchio Under the Sea, Gemma Rembadi, 1913, Macmillan, illustrations by Florence Wilde: $50.00

Heart of Pinocchio, Nipote, 1919, Harper, paste-on-pictorial hardcover, b/w illustrations by Flanagan: $50.00

Pinocchio's First Visit to America, Angelo Patri, 1928, Ginn, b/w illustrations by Sears Gallagher: $50.00

Pinocchio in America, 1928, Doubleday, Doran, blue hardcover, illustrated by Mary Liddell, with dust jacket: $150.00

PIPPI LONGSTOCKING SERIES, Astrid Lindgren, stories of a small girl with amazing strength, translated by Florence Lamborn, Viking, US editions, hardcover, b/w illustrations by Louis Glanzman, first US edition with dust jacket: $40.00

American titles:

Pippi Longstocking, 1950

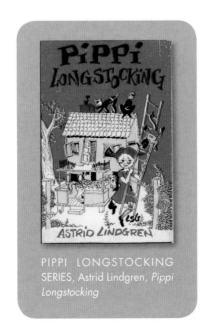

PIPPI LONGSTOCKING SERIES, Astrid Lindgren, *Pippi Longstocking*

Pippi Goes on Board, 1957

Pippi in the South Seas, 1959

Pippi on the Run, 1976

PIT DRAGONS TRILOGY, Jane Yolen, Delacorte, on a distant planet a bond boy secretly trains a fighting pit dragon.

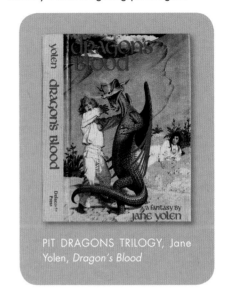

PIT DRAGONS TRILOGY, Jane Yolen, *Dragon's Blood*

Delacorte Press, US, first edition with dust jacket: $30.00

Dragon's Blood, 1982

Heart's Blood, 1984

Sending of Dragons, 1987

POGO BOOKS, Walt Kelly, comic strip character who lives in the Okefenokee swamp, titles include:

Pogo, Simon & Schuster, 1951, in dust jacket: $200.00

Uncle Pogo So-So Stories, Simon & Schuster, 1953, in dust jacket: $130.00

Songs of the Pogo, Kelley and Norman Monath, 1958, Simon & Schuster, over-size hardcover with gilt, illustrated endpapers, color illustrations, first edition with dust jacket: $150.00. Without dust jacket: $30.00

Pogo Sunday Parade, 1958, Simon & Schuster, hardcover, 127 pages, b/w illustrations, first edition: $30.00

POGO BOOKS, Walt Kelly,
Pogo Puce Stamp Catalog

Ten Ever-Lovin' Blue-Eyed Years with Pogo, Simon & Schuster, 1959, in dust jacket: $130.00

Pogo Puce Stamp Catalog, Simon & Schuster, 1963, pictorial cover, 93 pages: $100.00

Pogo, 1970s reprints, Gregg Press, Boston, with dust jackets: $40.00

Pogo

I Go Pogo

Potluck Pogo

Pogo Papers

Incompleat Pogo

Ungle Pogo So-So Stories

Pogo Peek-a-Book

Pogo Stepmother Goose

Gone Pogo

Pogo A La Sundae

Pogo, collection:

Best of Pogo, collected from the Okefenokee Star, edited by Mrs. Walt Kelly and Bill Couch, Jr., 1982, Simon & Schuster, with dust jacket: $40.00

POLLY BREWSTER SERIES, Lillan Elizabeth Roy, 1922 – 1932, Grosset & Dunlap, first edition with dust jacket: $30.00

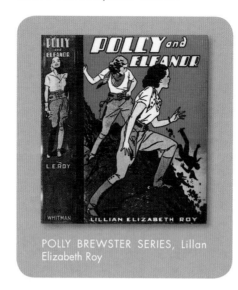

POLLY BREWSTER SERIES, Lillan Elizabeth Roy

POOKIE SERIES, Ivy L. Wallace, tales of a winged white rabbit. Collins, London, first edition, pictorial oversize hardcover, color and b/w illustrations, with dust jacket: $100.00. Without dust jacket: $40.00

Titles include:

Pookie and the Gypsies, 1947

Pookie Puts the World Right, 1949

Pookie Believes in Santa Claus, 1953

Pookie and the Swallows, 1955

Pookie at the Seaside, 1956

POOKIE SERIES, Ivy L. Wallace, *Pookie and the Gypsies*

POPEYE THE SAILOR MAN BOOKS, based on the famous spinach-eating cartoon character created by E. C. Segar.

Titles include:

Thimble Theatre Starring Popeye, 1935, Whitman Publishing, oversize, illustrated, first edition: $150.00

Popeye, Movie Book, 4 Big Reels, 1933, King Features, illustrated by Bud Segar, 5 x 3 inches, b/w flip-it, shows feature Popeye, Olive, Wimpy, and Popeye Knockout, was an Orbit Gum premium: $200.00

Adventures of Popeye, 1934, Saalfield, oblong hardcover: $50.00

Popeye in Puddleburg, 1934, Saalfield, oblong hardcover: $50.00

Popeye Starring in Choose Your Weppins, 1936, Saalfield, small Big Little Book style format, b/w cartoons: $150.00

Popeye, the Fighting Sailor Man, Segar, 1937, Whitman, oversize picture book with illustrated boards, b/w and color illustrations, with dust jacket: $200.00. Without dust jacket: $80.00

Popeye Borrows a Baby Nurse, Segar, 1937, Whitman, oversize picture book with illustrated boards, b/w and color illustrations, with dust jacket: $200.00. Without dust jacket: $60.00

Popeye and His Friends, Segar, 1937, Whitman, oversize picture book with illustrated boards, b/w and color illustrations: $80.00

Popeye and His Jungle Pet, Segar, 1937, Whitman, oversize picture book with illustrated boards, b/w and color illustrations: $50.00

Wimpy Tricks Popeye and Rough-House, 1937, Whitman: $100.00

Popeye, 1937, King Features, oversize picture book with linen-look cover: $75.00

Popeye the Sailor Man, Segar, 1937, Grosset & Dunlap, oversize picture book with illustrated boards, 31 pages, b/w and color illustrations, with dust jacket: $200.00. Without dust jacket: $100.00

Popeye the Sailor Man, Segar, 1940, Birn Bros. Ltd., UK, oversize picture book with illustrated boards, red cloth spine, b/w and color illustrations: $80.00

Popeye, Whitman Big Little Books, color illustrated cardboard cover, b/w illustrations:

Popeye Sees the Sea, 1936: $60.00

Popeye and the Jeep, 1937: $60.00

Popeye Raps a Rival, 1937: $40.00

Popeye Takes in Toar, 1937: $40.00

Popeye in Quest of his Poopdeck Pappy, 1937: $50.00

Popeye, Whitman Better Little Book, color illustrated cardboard cover, b/w illustrations:

Popeye and the Deep Sea Mystery, Segar, 1939: $75.00

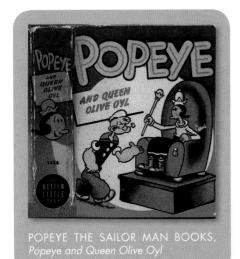

POPEYE THE SAILOR MAN BOOKS, *Popeye and Queen Olive Oyl*

Popeye and Queen Olive Oyl, Better Little Book, Bud Sagendorf, 1946: $40.00

Popeye Pop-Ups, Blue Ribbon, oversize book, color illustrations throughout and features three double-page pop-ups:

Popeye in Among the Savages, 1934: $400.00

Popeye with the Hag of the Seven Seas, 1935: $400.00

POPPY OTT SERIES, Leo Edwards, ca. 1926 – 1939, Grosset & Dunlap, advertised as "packed full of the side-splitting adventures which a group of 100% American boys share," first eight titles were illustrated by Bert Salg, first edition with dust jacket: $140.00. Later printings with dust jackets: $40.00

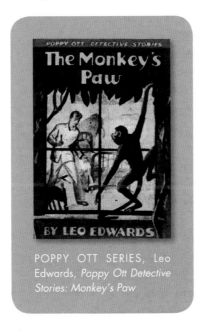

POPPY OTT SERIES, Leo Edwards, *Poppy Ott Detective Stories: Monkey's Paw*

Poppy Ott and the Stuttering Parrot, 1926

Poppy Ott's Seven League Stilts, 1926

Poppy Ott and the Galloping Snail, 1927

Poppy Ott's Pedigreed Pickles, 1927

Poppy Ott and the Freckled Goldfish, 1929

Poppy Ott and the Tittering Totem, 1929

Poppy Ott and the Prancing Pancake, 1930

Poppy Ott Hits the Trail, 1933

Poppy Ott & Co., Inferior Decorators, illustrated by Myrtle Sheldon

Poppy Ott Detective Stories: Monkey's Paw, 1938

Poppy Ott Detective Stories: Hidden Dwarf, 1939

PRINCE VALIANT SERIES, Hal Foster, 1951 – 1957, Hastings House, hardcover with dust jacket and pictorial endpapers. Stories adapted from the original Foster newspaper comic strip by Max Trell, one double-page color illustration plus b/w illustrations throughout. Reprinted by Nostalgia Press, starting in 1974.

Hastings hardcovers, first editions, with dust jackets: $50.00

Prince Valiant in the Days of King Arthur, 1951

Prince Valiant Fights Attila the Hun, 1952

Prince Valiant on the Inland Sea, 1953

PRINCE VALIANT SERIES, Hal Foster, *Prince Valiant on the Inland Sea*

Prince Valiant's Perilous Voyage, 1954

Prince Valiant and the Golden Princess, 1955

Prince Valiant in the New World, 1956

Prince Valiant and the Three Challenges, 1957

PRYDAIN CHRONICLES, Lloyd Alexander, Holt Rinehart Winston, folk tales set in Wales, hardcover, jacket illustrations and maps by Evaline Ness, first edition with dust jacket: $125.00

Book of Three, 1964

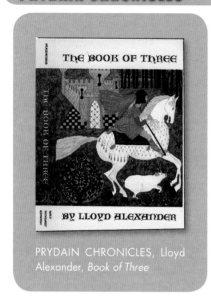

PRYDAIN CHRONICLES, Lloyd Alexander, *Book of Three*

Black Cauldron, 1965

Castle of Llyr, 1966

Taran Wanderer, 1967

High King, 1969 (Newbery winner)

Prydain Picture Books:

Coll and his White Pig, Lloyd Alexander, 1965, Holt, hardback, illustrated by Evaline Ness, short story related to character in *Prydain Chronicles,* color illustrations throughout, with dust jacket: $50.00

PRYDAIN CHRONICLES, Lloyd Alexander, *Foundling*

Truthful Harp, Lloyd Alexander, 1967, Holt, hardback, illustrated by Evaline Ness, short story related to character in *Prydain*

Chronicles, color illustrations throughout, with dust jacket: $60.00

Foundling, Lloyd Alexander, 1973, Holt, 73 pages, b/w illustrations by Margot Zemach, with dust jacket: $40.00

PURPLE PENNANT SERIES, Ralph Henry Barbour, Appleton, hardcover with paste-on-pictorial and gilt lettering, four two-color plates by Norman Rockwell, popular with both Barbour and Rockwell collectors: $100.00 up

Lucky Seventh, 1915

Secret Play, 1915

Purple Pennant, 1916

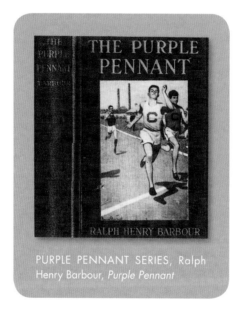

PURPLE PENNANT SERIES, Ralph Henry Barbour, *Purple Pennant*

■ ⋯⋯⋯⋯⋯ **R** ⋯⋯⋯⋯⋯ ■

RACKETTY-PACKETTY HOUSE SERIES, Frances Hodgson Burnett, Century and Warne. The second book of this series about interfering fairies is the best known and the most often reprinted. It deals with the rescue of the dollhouse dolls by the Queen of the Fairies.

Queen Silverbell, 1906, Century, small hardcover with paste-on illustration, color illustrations by Harrison Cady: $100.00

Racketty-Packetty House, As Told by Queen Crosspatch, 1906, Century, small

RACKETTY-PACKETTY HOUSE SERIES, Frances Hodgson Burnett, *Racketty-Packetty House*

hardcover with paste-on illustration, 130 pages, color illustrations by Harrison Cady: $100.00

Spring Cleaning, As Told by Queen Crosspatch, 1908, small hardcover with paste-on illustration, color illustrations by Harrison Cady: $100.00

Cozy Lion, As Told by Queen Crosspatch, 1912, Century, small hardcover, illustrations by Harrison Cady: $60.00

Troubles of Queen Silverbell, As Told by Queen Crosspatch, 1919, Century, small hardcover with paste-on illustration, color illustrations by Harrison Cady: $60.00

Racketty-Packetty, later edition:

Racketty-Packetty House and Other Stories, 1961, Scribner, illustrated by Harold Berson, with dust jacket: $40.00

RADIO BOYS SERIES, Allen Chapman (Stratemeyer Syndicate pseudonym), ca.1907 – 1915, Grosset & Dunlap, radio set design on blue hardcover, frontispiece, advertised as "Fascinating radio adventures founded on fact and containing full details of radio work. Each volume has a foreword by Jack Binns, the well known radio expert." First edition (list-to-title) with dust jacket: $75.00

Later printings with dust jacket: $40.00

RADIO GIRLS SERIES, Margaret Penrose (Stratemeyer Syndicate pseudonym), 1920s, Cupples & Leon, hardcover, b/w illustrations by Thelma Gooch, later reprinted as part of Goldsmith's CAMPFIRE GIRLS series with title changes, first edition with dust jacket: $85.00

RAGGEDY ANN SERIES, Johnny Gruelle, author/illustrator, see also ALL ABOUT SERIES, tales of a rag doll, her toy friends, and her little girl, Marcella. Gruelle designed the first dolls for Volland, and books and dolls continue to be produced. These popular books have been reproduced in many formats and combinations of titles. Many are still in print and can be found at reading copy prices.

The following is a partial list of highly collectible editions:

Raggedy Ann, Volland and Donohue editions:

Hardcover, color illustrations throughout by author. Volland books had a paper-over-board pictorial cover, illustrated endpapers, color illustrations throughout, and were usually sold in a matching cardboard box. Box lid shows front cover illustration.

Volland book with box: $200.00. Without box: $100.00

Donohue first editions with dust jackets: $100.00. Without dust jackets: $50.00

Later editions with dust jackets: $30.00

Raggedy Ann Stories, 1918

Raggedy Ann's Friendly Fairies, 1919

Raggedy Andy Stories, 1920

Raggedy Ann and Andy and the Camel with the Wrinkled Knees, 1924

Raggedy Andy's Number Book, 1924, a linen book for pre-schoolers

Raggedy Ann's Wishing Pebble, 1925

Raggedy Ann and the Paper Dragon, 1926

Raggedy Ann's Magical Wishes, 1928

Raggedy Ann Fairy Stories, 1928

Marcella: A Raggedy Ann Story, 1929

Raggedy Ann in the Deep Deep Woods, 1930

Raggedy Ann in Cookie Land, 1931

Raggedy Ann's Lucky Pennies, 1932

Raggedy Ann, Whitman, illustrated hardcover:

Raggedy Ann and the Left Handed Safety Pin, 1935, Whitman, small, illustrations by Johnny Gruelle, first edition: $65.00

Raggedy Ann in the Golden Meadow, 1935, Whitman, oversize, illustrations by Johnny Gruelle, first edition: $150.00

Raggedy Ann, Johnny Gruelle Company, illustrated by Johnny Gruelle's brother, Justin, or by Johnny Gruelle's son, Worth,

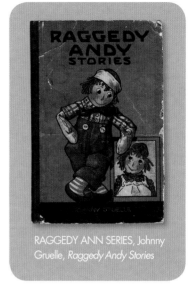

RAGGEDY ANN SERIES, Johnny Gruelle, *Raggedy Andy Stories*

pictorial paper-covered-boards, decorated endpapers, color illustrations throughout, first edition with dust jacket: $125.00. Without dust jacket: $50.00

Raggedy Ann in the Magic Book, 1939, illustrations by Worth Gruelle

Raggedy Ann and the Golden Butterfly, 1940, illustrations by Justin Gruelle

Raggedy Ann and Andy and the Nice Fat Policeman, 1942, illustrations by Worth Gruelle

Raggedy Ann and Betsy Bonnet String, 1943, illustrations by Justin Gruelle

Raggedy Ann in the Snow White Castle, 1946, illustrations by Justin Gruelle

Raggedy Ann, McLoughlin's "Westfield Classics" collection, ca. 1940, approximately 42 pages, hardboard covers with color illustrations, large easy-read print, b/w endpaper illustrations, b/w and color illustrations, also labeled as McLoughlin's Little Color Classics: $50.00

Raggedy Ann Helps Grandpa Hoppergrass

Raggedy Ann and the Hoppy Toad, illustrated by Justin Gruelle, 1943

Raggedy Ann in the Garden

Raggedy Ann and the Laughing Brook

RAGGEDY ANN SERIES, Johnny Gruelle. Volland cover, and Donahue endpapers and cover

Raggedy Andy Goes Sailing

Camel with the Wrinkled Knees

Raggedy Ann, 1944, Saalfield, Julian Wehr animation:

Raggedy Ann and Andy, red spiralbound with color illustrated hardcover, color illustrations, six pages of animations by Julian Wehr: $200.00

Raggedy Ann, Bobbs-Merrill:

Beloved Belindy, 1960, Bobbs-Merrill, hardcover, color illustrations, with dust jacket: $100.00

Raggedy Ann and the Wonderful Witch, 1961, Bobbs-Merrill, large yellow hardcover with paste-on illustration, color illustrations by Johnny Gruelle, Worth Gruelle, and Worth's daughter, Joni, 48 pages, with dust jacket: $150.00. Without dust jacket: $50.00

Raggedy Ann and the Happy Meadow, 1961, Bobbs-Merrill, hardcover, color illustrations by Worth Gruelle, with dust jacket: $100.00. Without dust jacket: $50.00

Raggedy Ann and the Hobby Horse, 1961, Bobbs-Merrill, hardcover, color illustrations by Worth Gruelle, with dust jacket: $100.00. Without dust jacket: $50.00

Raggedy Ann & Andy's Alphabet and Numbers, 1975, Bobbs-Merrill, hardcover, illustrated: $50.00

Raggedy Ann & Andy's Cookbook, 1975, Bobbs-Merrill, hardcover, illustrated: $75.00

Raggedy Ann & Andy's Green Thumb Book, 1975, Bobbs-Merrill, first edition, dark green hardcover, illustrated: $50.00

Raggedy Ann and Andy and Witchie Kissabye, 1975, Bobbs-Merrill, pictorial hardcover, illustrated: $50.00

Raggedy Ann and Andy and the Kindly Ragman, 1975, Bobbs-Merrill, pictorial hardcover, illustrated: $50.00

Raggedy Ann, Mary Perks editions, Famous Books for the Nursery, ca. 1945,

oversize, color illustrated cardboard cover, two-color illustrations, many by Mary and Wallace Stover: $35.00

Raggedy Ann in the Garden

Raggedy Ann and the Laughing Brook

Raggedy Ann Helps Grandpa Hoppergrass

Raggedy Ann and the Hoppy Toad

Raggedy Ann, novelties:

Raggedy Ann's Sunny Songs, author/illustrator Johnny Gruelle, music by Will Woodin, 1930, Miller Music, songbook with 16 illustrated songs: $110.00

Raggedy Ann Cut-Out Paper Dolls, 1935, Whitman, color paper doll book with artwork and poems by Johnny Gruelle, uncut: $125.00

Raggedy Ann's Joyful Songs, words and illustrations by Johnny Gruelle, music by Charles Miller, 1937, Miller Music Co., oblong songbook with 20 illustrated songs: $85.00

Raggedy Ann, reference:

Animated Raggedy Ann & Andy, John Canemaker, 1977, Bobbs-Merrill, oversize hardcover, 292 pages, b/w and color illustrations of film animations, first edition with dust jacket: $75.00

RAILROAD SERIES, Allen Chapman (Stratemeyer Syndicate pseudonym), ca. 1910 – 1930, Mershon, then Grosset & Dunlap; Chatterton-Peck, advertised as "Railroad stories are dear to the heart of every American boy. Ralph is determined to be a railroad man. He starts at the foot of the ladder but through manly pluck wins out."

Mershon and Chatterton-Peck editions, locomotive design printed on red hardcover, four b/w plates: $40.00

Grosset & Dunlap editions, light colored hardcovers with dust jackets: $45.00

RALPH THE MOUSE SERIES, Beverly Cleary, these popular stories are by the author of the *Ramona Quimby* and *Henry Huggins* books.

RALPH THE MOUSE SERIES, Beverly Cleary, *Ralph S. Mouse*

Morrow, first edition with dust jacket: $50.00

Mouse and the Motorcycle, 1965, b/w illustrations by Louis Darling

Runaway Ralph, 1970, b/w illustrations by Louis Darling

Ralph S. Mouse, 1982, illustrated by Paul O. Zelinsky

RAMBLER CLUB SERIES, W. Crispin Sheppard, 1910 – 1920, Penn Publishing, pictorial gray hardcover, b/w frontispiece and illustrations by author, first edition: $50.00

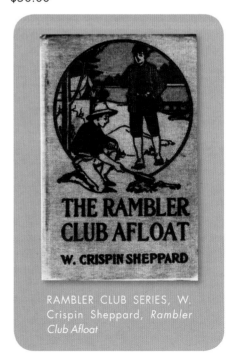

RAMBLER CLUB SERIES, W. Crispin Sheppard, *Rambler Club Afloat*

RAMONA QUIMBY SERIES, Beverly Cleary, Morrow, hardcover, b/w illustrations.

1955 – 1975, illustrations by Louis Darling, first edition with dust jacket: $60.00

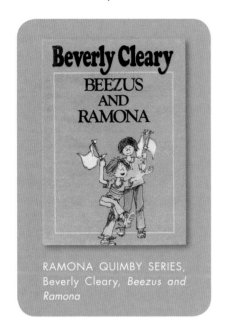

RAMONA QUIMBY SERIES, Beverly Cleary, *Beezus and Ramona*

Beezus and Ramona, 1955

Ramona the Pest, 1968

Ramona the Brave, 1975

1975 – 1984, illustrations by Alan Tiegreen, first edition with dust jacket: $35.00

Ramona and Her Father, 1975

Ramona and Her Mother, 1979

Ramona Quimby, Age 8, 1981

Ramona Forever, 1984

RANDOM HOUSE POP-UP BOOKS, undated, ca. 1960s, Random House, about 9½" x 6½", shiny hardcover, color illustrations, pop-ups and animations throughout, many were written by Albert Miller, designed by Paul Taylor, and illustrators include Tor Lokvig, Marvin Brehm, Dave Chambers, and Gwen Gordon. All pop-ups in good working condition: $40.00

Adventures of Dr. Dolittle

Animal Alphabet Book

RANDOM HOUSE POP-UP BOOKS, *Wishing Ring* and *Tournament of Magic*

Bennett Cerf's Pop-Up Limericks

Bennett Cerf's Silliest Riddles

Book of Left and Right

Color Book

Hide and Seek

Mother Goose

Night Before Christmas

Riddles, Sound-Alikes

Tournament of Magic

Wishing Ring

RAPHAEL TUCK GIFT BOOKS, undated, ca. 1900 – 1915, Raphael Tuck, UK, and David McKay, US, oversize, dark cover with gilt lettering, color plates plus b/w illustrations, 30 books. Titles include:

Animal Legends from Many Lands, Woolf, illustrated by Edwin Noble: $70.00

Children's Stories from French Fairy Tales, Ashley, illustrated by Mabel Lucie Attwell: $150.00

Children's Stories from Indian Legends, Belgrave and Hart, illustrated by Theaker: $120.00

Children's Stories from Italian Legends, Romano, illustrated by Howard Davie: $90.00

Children's Stories from Japanese Fairy Tales, N. Kato, illustrated by Harry G. Theaker: $130.00

Children's Stories from Longfellow, Doris Ashley, illustrations by Dixon, Copping and others: $70.00

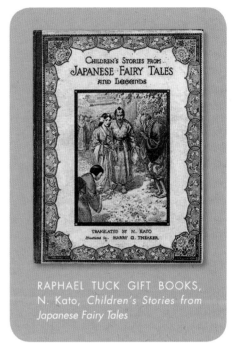

RAPHAEL TUCK GIFT BOOKS, N. Kato, *Children's Stories from Japanese Fairy Tales*

Children's Stories from the Northern Legends, Belgrave and Hart, illustrated by Theaker: $65.00

Children's Stories from Old British Legends, Belgrave and Hart, illustrated by Harry Theaker: $120.00

Children's Stories from Roumanian Fairy Tales, Gaster, illustrated by C. E. Brock: $90.00

Children's Stories from Russian Fairy Tales, Pulman, illustrated by Dixon: $65.00

Children's Stories from Scott, Doris Ashley, illustrations by Harold Earnshaw: $65.00

Children's Stories from Shakespeare, Nesbit, illustrations by Bacon, Davie and Copping: $65.00

Children's Stories from Tennyson, Chesson, illustrations by Bacon, Dixon, Copping: $65.00

Children's Stories from the Arabian Nights, Woolf, illustrations by Theaker: $130.00

Children's Stories from the Poets, Belgrave and Hart, illustrated by Frank Adams: $100.00

Curly Heads and Long Legs, stories by editors, illustrations by Agnew Richardson: $75.00

Golden Locks and Pretty Frocks, stories by editors, illustrations by Agnew Richardson: $75.00

My Book of Favourite Fairy Tales, Vredenburg, illustrated by Jennie Harbour: $150.00

Tales of King Arthur and the Knights of the Round Table, Ashley, illustrated by A. A. Dixon: $65.00

Tales of the Alhambra, Irving, illustrated by H. M. Brock: $75.00

Tinker, Tailor, Vredenburg, illustrations by Louis Wain: $65.00

RATS OF NIMH SERIES, award-winning first title by Robert O'Brien, the series was continued by his daughter, Jane Conly, from his notes after his death. Tales of the rats whose intelligence had been artificially enhanced by the National Institute of Mental Health, NIMH.

Mrs. Frisby and the Rats of NIMH, Robert O'Brien, 1971, Atheneum, hardcover, illustrated by Zena Bernstein, first edition with dust jacket: $75.00

Racso and the Rats of NIMH, Jane Leslie Conly, 1986, Harper & Row, hardcover, illustrations by Leonard Lubin, first edition with dust jacket: $35.00

R-T, Margaret, and the Rats of NIMH, Jane Leslie Conly, 1990, Harper & Row, hardcover, illustrations by Leonard Lubin, first edition with dust jacket: under $30.00

RED PLUME SERIES, Edward Williams, ca. 1925, Harper & Brothers, hardcover, two boys travel west with the cavalry, four b/w plates by Stinemetz, first edition: $30.00

Red Plume

Red Plume Returns

Red Plume with the Royal Northwest Mounted

RED RANDALL SERIES, R. Sidney Bowen, ca. 1940s, Grosset & Dunlap, hardcover, illustrated endpapers, frontispiece, illustrations by Ralph Smith, WWII adventures, with dust jacket: $30.00

Red Randall at Pearl Harbor

RED RANDALL SERIES, R. Sidney Bowen, *Red Randall on New Guinea*

Red Randall on Active Duty

Red Randall over Tokyo

Red Randall at Midway

Red Randall on New Guinea

Red Randall in the Aleutians

Red Randall in Burma

Red Randall's One Man War

REDWALL SERIES, Brian Jacques, 1987 – present, published by Hutchinson, UK, and sometimes dated one year later for Philomel or Penguin Putnam, US first edition, black and white chapter heading illustrations by Gary Chalk or Allan Curless, tales of the brave and adventurous creatures of the medieval Mossflower Woods. Collectors pay premium prices for first editions, first printings only (check number line

on copyright page to identify). Later editions in very good condition generally sell used at half to 75 percent of cover price.

Redwall, 1987, Hutchinson, UK first edition with dust jacket: $500.00

Redwall, 1987, Putnam, US first edition with dust jacket: $300.00

Mossflower, 1988, Hutchinson, UK first edition with dust jacket: $250.00

Mossflower, 1988, Putnam, US first edition with dust jacket: $100.00

Mattimeo, 1989, Hutchinson, UK first edition with dust jacket: $200.00

Mattimeo, 1990, Philomel, US first edition with dust jacket: $80.00

Mariel of Redwall, 1991, Hutchinson, UK first edition with dust jacket: $200.00. Philomel, US first edition with dust jacket: $80.00

Salamandastron, 1992, Hutchinson, UK first edition with dust jacket: $300.00. Philomel, US First edition with dust jacket: $80.00

Martin the Warrior, 1993, Hutchinson, UK first edition with dust jacket: $150.00. Philomel, US First edition with dust jacket: $60.00

Redwall titles, 1995 – 1999, Hutchinson, UK first edition with dust jacket: $80.00. Philomel, US first edition with dust jacket: $30.00

Bellmaker, 1995

Outcast of Redwall, 1996

Pearls of Lutra, 1996

Long Patrol, 1997

Marifox, 1998

Legend of Luke, 1999

Lord Brocktree, 2000, Hutchinson, UK first edition with dust jacket: $40.00. Philomel, US first edition with dust jacket: $30.00

Redwall, related title:

Redwall Abbey, 1998, Hutchinson, a craft book to build the abbey, also includes a story: $60.00

REED CONROY SERIES, Alan Gregg, 1940 – 1948, Doubleday, blue hardcover with gilt lettering, pictorial endpapers, first edition with dust jacket: $60.00

Winged Mystery, 1940

Hidden Wings Mystery, 1941

Skywinder Mystery, 1942

Mystery of the King Turtle, 1943

Mystery in the Blue, 1944

Mystery of Batty Ridge, 1946

Mystery of Flight 24, 1947

Flying Wing Mystery, 1948

RENFREW SERIES, Laurie York Erskine, 1922 – 1941, Appleton, hardcover, color frontispiece, with dust jacket: $40.00

Renfrew of the Royal Mounted, 1922

Renfrew Rides Again, 1927

Renfrew Rides the Sky, 1928

Renfrew Rides North, 1931

RENFREW SERIES, Laurie York Erskine, *Renfrew Rides North*

Renfrew's Long Trail, 1933

Renfrew Rides the Range, 1935

Renfrew in the Valley of the Vanished Men, 1936

Renfrew Flies Again, 1942

RESCUERS SERIES, Margery Sharp, 1959 through 1978, Little, Brown, US editions, Collins or Heinemann, UK editions. Two Disney animated films were based on the adventures of Miss Bianca and her loyal beau, Bernard.

RESCUERS SERIES, Margery Sharp, *Bernard the Brave*

Rescuers, 1959, Collins, London, first edition, illustrated by Judith Brook, with dust jacket: $50.00

Rescuers, 1959, Little, Brown, first edition, illustrated by Garth Williams, with dust jacket: $100.00

Miss Bianca, 1962, Little, Brown, illustrated by Garth Williams, first edition with dust jacket: $65.00

Turret, 1963, Little, Brown, illustrated by Garth Williams, first edition: $60.00

Miss Bianca in the Salt Mines, 1966, Little, Brown, illustrated by Garth Williams, first edition with dust jacket: $50.00

Miss Bianca in the Orient, 1970, Heinemann, UK, illustrations by Eric Blegvad, UK first edition with dust jacket: $40.00

Miss Bianca in the Antarctic, 1971, Little, Brown, first edition, illustrated by Eric Blegvad, with dust jacket: $30.00

Miss Bianca and the Bridesmaid, 1972, Little, Brown, illustrated by Eric Blegvad, first edition with dust jacket: $30.00

Bernard the Brave, 1977, Little, Brown, illustrated by Leslie Morrill, first edition with dust jacket: $45.00

Bernard into Battle, 1979, Little, Brown, or William Heinemann, illustrated by Leslie Morrill, first edition with dust jacket: $30.00

RICK AND RUDDY SERIES, Howard R. Garis, 1920s, Milton Bradley, tan hardcover, four b/w plates by Milo Winter, adventures of Rick and his dog, Ruddy, with dust jacket: $35.00

Rick and Ruddy

Rick and Ruddy in Camp

Rick and Ruddy Afloat

Rick and Ruddy Out West

Rick and Ruddy on the Trail

1930s editions, McLoughlin, 256 pages, wraparound color illustrations on cover boards, b/w frontispieces, same stories with new titles: $30.00

RICK AND RUDDY SERIES, Howard R. Garis, *Rick and Ruddy on the Trail*

297

McLoughlin titles:

Mystery of the Brass Bound Box

Swept from the Storm

Face in the Dismal Cavern

Secret of Lost River

On the Showman's Trail

RICK BRANT ELECTRONIC ADVENTURE SERIES or RICK BRANT SCIENCE-ADVENTURE SERIES, John L. Blaine (pseudonym for Harold Goodwin or Peter Harkins), 1947 – 1968, Grosset & Dunlap, 23 titles.

Rick Brant Electronic Adventure Series and *Rick Brant Science-Adventure Stories* both used by Grosset & Dunlap as series name. *Electronic Adventure* name was the earlier, but many books use both series designations in different places in the jacket or hardcover text. *Electronic Adventure* was dropped soon after the picture cover format was introduced. First editions were not identified by publisher, who kept the same copyright date for all. Most collectors consider the first two titles as probable first editions if the title listings do not exceed books published that year.

Rick Brant, 1947 – 1960, tweed hardcovers, illustrated endpapers, b/w frontispieces, with dust jackets that list to self: $50.00

Rocket's Shadow, 1947, probable first jacket lists to *Lost City*

Lost City, 1947

Sea Gold, 1947

100 Fathoms Under, 1947

Whispering Box Mystery, 1948

Phantom Shark, 1949

Smuggler's Reef, 1950

Caves of Fear, 1951

Stairway to Danger, 1952

RICK BRANT SCIENCE-ADVENTURE SERIES , John L. Blaine , *Veiled Raiders*

Golden Skull, 1954

Wailing Octopus, 1956

Electronic Mind Reader, 1957

Scarlet Lake Mystery, 1958

Pirates of Shan, 1958

Rick Brant, 1960 – 1962, hardcover, series titles list-to-self probable firsts with dust jacket: $100.00. Later printings with dust jacket: $40.00

Blue Ghost Mystery, 1960

Egyptian Cat Mystery, 1961

Flaming Mountain, 1962

Rick Brant, 1963 – 1968, pictorial hardcover, no dust jackets issued, series titles probable firsts, list-to-self. For some titles, only one or two printings were done.

Later printings: $35.00

Flying Stingaree, 1963, first edition: $75.00

Ruby Ray Mystery, 1964, first edition: $75.00

Veiled Raiders, 1965, first edition: $75.00

Rocket Jumper, 1966, first edition: $125.00

Deadly Dutchman, 1967, first edition: $125.00

Danger Below, 1968, first edition: $75.00

Rick Brant, related titles:

Rick Brant's Science Projects, 1960, Grosset & Dunlap, nonfiction, with dust jacket: $700.00

Deadly Dutchman, Mystery & Adventure, 1986 reprint, pictorial endpapers with map of world showing locales of Rick Brant's adventures: $75.00

Magic Talisman, 1989, Manuscript Press, manuscript written for, but never published by Grosset & Dunlap. Map of Spindrift Island on endpapers. Limited edition of 500 copies, hard to find.

RIDDLE-MASTER OF HED TRILOGY, Patricia A. McKillip, 1976 – 1979, Atheneum, hardcover, map endpapers or frontispiece, fantasy. Wraparound illustration on dust jacket by Michael Mariano.

Atheneum, first edition with dust jacket: $75.00

Sidgwick & Jackson, first UK editions with dust jackets: $30.00

Riddle-Master of Hed, 1976

Heir of Sea and Fire, 1977

Harpist in the Wind, 1979

RIDDLE-MASTER OF HED TRILOGY, Patricia A. McKillip, *Heir of Sea and Fire*

RING OPERA SERIES, based on the operas of Richard Wagner, illustrated by Arthur Rackham, Heinemann, London, and Doubleday, US. A first limited edition, now priced in the thousands, featured elaborate covers, mounted color plates with tissue overlays, and the artist's signature.

Ring, standard edition:

Rhinegold and the Valkyrie, 1910, brown buckram hardcover with gilt decoration, pictorial endpapers, English translation by Margaret Armour, oversize, 34 color plates, 14 black and white drawings: $400.00

Siegfried and Twilight of the Gods, 1911, brown buckram hardcover with gilt decoration, pictorial endpapers, English translation by Margaret Armour, oversize, 30 color plates plus b/w drawings: $400.00

Ring of the Nibling, undated edition, Garden City Publishing, Wagner's operas, brown boards, oversize, 24 of the Rackham plates: $25.00

RIVER MOTOR-BOAT SERIES, Harry Gordon, 1913 – 1915, Burt, frontispiece, with dust jacket: $50.00

River Motor-Boat Boys on the Amazon, or, *Secret of Cloud Island*

River Motor-Boat Boys on the Columbia, or, *Confession of a Photograph*

River Motor-Boat Boys on the Colorado, or, *Clue in the Rocks*

River Motor-Boat Boys on the Mississippi, or, *Trail to the Gulf*

River Motor-Boat Boys on the St. Lawrence, or, *Lost Channel*

River Motor-Boat Boys on the Ohio, or, *Three Blue Lights*

River Motor-Boat Boys on the Yukon, or, *Lost Mine of Rainbow Bend*

River Motor-Boat Boys on the Rio Grande, or, *In Defense of the Rambler*

ROCK TRILOGY, A. M. Lightner, Putnam, b/w illustrations by Denny McMains, science fiction, first edition with dust jacket: $40.00

Rock of Three Planets, 1963

Planet Poachers, 1965

Space Ark, 1968

ROCKET RIDERS SERIES, Howard R. Garis, 1933 – 1934, Burt, four titles, red hardcover, frontispiece by Warren also used on dust jacket, with dust jacket: $60.00

Rocket Riders Across the Ice, or, *Racing Against Time,* 1933

Rocket Riders Over the Desert, or, *Seeking the Lost City,* 1933

Rocket Riders in Stormy Seas, or, *Trailing the Treasure Divers,* 1933

Rocket Riders in the Air, or, *Chase in the Clouds,* 1934

ROCKY McCUNE SPORTS STORIES, Wilfred McCormick (see also BRONC BURNETT SERIES), 1955 – 1965, David McKay or Duell Sloan, early printings with dust jackets: $100.00

Man on the Bench, 1955

Captive Coach, 1956

Bigger Game, 1958

Hot Corner, 1958

Five Yards to Glory, 1959

Proud Champions, 1959

Automatic Strike, 1960

Too Many Forwards, 1960

Double Steal, 1961

Play for One, 1961

Five Man Break, 1962

Home Run Harvest, 1962

Phantom Shortstop, 1963

Two-One-Two Attack, 1963

Long Pitcher, 1964

Wild on the Bases, 1966

ROGER TEARLE SERIES, Scott Corbett, Little, Brown, five titles, hardcover, illustrations by Paul Frame, with dust jacket: $30.00

Case of the Gone Goose, 1966

Case of the Fugitive Firebug, 1969

Case of the Ticklish Tooth, 1971

Case of the Silver Skull, 1974

Case of the Burgled Blessing Box, 1975

ROLLO SERIES, Jacob Abbott (1803 – 1879), 28 titles, 1840s – 1860s, Reynolds and others, including J. Allen, Boston, first editions with cloth covers, gilt cover lettering, engraving illustrations, nursery tales possibly based on author's son: $50.00

ROOSEVELT BEARS SERIES, Seymour Eaton (1859 – 1916), oversize hardcovers with colorful paste-on-pictorials, stories told in verse, color plates plus b/w illustrations throughout by Floyd Campbell or R. K. Culver, Stern or Barse, early editions with dust jacket: $350.00. Without dust jacket: $200.00

Roosevelt Bears, Their Travels and Adventures, 1906, Stern, Philadelphia, oversize, dark hardcover with white lettering and color paste-on-pictorial, 180 pages, 16 color plates plus b/w text illustrations by Floyd Campbell, first edition: $400.00

More about Teddy B and Teddy G, the Roosevelt Bears, 1907, Stern, Philadelphia, oversize, hardcover with color paste-on-pictorial, 186 pages, 15 color plates plus b/w text illustrations by R. K. Culver, first edition: $400.00

Roosevelt Bears Abroad, ca. 1908, Barse & Hopkins, New York, Stern, Philadelphia, hardcover, 178 pages, 15 color plates plus hundreds of b/w text illustrations by Culver, first edition with dust jacket: $800.00. Without dust jacket: $300.00

Teddy B and Teddy G, the Bear Detectives, 1909, Barse & Hopkins, NY, 15 color plates by Francis Wightman and William Sweeney, first edition: $400.00

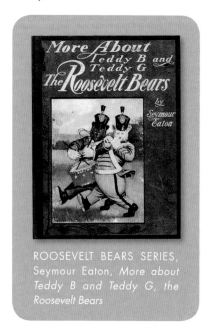

ROOSEVELT BEARS SERIES, Seymour Eaton, *More about Teddy B and Teddy G, the Roosevelt Bears*

ROUNDABOUT AMERICA SERIES, Lois Lenski, 1950s, J. B. Lippincott, hardcover, b/w illustrations by Lenski, who did several series based on historical and geographic themes, first edition with dust jacket: $125.00

We Live in the South, 1952

Peanuts for Billy Ben, 1952

We Live in the City, 1954

Berries in the Scoop, 1956

Little Sioux Girl, 1958

We Live in the Country, 1960

We Live in the Southwest, 1962

High-Rise Secret, 1966

ROVER BOYS SERIES, Arthur M. Winfield (Edward Stratemeyer), 1899 – 1926, Stitt,

also Grosset & Dunlap, and Whitman reprints, cloth-over-board cover, b/w illustrations.

Pre-1920 printings with dust jackets: $50.00

Later editions with dust jackets: $30.00

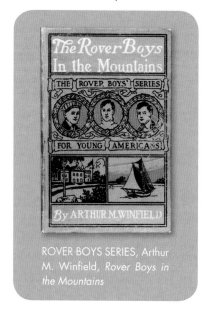

ROVER BOYS SERIES, Arthur M. Winfield, *Rover Boys in the Mountains*

ROY ROGERS SERIES, various authors, books feature the singing movie star and his wife, Dale Evans. In the 1950s Little Golden Books and Whitman hardcovers were plentiful and are still fairly easy to find.

Roy Rogers and the Gopher Creek Gunman, 1945, Whitman, with dust jacket: $40.00

Roy Rogers, coloring books, prices are for clean, uncolored books:

Roy Rogers Paint Book, 1944, Whitman, drawings by Betty Goodan: $45.00

Roy Rogers and Dale Evans Coloring Book, 1951, Whitman, cover features Roy, Dale, and Trigger, the horse, drawings by Peter Alvarado: $35.00

Dale Evans Coloring Book, 1957, Whitman, cover illustration of Dale on her horse: $35.00

RUPERT LITTLE BEAR SERIES, originated by Mary Tourtel, author/illustrator, series based on a daily pictorial series in the

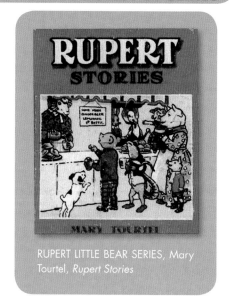

RUPERT LITTLE BEAR SERIES, Mary Tourtel, *Rupert Stories*

London Daily Express, continued by Albert Bestall, then by John Harrold.

Rupert Little Bear Library, 46 volumes, ca. 1930 – 1936, Sampson Low, Marston, London, pictorial boards, 62 pages, one shilling price on cover, each with dust jacket: $150.00. Without dust jacket: $60.00

Rupert and His Pet Monkey through *Rupert and the Magician's Umbrella*

Rupert, annuals: 1930s: $500.00. 1940s: $300.00. 1950s: $100.00. Annuals after 1960: under $30.00

Rupert, other:

Rupert, 1964, Daily Express, oversize glazed illustrated boards, 114 pages, short stories, activities, magic paintings: $90.00

Rupert, 1965, Daily Express, oversize glazed illustrated boards with illustration of Rupert carrying a Christmas tree, 115 pages, short stories, activities, magic paintings: $120.00

RUSS FARRELL SERIES, Thomson Burtis, 1924 – 1929, Doubleday, red hardcover, b/w frontispiece, airplane adventures, motion picture tie-in, with dust jacket: $50.00

RUTH DARROW FLYING STORIES, Mildred Wirt. Wirt was one of the best-known of the Nancy Drew authors and had a pilot's license. 1930 – 1931, Barse, with dust jacket: $200.00

Ruth Darrow in the Air Derby

Ruth Darrow in the Fire Patrol

Ruth Darrow in the Yucatan

Ruth Darrow and the Coast Guard

RUTH FIELDING SERIES, Alice B. Emerson (Stratemeyer Syndicate pseudonym), 1913 – 1930s, Cupples & Leon, printed illustration tan cover, frontispiece, mysteries for girls, at least 30 titles, beginning with *Ruth Fielding of the Red Mill.* Advertised as "Ruth Fielding was an orphan and came to live with her miserly uncle. Her adventures and travels make stories that will hold the interest of every reader."

The hardcover design was changed once, updating Ruth's costume to a shorter skirt in 1929. There were four dust jacket designs, one done by the well-known illustrator Clara Burd.

RUTH FIELDING SERIES, Alice B. Emerson, *illustration*

Ruth Fielding books, first editions with dust jackets: $80.00

■ · · · · · · · · · · · · · · · · · S · · · · · · · · · · · · · · · · · ■

SADLER'S WELLS SERIES, Lorna Hill, 1950 – 1964, Evans (American editions published by Holt), 14 titles. Ballet series based on the school experiences of the

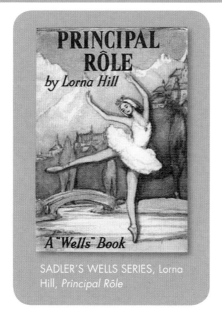

SADLER'S WELLS SERIES, Lorna Hill, *Principal Rôle*

author's daughter at Sadler's Wells, later called the Royal Ballet School, in London.

First edition with dust jacket: $40.00

Dream of Sadler's Wells, 1950

Veronica at the Wells, 1951

Masquerade at the Wells, 1952

No Castanets at the Wells, 1953

Jane Leaves the Wells, 1953

Ella at the Wells, 1954

Return to the Wells, 1955

Rosanna Joins the Wells, 1956

Principal Rôle, 1957

Swan Feather, 1958

Dress-Rehearsal, 1959

Back-Stage, 1960

Vicki in Venice, 1962

Secret, 1964

SALLY SMITH SERIES, Elizabeth Coatsworth, hardcover, Macmillan, b/w illustrations by Helen Sewell, adventures of an orphan in Colonial America, with dust jacket: $70.00

Away Goes Sally, 1934

Five Bushel Farm, 1939

Fair American, 1940

White Horse, 1942

Wonderful Day, 1946

SALLY SMITH SERIES, Elizabeth Coatsworth, *Away Goes Sally*

SAM PIG SERIES, Alison Uttley (1884 – 1976), 1940s, Faber and Faber, illustrated by Francis Cower, Cecil Leslie, or A. E. Kennedy, first edition with dust jacket: $30.00

Adventures of Sam Pig

Sam Pig and Sally

SAM PIG SERIES, Alison Uttley, *Sam Pig and the Hurdy-Gurdy Man*

Sam Pig and the Wind

Sam Pig at the Theatre

Sam Pig in Trouble

Sam Pig and the Singing Gate

Sam Pig Goes to Market

Sam Pig Story Book

Sam Pig and the Hurdy-Gurdy Man

SANDY COVE, Alice Dalgliesh, Macmillan, hardcover, illustrated by Hildegard Woodward, with dust jacket: $75.00

Blue Teapot, Sandy Cove Stories, 1931

Relief's Rocker, a Story of Sandy Cove and the Sea, 1932

Roundabout, Another Sandy Cove Story, 1934

SASEK SERIES, Miroslav Sasek, 1959 – 1974, Macmillan, oversize hardcover picture books, glossy illustrated cover, color illustrations throughout by author. The dust jackets have the same illustrations as the covers. Note different price on *This Is Cape Canaveral.*

Early edition with dust jacket: $40.00

This Is Paris, 1959

This Is London, 1959

This Is Rome, 1960

This Is New York, 1960

This Is Edinburgh, 1961

This Is Munich, 1961

This Is Venice, 1961

This Is San Francisco, 1962

This Is Israel, 1962

This is Cape Canaveral, published in 1963, first edition (later editions of this title are re-named *This is Cape Kennedy*), with dust jacket: $75.00

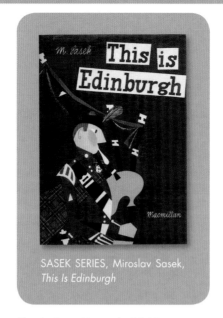

SASEK SERIES, Miroslav Sasek, *This Is Edinburgh*

This Is Cape Kennedy, 1963

This Is Ireland, 1964

This Is Hong Kong, 1965

This Is Greece, 1966

This Is Texas, 1967

This Is the United Nations, 1968

This Is Australia, 1970

This Is Historic Britain, 1974

SCIENTIFIC AMERICAN BOY SERIES, Russell Bond, Scientific American Publishing, hardcover with paste-on-pictorial, illustrated with line drawings and photos: $45.00

Scientific American Boy, or, Camp at Willow Clump Island, 1905

Scientific American Boy at School, 1910

With the Men Who Do Things, 1913

Pick, Shovel and Pluck, 1914

SCOUT DRAKE SERIES, Isabel Hornibrook, Little, Brown, hardcover, four plates by Gallagher, with dust jacket: $40.00

Drake of Troop One, 1916

Scout Drake in War Time, 1918

Coxswain Drake of the Seascouts, 1920

Drake and the Adventurer's Cup, 1922

SCRIBNER CLASSICS, listed on dust jackets as "Scribner Jr. Classics" and "Scribner Illustrated Classics" with crossovers in titles to both series, Charles Scribner's Sons, New York, color paste-on-pictorials on cloth hardcovers, color endpapers, color plate illustrations. First editions in this series are new editions of previously published books, some using illustrations from earlier editions, some using all-new illustrations. The Scribner Illustrated Classics series was advertised as "books of rare beauty and tested literary quality, presented in handsome format and strikingly illustrated in color by such famous artists as N. C. Wyeth, Maxfield Parrish, Jessie Willcox Smith and others – They are to be found in two groups – the Popular Group, issued at a remarkably low price, and the Quality Group, published at a higher but still very reasonable price." The higher priced books were printed on better quality paper and often contained 12 color plates. The lower priced books usually contained eight or less color plates.

See Book List by Author section for descriptions and values. Titles include:

Poems of Childhood, Eugene Field, 1904

Arabian Nights, edited by Kate Douglas Wiggin and Nora Smith, 1909

Treasure Island, R. L. Stevenson, 1911

Wind in the Willows, Kenneth Grahame, 1928

Hans Brinker, Mary Mapes Dodge, 1936

Yearling, Marjorie Rawlings, 1938

Boy's King Arthur, Sidney Lanier, 1947

SECKATARY HAWKINS SERIES, Robert Schulkers, 1921 – 1930, Robert F. Schulkers, Publisher, hardcover, illustrations by Carl Williams, this is a series of humorous newspaper stories about a boys' club that solves mysteries. The stories have appeared in several formats, with individual collections printed as single titles by other publishers.

Schulkers, publisher, hardcover, first edition starts at: $200.00

Seckatary Hawkins in Cuba, 1921

Red Runners, 1922

Stormie, the Dog Stealer, 1925

Gray Ghost, 1926

Knights of the Square Table, 1926

Ching Toy, 1926

Chinese Coin, 1926

Yellow Y, 1926

Herman the Fiddler, 1930

SERAFINA THE GIRAFFE SERIES, Laurent DeBrunhoff, see also BABAR SERIES.

Laurent DeBrunhoff inherited the *Babar* series from his father, Jean, who died in 1937 when Laurent was 12. Although Laurent studied to be a painter, he decided to continue his father's work while still in his twenties. He wrote and illustrated *Babar's Cousin: That Rascal Arthur* (1947), and continued to write and illustrate forty more picture books, most of which are still in print, including his own series, SERAFINA THE GIRAFFE.

Serafina titles, Methuen, London, pictorial hardcover, oversize, color illustrations on every page by the author, first edition with dust jacket: $100.00

Serafina the Giraffe, 1961

Serafina's Lucky Find, 1962

Captain Serafina, 1963

SEVEN CITADELS SERIES, Geraldine Harris, Greenwillow, US first edition with dust jacket: $40.00

Prince of the Godborn, 1982

Children of the Wind, 1982

Dead Kingdom, 1983

Seventh Gate, 1983

SHADOW SERIES, books are based on the radio mystery program, "The Shadow," and also done as a newpaper comic strip, crime fighter can "cloud men's minds," creating invisibility for himself.

Shadow, ca. 1940s, Better Little Books, Whitman, small, pictorial cardboard covers, b/w illustrations: $100.00

Shadow and the Living Death, 1940

Shadow, Master of Evil, 1941

Shadow and the Ghost Makers, 1942

SHADOW SERIES, *Shadow and the Living Death*

SHELDON SIX SERIES, Grace May Remick, 1920 – 1924, Penn, hardcovers with gilt lettering: $65.00

SHIRLEY TEMPLE EDITION BOOKS, ca. late 1930s – 1940s, Random House, hardcover with photo illustration of Shirley Temple in costume, interior b/w photo illustrations from movies based on these novels and starring Shirley Temple, with dust jacket: $40.00

1960s glossy illustrated hardcover reprints: $30.00

Heidi, Johanna Spyri, x-1

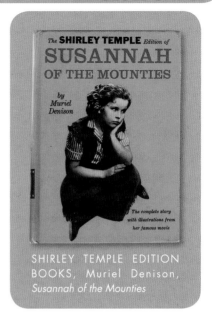

SHIRLEY TEMPLE EDITION BOOKS, Muriel Denison, *Susannah of the Mounties*

Littlest Rebel, Edward Peple, x-2

Rebecca of Sunnybrook Farm, Kate Douglas Wiggin, x-3

Susannah of the Mounties, Muriel Denison, x-4

Captain January, Laura E. Richards, and *Little Colonel*, by Annie Fellows Johnston, two novels in one book

Shirley Temple related book:

Shirley Temple Treasury, 1959, Random House, hardcover, illustrated by Robert Patterson, drawings and photographs from motion pictures featuring Shirley Temple, first edition with dust jacket: $65.00

SHOES SERIES, Noel Streatfeild, Random House, hardcover, b/w illustrations, eight of the books illustrated by Richard Floethe. British series released under other titles.

First edition with dust jacket: $50.00

Ballet Shoes, 1937

Circus Shoes, 1939

Theatre Shoes, 1945

Party Shoes, 1947

Movie Shoes, 1949

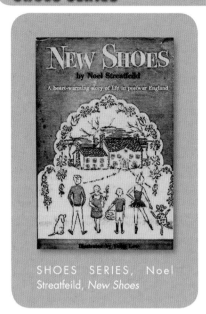

Skating Shoes, 1951

Family Shoes, 1954

Dancing Shoes, 1958

New Shoes, 1960

Travelling Shoes, 1962

Tennis Shoes, 1977

SKYLARKING COMRADES SERIES,
Delmore Marquith, ca. 1930, World
Syndicate Publishing, blue hardcover,
gilt lettering, paste-on-pictorial, with dust
jacket: $35.00

Border-Line Mystery

Flying Buddies of Texas

Flying in Southern Wilderness

Emerald Temple Air Mystery

SLIM TYLER AIR SERIES, Richard Stone
(Stratemeyer Syndicate pseudonym), ca.
1920s, Cupples & Leon, red hardcover,
frontispiece, with dust jacket: $40.00

Sky Riders of the Atlantic

Lost Over Greenland

Air Cargo of Gold

Adrift Over Hudson Bay

304

Airplane Mystery

Secret Sky Express

SLOTTIES TOY SERIES, hardcover, cardboard page with a punch-out toy to
construct.

Slotties, Rand McNally, with punch-outs
uncut and with dust jacket: $75.00.
Without dust jacket: $50.00. With Slottie
toy missing: $15.00

Elegant Elephant, Russell McCracken,
1944, illustrated by Susanne Suba

SLOTTIES TOY SERIES, Russell
McCracken, *Elegant Elephant*

Gentle Giraffe, Russell McCracken, 1945,
illustrated by Susanne Suba

Osbert, Noel Streatfeild, 1950, with a
punch-out Osbert, the poodle, and a
mirror, illustrated by Susanne Suba

Theater Cat, Noel Streatfeild, 1951, with a
punch-out cat, illustrated by Susanne Suba

Lazy Lion, Helen Wing, 1953, illustrated
by Jan B. Balet

Rosalinda, Helen Wing, 1952, illustrated
by Jan B. Balet

Slotties, Container Corp of America, 1954,
with punch-outs uncut and with dust jacket:
$50.00. Without dust jacket: $30.00

Columbine: The White Cat, Patricia Jones,
1955 French folk tale illustrated by Jan B. Balet

Papa Pompano, Martha Bennett King,
1959, 33 pages, illustrated by Jan B. Balet

SMILING POOL SERIES, Thornton W.
Burgess, 1920s, Grosset & Dunlap, small
size, paste-on-pictorial covers, color plate
illustrations by Harrison Cady, with dust
jacket: $75.00

Adventures of Jerry Muskrat

Jerry Muskrat at Home

Little Joe Otter

Longlegs the Heron

Smiling Pool, other:

At Smiling Pool, 1945, Little, Brown, hardcover with dust jacket: $40.00

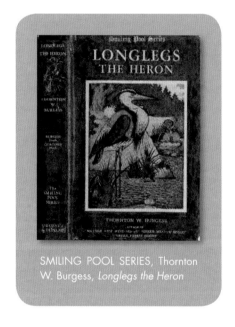

SMILING POOL SERIES, Thornton
W. Burgess, *Longlegs the Heron*

SNIPP, SNAPP, SNURR SERIES, written and
illustrated by Maj Lindman, 1932 – 1959,
Whitman, oversize books with bright colored cover illustrations, color illustrations
throughout.

First Whitman, US, oversize editions,
1930s and 1940s, with dust jacket:
$150.00. Without dust jacket: $80.00

8x10 reprints, ca. 1940s, Whitman, cloth-
over-board cover with paste-on-pictorial,
color illustrations throughout, with dust
jacket: $110.00. Without dust jacket:
$50.00

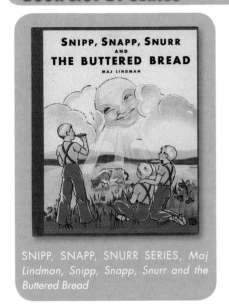

SNIPP, SNAPP, SNURR SERIES, *Maj Lindman, Snipp, Snapp, Snurr and the Buttered Bread*

First US editions published in the 1950s with dust jackets: $90.00. Without dust jackets: $50.00

Snipp, Snapp, Snurr and the Red Shoes, 1932

Snipp, Snapp, Snurr and the Buttered Bread, 1934

Snipp, Snapp, Snurr and the Magic Horse, 1935

Snipp, Snapp, Snurr and the Gingerbread, 1936

Snipp, Snapp, Snurr and the Yellow Sled, 1936

Snipp, Snapp, Snurr and the Big Surprise, 1937

Snipp, Snapp, Snurr and the Big Farm, 1946

Snipp, Snapp, Snurr Learn to Swim, 1954

Snipp, Snapp, Snurr and the Reindeer, 1957

Snipp, Snapp, Snurr and the Seven Dogs, 1959

SNUG AND SERENA SERIES, Alison Uttley (1884 – 1976), hardcover, 64 pages, illustrated by Katherine Wigglesworth.

1950 – 1963, Heinemann, British Book Center, five titles, UK first edition with dust jacket: $70.00

Bobbs-Merrill, first American edition with dust jacket: $40.00

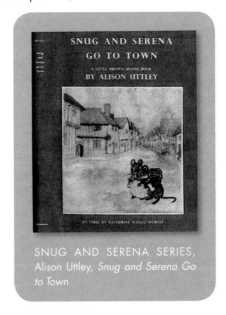

SNUG AND SERENA SERIES, Alison Uttley, *Snug and Serena Go to Town*

SONG OF THE LIONESS SERIES, Tamora Ann Pierce

Alanna: The First Adventure, 1983, Atheneum, hardcover, 240 pages, First edition with dust jacket: $150.00

Alanna: The First Adventure, 1984, Oxford University Press, UK first edition with dust jacket: $80.00

In the Hand of the Goddess, 1984, Atheneum, first edition with dust jacket: $150.00

Woman Who Rides Like a Man, 1986, Atheneum, first edition with dust jacket: $150.00

Woman Who Rides Like a Man, 1989, Oxford University Press, UK first edition with dust jacket: $80.00

Lioness Rampant, 1988, Atheneum, first edition with dust jacket: $100.00

SORAK SERIES, Harvey D. Richards, Cupples & Leon, red hardcover, black lettering, frontispiece by F. R. Schaare, adventures in the Malay jungle, with dust jacket: $35.00

SORAK SERIES, Harvey D. Richards, *Sorak and the Clouded Tiger*

Sorak of the Malay Jungle, 1934

Sorak and the Clouded Tiger, 1934

Sorak and the Sultan's Ankus, 1934

Sorak and the Tree-Men, 1936

SORCERY HALL TRILOGY, Suzy McKee Charnas. Tina, Valentine, Marsh and Joel battle magical dangers in modern Manhattan. First edition with dust jacket: $40.00

Bronze King, 1985, Houghton Mifflin

Silver Glove, 1988, Bantam

Golden Thread, 1989, Bantam

SOUTH TOWN SERIES, Lorenz Graham, Follett and Crowell, hardcover, dust jacket illustration by Ernie Crichlow, first edition with dust jacket: $40.00

South Town, 1958

North Town, 1965

Whose Town?, 1969

Return to South Town, 1976

SOU'WESTER SERIES, Arthur Baldwin, Random House, oversize hardcover, sailing adventures of two young brothers, blue and white pictorial endpapers, b/w

SOUTH TOWN SERIES, Lorenz Graham, *South Town*

illustrations by Gordan Grant. Early printings with dust jacket: $35.00

Sou'wester Sails, 1936

Sou'wester Goes North, 1938

Sou'wester Victorious, 1939

SPACEBREAD SERIES, Steve Senn, ca. 1980, Atheneum, hardcover, wraparound illustration dust jackets by the author. Spacebread is a space roving cat who travels around the galaxy in a spaceship. First edition with dust jacket: $75.00

Spacebread

Circle in the Sun

Born of Flame

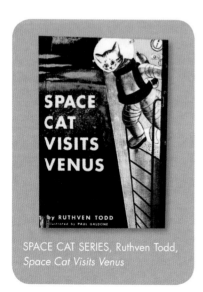

SPACE CAT SERIES, Ruthven Todd, *Space Cat Visits Venus*

SPACE CAT SERIES, Ruthven Todd, starring an astronaut cat, Scribner's, US and

306

Chatto & Wyndus, UK, hardcover, illustrations by Paul Galdone.

First edition with dust jacket: $100.00. Without dust jacket: $40.00

Later printings issued with pictorial hardcovers: $30.00

Space Cat, 1952

Space Cat Visits Venus, 1955

Space Cat Meets Mars, 1957

Space Cat and the Kittens, 1959

SPACE SHIP SERIES, Louis Slobodkin, Macmillan, b/w illustrations by author. Marty, the alien, and Eddie, earth boy, share space adventures.

First editions with dust jackets: $100.00

SPACE SHIP SERIES, Louis Slobodkin, *Space Ship in the Park*

SPACEBREAD SERIES, Steve Senn, *Born of Flame*

Later printings with dust jackets: $35.00

Space Ship under the Apple Tree, 1952

Space Ship Returns to Apple Tree, 1958

Three-Seated Space Ship, 1962

Round Trip Space Ship, 1968

Space Ship in the Park, 1972

STACY BELFORD SERIES, Lenora Mattingly Weber, Crowell, hardcover, another teen romance series (what else, with these titles?) by this popular writer. First edition with dust jacket by Robert Levering, start at: $200.00

How Long Is Always?, 1970

Hello, My Love, Good-bye, 1971

Sometimes a Stranger, 1972

STACY BELFORD SERIES, Lenora Mattingly Weber, *Hello, My Love, Good-bye*

STAMPKRAFT BOOKS, Barse & Hopkins, New York, series ca. 1920, oversize oblong paper-over-board hardcover, b/w illustrations with sheets of colored illustrations of stamps to paste on story pages, no author or illustrator identification: $45.00

Alice in Wonderland

Anderson's Fairy Tales

Cinderella

Favorite Rhymes from Mother Goose

Kiddie Kapers

King Parrot and His Court

Mother Goose and Other Rhymes

Puss in Boots

Stories from the Bible

Robinson Crusoe

Three Bears

Tiny Tot Rhymes

STAR KA'AT SERIES, Andre Norton and Dorothy Madlee, science fiction series for younger readers, featuring a cat.

Walker, first edition with dust jacket: $100.00

Star Ka'at, 1976

Star Ka'at World, 1978

Star Ka'at and the Plant People, 1979, illustrated by Jean Jenkins

Star Ka'at and the Winged Warriors, 1981

STAR KA'AT SERIES, Andre Norton and Dorothy Madlee, *Star Ka'at*

STAR TREK SERIES, books based on the TV series by Gene Roddenberry. Novels based on the *Star Trek* series were aimed

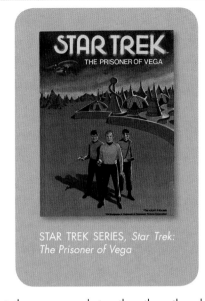

STAR TREK SERIES, *Star Trek: The Prisoner of Vega*

at the mass market rather than the children's market, and were originally released as paperbacks. Later, hardcover editions were published in extremely large runs and can be found at an average price of $20.00 with dust jacket.

Star Trek Pop-Ups:

Paramount Pictures Pop-Up Book, Star Trek — Giant in the Universe, 1967, Random House, pictorial hardcover, pop-ups: $50.00

Star Trek: Trillions of Trilligs, a Star Trek Pop-up, 1977, Random House, illustrated hardcover, color pop-ups. $40.00

ST. CLARE SERIES, Enid Blyton, ca. 1940s, Methuen, small hardcover, b/w illustrations, first edition with dust jacket starts at: $40.00

Twins at St. Clare's

O'Sullivan Twins

Summer Term at St. Clare's

Second Form at St. Clare's

Claudine at St. Clare's

Fifth Formers of St. Clare's

ST. DUNSTAN SERIES, Warren Eldred, sports stories, Lothrop, Lee and Shepard, red hardcover with paste-on-pictorial, gold lettering, b/w plates: $30.00

ST. CLARE SERIES, Enid Blyton, *Claudine at St. Clare's*

Crimson Ramblers, 1910

Camp St. Dunstan, 1911

Classroom and Campus, 1912

St. Dunstan Boy Scouts, 1913

STEVE CANYON, see TERRY AND THE PIRATES

STEVE KNIGHT FLYING SERIES, Ted Copp, Grosset & Dunlap, orange hardcover with black lettering and airplane illustration, frontispiece, with dust jacket: $35.00

Devil's Hand, 1941

Bridge of Bombers, 1941

Phantom Fleet, 1942

ST. MARY'S SERIES, William Heyliger, school sports, 1911 – 1915, Appleton, tan hardcover with impressed illustration, b/w plates, start at: $70.00

Bartley, Freshman Pitcher

Bucking the Line

Captain of the Nine

Strike Three

Off Side

Against Odds

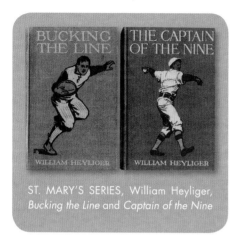

ST. MARY'S SERIES, William Heyliger, *Bucking the Line* and *Captain of the Nine*

SUE BARTON SERIES, Helen Dore Boylston

Little, Brown, cloth hardcover, color frontispiece, first edition with dust jacket: $100.00

Bodley Head, UK edition with dust jacket: $50.00

Sue Barton, Student Nurse, 1936

Sue Barton, Senior Nurse, 1937

Sue Barton, Visiting Nurse, 1938

Sue Barton, Rural Nurse, 1939, dust jacket by Major Felten

Sue Barton, Superintendent of Nurses, 1940

SUE BARTON SERIES, Helen Dore Boylston, *Sue Barton, Rural Nurse*

Sue Barton, Neighborhood Nurse, 1949

Sue Barton, Staff Nurse, 1952

SUNBONNET BABIES BOOKS, Eulalie Osgood Grover, illustrator Corbett created the unique shape of a small child in long dress and sunbonnet in these books. Her illustration became a favorite needlework design.

An illustration from SUNBONNET BABIES BOOKS, Eulalie Osgood Grover

Sunbonnet Babies' Primer, 1902, Rand McNally, Chicago, small illustrated hardcover, 100+ pages, illustrated endpapers, color illustrations throughout by Bertha Corbett: $100.00

Sunbonnet Babies: A First Reader, 1914, Rand McNally, small gray illustrated hardcover, color illustrations throughout by Bertha Corbett: $100.00

Sunbonnet Babies in Holland, 1915, Rand McNally, illustrated by Bertha Corbett: $100.00

Sunbonnet Bables in Mother Goose Land, 1927, Rand McNally, pictorial boards, full-color and b/w illustrations by Bertha Corbett Melcher, first edition: $100.00. Later editions: $40.00

Sunbonnet Babies A B C Book, 1929, Rand McNally, paste-on-pictorial on board covers, oversize, 64 pages, illustrated in b/w and color plates by Bertha Corbett Melcher, first edition with dust jacket: $400.00

SUNNY BOOKS SERIES, 1910 – 1930, Volland Publishers, Chicago (see also HAPPY CHILDREN BOOKS) small color

illustrated paper-over-board hardcovers, color illustrations throughout. Somewhat fragile books, beautiful color illustrated endpapers and color illustrations throughout, titles cross over and turn up in other Volland series, as well as in other publishers' editions. Volland books were often packaged in cardboard boxes with box lids matching the book cover, rather than in dust jackets. Individual titles are listed in the Author section of this book. Price varies by artist, but generally, with a good condition box: $150.00. Without box: $70.00

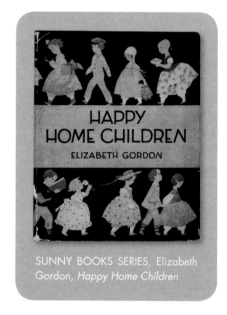

SUNNY BOOKS SERIES, Elizabeth Gordon, *Happy Home Children*

SUNNYBROOK MEADOW SERIES, Elsie M. Alexander, ca. 1920s, Burt, small hardcover, illustrated endpapers, color illustrations by Marie Schubert, with dust jacket: $30.00

SUSANNAH SERIES, Muriel Denison, this popular series was reprinted in a variety of formats. (See also SHIRLEY TEMPLE EDITION BOOKS).

1930s – 1940s, Dodd, Mead edition, hardcover, illustrated endpapers, b/w illustrations by Marguerite Bryan, with dust jacket: $40.00

Susannah of the Mounties, 1936

Susannah of the Yukon, 1936

Susannah at Boarding School, 1938

Susannah Rides Again, 1940

SUSANNAH AND LUCY MYSTERIES,
Patricia Elmore, 1980 – 1982, E. P. Dutton, three titles, hardcover, b/w illustrations by Joel Schick, first edition with dust jacket: $30.00

Susannah and the Blue House Mystery, 1980

Susannah and the Poison Green Halloween, 1982

Susannah and the Purple Mongoose Mystery, 1992

SUSANNAH AND LUCY MYSTERIES, Patricia Elmore, *Susannah and the Poison Green Halloween*

SWALLOWS AND AMAZONS SERIES,
Arthur Ransome (1884 – 1967), camping and sailing adventures of the Walker family and their catboat, Swallow, and the

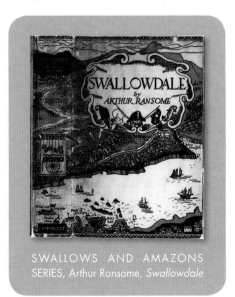

SWALLOWS AND AMAZONS SERIES, Arthur Ransome, *Swallowdale*

Blackett girls, these popular books were reprinted in various formats. More collectors seek the British first editions published by Jonathan Cape than the American editions from Lippincott or Macmillan.

Swallows reprints of the titles listed are:

Pre-1938, Cape, with Webb illustrations, with dust jacket: $200.00

Late 1930s, Cape, with dust jacket start at: $60.00

1940s and 1950s, Cape or American editions with dust jackets: $40.00 (slightly higher per book for a complete set)

Swallows first editions, Cape, UK, and Lippincott or Macmillan, US, prices start at:

Swallows and Amazons, 1930, Cape, no illustrations, jacket illustration and maps by Steven Spurrier (Ransome objected to Spurrier's illustrations so they were dropped from book. This edition is rare, but price at auction should be the same as or higher than 1931 first editions listed below.) Infrequent UK dealer listings start at: $12,000.00

Swallows and Amazons, 1931, Cape, illustrations by Clifford Webb, new dust jacket design (Again, Ransome objected to illustrations, finally having publisher substitute his own drawings for editions published after 1938). First edition without dust jacket: $2,000.00. With dust jacket starts at: $10,000.00

Swallows and Amazons, 1931, J. B. Lippincott, illustrations by Helene Carter, first edition without dust jacket: $2,000.00. With dust jacket: $10,000.00

Swallowdale, 1932, Cape, illustrations by Clifford Webb (Ransome's illustrations replaced Webb's drawings for editions published after 1938.) First edition: $2,000.00. With dust jacket: $6,000.00

Swallowdale, 1932, J. B. Lippincott, illustrations by Helene Carter (The first edition deleted the last three paragraphs of the text. First edition ended with "The Swallows and Amazons went down again into their

camp." Later editions end with "Isn't it a blessing to get home?"), US first edition: $250.00, with dust jacket: $500.00

Peter Duck, 1932, Cape, illustrations by Ransome (credited on dust jacket as "with illustrations mainly by themselves"), color map endpapers, first edition with dust jacket: $4,000.00

Peter Duck, 1933, J. B. Lippincott, illustrations by Helene Carter, US first edition: $250.00. With dust jacket: $500.00

Winter Holiday, 1933, Cape, illustrations by Ransome, first edition: $200.00. With dust jacket: $700.00

Winter Holiday, 1934, J. B. Lippincott, illustrations by Helene Carter, US first edition: $100.00. With dust jacket: $500.00

Coot Club, 1934, Cape, illustrations by Ransome, first edition: $100.00. With dust jacket: $500.00

Coot Club, 1935, J. B. Lippincott, illustrations by Helene Carter, US first edition: $100.00. With dust jacket: $500.00

Pigeon Post, 1936, Cape, first winner of Carnegie Medal for Children's Literature, first edition with dust jacket: $400.00

Pigeon Post, 1937, J. B. Lippincott, illustrations by Mary Shepard, US first edition with dust jacket: $100.00

We Didn't Mean to Go to Sea, 1937, Cape, illustrations by author, first edition with dust jacket starts at: $500.00

Secret Water, 1939, Cape, map endpapers, illustrations by author, first edition with dust jacket: $500.00

Secret Water, 1940, Macmillan, first edition with dust jacket: $50.00

Big Six, 1940, Cape, illustrations by author, first edition with dust jacket: $300.00

Big Six, 1941, Macmillan, first edition with dust jacket starts at: $50.00

Missee Lee, 1941, Cape, illustrations by author, semaphore mistakes corrected in

SWALLOWS AND AMAZONS SERIES, Arthur Ransome, *Secret Water*

SWORD OF THE SPIRITS TRILOGY, John Christopher, see also FIREBALL SERIES, TRIPODS SERIES

Hamish Hamilton, UK first edition with dust jacket: $45.00

Macmillan, US first edition with dust jacket: $35.00

Prince in Waiting, 1970

Beyond the Burning Lands, 1971

Sword of the Spirits, 1972, dust jacket by Emanuel Schongut

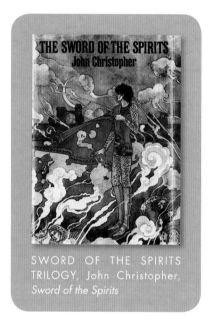

SWORD OF THE SPIRITS TRILOGY, John Christopher, *Sword of the Spirits*

■ ·············· T ·············· ■

TAHARA ADVENTURE SERIES, Harold M. Sherman, 1933, Goldsmith Publishing, Tarzan-type adventures, same dust jacket design for all books, with dust jacket by J. C. Gretta: $35.00

Tahara, Boy Mystic of India

Tahara among African Tribes

Tahara, Boy King of the Desert

Tahara in the Land of the Yucatan

TARZAN SERIES, Edgar Rice Burroughs. Tarzan was written for the adult market, but quickly became a favorite of young

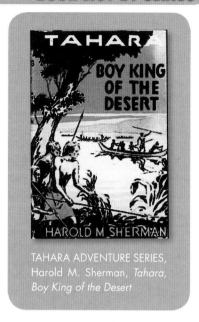

TAHARA ADVENTURE SERIES, Harold M. Sherman, *Tahara, Boy King of the Desert*

the illustration "Captain Flint's S.O.S." in later editions (after Ransome was informed of the error by a Brownie scout), first edition with dust jacket: $300.00

Missee Lee, 1942, Macmillan, first edition with dust jacket: $50.00

Picts and the Martyrs, 1943, Cape, illustrations by author, first edition with dust jacket: $300.00

Picts and the Martyrs, 1944, Macmillan, illustrations by author, first edition with dust jacket: $50.00

Great Northern?, 1947, Cape, illustrations by author, first edition with dust jacket: $300.00

Great Northern?, 1948, Macmillan, illustrations by author, first edition with dust jacket: $50.00

Swallows and Amazons, research:

Hardyment, Christine. *Arthur Ransome and Captain Flint's Trunk.* Cape, 1984. Research into the true locations used by Ransome for the *Swallows and Amazons* series (in print, updated editions are still available for retail price from the UK), first edition: $100.00

Hammond, Wayne. *Arthur Ransome: A Bibliography.* Oak Knoll Press, 2000.

readers. The following is a list of the first printings of first editions. Later editions are listed at the end of this section. These have become highly collectible, demand escalating prices, with wide variations due to availability. Later printings have less value. The Zeuschner reference listed below gives detailed descriptions of editions and printings.

Because the covers were not illustrated, and the dust jackets were highly decorative, a mint dust jacket of a first edition can increase the value about ten times or more. In this price range, remember that dust jackets are easy to reproduce, and should be examined carefully. Reproduction jackets (color photocopies of originals) are regularly listed for sale on such sites as eBay and Abebooks. Price for an edition with reproduction dust jacket is usually only $15.00 to $20.00 more than a similar quality first edition without dust jacket.

Wide fluctuations in price are due to the wide variety of print runs, making some books far easier to find than others. McClurg printed more than 75,000 copies total of *Jungle Tales of Tarzan,* but less than 8,000 copies total of their last book, *Tarzan, Lord of the Jungle.*

Tarzan first editions, in order of publication:

Tarzan of the Apes, 1914, McClurg, green cloth-over-board cover with gold lettering, eight sepia plates by J. Allen St. John, with dust jacket: $45,000.00 to $55,000.00. Without dust jacket: $1,000.00 to $2,500.00

Return of Tarzan, 1915, McClurg, green cloth-over-board cover with gold lettering, b/w illustrations by J. Allen St. John, the dust jacket has an N. C. Wyeth illustration and is extremely rare, although reproductions are available for about $25.00. Without dust jacket: $400.00

Beasts of Tarzan, 1916, McClurg, olive cloth-over-board cover with gold lettering, wraparound dust jacket illustration and interior b/w illustrations by J. Allen St. John, with dust jacket starts at: $3,000.00. Without dust jacket: $150.00

Son of Tarzan, 1917, McClurg, green cloth-over-board cover with gold lettering, b/w illustrations by J. Allen St. John, with dust jacket starts at: $5,000.00. Without dust jacket: $150.00

Tarzan and the Jewels of Opar, 1918, McClurg, dark green cloth-over-board cover with gold lettering, eight sepia plates by J. Allen St. John, with dust jacket starts at: $4,500.00. Without dust jacket: $200.00

Jungle Tales of Tarzan, 1919, McClurg, orange cloth-over-board cover (first printing used orange, later used green cloth), five sepia plates plus b/w drawings by J. Allen St. John, with dust jacket: $1,500.00. Without dust jacket: $150.00

Tarzan the Untamed, 1920, McClurg, olive cloth-over-board cover, nine sepia plates by J. Allen St. John, with dust jacket: $1,600.00. Without dust jacket: $150.00

Tarzan the Terrible, 1921, McClurg, red cloth-over-board cover, nine sepia plates by J. Allen St. John, plus a map and glossary by author, with dust jacket starts at: $1,000.00. Without dust jacket: $150.00

Tarzan and the Golden Lion, 1923, McClurg, mustard-yellow cloth-over-board cover, eight sepia plates by J. Allen St. John, with dust jacket starts at: $1,500.00. Without dust jacket: $250.00

Tarzan and the Ant Men, 1924, McClurg, brown cloth-over-board cover, b/w illustrations by J. Allen St. John, with dust jacket: $1,500.00. Without dust jacket: $150.00

Tarzan, Lord of the Jungle, 1928, McClurg, green cloth-over-board cover, five sepia plates by J. Allen St. John, plus a map by author, with dust jacket: $2,000.00. Without dust jacket: $150.00

Tarzan and the Lost Empire, 1929, Metropolitan, orange cloth-over-board cover, b/w frontispiece by A. W. Sperry, with dust jacket: $600.00. Without dust jacket: $100.00

Tarzan at the Earth's Core, 1930, Metropolitan, light green cloth-over-board cover, b/w frontispiece by J. Allen St. John, with dust jacket: $1,000.00. Without dust jacket: $250.00

Tarzan the Invincible, 1931, Edgar Rice Burroughs Inc., blue cloth-over-board cover with red lettering, b/w frontispiece by Studley Burroughs, with dust jacket: $900.00. Without dust jacket: $125.00

Tarzan Triumphant, 1932, Edgar Rice Burroughs Inc., blue cloth-over-board cover with red lettering, b/w frontispiece and five b/w plates by Studley Burroughs, with dust jacket: $500.00. Without dust jacket: $125.00

Tarzan and the City of Gold, 1933, Edgar Rice Burroughs Inc., blue cloth-over-board cover, five b/w plates by J. Allen St. John, with dust jacket: $500.00. Without dust jacket: $125.00

Tarzan and the Lion Man, 1934, Edgar Rice Burroughs Inc., gray cloth-over-board cover, five b/w plates by J. Allen St. John, with dust jacket: $500.00. Without dust jacket: $125.00

Tarzan and the Leopard Men, 1935, Edgar Rice Burroughs Inc., blue cloth-over-board cover with red lettering, four b/w plates by J. Allen St. John, with dust jacket: $500.00. Without dust jacket: $100.00

Tarzan's Quest, 1936, Edgar Rice Burroughs Inc., blue cloth-over-board cover, five b/w plates by J. Allen St. John, with dust jacket: $600.00. Without dust jacket: $125.00

Tarzan and the Forbidden City, 1938, Edgar Rice Burroughs Inc., blue cloth-over-board cover, color frontispiece and four b/w plates by John Burroughs, with dust jacket starts at: $400.00. Without dust jacket: $100.00

Tarzan the Magnificent, 1939, Edgar Rice Burroughs Inc., blue cloth-over-board cover, five b/w plates by John Burroughs, with dust jacket: $600.00. Without dust jacket: $250.00

Tarzan and the Foreign Legion, 1947, Edgar Rice Burroughs Inc., blue cloth-over-board cover, five b/w plates by John Burroughs, with dust jacket: $150.00. Without dust jacket: $50.00

Tarzan Series, A. L. Burt reprints:

1915 – 1928, A. L. Burt, plain hardback reprints of first five titles were published on poorer quality paper than the McClurg originals, but used the original McClurg interior illustrations and dust jacket

TARZAN SERIES, Edgar Rice Burroughs, *Beasts of Tarzan,* A.L. Burt; *Tarzan and the Foreign Legion,* W. H. Allen; *Tarzan Twins,* Volland; Grosset bookmark; *Tarzan and the Golden Lion,* Grosset photoplay

designs. As these are fragile books, condition causes a wide variation in price. Early Burt printings with very good condition dust jackets start at: $75.00. Without dust jacket: $20.00 to $30.00

Tarzan Series, 1920s, Grosset & Dunlap editions:

1920s editions, Grosset & Dunlap, plain cloth-over-board cover, about 400 pages, four b/w plate illustrations. Grosset & Dunlap editions use earlier illustrations from both the McClurg and the Metropolitan books, and also copied the original dust jackets, with the Grosset & Dunlap mark added to the spine. Dating is unclear, listing the original McClurg or Metropolitan date rather than the date of the Grosset & Dunlap printing. With dust jacket start at: $50.00. Without dust jacket up to: $30.00

Tarzan and the Golden Lion, 1929, Grosset Photoplay editions with four b/w stills from silent movie, orange cloth-over-board cover, dust jacket shows actor James Pierce (Burroughs' son-in-law) as Tarzan, with dust jacket: $300.00. Without dust jacket: $30.00

Tarzan Series, other books based on the series:

Tarzan Twins, 1927, Volland, Golden Youth Series, illustrated paper-over-board cover, 127 pages, illustrated endpapers, color and b/w illustrations by Douglas Grant, with dust jacket: $200.00. Without dust jacket: $100.00

Tarzan Twins, Volland, second edition in its original Volland box with cover illustration: $150.00. Without box: $65.00

Tarzan and the Tarzan Twins with Jad-Bal-Ja, the Golden Lion, 1936, Whitman, oversize, marked "Big Big Book," color illustrated paper-over-board cover, coloring book drawings by Juanita Bennett: $100.00

Tarzan Pop-Up:

New Adventures of Tarzan, 1935, Blue Ribbon, Chicago, hardcover with three double-page full-color pop-ups, Stephen

Slesinger illustrations, with good condition pop-ups start at: $500.00

Tarzan Series, ca. 1930s to 1940s, Big Little Books and Better Little Books, pictorial cardboard cover, b/w illustrations: $40.00 to $70.00

Tarzan Series, UK:

Methuen, UK, did early editions of many Tarzan titles with new dust jacket art. 1918 – 1930s, Methuen hardcovers with pictorial dust jackets: $150.00. Later Methuen reprints with dust jackets: $30.00

Tarzan Series, Canaveral reprints:

1960s, hardcover reissues of out-of-print Burroughs novels, often with new dust jacket design and interior illustration art, with dust jacket: $90.00

Hard-to-find Canaveral titles:

Tarzan and the Madman (1964 posthumous Tarzan story), illustrated by Reed Crandall, with dust jacket: $200.00

TARZAN SERIES, Edgar Rice Burroughs, *Tarzan and the Madman*

Tarzan and the Tarzan Twins, yellow hardcover, b/w illustrations by Roy G. Krenkel, with dust jacket: $150.00

Tarzan and *Mars* series illustrators:

St. John, James Allen (1872 – 1957, American) After resisting efforts by his

father to make him a businessman, St. John followed the footsteps of his maternal grandfather, Hilliard Hely, and chose art as his career. He worked as a portrait artist in New York but eventually moved to Chicago and took up residence in the "Tree Studio." This apartment complex for artists had a large studio attached to each residence. St. John worked for the Chicago publishers as a cover artist and illustrator for nearly 50 years as well as taught classes at the Art Institute and American Academy of Art. Through his association with the A.C. McClurg company, St. John received commissions to illustrate the work of Edgar Rice Burroughs. He painted full-color covers in oils as well as provided interior illustrations, usually done in pen and ink or gouache, for both the *Tarzan* and *Mars* series. In the early 1930s, when Burroughs took over publishing his own books, he decided that St. John's fees were too high and farmed out the art work to relatives Studley Burroughs and John Coleman Burroughs. St. John continued to teach as well as do science fiction magazine covers and illustrations through the 1950s.

Krenkel, Roy (1918 – 1983, American) Krenkel started out with EC Comics after World War II. Heavily influenced by J. Allen St. John, he won the assignment of creating new covers for the Ace paperback reissue of many Edgar Rice Burroughs titles. Besides winning the 1963 Hugo for his work, Krenkel also launched the paperback cover career of fellow EC Comics artist Frank Frazetta when he recommended Frazetta to editor Donald Wolheim.

Tarzan reference:

Edgar Rice Burroughs, the Exhaustive Scholars and Collectors Descriptive Bibliography, Robert B. Zeuschner, 1996, McFarland & Co., hardcover, 237 pages, b/w photos of book covers, complete explanations of editions.

Edgar Rice Burroughs Library of Illustration, Russ Cochran, publisher and editor, 1976 – 1985. Three volumes, limited edition of 2,000 copies, books reproduced original artwork that appeared in the *Tarzan* and *Mars* series as drawn from

Burroughs' private collection. Hardcover, folio, slipcase, set of three volumes: $800.00

TED AND NINA SERIES, Marguerite DeAngeli, Doubleday, four titles, small, illustrated endpapers, color illustrations by author, first edition with dust jacket: $100.00

Ted and Nina Go to the Grocery Store, 1935

Ted and Nina Have a Happy Rainy Day, 1936

Summer Day with Ted and Nina, 1940

Ted and Nina Story Book, 1965

TEENIE WEENIES SERIES, Wm. Donahey, Teenie Weenies was a Sunday comic page feature from 1914 through the 1960s, adventures of the miniature inhabitants of Teenie Weenie Town.

Original printings by Reilly & Lee, then Whittlesey, had cloth-over-board hardcovers, color plate illustrations by author. See title for value.

Ca. 1940s, Rand McNally, Jr. Edition reprints, color illustrated paper-over-board cover, small, color illustrations by author: $80.00. Titles include:

Adventures of the Teenie Weenies, ca. 1920, Reilly & Lee: $200.00

An illustration from the TEENIE WEENIES SERIES, Wm. Donahey

Teenie Weenies under the Rosebush, 1922, Reilly & Lee: $200.00

Teenie Weenies in the Wildwood, 1923, Reilly & Lee: $200.00

Teenie Weenie Land, 1923, Beckley: $100.00

Alice and the Teenie Weenies, 1927, Reilly & Lee: $200.00

Teenie Weenie Town, 1942, Whittlesey, with dust jacket: $200.00

Teenie Weenie Days, 1944, Whittlesey, without dust jacket: $100.00

Teenie Weenie Neighbors, 1945, Whittlesey, with dust jacket: $200.00

Teenie Weenies, reference:

Teenie Weenies Book, the Life and Art of William Donahey, Joseph M. Cahn, 1986, Green Tiger Press: $100.00

TERRY AND THE PIRATES, Milton Caniff, based on the newspaper comic strip characters.

Terry and the Pirates, Whitman hardcover:

April Kane and the Dragon Lady, a Terry and the Pirates Adventure, 1942, Whitman, hardcover, illustrated endpapers, b/w full-page illustrations, 248 pages, with dust jacket: $30.00

Terry and the Pirates, Whitman Big Little Books: $30.00

Terry and the Pirates, 1935

Terry and the Pirates and the Giant's Vengeance, 1939

Terry and the Pirates in the Mountain Stronghold, 1941

Terry and the Pirates Shipwrecked on a Desert Island, ca. 1940s

Terry and the Prates, related titles: STEVE CANYON series, Milton Caniff, based on the newspaper comic strip, 1959, Grosset & Dunlap, hardcover, with dust jacket: $50.00

TERRY AND THE PIRATES, Milton Caniff, *April Kane and the Dragon Lady*

Operation Convoy

Operation Snowflower

Operation Foo Ling

Operation Eel Island

TEXAN SERIES, Joseph Altsheler, 1912 – 1913, Appleton, hardcover, frontispiece and three plates, first edition with dust jacket: $200.00

1950s reprints with dust jackets: $30.00

Texan Star

Texan Scouts

Texan Triumph

THOMAS THE TANK ENGINE RAILWAY SERIES, Rev. Wilbert Awdry (1911 – 1997), tales of a train engine and his friends.

Awdry, a train buff from childhood, created the first story of the *Railway Series* to distract his son, Christopher, from a bout of the measles. Self-illustrated and starring a railway engine named Edward, the book was a favorite of the Awdry children and Mrs. Margaret Awdry suggested that her husband submit it to a publisher. By 1946, the series had become so popular that the author produced a book a year until 1972. In 1983, Awdry's son Christopher started a second series of books about

THOMAS THE TANK ENGINE RAILWAY SERIES, Rev. Wilbert Awdry, 1950s edition, with dust jacket

the trains of the Island of Sodor. In 1984, *Thomas the Tank Engine* became a popular BBC TV animation series and later printings emphasized the Thomas name rather than *Railway Series*. The books have been re-printed often and can be confusing to identify. The dates are sometimes changed with printings and the original date is not always indicated.

Thomas, original series, 1945 – 1972, published by Edward Ward, London, small hardcover, color illustrations by various artists. Starting with the third book in 1948, C. Reginald Dalby replaced the author as illustrator and his bright colors set the style for the series. In 1956 John T. Kenney became the illustrator and kept much of the Dalby style. In 1963 the illustration job went to Peter and Guvnor Edwards, a husband and wife team.

Thomas, values:

1940s and 1950s editions, with dust jacket: $100.00. 1960s editions, with dust jacket: $75.00

Three Railway Engines, 1945, illustrations by author

Thomas the Tank Engine, 1946, illustrations by author

Thomas the Tank Engine, circa 1948, illustration added to by Dalby

Illustrations by C. Reginald Dalby:

Three Railway Engines, circa 1948

James the Red Engine, 1948

Tank Engine Thomas Again, 1949

Troublesome Engines, 1950

Henry the Green Engine, 1951

Toby the Tram Engine, 1952

Gordon the Big Engine, 1953

Edward the Blue Engine, 1954

Four Little Engines, 1955

Illustrations by John T. Kenney:

Percy the Small Engine, 1956

Eight Famous Engines, 1957

Duck and the Diesel Engine, 1958

Little Old Engine, 1959

Twin Engines, 1960

Branch Line Engines, 1961

Gallant Old Engine, 1962

Stepney the Bluebell Engine, 1963

Illustrations by Peter and Guvnor Edwards:

Mountain Engines, 1964

Very Old Engines, 1965

Main Line Engines, 1966

Small Railway Engines, 1967

Enterprising Engines, 1968

Oliver the Western Engine, 1969

Duke the Lost Engine, 1970, small oblong, 56 pages, first edition with dust jacket: $60.00

Tramway Engines, 1972

Thomas, second *Railway Series*, Christopher Awdry, 14 titles, 1983 – 1996, used editions and reprintings easily available.

Thomas, other: According to a recent omnibus edition of the first 26 books, the *Thomas* stories have been reproduced in hundreds of other editions and formats since the animation series ran on the BBC. Some which vary from the standard baby board book are sought by collectors. Examples:

Awdry Railway Series Scenes from Tank Engine Thomas Again, Painting Book #1, 1950, Ward, oversize, 12 pages, color illustrations with matching b/w illustrated pages to paint: $60.00

Meet Thomas the Tank Engine and His Friends, Awdry, 1989, Random House, oversize pictorial hardcover: $40.00

Percy the Small Engine Takes the Plunge, pop-up book, 1992, Random House, hardcover with pop-up illustrations in color: $30.00

THOUSAND AND ONE NIGHTS, also known as *Arabian Nights*, tales and legends, many collected in Persia between the 980s and 1011 A. D., others collected throughout the Orient and translated to French by Antoine Galland, seventeenth century. Famous English translators of the nineteenth century include Edward Lane and Sir Richard Francis Burton. The stories were intended for adults and printed in volume sets. The colorful tales revolve around Queen Scheherazade, who tells a story each night to delay her own execution. The adventures include many with great appeal for children and became favorites of writers and illustrators of children's books.

Some early editions marketed for children include:

Thousand, collections:

Arabian Nights' Entertainments, 1821, London, leather cover over marbled boards, three volumes, 470 to 500 pages each, engraved illustration on frontispiece and title page. Set of three volumes: $300.00

Arabian Nights' Entertainments, 1877, George Routledge and Sons, decorated blue cloth-over-board hardcover with gilt, all page edges gilded, 796 pages, 150 illustrations by Thomas B. Dalziel: $80.00

Fairy Tales from the Arabian Nights, 1893, Dent, London, hardcover, plates and drawings by J. D. Batten: $150.00

Sinbad the Sailor and Other Stories from the Arabian Nights, 1914, Hodder & Stoughton, cloth-over-board with gilt, 223 pages, tipped-in color plates by Edmund Dulac, first edition thus: $600.00

Tales from the Thousand and One Nights, 1925, Dodd, Mead and Company, blue hardcover with paste-on-pictorial, 297 pages, color illustrations by E. J. Detmold: $150.00

Tales from the Arabian Nights, 1957, Golden Press, pictorial hardcover, 92 pages, color illustrations by Gustaf Tenggren: $40.00

Thousand, individual stories:

Aladdin, 1925, McBride, black hardcover, eight color plates plus b/w by S. G. Hulme Beaman, first edition with dust jacket: $150.00. Without dust jacket: $75.00

Aladdin and the Wonderful Lamp, 1935, Macmillan, oversize, hardcover, full-page and partial page color illustrations by Elizabeth MacKinstry, first edition with dust jacket: $100.00. Without dust jacket: $50.00

THURSDAY SERIES, Michael Bond, *Here Comes Thursday*

THURSDAY SERIES, Michael Bond (see OLGA DA POLGA SERIES and

PADDINGTON BEAR SERIES), adventures of a mouse.

Harrap, London, and Lothrop, Lee, US, first edition with dust jacket: $35.00

Later printings, with dust jacket: $20.00

Here Comes Thursday, 1966, illustrated by Daphne Rowles

Thursday Rides Again, 1969, illustrated by Beryl Sanders

Thursday Ahoy!, 1970, illustrated by Leslie Wood

Thursday in Paris, 1971, illustrated by Leslie Wood

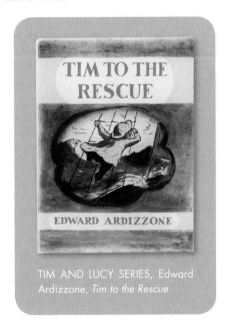

TIM AND LUCY SERIES, Edward Ardizzone, *Tim to the Rescue*

TIM AND LUCY SERIES, Edward Ardizzone, oversize hardcover, color illustrations throughout by author, Oxford University Press, London, first editions with dust jackets:

Little Tim and the Brave Sea Captain, 1936: $1,000.00

Tim and Lucy Go to Sea, 1938: $800.00

Tim to the Rescue, 1949: $500.00

Tim and Charlotte, 1951: $200.00

Tim in Danger, 1953: $200.00

Tim All Alone, 1956: $200.00

Tim's Friend Towser, 1962: $100.00

Tim and Ginger, 1965: $100.00

Tim to the Lighthouse, 1968: $100.00

Tim's Last Voyage, 1972: $100.00

Ship's Cook Ginger, 1977: $100.00

TINKER AND TANKER SERIES, Richard Scarry, author/illustrator, easy to read adventures of a hippo and a rabbit who are best friends, oversize easy-read picture books, color illustrated glossy paper-over-board cover, 96 pages, full-page color and b/w illustrations throughout by Scarry.

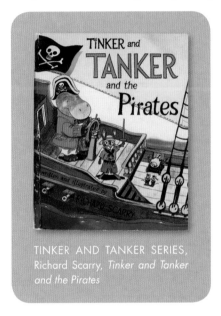

TINKER AND TANKER SERIES, Richard Scarry, *Tinker and Tanker and the Pirates*

1960 – 1963, Doubleday, first edition with dust jacket: $150.00. Without dust jacket: $80.00

Adventures of Tinker and Tanker

More Adventures of Tinker and Tanker

Tinker and Tanker and Their Space Ship

Tinker and Tanker Out West

Tinker and Tanker and the Pirates

More Adventures of Tinker and Tanker

Tinker and Tanker, Knights of the Round Table

Tinker and Tanker in Africa

315

Tinker and Tanker, other:

Tinker and Tanker Journey to Tootle Town and Build a Space Ship, 1961, Golden Press, oversize glossy illustrated cover, 72 pages: $100.00

Tinker and Tanker Travel Out West and to Africa, 1963, Golden Press, oversize glossy illustrated cover, 68 pages including color illustrations and b/w pages to color: $100.00

TINTIN SERIES, Herge (pseudonym of George Remi, 1907 – 1983), 1929 – 1975, 22 titles, Casterman French editions, Methuen, English, and others. The world-ranging adventures of the boy reporter Tintin, his dog Snowy and their friends mix fast action with exotic locations, science fiction gadgets, and political satire. Belgian cartoonist Herge's stories first appeared as black and white comic strips and were soon gathered into hardbound graphic novels. When Herge's Belgian/French publisher switched to an all-color format in the 1940s, Herge revised many of the 1930s adventures to fit into a shorter page count as well as to better reflect the sensibilities of the day. One adventure, *Land of the Black Gold,* was judged too political to be published in the German-occupied Belguim of 1940 and was abandoned until 1950. By the 1950s, the original French language books were so popular that the publishers decided to sell translation rights.

The English editions appeared first in the 1950s but in a different order than the French editions. Herge rewrote *Black Gold* again prior to translation into English in 1971. By the 1990s, *Tintin* had been translated into 50 different languages, starred in several animated films, a TV series, and a BBC radio program. Toys, clothes, dishes, and other items appeared and created whole stores devoted to nothing but Tintin.

Tintin titles:

The original adventures are listed in order of first publication. Original French language publication date listed in parenthesis with the date of any story revision. Date of first English translation by Leslie Lonsdale-Cooper and Michael Turner noted

TINTIN SERIES, Herge, *Shooting Star* and *Explorers on the Moon*

next. (See values under the publisher listings below.)

Titles:

Tintin in the Land the Soviets (1929), English translation, 1989

Tintin in the Congo (1930), English translation, 1991

Tintin in America (1931, revised 1946), English translation, 1978

Cigars of the Pharoah (1932, revised 1955) English translation, 1971

Blue Lotus (1934, revised 1946), English translation, 1983

Tintin and the Broken Ear (1935, revised 1943), English translation, 1975

Black Island (1937, revised 1966), English translation, 1966

King Ottokar's Sceptre (1938, revised 1947), English translation, 1958

Crab with Golden Claws (1940, revised 1943), English translation, 1958

Secret of the Unicorn (1941), English translation, 1961

Red Rackham's Treasure (1943), English translation, 1959

Seven Crystal Balls (1943), English translation, 1963

Prisoners of the Sun (1944), English translation, 1963

Land of Black Gold (written 1939, published 1950, revised 1971), English translation, 1971

Destination Moon (1950), English translation, 1959

Explorers on the Moon (1952), English translation, 1959

Calculus Affair (1954), English translation, 1960

Red Sea Sharks (1956), English translation, 1967

Tintin in Tibet (1958), English translation, 1968

Castafiore Emerald (1961), English translation, 1963

Flight 714 (1966), English translation, 1968

Tintin and the Picaros (1975), English translation, 1976

Tintin publishers:

Tintin, French editions, Les Editions Du Petit Vingtieme, 1929, 1930, b/w, limited editions, probably 500 copies were produced for Herge, fascimile copies by Casterman or Sundancer in the 1980s/1990s: $35.00

Tintin, French editions, Casterman, circa 1930s, hardbound, large, b/w format, 102 to 112 pages, are seldom available for sale.

1980s/1990s fascimile editions of the 1930s titles, French or English translation: $30.00

Tintin, French editions, color, Casterman, circa 1940s – 1970s, hardbound. In 1942, Casterman switched to an all-color format and asked Herge to limit each adventure to 62 pages to cut printing costs. All adventures originally published in the 1930s were revised to fit this format, except for *Soviets* (1929), which would not be reprinted until the 1980s.

1940s editions: $250.00

1950s editions: $175.00

1960s editions: $150.00

1970s first editions: $100.00

Later editions, hardbound: $35.00

Tintin, English editions, color, Casterman, 1952. To test the export waters, Casterman translated two adventures, *Secret of the Unicorn*, and *Red Rackham's Treasure*, then sold English rights to publisher Methuen.

Tintin, English editions, color, Methuen, UK, 1958 – present:

Methuen, 1950s first edition thus, pictorial hardcover: $250.00

Methuen, 1960s first edition thus, pictorial hardcover: $125.00

Methuen, 1970s first edition thus, glossy pictorial hardcover: $45.00

Methuen later editions, hardcover: $25.00 to $40.00

Tintin, first American editions, color, Golden Press, 1958 – 1960. Golden Press editions: $120.00

King Ottokar's Scepter, 1959, Herge, translated by Nicole Duplaix

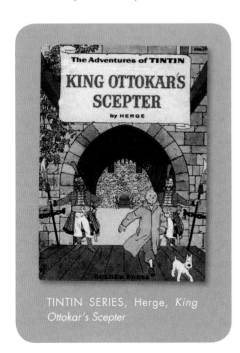

TINTIN SERIES, Herge, *King Ottokar's Scepter*

Crab with the Golden Claws, 1959, translated by Danielle Gorlin

Secret of the Unicorn, 1959, translated by Danielle Gorlin

Red Rackham's Treasure, 1959, translated by Danielle Gorlin

Destination Moon, 1960, translated by Danielle Gorlin

Explorers on the Moon, 1960, translated by Danielle Gorlin

Tintin, movie versions, color, Methuen/ Little, Brown, 1960 – 1973:

Tintin and the Golden Fleece, 1965, Methuen, pictorial hardcover, first edition: $125.00.

Tintin and the Blue Oranges, 1965, Methuen, UK, and Little, Brown, 1967, US, hard-to-find

Tintin and the Lake of Sharks, 1973, Methuen, pictorial hardcover, first edition: $100.00

Tintin and the Lake of Sharks, 1989, Little, Brown, pictorial hardcover, first edition: $100.00

Tintin, other books, 1980s – present. Tintin continues to inspire new adaptations. A selected few are:

Explorers on the Moon, Pop-Up Book, 1992, Methuen or Little, Brown: $35.00

Tintin and Alph-Art, 1990, Casterman. Publication of sketches and notes for Herge's final Tintin adventure, left uncompleted by his death: $100.00

Tintin: 60 Years of Adventure, 1980, Casterman: $50.00

Tintin and the World of Herge: An Illustrated History, Benoit Peters, 1992, Bullfinch Press, biography of Herge with bibliography, hardcover with dust jacket: $35.00

TISH STERLING SERIES, Norma Johnston, journals of a teenager in the Bronx,

Atheneum, early edition with dust jacket: $50.00

Keeping Days, 1973

Glory in the Flower, 1974, dust jacket by Velma Ilsley

Mustard Seed of Magic, 1977

Nice Girl Like You, 1980

Myself and I, 1981

TOBY HEYDON SERIES, Rosamund DuJardin, teen romance, Lippincott, first edition with dust jacket: $90.00

Practically Seventeen, 1949

Class Ring, 1951

Boy Trouble, 1953

Real Thing, 1956

Wedding in the Family, 1958

One of the Crowd, 1961

TOD HALE SERIES, Ralph Henry Barbour, school sports, of course, 1926 – 1929, Dodd, Mead, brown hardcover with paste-on-pictorial, four plates by Leslie Crump, first edition with dust jacket: $40.00

Tod Hale with the Crew

Tod Hale at Camp

Tod Hale on the Scrub

Tod Hale on the Nine

TOM CORBETT SPACE CADET SERIES, Carey Rockwell, based on radio and TV series, 1950s, Grosset & Dunlap, tweed hardcover, blue illustrated endpapers, b/w illustrations by Frank Vaughn, first edition with dust jacket: $50.00

Stand by for Mars!, 1952

Danger in Deep Space, 1953

On the Trail of the Space Pirates, 1953

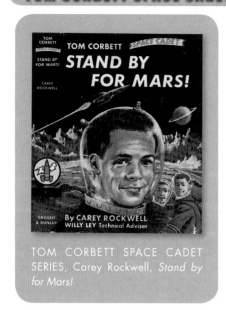

TOM CORBETT SPACE CADET SERIES, Carey Rockwell, *Stand by for Mars!*

Space Pioneers, 1953

Revolt on Venus, 1954

Treachery in Outer Space, 1954

Sabotage in Space, 1955

Robot Rocket, 1956

TOM QUEST SERIES, Fran Striker, Grosset & Dunlap, tweed hardcover, pictorial endpapers, frontispiece, first edition with dust jacket: $40.00

Sign of the Spiral, 1947

Telltale Scar, 1947

Clue of the Cypress Stump, 1948

Secret of the Lost Mesa, 1949

Hidden Stone Mystery, 1950

Secret of Thunder Mountain, 1952

Inca Luck Piece, 1955

Mystery of the Timber Giant, 1955

TOM SLADE SERIES, Percy Keese Fitzhugh, advertised as "endorsed by the Boy Scouts of America," ca. 1910 – 1930, Grosset & Dunlap, hardcover, photo illustrated endpapers, four b/w plates by Emmett Owen, several editions with some format variations, with dust jacket: $30.00

TOM SWIFT SERIES, Victor Appleton (Stratemeyer syndicate pseudonym), created by Stratemeyer, the books through ca. 1932 were probably written by Howard Garis, Grosset & Dunlap, several hardcover designs. In early books, Tom invented gadgets that were just slightly ahead of their time, obviously inspired by American inventor Thomas Edison as well as by the dime novel adventures of such boy inventors as FRANK READE. First editions are usually identified by list-to-self ads or title lists showing only titles from the original year of publication.

Tom Swift, 1910 – 1920, early editions, Grosset, tan cloth hardcover with red/ black quadrant design, b/w frontispiece, earliest dust jackets used same art as cover and were printed on uncoated brown paper. Later dust jackets printed on coated white paper with two-color illustrations.

Early edition with dust jacket: $400.00. Without dust jacket: $35.00

Tom Swift and His Motor Cycle, 1910

Tom Swift and His Motorboat, 1910

Tom Swift and His Airship, 1910

Tom Swift and His Submarine Boat, 1910

Tom Swift and His Electric Runabout, 1910

Tom Swift and His Wireless Message, 1911

Tom Swift among the Diamond Makers, 1911

Tom Swift in the Caves of Ice, 1911

Tom Swift and His Sky Racer, 1911

Tom Swift and His Electric Rifle, 1911

Tom Swift in the City of Gold, 1912

Tom Swift and His Air Glider, 1912

Tom Swift in Captivity, 1912

Tom Swift and His Wizard Camera, 1912

Tom Swift and His Great Searchlight, 1912

Tom Swift and His Giant Cannon, 1913

Tom Swift and His Photo Telephone, 1914

Tom Swift and His Aerial Warship, 1915

Tom Swift and His Big Tunnel, 1916

Tom Swift in the Land of Wonders, 1917

Tom Swift and His War Tank, 1918

Tom Swift and His Air Scout, 1919

Tom Swift and His Undersea Search, 1920

Tom Swift, 1920s, Grosset & Dunlap early editions, with dust jackets: $100.00

TOM SWIFT SERIES, Victor Appleton, 1911 cover, 1915 dust jacket, 1970s cover

Tom among the Fire Fighters, 1921

Tom Swift and His Electric Locomotive, 1922

Tom Swift and His Flying Boat, 1923

Tom Swift and His Great Oil Gusher, 1924

Tom Swift and His Chest of Secrets, 1925

Tom Swift and His Airline Express, 1926

Tom Swift Circling the Globe, 1927

Tom Swift and His Talking Pictures, 1928

Tom Swift and His House on Wheels, 1929

Tom Swift, 1930s and 1940s, Grosset & Dunlap early editions, with dust jacket: $75.00

Tom Swift, Whitman, Big Little Books and Better Little Books, small hardcovers with color illustrated covers, b/w drawings throughout: $200.00

Jack Swift and His Rocket Ship, 1934 a copy of the Tom Swift formula

Tom Swift and His Giant Telescope, 1939

Tom Swift and His Magnetic Silencer, 1941

New Tom Swift, Jr. Adventures Series, 1954 – 1971, Grosset & Dunlap, based on the *Tom Swift* series, Victor Appleton II (Stratemeyer pseudonym), probably a Harriet Adams idea and written by several authors, including Jim Lawrence, b/w illustrations by Graham Kaye. Once again, Tom's inventions are slightly ahead of their time. Now he invents rockets and ray guns instead of airplanes and telegraphs.

Cloth hardcover, blue and white scene endpapers (later editions use black & white endpapers), with dust jacket: $30.00

Tom Swift Jr., 1961 – 1969, Grosset & Dunlap, blue spine (one year only) or yellow spine pictorial hardcover, probable first editions: $25.00

Tom Swift, 1970s, Grosset & Dunlap, yellow spine, probable first editions: $100.00. Later printings: $30.00

Tom Swift and His Cosmotron Express, 1970

Tom Swift and the Galaxy Ghosts, 1971

Tom Swift Jr. Activity Book, 1978, Grosset & Dunlap, paperback, 8½" x11": $50.00

TOMMY ROCKFORD HAM RADIO MYSTERY SERIES, Walker A. Tompkins, Macrae, first three titles, hardcover with dust jacket: $50.00

SOS at Midnight, 1957

CQ Ghost Ship, 1960

DX Brings Danger, 1962

TOMMY TIPTOP SERIES, Raymond Stone (Stratemeyer pseudonym), 1912 – 1917, Graham and Matlock, hardcover, frontispiece and seven plates, with dust jacket: $35.00

Tommy Tiptop and His Baseball Nine, 1912

Tommy Tiptop and His Football Eleven, 1913

Tommy Tiptop and His Winter Sports, 1914

Tommy Tiptop and His Boat Club, 1915

Tommy Tiptop and His Boy Scouts, 1916

Tommy Tiptop and His Great Show, 1917

TOMORROW MOUNTAINS TRILOGY, Sylvia Louise Engdahl, fantasy set on a planet of another solar system.

This Star Shall Abide (UK title: *Heritage of the Star*) 1972, Atheneum, first edition with dust jacket: $150.00

Heritage of the Star, 1973, Gollancz, UK, hardcover, dust jacket by David Smee, first edition with dust jacket: $30.00

Beyond the Tomorrow Mountains, 1973, Atheneum, first edition with dust jacket: $80.00

Doors of the Universe, 1981, Atheneum, first edition with dust jacket: $80.00

TOMORROW MOUNTAINS TRILOGY, Sylvia Louise Engdahl, *This Star Shall Abide*

TORIN TRILOGY, Cherry Wilder, earth explorers change an ancient world, Atheneum, first edition with dust jacket: $40.00

Luck of Brin's Five, 1977

Nearest Fire, 1980

Tapestry of Warriors, 1983

TORIN TRILOGY, Cherry Wilder, *Luck of Brin's Five*

TORNADO JONES MYSTERY SERIES, Trella Dick, Follett, pictorial hardcover, b/w line drawings by Mary Stevens, with dust jacket: $40.00

Tornado Jones, 1953

Tornado Jones on Sentinel Mountain, 1955

Tornado Jones' Big Year, 1956

TOYTOWN SERIES, S. G. Hulme Beaman, stories of a town of wooden toys, illustrated by the author, and read aloud on the BBC's "Children's Hour" radio program in the 1930s. Titles include:

Tales of Toytown, 1928, Oxford University Press, illustrated boards, color plates, first edition: $100.00

Wireless in Toytown, ca. 1930, Collins, cloth hardcover with gilt, color plates: $50.00

Toytown Mystery, 1932, Collins, cloth hardcover with gilt, color frontispiece, line drawings: $50.00

Ernest the Brave and the Toytown Mystery, with Betty Beaman, 1957, Oldbourne, London, pictorial boards, illustrated endpapers, color illustrations, with dust jacket: $40.00

Dirty Work at the "Dog and Whistle," 1958, Oldbourne, London, pictorial boards, illustrated endpapers, color illustrations, with dust jacket: $40.00

Toytown Treasure, with Betty Beaman, 1961, Oldbourne, London, pictorial boards, illustrated endpapers, color illustrations by Kenneth Lovell, with dust jacket: $40.00

How the Radio Came to Toytown, with Betty Beaman, 1961, Oldbourne, London, pictorial boards, illustrated endpapers, color illustrations by Kenneth Lovell, with dust jacket: $40.00

Toytown Christmas Party, with Betty Beaman, 1962, Oldbourne, London, pictorial boards, illustrated endpapers, color illustrations by Kenneth Lovell, with dust jacket: $40.00

Pistols for Two, with Betty Beaman, 1962, Oldbourne, London, pictorial boards, illustrated endpapers, color illustrations by Kenneth Lovell, with dust jacket: $40.00

Toytown Pantomime, with Betty Beaman, 1963, Oldbourne, London, pictorial boards, illustrated endpapers, color illustrations by Kenneth Lovell, with dust jacket: $40.00

Arkville Dragon, 1963, Oldbourne, London, pictorial boards, illustrated endpapers, color illustrations by Kenneth Lovell, with dust jacket: $40.00

TRAVEL-TOT-TALES SERIES, 1920s, Reilly & Lee, oversize picture books with color illustrated paper-on-board covers, blue/white illustrations by Bess Devine Jewell: $30.00

TREASURE SEEKERS SERIES, Edith Nesbit, popular English novels about a Victorian family of inventive children. These are available in paperback and the stories have been adapted and made popular through TV productions. Early editions include:

Story of the Treasure Seekers, 1899, undated Stokes, apparent first American edition, green cloth with gilt and white decoration: $100.00

Story of the Treasure Seekers, 1926, Unwin edition, blue hardcover, color frontispiece, b/w line drawings: $30.00

Wouldbegoods, ca. 1900, undated Unwin, London, gilt decoration on red hardcover, early printing: $40.00

Wouldbegoods, 1901, Harper, first US edition, small decorated hardcover, Reginald Birch illustrations: $100.00

New Treasure Seekers, 1904, Unwin, first edition, gilt embossed red hardcover, engraved plates by Gordon Browne and Lewis Baumer: $100.00

Oswald Bastable and Others, 1905, Gardner Darton, red hardcover with gilt, plates by C. E. Brock and H. R. Millar, collection of 15 short stories with four about the Bastable children, first edition: $200.00

Complete History of the Bastable Family, 1928, Ernest Benn, London, red hardcover with gilt, collected edition of the three novels: $30.00

Bastable Children, 1928, Coward-McCann, first American edition, collection of three novels, preface by Christopher Morley, orange hardcover, illustrations: $150.00

TREEHORN SERIES, Florence Parry Heide, whimsical fantasies about a small boy, Holiday House, small oblong hardcover, b/w illustrations by Edward Gorey.

Shrinking of Treehorn, 1971, first edition with dust jacket: $60.00

Treehorn's Treasure, 1981, first edition with dust jacket: $40.00

Treehorn's Wish, 1984, first edition with dust jacket: $40.00

TREEHORN SERIES, Florence Parry Heide, *Treehorn's Wish*

TRIGGER BERG MYSTERY SERIES, Leo Edwards, ca. 1930s, Grosset & Dunlap, hardcover, illustrated endpapers, b/w plates by Bert Salg, wide range of value and condition, wide range of condition, probable first edition with dust jacket starts at: $200.00

Later editions with dust jackets: $50.00

Trigger Berg and the Treasure Tree

Trigger Berg and His 700 Mouse Traps

Trigger Berg and the Sacred Pig

Trigger Berg and the Cockeyed Ghost

TRIPODS SERIES, John Christopher, trio of teenage boys resist an alien invasion, first edition with dust jacket: $50.00

White Mountains, 1967, Macmillan

City of Gold and Lead, 1967, Macmillan

Pool of Fire, 1968, Macmillan

When the Tripods Came, 1988, E. P. Dutton

TRIPODS SERIES, John Christopher, *Pool of Fire*

TRIXIE BELDEN SERIES, Kathryn Kenny, pseudonyn, originated by Julie Campbell Tatham, literary agent, first title was published in 1948 by Whitman. Whitman and Golden Press are owned by Western Publishing, and the books appear under both names in different formats. 39 books

TRIXIE BELDEN SERIES, Kathryn Kenny, ca.1959, diamond pattern on spine

were published, written by Campbell and also by other authors who used the pseudonym Kathryn Kenny. This popular series was printed in several formats, including easy-to-find illustrated hardcovers.

Trixie Belden, Whitman, ca. 1948 – 1951, titles 1, 2, 3, wraparound illustration by Mary Stevens on dust jacket: $45.00

Trixie Belden, Whitman, ca.1959, diamond pattern on spine, illustrations by Mary Stevens, dust jacket illustration by Herbert Tauss: $30.00

TUCKER TWINS SERIES, Nell Speed, ca. 1915, Hurst, illustrated cloth-over-board cover, illustrated by Arthur Scott. Dust jackets all have same wraparound illustration, early edition with dust jacket: $30.00

TUFFY BEAN THE DOG SERIES, Leo Edwards, ca. 1931, Grosset & Dunlap, about 210 pages, 18 b/w line drawings by Bert Salg, advertised as "Something else to howl about..." With dust jacket: $200.00. Without dust jacket: $50.00

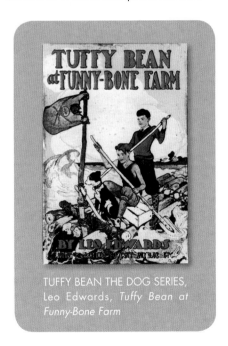

TUFFY BEAN THE DOG SERIES, Leo Edwards, *Tuffy Bean at Funny-Bone Farm*

Tuffy Bean's Puppy Days

Tuffy Bean's One-Ring Circus

Tuffy Bean at Funny-Bone Farm

Tuffy Bean and the Lost Fortune

TURF-CUTTER'S DONKEY SERIES, Patricia Lynch, magical adventures of Eileen, Seamus and Long Ears the Donkey are based on Irish mythology.

Turf-Cutter's Donkey, 1934, Dent, UK, and 1935, E. P. Dutton, US, illustrated by Jack B. Yeats, first edition with dust jacket: $100.00

Turf-Cutter's Donkey Goes Visiting, 1936, E. P. Dutton, illustrations by George Altendorf, first edition with dust jacket: $50.00

Turf-Cutter's Donkey Kicks Up His Heels, 1939, E. P. Dutton, b/w illustrations by Winifred Bromhall, US first edition with dust jacket: $100.00

TWINKLE TALES, Laura Bancroft (L. Frank Baum, see OZ BOOKS SERIES) ca. 1906, Reilly & Britton, small, illustrated cloth-over-board cover, approximately 62 pages, color illustrations throughout by Maginal Wright Enright, first editions: $3,000.00. Later editions: $100.00

Bandit Jim Crow

Mr. Woodchuck

Prairie-Dog Town

Prince Mud-Turtle

Sugar-Loaf Mountain

Twinkle's Enchantment

TWINKLE TALES, Laura Bancroft, *Bandit Jim Crow*

Policeman Bluejay, Twinkle Tales, 1907, Reilly & Britton, illustrations by Wright, first edition: $1,000.00

Babes in Birdland, 1911, Reilly & Britton, reissue of *Policeman Bluejay,* b/w illustrations, paste-on-pictorial: $300.00

Twinkle and Chubbins, Their Astonishing Adventures in Nature-Fairyland, 1911 Reilly & Britton, hardcover, full size novel similar in format to the *Oz* books, 380 pages, color plates and b/w illustrations by Maginel Wright Enright, continues the story of Twinkle and Chubbins: $200.00

TWINS OF THE WORLD SERIES, Lucy Fitch Perkins, 1911 – 1930, Houghton Mifflin, 25 books, educational series for schools, with dust jacket: $50.00. Titles include:

Dutch Twins, 1911

Japanese Twins, 1912

Eskimo Twins, 1914

Spartan Twins, 1918

Italian Twins, 1920

Puritan Twins, 1921

Colonial Twins, 1924

Indian Twins, 1930

TWO LIVE BOYS SERIES, Clarence Burleigh, 1906 – 1910, Lothrop, Lee and Shepard, pictorial hardcover with gilt lettering, eight b/w plates by Bridgman or 16 b/w photo plates by H. D. Edwards: $40.00

Camp on the Letter K, or, *Two Live Boys in Northern Maine*

Raymond Benson at Krampton, or, *Two Live Boys at Preparatory School*

Kenton Pines, or, *Raymond Benson at College*

All Among the Loggers, or, *Norman Carver's Winter in a Lumber Camp*

With Pickpole and Peavey, or, *Two Live Boys on the East Branch Drive*

Young Guide, or, *Two Live Boys in the Maine Woods*

■ ·················· **U** ·················· ■

UNCLE BILL SERIES, Will James, Scribner, hardcover, color frontispiece, b/w illustrations throughout by author, first edition with dust jacket: $300.00

Later reprints with dust jackets: $30.00

Uncle Bill, 1933

In the Saddle with Uncle Bill, 1935

Look-See with Uncle Bill, 1938

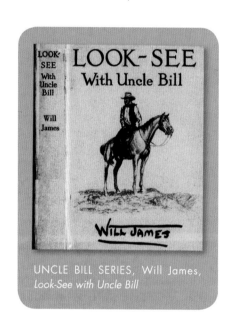

UNCLE BILL SERIES, Will James,
Look-See with Uncle Bill

UNCLE CLEANS SERIES, John Percival Martin, adventures of a millionaire elephant, illustrated by Quentin Blake.

Coward-McCann, US, first edition with dust jacket: $200.00

Later printings with dust jackets: $60.00

Uncle Cleans, 1964

Uncle Cleans Up, More Uncle Stories, 1965

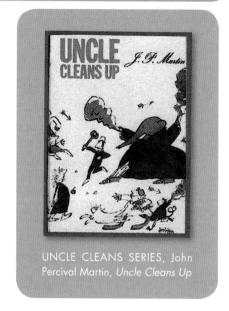

UNCLE CLEANS SERIES, John
Percival Martin, *Uncle Cleans Up*

Uncle Cleans and the Battle for Badgertown, 1967

UNCLE REMUS SERIES, Joel Chandler Harris (1848 – 1908), fictional Uncle Remus told stories, including the well-known tales of *Brer Rabbit* and *Brer Fox,* to the children on an old South plantation. Numerous reprints include picture books made of single stories taken from original text. Numerous revised editions. Harris died in 1908. Books after that date are collections and new editions of his earlier stories. Listed below is a sampling of the many early editions:

Uncle Remus, His Songs and His Sayings, 1881, Appleton, blue cover with gilt illustration of Brer Rabbit on cover, wood engraved text illustrations by Frederick Church and James Moser, patterned endpapers, probable first state: $2,000.00

Nights with Uncle Remus, 1883, Osgood, Boston, and 1884, Routledge, London, pictorial hardcover with gilt, first edition: $600.00

Daddy Jake the Runaway and Other Stories by "Uncle Remus," 1889, Century, illustrated hardcover, first edition with dust jacket: $2,000.00. Without dust jacket: $500.00

Daddy Jake the Runaway, 1890, T. Fisher Unwin, UK, hardcover, with gilt: $400.00

Uncle Remus and His Friends, 1892, Houghton Mifflin, green hardcover with

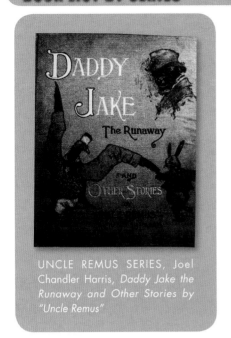

UNCLE REMUS SERIES, Joel Chandler Harris, *Daddy Jake the Runaway and Other Stories by "Uncle Remus"*

gilt, 357+ pages, 12 plates, illustrations by A. B. Frost: $250.00

Tar-Baby and Other Rhymes of Uncle Remus, 1904, Appleton, illustrations by A. B. Frost and Kemple: $75.00

Told by Uncle Remus, 1905, McClure, hardcover with gilt lettering and top page edges, 295 pages, 18 b/w plates, illustrations by Frost, Conde and Verbeck, first edition: $250.00

Uncle Remus and Brer Rabbit, 1907, Stokes, cardboard covers, 62 pages, color illustrations by Conde, first edition: $500.00

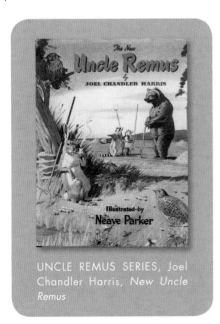

UNCLE REMUS SERIES, Joel Chandler Harris, *New Uncle Remus*

Uncle Remus and the Little Boy, 1910, Small, Maynard, hardcover with illustration: $100.00

Uncle Remus Returns, 1918, Houghton Mifflin, hardcover, illustrations by Frost, Conde: $150.00

Tales from Uncle Remus, 1935 edition, Houghton Mifflin, 62 pages, 12 color plates by Milo Winter: $40.00

Brer Rabbit, Song of the South, Whitman Big Little Book #1426, illustrated cardboard cover, b/w illustrations: $50.00

New Uncle Remus, 1956, Bruce & Gawthorn, UK, line drawings by Neave Parker, with dust jacket: $50.00

UNCLE TOOTH SERIES, Geoffrey Hayes, Uncle Tooth tells tall tales of adventure to his alligator nephew, illustrated by author, first edition with dust jacket: $30.00

Alligator and His Uncle Tooth: Novel of the Sea, 1977, Harper

Mystery of the Pirate Ghost, 1985, Random House

Secret of Foghorn Island, 1988, Random House

UNCLE WIGGILY SERIES, Howard R. Garis, copyright R. F. Fenno Publishers, Newark. Many of these stories first appeared in daily newspaper features and on a read-aloud radio show, before being compiled into individual books and series of books. The stories feature Uncle Wiggily, a "kindly old rabbit gentleman" with top hat and cane, and his woodland friends.

Uncle Wiggily Bedtime Animal Stories, printed with series designation, identified as *Bedtime Stories* on pictorial hardcover and *Uncle Wiggily's Bedtime Stories* on title page, eight color plate illustrations by Lang Campbell and 31 stories per book, a bedtime story per night for a month, ca. 1910 – 1915, A. L. Burt Publishers: $55.00

Uncle Wiggily and Sammie and Susie Littletail

Uncle Wiggily and Johnnie and Billie Bushytail

Uncle Wiggily and Lulu, Alice, and Jimmie Wibblewobble

Uncle Wiggily and Jackie and Petie Bow Wow

Uncle Wiggily and Buddy and Brighteyes Pigg

Uncle Wiggily and Joie, Tommie, and Kittie Kat

Uncle Wiggily and Charlie and Arabella Chick

Uncle Wiggily and Neddie and Beckie Stubtail

Uncle Wiggily and Bully and Bawly No-Tail

Uncle Wiggily and Nannie and Billie Wagtail

Uncle Wiggily and Jollie and Jillie Longtail

Uncle Wiggily and Jacko and Jumpo Kinkytail

Uncle Wiggily and Curly and Floppy Twistytail

Uncle Wiggily and Dottie and Willie Flufftail

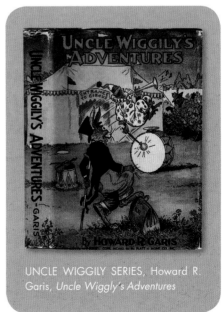

UNCLE WIGGILY SERIES, Howard R. Garis, *Uncle Wiggly's Adventures*

Uncle Wiggily and Dickie and Nellie Fliptail

Uncle Wiggily and Woodie and Waddie Chuck

Uncle Wiggily Bedtime Stories, printed with series designation, identified as *Bedtime Stories* on pictorial hardcover and *Uncle Wiggily's Bedtime Stories* on title page, eight color plate illustrations by Lang Campbell and 31 stories per book, a bedtime story per night for a month, ca. 1910 – 1915, A. L. Burt Publishers: $55.00

Uncle Wiggily's Adventures

Uncle Wiggily's Travels

Uncle Wiggily's Fortune

Uncle Wiggily's Automobile

Uncle Wiggily at the Seashore

Uncle Wiggily in the Country

Uncle Wiggily in the Woods

Uncle Wiggily on the Farm

Uncle Wiggily's Journey

Uncle Wiggily's Rheumatism

Uncle Wiggily and Baby Bunty

Uncle Wiggily in Wonderland

Uncle Wiggily in Fairyland

Uncle Wiggily's Airship

Uncle Wiggily Bedtime Stories and Bedtime Animal Stories, reprinted without the series designation, ca. 1940s, by Platt Munk, same or similar titles, new color plate illustrations by Elmer Rache, with dust jacket: $60.00

Uncle Wiggily, other editions, listed alphabetically:

Adventures of Uncle Wiggily, the Bunny Rabbit Gentleman with the Twinkling Pink Nose, 1924, Graham, New Jersey, oversize red cloth and paper over boards, 30

pages, illustrations by Lang Campbell, with dust jacket: $100.00

Uncle Wiggily and Alice in Wonderland, 1918, Donohue, Chicago, color plate illustrations by Edward Bloomfield: $60.00

Uncle Wiggily and His Flying Rug (1920), 1940 edition, Whitman, illustrated hardcover, 33 pages, illustrated endpapers, color illustrations by Lang Campbell, with dust jacket: $70.00

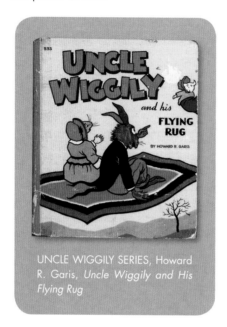

UNCLE WIGGILY SERIES, Howard R. Garis, *Uncle Wiggily and His Flying Rug*

Uncle Wiggily and His Funny Auto, 1940 edition, Whitman, illustrated hardcover, color illustrations by Lang Campbell, with dust jacket: $70.00

Uncle Wiggily and the Pirates, 1940 edition, Whitman, illustrated hardcover, 33 pages, illustrated endpapers, color illustrations by Lang Campbell, with dust jacket: $70.00

Uncle Wiggily at the Beach (1919), 1936 edition Whitman, illustrated hardcover, illustrations by Lang Campbell: $35.00

Uncle Wiggily Goes Camping, 1940 edition, Whitman, illustrated hardcover, 33 pages, illustrated endpapers, color illustrations by Lang Campbell, with dust jacket: $70.00

Uncle Wiggily Stories, 1965, Grosset & Dunlap, glossy pictorial hardcover, oversize, illustrations by Art Seiden, illustrated endpapers, 29 pages: $35.00

UNCLE WIGGILY SERIES, Howard R. Garis, *Uncle Wiggily at the Beach*

Uncle Wiggily's Arabian Nights, 1917, Donahue, paste-on-pictorial hardcover, color plates and endpapers by Edward Bloomfield: $100.00

Uncle Wiggily's Happy Days, 1947, Platt & Munk, color plate illustrations by Elmer Rache: $45.00

Uncle Wiggily, collection:

Uncle Wiggily's Library, 1939, Platt & Munk, boxed set of eight papercover books, complete set with box: $250.00 (individual books, $25.00 each)

Uncle Wiggily, Mary Perks editions, Famous Books for the Nursery, ca. 1945, oversize, color illustrated cardboard cover, two-color illustrations, many by Mary and Wallace Stover: $35.00

Uncle Wiggily Goes Berrying

Uncle Wiggily Helps Jimmie

Ungle Wiggily and the Baker Cat

Uncle Wiggily and the Picture Book

Uncle Wiggily, Mary Perks editions, Uncle Wiggily Stories, Howard R. Garis, ca. 1943, oversize, color illustrated cardboard cover, two-color illustrations by Mary and Wallace Stover: $35.00

Uncle Wiggily Starts Off

Uncle Wiggily and the Paper Boat

Uncle Wiggily and the Troublesome Boys

Uncle Wiggily and Granddaddy Longlegs

Uncle Wiggily and the Milkman

Uncle Wiggily and the Cowbird

Uncle Wiggily and the Starfish

Uncle Wiggily and the Red Monkey

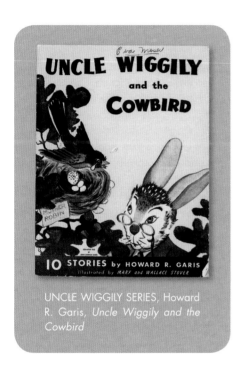

UNCLE WIGGILY SERIES, Howard R. Garis, *Uncle Wiggily and the Cowbird*

UNDERSEA SERIES, Jack Williamson with Frederik Pohl, Jim Eden adventures.

Gnome Press first edition with dust jacket: $100.00

Dennis Dobson, UK, first edition with dust jacket: $40.00

Undersea Quest, 1954

Undersea Fleet, 1956

Undersea City, 1958

UNITED STATES MARINE SERIES, Giles Bishop, 1921 – 1922, Penn Publishing, blue hardcover with paste-on-pictorial, frontispiece and four plates by Donald Humphreys: $50.00

UNITED STATES MIDSHIPMAN SERIES, Lt. Com. Yates Stirling, 1908 – 1913, Penn Publishing, green illustrated hardcover, white lettering, illustrated endpapers, frontispiece and plates by Ralph Boyer, first edition with dust jacket: $85.00

Later printings with dust jackets: $30.00

UNITED STATES SERVICE SERIES, Francis Rolt-Wheeler, 1909 – 1929, Lothrop, Lee & Shepard, hardcover with photo paste-on-illustration, illustrations include photographs and maps, with dust jacket: $35.00

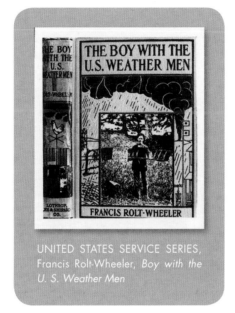

UNITED STATES SERVICE SERIES, Francis Rolt-Wheeler, *Boy with the U. S. Weather Men*

· · · · · · · · · · · · · · · **V** · · · · · · · · · · · · · ·

VERONICA SERIES, Roger Duvoisin (see PETUNIA, also the illustrations for HAPPY LION), Knopf, oversize hardcover, illustrated endpapers, color illustrations by author, adventures of a hippopotamus.

First edition, with dust jacket: $40.00

Veronica, 1962

Our Veronica Goes to Petunia's Farm, 1962

Lonely Veronica, 1963

Veronica's Smile, 1964

Veronica and the Birthday Present, 1971

VERONICA SERIES, Roger Duvoisin, *Veronica*

Veronica, other:

Veronica and Three Little Horses, ca. 1960s, Dandelion Library, two-books-in-one flip layout, illustrated hardcover: $30.00

VESPER HOLLY SERIES, Lloyd Alexander, nineteenth century girl investigates lost civilizations, elements of fantasy, Dutton, first edition with Trina Schart Hyman illustrated dust jacket: $30.00

Illyrian Adventure, 1986

El Dorado Adventure, 1987

Drackenburg Adventure, 1988

Jedera Adventure, 1989

Philadelphia Adventure, 1990

VICKI BARR FLIGHT STEWARDESS SERIES, Helen Wells and Julie Campbell Tatham, advertised as the Flight Stewardess Series, "fly to adventure with Vicki Barr."

Vicki Barr, 1947 – 1958, titles, Grosset & Dunlap, plain hardcover with dust jacket: $40.00

Silver Wings for Vicki, 1947

Vicki Finds the Answer, 1947

Hidden Valley Mystery, 1948

Secret of Magnolia Manor, 1949

Clue of the Broken Blossom, 1950

VICKI BARR FLIGHT
STEWARDESS SERIES, Helen
Wells, *Silver Wings for Vicki*

Behind the White Veil, 1951

Mystery at Hartwood House, 1952

Peril over the Airport, 1953

Mystery of the Vanishing Lady, 1954

Search for the Missing Twin, 1954

Ghost at the Water Fall, 1956

Clue of the Gold Coin, 1958

Vicki Barr, 1960 – 1962, titles, Grosset &
Dunlap, tweed hardcover, first edition with
dust jacket:

Silver Ring Mystery, 1960: $75.00

Clue of the Carved Ruby, 1961: $100.00

Mystery of Flight of 908, 1962: $150.00

■ ⋯⋯⋯⋯⋯ **W** ⋯⋯⋯⋯⋯ ■

WALLYPUG SERIES, G. E. Farrow (George
Edward), Victorian tales of the Kingdom of
Why, its ruler, and Girlie.

Wallypug Tales, 1898, Raphael Tuck &
Sons, Ltd., folio size, color illustrations
throughout by Alan Wright, green cloth
with stamped illustration, first edition:
$1,000.00

Wallypug of Why, 1895, Hutchinson,
London, hardcover, page illustrations by
Harry Furness and vignettes by Dorothy
Furness, 201 pages: $300.00

Adventures in Wallypug Land, 1898,
Metheun, UK, illustrations by Allan Wright:
$200.00

Wallypug in the Moon, 1907, Unwin,
hardcover with gilt, b/w illustrations by
Allan Wright: $75.00

Wallypug, Arthur Pearson early editions,
illustrations by Allan Wright: $150.00

Wallypug in London, or, His Badjesty,
1898

In Search of the Wallypug-land, 1903

Wallypug in Fogland, 1904

Wallypug, related title:

*Dick, Marjorie and Fidge, a Search for the
Wonderful Dodo*, Farrow, undated, ca.
1910, Burt edition, gilt lettering on spine,
269 pages, Allan Wright drawings, similar
type of nonsense fantasy as the Wallypug
stories: $30.00

WALTER CRANE'S PICTURE BOOKS, oversize, cloth-over-board hardcover, three or
four stories, eight color plates per story
by Walter Crane, engravings by Edmund
Evans. Stories originally appeared individually in paper wrappers with the beautiful
Crane illustrations, then were collected into
hardcover volumes combining four stories
in each volume.

Routledge, London and New York, ca.
1870s, oversize, 32 pages, color plates,
pictorial boards: $400.00

John Lane, London, ca. 1898, each
volume: $300.00

Lane, ca. 1910 edition: $150.00

Dodd, Mead & Company, US, ca. 1900
edition: $125.00

Blue Beard's Picture Book, includes
Bluebeard, Sleeping Beauty, and *Baby's
Own Alphabet*

Chattering Jack's Picture Book, includes
How Jessie Was Lost, Annie and Jack, and
Grammar in Rhyme

Cinderella's Picture Book, includes *Puss in
Boots, Valentine*, and *Orson*

Goody Two Shoes Picture Book, includes
Beauty and the Beast, Frog Prince, and
Alphabet of Old Friends

Mother Hubbard's Picture Book, includes
Three Bears and *Absurd A.B.C.*

Red Riding Hood's Picture Book, includes
Red Riding Hood, Jack and the Bean Stalk,
and *Forty Thieves*

Song of Sixpence Picture Book, includes
Princess Belle Etoile, and *Alphabet of Old
Friends*

This Little Pig Picture Book, includes *Fairy
Ship* and *King Luckieboy's Party*

WARTON THE TOAD SERIES, Russell E.
Erickson, seven titles, b/w illustrations by
Lawrence Di Fiori.

Lothrop, Lee, US first edition, with dust
jacket: $40.00

Hodder & Stoughton, UK first edition, with
dust jacket: $40.00

Toad for Tuesday, 1974

Warton and Morton, 1976

WARTON THE TOAD SERIES,
Russell E. Erickson, *Warton and
Morton*

Warton's Christmas Eve Adventure, 1977

Warton and the King of the Skies, 1978

Warton and the Traders, 1979

Warton and the Castaways, 1982

Warton and the Contest, 1986

WELLWORTH COLLEGE SERIES, Leslie Quirk, 1912 – 1916, Little, Brown, hardcover, b/w plates by Henry Watson, earliest editions had gilt lettering: $35.00

Fourth Down, 1912

Freshman Eight, 1914

Third Strike, 1915

Ice-boat Number One, 1916

WESTMARK TRILOGY, Lloyd Alexander, ca. 1980, E. P. Dutton, hardcover, fantasy novels, first edition with dust jacket: $50.00

Westmark

Kestrel

Beggar Queen

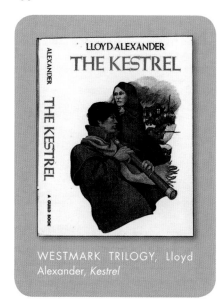

WESTMARK TRILOGY, Lloyd Alexander, *Kestrel*

WEST POINT, CLINT LANE SERIES, Colonel Red Reeder, Duell, Sloane and Pearce, gray hardcover, map endpapers, first edition with dust jacket: $75.00

WEST POINT, CLINT LANE SERIES, Colonel Red Reeder, *West Point Plebe*

West Point Plebe, 1955

Yearling, 1956

West Point Second Classman, 1957

West Point First Classman, 1958

2nd Lieutenant Clint Lane: West Point to Berlin, 1960

Clint Lane in Korea, 1961

WEST POINT, MARK MALLORY SERIES, Lt. Frederick Garrison (Upton Sinclair), 1903, Street & Smith, later editions by McKay or Federal Book, collected stories from earlier magazine serials, brown hardcover with gilt, frontispiece: $60.00

Off for West Point, or, Mark Mallory's Struggle

Cadet's Honor, or, Mark Mallory's Heroism

On Guard, or, Mark Mallory's Celebration

West Point Treasure, or, Mark Mallory's Strange Find

West Point Rivals, or, Mark Mallory's Stratagem

WEST POINT SERIES, Captain Paul B. Malone, 1904 – 1911, Penn Publishing, hardcover with gilt, illustrated endpapers, b/w plates: $60.00

Winning His Way to West Point, 1904

Plebe at West Point, 1905

West Point Yearling, 1907

West Point Cadet, 1908

West Point Yearling, 1909

West Point Lieutenant, 1911

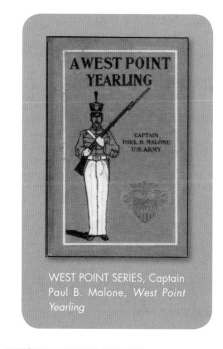

WEST POINT SERIES, Captain Paul B. Malone, *West Point Yearling*

WESTY MARTIN SERIES, Percy Keese Fitzhugh, ca. 1920s, Grosset & Dunlap, cloth-over-board cover, a Boy Scout series, with dust jacket: $30.00

WHITEY SERIES, Glen Rounds, Holiday House, hardcover, illustrations by author, first edition with dust jacket: $30.00

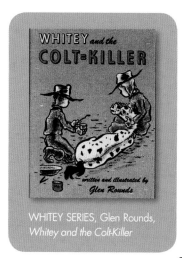

WHITEY SERIES, Glen Rounds, *Whitey and the Colt-Killer*

Whitey's First Round Up, 1942

Whitey's Sunday Horse, 1942

Whitey Looks for a Job, 1944

Whitey and Jinglebob, 1946

Whitey Takes a Trip, 1954

Whitey Ropes and Rides, 1956

Whitey and the Wild Horse, 1958

Whitey and the Colt-Killer, 1962

WHITMAN PILLOW BOOKS, 1960s, Whitman Publishing, small glossy hardcover with wraparound illustration, covers are slightly padded to make the book soft to the touch, color illustrations throughout, pre-school stories.

First printings: $35.00

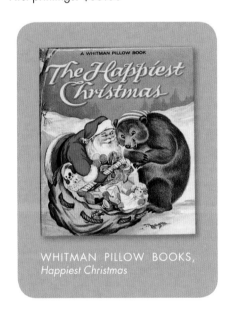

WHITMAN PILLOW BOOKS, *Happiest Christmas*

WILDWOOD SERIES, Ben Field, ca. 1928, A. L. Burt, small, color paste-on-pictorial cover, illustrated comic strip style endpapers, b/w/brown illustrations by Eloise Burns, with dust jacket: $50.00

WILLIAM BROWN SERIES, also called JUST WILLIAM, Richmal Crompton. Crompton worked as a school teacher until forced to retire by the onset of polio. This school series is based on her experiences and on the character of her brother, Jack, also an author.

WILDWOOD SERIES, Ben Field, *Exciting Adventures of Mr. Tom Squirrel*

George Newnes, UK, hardcover, illustrations by Thomas Henry and Henry Ford, gilt titles and gilt picture of William on spine.

William Brown, 1920s and 1930s, first editions with dust jacket: $300.00

1950s Newnes reprints, hardcover with black lettering, b/w illustrations throughout with dust jacket: $30.00

Just William, 1922

More William, 1922

William Again, 1923

William the Fourth, 1924

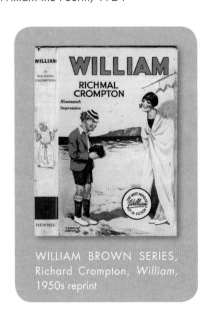

WILLIAM BROWN SERIES, Richard Crompton, *William,* 1950s reprint

Still William, 1925

William the Conqueror, 1926

William the Outlaw, 1927

William in Trouble, 1927

William the Good, 1928

William, 1929

William the Bad, 1930

William's Happy Days, 1930

William's Crowded Hours, 1931

William the Pirate, 1932

William the Rebel, 1933

William the Gangster, 1934

William the Detective, 1935

Sweet William, 1936

William the Showman, 1937

William the Dictator, 1938

William and the A.R.P. (also issued as *William's Bad Resolution*), 1939

William, 1940s first edition with dust jacket: $200.00 and up

William and the Evacuees, 1940 (also issued as *William the Film Star*)

William Does His Bit, 1941

William Carries On, 1942

William and the Brains Trust, 1945

Just William's Luck, 1948

William, 1950s and most 1960s, George Newnes, UK, hardcover, illustrations by Thomas Henry and Henry Ford, gilt titles and gilt picture of William on spine, first edition with dust jacket: $50.00

William the Bold, 1950

William and the Tramp, 1952

William and the Moon Rocket, 1954

William and the Space Animal, 1956

William's Television Show, 1958

William the Explorer, 1960

William's Treasure Trove, 1962

William and the Witch, 1964

William and the Pop Singers, 1965

William, last three titles (harder to find), first edition with dust jacket: $100.00

William and the Masked Ranger, 1966

William the Superman, 1968

William the Lawless, 1970

WINDEMERE BOOKS, Rand McNally, reprints of classics issued earlier by Rand, many of the original Rand editions appearing with tweed covers, paste-on pictorials, and 12 to 16 color plates.

The Windemere books have easily recognizable black covers with pictorial paste-on and bright silver gilt lettering and spine trim, five or six of the original full-page color illustrations, with dust jacket: $60.00. Without dust jacket: $45.00. Titles include:

Adventures of Perrine, Hector Malot, illustrations by Milo Winter

Adventures of Remi, Hector Malot, illustrations by Mead Schaeffer

Alice's Adventures in Wonderland, Lewis Carroll, illustrations by Milo Winter

Andersen's Fairy Tales, Hans Christian Andersen, illustrations by Milo Winter

Arabian Nights, illustrations by Milo Winter

Grimm's Fairy Tales, J & W Grimm, illustrations by Hope Dunlap

WINDEMERE BOOKS, *Tales of India* and *Arabian Nights*

Gulliver's Travels, Swift, 1912, illustrations by Milo Winter

Hans Brinker, Mary Mapes Dodge, illustrations by Winter

Heidi, Johanna Spyri, 1921, illustrations by Maginal Wright Barney

Ivanhoe, Sir Walter Scott, illustrations by Milo Winter

Jungle Babies, Edyth Kaigh-Eustace, illustrations by Paul Bransom

Kidnapped, Robert Louis Stevenson, illustrations by Winter

King Arthur and His Knights, edited by Philip Allen, illustrations by Schaeffer

Pinocchio, Carlo Collodi, illustrations by Esther Friend

Robin Hood, Edith Heal, illustrations by Dan Content

Robinson Crusoe, Daniel Defoe, illustrations by Winter

Swiss Family Robinson, Johann Rudolf Wyss, 1916, illustrations by Milo Winter

Tales of India, Rudyard Kipling, illustrations by Paul Strayer

Tanglewood Tales, Nathaniel Hawthorne, 1913, illustrations by Milo Winter

Three Musketeers, Alexandre Dumas, illustrations by Milo Winter

Treasure Island, R. L. Stevenson, illustrations by Milo Winter

Twenty-Thousand Leagues Under the Sea, Jules Verne, illustrations by Winter

Wonder Book, Nathaniel Hawthorne, 1913, illustrations by Milo Winter

WINDY FOOT SERIES, Frances Frost, published by Whittlesey House and illustrated by Lee Townsend, first edition with dust jacket: $60.00

Windy Foot at the County Fair, 1947

Sleigh Bells for Windy Foot, 1948

Maple Sugar for Windy Foot, 1950

Fireworks for Windy Foot, 1956

WINNIE-THE-POOH SERIES, A. A. Milne (Alan Alexander Milne, 1882 – 1956)

The four "Pooh" books, featuring Milne's son Christopher Robin and his toy animal friends, were issued by Methuen first in limited editions of 200 to 500 copies, the cloth-over-board hardcovers of each in a different color, blue, green, pink, maroon, plus gilt decoration and top edge gilt, illustrated endpapers, illustrations by E. H. Shepard. There were also other limited printings in different bindings including a Publisher's Deluxe Binding edition in morocco. Some special editions were boxed, some in wrappers, some numbered and signed. These limited editions are valued in the thousands. Other early editions include:

Methuen trade edition, first year, with dust jacket: $1,200.00

Without dust jacket: $400.00

E. P. Dutton, first US edition with dust jacket: $1,000.00

Without dust jacket: $400.00

The original four titles were:

When We Were Very Young, 1924, blue cover

Winnie-the-Pooh, 1926, green cover

Now We Are Six, 1927, maroon cover

329

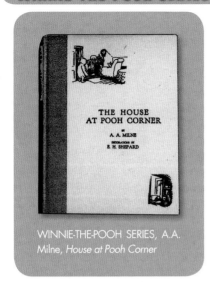

WINNIE-THE-POOH SERIES, A.A. Milne, *House at Pooh Corner*

House at Pooh Corner, 1928, pink cover

Winnie-the-Pooh, related titles:

Christopher Robin Story Book, 1926, London, blue hardcover with gold embossed illustration, b/w illustrations by E. H. Shepard: $400.00

Christopher Robin Verses, includes the first and third books in a combined edition, 1932, Methuen, hardcover, 12 color plates plus b/w illustrations by Shepard: $300.00

Winnie-the-Pooh, Related Song Books, ca. 1926, Methuen, London, publisher issued song books based on Milne's poems, music by H. Fraser-Simson, folio size, cream or brown boards, cloth spine, paste-on-label, illustrations by E. H. Shepard, with pictorial dust jacket: $300.00 to $500.00. Without dust jacket: $200.00

McClelland and Steward, Toronto, edition, ca. 1926, with pictorial dust jacket: $300.00. Without dust jacket: $200.00

E. P. Dutton, New York, edition, 9" x 12", hardcover with paste-on label, ca. 1926: $100.00

Fourteen Songs

King's Breakfast

Teddy Bear and Other Songs from "When We Were Very Young," 43 pages

Songs from "Now We Are Six," 33 pages

More Very Young Songs, 40 pages

Hums of Pooh, Lyrics by Pooh, 64 pages

Winnie-the-Pooh, related books, see ELLISON, Virginia H., in Book List by Author section.

WINSTON SCIENCE FICTION CLASSICS,

circa 1953 – 1961, 36 titles. Novels by the authors Arthur C. Clarke, Jack Vance, Lester DelRey, Ben Bova, and others. Most were stand-alone books which previously appeared in other formats but a few had continuing characters. These hardcover books with colorful dust jackets were marketed to libraries and served as an introduction to science fiction for young readers. Dust jackets in good condition generally triple the value, with the highest prices paid for known authors such as Clarke or Bova.

Hardcovers with dust jacket: $50.00 to $100.00

Ant Men, Eric North, dust jacket art by Paul Blaisdell

Attack from Atlantis, Lester DelRey, dust jacket art by Kenneth Fagg

Battle on Mercury, Erik Van Lhin (pseudonym of Lester DelRey), dust jacket art by Kenneth Fagg

Danger: Dinosaurs!, Richard Marsten (also wrote as Ed McBain), dust jacket art by Alex Schomburg

Earthbound, Milton Lesser, dust jacket art by Peter Poulton

Find the Feathered Serpent, Evan Hunter, dust jacket art by Henry Sharp

Five Against Venus, Philip Latham, dust jacket art by Virgil Finlay

Islands in the Sky, Arthur C. Clarke, dust jacket art by Alex Schomburg

Lost Planet, Paul Dallas, dust jacket art by Alex Schomburg

Marooned on Mars, Lester DelRey, dust jacket art by Paul Orban

Missing Men of Saturn, Philip Latham, dust jacket art by Alex Schomburg

Mission to the Moon (Jim Stanley Series), Lester DelRey, dust jacket art by Alex Schomburg

Mists of Dawn, Chad Oliver, dust jacket art by Alex Schomburg

Moon of Mutiny (Jim Stanley Series), Lester DelRey, dust jacket art by Ed Emshwiller

Mysterious Planet, Kenneth Wright (pseudonym Lester DelRey), dust jacket art by Alex Schomburg

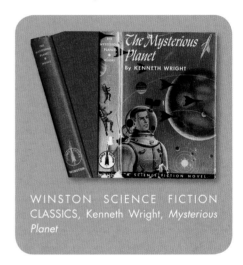

WINSTON SCIENCE FICTION CLASSICS, Kenneth Wright, *Mysterious Planet*

Mystery of the Third Mine, Robert W. Lowndes, dust jacket art by Kenneth Fagg

Planet of Light (Clonar Series), Raymond F. Jones, dust jacket art by Alex Schomburg

Rocket Jockey, Philip St. John, dust jacket art by Alex Schomburg

Rocket to Luna, Richard Marsten, dust jacket art by Alex Schomburg

Rockets to Nowhere, Philip St. John, dust jacket art by Alex Schomburg

Rockets through Space, Lester DelRey, dust jacket art and illustrations by James Heugh

Secret of the Ninth Planet, Donald A. Wollheim, dust jacket art by James Heugh

Secret of Saturn's Rings, Donald A. Wollheim, dust jacket art by Alex Schomburg

Secret of the Martian Moons, Donald A. Wollheim, dust jacket art by Alex Schomburg

Son of the Star (Clonar Series), Raymond F. Jones, dust jacket art by Alex Schomburg

Sons of the Ocean Deeps, Bryce Walton, dust jacket art by Paul Orban

Spacemen, Go Home, Milton Lesser, dust jacket art by Ed Emshwiller

Stadium Beyond the Stars, Milton Lesser, dust jacket art by Mel Hunter

Star Conquerors, Ben Bova, dust jacket art by Mel Hunter

Star Seekers, Milton Lesser, dust jacket art by Paul Calle

Step to the Stars (Jim Stanley Series), Lester DelRey, dust jacket art by Alex Schomburg

Trouble on Titan, Alan E. Nourse, dust jacket art by Alex Schomburg

Vandals of the Void, Jack Vance, dust jacket art by Alex Schomburg

Vault of the Ages, Poul Anderson, dust jacket art by Paul Orban

World at Bay, Paul Capon, dust jacket art by Alex Schomburg

Year after Tomorrow, edited by Lester DelRey, dust jacket art and illustrations by Mel Hunter

Year When Stardust Fell, Raymond F. Jones, dust jacket art by James Heugh

WIRRUN TRILOGY, Patricia Wrightson, stories based on Australian Aborigine legends.

Ice Is Coming, 1977, Hutchinson, hardcover, 223 pages, map endpapers, first edition with dust jacket: $40.00

Dark Bright Water, 1978, Hutchinson, hardcover, first edition with dust jacket: $30.00

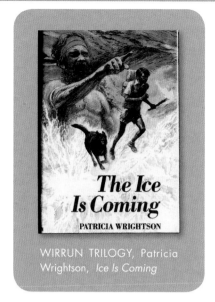

WIRRUN TRILOGY, Patricia Wrightson, *Ice Is Coming*

Journey Beneath the Wind, 1981, Atheneum, hardcover, US first edition with dust jacket: $35.00

WISHING STONE SERIES, Thornton W. Burgess, 1921, Little, Brown, hardcover with paste-on-pictorial, color plates by Harrison Cady, stories of a boy who finds magic, first edition: $75.00

Tommy and the Wishing Stone

Tommy's Wishes Come True

Tommy's Change of Heart

WITCH SERIES, Ruth Chew, author/illustrator, dust jacket and b/w illustrations by author. The series has continued in Scholastic's paperback line.

First edition hardcover with dust jacket: $50.00

Later editions with dust jackets: $30.00

Wednesday Witch, 1969, Holiday House

No Such Thing as a Witch, 1971, Hastings House

What the Witch Left, 1973, Hastings House

Witch's Buttons, 1974, Hastings House

Witch in the House, 1975, Hastings House

WITCH SERIES, Ruth Chew, *Witch's Garden*

Would-Be Witch, 1977, Hastings House

Witch's Broom, 1977, Dodd, Mead & Company

Witch's Garden, 1979, Hastings House

WITCH SERIES, Phyllis Reynolds Naylor, Lynn and Mouse combat the dangerous Mrs. Tuggle.

Atheneum, illustrations by Gail Owens, first edition of 1970s titles with dust jacket: $40.00

Witch's Sister, 1975

Witch Water, 1977

Witch Herself, 1978

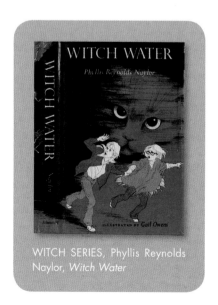

WITCH SERIES, Phyllis Reynolds Naylor, *Witch Water*

Witch, continuing titles, Delacorte Press, illustrations by Joe Burleson, used editions available at cover price or less:

Witch's Eye, 1990

Witch Weed, 1991

Witch Returns, 1992

WITCH WINNIE SERIES, Lizzie Champney (1850 – 1922)

Dodd, Mead & Company, hardcover with gilt, illustrations by J. Wells Champney: $50.00

Hurst editions, ca. 1910, b/w drawings: $30.00

WITCH WORLD SERIES, Andre Norton, see also GRYPHON SERIES and HIGH HALLECK SERIES, 1963 on, various publishers, this is one of those series that kept growing, crossing over, and inspiring other series until it became a bibliographer's nightmare. Like many works listed here, Norton's books appear under the label of "adult" or "young adult," depending on her publisher's whims. Her books appeal to teens or younger readers as well as to adults. Starting in the 1980s, a number of other authors contributed stories to the series, often citing how they'd been inspired by these books as children. The first six books of the *Witch World Series* follow the adventures of Simon Tregarth and his descendents in the region known as Estcarp. Originally published in paperback by Ace or DAW, they were reissued in hardcover by Gregg in 1977 (dates shown are for the original copyright).

1977 Gregg hardcover reprints with dust jackets: $100.00

Witch World, 1963

Web of the Witch World, 1964

Three against the Witch World, 1965

Warlock of the Witch World, 1967

Sorceress of the Witch World, 1968

Spell of the Witch World, 1972

WITCH WORLD SERIES, Andre Norton, `Ware Hawk

Trey of Swords, 1977, Grosset & Dunlap, hardcover with copper foil lettering, first edition with dust jacket: $50.00

Gate of the Cat, 1978, Ace, hardcover, first edition with dust jacket: $20.00

`*Ware Hawk,* 1983, Atheneum, hardcover, dust jacket by Jack Gaughan, first edition with dust jacket: $50.00

Witch World, short story collections, featuring other writers than Norton:

Four from Witch World, 1989, TOR, dust jacket by Victoria Poyser, first edition with dust jacket: $40.00

Tales of the Witch World, 1987, TOR, metallic dust jacket, first edition with dust jacket: $30.00

Tales of the Witch World 2, 1988, TOR, first edition with dust jacket: $30.00

WITH THE STARS AND STRIPES OVER THERE SERIES, William James, 1919, Platt & Nourse, hardcover, World War I novels: $35.00

WOLVES CHRONICLES, Joan Aiken, 1960s, various illustrators. Aiken's spoof of the Victorian melodrama takes place in the time of James III, a Stuart king who never was, ruling a Dickensian England.

The most popular character in the series, Dido Twite, and her family continued to inspire new novels into the 1990s. The original series deals with the wicked plots of the Hanoverians bent on overthrowing the Stuart monarchy.

Wolves of Willoughby Chase, 1962, b/w illustrations by Pat Marriot, Jonathan Cape first edition with dust jacket: $100.00. Doubleday edition with dust jacket: $50.00

Black Hearts in Battersea, 1964, b/w illustrations by Robin Jacques, Jonathan Cape and Doubleday edition with dust jacket: $50.00

Nightbirds in Nantucket, 1966, map endpapers, b/w illustrations by Robin Jacques, with dust jacket: $30.00

Cuckoo Tree, 1971, Cape, illustrated by Pat Marriott, and Dutton, b/w illustrations by Susan Obrant, with dust jacket: $30.00

Stolen Lake, 1981, Delacorte Press, with Edward Gorey dust jacket: $30.00

Dido and Pa, 1986, Delacorte Press, with Edward Gorey dust jacket: $30.00

Is Underground, 1995, Delacorte Press, with Edward Gorey dust jacket: $50.00

Cold Shoulder Road, 1995, Delacorte Press, with Edward Gorey dust jacket: $30.00

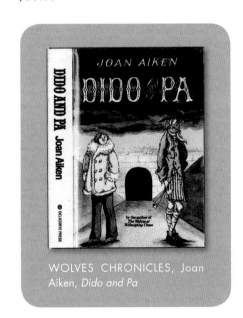
WOLVES CHRONICLES, Joan Aiken, *Dido and Pa*

Dangerous Games, 1999, Bantam/Doubleday, hardcover with dust jacket: $20.00

Wolves, related:

Whispering Mountains, 1968, Cape, UK, some crossover characters, first edition with dust jacket: $70.00

WOODCRAFT SERIES, Lillian Elizabeth Roy, 1868 – 1932, ca. 1920s, Doran, 1930s, Grosset & Dunlap, crossover titles used in Grosset & Dunlap GIRL SCOUTS series, hardcover: $35.00

WORLD FAIRY TALE COLLECTIONS, ca. 1960s, Follett, illustrated hardcover with same-as-cover dust jacket, b/w illustrations by Harry and Ilse Toothill, with dust jacket: $35.00

Burmese and Thai Fairy Tales, Eleanor Brockett

Danish Fairy Tales, Inge Hack

Fairy Tales from Bohemia, Maurice and Pamela Michael

Fairy Tales from Sweden, Irma Kaplan

German Folk and Fairy Tales, Maurice and Pamela Michael

Greek Fairy Tales, Barbara Ker

Italian Fairy Tales, Peter Lum

WORLD FAIRY TALE COLLECTIONS, Peter Lum, *Italian Fairy Tales*

Japanese Fairy Tales, Juliet Piggott

Persian Fairy Tales, Eleanor Brockett

Portuguese Fairy Tales, Maurice and Pamela Michael

WORLD WAR SERIES, Joseph Altsheler, 1915, Appleton, hardcover, early editions with dust jacket: $150.00. Without dust jacket: $50.00

Guns of Europe

Hosts of the Air

Forest of Swords

WORRALS SERIES, Captain W. E. Johns, Lutterworth Press. Johns created Worrals, a teenage female pilot, to encourage women to join the war effort in World War II. Worrals joins the Womens Auxiliary Air Force (WAAF) and defeats various Nazi plots. When WWII ended, Worrals and her younger friend Frecks continued to solve mysteries and have adventures. See also BIGGLES SERIES.

1940s Lutterworth editions with dust jackets: $55.00

1950s Hodder editions with dust jackets: $40.00

Worrals of the WAAF, 1941

Worrals Flies Again, 1942

Worrals Carries On, 1942

Worrals on the Warpath, 1943

Worrals Goes East, 1944

Worrals of the Islands, 1945

Worrals in the Wilds, 1947

Worrals down Under, 1948

Worrals Goes Afoot, 1949

Worrals in the Wastelands, 1949

Worrals Investigates, 1950

WORRALS SERIES, Captain W. E. Johns, *Worrals down Under, Worrals on the Warpath*

X

X BAR X BOYS SERIES, James Cody Ferris (Stratemeyer Syndicate pseudonym), ca. 1926 – 1942, Grosset & Dunlap, advertised as "These thrilling tales of the Great West concern the Manley boys, Roy and Teddy. They know how to ride, how to shoot, and how to take care of themselves." Several were written by Roger Garis. With dust jacket: $50.00

Hamlyn Westerns, UK, ca. 1950s, with dust jacket: $60.00

X BAR X BOYS SERIES, James Cody Ferris, *Hamlyn Westerns, Thunder Canyon*

Y

YARDLEY HALL SERIES, Ralph Henry Barbour, 1908 – 1920, Appleton, more school sports from the master of the genre, hardcover with paste-on-illustration, four two-color plates by Charles Relyea, first edition with dust jacket: $60.00

Winning His "Y," 1910

For Yardley, 1911

Change Signals, 1912

Forward Pass, 1912

Around the End, 1913

Double Play, 1914

Guarding His Goal, 1919

Fourth Down, 1920

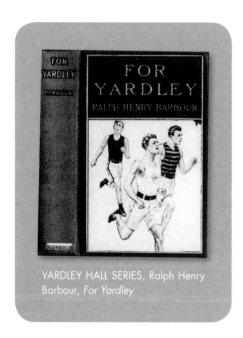

YARDLEY HALL SERIES, Ralph Henry Barbour, *For Yardley*

YORK TRILOGY, Phyllis Reynolds Naylor, Dan Roberts time travels to fourteenth century Britain.

Atheneum, first edition with dust jacket: $50.00

Shadows on the Wall, 1980

Faces in the Water, 1981

Footprints at the Window, 1981

YOUNG ALASKANS SERIES, Emerson Hough, ca. 1910 – 1920, Harper & Brothers, decorated hardcover, photo illustrations: $35.00

YORK TRILOGY, Phyllis Reynolds Naylor, *Shadows on the Wall*

Young Alaskans

Young Alaskans on the Trail

Young Alaskans in the Rockies

Young Alaskans in the Far North

Young Alaskans on the Missouri

YOUNG BIRDMEN SERIES, Keith Russell, ca. 1929, Sears, hardcover, illustrated by Richard Rodgers, with dust jacket: $60.00

Young Birdmen on the Wing, or, *Rescue at Greenley Island*

Young Birdmen Across the Continent, or, *Coast-to-Coast Flight of the Night Mail*

Young Birdmen Up the Amazon, or, *Secrets of the Tropical Jungle*

YOUNG CONTINENTALS SERIES, John Thomas McIntyre, 1909 – 1912, Penn Publishing, hardcover. Early editions with dust jackets: $85.00

Young Continentals at Lexington, 1909

Young Continentals at Bunker Hill, 1910

Young Continentals at Trenton, 1911

Young Continentals at Monmouth, 1912

YOUNG FOLKS TREASURY, 12 volumes, edited by Hamilton Wright Mabie and Edward Everett Hale, ca. 1910 – 1920, University Society, New York, color plate illustrations, each book: $30.00

YOUNG MINERALOGIST SERIES, Edwin James Houston, 1910 – 1912, Griffith & Rowland, hardcover: $40.00

Chip off the Old Block, or, *At the Bottom of the Ladder*

Land of Drought, or, *Across the Great American Desert*

Jaws of Death, or, *In and around the Canyons of the Colorado*

Yellow Magnet, or, *Attracted by Gold*

Land of Ice and Snow, or, *Adventures in Alaska*

■ ···················· **Z** ···················· ■

ZIGZAG JOURNEYS SERIES, Hezekiah Butterworth, travels of the fictional Zigzag Club. The stories were written originally for *Youth's Companion* periodical, then published in book format. The price range is extremely wide for these books, probably because the books are heavy and the covers are often torn away from the spine, making it difficult to find books in good condition.

Estes, Boston, ca. 1882 – 1895, oversize, dark cloth with gilt decoration, 300+ pages, map endpapers, numerous b/w illustrations: $65.00 to $200.00

Estes & Lauriat, Boston, ca. 1880s – 1890s, oversize, colorfully illustrated paper-overboard hardcovers, some with gilt, 300+ pages, b/w illustrations: $40.00

ZIGZAG JOURNEYS SERIES, Hezekiah Butterworth, *Zigzag Journeys in the Orient*, Estes & Lauriat, Boston

Collecting Medal Winners

There are many different prizes given to children's books and many collectors like to build a collection with all or most of the winners of a particular prize. The two prizes best known to American book collectors are the Newbery Medal and the Caldecott Medal. Following are complete listings for these two prizes.

Newbery Medal Winners, 1922 – 2008

The Newbery Medal goes to the author of the book and is awarded after the book is published. Collectors of Newbery Medal books pay more for first editions sold before the Newbery was awarded (i.e., first issue of the book with a dust jacket not displaying the medal). Collectors also look for first editions with dust jackets displaying the medal with the price paid for books dropping considerably for later printings. Prices for several highly collectible individual titles may be found in the Author section. Most Newbery Medal titles were reprinted frequently and are readily available in the secondary market.

1922: *The Story of Mankind,* by Hendrik Willem van Loon, Liveright

1923: *The Voyages of Doctor Dolittle,* by Hugh Lofting, Stokes

1924: *The Dark Frigate,* by Charles Hawes, Little, Brown

1925: *Tales from Silver Lands,* by Charles Finger, Doubleday

1926: *Shen of the Sea,* by Arthur Bowie Chrisman, E. P. Dutton

1927: *Smoky, the Cowhorse,* by Will James, Scribner

1929: *The Trumpeter of Krakow,* by Eric P. Kelly, Macmillan

1928: *Gay Neck, the Story of a Pigeon,* by Dhan Gopal Mukerji, E. P. Dutton

1930: *Hitty, Her First Hundred Years,* by Rachel Field, Macmillan

1931: *The Cat Who Went to Heaven,* by Elizabeth Coatsworth, Macmillan

1932: *Waterless Mountain,* by Laura Adams Armer, Longmans

1933: *Young Fu of the Upper Yangtze,* by Elizabeth Lewis, Winston

1934: *Invincible Louisa: The Story of the Author of Little Women,* by Cornelia Meigs, Little Brown

1935: *Dobry,* by Monica Shannon, Viking Press

1936: *Caddie Woodlawn,* by Carol Ryrie Brink, Macmillan

1937: *Roller Skates,* by Ruth Sawyer, Viking Press

1938: *The White Stag,* by Kate Seredy, Viking Press

1939: *Thimble Summer,* by Elizabeth Enright, Rinehart

1940: *Daniel Boone,* by James Daugherty, Viking Press

1941: *Call It Courage,* by Armstrong Sperry, Macmillan

1942: *The Matchlock Gun,* by Walter Edmonds, Dodd

1943: *Adam of the Road,* by Elizabeth Janet Gray, Viking Press

1944: *Johnny Tremain,* by Esther Forbes, Houghton Mifflin

1945: *Rabbit Hill,* by Robert Lawson, Viking Press

1946: *Strawberry Girl,* by Lois Lenski, J. B. Lippincott

1947: *Miss Hickory,* by Carolyn Sherwin Bailey, Viking Press

1948: *The Twenty-One Balloons,* by William Pène du Bois, Viking Press

1949: *King of the Wind,* by Marguerite Henry, Rand McNally

1950: *The Door in the Wall,* by Marguerite de Angeli, Doubleday

1951: *Amos Fortune,* Free Man, by Elizabeth Yates, E. P. Dutton

1952: *Ginger Pye,* by Eleanor Estes, Harcourt Brace

1953: *Secret of the Andes,* by Ann Nolan Clark, Viking Press

1954: *...And Now Miguel,* by Joseph Krumgold, Crowell

1955: *The Wheel on the School,* by Meindert DeJong, Harper

1956: *Carry On, Mr. Bowditch,* by Jean Lee Latham, Houghton Mifflin

1957: *Miracles on Maple Hill,* by Virginia Sorensen, Harcourt Brace

1958: *Rifles for Watie,* by Harold Keith, Crowell

1959: *The Witch of Blackbird Pond,* by Elizabeth George Speare, Houghton Mifflin

1960: *Onion John,* by Joseph Krumgold, Crowell

1961: *Island of the Blue Dolphins,* by Scott O'Dell, Houghton Mifflin

1962: *The Bronze Bow,* by Elizabeth George Speare, Houghton

1963: *A Wrinkle in Time,* by Madeleine L'Engle, Farrar

1964: *It's Like This, Cat,* by Emily Neville, Harper

1965: *Shadow of a Bull,* by Maia Wojciechowska, Atheneum

1966: *I, Juan de Pareja,* by Elizabeth Borton de Trevino, Farrar

1967: *Up a Road Slowly,* by Irene Hunt, Follett

1968: *From the Mixed-Up Files of Mrs. Basil E. Frankweiler,* by E. L. Konigsburg, Atheneum

1969: *The High King,* by Lloyd Alexander, Holt

1970: *Sounder,* by William H. Armstrong, Harper

1971: *Summer of the Swans,* by Betsy Byars, Viking Press

1972: *Mrs. Frisby and the Rats of NIMH,* by Robert C. O'Brien, Atheneum

1973: *Julie of the Wolves,* by Jean Craighead George, Harper

1974: *The Slave Dancer,* by Paula Fox, Bradbury

1975: *M. C. Higgins, the Great,* by Virginia Hamilton, Macmillan

1976: *The Grey King,* by Susan Cooper, McElderry/Atheneum

1977: *Roll of Thunder, Hear My Cry,* by Mildred D. Taylor, Dial Press

1978: *Bridge to Terabithia,* by Katherine Paterson, Crowell

1979: *The Westing Game,* by Ellen Raskin, E. P. Dutton

1980: *A Gathering of Days: A New England Girl's Journal, 1830 – 1832,* by Joan W. Blos, Scribner

1981: *Jacob Have I Loved,* by Katherine Paterson, Crowell

1982: *A Visit to William Blake's Inn: Poems for Innocent and Experienced Travelers,* by Nancy Willard, Harcourt Brace

1983: *Dicey's Song,* by Cynthia Voigt, Atheneum

1984: *Dear Mr. Henshaw,* by Beverly Cleary, Morrow

1985: *The Hero and the Crown,* by Robin McKinley, Greenwillow

1986: *Sarah, Plain and Tall,* by Patricia MacLachlan, Harper

1987: *The Whipping Boy,* by Sid Fleischman, Greenwillow

1988: *Lincoln: A Photobiography,* by Russell Freedman, Clarion

1989: *Joyful Noise: Poems for Two Voices,* by Paul Fleischman, Harper

1990: *Number the Stars,* by Lois Lowry, Houghton Mifflin

1991: *Maniac Magee,* by Jerry Spinelli, Little, Brown

1992: *Shiloh,* by Phyllis Reynolds Naylor, Atheneum

1993: *Missing May,* by Cynthia Rylant, Jackson/Orchard

1994: *The Giver,* by Lois Lowry, Houghton Mifflin

1995: *Walk Two Moons,* by Sharon Creech, HarperCollins

1996: *The Midwife's Apprentice,* by Karen Cushman, Clarion

1997: *The View from Saturday,* by E. L. Konigsburg, Jean Karl/Atheneum

1998: *Out of the Dust,* by Karen Hesse, Scholastic

1999: *Holes,* by Louis Sachar, Frances Foster

2000: *Bud, Not Buddy,* by Christopher Paul Curtis, Delacorte Press

2001: *A Year Down Yonder,* by Richard Peck, Dial Press

2002: *A Single Shard,* by Linda Sue Park, Clarion Books/ Houghton Mifflin

2003: *Crispin: The Cross of Lead,* by Avi, Hyperion Books for Children

2004: *The Tale of Despereaux: Being the Story of a Mouse, a Princess, Some Soup, and a Spool of Thread,* by Kate DiCamillo, Candlewick Press

2005: *Kira-Kira,* by Cynthia Kadohata, Atheneum Books for Young Readers/Simon & Schuster

2006: *Criss Cross,* by Lynne Rae Perkins, Greenwillow Books/HarperCollins

2007: *The Higher Power of Lucky,* by Susan Patron, Simon & Schuster/Richard Jackson

2008: *Good Masters! Sweet Ladies! Voices from a Medieval Village,* by Laura Amy Schlitz, illustrated by Robert Byrd, Candlewick Press

Caldecott Medal Winners, 1938 – 2008

The Caldecott Medal goes to the illustrator of the picture book. Like Newbery collectors, Caldecott collectors pay more for first editions sold before the Caldecott was awarded (i.e., first issue of the book with a dust jacket not displaying the medal). Collectors also look for first editions with dust jackets displaying the medal. Prices for several highly collectible individual titles may be found in the Book List by Author section. Most Caldecott winners were reprinted frequently and are readily available in the secondary market. Caldecott winners are listed below with the illustrator shown first and the author second. For titles which say only "by" followed by a name, the illustrator also provided the text, i.e., *Make Way for Ducklings* was written and illustrated by Robert McCloskey.

1938: *Animals of the Bible, a Picture Book,* illustrated by Dorothy P. Lathrop, written by Helen Dean Fish, J. B. Lippincott

1939: *Mei Li,* by Thomas Handforth, Doubleday

1940: *Abraham Lincoln,* by Ingri and Edgar Parin d'Aulaire, Doubleday

1941: *They Were Strong and Good,* by Robert Lawson, Viking Press

1942: *Make Way for Ducklings,* by Robert McCloskey, Viking Press

1943: *The Little House,* by Virginia Lee Burton, Houghton Mifflin

1944: *Many Moons,* illustrated by Louis Slobodkin, written by James Thurber, Harcourt Brace

1945: *Prayer for a Child,* illustrated by Elizabeth Orton Jones, written by Rachel Field, Macmillan

1946: *The Rooster Crows,* by Maud and Miska Petersham, Macmillan

1947: *The Little Island,* illustrated by Leonard Weisgard, written by Golden MacDonald (Margaret Wise Brown), Doubleday

1948: *White Snow, Bright Snow,* illustrated by Roger Duvoisin, written by Alvin Tresselt, Lothrop, Lee & Shepard Company, Inc.

1949: *The Big Snow,* by Berta and Elmer Hader, Macmillan

1950: *Song of the Swallows,* by Leo Politi, Scribner

1951: *The Egg Tree,* by Katherine Milhous, Scribner

1952: *Finders Keepers,* illustrated by Nicolas (Nicholas Mordvinoff), written by Will (William Lipkind), Harcourt Brace

1953: *The Biggest Bear,* by Lynd Ward, Houghton Mifflin

1954: *Madeline's Rescue,* by Ludwig Bemelmans, Viking Press

1955: *Cinderella, or, the Little Glass Slipper,* by Marcia Brown, Scribner

1956: *Frog Went A-Courtin',* illustrated by Feodor Rojankovsky, retold by John Langstaff, Harcourt Brace

1957: *A Tree Is Nice,* illustrated by Marc Simont, written by Janice Udry, Harper

1958: *Time of Wonder,* by Robert McCloskey, Viking Press

1959: *Chanticleer and the Fox,* by Barbara Cooney, Crowell

1960: *Nine Days to Christmas,* illustrated by Marie Hall Ets, written by Ets and Aurora Labastida, Viking Press

1961: *Baboushka and the Three Kings,* illustrated by Nicolas Sidjakov, written by Ruth Robbins, Parnassus

1962: *Once a Mouse,* by Marcia Brown, Scribner

1963: *The Snowy Day,* by Ezra Jack Keats, Viking Press

1964: *Where the Wild Things Are,* by Maurice Sendak, Harper

1965: *May I Bring a Friend?,* illustrated by Beni Montresor, written by Beatrice Schenk de Regniers, Atheneum

1966: *Always Room for One More,* illustrated by Nonny Hogrogian, written by Sorche Nic Leodhas, Holt

1967: *Sam, Bangs & Moonshine,* by Evaline Ness, Holt

1968: *Drummer Hoff,* illustrated by Ed Emberley, adapted by Barbara Emberley, Prentice-Hall

1969: *The Fool of the World and the Flying Ship,* illustrated by Uri Shulevitz, written by Arthur Ransome, Farrar

1970: *Sylvester and the Magic Pebble,* by William Steig, Windmill Books

1971: *A Story A Story,* by Gail E. Haley, Atheneum

1972: *One Fine Day,* by Nonny Hogrogian, Macmillan

1973: *The Funny Little Woman,* illustrated by Blair Lent, written by Arlene Mosel, E. P. Dutton

1974: *Duffy and the Devil,* illustrated by Margot Zemach, written by Harve Zemach, Farrar

1975: *Arrow to the Sun,* by Gerald McDermott, Viking Press

1976: *Why Mosquitoes Buzz in People's Ears,* illustrated by Leo and Diane Dillon, written by Verna Aardema, Dial Press

1977: *Ashanti to Zulu: African Traditions,* illustrated by Leo and Diane Dillon, written by Margaret Musgrove, Dial Press

1978: *Noah's Ark,* by Peter Spier, Doubleday

1979: *The Girl Who Loved Wild Horses,* by Paul Goble, Bradbury

1980: *Ox-Cart Man,* illustrated by Barbara Cooney, written by Donald Hall, Viking Press

1981: *Fables,* by Arnold Lobel, Harper

1982: *Jumanji,* by Chris Van Allsburg, Houghton Mifflin

1983: *Shadow,* translated and illustrated by Marcia Brown (from the French story by Blaise Cendrars), Scribner

1984: *The Glorious Flight: Across the Channel with Louis Bleriot,* by Alice and Martin Provensen, Viking Press

1985: *Saint George and the Dragon,* illustrated by Trina Schart Hyman, written by Margaret Hodges, Little, Brown

1986: *The Polar Express,* by Chris Van Allsburg, Houghton Mifflin

1987: *Hey, Al,* illustrated by Richard Egielski, written by Arthur Yorinks, Farrar

1988: *Owl Moon,* illustrated by John Schoenherr, written by Jane Yolen, Philomel

1989: *Song and Dance Man,* illustrated by Stephen Gammell, written by Karen Ackerman, Knopf

1990: *Lon Po Po: A Red-Riding Hood Story from China,* by Ed Young, Philomel

1991: *Black and White,* by David Macaulay, Houghton Mifflin

1992: *Tuesday,* by David Wiesner, Clarion Books

1993: *Mirette on the High Wire,* by Emily Arnold McCully, Putnam

1994: *Grandfather's Journey,* by Allen Say, written by Walter Lorraine, Houghton Mifflin

1995: *Smoky Night,* illustrated by David Diaz, written by Eve Bunting, Harcourt Brace

1996: *Officer Buckle and Gloria,* by Peggy Rathmann, Putnam

1997: *Golem,* by David Wisniewski, Clarion

1998: *Rapunzel,* by Paul O. Zelinsky, E. P. Dutton

1999: *Snowflake Bentley,* illustrated by Mary Azarian, written by Jacqueline Briggs Martin, Houghton Mifflin

2000: *Joseph Had a Little Overcoat,* by Simms Taback, Viking Press

2001: *So You Want to Be President?,* illustrated by David Small, written by Judith St. George, Philomel Books

2002: *The Three Pigs,* by David Wiesner, Clarion/Houghton Mifflin

2003: *My Friend Rabbit,* by Eric Rohmann, Roaring Brook Press/Millbrook Press

2004: *The Man Who Walked Between the Towers,* by Mordicai Gerstein, Roaring Brook Press/Millbrook Press

2005: *Kitten's First Full Moon,* by Kevin Henkes, Greenwillow Books/HarperCollins Publishers

2006: *The Hello, Goodbye Window,* illustrated by Chris Raschka, written by Norton Juster, Michael di Capua/Hyperion

2007: *Flotsam,* by David Wiesner, Clarion

2008: *The Invention of Hugo Cabret,* by Brian Selznick, Scholastic Press

Glossary and Abbreviations

Glossary

Annuals: Books issued once a year that collected the works published in a magazine or newspaper comic strip.

Backlist: Refers to a publisher's catalog of titles in print or out-of-print. Often the most valuable asset of a publisher's business, backlists were often sold to pay off debts or reorganize a business. Frontlist refers to the books that a publisher has bought but has not published or is in the process of publishing.

Board: Paste-boards were covered with another material to form the hardcover of a book, leading to terms such as "cloth bound" or "paper over board."

Board books: These were originally designed for very small children. Each page is made of a stiff "board" material that babies and toddlers can handle without tearing.

Cloth binding, cloth hardcover, clothbound: Cloth wrapped around a "board" (usually paste-board or another stiff base) and glued on the edges to form a cover. See also "pictorial cover" and "laminated cover."

Color plate: Color plates are colored pictures printed on a glossy paper that is different from the paper used for the text.

Copyright date: The copyright date indicates when the publisher or author registered the copyright for a work, but not necessarily the date that the book was printed. For example, most Grosset & Dunlap series books show the original date that the book was copyrighted and not necessarily the date that it was issued. See also first edition.

Copyright page: Generally, the copyright page is located on the back of the title page. However, this term will be used for any page that shows the copyright information. Some publishers, such as Garden City, put this information on the title page. Picture books may have this information on the title page, the endpapers, or hidden somewhere in the back, depending on the design of the book.

Dust jacket, dust wrapper, dust cover: The loose paper cover used to both protect and advertise the book's contents. See also "pictorial hardcover" and "laminated cover."

Edition: see "first edition."

Endpapers: The double leaves (pages) added at the front and back during the binding process. The outer leaf is pasted down to the inner surface of the cover, while the inner leaf forms the first or last page of the book. Endpapers can be plain or form a double page illustration related to the text. Sometimes they are called endleaves. See also "flyleaf."

Errata: Errors made in the printing or binding of the book. Sometimes, the errata can be used to identify first editions as such mistakes are usually corrected by the publisher as soon as possible.

Ex-library: This term applies to a book that has been removed from the collection of a public library. Ex-library editions are usually priced far less than originals because they have been altered or marked by the library. They might be re-bound by the library, have cards pasted over the endpapers, or be stamped with the library's name throughout the text. See also "library binding."

First edition: A first edition is generally defined as the first time that a book appears in print.

Flyleaf: The blank loose page found in the front or back of the book. See also "endpapers."

Folio: The largest size of a paper sheet used by printers to make a book. The term is also used by book dealers to designate books that are over 13 inches in height. See also "size."

Frontispiece: This illustration faces the title page of the book.

Gilt edges, gilt lettering: When the letters are printed with gold-colored, metallic ink, the book has "gilt lettering." Gilt lettering usually appears on the cover. Gilt edges refer to pages with gold decoration on the edge of the paper.

Hardcover, hardback: A book with a stiff cover created from "boards." Almost all the prices in this guide refer to hardcover editions of a title (this book is a hardcover).

ISBN: The International Standard Book Number (ISBN) system was adopted between 1967 and 1969 by publishers in Great Britain and North America. Each book is assigned a unique series of digits, such as 0-89145-717-8 (the ISBN for our first book). This information is usually printed on the copyright page and also the dust jacket. The number is changed when the publisher changes the binding (a paperback is assigned a different number from the hardback edition). The number will also be changed when the book is reprinted by another publisher (the Macmillian edition would have a different number from the Grosset & Dunlap edition of the same title). A new ISBN will be assigned if the book goes through a rewrite or other changes that make the book a new "edition" from the publishers' point-of-view. The ISBN does not usually change between printings. RR Bowker assigns and tracks the ISBN for American publishers. The Standard Book Numbering Agency, Ltd. in the United Kingdom tracks the British ISBN. See also "Library of Congress" and "SBN."

Laminated covers: Pictorial hardcovers laminated with a shiny clear gloss coating. Many of the Whitman books were issued with laminated covers. See also "pictorial hardcover."

Library binding: As books become worn by library patrons, they may be rebound. These library bindings replace the original binding, and often require the page edges to be trimmed slightly from the original size. Library bindings are usually easy to spot as they are of a thicker, more durable material than regular book covers (bright orange seems a popular color). The library bindings do not have the usual publisher marks on the spine and cover. They also considerably reduce the value of the book (see also "ex-library"). Sometimes, library binding may also refer to the reinforced binding used by the publishers — this type of binding does not reduce the value of the book as it generally looks just like the regular trade edition.

Library of Congress catalog card number, LOC number: The card number assigned by the Library of Congress started appearing regularly in books around 1960. Eventually this information was replaced by the Library of Congress Cataloging-in-Publication Data (a paragraph that looks like a library card) in the late 1970s. This information appears on the copyright page and is just one of the many "clues" that can be used to date a book when the date of printing is unclear. Publishers of childrens' books were very inconsistent during the early days of this system (and the SBN), so these dates should be used as a general guideline only.

Limited edition: an edition of a book issued in a "limited" number of copies.

List-to-self or List-to-title: On the dust jacket flap, or on an interior advertising page in a series book, titles of other books in the series may be listed. If the book's title is the last title on the list, this is called a "list-to-self" book. Because this information is not 100% reliable, collectors and dealers refer to such a book as a "probable first."

List-to-year: Like list-to-self, this is a method of determining a probable first edition of a series book. The titles on the dust jacket or advertising page may go past the volume's title, but only to include other titles released the same year, and therefore the book may still be a probable first. If titles for other series are included on the dust jacket or advertising pages, and their titles end with titles published the year of the volume's release, this is another helpful hint.

No date/undated: In this guide and in most dealer catalogs, "no date" or "undated" means a book that has no date of publication printed on the copyright or title page.

Paperback: A small book issued with a soft cover is usually called a paperback. The standard size is approximately 4¼" by 6½", but children's books, such as the Scholastic paperbacks, may be slightly larger. Unless specifically noted, we did not price paperbacks in this guide. See also "softcover."

Paper boards, paper covered: The paper boards are the stiff material that forms the outer cover of a book. Generally, these are made from paste boards (layers of paper). When used by a dealer to describe the cover of a book, this generally means that the boards are plain and not covered by cloth. This is different from a paperback (see also "softcover").

Pictorial hardcover: A hardcover, usually issued without a dust jacket, decorated with a printed picture on the front cover. The 1960s NANCY DREW books were issued as pictorial hardcovers. Many picture books were printed as pictorial hardcovers but issued with dust jackets. If the dust jacket and cover have the same illustration, the hardcover is often referred to as "same as" pictorial cover. See also "laminated cover" and "dust jacket."

Picture book: In this text, a picture book is a book that relies mostly on pictures to convey the story to very young readers.

Price clipped: In many cases, dust jackets had the price clipped off them before being given as gifts. Some collectors are looking for completely intact dust jackets, some don't care if the price is clipped as long as it doesn't affect the look of the dust jacket. Generally this is considered a minor fault on dust jackets, but something that should be noted if you are selling a book.

Printer: The company that actually operates the press or other equipment needed to print a book. Many early publishers operated as both printers and publishers.

Provenance: The pedigree of a book's ownership presented by a dealer. We did not look at the provenance of books when creating this guide and this type of information should be treated like an author's signature — something that takes the book outside the normal realm of pricing.

Publisher: The company that purchases the rights to print and market a book. Some early publishers started out as printers, but by the mid-twentieth century, most publishers farmed out their printing to other companies.

Re-backed: When the spine or backstrip of a book has been replaced, the book is said to be "re-backed."

SBN: Standard Book Number (SBN), the forerunner of the ISBN that appeared on copyright pages mostly in the mid-1960s. See also "ISBN."

Series: A set of books with an ongoing theme, a continuation of stories about specific characters, or a label put on a set of books by a publisher.

Set: Several books meant to be sold together, typically in sets of six or 12 volumes.

Size: In this guide, we've tried to stay with general terms like "oversize" or "small." Some dealers use "folio" or "quarto" to refer to size. These terms originally referred to the size of the paper sheet on which the book was printed and the number of times that sheet was folded to form the book. There is much debate over the proper use of these terms, so we have avoided them whenever possible. See also "Abbreviations" below.

Softcover: A "softcover" book is one that is issued with a soft outer cover but is larger than the standard paperback. Today, booksellers and publishers may use the term "trade paperback" to refer to softcovers of a medium size (approximately six inches by nine inches). Unless specifically noted, we did not price softcovers in this guide.

Spine: The spine is the part of the book which is visible when the book is closed and placed on the shelf.

Volume: As used in this guide, a volume generally means one book in a set, such as a volume in a set of encyclopedias.

ABBREVIATIONS

Many dealers use abbreviations to describe books and their conditions in their catalogs and Internet listings. The abbreviations listed below seem to be the most commonly used, but be aware that dealers often invent their own abbreviations or use a standard abbreviation for another meaning. When in doubt, query first, especially if this information makes a difference in the desirability of the book for you.

4to: Quarto, usually meaning quarto sized (approximately 12" tall).

8to: Octavo, usually meaning octavo sized (approximately 9" tall).

12mo: Twelvemo or duodecimo, usually meaning approximately 7" tall.

16mo: Sixteenmo, usually meaning 5½" tall.

(Special note on sizes: librarians, bibliographical references, and many antiquarian booksellers use 4to, etc., to refer to the original size of the paper and the number of folds taken by the printer, rather than the height of the book. It is wise to check how a particular dealer is using the term.)

Anon., anony.: Anonymous author.

BCE: Book club edition.

Bndg.: Binding.

BW, b/w: Black-and-white, as in black-and-white illustrations.

C.: Copyright date (c. 1967) or "circa," meaning "about" that time (c. 1970s). One of those abbreviations that you want to double check. To avoid confusion, we have used "ca." to mean circa.

Ca.: Circa (approximate date or era).

Cond.: Condition as in "good cond."

CP: Copyright page.

DJ, dw, dc: Dust jacket, dust wrapper, or dust cover.

Ed.: Editor or edited by as in "short stories ed. Andre Norton."

Ex. lib., exlib, ex-lib: Ex-library.

F.: Fine as in "f. condition."

FAE: First American Edition.

FE: First Edition rather than fine edition (but double check if unsure).

Fly, fr. fly, r. fly: Flyleaf, front flyleaf, rear flyleaf.

Fr.: Front or frontispiece.

G, gd: Good as in "g. condition."

Ill., illus.: Illustrated or illustrations: "illus. by M Sendak."

Lg., lge.: Large

Lt.: Light as in "lt. marks on dust jacket."

Ltd.: Limited as in "ltd. edition"

Med.: Medium size.

NAP: No additional printing, i.e., no additional printings shown on copyright page.

ND, nd: No date, usually means no date of printing available

Obl.: Oblong, as in a book that is wider than it is tall.

O.P., OOP: Out of print.

PC, p.c.: Price clipped as in "dust jacket pc"

Phots., photos: Photographs as in "illustrated w/phots."

Pg., pgs.: Page, pages

Prtg.: Printing such as "first prtg."

Pub., pu.: Published, as in "pu. 1967" or publisher as in "pub. Random House."

Qto.: Quarto, often used for quarto-sized (approx. 12" tall).

Rev.: Revised as in "rev. edition."

Rpt.: Reprint or reprinted as in "rept. by G&D" (reprint by Grosset & Dunlap).

Sigd., sgd., /s/: Signed as in "sigd. by author." May also use "sig." for signature.

Sm.: Small.

Sp.: Spine as in "dust jacket sp torn."

SS, ss: short stories as in "ss by various authors."

TP: Title page.

Trans.: Translator or translated by.

V., v.: Very

VG, vg: Very good as in "vg dust jacket."

VG/VG, G/VG, etc.: Refers to the condition of the book and dust jacket. The first is used for a very good edition, very good dust jacket. A reference like VG/0 usually means that there is no dust jacket available, but this is one of those abbreviations that it is wise to double check.

Vol.: Volume as in "8 vol. set."

W/ or w/o: With or without as in "w/dust jacket" or "w/o dust jacket."

Bibliography

Arbuthnot, May Hill, *Arbuthnot Anthology of Children's Literature,* 1961, Scott Foresman and Co.

Allen, Douglas, *N. C. Wyeth: The Collected Paintings, Illustrations and Murals,* 1996, Grammercy

Anderson, Vicki, *Fiction Sequels for Readers 10 to 16,* 1998, McFarland

Axe, John, *Secret of Collecting Girls' Series Books,* 2000, Hobby House Press

Bader, Barbara, *American Picturebooks from Noah's Ark to the Beast Within,* 1976, Macmillan

Baum, Roger and Russell P. MacFall, *To Please a Child,* 1961, Reilly & Lee

Billman, Carol, *Secret of the Stratemeyer Syndicate,* 1986, Ungar Publishing

Blanck, Jacob, *Harry Castlemon, Boys' Own Author,* 1941, Bowker

Burke, W. J., *American Authors and Books,* 1962, Crown

Cahn, Joseph M., *Teenie Weenies Book, the Life and Art of William Donahey,* 1986, Green Tiger Press

Cech, John, *American Writers for Children: 1900 – 1960,* 1983, Gale Research

Dartt, Captain Robert L., *USNR/R, G. A. Henty, a Bibliography,* 1971, Dar-Web Incorporated

Doyle, Brian, *Who's Who of Children's Literature,* 1968, Schocken Books

Feaver, William, *When We Were Young: Two Centuries of Children's Book Illustration,* 1977, Holt, Rinehart and Winston

Fisher, Margery, *Who's Who in Children's Books,* 1975, Holt, Rinehart and Winston

Garis, Roger, *My Father Was Uncle Wiggily,* 1966, McGraw-Hill

Gale Editiorial, *Yesterday's Authors of Books for Children, volumes 1 and 2,* 1978, Gale Research

Greene, Douglas and Peter Hanff, *Bibliographia Oziana,* 1976, International Wizard of Oz Club

Hall, Patricia, *Johnny Gruelle, Creator of Raggedy Ann and Andy,* 1993, Pelican

Hammond, Wayne, *Arthur Ransome: A Bibliography,* 2000, Oak Knoll Press

Haviland, Virginia (ed.), *Children's Literature,* 1966, Library of Congress

Hinke, C.J., *Oz in Canada,* 1982, Hoffer

Horne, Alan, *Dictionary of 20th Century British Book Illustrators,* 1994, Antique Collector's Club

Houfe, Simon, *Dictionary of British Book Illustrators and Caricaturists 1800 – 1914,* 1981 (revised edition), Antique Collector's Club

Irene, Joyce and Tessa Rose Chester, *History of Children's Book Illustration,* 1988, John Murray Ltd.

Jacobs, Larry, *Big Little Books,* 1996, Collector Books

Johnson, Deidre, *Stratemeyer Pseudonyms and Series Books,* 1982, Greenwood Press

Kismaric, Carole and Marvin Heiferman, *Growing up with Dick and Jane,* 1996, Collins

Lanes, Selma G., *Art of Marice Sendak,* 1980, Harry N. Abrams, Inc.

Linder, Leslie, *History of the Writings of Beatrix Potter,* 1971, Warne

Lynn, Ruth Nadelman, *Fantasy Literature for Children and Young Adults: An Annotated Bibliography,* 4th edition, 1995, R. R. Bowker Company

Mahoney, Bertha and Elinor Whitney, *Realms of Gold in Children's Books,* 1930, Doubleday

Madison, Charles A., *Book Publishing in America*, 1966, McGraw-Hill

Marcus, Leonard, *75 Years of Children's Book Week Posters*, 1994, Alfred A. Knopf

McBride, Bill, *Pocket Guide to the Identification of First Editions*, 1995, McBride/Publisher

McBride, Bill, *Points of Issue*, 1996, McBride/Publisher

Meyer, Susan E., *America's Great Illustrators*, 1978, Harry N. Abrams

Miller, Betha E. Mahoney (ed.), *Illustrators of Children's Books, 1744 – 1945*, 1947, Horn Book

Morgan, Judith and Neil, *Dr. Seuss & Mr. Geisel: A Biography*, 1995, Random House

Mott, Frank Luther, *Golden Multitudes: Story of Best Sellers in the United States*, 1947, Macmillan

Pitz, Henry Clarence, *Treasury of American Book Illustration*, 1947, American Studio Books and Watson-Guptill Publications, Inc.

Plunkett-Powell, Karen, *Nancy Drew Scrapbook*, 1993, St. Martin's Press

Quayle, Eric, *Collector's Book of Children's Books*, 1971, Clarkson Potter

Reynolds, Quentin, *The Fiction Factory (100 Years of Publishing at Street & Smith)*, 1955, Random House

Riall, Richard, *New Bibliography of Arthur Rackham*, 1994, Ross Press

Roy, John Flint, *Guide to Barsoom*, 1976, Ballantine

Santi, Steve, *Collecting Little Golden Books*, 1989, Books Americana

Schuster, Thomass and Rodney Engen, *Printed Kate Greenaway: A Catalogue Raisonné*, 1986, T. E. Schuster

Silvey, Anita (ed.), *Children's Books and Their Creators*, 1995, Houghton Mifflin

Tebbel, John, *History of Book Publishing in the United States (four volumes)*, 1981, R. R. Bowker Company

Tillman, Albert, *Pop-Up! Pop-Up!*, 1997, Whaleston Farm Publications

Ward, Martha Eades, *Authors of Books for Young People*, 1971, Scarecrow Press

Weinberg, Robert, *A Biographical Dictionary of Science Fiction and Fantasy Artists*, 1988, Greenwood Press

Whalley, Joyce Irene and Tessa Rose Chester, *History of Children's Book Illustration*, 1988, John Murray Ltd.

Younger, Helen and Marc, and Dan Hirsch, *First Editions of Dr. Seuss Books: A Guide to Identification*, 2002, Custom Communications

Zeuschner, Robert B., *Edgar Rice Burroughs, the Exhaustive Scholar's and Collector's Descriptive Bibliography*, 1996, McFarland & Co.

Zillner, Dian, *Collecting Coloring Books*, 1992, Schiffer Publishing Ltd.

MAGAZINES

We have found articles and auction reports in the following magazines to be very helpful for the collector. Both magazines maintain websites where past issues can be purchased and articles are posted for collectors.

Fine Books & Collections (formerly *OP Magazine*), www.finebooksmagazine.com

Firsts: The Book Collector's Magazine, www.firsts.com